READINGS

IN THE

MAKING OF

American Foreign

Policy

ANDREW M. SCOTT

RAYMOND H. DAWSON

Department of Political Science
The University of North Carolina

THE MACMILLAN COMPANY

New York

COLLIER-MACMILLAN LIMITED

London

SECOND PRINTING, 1966

Library of Congress catalog card number: 65–13587
THE MACMILLAN COMPANY, New York
COLLIER-MACMILLAN CANADA, LTD., Toronto, Ontario
PRINTED IN THE UNITED STATES OF AMERICA

PREFACE

FOREIGN policy can never properly be studied in isolation from the internal environment in which it arises and the complex process that gives it form and substance. The nature of that environment and of that process will necessarily affect the quality and character of policy decisions. For example, one can scarcely understand the design and working of contemporary United States foreign aid programs if one is unaware of the role of Congress and its committees in shaping these programs. Substance and process, ends and means, are bound together, and the origins of a policy are commonly reflected in its content.

This volume is concerned with the formulation of American foreign policy and it treats matters of substance only incidentally. It is designed to bring together many of the best and most suggestive materials dealing with the making of American foreign policy in the present era. The editors, in teaching courses in this field, encountered difficulty in developing a satisfactory body of reading. The literature on foreign policy deals more abundantly with content than with process and students were required to search through a variety of sources—books, journals, public documents, and periodicals—for assigned materials. It proved a cumbersome, inefficient procedure.

As all source books must, this volume reflects the interests and the approach of its editors. It is analytic in its orientation, since the greatest need is for interpretive materials that will help the student understand the complexity and workings of the foreign policy process. It presents divergent views because the views of qualified observers are, in fact, divergent. Its conception of the foreign policy process is broad and is not restricted to the State Department or even to the Executive Branch as a whole. The press, public opinion, and nongovernmental groups are as much parts of the foreign-policy process, as is the Secretary of State. To ignore the one would be as mistaken as to ignore the other. By the same token, in a period in which national security issues are of central importance, it would be a mistake to think of foreign policy exclusively in political terms and to ignore the powerful role of the Defense Department and defense considerations. The editors hope that the approach used will make the volume useful for others besides themselves.

ANDREW M. SCOTT
RAYMOND H. DAWSON

CONTENTS

Contents

V

The Overseas Administration of American Foreign Policy

I

United States Foreign Policy and the World Revolution

INTRODUCTION

LESS than thirty years ago Congress enacted a statute called the Neutrality Act. This law was designed to insulate the United States from any involvement in another war in Europe. It symbolized a general national feeling that the American participation in World War I had been a mistake, and, worse, that it was the product of the clever trickery of European diplomats and the machinations of bankers, munitions makers, and others who reaped financial gain from Europe's agony, serving no American interest or purpose.

It would be a gross distortion of American diplomacy and history to represent the Neutrality Act, and the spirit of the 1930's which nurtured it, as characteristic of the national tradition in foreign policy. Like any policy, the policy of neutrality, as defined in that era, was a product of circumstances peculiar to those years. It was a time of peculiar disenchantment with foreign affairs, marked by almost bitter disillusionment in the aftermath of the war to "make the world safe for democracy." Further, the nation was caught in the throes of a terrible depression, and its people were preoccupied with domestic problems of unemployment, bank failures, mortgage foreclosures, and falling farm prices.

For all that, the neutrality legislation of the 1930's marked the passing of a time when the United States could feel that its active participation in world affairs was itself a debatable question. It had emerged as a world power at the turn of the century, and had consciously sought to demonstrate that emergence in the "spendid little war" with Spain. It had planted the flag as far away as the Philippines, and had built a formidable Navy. It had participated in the resolution of a major crisis in Europe, concerning the status of Morocco, and its President had acted as mediator to end a war between Russia and Japan. Finally, it threw its great strength to the side of the Allied Powers in 1917 and went to war with Imperial Germany. Its entry into the Great War guaranteed an Allied victory, and its President became the foremost spokesman of the aspirations for peace in a world sickened by four years of unconscionable slaughter. Certainly these were the acts of a front-rank power, deeply involved in the affairs of the entire world.

Almost at the very moment of victory, however, America retreated from the world scene. The Covenant of the League of Nations was repudiated, and while the United States continued to play an important part in various disarmament efforts and in the restoration of German and European finance, it determinedly pursued a policy of eschewing any commitments and entanglements outside the Western Hemisphere. Based on the premise that if warring nations in Europe were denied access to the United States for the purchase of munitions and supplies in the event of war, and if Americans stayed far away from "war zones" in the event of hostilities, then the events of 1914–17 could not be repeated, the Neutrality Act was voted to insure that it "would not happen again." The obvious assumption was that another war, great or small, but did not really concern the United States or impinge upon its interests. If it kept to itself and managed its own affairs, it could live in security behind the great ocean barriers. When President Roosevelt suggested in a speech in Chicago in 1937 that the aggressive actions of the totalitarian dictatorships threatened the fabric of world order, and thereby menaced the United States, there was a sharp adverse reaction in Congress and from the public. In the summer of 1939, as the European democracies moved closer to a trial by arms with the Axis, the President and the Secretary of State met at the White House with Congressional leaders and tried to persuade them that the arms embargo provisions of the Neutrality Act should be repealed, at least to the extent of permitting the democracies to buy vitally needed arms and supplies in the United States on a straight cash-and-carry basis. The legislative leaders were not convinced. One isolationist Senator blandly assured Secretary of State Hull that the State Department was misinformed, that his own sources of information provided firm evidence that there would be no war. In any event, nothing could convince the isolationist leaders that American power and resources should be committed in even an indirect fashion to the task of shaping the outcome of the world crisis.[1] When in fact

[1] See the account of this confrontation with isolationist leaders in Robert E. Sherwood, *Roosevelt and Hopkins: An Intimate History* (New York: Bantam Books, 1950), Vol. I, pp. 161–162.

Europe was plunged into war, the embargo was lifted, but there was no lessening of the general popular determination to stay out of it. Not until the fall of France in the spring of 1940 did the American people visibly begin to act and talk in terms of a concrete national interest in insuring the victory of Great Britain over Nazi Germany. This marked the turning point—the "point of no return" in American foreign policy. The experience of World War II, the revolution in military technology symbolized by the heavy bomber of that war and then by the atomic bomb, drove home the unmistakable fact that the security and well-being of the United States, even its very survival as a free nation, was dependent upon the utilization and application of its power to shape the international environment in a manner compatible with American interests and security. What William G. Carleton has so aptly called "the revolution in American Foreign Policy" had begun.[2]

The Age of Concurrent Revolutions

It is not our purpose here to recount the events and trace the developments of this new departure in American foreign policy. Our interest and our objective, as we have noted, is the analysis of the process by which foreign policy is made. Our consideration of this process must be preceded, however, by some discussion of the context in which the decisions which aggregate "policy" are formed. The process of policy-making, in other words, cannot be understood in isolation from the political context in which it occurs. Briefly, then, we will attempt to characterize the international and the national contexts of foreign policy decision-making.

Probably every generation in history is inclined to view the problems with which it must wrestle as unique in their complexity and perils. Yet it is no exaggeration to say that the adjectives "complex" and "dangerous" were never more accurately used to describe the human predicament that they are in our time. This is not to suggest that foreign policy in the days of Hull, or even of Seward or of John Quincy Adams or of Thomas Jefferson, was a simple proposition. These men all faced crises that taxed their ingenuity and their courage, and which posed grave dangers to the security of the American Republic. But for all that, they never experienced the existence of thermonuclear weapons, intercontinental ballistic missiles, astronauts and cosmonauts, or the upheavals of political and social revolution that have transformed the face of three continents in a single decade. The nature of our problem today—of developing foreign policy to cope with continuing crises and revolution—can be better understood if we think in terms of our generation's witnessing and experiencing

[2] William G. Carleton, *The Revolution in American Foreign Policy: Its Global Range* (New York: Random House, 1963).

a series of *concurrent revolutions,* each one of which has created issues of peculiar complexity for the policymaker to contend with.

1. A Structural Revolution in the International System. The first of these revolutions we may designate as a structural change in the international system. Charles Burton Marshall has observed that barely one generation ago the American policy-maker had only to concern himself with the development of American policy toward a relative handful of other national governments. World politics was dominated by a club of great powers, most of them in Europe, and a small core of these were centers of great imperial systems. Thus, in the 1920's, to cite one example, relations with Africa were largely subsumed in the conduct of American relations with Britain, France, and a few other European powers.

The first element in this structural revolution, then, has been a "population explosion" in national states. Nationalism and national self-determination have truly encompassed the globe, and the United States now maintains relations with over a hundred individual governments. The problems of coordination have multiplied, and the sheer burden of "business" has increased many times over.

The structure of the international system has also been revolutionized by the development of a variety of international and supranational organizations. In addition to the management of its affairs through direct, bilateral relationships with individual nations, the United States participates in the political organs and specialized agencies of the United Nations, and in several multinational alliance organizations—most notably NATO—which have quite complicated institutional arrangements, to name only two kinds of examples. While this institutionalization of the international system has certainly not pushed into obsolescence the vital process of "traditional" diplomacy, it clearly constitutes an important new element in the conduct and formulation of foreign policy. In fact, it adds far more than merely another procedural channel for international politics. The institutionalization of the system has brought an entirely new dimension to the conduct of foreign policy. The development of policy toward supranational communities such as the European Economic Community (the Common Market), or such international organizations as the International Atomic Energy Agency, and the participation in a fifteen nation alliance such as NATO, have involved the development of novel techniques and have created problems and issues for the policymaker that would have been quite unfamiliar to the diplomat of even a generation ago. This flowering of organizations has been encouraged and has, to some extent, been a central objective of United States foreign policy. Future historians will undoubtedly mark it as an important transitional stage in the emergence of an international community. Nevertheless, the fact that it imposes additional problems and demands cannot be blinked. Progress has its price.

Another element in this structural revolution has been a process we will call cultural diffusion and ideological proliferation. The diplomatist and policy-maker of the 19th century operated in an international system clearly dominated by the West. Each of the major powers looked back upon a cultural heritage and tradition which had much in common with that of the other major powers. The twentieth century has witnessed the passing of this Western hegemony and the arrival upon the world stage of independent national societies representing a tremendous diversity of cultural backgrounds. In addition, it has been a century in which militant ideologies have harnessed whole national societies for frontal assaults upon the value system and political institutions of the Western world. National competition and conflict has thus been joined to ideological struggle—or vice versa—and has added another significant and new dimension to international politics.

2. *The Revolution in Technology.* Even more dramatic in its consequences for international relations than these structural upheavals has been the revolution in technology in the twentieth century. The military applications of technology, and particularly the development of nuclear weapons and ballistic missiles, have been the most spectacular—and ominous—benchmarks of the revolution. During the Venezuelan boundary crisis in the second administration of President Cleveland, the Secretary of State asserted to Britain that the United States is "practically sovereign" in this Hemisphere, because "its infinite resources combined with its isolated position render it master of the situation and practically invulnerable as against any or all other powers." And for all its bombast, there was a ring of truth in this assertion of invulnerability. During the week of September 18, 1963, by contrast, the completion of the Ballistic Missile Early Warning System was announced by the Pentagon. In the event of a missile attack on the United States launched over the northern polar regions, this system is expected to give approximately *fifteen minutes warning.* This warning is to enable the launching of a retaliatory strike by U.S. forces, but there is no defense against a missile attack other than this retaliation. Foreign policy today is thus shaped in a context in which the risks that may be taken are literally incalculable. The possibility of catastrophic destruction, inflicted by accident, by miscalculation, or by deliberate intent, is only minutes away.

Nor do these developments in military technology even begin to exhaust the revolution we are discussing. Communications, automation, and space exploration provide us with equally spectacular examples. The policy-maker is faced with a virtually impossible task in developing concepts and doctrines to keep pace with this revolutionary process, and the rate of scientific and technological advance is quickening.

3. *The Revolution in Rising Expectations.* The third of the concurrent revolutions of the twentieth century has been termed the "revolution in

rising expectations." Essentially, we may describe it as the leap of hitherto backward, traditional societies in Asia, Africa, and Latin America into the modern world of industrialization and technical innovation. It is a revolution in expectations in that these societies are engaged in a determined drive to modernize their economies and to gain status and prestige as well as higher levels of productivity. As such, they have succeeded in overthrowing, for the most part, the external colonial rule, but few of them have managed to establish any significant degree of political stability. Such stability as has been achieved is generally in the direction of what Robert Heilbroner calls "leftist authoritarianism." [3] The future development of these societies is of the greatest importance to the long-term interests of the United States, and this interest has necessitated the formulation of vast economic and military assistance operations by American policy-makers. In Latin America, to take the most notable example, the United States is committed to the promotion of internal social and political change through the Alliance for Progress, but the management of change in such a fluid, unstable environment poses uniquely difficult choices and decisions. The United States has an active interest in the development process there, as well as in the emerging nations of Asia and Africa, and it has made significant commitments of its resources to underwriting social, economic and political progress. Its ability to shape and guide this process of change, however, is severely circumscribed.

The political consequences of each of these concurrent revolutions interact and serve as catalysts for one another, so that we have grossly simplified the reality of the international context of American foreign policy in resorting to a scheme of classification such as this. The swift advance in science and technology, as applied to public health and medical care, for example, has so dramatically reduced the death rate in the developing nations that those societies are experiencing a population "explosion." For the immediate future, this explosion makes far more difficult the whole program of economic development in these nations, and thus constitutes a policy problem of the first magnitude. The long-run consequences of this explosion we have not even begun to understand, beyond recognizing that they exist.

This interaction of concurrent revolutions, moreover, has transformed the scale and level of political interaction between national societies. A riot in Jakarta, a student demonstration in Tokyo, a military coup in Peru, a civil war in the Congo, or a sit-in in Birmingham sends political reverberations throughout the world. There is an immediacy of events, a technological fusion of the international system, which creates a seamless web in which national decision-makers must act.

[3] See Robert Heilbroner, *The Future as History* (New York: Grove Press, Inc., 1959), Chapter II.

The rate of scientific and technological development is already breath-taking, yet that rate is steadily increasing. The body of scientific knowledge now doubles, so it is said, every fifteen years. Much of this increase has been as a consequence of the boost to research and development given by the massive programs receiving federal support. Yet both the total figure and percentage of research and development financed by the Federal government are likely to increase still further during the next few years.

Directly or indirectly, a great many developments in science and technology have implications for foreign policy. It is rarely easy to examine a research finding, however, in the first instance, and perceive its foreign policy implications. Foreign policy-makers are often slow to perceive the implications of something as closely related as a development in military technology. Communications technology is one step further removed from foreign policy, so that it is even harder for a foreign policy specialist to grasp the significance for his field of, let us say, the increasing diffusion of transistor radios in other lands, the advent of communications satellites, or the development of high-speed automatic translating machines. The difficulty of anticipating foreign policy implications is increased by a factor of two or three when one moves outside the fields of weapons and communications technology. What would be the implications of an inexpensive process of converting sea water to fresh water, perhaps using solar energy? Given the population problems of the world, what are the political implications in the development of a simple, effective oral contraceptive, a breakthrough in the understanding of photosynthesis, or a way to develop edible carbohydrates from cellulose sources? What consequences must be expected from the spread of nuclear fission as a source of energy or the development of significant new materials from coal, air, and water to replace those now being rapidly depleted? What types of foreign policy problems will be associated with the spread of automation?

"If we could first see where we are and whither we are tending," observed Lincoln in his "House Divided" speech, "we could better judge what to do and how to do it." This is a plane of wisdom that fallible men charged with the formulation and execution of American foreign policy have never been able to attain. Our point here is that the process of concurrent revolutions has made the task of judgment, choice, and decision in the shaping of foreign policy incalculably more difficult. An incisive observation made several years ago by Whitehead sums up our contemporary predicament very well. He commented that, throughout previous times, an important stabilizing element in human experience was the fact that "the timespan of important change was considerably longer than that of a single human life." Men were therefore able to adapt themselves to conditions and situations which seemed relatively fixed. "But today," Whitehead continued, "the timespan [of important change] is considerably shorter than that of a human life, and accordingly our training must prepare individuals to face a novelty of conditions." [4] Our problem, in other words, is in part to expect the unexpected and to have the capacity for innovation and flexibility to contend with the novel conditions growing out of these revolutions.

American Foreign Policy: The National Context

It is not surprising that the United States—thrust into the role of great power and world leader in a time of historic change—has had to feel its way, to experiment, and to improvise. This process of experimentation and improvisation has characterized not only the content and substance of American foreign policy decisions. It has equally characterized the American effort to develop a policy-making structure and organization adequate to cope with the demands of leadership and of survival in the midst of concurrent revolutions.

This process of organizational response to the international environment and the conflicts of the Cold War began almost immediately after World War II. There was an overwhelming consensus, driven home by the experiences of that war and the glimpse into the future that the atomic bomb portended, that the jerry-built structure of decision-making hastily put together to meet the demands of war was insufficient. America's interests, commitments, and responsibilities were recognized as necessitating major organizational and administrative adaptation and innovation if the transition from isolation to leadership was to be made. The Foreign Service was reorganized, the entire structure of the military establishment was redrawn, new agencies were created, and the Department of State entered into a long period of organizational change and adjustment.

It would be pointless, and frustrating, to attempt to detail this process of departmental and agency reorganization. Three general observations need to be made, however, in order to indicate the framework within which our examination of how foreign policy is made will proceed:

First, we must keep in mind that the American governmental system is characterized by a dispersion of decision-making power. Power to influence and to shape the content of policy, in other words, is divided between the two political departments of government—executive and legislative—and, within each of these, between various departments, agencies, bureaus, and committees, all representing particular interests

---

[4] Quoted in Stanford Research Institute, *Possible Nonmilitary Scientific Developments and Their Potential Impact on Foreign Policy Problems of the United States* (A Study Prepared for the Senate Committee on Foreign Relations, Washington: Government Printing Office, 1961), p. 183.

growing out of their functional responsibilities and clienteles. Inevitably, these interests, jurisdictions, and particular points of view will compete and conflict, as well as coincide. In part because of the overlapping of concerns and responsibilities, one of the major tasks of policy-making organization in recent years has therefore been the creation of regular institutional arrangements for the coordination and integration of departmental operations, so that the over-all foreign policy effort can be orchestrated into a unified, concerted whole. The most noteworthy example of this particular kind of institution is the National Security Council, created in 1947.

Second, the task of coordination and the problem of policy formulation have been complicated by the necessity to develop new operational agencies to perform specialized functions in the implementation of American foreign policy, which do not fit within the structural framework of established departments and agencies. Several examples come readily to mind. In 1948 the United States initiated the European Recovery Program, one of the historic policy undertakings of our era. Designed to operate over a period of years, and involving the outlay of billions of dollars for the rehabilitation and recovery of Western Europe, a new agency was established for the administration of the program. The agency, the Economic Cooperation Administration, was an administrative response —and a political response—to a novel foreign policy situation. The European Recovery Program was only the beginning, of course, of a vast American undertaking in economic assistance, now directed chiefly toward the economic development of the emerging nations. It became, in turn, the Mutual Security Agency, the Foreign Operations Administration, the International Cooperation Administration, and now the Agency for International Development. Cynics might observe that this confirms the theory of the immortality of a government bureau. A more meaningful observation, however, would be that it represents an attempt to organize the national response to the unprecedented foreign policy demands of the nuclear age. The same could be said of the establishment of the United States Information Agency, signifying yet another functional aspect of foreign policy which could not be fitted into the mold of past organization and experience, or of the Arms Control and Disarmament Administration. The point to keep in mind is that the input of new kinds of functional policy questions, and the new forms and character assumed by older kinds of policy questions that appear in new and more urgent ways, have led to organizational growth and proliferation, intensifying the problems of concerting American policy-making and policy implementation.

Third, we must remember that making foreign policy is a political process. As Roger Hilsman has observed in an illuminating essay on the formulation of American foreign policy, this means that the process has these characteristics: (1) In confronting a problem that calls for a policy decision, there will be a multiplicity of goals and values and of alternative policy responses. (2) The multiple goals, values, and alternatives will be identified with and represented by competing groups who advance the alternatives. These groups may be inside the governmental structure, or in some instances they may be outside that structure but can gain access into it. (3) The policy outcome (decision) in such a process will therefore reflect the relative power of these participants as much as, or more than, the relative logic and wisdom with which they present the case for some choice.[5]

These qualities of a political process clearly indicate the disparity between the "real world" of policy-making, where officials "muddle through," and the tidy model of rational decision-making.[6] Such a model would describe the process as consisting of a series of logical, sequential steps, following in a pattern of this nature: First, the determination of the values the United States wishes to advance and protect, and the definition of guiding concepts of national purpose and national interest. Second, in the light of the above, and of accepted norms and principles of conduct, the selection of alternative policies for the achievement of these ends. Third, a determination of the necessary allocations of resources for the existing alternatives, and a decision on the preferred policy choice. Fourth, the allocation of the required resources, and the establishment of whatever institutional or other requirements may be needed for the implementation of the decision reached.

In actuality, the policy-maker can only dimly approximate this kind of model. The model is valuable to our understanding and analyzing the process, but policy has to emerge out of ambiguous situations, contradictory pressures emanating from both the international environment and the American political system itself, and conflicting sets of priorities. Ends and means, goals and values, become mixed together.

All this is not said to uphold the existing organization and process for policy-making as the best attainable. In the ensuing sections of this book we will be confronted with very serious criticisms of its adequacy to meet the requirements of the nuclear-missile age. Undoubtedly it is a cumbersome process, with certain inbuilt characteristics which can be debilitating or even stultifying to the need for imagination and innovation that such a dangerous time imposes. Two comments may provide us with some perspective in approaching these tangled problems. The first is that our political system and political tradition have a notable propensity to focus attention on organizational failings when events are not to our liking,

5 Roger Hilsman, "The Foreign-Policy Consensus: An Interim Research Report," *Journal of Conflict Resolution,* **III** (1959), p. 365.

6 Charles E. Lindblom, "The Science of 'Muddling Through,'" *Public Administration Review,* **XIX** (Spring 1959), pp. 79–88, is an exceptionally able analysis.

rather than on the substance of the policy involved. Looking back on the events that followed the launching of the Sputniks by the Soviet Union in the fall of 1957, for example, one is struck by the extent to which the ensuing debate about the American missile effort and space program was directed toward the question of the proper organization of these efforts, rather than the question of the nature and extent of these efforts. Organizational changes ensued, which were undoubtedly called for and probably long overdue, but reorganization of the policy-making structure does not of itself solve the substantive issues involved.

In the second place, organizational change, no matter how significant, must be developed and shaped in the context of the political system. Shortcuts to the rational model are hard to come by when one must cope with the built-in inertial qualities of a vast executive bureaucracy and legislative process. In a celebrated speech at the National War College in April of 1959, Senator Henry Jackson offered a cogent critique of the shortcomings of America's organizational response to the demands of the cold war. Shortly thereafter he was named chairman of a Senate sub-committee which proceeded, over the ensuing two years, to make one of the most searching and constructive analyses of the policy-making process in the history of the nation. We shall, in this book, draw upon this quite remarkable study, and will be referring to it many times. For the moment, it is instructive to note that out of this study came no major recommendations for organizational change. The recommendations, in fact, strongly opposed such sweeping proposals as the creation of a "super-cabinet officer," and confined themselves principally to suggesting more effective and efficient uses of existing structures, and to the possibilities for simplifying that structure by eliminating some committees and subagencies which seemed duplicative. This suggests the durability of established patterns of policy-making, and the fact that these patterns are deeply rooted in the very nature of the American political system.

W. W. Rostow

THE AMERICAN AGENDA

THE generation of eighteenth-century men who founded the nation was part of an international philosophic tradition of considerable sophistication

FROM *The United States in the World Arena* by W. W. Rostow. Copyright © 1960 by Massachusetts Institute of Technology. Reprinted by permission of Harper & Row, Publishers, Incorporated.

which placed a high premium on formal thought and its precise articulation. However hardheaded and pragmatic the Founding Fathers were as working politicians, they were notably unembarrassed in the face of abstraction. And they brought the facts they perceived into an orderly relation to the abstractions which framed their thought.

As the nation moved forward into the nineteenth century, however, it developed a more distinctive style, acutely empirical, geared to facts and to the job in hand on the unfolding American scene. American empiricism was joined to a tendency to seek order among the perceived facts by loose generalizations. This splayed approach to the universal dilemma of theory and fact concentrated at the two extremes of the spectrum of abstraction, with the intermediate connections left vague—or not examined.

The predominant American way of looking at and dealing with the world linked naturally with elements of the German intellectual and educational tradition of the nineteenth century and helped the nation to emerge with universities devoted to high degrees of specialization, training their men narrowly in rigorous empirical exercises, the conclusions of which were hastily drawn (often in the short last chapter of doctoral theses) by the method Tocqueville long before had identified as distinctively American: the method of explaining "a mass of facts by a single cause."

This method marked, for example, the institutionalist school which began to emerge as the special American contribution to the analysis of society in the first quarter of the twentieth century. The United States was in the midst of an effort to assess the transitional process through which it was passing and to establish what should be done to mitigate its evils. As Riesman has pointed out, the kind of thought represented by Thorstein Veblen and Alvin Johnson "was, along with the Sherman Act and the Wobblies, a response of a once rural society to the changes brought about by industrialization—changes that could not be understood simply through analyzing their exchanges and transactions, by following the flow of goods and credits." [1] A similar philosophic bias shaped, for example, Beard's economic determinism, the frontier thesis school of American history, and Wesley Mitchell's passionate empirical investigations.

In natural science, too, from the Morrill Act forward, Americans in dealing formally with physical reality were, with a few notable exceptions, mainly engineers rather than scientists. The first generation of American scientists to emerge in the twentieth century, moving beyond skillful engineering, were, like the institutionalists, strongly empirical—for example, Michelson and Millikan who, without actively rejecting the relevance of theory, made their mark by imaginative, energetic experiment.

Between the wars, the balance of American intellectual life began to

---

[1] D. Riesman, *Constraint and Variety in American Education* (Garden City, N.Y.: Doubleday Anchor Books, 1958), p. 71.

shift away from this empirical and experimental pattern. That shift appears to have resulted from several converging forces. For one thing, the younger generation of scholars, born into an amplitude of statistics and descriptive monographs, behaved in the eternal manner of a new generation: they took for granted what they had and began to devote themselves in higher proportion to what was missing in American thought, that is, to formal theory.

In this development the economists were strengthened between the wars by the rise in the influence of the British school. In the other social sciences, the theories of Freud, Weber, and Durkheim gave to American thought about society a stimulus parallel to that of Pigou, Keynes, and Robertson in British economics.

In addition to such new transatlantic influences and the natural contrariness of a new generation, the Great Depression and Hitler played a role in shifting the balance of American intellectual life. The Great Depression obviously violated the continuity of American institutional development. It was an unexpected event, not to be understood by a simple examination of facts or a projection of slow-moving trends. Moreover, the British in particular had been developing between the wars, in response to their chronic problem of unemployment, theoretical structures which were immensely helpful. The Great Depression thus stirred up in economics and the social sciences generally a wave of new theoretical speculation. Hitler's contribution was even more direct. His policies drove or detached from Europe a substantial number of scholars who, whatever their particular intellectual tradition, brought into the heart of American universities a respect for theoretical concept and virtuosity.

Thus, before the Second World War, there was a vigorous development of theory and theorists in the social sciences directly linked to intellectual developments in Europe.

There was a similar process, under somewhat different stimuli, in the natural sciences. Large numbers of the newer generation of the interwar years—the postexperimentalists—traveled and studied abroad, where they were caught up in the excitement of the revolutionary development stemming from the work of Rutherford, Einstein, Bohr, and the others. The new physics was, in a sense, the equivalent of interwar monetary and income analysis for the new generation of economists. And in the 1930's American natural science—even more than social science—was strengthened by the inflow of Europeans seeking refuge.

The America that entered the Second World War was thus reinforced by the presence in the society of a good many European theorists, some of whom were of first quality, plus a younger generation in both the social and natural sciences trained in, comfortable with, and respectful of theoretical constructs. In many dimensions—from the Manhattan Project to the administration of the war economy, from the development of radar to the design of the Bretton Woods institutions, from the choice of strategic bombing targets to the psychological testing of officer candidates—this new generation of American theorists left their mark. In the various wartime enterprises, men were effective in part because they were intelligent, strongly motivated, and adaptable; but the relative success of the nation in rapid innovation during the Second World War was in part also due to the fact that the qualities of the good theorist were brought to bear on new practical questions.

The empiricist, the student of institutions, and the engineer may well be the best men to work out the next stage in a process of gradual piecemeal change; but the theorist, used to constructing and manipulating radically different models of reality, can enormously accelerate the innovational process. It is out of new ways of looking at things that new questions are posed; and it is through posing new questions that problems are solved. By the nature of his profession, the man trained to deal with abstractions thus often finds himself reasonably at home in practical situations of rapid change.

The Intellectual in the Bureaucracy

Contrary to a widely held view, the intellectual continued to occupy an elevated public role in American life in the postwar years. In industry there was a radical enlargement of funds available for research; and a new high status came to be accorded not only the natural scientist and engineer but also the economist, the psychologist as personnel expert, and the sociologist or social psychologist willing to apply his skills to market research and labor relations. American business had come to take an increasingly explicit view of its relation to the economy and to the whole society of which it is a part. Industrial economists examine long-period trends in population, income, and tastes, seeking to deduce the trend in demand for their firm's output and, thus, the appropriate rate of investment. They study their firm's relations to the public and to the political process in much the same way.

The American business firm is no longer an atomistic unit concentrated on the current behavior of its prices and its costs, guessing as shrewdly as it can its future prospects, making relatively simple profit-maximizing decisions, with its only communal concern to ensure that its officers keep out of jail. It is a self-conscious unit in a complex, interacting society, trying to understand how to exploit its environment, trying to influence (if not fully to determine) its own technological, social, and political setting. This new role has required businessmen to deal with the world about them with increased intellectual sophistication; and this, by and large, they have done.

There has been a parallel revolution in the institutions and attitudes of the national government, notably in national security policy. During the Second World War (quite aside from the atomic bomb) all three military services found that the natural scientist, the economist, the psychologist, and even the psychiatrist had important uses. And the post-1945 soldier retained a new degree of respect for the intellectual and the theorist, reflected, for example, in the remarkable elevation in the quality and level of military education. By the mid-1950's the Federal government had become the sponsor of intellectual effort, basic and applied, on a mammoth scale, providing about half the funds for research and development in industry in 1956 (about $3 billion) and a high proportion of university research funds as well.

The nation's intellectual structure and balance have thus changed in directions which should permit the society to deal with its environment in more responsive ways, transcending more swiftly than in the past the limits imposed by a vision of reality focused on a static or slowly changing *status quo*. . . .

Bureaucracy, Innovation, and the Individual

The need for higher orders of intellectual synthesis and the need for the cultivation of excellence which arise from the nation's enlarged innovational requirements have this in common: they place a new premium on individuals and on the expression of individuality in the context of public organization and public problems. Intellectual excellence of the first order is the gift of a few among millions; the act of synthesis is a creative experience uniquely achieved. The need to cherish them in the common interest sets up imperatives which, while consonant with certain old American values, run counter to modes of thought and organization which have come to develop in a society much of whose business—even its intellectual and artistic business—is conducted by large-scale bureaucracies. . . .

The problem of innovation and change is, indeed, treated to a degree by American administrative analysts; but it tends to be subsumed in a rather abstract way in the concept of "the choice among alternatives," just as modern economic theory assumes that entrepreneurs choose the most profitable technique available from a given "state of the arts." This is a gross evasion; for the very heart of the decision-making process is the posing of the alternatives. Innovation—creativeness—consists in thinking up an alternative which hasn't been thought of before. The good executive knows that one of his major tasks is to ensure that all the conceivable alternatives are explored and available to him, not merely those which his operating subordinates or staff men think up, agree upon, and regard as appropriate to place before him.

By making the act of decision the center of the job—and deflating the problem of formulating alternatives—concepts of the administrative process emerge which are attuned, at best, to modest, slow-moving innovation. When, for example, Simon and his colleagues treat such issues as "the growth of administration," "how problems give rise to administrations," and "the strategy of planning," their examples derive from American domestic life in which innovations are seen to arise from a slowly accumulating sense of an unresolved problem, gathering popular momentum until a political consensus is reached and action is taken. Subsequently, the planning process is seen as the projection out to the future of familiar ongoing processes and trends. The classic American table of organization for staff work consists of a hierarchy of specialized experts, each surveying a sector of operations, passing his recommendations for marginal change upward to be considered by the responsible executive in his "choice among alternatives." There is no perception—until very recent years—that the definition of alternatives in a rapidly changing field for action is, in itself, a powerful creative act most unlikely to be generated by specialized bureaucrats.

Innovation by Bureaucracy: The Unsolved Problem

The cumulative national experience and American thought about it have left this central problem unsolved: How shall change be instituted to meet new circumstances in large-scale units which, because they are committed to comparatively static standards of efficiency, limit the capacity of those relatively few creative men capable of innovation and leadership? [2] In dealing with this problem, the nation is inhibited in both business and government by the following characteristics of the national style:

1. An empirical approach that tends to discount the reality of problems defined by imaginative projection of trends until the problems have reached a stage so acute that they obtrude on the field of vision of responsible operators: in government, over the incoming cables, or voting shifts in the electorate; in business, on current income accounts; in war, by initial defeat in the field.

2. A related tendency to organize staff work on highly specialized lines which make difficult the development of an over-all view of the problems confronted by any major institution.

3. In consequence of overspecialization, the tendency to overman staff work units in such a way as to minimize the amount of time available to any responsible figure for coherent thought and reflection, and to dilute the insights and views of knowledgeable specialists as they pass upwards through bureaucratic hierarchies.

4. A tendency, in the interests of organizational cohesion, to accord all units in an organization a voice in major decisions touching their area of operation.

5. As a result, fundamental policy decisions which take the form of compromise among responsible operators, strengthening the inertia innate to any large-scale unit.

[2] For a classic exploration of this problem, see E. E. Morison, "A Case Study of Innovation," *Engineering and Science Monthly* (April 1950).

Under these circumstances, the concept of a high executive has ceased to be that of the creative innovator or forceful leader and has become that of the negotiator of successful compromise.[3]

In domestic politics the process of innovation is powerfully checked and governed by the sensitive market of the polling booths; and in business by the equally powerful pressures of competition and profit margin shifts. In both areas the rate of innovation required for the vitality and quality of American society is certainly increasing; but it can be handled tolerably well by the processes of institutionalized innovation which have been evolving when strengthened by enlarged political staffs, outside trouble-shooters, efficiency experts, and idea men.

In military and foreign policy, however, neither the domestic political process nor the competitive marketplace of power operates sensitively until acute crises have arisen; and the character of innovation required to deal with reality is more radical.

The two great institutions designed to synthesize a view of national problems in security and foreign policy—the National Security Council and the Joint Chiefs of Staff—have been in their first decade of life essentially committees of operators. There the bureaucratic chieftains meet, each freighted with large vested interests to protect, each biased heavily toward the *status quo*—as, indeed, operators must be. Under such circumstances these institutions have been unable to survey in a systematic way the horizons of the national position and formulate policies which effectively unified day-to-day operations.

High-level policy has tended to emerge in one of two forms: either as general statements so broad that operators could go on doing what they were doing and interpreting policy statements as they wished, or as tough practical compromises, allocating money or other scarce resources, in which the pattern of policy is much less important to the outcome than the bargaining weight of the negotiators.

What is the result? Policy-making has consisted in a progression of reactions to major crises. Having failed to define, to anticipate, and to deal with forces loose in the world, having tried merely to keep the great machine of government ticking over from day to day in the face of issues even operators could not ignore, at last the problems either never recognized or swept under the rug came ticking in over the incoming cables. Then, at last, the reality of the matter was recognized, but at a time when the options were narrowed. Emergency efforts—often bypassing all the bureaucratic machinery created to deal with national affairs—were hastily launched; and

---

[3] Compare, for example, D. Eisenhower, *Crusade In Europe* (Garden City, N.Y.: Doubleday, 1948), pp. 74–76, on the task of a modern military commander; and M. Newcomber, *The Big Business Executive and the Factors that Made Him, 1900–1950* (New York: Columbia U. P., 1955), pp. 20–23, on the functions of a modern business executive.

these became the working norms of policy until the next crisis came along. As a first approximation it is quite accurate to say of any moment over the period 1940–1958 that current military and foreign policy was a bureaucratized version of that created *ad hoc* to deal with the last crisis.

The nation has thus far been saved because Americans do not respect tables of organization nearly so much as would appear. A battalion in the field, a firm in trouble, or the White House at a moment of national crisis has its decisions made for it by the few men who really matter and who are rallied round for the occasion by the responsible officer who seizes personal command. Everyone knows that the vitality of even the largest of institutions hinges on a few key men. But the nation has found it difficult to acknowledge that the qualities of a few men matter so much when institutions are designed or their workings formally described.

The Character of a Solution

How can the quality of individual creativeness be woven back into the fabric of a society much of whose business must continue to be conducted by great bureaucratic structures embracing and seeking to organize coherently many highly specialized skills? There is, of course, no simple answer. The struggle between staff and line, between the inertia of operators and the perception of the need for change, will go on; but the balance can and must be tilted in ways which favor the process of innovation.

Each institution will have to fight out its own battles, find its own improved balance. There are, nevertheless, four things which can usefully be said in general.[4]

First, the reality of the problem should be recognized. The notion that American society is competent in the field of administration must give way to a skeptical analysis of the extent to which the pace of innovation is sacrificed to essentially static concepts of order. The problem of inevitable conflict between the canons of order and those of creative change must be accepted as one which can be resolved only by uneasy, endless struggle and balance.

Second, staff structures should be re-examined on the presupposition that they are likely to be too large, burdening the ablest men with tasks of human organization and manipulation to the point of diluting their knowledge of the substance of problems and their time to think.

Third, within staff administration, the role of the committee as an instrument for defining alternatives and arriving at decisions must be reviewed.

---

[4] For analysis and prescription along these lines, see E. E. Morison (ed.), *The American Style* (New York: Harper, 1958), chapter by George Kennan and the commentary on Kennan's essay by Richard M. Bissell, Jr.

The checks and balances which must inevitably operate when many factors and interests bear on a given decision cannot be eliminated even if that were desirable. But individual men can be assigned responsibility to formulate the alternatives and to propose an answer to problems, bearing with that assignment the responsibility of consulting legitimately interested parties. The essential point is this: the performance of the same individual as the member of a committee bearing a dilute communal responsibility and his performance when faced with an unambiguous personal assignment to do a job is remarkably different.

Fourth, in industry as well as in government, the technique of decentralization of operating function appears capable of further extension. In the end, in all bureaucracies the unity and the coordination of parts must be achieved; but it well suits a nation constructed politically by making an art of federalism to find new and economical ways of maintaining unity on minimum essential issues while still permitting large areas of responsibility and choice to elements within the large organization.

The argument here, then, is that, although large-scale organizations inevitably place the individual in a setting different from that of a farmer who owns his own land, the man who sets up his own small business, or even the scholar writing his book alone in the library, the loss of connection between what a man does and the larger purposes of the organization of which he is a part has been excessive. It is not beyond the wit of man to devise better ways of reconciling the imperatives of large-scale organization with those personalized challenges and incentives on which the best human performance depends.

In Washington, aside from new administrative procedures and balances like those going forward slowly in the Pentagon, a change of spirit is required. The individual human beings in the great bureaucracies must be encouraged to think, to throw out new ideas, to debate openly. The illusion that the nation's affairs can successfully be handled by negotiating minimum consensus in layer after layer of interdepartmental committees must be broken. The government must recapture a sense that creation is something the nation badly needs; and that creation is a job of individuals backing their play with integrity. This spirit must suffuse the whole apparatus from the Office of the President to the lowest GS-5.

The interdepartmental machinery of negotiation and consensus will continue to grind along. Bureaucracy will not end. But its processes must be made to grind on something other than departmental vested interests and the precompromised views of men anxious above all to avoid controversy and trouble.

A systematic counterattack on prevailing administrative theory, bureaucratic structure, and organizational spirit appears to be in order, not only to salvage for American citizens a wider range of individual responsibility and expression but also to give increased play to those forces of creation and innovation on which the survival of American society—as well as its quality—increasingly depend.

Henry A. Kissinger
REFLECTIONS ON AMERICAN DIPLOMACY

I T is understandable that a nation which for a century and a half had been preoccupied with its domestic affairs should seek to apply the pattern of these to international affairs. But the very success of the American experiment and the spontaneity of our social institutions have served to emphasize the dilemma faced at some stage by every country: how to reconcile its vision of itself with the vision of it as seen by others. To itself, a nation is an expression of justice, and the more spontaneous has been the growth of its social institutions the more this is true; for government functions effectively only when most citizens obey voluntarily and they will obey only to the extent that they consider the demands of their rulers just. But to other nations, a state is a force to be balanced. This is inevitable because national strategy must be planned on the basis of the other side's capabilities and not merely a calculation of its intentions. There exists a double standard, therefore, in all foreign policy: internally, foreign policy is justified like all other policy in terms of an absolute standard; but abroad, what is defined as justice domestically becomes a program to be compromised by negotiation. If the institutions and values of the states comprising the international order are sufficiently similar, this incommensurability may not become apparent. But in a revolutionary period like the present, it affects profoundly relationships among states.

Foremost among the attitudes affecting our foreign policy is American empiricism and its quest for methodological certainty: nothing is "true" unless it is "objective" and it is not "objective" unless it is part of experience. This makes for the absence of dogmatism and for the ease of social relations on the domestic scene. But in the conduct of foreign policy it has pernicious consequences. Foreign policy is the art of weighing probabilities; mastery of it lies in grasping the nuances of possibilities. To attempt to conduct it as a science must lead to rigidity. For only the risks are certain; the opportunities are conjectural. One cannot be "sure" about the implications of events until they have happened and when they have occurred

F R O M *Foreign Affairs*, **35** (1956), 37–56. Copyright 1956 by the Council on Foreign Relations, Inc., New York. Reprinted by permission of the author and publisher.

it is too late to do anything about them. Empiricism in foreign policy leads to a penchant for *ad hoc* solutions; the rejection of dogmatism inclines our policy-makers to postpone committing themselves until all facts are in; but by the time the facts are in, a crisis has usually developed or an opportunity has passed. Our policy is therefore geared to dealing with emergencies; it finds difficulty in developing the long-range program that might forestall them.

A symptom of our need for methodological certainty is the vast number of committees charged with examining and developing policy. The very multiplicity of committees makes it difficult to arrive at decisions in time. It tends to give a disproportionate influence to subordinate officials who prepare the initial memoranda and it overwhelms our higher officials with trivia. Because of our cult of specialization, sovereign departments negotiate national policy among each other with no single authority able to take an over-all view or to apply decisions over a period of time.[1] This results in a hiatus between grand strategy and particular tactics, between the definition of general objectives so vague as to be truistic and the concern with immediate problems. The gap is bridged only when a crisis forces the bureaucratic machinery into accelerated action, and then the top leadership has little choice but to concur in the administrative proposals. In short, we are trying to cope with political problems by administrative means.

The temptation to formulate policy administratively is ever present in a government organized, as ours is, primarily for the conduct of domestic affairs. But the spirit of policy and that of bureaucracy are fundamentally opposed. Profound policy thrives on creativeness; good administration thrives on routine—a procedure which can assimilate mediocrity. Policy involves an adjustment of risks; administration an avoidance of deviation. The attempt to formulate policy administratively leads to the acceptance of a standard which evaluates by mistakes avoided rather than by goals achieved. It is no accident that most great statesmen were opposed by the "experts" in their foreign offices, for the very greatness of the statesman's conception tends to make it inaccessible to those whose primary concern is with safety and minimum risk.

Our methodological doubt makes for vulnerability to Soviet manœuvres in two ways: on the one hand, every Soviet change of line is taken at least in part at face value, for we cannot be certain that the Soviets may not "mean" it this time until they have proved they do not; and they will try their best not to prove it until the tactic has served its purpose. On the other hand, we have found it difficult to adjust our tactics to new situations, so that we always tend to speak in the categories of the most recent threat but one. The paradoxical result is that we, the empiricists, appear to the world

---

[1] This is true despite the National Security Council. Since the N.S.C. is composed mainly of department heads overwhelmed with administrative responsibilities, all the pressures make for a departmental outlook and a concern with immediate problems.

as rigid, unimaginative and even somewhat cynical, while the dogmatic Bolsheviks exhibit flexibility, daring and subtlety. This is because our empiricism dooms us to an essentially reactive policy that improvises a counter to every Soviet move, while the Soviet emphasis on theory gives them the certainty to act, to manœuvre and to run risks. The very fact of action forces us to assume the risks of countermoves and absorbs our energies in essentially defensive manœuvres.

The willingness to act need not derive from theory, of course. Indeed, an overemphasis on theory can lead to a loss of touch with reality. In many societies—in Great Britain, for example—policy developed from a firmly held tradition of a national strategy. Throughout the nineteenth century it was a tenet of British policy that Antwerp should not fall into the hands of a major Power. This was not backed by an elaborate metaphysics but simply by a tradition of British sea power whose requirements were so generally understood that they were never debated. It is the absence of a tradition of foreign policy which exaggerates the biases of our empiricism and makes it difficult to conduct our policy with a proper regard for the timing of measures. It causes us to overlook the fact that policy exists in time as well as in space, that a measure is correct only if it can be carried out at the proper moment. To be sure, our cumbersome administrative mechanism adds immeasurably to the problem. But in addition, our deliberations are conducted as if a course of action were eternally valid, as if a measure which might meet exactly the needs of a given moment could not backfire if adopted a year later. For this reason our policy lacks a feeling for nuance, the ability to come up with variations on the same theme, as the Soviets have done so effectively. We consider policy-making concluded when the National Security Council has come to a decision. And in fact, the process of arriving at a decision is so arduous and a reappraisal is necessarily so "agonizing" that we are reluctant to reëxamine policies after they have outlived their usefulness.

But a written statement of policy is likely to amount to a truism; the real difficulty arises in applying it to concrete situations.

• • •

Related to this problem is our reluctance to think in terms of power. To be sure, American expansion both economic and geographical was not accomplished without a judicious application of power. But our Calvinist heritage has required success to display the attribute of justice. Even our great fortunes, however accumulated, were almost invariably held to impose a social obligation; the great foundation is after all a peculiarly American phenomenon. As a nation, we have used power almost shamefacedly as if it were inherently wicked. We have wanted to be liked for our own sakes and we have wished to succeed because of the persuasiveness of our prin-

ciples rather than through our strength. Our feeling of guilt with respect to power has caused us to transform all wars into crusades, and then to apply our power in the most absolute terms. We have rarely found intermediary ways to apply our power and in those cases we have done so reluctantly.

But international relations cannot be conducted without an awareness of power relationships. To be sure, the contemporary revolution cannot be managed merely by an exercise of force. But unless we maintain at least an equilibrium of power between us and the Soviet bloc we will have no chance to undertake any positive measures. And maintaining this equilibrium may confront us with some very difficult choices. We are certain to be confronted with situations of extraordinary ambiguity such as civil wars or domestic coups. Every successful Soviet move makes our moral position that much more difficult: Indochina was more ambiguous than Korea; the Soviet arms deal with Egypt more ambiguous than Indochina; the Suez crisis more ambiguous than the arms deal. There can be no doubt that we should seek to prevent such occurrences. But once they have occurred, we must find the will to act and to run risks in a situation which permits only a choice among evils. While we should never give up our principles, we must also realize that we cannot maintain our principles unless we survive.

Consistent with our reluctance to think in terms of power has been our notion of the nature of peace. We assume that peace is the "normal" pattern of relations among states, that it is equivalent to a consciousness of harmony, that it can be aimed at directly as a goal of policy. These are truisms rarely challenged in our political debate. Both major political parties maintain that they work for a lasting peace, even if they differ about the best means of attaining it. Both make statements which imply that on a certain magic day, perhaps after a four-power conference, "peace will break out."

No idea could be more dangerous. To begin with, the polarization of power in the world would give international relations a degree of instability even if there were no ideological disagreement, and the present volatile state of technology is likely to compound this sense of insecurity. Moreover, whenever peace—conceived as the avoidance of war—has become the direct objective of a Power or a group of Powers, international relations have been at the mercy of the state willing to forego peace. No statesman can entrust the fate of his country entirely to the continued good will of another sovereign state, if only because the best guarantee for the will remaining good is not to tempt it by too great a disproportion of power. Peace, therefore, cannot be aimed at directly; it is the expression of certain conditions and power relationships. It is to these relationships—not to peace—that diplomacy must address itself.

Stanley H. Hoffmann

RESTRAINTS AND CHOICES IN
AMERICAN FOREIGN POLICY

NOT long ago Henry A. Kissinger commented: "The stagnation of our policy is often ascribed to the fact that our best people are not in government service. But the more serious and pertinent question is how qualified our eminent men are for the task of policy-making in a revolutionary period." Since those words were printed, a new administration has done its best to harness "our best people" to American foreign policy, and Mr. Kissinger's question is more pertinent than ever.

It would take a volume to analyze why policy-making is so frustrating a task in today's America. The purpose of this article is to discuss the most important constraints that restrict the policy-makers' liberty of action, and to see how narrow or how broad a margin remains for choice. Such an attempt is worth while from at least two viewpoints. On the one hand, recent theories of international politics seem to divide into opposite extremes. Some focus on the international system; they tend to describe it as a compelling, even tyrannical, sociological divinity. Others scrutinize national decision-making; they patiently list all the organs that take part in it and all the "inputs" that go into decisions. Theories of the former type have not yet examined carefully enough the weight with which the system presses on various kinds of states at different times; theories of the latter type tend to be casual about the environment. A study of the restraints and margins of choice may be useful to both groups of theories, and even begin to build a necessary bridge between them.

On the other hand, such a study may also be of interest to the observer, often baffled and generally critical of American foreign policy. What baffles him is the massive continuity of American policy, despite its innumerable verbal clashes, its promises of drastic reform, the temporary oscillations around the main trends, and the headlines announcing crises and bankruptcy. The wrapping changes: the substance remains much the same. Images multiply, but the reality they mirror is monotonous. Consequently, there is a constant clamor for change. The best way of trying to find out why there seems to be a curse of continuity, and to what extent it is

FROM *Daedalus,* Journal of the American Academy of Arts and Sciences (Fall 1962). Reprinted by permission of the author and publisher.

legitimate to suggest alternatives, consists in analyzing the restraints that constrict American policy.

Now, various distinctions can be made. Certain restraints operate as prohibitions, others as imperatives: the study of the former tells us what cannot be done; the study of the latter tells us what has to be done. Certain restraints (prohibitions or imperatives) delimit what United States foreign-policy proposals can try to accomplish; others delineate what kinds of proposals United States policy-makers can put forward. To take the case of prohibitions, let us say that what cannot be accomplished should not be requested (except for propaganda reasons), but what cannot even be formulated should be expected even less. The most basic distinction, with which this article deals, is of a different kind. Its criterion is in the origin of the restraints. Some are provided by the international system. The system, of which the United States is but one element, rules out certain policies and dictates others, but it does not annihilate all freedom of choice. Other limits must be taken into account. They stem from the nature of the United States as a political community; either they rule out actions that the international system does not exclude, or else they push the nation into decisions that on surface may appear as shining examples of free choice but are actually, in a deeper sense, domestic compulsions. Many critics blame the nation or its leaders for what is the fault of the international system; others indict the system for evils that must be traced to the nation. The vultures that attack Prometheus may be the gods', but the ties that bind him to the rock may be his own.

The Impossible and the Necessary

Sensitive souls often object to describing international politics as a game —whether chess, poker, or the complicated play of game theory; but the metaphor has its usefulness. As Raymond Aron keeps telling us, the nations play a game in which payment is in blood, not only cash. The restraints the players must observe are of two kinds. Some are inherent in the distribution of the cards among the players; others result from the rules of the game, which even those players who want better cards must respect. Whether he seeks a better distribution of new rules, the player must exercise self-restraint lest he lose. What those limitations are and to what extent they can be overcome depend on the concrete circumstances of the system and the player.

Let us start with the cards, that is, the basic elements of the present system as they must appear to the United States. The first element is bi-polarity. America's power has not been America's choice. As long as the international order could be left in the hands of Britain and France, the United States chose isolation; but the United States emerged from World

War II as the only nation that could counterbalance the might of the Soviet Union. The United States had literally no choice, unless one called abdication from politics and escape from history a genuine alternative. There is a difference between a mistake and a mirage; those who in the 1920's encouraged Americans to cultivate their model gardens may have been wrong, but those who suggest today that the United States practice "self-commitment and self-containment" before trying to deal with others live in an anachronism. The old choice between isolation and involvement is dead; there remains only the purely academic choice between historical sleep and the dangerous life of a great power. The fact that the latter often seems a nightmare does not make escape into untroubled dreams the alternative.

It is significant that at the close of World War II the United States behaved as if the old choice still existed. It opted for a kind of disengagement that did not amount to isolation but behind which there was the expectation of a world without a bipolar struggle, or one in which other people's conflicts could be arbitrated by the United States. But bipolarity by definition rules out arbitration and entails conflict. On the world scene, Bertrand de Jouvenel's distinction between *dux* and *rex* is never really valid. In the nineteenth century the British *rex* had to behave as *dux* more often than theoreticians of the balance of power like to admit; in a bipolar world, there is a clash of *duces*, and no *rex*.[1] Consequently, when the nature of Soviet power and policy and the crumbling of British strength became obvious, the United States simply had to fill the vacuum. The freedom of choice President Truman had was strictly limited: it concerned the moment and the manner in which America's taking up the challenge would be demonstrated. Even in this respect, the margin of choice was narrowed by the development of the crisis in Greece. Thus it is true to see in the great decisions of 1947 supremely creative acts of statesmanship; but it is also true to describe America in Malraux's terms as the nation "that has won the greatest power in the world but not sought it." Rarely has freedom been more clearly the recognition of necessity, and statesmanship the imaginative exploitation of necessity. America rushed to those gates at which Soviet power was knocking. Part of the trouble, as we shall see, has been that so many unexpected challenges to America's power have appeared ever since on the Western side of the gates.

Among the various consequences of bipolarity, two deserve mention: one is the risk of general war; the other is the scramble for allies. Critics occasionally argue as if a specific wickedness of American policy-makers were responsible for the climate of tension and for "pactomania." But the dialectic of reciprocal fear, which accounts for both, appears whenever the game has only two major players. It is legitimate to ask whether each

[1] Bertrand de Jouvenel, *Sovereignty: An Inquiry into the Political Good* (Chicago: University of Chicago Press, 1957).

one does all he can to make the atmosphere less electric and to select only those allies worth being defended. In those respects there may indeed remain some freedom of choice, but it is a very limited freedom, both because bipolarity sets the stage for a pugnacious competition and because of other restraints to which we now turn.

A second fundamental constraint in the postwar international system is that system's ideological character. To make things worse, there are two ideological battles in progress. As is well known, the bipolar struggle is a contest for the minds of men at least as much as a fight for men, markets, resources, or space. What is at stake is how both domestic politics and the international order are to be organized. In any nonideological struggle (even if it is bipolar), pauses and compromises are much more likely, because their implications are less damaging to the players. In an ideological contest, the psychological repercussions of minor defeats, the use of temporary advantages as springboards, the symbolic nature of every test of will, and the unlimited character of the final objective (however limited the subject matter of a particular crisis) almost condemn the world political scene to being a desert without oases. Concessions do not disarm hostility, and may indeed infect the adversary with the exhilaration of success. Thus it becomes almost impossible (and not for domestic reasons alone) to recognize Red China. A small concession in Berlin may undo the whole tapestry; an East-German agent in an international control commission adds nothing to Soviet material power—his only value is symbolic— but this is precisely what the battle is about. In such a context, even mild conditions put by each camp to the signing of agreements with the other tend to be interpreted as death warrants. To ask that West Berlin stop being a teeming nest of subversive activities aimed at East Germany is tantamount to undermining the freedom of thought and speech that are the pride of the West. To ask that the Soviet Union stop bringing aid and comfort to Communist parties or guerrillas outside the Soviet camp is to ask the Communist bloc to give up the proselytizing that is its cement. In such a climate the traditional tricks of diplomacy (the neutralization or internationalization of certain areas, the political armistices that delineate spheres of influence) lose their justification. Domestic affairs cannot be insulated from the competition any more than specific areas can. As the old techniques become useless, new methods of intervention become unavoidable, and thus restraints and compulsions converge to decrease freedom of choice.

The other ideological contest, which opposes the anticolonial forces and their former masters, operates primarily as a restraint on the United States because of the link between the cold war and the nationalist revolution. The United States is not free to give full endorsement to this revolution, whereas the Soviet Union can do so; for, in the scramble for allies, the United States has lined up with all the colonial powers. Moreover, despite North American reluctance at considering United States-Latin American relations as in any way colonial, the danger of anticolonial nationalism reaching Latin America and hitting United States positions is not fictitious. Nor is the United States free to ignore or resist the winds of change, for nothing could be more calculated to turn them into hurricanes spreading Communism. This is particularly true in Latin America, for should the United States oppose all manifestations of nationalism aimed at American interests and influence there, the nationalists would have no place to turn to but Moscow, whereas African and Asian nationalists in revolt against Europe have a broader choice.

The two ideological conflicts have one important characteristic in common: asymmetry. One side is on the offensive, one on the defensive —and in both cases it is the West that is on the defensive. It takes only one nation to start a war; it takes only one camp to launch an ideological contest; the adversary has no choice but to pick up the challenge, however distasteful, unless he is resigned to defeat at the outset. The United States is an ideological contender by necessity rather than by choice: in the bipolar struggle, the United States "ideology" (to be examined later) consists of a set of views-on-things rather than of a doctrine (however vague) about the direction of history and rather than of instructions for pushing the world along its due course. In the anticolonial revolution the United States finds itself on the defensive, not because of its "public philosophy," but largely because this "philosophy," which is a set of anticolonial reflexes, is neutralized by America's alliances.

Such asymmetry immeasurably complicates America's problem of action. The United States must first try to gain some sort of initiative in the midst of a generally defensive strategy: in other words, all too often the site and the moment of the battle are selected by the other camp, and the United States' freedom of choice is more tactical than strategic. Second, whereas the side that is on the offensive can choose to provoke a limited and localized crisis, the United States cannot apply the traditional Cartesian method of subdividing the issue into its component parts so as to try to resolve them one by one; for such a method would lead to precisely the kind of piecemeal retreats that the adversary wants to impose. Third, because of the absence of a genuine national ideology, and because of the conflict between anticolonial feelings and colonial alliances, the way in which the United States can wage the battle for the minds of men remains strictly limited: characteristically, the proponents of a "forward strategy" do not do much more than ask for greater vigor in American propaganda activities—and there are other restraints that operate here.

The third basic aspect of the international system is the one most widely discussed: nuclear power. It is also one of the sharpest restraints with which great powers have ever had to cope. Does not the possession of the most formidable weapons in history increase the freedom of movement of its

possessors? Reality, for better or worse, is more complicated. Such possession is a prerequisite of great power status, but today, because of nuclear
weapons, the discretion of a great power is much more sharply limited
than before. A great power is like Baudelaire's albatross: *Ses ailes de géant
l'empêchent de voler*—because those wings are nuclear. It may be argued
retrospectively that in the days of its monopoly the United States had a
freedom of action that it wasted out of timidity; but in the age of nuclear
stalemate and nuclear plenty, surely the restraints on the actual use of
nuclear weapons are decisive.

What of the threat to use such weapons? If their invention has virtually
abolished certain kinds of war as rational instruments of foreign policy,
does not the possession of a nuclear arsenal increase the state's saber-
rattling possibilities in peacetime? Here two different restraints weigh on
the United States. First, the more the "balance of terror" tends toward
stability, the less the threat becomes credible. Indeed, we have reached
the stage when Europeans and Americans both wonder whether the threat
of a United States first strike against the Soviet Union, in the case of a
Soviet conventional attack in Europe and in the absence of a conventional
NATO army large enough to be a deterrent force all by itself, has not
ceased to be plausible. There may still be psychological advantages resulting from a militarily implausible threat, precisely because of the ideological
dimension of the contest; and the Soviet Union has shown (in 1956 at
the time of Suez or in 1961 for the "protection" of Cuba) that it was not
ready to throw away the benefits of bluff. Here is where the second handicap appears: it applies only to the United States, because of the asymmetry
I have discussed. A nation whose position in a contest is essentially defensive *can* use the *threat* of force defensively, for the protection of vital interests and stakes—indeed, it often *has* to resort to such a threat when only
the prospect of having to fight a battle may still deter the enemy. But a
defensive power finds it much more difficult to use saber-rattling imaginatively in order to put the enemy on the defensive. Not only does the threat
have little military credibility, but one way in which the defensive power
in an ideological contest can try to win the minds of men is to stress the
innocence of being on the defensive. The offensive power by definition
uses all possible techniques in order to push ahead: ideological appeals,
subversion, and also fear. The defensive power gains by appearing as the
mighty champion of the frightened. To frighten back has more drawbacks
than advantages.

One question may be raised—it has been raised many times. If these
are the disadvantages of the defensive, is the United States not free to
switch to the offensive? We must look for the last time at the way in
which the cards were distributed at the end of World War II. There
is no doubt that the challenge was cast by the Soviets and that Western
positions have been besieged (indeed, often conquered) either by the

Communists or by the nationalists in the underdeveloped countries. Nor is there any doubt that the West has nowhere tried to roll back the iron curtain. In order to preserve its position, the West will have to do infinitely more than sit and wait behind radar screens and barbed wire; but until and unless the world stops being bipolar and the Soviets' ideological drive loses its force, either because of domestic "thawing" or because of failure abroad, the basic conditions of the game will keep the United States in a defensive position vis-à-vis the Soviet Union.

Other restraints and necessities result from the rules of the game. For the United States, foreign policy in a bipolar, ideological, and nuclear contest raises four types of problems. First, there are sharp limits to United States freedom of action in East-West relations, owing to two kinds of asymmetry. On the one hand, the ideological asymmetry discussed above not only narrows the range of common interests; it also makes the translation of such interests into explicit agreements very difficult. The fundamental difference between the two political regimes is the major component of ideological asymmetry, and the main reason why this translation appears so unlikely. The most obvious example is the spectacular failure of attempts to get a Soviet-American consensus against nuclear war and nuclear diffusion expressed in any treaty. Soviet disarmament proposals are tactical constructs. They give propaganda advantages to the Soviets if they are rejected, and they would benefit the Soviet Union by destroying the barrage of Western force that keeps Russia away from Western Europe, and China from Formosa and Southeast Asia, should the proposals be adopted. United States schemes for disarmament and arms control tend to keep the Western barrage intact. They inevitably raise the formidable question of inspection, and they give a kind of priority to the problem of surprise attack, which is not really the Soviet major fear, since the likelihood of a United States switch to the military offensive is small.

Another example of the limits that ideological asymmetry imposes on American foreign policy concerns negotiation tactics. It is easy for the Soviet Union to start a diplomatic campaign with thoroughly unreasonable and outrageous demands, which will be gradually toned down in such a way that the outcome will be either no agreement at all, and consequently a Soviet possibility of reopening the matter at any time, or an agreement in which the Soviets will have made some gain. It is much more difficult for the United States, given its regime and the vision of world order it tries to promote, to retaliate with equally extreme suggestions. The Soviets can ask Western forces to get out of West Berlin. The best the West can do in return is to ask for a plebiscite in West and East Berlin. The Soviets can insist on a *troika* in the secretariats of international organizations. The range of United States alternatives goes from a flat "no" to some compromise.

The other limit imposed on the United States in East-West relations comes from geographical differences rather than ideological asymmetry. Even if nuclear diffusion made it easier for the United States and the Soviet Union to agree on formulas of arms control and disarmament that would be politically neutral, that is, would not conceal advantages won by one side, negotiators would still have to cope with the fact that they are not dealing with abstract units but with one land mass and one sea power. Even in the nuclear age of permeable territorial states, geography retains some importance: the United States in its struggle needs a minimum of bases and supporters outside the Western hemisphere in order to deploy its strength and to deter or stop the advances of Communist nations. Even if the contest were not an ideological one that makes compromises difficult, the geopolitical conditions would make it disadvantageous for the United States to let too many zones in the world be neutralized. In a thoroughly disarmed world, such a liability would disappear; but what is in question is not the bliss in the millennium, it is how one gets there. Geography restricts the range of concessions the United States can make in arms negotiations; the combination of geographical position and ideological defensive compels the United States to defend the allies it needs to contain the Soviet bloc. Once again, freedom of action is limited to a choice of scope and means within a context of necessity.

A second set of problems arises from the nature of American alliances. *Any* alliance restrains the freedom of movement of every partner, including the senior one. Not even the Soviet Union can sacrifice the interests of East Germany without damaging its own; it was much easier for an isolated Russia in 1939 to reverse its policy than it is now for the leader of the socialist camp. Yet an alliance of *autonomous* nations, however unequal in power, introduces even more stringent constraints on the senior partner when he is locked in a bipolar and ideological struggle. The Western alliances are of course the prime example: the United States may be preponderant, but in almost no place are the local leaders simply puppets manipulated by the United States. In the Soviet camp, the satellites are not autonomous, but China is. The senior partner wants and needs allies; should he disagree with them because they are getting tired of the struggle, to mistreat them would push them out of his camp, unless he were willing to use force against them, as the Soviets did in Hungary. It is hard to imagine the United States compelling a reluctant ally by force, unless a case could be made to show that this ally had already become the tool of Communism. The United States could put pressure on France to consent to German rearmament, but it could not compel France to ratify the European Defense Community.

Should the senior partner disagree with his ally because the latter resisted concessions the boss wanted to make to the common enemy, then the combination of a world struggle and of the "non-directive" nature of the alliance gives the weaker partner an almost unbeatable weapon. It is not only in the United Nations that the cold war reverses the traditional hierarchy between the weak and the strong. The blackmail of the weak who appeal to the spirit of the alliance has been one of the most serious restraints on United States freedom of movement; for the United States can literally do very little about it, unless the Soviets become cooperative. To coerce one ally in order to please the enemy is not the best way of keeping one's other allies. The United States cannot recognize East Germany as long as West Germany objects so strenuously that a United States dismissal of West German objections might destroy West German confidence in the alliance. It is false to say that in a bipolar struggle one's ally has "nowhere else to go." Nor can the United States compel Chiang to give up Quemoy and Matsu as long as the Chinese make it clear that they would interpret any concession as a sign of weakness and an incentive to push harder. Nor can the United States by itself even oblige Laotian right-wing forces to stop blocking the formation of a coalition government. If there is anything more startling than the failure of extremely strong United States pressures, it is the fact that what has finally coerced the Laotians is the Communist use of force. Whether it is in the United States' interest to have the *other* camp provide the means of compelling the Laotian allies of the United States is something else again. Hans Morgenthau has sharply criticized the United States' failure to impose its political will on its allies, but the limits are set by the nature of the competition and of the alliance, rather than by deficiencies of will on the part of the United States. The major complaint from the United States' allies has not been the absence of its leadership, except in the final phase of the second Eisenhower administration.

Often, precisely because of what is at stake in the East-West contest, "it is not wise to scrap alliances which it was unwise to form," or to evacuate bases that have lost their military usefulness (except if the nation on whose territory they are should ask for their removal). One is bound by one's commitments; one is committed even by one's mistakes. The United States may be free to avoid new and mistaken entanglements in the future. It is not free to tear out of its scrapbook the political misjudgments of the past. Nor is it free to avoid entanglements altogether (the mediocrity of SEATO as an instrument of foreign policy has led, not to a United States withdrawal from the defense of Southeast Asia, but to a downgrading of this particular alliance in favor of direct United States involvement). Once more, freedom of action shrinks to mitigating the bitterness of the unavoidable.

A third set of limits greatly resembles the previous ones, but the degree of inevitability strikes me as much lower. I am referring to the restraints the United Nations imposes on United States foreign policy. As in the case of American alliances, the limits result from one's entanglements. But whereas the need for alliances is questioned only by utopians, the need to let the United Nations be a major determinant of United States foreign policy is much more debatable. This is not the place to pursue the debate, but a few statements are in order. First, it is quite impossible for the United States to ignore the United Nations. In the recent contest between East and West, one that sharply curtails military conquest, the allegiance of the "third world" (so spectacularly represented in the United Nations) is an important stake. Also, the principles of the Charter reflect the vision of world order that Western nations propose to the rest of the world. In other words, the United States cannot bypass the United Nations as a forum and as an ideal; nor can the United States let the Soviet Union turn the United Nations into an instrument of Communist strategy. The United Nations cannot help being a stake.

Second, however, it is not at all clear that the United States is obliged to try to use the United Nations as an instrument of its own: for if the stake becomes a force, this force may well have a will that conflicts with United States interests or is plagued by internal dissensions and institutional weaknesses, and to ameliorate these may require of the United States more energy and more concessions than the benefits to be derived from such a force would justify. My point is that at various times in the past the United States has deliberately chosen to increase the role of the United Nations as a force in world affairs and that, although the United States' freedom of choice in the future persists, precedents have narrowed it, because of the same dialectic of commitment to which I have referred in the case of alliances. It may have been unwise at times to try to win friends and influence people through the one mechanism in which those friends and people are numerically in command; for in the attempt one puts a real, not just a paper, club into their hands. Having done it so often, however, to reverse the policy in the hope of regaining some of the influence one has already lost may be a sure way to undermine drastically the influence one still has.

A final set of limits appears in United States relations with other non-Communist nations in general and with the underdeveloped countries in particular. It is another consequence of ideological asymmetry, and a restraint for which it would be foolish to blame the United States. Almost by definition, the United States must deal with officialdom. Even when the United States believes that officialdom is corrupt, digs its own grave, and endangers the position of the West by throwing reformers into the arms of the Communists, it is officialdom that the United States must convince. This restraint can be traced to liberalism only if one makes it clear that liberalism here means, not the Wilsonian view of world politics, but what is the essence of Western political regimes and of Western international law. It is not only the United States that has "failed" to organize abroad parties that would be instruments of Western interests. To say that the United States must deal with officialdom does not mean that the United States cannot keep in touch with opposition parties, or encourage reformers, or frown officially on gravediggers in power. Indeed, it may well be that the United States has been much too shy in all these respects. But even if the United States became a virtuoso in the difficult art of combining diplomatic correctness with subdiplomatic manipulation, there would still remain sharp limits to what a nontotalitarian power can achieve. There is more than a difference of degree between the Central Intelligence Agency and the Communist International.

Given such a limit, one should avoid two mistakes of judgment. When, behind the gates to which America rushed in 1947–1948, political developments destroyed or weakened the hold Western nations had kept on Asia and Africa, when change began to shake Latin America as well, Americans complained about having "lost" areas that were never theirs to lose. It would be quite as serious a mistake for them to believe that, because France or Britain has gone from many areas, United States influence will spread more easily there: for better and for worse, America's instruments of influence are limited. The limits are set by the international system; the expectations from and disappointments with American omnipotence are peculiarly American.

Blinders, Reflexes, Hedges

The prism through which every nation looks at the outside world has been shaped by its own experience. For a policy-maker, there is as much truth in T. S. Eliot's "Hell is ourselves," as in Sartre's "L'enfer, c'est les autres." The way in which the same challenge (say, decolonization) is met by France or Britain tells us much more about the domestic values and political habits of each nation than about the particular external circumstances that distinguish the French from the British problem. Any study of foreign policy that sets goals which cannot be reached as long as the nation has not changed its skin and its soul is of limited worth. As in the case of every political community, the limits set by the experience of the United States can be divided into two kinds: those that derive from the nation's political style and culture, and those that result from its system of government.

The *political style* of the United States has been subjected in recent years to so many searching investigations that one need only restate the familiar. I do not suggest that the elements of this style are immutable; the way in which they have been affected by America's involvement in postwar world affairs has been shown often and well. However, there always remains a lag between age-old blinders and reflexes, and new (especially external) pressures that make them obsolete. To the extent of this lag, the heritage of the past remains. Often, responses that at first might appear to be unprecedented can be shown to be nothing but the application of the old habits of thought and action to a new problem. The "axiomatic" policies analyzed by Ernest May are the instinctive re-actions that express the nation's style.

There are three elements in America's experience that are relevant to its foreign policy. One is America's liberalism; the second, what one may call American conservatism; the third, America's peculiar experience in past world politics. The most familiar ingredient is the liberal tradition, well documented by Louis Hartz. It continues to operate as a filter of American attitudes in a variety of ways, which can be summed up as the "sin of transposition," the mistake of projecting into world affairs a vision of public life derived from the experience of the Liberal *Rechtsstaat*. What flows from such a vision is the expectancy of ultimate accommodation: even the "realist" school of international politics places in diplomacy and compromise a faith that, given the present international system, might be called *l'espoir des désespérés*, or the last straw of the tough-minded liberal. A liberal community is one in which rifts can be reconciled, or at least one in which the contenders entrust the procedures of government with the task of finding a formula for coexistence; diplomacy is supposed to be its international equivalent, and negotiated agreements tend to be seen in the same light as laws. . . .

The depreciation of the hidden role of force in a liberal community en-tails a depreciation of other, more subtle forms of coercion as well, and a tendency to underrate the element of struggle that persists in any political system. The basic tenets of liberal faith remain the gradual triumph of public opinion, the conciliating and unifying role of trade and industry, the civilizing and refining of power through law and legal institutions. All those tenets have left their mark on the American approach to foreign policy. They do not operate as absolute obstacles to a more effective ap-proach, but as blinders that always take years and the successive shocks of unfortunate experiences to discard. The first mental reflex consists in trusting the General Assembly as the expression of world public opinion; in hoping that economic aid will produce social and political progress in stability; in believing that deep conflicts of interest can be transcended through institutional changes (multiplying Peace Observation Committees in the United Nations or consultation committees in NATO); in being convinced that a dictator such as Castro simply cannot be supported by his people and that he is merely a vermin which it is legitimate to de-stroy by force. Gradually, one learns; but the pattern is always the same— illusions are not so much lost as frustrated. The normal expectation is problemless peace or uninhibited war; but experience tells us that peace is full of troubles and that war must be limited if the world is to survive; to the liberal, however, experience is a bitter pill.

•   •   •

The way of life reflects a domestic experience that is so singular that it amounts to "a severance of communications" between the United States and the outside world. The elements of this experience are well known. There is a long tradition of equality in affluence that has made class struggle *à l'européenne* unnecessary. But it has also made it difficult for Americans to understand and sympathize with such struggles, and it has reduced the possibilities of America's "people of plenty" for influencing the underprivileged. The amount of available aid is one thing; the amount of influence, quite another.

The United States has a long experience in social and political integration, which its social science reflects only too well. In many other countries there are both an evidence of ideological conflict and a discontinuity between society and the political system; integration may or may not be the goal, but it is not the norm. United States' policy-scientists and policy-makers have few answers to the problem of integrating dislocated communities, not only because of the limits on America's capacity for intervening in the domestic affairs of others, but also because of a lack of intellectual familiarity; it is difficult for Americans to understand an ideological mode of argument, unless it be the liberal one that plays conflict down, not up.

Nothing has contributed more to the "severance of communications" than the fact that is taken to be the very touchstone of conservatism almost anywhere else: the favor shown private interests, especially business interests, because their part in the making of America has on the whole been beneficial. This attitude has weighed on American foreign policy in two ways. On the one hand, it has broadened the intellectual gap discussed above, since the United States' experience has been so different from that of Europe, Latin America, or Asia, where private interests (even national ones) have often served only to preserve and increase the privileges of the elite. On the other hand, the expansion of United States' business interests abroad creates a unique problem. No Western government reacts with pleasure to the expropriation of Western private interests by nations that see in those firms either instruments of colonial exploitation or obstacles to domestic planning. But the link in the United States between those interests and the government is stronger than in any other country. This is so, not because of any "power elite" conspiracy on Populist or Marxist lines, but because of the material importance of those interests abroad, and as a result of the national ethos. Here again, we are faced with a limit which is flexible, as increasing official United States support for "socialistic" governments indicates. Yet, especially in its relations with Latin America, the United States reflex continues to be one of hostility to nationalizations, and however fast the Executive may learn, Congress in this respect serves as the thermos bottle of American resentment. It is too much to expect the United States to swallow its ethos and to accept expropriations gracefully, but since these are quite likely, the United States faces in this area one of its major difficulties.

It was fashionable not very long ago to ask for a renewal of the United States' national purpose. Even if America begins to "move again," it is unlikely that the gap between its domestic experience and that of the outside world will be closed. If a "new America" merely strengthens its tradition of equality in plenty, then the gap may even be widened. It is the domestic success of their way of life which makes Americans conservative amid a revolutionary world—and the goal of the new frontier is certainly not to impair this success in order to make them less so.

The other aspect of the Americans' conservatism concerns their approach to the solution of problems, including those problems of foreign policy which their way of life throws up. It may be called, in Walt W. Rostow's terms, "the operator's way," or it may be termed pragmatism; I would call it the engineering approach. For it is a peculiar kind of operation or pragmatism. It is not steeped in history or in psychology, which are sciences (or arts) of the complex and the uncertain. It too is reflected in American social science, with its passionate search for general laws, its preference for deductive models over inductive generalizations from history, its quest for mathematical formulas that tend to give a reassuring sense of certainty even when they measure the immeasurable.

The engineering approach has three drawbacks that operate as blinders on United States policy-making. First, the drive toward certainty is often carried too far. Either it distorts the importance of those limited areas of policy in which calculable certainty appears to exist (hence the enthusiasm for strategy in a nation that is so reluctant to initiate the use of force). Or else the quest is carried into areas where there is no certainty. Even military policy is too tricky a matter to be left to IBM machines, however well-fed with variables. In a world in which irrationality exists, the search for a thoroughly rational policy is both a mistake and a delusion. As Aron has written, in the game of international politics, whose objectives are multiple and whose rules are uncertain, there may be *reasonable* policies and *unreasonable* ones, but there cannot be one *rational* conceptualization, least of all when the game itself, because of nuclear weapons, has become unreasonable. Oversimplification and the overrating of purely technical but calculable elements over intangible ones are the by-products of a misplaced faith in human engineering.

A second flaw is discontinuity. The engineering approach is a piecemeal approach; one takes up the problems as they come. If game theory reflects the longing for certitude, decision-making theory expresses this other aspect of pragmatism. It strikes me even more as numbing. It concentrates thought and research on the immediate, which is not always the essential. For there is a double price one has to pay for waiting until the problems appear: first, one must repair what one has not prevented—the price of tardiness; second, there is the price of retrospective reflection—the remedies one discovers for the future are all too often patterned on the crisis that gave impetus to the search, a crisis not at all certain to be recurrent. Studies of limited war flourished after Korea. It is only now that one pays sufficient attention all of a sudden to "counter-insurgency." The tendency of United States newspapers to explore foreign countries after a crisis has exploded is characteristic. The "discovery" of Africa since 1960 (by the mass media as well as by the policy-makers) may be explained in part by the fact that the dark continent had been the preserve of our allies. The late discovery of Latin America after Castro has no similar justification.

Discontinuity also leads to the improvisation of measures, or to the accumulation of *ad hoc* researches, which so busily focus on the issue at hand that they neglect the deeper structural causes of the momentary trouble. The tendency to present foreign aid in terms of a shopping list of separate and limited projects obscures the fact that there are few areas of policy in which success requires more time and depends on more prerequisites which the donor cannot provide.

The third drawback of the engineering approach is the American tendency to support the status quo—not because of sympathy with it, but because it would take far more time to change it than the emergency allows the policy-maker. Franklin Roosevelt's deal with Darlan and United States policy in South Vietnam since 1954 are good examples. Foreign observers often make the mistake of reading an ideological conservatism into such behavior. All that is involved is a kind of scientific conservatism—the engineer who is asked to build a bridge does not start by questioning whether there is a need for it.

Consequently, a sharp contrast appears between the American approach to foreign policy and, say, the style of General de Gaulle. The latter sees in policy a continuous process. He has a *vision* (more or less debatable) of the distant future, of Europe's role in it, of France's rank, etc. He has what one might call middle-range *objectives*, such as the Algerian settlement, the organized political cooperation of Europe, an autonomous French military policy. The *tactics* to be adopted toward those objectives depend on the circumstances, and are sometimes quite baffling; but the objectives are relentlessly pursued. In the case of United States policy, the observer often has the feeling that there is an enormous gap between the over-all vague vision of a world consonant with United States values and interests, and the daily tactical maneuvers. From time to time, a grand announcement seems to mark a milestone: at best, it is a program, such as Lend-Lease and the Marshall Plan, which sets a definite objective and can become the object of a quasi-military campaign. At worst, it is an empty gesture—and as Hedley Bull has observed, a policy of gestures is the opposite from international politics. Too often United States policy gives the impression of men who worry about what to do tomorrow, and who also know what they would like the world to be at the end of its political history. Their ideals have little operational (though high inspirational) value; their operational concepts are of excessively short-range value. To take each issue "on its merits" may not be the best way of doing it justice; "problem solving" may be the worst approach to the solution of problems, although it may be the most drastic method of discovering how intractable they are.

The last element in the American experience is separate from United States liberalism and conservatism, although it has accentuated their impact on the American approach to foreign policy. I refer to the unique position of the United States in world affairs before World War II. The United States was not a major power in the game; but it was not a stake either. Usually it was not deeply involved; but when it wanted to act on the world stage, its geographic position and its power allowed it to respond to challenges in what Hans Morgenthau has called "unequivocal acts" depending on the United States alone. Two attitudes have resulted from such a happy course. One is impatience—a lack of understanding of the virtue of time, a perpetual fear of the fragility and instability of certain situations, which makes many Americans want to destroy them right away because they may be undermined in the long run (for instance, West Germany's links to the West). American liberalism and American conservatism are equally marked by such impatience, which reinforces both the liberal desire to reach the Erewhon of reconciliation as soon as possible and also the conservative tendency to plan piecemeal solutions to be enforced by brushing aside all human obstacles. The other attitude is the familiar faith in American omnipotence. When impatience and the illusion of omnipotence coincide, the result is the relentless drive to rearm Germany in 1950–1951, or the Cuban invasion in 1961.

United States liberalism hampers its foreign policy because it sees the world in colors much rosier than those the world displays. United States conservatism limits its foreign policy because it makes the world look infinitely less complex than it is. The heritage of America's sheltered past weighs on United States foreign policy because it really amounts to wishing the world away whenever its imperfections and complications become too blatant. It can be argued that the Korean War or the handling of the Congo crisis indicates how much United States policy-makers have learned. However, public opinion has shown alarming signs of impatience and of a continuing belief in omnipotence, and the policy-makers are caught between what they know of the outside world and their fears of domestic reactions. For there are other handicaps still.

Thus we reach the obstacles provided by *the political system*. This is not the place to discuss to what extent any democratic system restricts the freedom of action of foreign policy-makers. (Indeed, at such a level of generality the subject is not of great interest.) But three characteristics of United States democracy curtail this freedom in important ways.

A first one has already been mentioned: the amorphous brooding omnipresence of public opinion in the democratic sky. Some very different generalizations about public opinion in democracies seem to be valid. One, it is quite malleable and responsive to strong leadership; in this respect, it is an opportunity rather than a restraint. Second, democratic leaders tend to overestimate the conservatism of public opinion and to exaggerate the gap between what they would like to do and what they believe the public will accept—be it a leap into supranationality, or a retreat from Empire, or the recognition of Red China. Third, even with strong leadership, whenever the gap between traditional expectations and present experience widens so that feelings of frustration or humiliation spring from it, public opinion tends to be not a mere wind to which leaders would be wise to bend, but a real twister. First, it destroys the leaders when they are blamed for disappointments, rarely of their own making; then it continues to inhibit the formulation of foreign policy long after the hurricane has vanished. What happened in the United States in the last years of Mr. Acheson's tenure and in the early years of Mr. Dulles' has been well documented. When such a hurricane develops, it becomes impossible for the policy-makers to pursue the objectives that ought to be pursued, and necessary to state objectives that obviously cannot be achieved.

A second characteristic is the presidential system. The fact that the Chief Executive is elected by universal suffrage and that he normally converses not with the nation's representatives but with the public which elects him is of considerable importance to the formulation and presentation of foreign policy. A parliamentary premier addresses the nation and converses with parliament. The President converses with the public and addresses Congress. The advantages are different in each case. In the former, the more or less brute reactions of public opinion are filtered through parliament; but when parliament, as under the French Fourth Republic, expresses only too articulately the divisions of the nation, foreign policy may be paralyzed. At any rate, the premium is on moderation, the stress, on continuity. The American system reinforces (and has to a large extent engendered) the flaws of the American style; here the emphasis is on the dramatic and the new. Even though opportunities for undiluted leadership are greater in a system in which the link between the Executive and the people is direct, inevitably much of the effort of the leader goes into the creation of an image instead of into the definition of the substance. The more intractable are the external limits imposed by the international system, the more frantic is the attempt to make shifts in tone, switches in style, and changes in personality pass for revolutions in policy. The temptation would be less irresistible if the trend of the political system did not slope in that very direction.

The habit of expecting the dramatic perpetuates not only the panting rhythm of United States policy-making but also the illusion of omnipotence, as well as national impatience; consequently, the lag between public reflexes and external realities persists. The leader's hunch that public opinion remains sluggishly far behind him, therefore, remains justified; and whenever the public realizes that the image mirrors nothing and that the new plan is a gimmick, a crisis of frustration assails foreign policy. It is a vicious circle. As such, it encourages another effect of the Presidential system: the tendency to lead, not through rational argument (too easily dismissed as an academic exercise which passes above the voters' heads), but through inspirational exhortation. Pulpitry replaces education; sermons substitute for explanations. Persuasion through ritual formulas and the invocation of national (or party) clichés is easier than persuasion through demonstration, which other systems of leadership often require. Not only does the necessary adjustment of the political culture to a revolutionary world thus get slowed down. This style of leadership also produces an insidious self-intoxication of the leaders. It is more usual in books about politics than in politics itself that the leaders are both cynical enough to make the distinction between rhetoric and conviction, and humble enough to realize that what they say is trash. Parliamentary leaders may be cynical, but they are rarely humble. Presidents are sometimes modest men, but hardly ever cynics.

The stress on image and innovation appears as a compensation, and often as a pitiful cover, for a third feature of America's political system: the dispersion of governmental power. It makes the definition of a substantive policy an ordeal that would have tried the patience of Penelope, and rapid innovation is an outcome so unlikely that it appears only in major emergencies. New teams of men come to Washington full of long repressed convictions about how to make foreign policy "right," or overflowing with ideas about how to make foreign policy sophisticated. Their emotions and their ideas soon get caught in the "thorns and branches and twigs of the governmental tree." As a result, continuity in the substance of policies is preserved, but discontinuity in handling issues is not eliminated.

It is not in the United States that Parkinson's law was conceived; but the United States combines three forms of proliferation. There is the fragmentation of power which the separation between the Presidency and Congress entails. There is the dispersion that results from the increasing importance of the House of Representatives in the control of foreign policy. There is the mushrooming of Executive agencies, which insist on participating in the definition of foreign policy—sometimes on an equal footing with the State Department, often on behalf of particular domestic-interest groups in their constituency. If one also takes into account the proliferation of experts who work as consultants for all those institutions, and the press (which is both a sounding board for the various organs and a power of its own), one gets an awe-inspiring picture of government by interagency and interbranch compacts, government by leaks and subcontracts.

The search for a consensus is one of the more damaging by-products of such fragmentation. It involves an erosion of substance and the wearing out of initiatives, ideas, and people. It has its advantages—what one might call, with a backward glance at the Republicans who came to power after twenty years in 1952, the taming of the wild. But the disadvantages have also become apparent. It is not only innovation that is made difficult— after all, the constraints of the international system do not allow much of it; it is precisely the concern for the middle-range objectives, half-way between distant dreams and daily diligence, which gets corroded. Finally, even the margins of choice that the external system and the domestic culture still provide are interpreted restrictively. There have been recent examples of the taming of the shrewd.

Another by-product affects less directly the substance of policy, and more obviously its presentation: there is a necessity for talking different languages to the different "publics," such as the electorate, the Congress, individual foreign nations, and foreign dignitaries within the United Nations. The resulting confusion may not impair the judgment of the policy-maker, who is usually aware of which is substance and which is wrapping. Yet, by increasing at times the suspiciousness of Congress, or the reluctance of other nations to accept United States policies, such a wealth of communications may result in no communication at all; for it is likely that the various listeners will compare notes at some point. The dilemma in which the policy-maker finds himself is embarrassing: if he tries for a consensus among the various publics, the policy he formulates may well be so pale as to be ineffective; if he attempts to push a more daring one but cannot sell it to all under the same cover, he may find no buyers.

Both the search for consensus and the concern for presentation heighten the tendency to discuss issues, not so much intrinsically as in terms of personalities. The more fragmented the system of power, the more the political universe becomes a stock market of reputations and influence. The merits on which problems are tackled become the merits of the men engaged in policy-making, and those men represent not so much ideas as tangible bits and pieces of power.

II

The Policy-Making Environment

INTRODUCTION

In his book, *The Public Philosophy,* Walter Lippmann laments what he feels to be one of the great evils of the time—the domination of government by mass opinion. "The record shows that the people of the democracies, having become sovereign in this century, have made it increasingly difficult for their governments to prepare properly for war or to make peace." [1] When public opinion has been inattentive, responsible officials have been able to promote wise policies, but as public opinion becomes aroused democratic officials "have been compelled to make the big mistakes that public opinion has insisted upon." [2]

A quite different and more flattering evaluation of the role of public opinion is offered by W. W. Rostow.

> The essence of what was done on occasions such as the Lend-Lease or Marshall Plan debates is precisely the opposite of what one would deduce from the literature of pessimism on democracy and foreign affairs. The key to action lay not in insulating a knowledgeable elite from popular pressure but in a widespread sharing of responsibility for the nation's decision. [3]

If the role of public opinion in the foreign policy process is to be understood, however, assertion must be supplanted by empirical data and analysis. The pioneer in this field was Gabriel Almond. His book, *The American People and Foreign Policy,* [4] was one of the first serious

---

[1] Walter Lippmann, *The Public Philosophy* (Boston: Little, Brown, 1955), p. 24.
[2] *Ibid.*
[3] W. W. Rostow, *The United States in the World Arena* (New York: Harper & Row, 1960), pp. 509–510.
[4] Gabriel Almond, *The American People and Foreign Policy* (New York: Harcourt, Brace, 1950).

efforts to illuminate the way that public opinion related to foreign policy. Almond introduced the notion of the "attentive public," distinguished four different types of elites, stressed the importance of "mood" in analyzing public opinion, and suggested the way that these and other elements might be thought of as working together.

James N. Rosenau in *Public Opinion and Foreign Policy* and *National Leadership and Foreign Policy* [5] carried the analysis somewhat farther. He tried to make operative the concepts of "mass public," "attentive public," and "opinion-making public." He also distinguished the opinion-making process from the opinion-submitting process and suggested a variety of possible patterns of opinion flow.

Lippmann implies that the public has a more or less continuing influence over foreign policy, while the picture that emerges from the writings of Almond and Rosenau is that of a general public that participates in foreign policy-making only in indirect and passive ways. The conflict between these opposed views becomes less sharp, however, as soon as one distinguishes different levels in the generality of the issue involved. On issues of first importance—Marshall Plan, attitude toward the Soviet Union, participation in the U.N.—decision-makers do not really have the option of side-stepping a debate. Without the development of a substantial body of supporting opinion any new policy would necessarily be tentative and liable to later repudiation. These periodic "great debates" establish the framework within which lesser policy issues are determined. After a consensus has been developed on the major outlines of foreign policy, the decision-makers will normally have a degree of freedom of action on issues of second-level importance and even greater freedom on tertiary issues. The extent to which the mass public participates in foreign policy decision-making, therefore, depends on the type of issue referred to.

However much Lippmann, Almond, and Rosenau may differ on the question of the influence the public *does* have, all appear agreed that it *ought not* to have a significant influence. In Rosenau's words:

> On the rare occasions when it does awaken from its slumber, the mass public, being no more informed than previously, is impulsive, unstable, unreasoning, unpredictable, capable of shifting direction or of going in several contradictory directions at the same time. . . . Instability and irrationality enter the policy-making process as both decision-makers and opinion-makers seek to cope with the changing moods and tempo of mass opinion. Hence it would seem that, given these conditions as the alternative to indifference, the

[5] James N. Rosenau, *Public Opinion and Foreign Policy* (New York: Random House, 1961); *National Leadership and Foreign Policy* (Princeton, N.J.: Princeton University Press, 1963).

prevalence of the mass public's passive mood introduces a factor of stability into the foreign policy-making process.[6]

A determination of the proper role of the public in foreign policy is usually based partly on an interpretation of the public's performance of this role in the past and partly on sheer preference. There seems to be as much evidence supporting the optimists' position as the pessimists', and when analysts divide sharply on the merits of the public's participation, we can usually assume that they have slid gently from the empirical into the normative realm on this question. The dispute is often somewhat artificial in the terms in which it is argued. How effective a role one judges the public to have played over the past two decades, let us say, depends on what areas one chooses to examine. When the public became involved in lesser issues it did not cover itself with glory, and would have been better advised to have left these matters to the professionals. On broad issues, however, the record of the public is defensible.

If there has been a distinct shortage of analytic and empirical research on the role of the public in the making of foreign policy, the situation has been only slightly better as regards the role of organized interest groups. The belief that interest groups play a key part in the making of foreign policy, and perhaps a commanding part, has been accepted as conventional wisdom by a great many Americans. An isolated example of interest-group influence, perhaps in a restricted field, will be used to justify broad generalizations about the role of interest groups across the entire foreign policy spectrum.

Academic writing is also prone to accept this belief and too often overlooks the vast realm in which foreign-policy makers move with relatively little restriction. There are countless issues concerning which organized interest groups have a negligible influence. For this reason, it is particularly important that the questions raised by Bernard Cohen, in his pamphlet on "The Influence of Non-Governmental Groups on Foreign Policy," be brought to the forefront.

One area that needs research relates to the communications of organized interest groups. How effective is the access of this or that group to the decision-making process? What facilitates and what impedes access? What is the relative advantage of access at one point compared to access at another point? Under what conditions can access be translated into genuine influence on the decision-making process?

Communication is, of course, vital to the operation of virtually every aspect of the making of foreign policy. Foreign-policy making might, indeed, be approached as a study of communication. It is not possible to

[6] James N. Rosenau, *Public Opinion and Foreign Policy* (New York: Random House, 1961), pp. 36–37.

examine all aspects of the complex pattern of communications affecting foreign policy, but the vital role of the press must certainly be noted. The role of the press in Washington, D.C., is of particular interest.

The individual concern with the making of foreign policy lives amidst a flow of incoming messages dealing with the news of the world. These messages, concerning events abroad and in the United States, help shape the way that he will view the unfolding picture. By reacting in simple or complex ways to this flow of information and interpretation, policy-makers determine the initiatives and responses that will be used to meet the changing situation.

The newspaper is in many cases the most important medium by which these events are brought to the policy-maker. The press serves as a communication channel that supplements official channels and sometimes ranks with the latter in importance. Since virtually everyone in Washington associated with foreign policy reads *The Washington Post* or *The New York Times,* or both, these newspapers can convey information throughout the city far more effectively than could any town crier. These newspapers provide a common basis of assumed fact and a common body of interpretation. An emerging policy, a shifting outlook, a changed personal relationship is telegraphed through the reaches of the bureaucracy and the committees of Congress by breakfast time. To the neophyte, to be sure, little may be conveyed beyond the sheer facts, but to the initiate the same pages may say a great deal. It is a form of esoteric communication.

> These papers are, in effect, an internal system of foreign policy communication in a widely decentralized policy-making structure. These are the channels through which the official participants in the process talk to and debate with one another, reasonably rapidly and in a way that lets interested third parties know what has been said.[7]

If one thinks of the Washington press as somewhat analogous to a central nervous system, as Cohen goes on to suggest, it is easier to understand the remarkable access to decision-makers that certain syndicated columnists have. A significant column written by Walter Lippmann, James Reston, or Joseph Alsop on Monday will have been discussed throughout Washington by noon Tuesday. No one within the formal policy-making structure, including the President, has a comparable opportunity to present his views to the assembled policy-makers day in and day out.

The press can be used for an almost limitless variety of purposes—to punish, to reward, to threaten, to inform, to convince, and to raise doubt.

[7] Bernard C. Cohen, "The Present and the Press," *World Politics,* **XIII** (October 1960), p. 172.

Because it offers an unparalleled opportunity for communication, individuals and organizations wishing to influence some aspect of foreign policy will seek to use it on a continuing or recurring basis. Some groups, agencies, and individuals find it easier to use the press than do others, but on the whole the press is remarkably accessible. No group possesses a monopoly of access.

Since an important aspect of the President's leadership task is persuasion, it is natural that he should take particular pains to use the news media as an instrument of his leadership. During the first two years of the Kennedy Administration the relationship between President and press was particularly close. There were perhaps a dozen newsmen who had easy access to the President, and a number of background stories that were attributed to "authoritative administration sources" had the President as the real source. So close was this relationship that some observers felt the Washington press was on its way to becoming a public relations adjunct of the Administration. They argued that this endangered the traditional role of the press as critic. By the time of the President's assassination in November 1963, however, the honeymoon between President and press was already drawing to a close and a more normal relationship was being developed.

The noisy little debate early in 1963 over the "management of the news" must be seen against the background of Presidential success in aligning press support. When Assistant Secretary of Defense for Public Affairs Arthur Sylvester declared during the Cuban missile crisis that "news flowing from actions taken by the government is part of the weaponry" of the government, there was an outcry in Congress. Presumably the Congressmen who were troubled by this statement had never themselves released news with an eye to the effect it might have on an audience. The error lay not in the way the news was handled but in an official acknowledgment of the policy underlying its handling. Mr. Sylvester disturbed the illusion that there was a real choice between managed news (bad) and unmanaged news (good).

That cannot possibly be the real choice, since "news" does not gather itself, write itself, release itself, interpret itself, print itself, and give itself front- or back-page treatment. It is not a product that can be advertised as "untouched by human hands." The relevant questions are: How much management? By whom? In accordance with what principles? And with what purposes in mind?

Anything that was said by an official spokesman to the American people about the Cuban crisis was certain to be overheard by those abroad. A spokesman would be foolhardy if he did not realize this and take it into account in calculating what he was to say. When an information officer for a governmental agency distributes a news release to reporters, as is done scores of times every day, he is trying to manage the news. That is his job. He is employed to sell the agency and its program to the press, the public, and Congress and the rest of the Administration. His employer has a vested interest in what is released and how and when it is released. Only if the information officer felt his hand was being forced would he normally release information that would harm his agency or present it in an unfavorable light. The danger is not that news will be "managed," for that is unavoidable, but that it will be managed in too zealous and shortsighted a manner. Officials might be so intent on the interests of the agency they could lose sight of a more inclusive interest, such as that of the Administration as a whole or the national interest.

The problem of managed news should not be debated in the abstract but should be viewed in the light of an opposite and, to some extent, off-setting problem. The American government normally operates in a gold-fish bowl. News is the livelihood of Washington newsmen, and prestige is acquired by those who are the most successful in the competitive effort to discover the news before it happens. Power is fragmented in Washington; hence when several hundred energetic and knowledgeable men are turned loose on the city with a license to hunt out emerging policies, the problem is as often one of maintaining sufficient secrecy as it is of maintaining too much secrecy.

Sometimes the lines are nicely drawn, with the bureaucracy mobilized to protect its secrets and with the press trying to ferret them out. More often, however, the bureaucracy is not monolithic. Policy often emerges from inter-agency or intra-agency combat, so that on almost any policy issue one can assume there is a dissident bureaucratic element that feels the policy is unwise. Given the accessibility of the press, the discontented are often tempted to try to use the press, to "manage" it, in an effort to win the dispute. A battle that cannot be won within the confines of the Executive Branch may take on a different appearance if the arena of combat is enlarged to include Congress, the opinion elites, and non-governmental organizations. The first shot in the battle might take the form of a "leak" of information favorable or unfavorable to the project in question.

To speak of groups and individuals "using" the press must not be understood to imply that the press is itself inert. Those who are associated with the press—the foreign press corps, syndicated columnists, reporters for weeklies, wire service reporters, those who work for the Washington bureaus of various papers, and a variety of special reporters—are not passive observers of the foreign policy scene. If others try to manage the news, the press manages the news whether they try to or not. The net result of its operation may be to give greater prominence to one program than another, to support one policy and undermine another, to present one set of facts accurately and to distort another, and to favor one individual over another. The extremely favorable press reaction to Senator Vandenberg's first tentative postwar moves away from isolation apparently encouraged him to move farther in this direction. The interest of newsmen in the Marshall Plan and their treatment of it helped create a body of opinion in favor of a foreign aid program. The fascination of the press with Senator McCarthy helped create McCarthyism with all its baneful affects on foreign policy. The lukewarm feelings of many newsmen toward Richard Nixon and their enthusiasm for John Kennedy undoubtedly had an effect on the 1960 election.

If the press treats an issue as important over a period of time it may make that issue important. Its power in this respect is not unlimited, however. There are some matters that the public is unlikely to become aroused about regardless of their treatment by the press. Conversely, newsmen might play down an event, and yet that event might be news despite everything they could do. The press influences the thinking of the various publics, but it operates against the background of a reservoir of pre-existing attitudes and concerns. A great deal remains to be learned about the role of the press in foreign policy, but books such as Bernard Cohen's *The Press and Foreign Policy* [8] and Douglass Cater's *The Fourth Branch of Government* [9] have carried analysis a long step forward.

Press, nongovernmental organizations, elites of one kind and another, the attentive public, mass public—all are parts of the environment in which foreign policy is produced. Indeed, their connection with foreign policy is sometimes so intimate that they become a part of the process itself and not merely part of the environment.

[8] Bernard Cohen, *The Press and Foreign Policy* (Princeton, N.J.: Princeton University Press, 1963).

[9] Douglass Cater, *The Fourth Branch of Government* (Boston: Houghton Mifflin, 1959).

Public Opinion, Opinion-Makers, and Foreign Policy

Gabriel A. Almond
AMERICAN CHARACTER AND FOREIGN POLICY

ATTITUDES and opinions toward foreign policy questions are not only to be understood as responses to objective problems and situations, but as conditioned by culturally imposed qualities of character. These largely unconscious patterns of reaction and behavior strongly influence the perception, selection, and evaluation of political reality. At the level of mass opinion these "psycho-cultural" characteristics condition patterns of thought and mood on foreign policy problems. At the elite level they affect patterns of policy-making. . . .

1. *General Value Orientation.* The characteristic American value orientation would appear to consist of the following interrelated traits.

a. The degree of atomization in the United States is perhaps greater than in any other culture. The American is primarily concerned with "private" values, as distinguished from social-group, political, or religious-moral values. His concern with private, worldly success is his most absorbing aim. In this regard it may be suggested by way of hypothesis that in other cultures there is a greater stress on corporate loyalties and values and a greater personal involvement with political issues or with other-worldly religious values.

b. The "attachment" of the American to his private values is characterized by an extreme degree of competitiveness. He views himself and his family as in a state of competition with other individuals and families for success and achievement. American culture tends to be atomistic rather than corporate, and the pressure of movement "upward," toward achievement, is intense. Here again a hypothesis might be proposed that in other cultures individual competition for success tends to be more localized within specific classes or regions, tends to be subordinated to, or assimilated in, political competition, and tends to be muted by religious conceptions of life.

c. The American views himself and his family as in a state of competition with other individuals and families for values which are largely "material" in character. What he appears to want are the material evidences of success —money, position, and the consumer-goods of the moment. While the stress is toward money, or what money can buy, the important thing is not the money itself, but the sense of accomplishment or fulfillment which it gives. This sense of accomplishment rests on matching and exceeding the material standard of community and social class; it requires external approval and conformity. Because of the stress in the American value system on having what others want, and because of the great emphasis on the elaboration of material culture, the American tends to be caught up in an endless race for constantly changing goals—the "newest" in housing, the "latest" in locomotion, the most "fashionable" in dress and appearance. This love of innovation, improvement, and change tends to be confined to the material culture. Attitudes toward human and social relations tend to be more conservative. By way of hypothetical comparison it may be said that in other cultures the criteria of accomplishment are more stable. Religious salvation and political resentment provide greater consolation for the poor and the failures. The material culture tends to be hemmed in by tradition. The criteria of achievement have a more stable subjective basis in the sense of craftsmanship, esthetic and intellectual subtlety, and the fulfillment of social and religious routines.

d. There are certain derivative elements of this general value orientation which call for comment. First, intense individualistic competitiveness, in which the primary aim is to get more of what other people want, produces diffuse hostile tension and general apprehension and anxiety, which pervades every aspect of the culture including the competing unit itself, the family. The fear of failure and the apprehension over the hostility which is involved in one's relations with other persons produce on the one hand an extraordinary need for affection and reassurance, and on the other, an extraordinary tendency to resort to physiological and spiritual narcosis. In other words, as a consequence of being impelled by cultural pressure toward relationships in which one is aggressively pitted against others, the resulting unease and apprehension is characteristically mitigated by demands for external response, attention, and warmth, or by resort to escapism. Thus an excessive concern with sexuality, an excessive resort to alcohol, and, what is a uniquely American form of narcosis of the soul—the widespread addiction to highly stimulating mass entertainment, the radio, movies, comics, and the like—provide culturally legitimate modes of discharging hostility and allaying anxiety.

Thus, by way of summary, the value orientation of the American tends to be atomistic rather than corporate, worldly rather than unworldly, highly mobile rather than traditional, compulsive rather than relaxed, and externally directed rather than autonomous. Needless to say, these are presented as hypothetical tendencies, which are supported only by an inadequate and quite heterogeneous body of evidence.

2. *Value Expectations.* The American is an optimist as to ends and an improviser as to means. The riches of his heritage and the mobility of his social order have produced a generally euphoric tendency, that is, the expectation that one can by effort and good will achieve or approximate one's goals. This overt optimism is so compulsive an element in the American culture that factors which threaten it, such as failure, old age, and death, are pressed from the focus of attention and handled in perfunctory ways. This belief that "things can be done" is coupled with a faith in common sense and "know-how" with regard to means. The American has a double approach to complex reasoning and theory. He has great respect for systematic thinking and planning in relation to technological and organizational problems. But even this type of intellectualism is brought down to earth by referring to it as "know-how." Know-how implies both the possession of formal technical knowledge and the capacity to improvise and overcome obstacles on the basis of a "feel" for the problem or the situation. In complicated questions of social and public policy there is a genuine distrust of complex and subtle reasoning and a preference for an earthy "common sense." Thus, in these important areas his compulsive optimism, his anti-intellectualism, and his simple rationalism leave the American vulnerable to deflation and pessimism when his expectations are thwarted and when threats and dangers are not effectively warded off by improvisations. This vulnerability is, to be sure, balanced by a certain flexibility and experimentalism, a willingness to try new approaches. If Americans typically avoid the rigidity of dogma in dealing with new problems, they also typically fail to reap the advantages of thoughtful policy-planning. What is involved here is not so much a net loss, but rather the failure to realize the net gain that would result from a greater intellectual discipline.

3. *Attitudes Toward Authority and Morality.* The American tends to "cut authority down to his own size." He has a respect for achievement and a toleration of order-enforcing agencies, but a distrust of arbitrary or traditional authority. This attitude toward authority also carries over into the field of tradition and custom. Certainly the urban American, and many of the rural ones as well, are not seriously limited by traditional methods of doing things. They are iconoclasts with respect to earlier aspects of culture, and conformists in relation to the most recent value changes. They reject what was done in the past, and they conform to the new things that are being done *now*. But again this iconoclasm is especially noticeable in the

sphere of material culture. A greater conservatism obtains in relation to social and political matters. This social and political conservatism is not unique to Americans. What seems to be unique is this combination of mobility of material values and fundamentalism with regard to social and political values.

Similar trends are observable in American attitudes toward moral norms. The norms of Christianity still constitute an important theme in contemporary American culture. Since these moral standards are in obvious and continual rivalry with the competitive ethic, Americans tend to suffer from ambivalence and conflicts in determining what is "proper." Under normal circumstances this conflict does not appear to have a seriously laming effect. It tends to be disposed of by adding a moral coloration to actions which are really motivated by expediency, and an expediential coloration to actions which are motivated by moral and humanitarian values. These tendencies are related to a rather widespread naïve belief in the compatibility of morality and expediency. While this ambivalence is a factor which generally affects American behavior, there is also a characteristic pendulum movement between the two ethics. Thus, if generous actions, motivated by moral and humanitarian considerations, are accepted without gratitude, are misinterpreted, or are unrequited, a "cynical" rejection of humanitarianism may follow, resulting from the humiliation at having been "played for a sucker." To yield to humanitarian impulses in the "market place" or to moderate one's own demands in the light of "Christian" considerations, to give without the expectation of receiving, to suffer injury without retaliation—these are impulses which have a partial validity; but it is dangerous to give way to them since they dull the edge of competitiveness, confuse and retard the forward course of action.

Mood Versus Policy

Since Americans tend to exhaust their emotional and intellectual energies in private pursuits, the typical approach to problems of public policy is perfunctory. Where public policy impinges directly on their interest, as in questions of local improvements, taxation, or social security policy, they are more likely to develop views and opinions resting on some kind of intellectual structure. But on questions of a more remote nature, such as foreign policy, they tend to react in more undifferentiated ways, with formless and plastic moods which undergo frequent alteration in response to changes in events. The characteristic response to questions of foreign policy is one of indifference. A foreign policy crisis, short of the immediate threat of war, may transform indifference to vague apprehension, to fatalism, to anger; but the reaction is still a mood, a superficial and fluctuating response. To some extent American political apathy is a consequence of the compulsive absorption of energy in private competitiveness.

To inform oneself on public issues, to form policies on the basis of careful thought-taking, is hardly a task that is beyond the intellectual competence of a large proportion of the population. The intellectual demands of business life are in some respects as complicated as those of foreign policy. But the American has a powerful cultural incentive to develop policies and strategies relating to his business and professional career, and little incentive, if any, to develop strategies for foreign policy.

The orientation of most Americans toward foreign policy is one of mood, and mood is essentially an unstable phenomenon. But this instability is not arbitrary and unpredictable. American moods are affected by two variables: (1) changes in the domestic and foreign political-economic situation involving the presence or absence of threat in varying degrees, (2) the characterological predispositions of the population. Our knowledge of American character tendencies, meager as it may be, makes it possible to suggest potential movements of opinion and mood which may have significant effects on foreign policy.

1. *Withdrawal-Intervention.* Given the intense involvement of most Americans with private interests and pursuits, the normal attitude toward a relatively stable world political situation is one of comparative indifference and withdrawal. This was the case throughout the greater part of the nineteenth century, in the period between World War I and II, and as we shall show in a later chapter, in the period immediately following World War II. The existence of this cyclical withdrawal-intervention problem suggests at least two serious dangers for foreign policy decision-making: (1) possible overreactions to threat; (2) possible overreactions to temporary equilibria in world politics. Under ordinary circumstances American emotion and action are directed with considerable pressure in the normal orbits of private competition. However, when threats from abroad become grave and immediate, Americans tend to break out of their private orbits, and tremendous energies become available for foreign policy. Thus, we see the explosions of American energy in World Wars I and II when, after periods of indifference and withdrawal, exceptional feats of swift mobilization were achieved. There is some evidence to suggest that the Russian threat may, if carelessly handled, produce dangerous overreactions. Thus the press conference of Secretary of State Marshall in the spring of 1947, in which he urged the American people to "keep calm," produced what amounted to a war scare. The volatility and potential explosiveness of American opinion must be constantly kept in mind if panic reactions to threat are to be avoided.

The danger of overreaction to threat is only one aspect of this withdrawal-intervention tendency of American opinion. Equally serious is the prospect of overreaction to temporary stabilizations in the world crisis. Because of the superficial character of American attitudes toward world politics, American opinion tends to react to the external aspects of situations. A temporary Russian tactical withdrawal may produce strong tendencies toward demobilization and the reassertion of the primacy of private and domestic values. The pull of "privatism" in America creates a strong inclination to self-deception. And while this is less characteristic of the informed and policy-making levels, it undoubtedly plays an important role here as well. The great American demobilization of 1945, both in the military establishment and in the civilian bureaucracy, and the hasty dismantling of war agencies and controls reflected the overwhelming eagerness to withdraw to private values and normal conditions. This movement was not based on a sober evaluation of the foreign situation and what this might require in military and political terms, but was a response to the overwhelming urge to have done with alarms and external interruptions and get back to the essential and important values.

2. *Mood-Simplification.* Closely connected with the withdrawal-intervention pattern is a tendency which has to do with characteristic changes in the internal structure of American foreign policy moods. It has already been pointed out that under conditions of political equilibrium American attitudes toward world politics tend to be formless and lacking in intellectual structure. We define policy, as distinguished from mood, as consisting of a relatively stable intellectual structure including (1) explicit assumptions as to the values involved in domestic or international political conflict, (2) explicit evaluations of the relative costs and efficiency of alternative means of maximizing the value position of one's own country or political group. From the point of view of this criterion, American attitudes tend to range from unstructured moods in periods of equilibrium to simplification in periods of crisis. So long as there is no immediate, sharply defined threat, the attitude is vague and indefinite—e.g., apathetic, mildly apprehensive, euphoric, skeptical. When the crisis becomes sharpened American responses become more specific. Here American distrust of intellectualism and subtlety, the faith in "common sense," and the belief in simple answers lead to oversimplifications of the threat and the methods of coping with it.

.   .   .

It would, of course, be an exaggeration to attribute the same degree of "simplism" to policy-makers as might be expected of the "man in the street." But there can be little doubt that the process of foreign policy making is strongly influenced by this common-sense, improvisational tendency. Faith in policy-planning (which means in simple terms, taking the "long view," acquiring sufficient reliable information on which sound policy can be based, weighing and balancing the potential value of military, political, diplomatic, and psychological means in relation to proposed courses of action) has hardly taken root in the American policy-making process.

3. *Optimism-Pessimism.* The problem of shifts in mood from euphoric

to dysphoric expectations is clearly related to those aspects of American opinion already described. The involvement in private concerns, coupled with an optimistic faith in good will, common sense, and simple answers, renders the American public vulnerable to failure. This reaction tends to result from the frustration of successive improvisations, none of which have been adapted to the complex character of the problem. Under these circumstances there are two possible dangers: (1) withdrawal reactions; (2) hasty measures motivated by irritation and impatience. The development of American attitudes toward Russia since the end of the war is an excellent illustration of this problem. During the war and in the period immediately following its termination there was a widely shared belief among Americans and among American policy-makers that the Russian problem could be readily solved by good will and the "man-to-man" approach. The continued thwarting of American overtures and concessions to the Russians now seems to have produced an attitude of hopeless pessimism. Pessimism certainly seems to be justifiable on the basis of the facts, but the negativism which has resulted may possibly constitute a danger if negotiation and bargaining with the Russians in principle is interdicted. The objective problem would seem to be one of choosing the time, the occasion, and the conditions when negotiation might lead to advantage. There is a similar danger of excessive pessimism in relation to potential allies. Perhaps there is a tendency toward a premature "writing off" of peoples whose social and political structures are unstable, countries which don't react with "American speed" to American proposals or which are not ready to commit themselves to the American "side" in as whole-hearted a fashion as we might desire.

4. *Tolerance-Intolerance.* The point has already been made that the American attitude toward authority, toward moral and ideological norms, contains conflicting elements. On the one hand, the American is not hemmed in by the mores and morals of "the horse and buggy days," and at the same time he is a conformist, a value-imitator. He is ready to try new things and new methods, but not if they make him look "different" or "peculiar." The truth of the matter would seem to be that, while he has loosened himself from the bonds of earlier moral standards and beliefs, he has not replaced these guides for conduct with any other set of principles. The autonomous conscience of Puritanism has been replaced by the "radar-directed" conduct of the "marketer." He tends to take his judgments as to what is right and wrong, proper and improper, from the changing culture as it impinges on him through the various social institutions and media of communication. This makes for a certain flexibility in attitudes toward other cultures and ideologies. But the flexibility is negative rather than positive. That is, the American has moved away from older moral and traditional norms without acquiring new bases of judgment. His toleration of difference therefore is unstable, and there is a substratum of ideological

fundamentalism which frequently breaks through the surface and has an important impact on foreign policy. Thus in our efforts to stabilize the weakened and chaotic areas of Western Europe we have been prepared to go a long way in aiding "Socialist Great Britain" and the left-inclined powers of Western Europe. But there is a continual sabotage of this tolerance, frequent efforts at ideological imperialism, even occasional interferences at the administrative level, which are motivated by ideological fundamentalism.

In general, this intolerance of difference is more clearly expressed in periods of normalcy. Thus, even though the possibility appears to be remote, the prospect of a recrudescence of isolationism cannot be excluded. A tactical cessation of Russian pressure might produce just this kind of demobilization and withdrawal reaction and the reassertion of older principles of conduct. This is not to say that such a reaction would be decisive so far as policy is concerned; but it is a prospect which sound policy-planning should anticipate.

5. *Idealism-Cynicism.* In still another respect American moral predispositions may have consequences for foreign policy. The annoyance and irritation of the peoples of foreign countries over American self-righteousness is, on the whole, a relatively minor source of difficulty. Americans would appear to be happiest when they can cloak an action motivated by self-interest with an aura of New Testament selflessness, when an action which is "good business," or "good security" can be made to "look good" too. Similarly there is resistance among Americans over the straightforward expression of conscience-motivated behavior. What is "good" has to be represented as satisfying the criteria of self-interest. They are happiest when they can allay the Christian conscience at the same time that they satisfy self-interested criteria. In this regard the peoples of foreign countries are well protected, perhaps overprotected, by their own cynicism.

But there are a number of respects in which this moral dualism may produce more serious problems for the policy-maker. There would appear to be a certain cyclical trend in American moral attitudes. The great wave of idealism in the first world war gave way to the cynicism about foreign countries of the 1920's. The friendliness for our British and French allies of World War I gave way to bitterness over their defaults on their indebtedness. A little more than a decade ago the little country of Finland had a place at the very center of the American heart because she had kept up her payments on her war debts, while the European powers which had defaulted, and on the fate of which our security rested, were prevented from borrowing money in the American capital market. The chiliastic faith in the reasonableness of the Russians has now been supplanted by deep resentment over their base ingratitude.

American generosity and humanitarianism is a tentative phenomenon. Along with impulses toward good will and generosity, there is a deep-seated suspicion that smart people don't act that way, that "only suckers are a soft touch." In this connection a recent study which appeared in a popular magazine is of considerable interest. This investigation, claiming to have been based on "reliable sampling procedures," reflected a degree of religious piety among Americans considerably greater than had previously been estimated. Of greatest interest was its description of American attitudes toward ethics. It would appear that almost half of the sample was sharply aware of the conflict between what was "right" and the demands of secular life. A somewhat smaller proportion considered that religion influenced their activities in business, political and social life. Considerably more than half felt that their conduct toward neighbors was governed by the golden rule; but more than 80 per cent felt that their neighbors fell considerably short of the golden rule in their conduct toward their fellowmen.

Quite aside from the question of the full reliability of a study asking such "loaded" and personal questions, there seems to be confirmation here for the proposition regarding the moral dualism in the American character. The aspiration to conform to Christian ethical ideals is clearly present among most members of the culture, but there would appear to be a strong apprehension that such standards of conduct are inapplicable because the outside world does not behave that way. Hence any impulse toward ethically motivated generosity is impaired not only by the feeling that it will go unrequited, but that one's neighbors will ridicule it or attribute it to some concealed, self-interested motive.

It would appear to be a reasonable speculation from the foregoing findings that any action involving the giving or loaning of American wealth to foreign peoples, even though it be motivated by calculations of self-interest, activates this fear that "only a sucker is a soft touch." Under conditions of threat, such as those of the present, these doubts and suspicions about "giving things away" have been kept within manageable proportions. But in a period of temporary stabilization when the superficial aspect of the foreign situation encourages withdrawal reactions, these feelings may play a role of some significance.

6. *Superiority-Inferiority*. In a sense America is a nation of parvenus. A historically unique rate of immigration, social, and geographic mobility has produced a people which has not had an opportunity to "set," to acquire the security and stability which come from familiar ties, associations, rights, and obligations. It is perhaps not accidental that in the vulgarization of psychoanalytic hypotheses in America in the last decades one of the first to acquire popular currency was the "superiority-inferiority" complex. In more stably stratified societies the individual tends to have a greater sense of "location," a broader and deeper identification with his social surroundings. He has not *made* his own identity, while in America a large proportion of each generation is *self-made*. Being self-made produces a certain buoyancy,

a sense of mastery, but it leaves the individual somewhat doubtful as to his social legitimacy. This sense of insecurity and uncertainty may add a strident note to American claims for recognition. This may explain the stereotype of the American abroad, confronted with complex and ancient cultures, taking alcoholic refuge in assertions of American moral, political, and technical virtue. It may also account for a feeling in the United States that American diplomats are no match for the wiliness and cunning of Old World negotiators. In other words, Americans typically overreact in their self-evaluations. They over- and under-estimate their skills and virtues, just as they over- and under-estimate the skills and virtues of other cultures and nations. . . .

Conclusion: The Many Faces of America

It would be unfortunate if the preceding analysis conveyed the impression of a neat periodicity of American foreign policy moods. Actually the American approach to foreign policy problems at any given time is a historically unique phenomenon. It is influenced not only by these (and other) ambivalences in the American character, but by the immediate historical background and the specific content of the foreign policy problem. While it is useful analytically to talk about the alternation of "normalcy" and "crisis" moods, it must be recognized that crises differ from one another, just as do periods of normalcy, and that the American character is undergoing continual change. Thus from one era to the next, both the subjective and objective components of foreign policy moods may greatly change.

In the period before World War II, the dominant and overt foreign policy mood was a composite of withdrawal impulses, cynicism about power politics, intolerance of foreign peoples and cultures, and pessimism about the prospects of idealistic internationalism. Many experiences had combined to produce this state of mind. The development of a power structure in Europe which did not immediately and overtly threaten the United States provided a plausible justification for isolationism. Disillusionment over the collapse of the high moral purposes of the Allies in World War I provoked a cynical and pessimistic reaction which strengthened the withdrawal trend. The default on Allied war debts contributed to American arrogance with regard to the inefficiency and lack of integrity of foreign governments.

The growing threat to American security began to undermine this withdrawal mood in the late 1930's. But it took the catastrophe of Pearl Harbor to produce a broad interventionist consensus. American intolerance of foreign countries and social systems was supplanted by a tolerance of actual and potential allies. Cynicism and pessimism about international power politics were supplanted by moderately idealistic aspirations and somewhat optimistic expectations of peace and international amity.

This mood pattern lasted through the latter years of the war and the brief period of Allied amity which followed it. But as specific conflicts with the Soviet Union broadened into the general impasse of the Cold War, the American foreign policy mood changed again. Optimism about the future of peace gave way to pessimism. Idealist internationalism faded into "security realism." Overtones of impatience and intolerance began to emerge in public reactions to our relations with the Soviet Union, England, China; but the continuance of threat precluded an unequivocal expression of these reactions.

There is some value for the purposes of foreign policy planning in recognizing that an overtly interventionist and "responsible" United States hides a covertly isolationist longing, that an overtly tolerant America is at the same time barely stifling intolerance reactions, that an idealistic America is muttering *sotto voce* cynicisms, that a surface optimism in America conceals a dread of the future. Understanding of these ambivalences might save statesmen periodic shocks at the sequences of American moods. One must always take into account the fact that Americans in this period of their development are both responsible and irresponsible. A momentary rift in the clouds brings the irresponsible trends to the surface; an intensification of threat brings out a sober readiness to sacrifice.

America's contemporary role in world politics is hardly more than a decade old. Other nations have had generations to assimilate their great political lessons. That America has begun to assimilate some of its political lessons is suggested by the widespread resolution that it can no longer tolerate the degree of economic instability which has characterized the past. This rejection of the inevitability of the severe shocks of the business cycle is matched in the political sphere by a growing acceptance of our foreign policy status and the sacrifices it imposes. But with regard to the foreign policy cycle, as well as the business cycle, a confident sense of self-mastery is still lacking.

Another impression which analysis of American moods may have conveyed is that these reactions are equally distributed among the entire population. We shall have the occasion to observe at a later point that there are substantially different mood susceptibilities at different points in the social and political structure. Social classes, age groups, men and women, and the various educational levels approach foreign policy problems from different emotional and intellectual starting points. The fact that there are so many different Americas is not only attributable to attitude instability *through time,* but also to the fact that *at any given time* there is a bewildering variety of moods and foreign policy proposals. . . .

THE FOREIGN POLICY CONSENSUS

WHILE the policy disunity and conflicts of the American elites are in sharp contrast to the compulsive ideological homogeneity of the Communist elites, there is, nevertheless, a general ideological consensus in the United States in which the mass of the population and its leadership generally share. At the level of basic attitudes this is largely an unconscious consensus of feeling with regard to values and of reactions regarded as suitable in response to certain political cues. There are underlying assumptions as to the inherent propriety of such values as mass material welfare and freedom and of certain modes of resolving political differences. At the level of general opinion on public policy, one may speak of a consensus of mood, of shared emotional states in response to changes in the domestic and foreign arenas. At the level of articulate elite policy formulation there is a broad consensus of policy. Neither in foreign nor in domestic policy is this to be understood as full agreement on principles or on details, but rather as an adherence to a broad compromise on political procedures and policies. Such adherence ranges from unqualified enthusiasm to a mere readiness to tolerate.

The foreign policy consensus is full of unilateral reservations, special emphases, and actual and potential conflicts of both an ideological and an interest character. Furthermore, the breadth and solidity of this consensus must be understood as having been produced by the circumstance of an external crisis combined with a fairly satisfactory internal situation. How stable this consensus is likely to be under other circumstances is discussed at a later point.

What distinguishes the foreign policy consensus from the deviational foreign policy positions discussed in the following chapter is agreement on the main themes of contemporary foreign policy—resistance to Communist expansion by economic, diplomatic, propaganda, and, if necessary, military means, and the establishment of a peaceful and legal international order in which American material and security interests would be protected. More basically, this foreign policy consensus is founded upon a consensus of fundamental attitudes and ideology which may be described in two dimensions—values and means. The advocates of the American foreign policy consensus are, in general, agreed that the primary aims of American policy, both domestic and foreign, should turn on a reconciliation of individual freedom and mass welfare of a primarily material kind. This is a broad substratum of agreement on which such divergent groups as Republicans and Democrats, laborites and capitalists, and the various cultural, regional, and religious groupings take a common stand, even though this agreement is obscured at the level of overt policy by the clamor and demagogy of special interest representation. The foreign policy consensus is also characterized by a basic agreement on means. There is a kind of rational eclecticism as to means; there is no rejection of coercion as such or of security diplomacy based on the threat of coercion, as is the case with such deviational groups as pacifists and certain of the internationalists. As a type of social action the foreign policy consensus approximates Max Weber's "instrumental rationality." Attitudes toward ends and means are contingent rather than absolute. In contrast, the foreign policy counter-elites discussed in the next chapter approximate the type of "absolute value rationality," in rejecting unconditionally certain policy ends or means and asserting certain others in a rigid manner. . . .

CONSENSUS IN A WORLD OF CRISIS

THE "crisis of Western man" has become a common theme among learned men. Theologians decry the secularization of modern life, the decline of religious feeling, and the rise of materialism and "scientism." College presidents deplore the rise of vocationalism and the decay of humanist cultural ideals. Critics of the arts struggle against the domination of "mass" standards of taste and the crumbling of esthetic discrimination. Sociologists and social philosophers are troubled by the breakdown of older forms of community relations and the costs of urban industrial civilization in human isolation and insecurity. Business leaders and economists caution against the consequences of the decline of the risk-taking mentality and the emergence of security as a dominant social value. Psychiatrists and psycho-anthropologists comment on the competitiveness of modern life and the impairment of human relations which it entails. This is but a partial summary of the modern jeremiad.

One of the most interesting interpretations of the modern crisis of the spirit, an interpretation which brings into focus many of the problems with which we have thus far been concerned, is the "privatization" hypothesis of Ernst Kris and Nathan Leites. These writers propose that in the mass societies of the twentieth century, politics and public affairs have come to impinge ever more closely on the life of the common man. In a formal sense, the masses determine the basic political decisions which affect them, and they are encouraged by their leaders to believe that they actually exercise such power. But the complexity of modern economic and political decisions and the professionalization of the decision-making process has created the feeling that in actuality the masses can neither "*understand* nor *influence* the very events upon which their life and happiness is known to depend." There has been, according to this view, an increasing sense of "incompetence" among the masses. Thus, in contrast to the era of political decentralization, when the average man is said to have had a sense of relatedness to, and understanding of, politics, contemporary Americans (and Western Europeans) have a sense of dependence upon, and distrust of, remote elites and decision-makers. This sense of powerlessness and suspicion is not discharged constructively in the form of "critical distrust" and critical evaluation of policy proposals and decisions. It cannot be expressed in constructive ways because the ordinary individual lacks the knowledge and analytical ability to evaluate policy in an age of complex interdependence. "He [the common man] therefore regressively turns to projective distrust: He fears, suspects and hates what he cannot understand and master." He projects his own feelings of hostility and resentment, continually fed by his sense of powerlessness and of being a tool manipulated for purposes other than his own, on his leaders. In the mind of the common man the leadership groups become malevolent, cynical, self-seeking and corrupt. In conclusion, these writers suggest that if "the appropriate education on a vast enough scale and at a rapid enough rate is not provided for, the distrust and privatization of the masses may become a fertile soil for totalitarian management."

In the present state of knowledge it is impossible to accept or reject such a hypothesis. We have already seen that, particularly in relation to foreign policy, the feeling of powerlessness among Americans is widespread. But these feelings of powerlessness were most marked among the lower-income and lower-educational strata. They are less characteristic of the "attentive public" which feels itself capable of exercising in some measure the kind of "critical distrust" which represents a sound response to the modern political division of labor. Instead of withdrawing into private rancor and suspicion, the attentive public subjects policy to more- or less-informed criticism. Furthermore, with the broadening of educational opportunity and the general rise in the standard of living in the course of the past decades, it would seem that this attentive public has expanded.

It is indeed an arguable point as to whether Americans have been withdrawing from political involvement. In some areas we may perhaps speak of an increasing sense of political involvement and relatedness. Thus if we take the moral tone of American political life in the past half century, we find a genuine decline in the cruder forms of corruption and manipulation. The urban public of today is more effectively related to urban politics than was the case in the era of the "shame of the cities." But it is not related to politics in any direct sense of the term. It is related to politics through a *division of labor*. What broke the hold of the older and grosser forms of urban political corruption was the rise of effective civic elites capable of competing with the politicians, and the broadening of the attentive public through educational opportunity and rising standards of living.

There is a certain tendency to treat the nineteenth century in the United States as a utopian age of mass political involvement. Actually this was the era during which de Tocqueville called the United States "blessed" because it did not need a foreign policy. In his judgment, had the United States been involved in world politics, her survival would have been seriously threatened by the instability of the American democracy, its intense involvement in private affairs, and its proclivities for evangelistic interventions. The nineteenth century also was the era of the great waves of evangelism and complacency in urban politics. This was attributable to a kind of privatism which was perhaps stronger in the nineteenth century than it is today.

Actually political involvement in the United States in the era before the first world war tended to take the form either of evangelistic political religiosity or hard and narrow interest calculation. There was, as we have already seen, a certain cyclical fluctuation from the one mood to the other. What seems to be developing today is a disenchantment with all sweeping ideals and, in addition, a rejection of the older forms of narrow interest calculation. Thus in the first world war the United States joined the Allies in a mood of sweeping idealism. The disenchantment that followed in the next decade was in part a consequence of the collapse of these exorbitant hopes. In the second world war a more wary people rejected millennial aspirations. There was less willingness to accept general slogans and a greater resistance to propaganda. The mood responses of soldiers asked to fight, and of civilians asked to sacrifice, were generally couched in simple terms of defense against aggression.

In this, as in other areas, there has undoubtedly been a decline in belief in general principles and ideals and a preference for interest calculation with the self as the starting point. But this tendency does not necessarily lead to political withdrawal and bitterness. It may lead into a broadening rationality in which the interdependence of individual and social action is recognized and in which there is a sober respect for the inevitability of division of labor in the making of complex policy decisions. Those writers who view the political apathy of the masses as a simple manifestation of social pathology have perhaps overlooked a number of essential aspects of the problem.

If we take any of the great problems of American foreign policy—such as the control of atomic energy, or the problem of Western European or Far Eastern stability and security—we have to recognize that even the most highly trained specialists have to act in the dark and on the basis of anxious guess-work. There is indeed, as we have already stressed, a constructive sense of economy of effort in the reaction of the "common man" who refuses to involve himself and to accumulate knowledge about these problems. Would he be in any better position to evaluate policy if he were able to pass the information tests posed by the public opinion researchers? Suppose all adult Americans knew the name of their Secretary of State, could locate Iran on a blank map, could identify the raw materials from which fissionable materials are derived, and could list the permanent members of the Security Council in alphabetical order, could they then make a sound decision whether military aid under the North Atlantic Pact should be a billion dollars or a billion and a half? This approach to the problem of public information operates on a kind of "Quiz Kids" standard. Anyone who has gone through the experience of trying to analyze a policy is aware of the fact that in the first period of concentrated effort, increased knowledge results in increased confusion and indecision. Since the great mass of the public lacks the time, energy, and training necessary for more than the most superficial consideration of foreign policy problems, widespread mass ignorance and indifference are hardly to be viewed as simple pathologies.

Mass indifference toward problems of foreign policy is partly justified by the great proliferation of interest organizations in the past fifty years or so. The public is not only represented in the formal political sense by a variety of elected officials, but there are few groups of any size in the United States today which do not have their interest representation. *Mass inattention* to problems of public policy is accompanied by the *accentuation* of *elite attention.* The trade-union leader, the agricultural lobbyist or propagandist, the official of the Chamber of Commerce is "paid" to look out for the interests of the worker, farmer, or businessman. There is, undoubtedly, considerable distrust among the masses of their political and interest representation, a distrust which is largely sound and healthy. Pressure group leaders are agents, and there can be little question that they bear watching. Anyone who has had experience with agency relationships becomes aware of the constructive value of distrust and lack of confidence.

In the last half century the American population has developed a political structure adapted to an era of mass democracy and social interdependence. The implications of these developments have been accepted with great reluctance and in the form of an "under-the-counter" transaction. The myth of democratic spontaneity and mass control still holds sway "above the counter," only to trouble the literal minds of young people, and older people who have resisted the impact of experience.

These considerations are of significance for public information policy. Only recently an analysis of the results of a foreign information campaign in Cincinnati showed that even a heavy concentration of information through the mass media of communication had no perceptible effects. According to the criteria used by the polling organization, approximately the same percentages of respondents were informed and ignorant after the campaign, as before.

What accounts for this mass immunity to information on foreign policy problems? The public information specialist who operates through the mass media reasons by analogy from the success of advertising. Advertisers get enormous results from radio, newspaper and periodical advertising, while information on the United Nations distributed through the same media appears to get no results at all. The point seems to be that the masses are already predisposed to want automobiles, refrigerators, and toothpaste, but they are not predisposed to want information about the United Nations or the control of atomic energy. Such information has no immediate utility or meaning.

What this and other studies suggest is that there is no mass market for detailed information on foreign affairs. The general public looks for *cues* for *mood responses* in public discussion of foreign policy. It does not listen to the content of discussion but to its tone. A presidential statement that a crisis exists will ordinarily be registered in the form of apprehension. A reassuring statement will be received with complacency reactions. In both cases the reaction has no depth and no structure.

But if there is no "quantity" market for information about foreign affairs, there is an important quality market. And it is through this quality market that an articulate and broad foreign policy consensus can be shaped and maintained. Through a disciplined democratic elite and a broad attentive public, foreign policy moods may be contained and gross fluctuations in attitude checked. No slick public relations campaign will "do the trick." The side-show barker who can appeal to well-established appetites will get the "cash," but little more than self-intoxication results from a grass roots campaign in Middletown, Ohio, "to relate Middletowners to the world in which we live." We are dealing with a complex political structure which has special points of access. If we shout at the wall, we can take a certain satisfaction in a ringing echo. But if we come up closer, we can find openings through which a quiet word might reach a listening ear.

An effective approach to public information on foreign policy questions will therefore be selective and qualitative. It will be directed toward enlarging the attentive public and training the elite cadres. This is not to suggest that the mass public is to be overlooked or neglected. A sound information program will confront the common man continually with opportunities to be informed and involved in foreign policy decisions. There should be a standing invitation for him to join the attentive public if and when he is ready to make the essential sacrifices of time and energy. The repetition of slogans and occasional promotional campaigns directed at the mass public through the mass media have the primary consequence of minimizing the complexities of the problem and encouraging self-deception.

The containment of mass moods and the broadening and qualitative improvement of the attentive public may be approximated through a bettering of elite selection and training. Our efforts ought to be directed toward the articulate points in the political structure. Both a democratic and effective foreign policy may be shaped and maintained as long as we have trained and disciplined elites competing for influence before an attentive public. These elites constitute an elaborate system of representation; they are (although in quite different ways and degrees) responsible to mass constituencies.

James N. Rosenau

THE OPINION-POLICY RELATIONSHIP

I T is useful to view the relationship between public opinion [1] and foreign policy as being composed of three distinctly different, but closely related, social processes—that is, as three separate systems of interaction between discrete individuals. One is the *governmental decision-making process* through which foreign policy is formulated and into which existing public opinion is integrated by the officials responsible for the conduct of policy (henceforth designated as the decision-makers or policy-makers). Another is the *opinion-submitting process* that occurs whenever opinions are conveyed to or impressed upon decision-makers by individual members or segments of the public (hereafter called the opinion-submitters). And thirdly, there is the *opinion-making process* whereby ideas about foreign-policy issues are formed and circulated in American society (through the interaction of what shall be referred to as opinion-holders and opinion-makers, the former being the entire citizenry and the latter those citizens who introduce opinions into the impersonal channels of the communications system).

It must be emphasized that the first and the last of these processes are independent systems of interaction, which is to say that both can occur irrespective of any linkage with the other. Opinions about foreign-policy issues can be and are circulated without coming to the attention of decision-makers. Because the opinion-submitting process is not always initiated, government does not necessarily experience every throb in the circulatory system whereby opinions are disseminated throughout the society. Likewise,

---

[1] As indicated below, the "public" is not equated with the citizenry of the nation. Rather, only those who hold opinions about an issue are considered to constitute the "public" with respect to that issue. . . . Hence the phrase "public opinion" is used to refer generally to the different publics that have formed around the various issues preoccupying the nation at any moment.

F R O M *Public Opinion and Foreign Policy,* by James N. Rosenau. © Copyright 1961 by Random House, Inc. Reprinted by permission.

decision-makers can and do conduct their deliberations and arrive at foreign-policy decisions without knowledge of the existing state of public opinion, either because the latter has not been conveyed to them or because, in the absence of an opinion-submitting process, they do not, consciously or otherwise, perceive its existence.

The opinion-submitting process, then, derives from the other two processes. If the decision-making process is inaccessible, or if the opinion-making process is quiescent or not governmentally oriented, there can be no opinion-submitting process. In this dependent sense, of course, the opinion-submitting process is merely an aspect of the opinion-making process. Yet, by analyzing it separately, constant attention is drawn to the crucial fact that the other two processes can operate independently of each other.

Why is the independence of the decision-making and opinion-making processes so crucial? Precisely because the opinion-policy relationship is defined in terms of a linkage between these two processes. Their interdependence, as distinguished from independence, is necessary for the relationship to exist at any particular moment. This analytic definition, while lacking an operational basis, has the advantage of freeing us from the value definition that opinion and policy *ought* to be articulated in harmony with each other. It forces us to posit the existence of the relationship as a hypothesis that has to be tested, rather than as an existing situation which calls only for description.

Having conceptually (but not empirically) established that the opinion-policy relationship can cease to exist even as its components continue to function, let us turn to its actual operation, to the varying linkages and sequences through which the relationship is formed and sustained. It must first be noted that the definition above does not posit a relationship in which policy is always a reflection of opinion. The definition merely asserts that the relationship cannot exist unless the two processes are linked together in some fashion. As can be seen in the diagrammatic presentation of the relationship (p. 70), linkage can occur in several other sequences besides the one which reflects classical democratic theory ($8\rightarrow9\rightarrow10$ on the diagram). Moreover, policy may not reflect opinion even if such a sequence is initiated; the resulting linkage might be an entirely negative one in which decision-makers reject the policy alternatives presented by the other two processes.

Nor does the opinion-submitting process have to intervene for linkage to occur. The definition also makes allowance for the special sequence whereby decision-makers, consciously (linkage 1) or otherwise (2), circumvent the opinion-submitting process by engaging in their own estimates of the prevailing state of opinion. Indeed, it may well be that the intervention of the submission process is more atypical than typical. Conceivably the perceptual antennae of decision-makers are more sensitive to unsolicited evidences of opinion than to representations made by opinion-submitters.

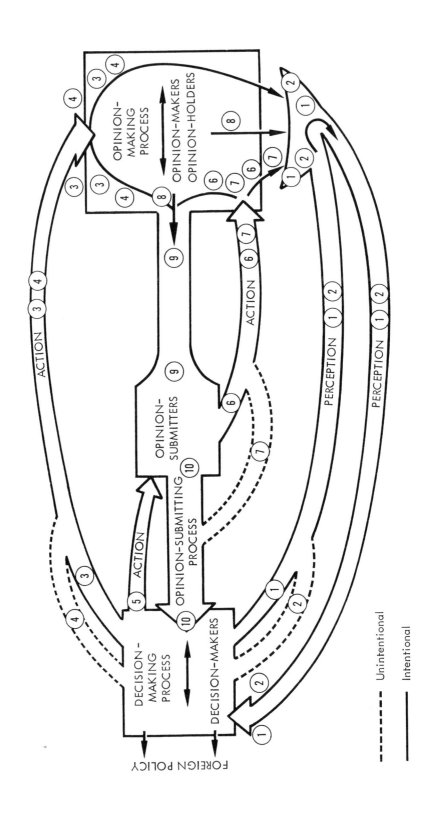

OPINION-MAKING PROCESS

OPINION-MAKERS
OPINION-HOLDERS

ACTION

ACTION

PERCEPTION

PERCEPTION

OPINION-SUBMITTERS

OPINION-SUBMITTING PROCESS

ACTION

DECISION-MAKING PROCESS

DECISION-MAKERS

FOREIGN POLICY

Unintentional

Intentional

Recent history is filled with instances in which decision-makers appear to have taken into account a larger "climate" of opinion that, rightly or wrongly, they somehow perceived to be operative as latent public attitudes or as manifest but unstructured majorities which opinion-submitters failed to articulate. In other words, opinions do not have to be submitted for policy to be linked to them. Contrary to the simple model of democratic value theory ($8 \rightarrow 9 \rightarrow 10$), the opinion-policy relationship can be initiated by, and even confined to, the perceptions of decision-makers (1 or 2).

There is still another way in which decision-makers can initiate the relationship. Besides perceptual circumvention of the opinion-submitting process, they can also activate a sequence that runs from decision-making to opinion-making to opinion-submitting to decision-making ($3, 4 \rightarrow 8 \rightarrow 9 \rightarrow 10$). This major variation from the democratic-value model centers around the fact that the federal government is itself a primary contributor to the opinion-making process. The speeches of Congressmen, the messages of the President, and the press releases of various departments and agencies are but a few of the many ways in which opinions are fed to the public. Decision-makers, in other words, often become opinion-makers. This multiplicity of roles may result from the unintentional contribution which decision-makers make to the opinion-making process (4) by virtue of their participation in the decision-making process; that is, interaction among them which occurs in public, as in legislative hearings or Congressional debates, can serve an unanticipated opinion-making function. Or, as is perhaps more often the case, the shifting of roles can be the consequence of intentional efforts by decision-makers to shape the direction and intensity of public opinion (3). The conviction that the success of a particular policy depends upon the degree of public support it enjoys, or at least upon the extent to which public opposition is minimized, leads decision-makers to assume the role of opinion-makers in order to facilitate the subsequent performance of their tasks as decision-makers. They may simply attempt to foster a "climate" of opinion more favorable to their contemplated policy, hoping in this way to affect the perceptions of other decision-makers who are either opposed to the projected proposal or not yet persuaded of its wisdom ($4 \rightarrow 1,2$). Or, they may try to convince their colleagues by engaging in opinion-making designed to alter the opinion-submitting process in such a way as to reduce the volume of negative submissions or to increase the flow of positive submissions ($4 \rightarrow 8 \rightarrow 9 \rightarrow 10$). Rivalry and disagreement between the legislative and executive branches of the government is frequently channeled along these circuitous opinion-making routes, each branch seeking to prove to the other that its position is supported or accepted by the "public."

While decision-makers can promote the submissions process indirectly by acting as opinion-makers, they cannot, by definition, shift into the opinion-submitting role itself. This would, so to speak, involve them in making representations to themselves or to each other, an activity which is virtually the essence of decision-making and thus cannot usefully be construed as opinion-submitting. There is, however, one way in which decision-makers can initiate the submission of opinions directly, namely by soliciting them (5→10). As illustrated by the Congressman who takes a poll of his constituency, or by the agency head who calls in outsiders for advice, decision-makers can cause opinion-holders to become opinion-submitters even if they cannot shift into this role themselves. At least three reasons would seem to lead decision-makers to solicit opinions in this direct fashion: (1) In the absence of any other linkages, they may want to create (or maintain) the opinion-policy relationship because of a conviction that it ought to exist. (2) Distrustful of their own capacity to perceive accurately the inarticulate "climate" of opinion, yet doubtful of the representativeness of the "self-interested" opinions currently being submitted, they may turn to the solicitation of "disinterested" opinion. (3) They may want to bolster a particular position they may have taken in the decision-making process by citing otherwise unattainable evidence that the "public" shares their viewpoint.

Normally, of course, the submission of opinions is not so much a response to the solicitations of decision-makers as it is a process initiated voluntarily (9→10), either by professional opinion-submitters or by opinion-holders temporarily performing this role. The latter type refers to those members of the public who write letters to decision-makers or in some other way submit their personal opinions. They speak for themselves alone and only on irregular occasions. Once their views have been submitted, they return immediately to opinion-holding, until such time as circumstances (including the urgings of opinion-makers) again move them to shift roles. Professional opinion-submitters, on the other hand, are continuously attempting to establish contact with decision-makers. They submit opinions on behalf of large aggregates or organizations, either because they are specifically employed to do so (as lobbyists) or because their responsibilities include representing the organizational interests in the halls of government (as, say, presidents or chairmen).

The professional submitters are thus a vital link between the public and the decision-makers, introducing meaning and reality into the classic democratic model (8→9→10). But their activities are not limited to those of mere middlemen. They too can initiate a sequence in the opinion-policy relationship, one that runs from opinion-submitting to opinion-making, and thence back to decision-making via any of the linkages previously described (6,7→8→9→10 or 6,7→1,2). Such a sequence develops when professional submitters assume the role of opinion-makers. Like decision-makers, and for similar reasons, they frequently make this shift, either unintentionally or purposely. As occupants of organizational positions that command respect among segments of the public, professional submitters may unintentionally foster opinion-making (7) whenever they employ public rather than private means of participating in the opinion-submitting process. Under these circumstances their audience is not necessarily confined to decision-makers, so that their statements may have unanticipated opinion-making consequences. It may even be that the views they express in such open and publicized forums as legislative hearings have a greater impact upon members of the public than upon the decision-makers for whom they were intended.

More frequently, professional submitters intentionally turn to opinion-making (6). Persuaded that decision-makers will heed them more closely if they can provide evidence of support for their positions, professional submitters easily become accustomed to stepping into the role of opinion-makers. Moreover, because of their organizational affiliation, a wide variety of opinion-making techniques are at their disposal. Through publicity releases, they may attempt to alter the "climate" of opinion in such a way that decision-makers who perceive it will be more receptive to their subsequent submissions (6→8→1,2). Or they may try to extend the opinion-submitting process itself by encouraging a temporary shift in role on the part of opinion-holders (6→8→9→10). They may even facilitate such a shift by providing opinion-holders, especially those within their own organizations, with mimeographed letters that have only to be signed and mailed to decision-makers. In short, the professional opinion-submitter often deliberately becomes a well-equipped opinion-maker in order to make himself more effective in the former capacity.

Thus far, attention has been focused on the varying sequences and role shifts through which the decision-maker and the opinion-submitter initiate the opinion-policy relationship. Now we must turn to the opinion-makers and the opinion-holders, without whom the relationship cannot be consummated. We need to clarify the distinction between them, to differentiate various types within each group, and to delineate the several channels through which opinions circulate and come to be held.

. . . Americans differ widely in the manner and extent of their participation in the opinion-making process. Differences in the *manner* of participation can be traced along a motivation-information scale ranging from opinion-holders who are totally unconcerned and uninformed about world affairs to those who are greatly concerned and well-informed about such matters. Differences in the *extent* of participation can be analyzed in terms of accessibility to the personal (face-to-face) and impersonal channels that form the communications system through which opinions circulate. The accessibility scale is conceived to range from opinion-holders who are unable to transmit opinions beyond the circle of their acquaintances to those who can disseminate their views widely among persons whom they do not know. These two scales form the basis of the stratification of the public developed below. First the accessibility scale is used to draw a distinction between opinion-holders and opinion-makers. The motivation-information scale is then employed as a means of distinguishing between two basic types of opinion-holders. Subsequently we shall return to the accessibility scale and use it to differentiate between sixteen main types and many secondary types of opinion-makers.

Opinion-holders are those persons in the society who, on a given issue or in general, cannot circulate opinions to persons with whom they are not acquainted. They may disseminate opinions on a face-to-face basis, but they have no access to the impersonal channels of the circulatory system. *Opinion-makers*, on the other hand, are those who, by virtue of their position of leadership in the society, have access to the impersonal channels. Opinion-makers may vary considerably in the extent of their access, and in respect to the number of issues about which they can circulate opinions to unknown persons, but on a particular issue all of them are above the zero point on the accessibility scale. While it follows that some persons may be opinion-holders on some issues and opinion-makers on others, the ensuing discussion is based on the premise that the vast majority of opinion-holders are not able to shift into an opinion-making role at any time. . . .

In equating opinion-making with access to the impersonal channels, we do not mean to minimize the importance of face-to-face communication or to deny the substantial evidence that it is a highly effective form of communication. On the contrary, there is every reason to emphasize that the processes of influence have been found to operate more extensively in face-to-face situations than in impersonal ones,[1] and that therefore the opinions which opinion-holders internalize and adopt are usually those which were transmitted to them through some personal means. In other words, we do not deny that every opinion-holder has some access to the circulatory system in the sense that potentially he can perpetuate the flow of opinion by merely expressing himself in the presence of others. Indeed, it is quite appropriate that opinion-holders who sustain the circulation of opinion in this manner be regarded as "opinion leaders," a designation which stresses the central role played by those who relay ideas and information from the impersonal channels to the personal ones.[2]

Notwithstanding the centrality of their role, however, it seems preferable not to view opinion leaders as opinion-makers nor to designate as opinion-making the communicative activity of those persons whose access is limited

[1] Elihu Katz and Paul F. Lazarsfeld, *Personal Influence* (Glencoe, Ill.: Free Press, 1955), Ch. 2.

[2] The designation "opinion leader" has been explicitly applied to performers of this relay function by Elihu Katz and Paul F. Lazarsfeld, *Personal Influence: The Part Played by People in the Flow of Mass Communications* (Glencoe, Ill.: Free Press, 1955), pp. 137–138, and it is in this sense that we shall use the designation on the few occasions when we need to take note of face-to-face communication among opinion-holders. If opinion-holders were more central to our focus, it would probably be necessary to develop new terminology (including, say, "opinion-relayer"), so as to delineate more clearly the various types of access to personal channels.

to the personal channels of the circulatory system. Two major considerations make it advisable to restrict the definition of opinion-making to the activity of those individuals who have access to impersonal channels. In the first place, it will be recalled that we are concerned here with charting how and where opinions flow through the communications system, not with depicting how and where they come to be held. In this sense it is the impersonal channels that constitute the main arteries of the circulatory system. Through them, opinions are distributed throughout the society regardless of whether they are picked up and internalized by individual opinion-holders. Opinions will not circulate very far, on the other hand, if those expressing them fail to modify—that is, influence—the viewpoints of their listeners. Through the personal channels may flow important pulsations of influence, but, from the point of view of opinion circulation, they are, so to speak, the small vessels which carry the blood to the extremities of the organism.

A second and closely related reason why those who transmit opinions exclusively by face-to-face means are not considered opinion-makers stems from the conception that the circulatory system functions via a "two-step flow," in which opinions first move through its impersonal channels and are then passed on through personal channels. If this is the case, and all the evidence justifies such a conception, it then follows that those who initiate the first step of the sequence are also those who give structure, informational content, and judgmental direction to the opinions which enter the communications system. In other words, the opinions which circulate are given form—are "made"—by those who introduce them into the impersonal channels. Hence it is appropriate to designate persons who have access to these channels as opinion-makers, and to regard everyone else as opinion-holders—that is, as potential recipients of the opinions which circulate.[3]

To be sure, opinion-holders can be said to form or "make" opinions whenever they dip into the circulatory system and internalize as their own one set of opinions rather than another. Opinions which become internalized in this fashion, however, already possess structure, content, and direction, so that opinion-forming in the creative sense does not accompany the process by which most opinion-holders develop their opinions. Similarly,

---

[3] At this point, I make no distinction between nonopinion-makers who have highly structured opinions about a particular foreign-policy issue and those who have no opinions whatsoever. Both are considered opinion-holders in order to emphasize that those who lack opinions may be just as relevant to the opinion-policy relationship as those who adhere to a point of view. In this sense, lack of ideas or information about an issue is considered to be a form of opinion. Moreover, by designating all nonopinion-makers as opinion-holders, we also make the point that behavior has to occur for opinions to be acquired, that potentially all citizens may be aroused to dip into the circulatory system for ideas and information. Of course, the distinction between the two types of opinion-holders cannot be entirely overlooked; it is accounted for below by an application of the motivation-information scale in which the opinion-holding public is subdivided into the attentive and mass publics.

the "making" of opinion does not necessarily occur when, say, two opinion-holders argue about which of several alternatives should be followed with respect to a particular foreign-policy issue. Even if one of them is ultimately convinced by the other in this face-to-face situation, such a debate does not constitute opinion-making because ordinarily the disputed alternatives have been previously formulated and have reached the disputants through prior throbs of the circulatory system. In short, it is henceforth assumed that opinions are formed *before* they circulate widely; that only opinion-makers formulate the opinions which are widely disseminated; and that little modification occurs in the structure, content, and direction of opinions once they circulate beyond the ranks of opinion-makers.[4]

This does not mean that opinion-makers are necessarily more influential than the opinion leaders who subsequently reroute their opinions from the impersonal to the personal channels of communication. As previously noted, influence is considered to be a process of interaction in which the behavior of the influencer modifies the behavior of the influence. In this sense, those who are responsible for the way in which opinion-holders internalize opinions may be just as influential as those who are responsible for the introduction of opinions into the circulatory system. Opinion-makers may often, but not always, perform the former as well as the latter function. The exercise of influence is not, to repeat, an automatic derivative of participation in the opinion-making process.

Nor does the distinction between opinion-makers and opinion-holders necessarily mean that the former are more knowledgeable about world affairs than the latter. The fact that many opinion-holders are dependent upon them for ideas and information does not necessarily lead opinion-makers to formulate sound or elaborate opinions. In some cases such a dependence may even require the formulation of opinions which, to the outside observer, seem to have little relevance to the world scene. Thus, depending upon the particular positions they occupy, some opinion-makers appear to be well informed and others uninformed. In their opinions, some may reflect the world they see while others may reflect the world they believe ought to exist. Some will advance their opinions as tentative formulations; others will insist that they have developed a blueprint for immediate action. Some may circulate opinions about every major issue, while others

---

[4] This point suggests that the opinion-making process is composed of two subprocesses: opinion-forming and opinion-circulating. The former refers to the interaction which takes place between opinion-makers (either through personal or impersonal channels) and which results in the development of diverse interpretations and judgments of particular issues. The latter refers to the communicative activity of opinion-makers whereby they introduce opinions into the impersonal channels that extend beyond their ranks. Although we shall have occasion to note that opinion-forming may not be followed by opinion-circulating, it is assumed that normally the two subprocesses overlap and unfold sequentially. Accordingly, so as to avoid unnecessary complexity, this breakdown of the opinion-making process has not, except as otherwise noted, been made a part of the ensuing analysis.

may confine their opinion-making activity to selected issues, either because they choose to do so or because their positions limit their access to the impersonal channels. Some may not purposely utilize their access to the impersonal channels, but may unintentionally have their opinions circulated because others, such as journalists, specialize in circulating the views of all opinion-makers as well as their own. In other words, opinion-makers are not homogeneous in either outlook or behavior.

Having used the accessibility scale to identify the opinion-makers, we are now in a position to complete the stratification of the public by introducing the motivation-information scale and differentiating between two basic types of opinion-holders. This latter distinction leads to a conception of American society that places all of its members in one of three strata. Together, these strata form a pyramidal structure that constitutes the "public" for any foreign-policy issue at any moment in time. While the composition and size of each stratum may vary somewhat as the issues vary through time,[5] all three will be present in a hierarchical arrangement whenever the opinion-policy relationship is activated and a public forms around a particular issue. As previously implied, opinions relative to the issue will circulate both vertically between the strata and horizontally within them. We shall return to these downward and sideward channels of communication after we have examined the characteristics of each stratum.

At the base of the pyramid, and comprising the greater part of its volume, is the *mass public*, composed of opinion-holders who have neither the opportunity nor the inclination to participate in the opinion-making process. Members of the mass public, in other words, fall at the lower end of both the accessibility and the motivation-information scales. The middle stratum, located near the top of the pyramid, is the *attentive public*, consisting of opinion-holders who are inclined to participate but lack the access or opportunity to do so. Attentive opinion-holders are thus those who fall at the lower end of the accessibility scale and the upper end of the motivation-information scale. At the very tip of the pyramid is the *opinion-making public*, composed of those who are, as indicated, located above the zero point on both scales.[6]

The notion of a stationary pyramid is perhaps a poor way of introducing behavioral differences among the three strata of the public. A more appropriate analogy is that of a gigantic theater, with a tense drama unfolding

---

[5] For a more elaborate analysis of this conception of the varying composition of the "public," see Harvey Glickman, "Viewing Public Opinion in Politics: A Common Sense Approach," *Public Opinion Quarterly*, 23 (Winter 1959–1960), pp. 498–501.

[6] This pyramidal conception, as well as the analysis of the mass and attentive publics which follow, has been derived from Gabriel Almond's formulation of the opinion-policy relationship (in particular see his *The American People and Foreign Policy*, pp. 138–139). The only major innovation is the labeling of the opinion-making public, which Almond regards as the elite groups. The reasons for this terminological alteration are noted in Chapter 5.

on the stage.[7] The mass public, occupying the many seats in the balcony, is so far removed from the scene of action that its members can hardly grasp the plot, much less hear all the lines or distinguish between the actors. Thus they may sit in stony silence or applaud impetuously, if not so vigorously as to shake the foundations of the theater. Usually, however, they get thoroughly bored and leave, declining as they go invitations to occupy the empty seats in the orchestra. The attentive public, on the other hand, is located in the few choice orchestra seats. Its members can not only hear every spoken line clearly, but can also see the facial expressions of the actors. Thus they become absorbed in the drama, applauding its high spots and disparaging its flaws. Indeed, their involvement is such that during the intermission they make their views known to any occupants of the balcony who may have wandered into the lobby. As for the members of the opinion-making public, they are the actors on the stage, performing their parts with gusto and intensity, not infrequently in an effort to upstage each other. Many are directing their performance at some specific portion of the orchestra audience. Others, those with especially strong vocal cords, try to make themselves heard as far as the balcony. All are keenly aware that the quality of their performance will greatly affect their bagaining power when they seek higher salaries or better parts in future productions.[8]

The Mass Public

Let us look more closely at the largest stratum. By almost any yardstick, the mass public includes a preponderant majority of the nation. Estimates of its size vary from 75 to 90 per cent of the adult population. The mass public is uninformed about either specific foreign-policy issues or foreign affairs in general. Its members pay little, if any, attention to day-to-day developments in world politics. Being uninformed and without initiative,

---

[7] Elmo Roper uses still another analogy, that of concentric circles, as a means of developing "the hypothesis that in so far as the flow of ideas is concerned, the entire American public can be stratified into six groups." Moving outward from the inner circle, Roper designates his six publics as the "Great Thinkers," the "Great Disciples," the "Great Disseminators," the "Lesser Disseminators," the "Participating Citizens," and the "Politically Inert" ("Who Tells the Story-tellers," *Saturday Review* (July 31, 1954), and the Foreword, in Katz and Lazarsfeld, *op. cit.*, pp. xv–xix). The last two of Roper's categories are roughly the equivalent of the attentive and mass publics, while his two groups of disseminators approximate what we have called the opinion-making public. Our conceptualization is not so explicit about the two innermost circles of Roper's scheme, but the few persons to which they apply also come under our definition of opinion-makers.

[8] Anticipating distinctions we shall later make between national and local opinion-makers, and between multi-issue and single-issue opinion-makers, this analogy can be carried further by noting that some occupants of the orchestra seats are members of the show's road company and are attending the performance with a view to learning their parts.

they lack structured opinions—that is, they are short of the cognitive and evaluative equipment which facilitates comprehension of the ideas and information that are flowing through the circulatory system. Thus their response to foreign-policy matters is less one of intellect and more one of emotion; less one of opinion and more one of mood, of generalized, superficial, and undisciplined feelings which easily fluctuate from one extreme to another—from tolerance to intolerance, optimism to pessimism, idealism to cynicism, withdrawal to intervention.

The most predominant mood of the mass public is, of course, indifference and passivity. Except for acute peace-or-war crises (and not always then), the mass public is usually unmoved by the course of world events. Few of its members are likely to have more than headline acquaintance with public discussions of foreign-policy issues or be willing to listen to more than truncated news broadcasts over radio and television. And even when contact is made with more substantive programs, the mass public "does not listen to the content of discussion but to its tone." In its passive mood, the mass public resists the prodding of opinion-makers, who are not content to let a slumbering giant rest. Few members of the mass public are likely to be activated into the temporary role of amateur opinion-submitters. Even fewer are likely to be enticed into permanent membership in the attentive public. As a passive mass, in other words, the mass public lies virtually outside the opinion-policy relationship. Its only function is that of setting, through the potentiality of its more active moods, the outer limits within which decision-makers and opinion-makers feel constrained to operate and interact. Since these limits are very broad, and since the mood of passivity prevails most of the time, it is the more structured and informed opinions of the attentive and opinion-making publics that usually determine the context within which the opinion-policy relationship functions.

On the rare occasions when it does awaken from its slumber, the mass public, being no more informed than previously, is impulsive, unstable, unreasoning, unpredictable, capable of suddenly shifting direction or of going in several contradictory directions at the same time. The nation's reactions to Russia's launching of the first earth satellite in October 1957, or to the advent of Red China's entry into the Korean War in November 1950, might be cited as recent examples of this type of aroused behavior on the part of the mass public. At such times, its members turn more frequently to opinion-submitting, either through their own amateur efforts or through more active support of their representatives in the opinion-making public. An air of uncertainty and intolerance is introduced into the "climate" of public opinion. The area of decision-making permissiveness is narrowed as the mass public moves closer to the center of the opinion-policy relationship. Instability and irrationality enter the policy-making process as both decision-makers and opinion-makers seek to cope with the changing moods and tempo of mass opinion. Hence it would seem that, given these conditions as the alternative to indifference, the prevalence of the mass public's passive mood introduces a factor of stability into the foreign policy-making process.

The respective consequences of the mass public's passive and active moods are amply illustrated by what has been called "attention groups." These are unorganized segments of the mass public, such as ethnic minorities, which are normally passive and disinterested, but which acquire structure as an aroused group whenever an issue arises that directly affects their common interests—for example, the liberation of Eastern Europe. Their entrance into public debate is then sudden and impulsive, and confined exclusively to the single issue which provoked them. Their recommendations concern only that issue, unmodified by and irrespective of the requirements of any other policy considerations. Once the issue has subsided, these attention groups disband (in so far as foreign policy is concerned), returning to the status of unorganized and passive segments of the mass public. Their cumulative effect "can be understood in terms of the analogy of loaded pistols which are triggered off by special issues which bring generally inattentive and uninformed groups into a sudden impact on the policy-making process."

Attention groups emphasize the heterogeneous composition of the mass public. They come into being because members of the mass public have a variety of political, economic, and social affiliations which can form the basis of temporary emergence from passivity. Some of these affiliations derive from organizational membership, as in a union, a trade association, or a religious club. Others are derived from reference group membership, as in a social class, an occupational field, or a religious denomination. The net result of both types of affiliation is a mass public of enormous diversity, of disparate and crisscrossing segments that have in common only a passivity and moodiness toward foreign-policy issues. Each affiliative segment, moreover, tends to have spokesmen in the opinion-making public, a linkage which, as will be seen, constitutes a major impersonal channel of communication in the circulatory system. In short, contrary to the impression conveyed by our reference to the mass public as an *it* that awakes or slumbers or feels or sets limits, neither most Americans nor their leaders are joined together in a grand and homogeneous organization that *does* things. By "mass public" we do not mean an identifiable actor; rather, the term and the action verbs associated with it are a shorthand method of describing the combined *effect* of unrelated actions or opinions (or inaction or nonopinion) which are undertaken or held by countless persons and groups that are ordinarily inattentive to international affairs.

Nor does our definition of the mass public contain an implicit explanation of its behavior. To say that the mass public includes those who have neither the inclination nor the opportunity to participate in the opinion-making process is not to say that the former characteristic is a consequence of the latter, or that members of the mass public are passive and moody because they lack a chance to be active participants in the public debate over foreign-policy issues. If this were the case, there would be no conceptual room for the empirical fact that some persons, the attentive public, *do* possess an interest in and structured opinions about such matters, despite a similar lack of access to the opinion-making process. The opportunity to participate through occupancy of certain leadership positions does, to be sure, foster an inclination to do so. If members of the mass public were to move into these opinion-making positions their passivity toward foreign affairs would probably change. But the holding of such a position is not necessarily prerequisite to an active interest in foreign policy, as the attentive public demonstrates. The definitions of the three publics, in short, are empirical and not causal. Obviously, the reasons for the passivity of most Americans are more complex than simply the scarcity of opportunities to join the ranks of opinion-makers.

The Attentive Public

As the foregoing implies, in some respects the attentive public closely resembles the mass public. It too is an unorganized cross section of the nation. Its members may have higher incomes and more formal education than those of the mass public, but, taken as a whole, they hardly represent a homogeneous stratum of American society. Indeed, being composed of individuals with structured opinions, the attentive public probably encompasses greater diversity of outlook than does the mass public with its unstructured moods. A second similarity between the two is, of course, one of definition: in neither case do members of these publics occupy leadership positions which provide their occupants with access to the impersonal channels of the communications system. As noted below, the role of the attentive public in the opinion-making process is highly significant, but it does not include participation in the opinion-making process itself.

Nevertheless, these similarities between the attentive and mass publics are far less important than the several ways in which they differ. One distinguishing feature of the attentive public is its size, which, though variously estimated, is small by almost any standard. Based on the circulation figures of the "quality media," [7] the attentive public is probably no larger than 10 per cent of the population, and possibly much smaller. Elmo Roper estimates that this stratum, which he calls the "Participating Citizens," is composed of "as many as ten to twenty-five million Americans." Another observer suggests that the attentive public may be constantly "increasing in size and in discrimination" because the universities, the quality media of communication, and the civic interest groups are more effectively stimulat-

---

[7] These are the channels through which members of the attentive public tend to acquire their opinions about foreign-policy issues.

ing more persons to maintain an interest in foreign affairs. Whatever the trend, however, in the foreseeable future the attentive public will remain minute in comparison to the mass public.

A second and much more important difference between the two publics is that members of the attentive public are more inclined to participate in the opinion-making process even though they have no opportunity to do so. Being continuously interested in foreign-policy matters, they are aware of the major issues and well informed with respect to them. Consequently the opinions which they internalize have structure and depth. While they too may occasionally respond to crises in an impetuous and moody way, members of the attentive public are not likely to persist in such behavior for very long. Their high level of interest and information serves to check the growth and maintenance of moods. In terms of concrete action, probably a substantial proportion of the attentive public frequently writes to decision-makers or engages in other forms of amateur opinion-submitting. Presumably it is also comprised of persons who constitute the active membership (though not the leadership) of voluntary associations. Although members of the mass and attentive publics may have their names side by side on associational rosters, it is the latter who are more likely to attend meetings and otherwise support associational efforts and policies.

Of course, the factors which lead to attentiveness are no less complex or easy to explain than those which produce indifference and passivity. Here we shall have to content ourselves with the simple conclusion that permanent members of the attentive public, as distinguished from members of the mass public who are temporarily activated by the special interests of an attention group, find intellectual stimulation and satisfaction in matters pertaining to foreign policy. The behavioral consequences of this intellectual hobby amount to a crucial role for the attentive public in the opinion-making process. Not only does this public constitute one of the key links in the vertical channels of communication between the opinion-making and mass publics, but, more important, the attentive public serves as a critical audience for opinion-makers as they discuss and debate foreign-policy issues. Such an audience, alert to the intricacies of day-to-day policy situations, tends to offset the irrational impact of mass moods and to fill the vacuum which exists when indifference is the prevailing mood. Members of the attentive public provide, in effect, a forum in which foreign-policy controversy among opinion-makers can occur openly and in specific rather than superficial terms. Thus, as the stratum of society to which opinion-makers make special appeals for support, the attentive public introduces a more effective measure of democratic control into the opinion-policy relationship than does the mass public. If the latter sets the outer limits beyond which policy choices cannot be made, then the former can be said to determine the inner limits within which the opinion-policy relationship operates.

Non-Governmental Groups and Foreign Policy

Gabriel A. Almond
THE ELITES AND FOREIGN POLICY

THE term "elite" acquired its modern sociological connotation in the writings of Vilfredo Pareto. Pareto was one of the most original and systematic thinkers in the late nineteenth- and early twentieth-century school of disillusionment and "scientism" which produced so many brilliant insights into, and so many distorted interpretations of, human and social behavior. Their hearts hardened by the fate of nineteenth-century liberal and socialist idealism and thrilled by the achievements of the physical and biological sciences, these intellectuals put on the white coats of the laboratory and fell to work dissecting the social organism and analyzing the physics of the soul. Their iconoclasm and detachment were somehow a suitable answer to Victorian morality and cosmology. Not many social scientists today can write of themselves as Pareto did in the opening words of his theoretical introduction: "This book is written for an exclusively scientific end. . . . I have no other purpose but objectively to seek the truth." The illusion of scientific precision and theoretical comprehensiveness was often created by the application of natural science concepts to social and psychological phenomena, as in Pareto's physiological interpretation of social mobility, or in Freud's physical and biological psychology.

The shortcomings of Pareto's elite theory resulted in part from his cynicism, and in part from his physiological bias. His doctrine rules out the possibility of a relationship of responsibility between elite and rank and file; the only possible relationship is one of coercion and manipulation. Humanitarianism in Pareto is treated as a symptom of elite degeneracy. A new elite capable of ruthlessness will soon supplant it. He also greatly oversimplified the processes of social and political mobility. He likened the "circulation of the elite" to the circulation of the blood. One gets the im-

F R O M *The American People and Foreign Policy* by Gabriel A. Almond, copyright, 1950, by Harcourt, Brace & World, Inc. and reprinted with their permission.

pression of a homogeneous substance, following certain natural laws of movement in which there is no place for the category of rational control and policy-making.

The concept of the elite as used here is not inconsistent with democratic or any other forms of control. It rests upon the insight so well established in political and sociological theory that any social form of action involves division of labor and division of influence. The influential are the elite. In a democratic society most adult persons have formally an equal share of influence. The distribution of power thus involves a gradation of influence in which there is no "non-elite" in the formal sense.

Both the "elitists" and their democratic critics have created serious confusion: the first, by the rejection of the possibility of a form of political division of labor in which the people have an effective share of influence; the second, by slurring over the reality of the political and social stratification of influence and perpetuating the myth of the active "demos." A genuine understanding of the political process requires the elimination of both of these normative inhibitions and the acceptance of structural conceptions. Much of the contemporary writing on public opinion and foreign policy falls into the democratic error of minimizing the inherent social and political stratification of influence. The tendency is to pose the problem in terms of an interplay between an official democratically selected leadership and an undifferentiated public. The types of problems treated fall into two categories: first, how to make the official leadership responsible to the public; and second, how to make the public alert, informed, and active in policy-making.

Actually the problems of public opinion and foreign policy are a good deal more complex than is suggested in the recent literature. As a crude approximation of political reality one might suggest four principal factors in the opinion and policy process. One may speak of a "general public" if one keeps in mind that while it is characterized by a sense of identification and reacts to general stimuli, it also contains a variety of interests and groupings which are affected differentially by both general and specific stimuli. Second, there is an "attentive public" which is informed and interested in foreign policy problems, and which constitutes the audience for the foreign policy discussions among the elites. Third, one may speak of the policy and opinion elites, the articulate policy-bearing stratum of the population which gives structure to the public, and which provides the effective means of access to the various groupings. One might almost say "who mobilizes elites, mobilizes the public." Such a formulation would be closer to the truth than some of the more ardent claims of democratic ideologues. Finally, within the elite formations one would have to single out the legal or official policy leadership—executives, legislators, civil servants—the mode of selection and role of which are more widely understood.

With this fourfold classification of factors we can begin to understand the democratic policy-making process. In this process the general mass of the population is neither interested nor informed, and is unable continuously to be active in policy-making. If interest, knowledge, and constant participation on the part of the mass were our criteria, we would have to write off all historic democracies as something other than democratic.

There are perhaps three essential criteria of a democratic policy-making process. First, there is the requirement of formal opportunity for mass participation. Second, there is the requirement of genuine autonomy and competition among the elites. Third, there is the requirement of an attentive public—an informed and interested stratum—before whom elite discussion and controversy take place. The various elites exercise different types of power in the policy-making process and have different types of relationships with their "constituencies." They impinge on policy-making at different points; and they are subject to popular control in differing degrees. The "masses" participate in policy-making in indirect and primarily passive ways. Their moods, interests, and expectations set limits on the discretion of their representatives—those exercising influence within private organizations and institutions and in the media of communication, as well as those holding public office. The public also affects the selection of elites through the public electoral process, the private electoral process of interest groups, or through "buying" or refusing to "buy" the policy recommendations of the communications elites.

Types of Foreign Policy Elites

The elite groups which share in the process of policy initiation and formation may be classified functionally under four main headings.

1. The *political elites* which include the publicly elected, high appointive, as well as the party leaders. The official political elite, of course, is subdivided according to its position in the policy-making process (i.e., legislative, executive, judicial) and according to the policy subject matter with which it is charged (e.g., in the foreign policy field, the Department of State and the foreign affairs committees of the House and Senate).

2. The *administrative* or *bureaucratic elites* which include the professional corps of the executive establishment who enjoy special powers by virtue of their interest in and familiarity and immediate contact with particular policy problems.

3. The *interest elites* which include the representatives of the vast number of private, policy-oriented associations, ranging from huge nation-wide aggregations to local formations and organized around aims and objectives which in their variety reflect the economic, ethnic, religious, and ideological complexity of the American population. Here too, as with the *political elites*, we may distinguish between the *elected* or *political interest*

elites and the *bureaucratic staffs* which have an importance in the field of interest group activity comparable to that of the governmental bureaucracy in official policy-making. They too are on the daily firing line of decision-making and enjoy powers in practice which are not formally recognized in the legal distribution of authority.

4. Finally, there are the *communications elites*, the most obvious representatives of which are the owners, controllers, and active participants of the mass media—radio, press, and movies. Careful analysis, however, indicates that the swift development and prominence of the mass media have tended to obscure the continued decisive importance of more intimate forms of communication in the shaping of popular attitudes. Perhaps the most effective opinion leaders are the vast number of vocational, community, and institutional "notables," known and trusted men and women —clergymen and influential lay churchmen, club and fraternal order leaders, teachers and the like—with personal followings. It may even be said that mass communication becomes more effective in the degree that it approximates the more intimate relationship between a personally known leader and his following. Thus, the "fireside chat," and the favorite columnist almost succeed in dissociating themselves from the impersonality and superficial impact of the mass media.

Any simple description of the structure of communications necessarily does violence to its variety and complexity. It overlaps with the political, bureaucratic, and interest group elites—all of whom compete for the attention of various publics via the media of communication. In this classification, however, the communications elites are limited to the *specialists* in communication—newspapermen, radio and movie personnel, teachers, clergymen, publicists, and the like.

Another method of elite classification might be based on policy interests and specializations. Thus one might speak of the foreign policy elite as having a political sector including the elected officials and their advisers especially charged with foreign policy decisions, the bureaucratic sector which includes the professional administrative personnel in and outside the State Department who deal with foreign policy questions, the interest group sector which includes the leadership of "foreign policy associations" as well as the foreign policy specialists within the more general interest organizations, and finally the communications sector which includes among others, publishers, editors, journalists, publicists, commentators, and teachers who are partly, primarily, or entirely devoted to foreign policy problems.

These various elites have quite different relationships with their followings. In some cases the system of selection facilitates intra-elite competition and rank-and-file control; in others, popular control and competition are minimized. Also, the degree to which publics are interested in "controlling" the policy decisions of their leadership varies with the nature of the issue and the pressures of the time.

All of these factors combine to reduce popular control to the status of a crude and primarily passive instrument. But this does not by any means suggest that its role in policy-making is insignificant. The various policy and opinion elites are continually, and more or less freely, recruited from the rank and file and consequently share in its prejudices and preferences. In addition they compete with one another in the "opinion markets" for the "sale" of policies. In most cases the influential policy alternatives placed before the public, or its constituent parts, represent in more or less articulate form the vaguer impulses and preferences of the masses.

But even this degree of popular control over the opinion and policy leaderships presupposes a measure of interest in, and awareness of, the issues on the part of the public. An obvious principle may be advanced in this connection that the influence of elite and minority groups in policy-making varies with the level of public concern with the issue. There are situations in which public predispositions set up a stony resistance to all appeals for change—widespread preferences or prejudices on which the hopes of propagandists are repeatedly crushed. There are other situations in which significant decisions fail to activate recognition or emotion among the public, and in which a free channel of decision is accorded to interested groups. It can hardly be said that these moods of public interest and apathy follow any rational pattern. For an issue which is met with indifference today may tomorrow provoke grave public concern. In this connection, a second principle may be hazarded that the public does not see the interdependence of decisions and policies. Only those aspects of the policy-making process really impinge on the public which directly involve immediate and observable interests.

The converse of this principle has a special bearing on the problem of public opinion and foreign policy. In the degree to which issues and decisions are remote, the incapacity of the public to grasp the issues and its consequent indifference accords a special importance to the initiatives and pressures of interested elite and minority groups. Under circumstances of peace or of only moderate international tension, most of the daily decisions of diplomacy and foreign policy are "remote." They involve little known peoples in far-away countries, or highly technical problems such as boundary settlements, international trade, and the complex issues of foreign loans and foreign economies. They are, indeed, the stuff out of which war and peace, victory and defeat, are made. But foreign policy is a tapestry of infinite complexity, and even the expert can only hope to achieve familiarity with a part of its intricate designs.

James N. Rosenau
THE ROLE OF NATIONAL LEADERSHIP

With the identity of national leaders in mind, let us turn now to constructing a model of their role in the foreign policy-making process. Extrapolating from studies of leadership in local communities, it seems clear that the main function of nongovernmental leaders at the national level is one of supporting or vetoing policy alternatives developed by their colleagues in the federal government. The former do not have the information, time, and other policy-making resources which the latter can employ to refine and translate initial ideas into workable and concrete alternatives. Nor do they have the formal authority to select a particular course of action. They can, however, react to alternatives proposed by policy-makers. Indeed, their responsibilities as leaders of segments of the mass public require them to judge government proposals—to "make" opinions—that are relevant to the area in which they exercise leadership.

Nor are the responsibilities of national leadership fulfilled after alternatives have been evaluated. Nongovernmental opinion-makers are then obligated to pronounce their judgments—to articulate the interests of those in the mass public for whom they are leaders. In this way both their followers and their colleagues in government are informed as to whether a proposal is acceptable, or at least not objectionable. Because they are spokesmen for diverse segments of the public, in other words, national leaders have an informal authority which the ordinary citizen does not possess, which officialdom cannot ignore, and which thus enables them to prevent or permit the selection of alternatives that are formulated, modified, and proposed by government leaders. American policy toward Communist China in the 1950s and United States adoption of the Marshall Plan in 1947 illustrate, respectively, the preventive and permissive versions of this national leadership function.

Like their counterparts at the local level, in short, national leaders serve as a key link between officialdom and the citizenry. They guide and mold mass opinion and they also reflect it, and in this dual capacity the flexibility, intensity, and depth of their opinions constitute the essential subsoil in which foreign policy alternatives must be rooted. As V. O. Key puts it, the ranks of national leadership—"the talkers, the persuaders, the speculators,

Reprinted from *National Leadership and Foreign Policy* by James N. Rosenau by permission of Princeton University Press. Copyright 1963, Princeton University Press.

the philosophers, the advocates, the opponents—mediate between the world of remote and complex events and the mass of the public." [1]

While the veto-support function of nongovernmental opinion-makers is the main focus of this inquiry, we need to differentiate it from another important role of national leadership—from what might be called the advisory function which some nongovernmental leaders perform when they respond to officialdom's requests for technical advice. As a dynamic technology renders world affairs more and more complex, government leaders have increasingly sought the expertise of private citizens in order to cope with the technical aspects of policy alternatives under consideration. The contribution of university scientists to decisions on nuclear testing is a good example of the advisory role played by nongovernmental leaders.[2] It is, however, very different from the veto-support function. The difference is unmistakable in the typical case of the opinion-making public vetoing or supporting a policy alternative *after* it has been formulated and proposed. Less clear are the cases when national leaders are "consulted" and "informed" about governmental thinking on a problem during the development of a policy and *prior* to the selection of an alternative. Under these circumstances a certain amount of expertise may be supplied officials, but frequently this is incidental to the main purpose of contacting and informing nongovernmental leaders. Often the primary aim of bringing interested leadership groups into policy deliberations at a pre-decisional stage is that of ensuring support when an alternative is finally adopted. It is presumed that if these groups are kept abreast of the deliberations and any major objections they may register taken into account, then they will be more likely to approve of the final decision and thus provide it with a legitimacy which it might not otherwise have. In short, because the veto-support function can, in effect, be performed at a pre-decision stage, there may be occasions when it appears indistinguishable from the advisory role of national leadership. Yet, the manner in which consultation between governmental and nongovernmental leaders occurs and the composition of the groups consulted should permit clear differentiation of the two roles.[3]

Closely related to the foregoing is still another function of nongovernmental leaders, which we shall call the issue-making function. While the

---

[1] V. O. Key, Jr., *Public Opinion and American Democracy* (New York: Alfred A. Knopf, 1961), p. 261.

[2] For a stimulating discussion of the advantages and difficulties attendant upon the performance of this advisory function, see Henry A. Kissinger, "The Policymaker and the Intellectual," *The Reporter*, 20 (March 5, 1959), pp. 30–35.

[3] Under special circumstances, of course, the two roles may be performed simultaneously, thereby greatly complicating the task of distinguishing between them. An excellent account of one such situation will be found in Morton H. Halperin, "The Gaither Committee and the Policy Process," *World Politics*, XIII (April 1961), pp. 360–84. A more general analysis of the overlap between the advisory and veto-support functions will be found in Harlan Cleveland, "Inquiry Into Presidential Inquiries," *New York Times Magazine*, August 14, 1960, pp. 12, 92–93.

task of developing, refining, and choosing policy alternatives is performed by government officials, other national opinion-makers can contribute to the process whereby policies do or do not become the center of public attention. If key groups of leaders do not, perhaps for a variety of reasons, become interested in a situation abroad and engage in opinion-making with respect to it, then the situation is not likely to take hold and acquire status as an "issue." To be sure, if the President or ranking members of Congress press the matter, it will receive a public airing. But it will not remain long in the limelight if concern about the situation is confined to officialdom.[4] Contrariwise, foreign policy issues come into being and persist when situations abroad arouse opinion-makers and become the subject of a continuing dialogue between them.

How many opinion-makers have to be activated to create and sustain an issue? Extrapolating from local community studies, it can be assumed that although an "issue can hardly be said to exist unless and until it commands the attention of a *significant segment*" of the opinion-making public, "whenever a *sizable minority* of the legitimate elements" of the leadership structure "is determined to bring some question to the fore, the chances are high that the rest" of the leadership groups "will soon begin to pay attention."[5] Once this happens, of course, the issue-making and veto-support functions merge into one. Irrespective of whether nongovernmental opinion-makers create an issue before or after officialdom becomes sensitive to the situation (and usually governmental sensitivity precedes issue-making), the more they concentrate attention on the situation, the more they engage in a process of vetoing or supporting alternative policies toward it. This fusing of the two functions also occurs whenever governmental responses to situations do *not* provoke debate among opinion-makers. In such instances—what might be called "unmade" issues—the lack of controversy among leadership segments constitutes, in effect, passive support for the decisions and actions of officials.

The veto-support function performed by nongovernmental leadership has long been explicitly recognized by officialdom at the local level. Convening a conference of "distinguished citizens" from all walks of life for the purpose of discussing and advising on particular problems facing a community is a commonplace practice of city mayors and state governors. Indeed, this technique is frequently institutionalized through the establishment of "citizens committees" of prominent leaders upon whom officials can "rely" for guidance. Dahl reports, for example, that without the creation of such a group, the Citizens Action Commission, officials in New Haven

---

[4] For a case study of a foreign policy problem which never became a full-fledged issue, see Bernard C. Cohen, *The Political Process and Foreign Policy: The Making of the Japanese Peace Settlement* (Princeton: Princeton University Press, 1957).

[5] Robert A. Dahl, *Who Governs? Democracy and Power in an American City* (New Haven: Yale University Press, 1961), p. 22 (italics added).

would never have been able to carry through a vast urban redevelopment program.[6] One might almost say that nongovernmental leaders give a *tri-cameral* quality to the policy-making process, that they constitute a "third chamber" of the legislature in which executive agencies must win support, or at least avoid defeat, even though votes are never actually tabulated.[7]

Nor have federal officials been unmindful of the role of nongovernmental leadership. Periodically, for example, President Eisenhower invited various national opinion-makers to "stag dinners" as a means of exchanging ideas on international and national problems. Similarly, President Kennedy has systematically played host at "luncheons" for publishers and editors from the various states in order to discuss with them matters of mutual concern.[8] Furthermore, in recent years leadership conferences and committees have been used as a policy-making technique by federal officials with increasing frequency and in an ever-widening number of issue-areas. Like their counter-parts at the local level, heads of federal agencies have reasoned that if a diverse and bipartisan group of leaders approve a proposed program, or if they do not object to it, opposition to the proposal will not easily coalesce and might even be nullified. In effect, by institutionalizing the veto-support function officials of the executive branch create their own legislature—"third chambers" which can rival, and thus pressure, the two houses of Congress.[9]

Abundant evidence could be marshalled to demonstrate the importance and institutionalization of the veto-support function at the national level. Indeed, its importance has been directly and publicly called to the attention of the Congress. In reporting to the Senate Foreign Relations Commit-

[6] *Ibid.*, p. 133.

[7] Or, if one wished to emphasize that leaders appointed to advisory boards and citizens' commissions constitute an extension of the work and scope of government, the institutionalization of their role might be viewed as the creation of an "external bureaucracy." This formulation has been impressively developed by Chadwick F. Alger, who refers "to these inhabitants of both the private and public worlds as external bu-reaucrats" because of the difficulty of classifying them "as either private citizens or government officials." See his "The External Bureaucracy in United States Foreign Affairs," *Administrative Science Quarterly*, 7 (June 1962), pp. 50–78.

[8] For a full account of the purposes and procedures of these luncheons, see the *New York Times*, October 22, 1961.

[9] Nor is the executive branch the only creator of "third chambers." Some private organizations have also regularly convened diverse groups of nongovernmental leaders with a view to discussing public problems and recommending solutions to them. The semi-annual meetings of the American Assembly are perhaps the most notable and publicized "third chamber" of this sort, but similar conferences are sponsored as annual or periodic events by such organizations as the Standard Oil Company of New Jersey, the Council on Religion and International Affairs, and the American Federation of Labor and Congress of Industrial Organizations. Indeed, even the U.S. Congress has conferred legitimate status upon "third chambers." In this case, however, the purpose is not that of implementing the veto-support function. Rather Congress tends to set up public advisory committees such as the International Development Advisory Board or the Advisory Committee on Educational Exchange in order to maintain a check over the work of the Executive . . .

tee, the Brookings Institution suggested that *both* the legislative and the executive branches should employ a variety of techniques to institutionalize the role of nongovernmental leaders. While not ignoring the need to inform the general public, the Brookings report stressed that

> a more systematic and energetic effort should be made to bring leaders of public opinion into closer touch with the officials and processes that shape U.S. foreign policy. These leaders are extremely important in informing and mobilizing the public and are most likely to make the best use of such an opportunity.
>
> Many devices could be used to implement this . . . alternative. More high-level briefings might be conducted by the executive departments for selected groups. Some agencies, such as the Industrial College of the Armed Forces, have devised programs for Reserve officers and private citizens in various cities which could serve as models for the foreign affairs field. More opportunities might be given to leading individuals to take part in the policy process as consultants, temporary staff members, delegates, or visitors abroad. Arrangements to provide information and other services for groups conducting programs in world affairs could be strengthened. The Congress could contribute by reinforcing its relations with special groups and the media that reach these groups. Hearings could be held in various parts of the country, and Members of Congress might more frequently form bipartisan teams to explain aspects of foreign policy and sample attitudes. A few Members have already performed valuable services in this regard and have developed effective means of discussing the essence of policy with community audiences.[10]

That such techniques are in fact being employed with increasing frequency in different foreign policy areas is indicated by such recently established organizations as the National Advisory Council for the Peace Corps, the Citizens Committee for International Development, the Freedom From Hunger Foundation, the General Advisory Committee of the United States Arms Control and Disarmament Agency, and the United States Advisory Commission on International Educational and Cultural Affairs.[11] That such groups can play a supportive role at the national level is suggested by the activities in 1947 of the Committee for the Marshall Plan. Just as Dahl attributes acceptance of urban redevelopment in New Haven to the

[10] *United States Foreign Policy: Compilation of Studies, Prepared under the Direction of the Committee on Foreign Relations, United States Senate*, 87th Congress, 1st Session (Washington, D.C.: U.S. Government Printing Office, 1961), p. 823.

[11] Accounts of the establishment and membership of these committees will be found, respectively, in the *New York Times* of March 31, July 11, and November 23, 1961, and March 2 and April 6, 1962. For a more elaborate analysis of the structure, functioning, and role of committees such as these, see David S. Brown, *The Public Advisory Board in Government: An Administrative Analysis of Several Boards with Particular Attention to the Public Advisory Boards of the Economic Cooperation Administration and the Mutual Security Program* (Ph.D. Dissertation, Syracuse University, 1954), and Chadwick F. Alger, *The Role of Private Experts in the Conduct of American Foreign Affairs* (Ph.D. Dissertation, Princeton University, 1958).

role of the Citizens Action Commission, so has the adoption of the Marshall Plan been described as partly a consequence of the activity sparked by "the remarkable array of bankers, lawyers, trade unionists, and editors" who comprised this committee.[12]

Nor is the utility of such techniques confined to issues of foreign policy. An innovative instance of their application to domestic policy areas occurred in the fall of 1961, when five members of the President's Cabinet went "on the road" to explain their policies to and receive advice from groups of "state and municipal officials, special civic groups, and interested citizens." Convened for two days in each of ten cities, the events were called White House Regional Conferences and they focused on such topics as agricultural surplus, conservation policy, economic growth, community development, juvenile delinquency, education, recreation, metropolitan planning, fiscal and monetary policies, minimum wages, and physical fitness.[13] Similarly, six months later President Kennedy heeded the advice of his Advisory Committee on Labor-Management Policy and brought 250 business, labor, and academic leaders to Washington for two days of discussions at the White House Conference on National Economic Issues.[14]

The large extent to which the role of nongovernmental leaders has been institutionalized at the national level is also evident in the fact that presidential orders have had to be issued governing the procedures and membership of certain types of advisory committees. Issued in February 1959 and revised and extended in February 1962, the orders have sought to avoid conflicts of interest on the part of committee members and to establish standards for the content, conduct, and records of committee meetings. In the revised order an "advisory committee" was defined as "any group formed or used by a Government agency for obtaining advice and recommendations, and not wholly composed of officers or employees of the Government."[15]

Some observers are inclined to regard the institutionalization of the veto-support function less as an aspect of the policy-making process and more as a formality to which deference must be paid. Even as he stresses the importance of the Citizens Action Commission in New Haven, for example, Dahl describes its formation and role as "democratic ritual."[16] But such a characterization is somewhat misleading. It implies that officials will necessarily obtain the policies they seek if they observe "third chamber" formalities. In fact, however, ritualistic creation of leadership committees does not

[12] Richard E. Neustadt, *Presidential Power: The Politics of Leadership* (New York: John Wiley & Sons, 1960), pp. 49–50.

[13] Accounts of, and reactions to, these conferences are reported in the *New York Times* of October 5 and November 26, 1961.

[14] See the account of the proceedings in the *New York Times* of May 22 and 23, 1962.

[15] *New York Times*, February 28, 1962.

[16] Dahl, *op. cit.*, p. 130.

automatically guarantee public acceptance of policy proposals. Nongovernmental leadership groups must be won over. If they are divided among themselves, then a consensus has to be fashioned. Or at least the recalcitrant groups must be persuaded not to exercise a veto. Thus, irrespective of whether the efforts to build consensuses within and among leadership groups are institutionalized or carried out informally, they must be viewed as important features of the policy-making process and not as appendages to it.

Of course, in attempting to build consensuses officials seek to implement the support function of national leadership. It should be noted, however, that consensus within the opinion-making public can also be negative and preventive. The veto function, in other words, can be performed when the opinion-making public is united as well as when it is divided. Widespread leadership opposition in the 1950's to the recognition of Red China stands out as an example of a consensus which prevented rather than facilitated government action.[17] Stated differently, there are two forms of the veto function. Either the opinion-making public can be so divided that a few key leadership groups are able to prevent the selection of one alternative, or it can be so united in a negative direction as to prevent the adoption of an alternative. If United States policy toward Communist China is an instance of the latter type of veto role, the former type is illustrated by the cancellation, after protests by a few key segments of the leadership structure, of a proposed visit to the United States in 1957 by Yugoslavia's President Tito.[18]

Having taken note of negative consensuses, henceforth the analysis will focus on the more numerous and complex situations in which the national leadership is either unified in support of the goals and actions of officialdom (positive consensus) or divided with respect to a policy (no consensus). Unless otherwise indicated, therefore, "consensus" is hereinafter used in the positive sense of widespread agreement within the ranks of nongovernmental leaders. Furthermore, whether a consensus takes the form of active support or passive permissiveness, it is conceived to exist whenever agreement exceeds, say, 75 per cent of the opinion-making public.[19]

---

[17] A measure of this consensus is provided by the results of a nationwide survey which the Council on Foreign Relations made in 1954 of "800 businessmen, lawyers, educators, editors, and other community leaders of other occupations." Prevailing U.S. policies toward Communist China were approved by 78 per cent of the respondents. *New York Times*, April 15, 1954.

[18] See James Reston, "A Policy Boomerangs," *New York Times*, February 4, 1957.

[19] This percentage is derived from the reasoning of Prothro and Grigg, who note that, "Logically, perfect consensus represents one extreme of an opinion continuum and perfect discord the other extreme. Any degree of agreement on a problem within a given universe that is less than 75% is accordingly closer to perfect discord than to perfect consensus." James W. Prothro and Charles Grigg, "Societal Coordination by the Educated Minority," *PROD*, **III** (January 1960), p. 7.

Regardless of the percentage of agreement that obtains with respect to any issue-area, however, the veto-support function of national leadership is clearly an extremely important one. For it follows from the foregoing discussion that American foreign policy will be more effective the greater the degree of consensus which prevails among national leaders. If the nation's business, labor, communication, religious, educational, agricultural, associational, and political leaders are united in their perceptions and judgments of events and trends abroad, then officialdom is free to formulate sound, creative, and consistent policies to cope with the international scene. Contrariwise, if the leadership structure is marked by dissension rather than consensus—by conflicting perspectives which foster different assessments and thereby lead to contradictory solutions and recommendations—then the American response to developments abroad is likely to be confused, vacillatory, and inadequate as officials move warily on the fissured subsoil of leadership opinion.

The preceding paragraphs also suggest that the followership of the nation—the mass public—plays a negligible role in the policy-making process. If the foregoing formulation is correct, plainly the mobilization of public opinion in support of a foreign policy does not involve informing and activating the mass public so much as it requires the fashioning of a consensus within the leadership structure.[20] Such a conclusion can also be derived from the abundant empirical data which bears on the role played by the mass public. All the evidence indicates that a large majority of the citizenry is not particularly concerned about international affairs. Reviewing the survey data, one commentator notes that "only three out of ten voters are aware of the major problems in foreign affairs [and] that only twenty out of 100 voters can be considered reasonably well informed."[21] It is hardly possible, in other words, to

> . . . underestimate the public's power to ignore, to acquiesce, and to forget, especially when the proceedings seem incalculable or remote from private life. Unless the shooting starts a Lebanon may be remote, a Berlin seems incalculable, sputniks overhead become routine. But paychecks, grocery

[20] This is not to imply, however, that the mass public is entirely homogeneous in its approach to foreign policy. Obviously a number of attitudinal and motivational distinctions would have to be made if it were a major focus of this inquiry. It has become commonplace, for example, to differentiate between the attentive and inattentive members of the mass public. However, since our concern is with the leadership stratum of the society, we have not attempted here to delineate the various segments of the mass public. For a recent effort to identify and differentiate these segments empirically, see Paul A. Smith, "Opinions, Publics, and World Affairs in the United States," *The Western Quarterly,* **XIV** (September 1961), pp. 698–714.

[21] Lester Markel, "What We Don't Know Will Hurt Us," *New York Times Magazine,* April 9, 1961, p. 9. For a full and careful analysis of all the available data on the mass public and its orientations, consult Alfred O. Hero, *Americans in World Affairs* (Boston: World Peace Foundation, 1959).

bills, children's schooling, sons at war are quite distinctly matters of real life.[22]

It follows that by exercising their "power to ignore, to acquiesce, and to forget," most citizens delegate, knowingly or otherwise, their voice in foreign affairs to those leaders—both in and out of government—who can effectively claim to speak for them. To be sure, like his colleagues in government, the nongovernmental leader cannot afford to stray too far beyond the interests of his segment or "constituency" in the mass public. He must maintain support among at least the more attentive elements of the groups from which he derives his leadership. However, since the mass public is predominantly uninterested in international affairs, the nongovernmental opinion-maker enjoys wide latitude within which to exercise his leadership on such matters. Thus, except perhaps when mass passivity diminishes in extreme emergencies or when votes are cast in elections, the views of national leaders *are* public opinion insofar as foreign policy issues are concerned. As one astute observer has noted, "Who mobilizes elites, mobilizes the public."

Bernard C. Cohen

THE INFLUENCE OF NON-GOVERNMENTAL
GROUPS ON FOREIGN POLICY-MAKING

FOR many years American political scientists have been deeply interested in exploring the nature and dimensions of the influence that is brought to bear on public policy by private (non-governmental) individuals and groups. A great many studies have been made of various aspects of this subject, aided from time to time by official investigations into "pressure politics" and its alleged abuses. . . .

Our purpose here is to review and evaluate this material—to ask ourselves, "What do we really know about the dimensions of group (and individual) influence on the formulation and execution of foreign policy?" A candid summary answer would have to be: not very much. . . .

The relevance of analyses of policy formation increases markedly as they come to deal with the post-World War II period, when the "revolution in American foreign policy" was already under way. But it would be very

---

[22] Richard E. Neustadt, *Presidential Power: The Politics of Leadership* (New York: John Wiley and Sons, 1960), pp. 97–98.

---

misleading to imply that the literature of the last fifteen years or so is uniformly instructive. In the first place, most of the studies of group interests and public policy deal with foreign policy in the barest fashion—if indeed they treat it at all. . . .

A substantive and thus more serious weakness in this body of literature is that very little of it is the product of empirical research, or deals with concrete evidence; instead, most of it rests on or reflects traditional opinion and interpretation—academic as well as public—in assigning weights to various types of organized groups. As a result, a "legend" of pressure group potency in foreign policy appears to be accepted and passed on without evidence to new generations of students and researchers. For example, William Y. Elliott writes, in *United States Foreign Policy: Its Organization and Control:* "Domestic pressure groups have a great influence on our foreign policy." . . . And Robert A. Dahl writes, in *Congress and Foreign Policy:* "The strength of pressure groups in the determination of legislative policy is no less evident in foreign than in domestic affairs. . . . The arena in which foreign policy is fought out is noisy with the jangle of pressure groups. . . . Nor is it merely the old-fashioned and perennial pressures of economic interest groups that are important today." . . . But the data that would be required to sustain interpretations of this kind have never been part of the literature.

An even greater substantive failing in the literature of pressure groups and foreign policy, however, is the repeated discussion of the interests, intentions, or actions of specific pressure groups in lieu of any specific discussion about, or investigation into, their *actual* effects. Policy effectiveness may thus be suggested merely by the circumstance that an author chose to discuss the policy interests of a particular group. This approach to the subject is particularly misleading because the interest groups themselves seem generally willing to foster the belief that their opinions or actions have in fact had some important effect on policy. This apparent equation of interest and activity with influence is found frequently in basic texts in the field. . . .

The available literature, in other words, does not seem to promise very much in the way of pertinent findings. But, in extenuation, it should be emphasized that there are some persistent analytical or conceptual difficulties that tend to hinder the accumulation of directly relevant evidence. The very question being asked is deceptively simple: what non-governmental groups or individuals have major effects on the making and execution of foreign policy?

In the first place, it is not always easy to make an operational distinction between "groups" and a more widely defined "public." Some of the more important foreign policy interest groups in our recent past have been *ad hoc* "Committees." (e.g., "Citizens Committee for the Marshall Plan," "Committee on the Present Danger") organized on a wide public base, generally for the pursuit of limited objectives, and striving to achieve a genuinely mass rather than a highly specialized character. The more successful this type of organization is in stimulating a broad support for policy, the harder it becomes to distinguish the organization from the larger stream of public opinion. A good example is the pre-World War II Committee to Defend America by Aiding the Allies: The Committee was so large and its affiliations so widespread that it became a kind of focal point for the many millions of Americans who favored a policy of assistance to Britain and France.[1] The difficulty in maintaining an operational distinction between specific groups and general public opinion in this same historical context may be noted in one of the conclusions reached by John Masland: "Did these (pre-World War II) pressure groups influence policy? Yes, they did, because policy formers were highly sensitive to public opinion. Policy had to stay within the bounds of toleration set by opinion." [2] To avoid this kind of difficulty in the present paper, and to increase the utility of whatever conclusions we may be able to draw about the influence on policy of non-governmental individuals and groups (as against a study of the influence of public opinion in the large), we shall try to maintain here the distinction between the discernible and traceable impact on policy of a discrete group or organization, and the diffuse, generalized influence on political decision-making of a large segment of the body politic. The latter is important, to be sure, but it does not fall within the purview of this paper.

Secondly, it is not always easy to draw a clear and useful line of demarcation between foreign policy and domestic policy. The distinction may perhaps have been somewhat easier to maintain through the first third of this century, when our foreign relations were chiefly concerned with political-diplomatic and occasionally military matters. In our own time, however, the enlargement of our world interests, which began in the 1930's, has been consummated: those interests now span the globe and cover such an extensive variety of relationships—economic, scientific and cultural, psychological, etc., as well as political and military—as to involve all the realms of public policy. Our foreign relations today are constantly affecting or being affected by issues of "domestic" policy—desegregation, for example, with its important political and psychological repercussions in the non-white world; or reciprocal trade legislation, which has so many domestic economic implications, and which is even handled by the House Ways and Means Committee and the Senate Finance Committee rather than by the foreign policy committees in the Congress; or the so-called "crisis in American education": clearly the provision of first-rate intellectual skills in adequate amounts is of prime importance to the United States in its long run political

[1] See Walter Johnson, *The Battle Against Isolation* (Chicago, 1944).
[2] John Masland, "Pressure Groups and American Foreign Policy Preceding Pearl Harbor," *Public Opinion Quarterly*, Vol. 6, No. 1 (Spring 1942), p. 122.

competition with the Soviet Union, but, apart from a relatively modest education bill at the national level, the subject is chiefly a matter for debate among educators, school boards, and parent-teachers' associations, rather than among policy-makers concerned with long range security planning.

To try to draw new and fine distinctions between foreign and domestic policy to suit our present purposes would be ineffectual and unrewarding. The best we can hope to do in this short compass is to rely on common usage, which now includes under foreign policy most aspects of U. S. economic, political and even social and cultural policy [e.g., participation in international expositions] which directly involve us with one or more other countries.

In the third place, it is exceedingly difficult to define what we mean by "major influence" or "major effects" in such a way that one cannot only recognize those effects, but also know how to organize a search for them. Most groups which are concerned with problems of foreign affairs have set themselves the task of influencing public opinion rather than policy in the first instance; by changing the political climate or by creating an articulate public opinion, they hope eventually to exert an influence upon policy makers. In these cases, however, it is virtually impossible to trace major policy influence. So many different factors are involved in the making and execution of foreign policy that a roundabout effort of this kind merges into a larger political process, losing the crucial aspects of its identity. This is no doubt true even of group efforts on a very large scale, such as those preceding World War II. The following observation illustrates this problem: "Domestic groups outside the government are also operative [in the making of foreign policy], but with what effect it is hard to say. In 1940, in the exchange of British bases for American destroyers, for example, the weight to be attached to the America First Committee, which opposed the deal, and the Committee to Defend America by Aiding the Allies, which advocated it, is not known. Both were active in creating 'public' opinion, both had access to the White House, both were able to generate considerable newspaper support for their respective points of view. Yet, simply because the deal was made, it would be less than accurate to assert that the latter was more influential as a pressure group than the former, given the many other factors which are known to have operated . . ." [3].

Furthermore, the distinction between mere "support" of a policy by an interest group and the exertion of a major influence on policy by the group may disappear in certain cases where a large number of major national organizations are united in support of a given foreign policy. This might be true, for example, where evidence of such support was more than sufficient to counterbalance the force of special interests being exerted on policy makers in more intimate fashion. In this sense, perhaps, one might even

[3] Donald C. Blaisdell *American Democracy Under Pressure* (New York, 1957), pp. 168–169.

define "effects" not as influencing policy in a specific direction to conform to the desires of an interest group, but rather as encouraging (or discouraging) policy makers in proceeding along self-chosen lines. But this is not an operational definition for our present purposes, since all groups can thus be said to have major effects on policy so long as they come out in support of a policy which is also supported by many other groups.

A similar difficulty is encountered in the fact that interest groups may have important effects on foreign policy even when they remain silent. In some cases the silence of major interest groups that are ordinarily quick to take a policy stand may be construed as acquiescence in the course of policy being pursued by the government.[4] Or words may not be required to make clear the feelings of a group: its position on a particular area of policy may be so well known and so important to the policy makers that they are constrained to take it into account in their first formulations of policy. This is one of the hardest kinds of influence for the casual or remote observer to discern; yet it is a type of influence with which we are, or ought to be, interested.[5]

In view of all the complications, perhaps the most meaningful definition of "effects" is one which differentiates direct from indirect effects, no matter what the manner of political expression. This will allow us to concentrate our attention on the evidence of direct, purposeful, immediate influence of interest groups on policy makers and their policy products, without becoming involved in the much more elusive problem of trying to weigh or measure the indirect effects on policy of group participation in the larger political processes of opinion formation.

By way of conclusion here, it is important to keep in mind that the evidence in respect of the effectiveness of particular groups or kinds of groups is rather slight and insubstantial; it consists more often of interpretations or impressions about the processes involved than of objective and systematic observations of political events and relationships. Yet enough is available to enable us to make some tentative generalizations about group influence. And as a starter we might observe, despite frequent assumptions to the contrary, that interest groups seem to have considerably less effect on foreign policy than they do in the domestic realm. This is indeed not a really new conclusion, having been suggested by several analysts on different occasions during the last twenty-five years.[6]

---

[4] *See* Bernard C. Cohen, *The Political Process and Foreign Policy: The Making of the Japanese Peace Settlement* (Princeton, N.J.: Princeton University Press, 1957).

[5] *See* Herbert A. Simon, "Notes on the Observation and Measurement of Political Power," *Journal of Politics*, **15**, 4 (November 1953).

[6] Harold Sprout, "Pressure Groups and Foreign Policies," *The Annals of the American Academy of Political and Social Science* (May 1935); John Masland, "Pressure Groups and American Foreign Policy Preceding Pearl Harbor," *op. cit.*; Donald Blaisdell, *American Democracy Under Pressure*; and Roger Hilsman, "Congressional-Executive Relations and the Foreign Policy Consensus," *The American Political Science Review*, **LII**, 3 (September 1958).

II. Effective Groups and Individuals

Turning first to the question of which groups have important direct effects on foreign policy, there is very widespread agreement that the most influential interest groups in the foreign policy field, as in the domestic arena, are economic interest groups—business organizations, trade associations, and the like. Some observers include labor organizations in this category of economic interest groups, while others would rank them a very close second. While this represents the considered judgment of a number of participants and observers, it is important to repeat here that the evidence to back up these generalizations is not abundant. Thus Franklin L. Burdette writes: "the most powerful domestic pressures which Congress encounters in the field of foreign policy . . . come from groups which expect to gain or lose financially from alternative courses of action. These economic interests have enough at stake to afford expensive participation in the legislative process. . . . Among the most influential of the economic groups in the determination of foreign policy are organized farmers, shippers, labor, and trade associations." [7] Donald Blaisdell's conclusion—no doubt influenced by his earlier monograph, *Economic Power and Political Pressures*, written for the Temporary National Economic Commitee, is this: "As shown in legislation passed or defeated, pressure politics is largely concerned with economics. This is not wholly the case, as the Chinese Exclusion Act repeal, . . . and the failure to admit Hawaii and Alaska testify. . . . But even in these, economics is by no means lacking." [8] Roger Hilsman also accords first place to what he calls "producers' groups." [9]

What are the particular business and trade groups which are influential on foreign policy subjects? It is impossible to give an adequate answer to this question. Trade associations alone number well into the thousands in the United States, and the task of observing and comparing their activities —not to speak of the activities of related business groups—is enough to discourage even the most ambitious analyst. Certain things can be said, however, even though they cannot claim to be any more than partial answers. The shipping lobby, for instance, must be rated as very effective in those areas of foreign policy which involve ocean transport: witness the success of the maritime unions and the National Federation of American Shipping in gaining and subsequently maintaining the legislative requirement that one-half of the cargoes financed by American aid be shipped to other countries in American vessels.[10] This subject has been explored in an un-

---

[7] "Influence of Non-congressional Pressures on Foreign Policy," *The Annals of the American Academy of Political and Social Science* (September 1953), p. 92.

[8] *Op. cit.*, p. 72.

[9] *Op. cit.*, pp. 727–728.

[10] David B. Truman, *The Governmental Process*, p. 364; Holbert N. Carroll, *The House of Representatives and Foreign Affairs*, pp. 64ff. This subject has been explored

published manuscript: "When questioned about the reasons for the effectiveness and the success of the shipping lobby, a State Department officer commented: The shipping lobby is without exception the strongest lobby there is. As a partial explanation its strength is derived from its ability to hide its own desires behind the emotional appeal of a national security—national defense argument; except for a few people on the coasts, no one sees the money that is spent subsidizing the merchant marine so there is no organized opposition; the seamen's unions are extremely powerful and when they joined with management, the combination was unbeatable. Another officer in the Department indicated that the Executive has conceded defeat on the 50–50 shipping clause. Sometimes the clause is written by State, sometimes it is left out with the knowledge that the shipping Congressmen will gladly take care of the oversight." [11]

Another effective interest group is the West Coast fishing industry, whose interest in the matter of tuna imports alone has repeatedly affected our relations with Japan and Peru; the influence of this well-organized industry on the negotiation of a fisheries settlement with Japan after World War II is set forth in Bernard C. Cohen, *The Political Process and Foreign Policy*. There are other instances where business groups seem to have put their effective mark upon international policy, which are, regrettably, mentioned only in passing in this literature. For example, Dayton McKean, in *Party and Pressure Politics*, calls the United States Beet Sugar Association the leading pressure group in the sugar bloc. "The sugar interests strove for years to obtain independence for the Philippines. The Costigan Act and the Sugar Act of 1947 are other examples of their victories." [12]

Admittedly, this is inadequate evidence to sustain the proposition that business and trade associations are the most influential groups with respect to foreign policy—or rather, with respect to foreign economic policy, which seems to be the aspect of foreign policy most susceptible to the pressures of non-governmental groups.[13] But inconclusive though it is, the evidence at least provides us with a relatively unambiguous hypothesis that could be tested if sufficient resources were ever to be put into the effort to uncover and describe a wider range of instances of group influence. We will explore later some of the reasons that may lie behind the influence of business groups, when we come to discuss why other groups are ineffective; but we

---

in an unpublished manuscript by Holsey Handyside, *The European Recovery Program: A Case Study*, Public Affairs 520-D, Woodrow Wilson School of Public and International Affairs (Princeton University, 1952).

[11] *Ibid.*, p. 35.

[12] *Op. cit.*, p. 456. For other brief references to the achievements of the "wool interests," the "farm interests," and other similar groups, see, e.g., Holbert N. Carroll, *op. cit.*, esp. Chapter 4: "The Committees and Foreign Economic Policy"; Holsey Handyside, *op. cit.*, p. 32; and William W. Marvel, *Foreign Aid and United States Security*, unpublished Ph.D. dissertation, Princeton University, 1951, esp. Appendix: "Cases of Special-Interest Demands."

[13] See Holbert N. Carroll, *op. cit., passim.*

may perhaps anticipate that discussion to the extent of noting here the apparent existence among government officials, not of a pro-business bias, but rather of a pro-business orientation—an assumption, in other words, that these policy matters are properly within the sphere of interest and competence of businessmen.[14]

Next to business groups, there seems to be most agreement that ethnic or minority groups are particularly influential in matters of foreign policy. Dahl writes: "Some minority groups—historically the most important, perhaps being the Irish, the Italians, the Poles, the Germans, and among the religious groups, the Catholics—influence American foreign policy out of all proportion to the size of the group. . . ." Then he adds, "The rising concern of the Jewish minority with the fate of the Jews in Palestine and in European displaced persons' camps is only the latest of a long series of similar actions by other ethnic or religious groups." [15] The weight of the opinion of others seems to be that this latest in the series represents the most important contemporary element in ethnic interest in or influence on American foreign policy. Franklin Burdette writes, "The Jewish interest in Israel has in recent years represented one of the most important special claims upon American foreign policy." [16] Hilsman similarly concludes that "in general it seems to be only on policy toward the Middle East that is subject to the kind of special interest pressures that are applied as a matter of course to domestic policy." [17]

Other than the above groups, however, there are discouragingly few generalizations that one can make about group influence on foreign policy. To be sure, one can find many occasions where specific groups seem to have exerted a specific influence on the course of foreign policy, but these cases seem to be time- and situation-bound instances of influence, too discrete to permit one to draw any generalizations about the past, present, or future political behavior of these groups. A sample of these is included here (although it is impossible to vouch for the accuracy of these mostly outdated claims of group effectiveness) to indicate the limited utility of this *kind* of evidence:

1) In 1925 the Geneva Protocol outlawing the use of poison gas was opposed by the American Chemical Society, the American Legion, the Association of Military Surgeons, and the National Association for Chemical Defense. Donald Blaisdell writes, "In the face of this opposition not even the support of President Coolidge, Secretary Kellogg, and General Pershing, to say nothing of the National Women's Conference on the Cause and

---

[14] As an illustration, see the tenor of interviews with Congressmen on the subject of reciprocal trade, as summarized by Frank Bonilla, "When is Petition 'Pressure'?" (*Public Opinion Quarterly*, 20, 1, Spring 1956).

[15] *Op. cit.*, pp. 55–56.

[16] *Op. cit.*, p. 94.

[17] *Op. cit.*, p. 728.

Cure of War, was sufficient to gain Senate approval." The treaty was sent back to the Foreign Relations Committee.[18]

2) In 1935 this country signed an Argentine Sanitary Convention, which would have permitted the importation of fresh meats from regions in Argentina that may be determined to be free of hoof-and-mouth disease. "For years the opposition of farm and ranch interests has been successful in preventing ratification by the Senate." [19]

3) "Occasionally one of . . . [the] professional peace groups exerts appreciable force on policy determination. This was the case with the 1935 Neutrality Act which grew out of the reports and recommendations of the Senate Munitions Investigation Committee. Committee Chairman Nye (North Dakota) was persuaded to initiate this investigation by Miss Dorothy Detzer, lobbyist for the Women's International League for Peace and Freedom. The National Council for the Prevention of War claims to have been responsible for cutting the 1929 naval expansion program to a third of the size originally planned. The same group took the initiative in 1928 in putting pressure upon Congress to adopt a resolution favoring arbitration of the dispute with Mexico, growing out of the passage there of a statute confiscating all oil lands held by aliens." [20]

4) "In February, 1939, the National Council for Prevention of War was able to challenge successfully the Administration's Far Eastern policy by clever exploitation of an obscure naval base bill item for harbor improvements at our Pacific outpost of Guam. It is probable that the Guam appropriation would have been voted had not the Council made a public issue of it. Through connections with minority members hearings were arranged before the House Naval Affairs committee, with the Council securing opposition witnesses. As a result of these hearings Guam became a front page issue across the country. Popular opposition was aroused and the item was defeated by the House." [21]

5) There are more recent examples, also: One finds many references to the "China lobby" as the only pressure group having had any real influence on America's China policy.[22] American labor unions have participated in various advisory capacities in the post war aid programs, presumably having some influence on the execution of policies. One can also recall Protestant opposition to President Truman's proposal to establish diplomatic relations with the Vatican, as well as Catholic efforts to establish a program of

---

[18] *Economic Power and Political Pressures*, TNEC Monograph No. 26, pp. 59–60.
[19] *Ibid*, p. 60.
[20] *Ibid*., p. 166.
[21] John Masland, *op. cit*., p. 121.
[22] See Daniel S. Cheever and H. Field Haviland, Jr., *American Foreign Policy and the Separation of Powers* (Cambridge, Mass., 1952), pp. 155–156; Nicholas V. McCausland, *Aid to China, 1948: A Case Study*, unpublished manuscript, Public Affairs, 520-D, Woodrow Wilson School of Public and International Affairs, Princeton University, 1952; also. "The China Lobby," *The Reporter*, 6, 8, 9 (April 15, 29, 1952).

American aid to Spain. There are also cases of *ad hoc* interest groups being established on the initiative of Executive agencies. "For example, during the Eightieth Congress the Committee on the Marshall Plan [the Citizens Committee for the Marshall Plan to Aid European Recovery] and the Committee on Peacetime Selective Service played an invaluable role in spearheading the legislative campaign on behalf of the Economic Co-operation Act and the Selective Service Act of 1948." [23]

So far we have been looking at the evidence pertaining to the foreign policy effectiveness of organized groups. But what about what Franklin Burdette calls the "persistent individual" with policy influence? One can find references to individuals who have had influence on certain aspects of American foreign policy, but these references fall far short of the abundant and systematic accumulation that would be required before we were in a position to draw any useful conclusions from them. No doubt there are always private individuals whose voices carry weight; we have taken notice of prominent persons with national reputations like William Allen White and of professional lobbyists who work without much publicity for various causes, such as Dorothy Detzer. Others work hard for their own interests: an interesting example is the case of Robert E. Rodes, who in 1949 was commander of the Casablanca American Legion Post and president of the American Trade Association of Morocco, an organization of 37 American businessmen in Morocco. Claiming that the French in Morocco were discriminating against the American businessmen there, the American Trade Association of Morocco sought an amendment to the bill extending ECA which would have cut off aid to France unless the alleged discrimination ended. By securing the support first of Senator Richard Russell and then of Senator Hickenlooper, Mr. Rodes had his claim advanced to the point where the French Government announced that it would present the whole matter of discrimination in violation of treaty rights to the Court of International Justice for a decision.[24] While these examples serve to illustrate the possibilities of individual participation in the foreign policy making process, they do not permit us to draw any important generalizations about individual influence on foreign policy.

On a different level from these anecdotal accounts of individual accomplishment in the policy making realm, one finds highly generalized descriptions of "individual influentials" which, although not operationally useful, are sufficiently suggestive of research possibilities to warrant brief mention. In a recent article based on an analysis of 39 persons of "above-average influence" [selected according to criteria that would probably not satisfy all tastes] living in a suburb of Chicago, Kenneth P. Adler and Davis Bobrow have drawn a portrait of the "non-governmental influential in foreign

[23] Bertram Gross, *The Legislative Struggle* (New York, 1953), p. 229.
[24] William W. Marvel, *op. cit.*, pp. 718–722.

affairs." [25] They found, for example, that the "influential" (as distinguished from the merely "interested") is highly educated, wealthy, Protestant, Anglo-Saxon, and in a professional-technical or managerial occupation. His influence is often based on high standing in the legal profession or high executive position in industry, banking, or commerce. Foreign travel is nearly universal among these suburban influentials, who are linked to Chicago, to other metropolitan areas, and to Washington by both business connections and personal friendships.[26] No claim is made, of course, that the community involved in this study is typical, or that the 39 persons are representative of persons with contemporary influence on foreign policy. It may even be that Adler and Bobrow have described only *one type* of foreign policy influential and that there are many other types to be found in other environments. In any case, the problem of personal or individual influence on foreign policy is a fertile field for future explorations.

Up to this point we have asked the question, "What groups and individuals have important direct effects on foreign policy." Now we shall explore the nature of those effects, and the policy circumstances in which they become evident. Many of the specific effects that have been achieved by identifiable groups have been mentioned in passing in the prior discussion; it might be useful here, perhaps, to try to draw some very tentative and low level] generalizations from this all-too-incomplete evidence.

While interest groups follow the whole range of American foreign policy, taking positions and expressing opinions on all aspects of it, the area of direct and significant influence seems to be mostly the protection or advancement of those particular interests which are the *raison d'être* of the interest groups. This pursuit of essentially private rather than public interest—whether or not it is in the guise of public interest—takes place through whatever policy means are at hand, or which have already been initiated or activated by the government itself. For example, international economic policy may be affected by the pursuit of private gain through tariff provisions or aid legislation; both economic interests and ethnic or minority interests can be achieved by trying to affect relations with particular countries or areas; or effects may be had by the processes of delaying or causing the rejection of whatever kinds of legislation the policy makers have seen fit to introduce.

It is less easy to generalize about the circumstances under which interest groups may have an influence upon policy. But the evidence available here suggests that particular groups are perhaps most effective on an individual basis when the policy issue in which they are interested is, for whatever reason, not in the public eye. There may be general public disinterest in a policy matter for a variety of reasons: it may deal, for example, with only a

<hr>

[25] Kenneth P. Adler and Davis Bobrow, "Interest and Influence in Foreign Affairs," *Public Opinion Quarterly*, 20, 1 (Spring 1956).

[26] *Ibid.*, pp. 92–93.

very narrow subject matter or with technical rather than political issues, or it may suffer the accident of having to compete for dramatic interest with more spectacular and compelling issues of domestic or perhaps even foreign policy. Whatever the reason, however, it would appear that when the "attentive public" is very small, it is much easier for specific interest groups to establish their position as the representatives of the only sectors of the public that are vitally concerned about the policy in hand. But these same circumstances can sometimes be exploited for quite opposite purposes: When there seems to be very little public interest in a policy issue, as in the case of the naval appropriations for Guam in 1939, an organization like the National Council for the Prevention of War can be effective by drawing press and public attention to the problems involved, thus delaying formal action on the matter and ultimately securing a reconsideration.

About the only conclusion to be drawn from all this in which one can have any confidence whatever is that the available information is much too fragmentary and unsystematic to sustain any sure conclusions. The best that can be done is to phrase the experience of one or two cases into the language of a general hypothesis; but it must be understood that the reason for doing so is not to suggest definite conclusions but rather to give some form of organization to the search for additional and more useful information.

On how broad a range of issues does a given group exert an important direct influence? The written record permits a more confident answer to this question. In general, the span of influence of specific groups seems to be limited to the area of their special policy interest; this limitation seems to hold even though an organization may take an articulate public position on the entire range of foreign policy issues. As Bertram Gross put it: "Strategic positions [occupied by non-governmental organizations], however, are only a source of generalized power. The American Medical Association can swing considerable weight to the subject of Government health policies, but its closest friends in Government would not give it much attention on foreign policy." [27] In the same way, the commodity groups have no effect on foreign policy beyond whatever arrangements they are able to make respecting the treatment of their particular commodities in international trade or a foreign aid program. Ethnic groups have no influence on policy with respect to areas of the world other than those to which they have a direct connection. Trade unions have little influence outside of matters involving international labor. Religious influence on foreign policy seems to be limited to sectarian interests. Perhaps the only major exception to this point is to be found among the general business groups. While their influence may be regarded as highest when it comes to matters of international economic policy, in our contemporary society the businessman is

[27] Bertram Gross, *The Legislative Struggle* (New York, 1953), p. 147.

frequently called upon for his advice and administrative experience in a wider range of foreign policy matters. But this exception aside, the general point here is interesting and important: it suggests that an easily identifiable division of labor—more accurately, a division of influence—exists, which is imposed by policy makers themselves whenever there might be temptations to violate it by interest groups.

Finally, what can one say about the ways in which influential groups approach the political process and use it effectively? There are, obviously, a host of political avenues that may be traversed in the effort to exert policy influence. Partly because of the interests of scholars and partly because of the ease of access, to the legislative process, the available material on this subject informs us most of all on the avenue to effectiveness through gaining the support of one or more members of Congress. According to V. O. Key, Jr., "Pressure groups are most conspicuous in their activities in support of and in opposition to legislative proposals." [28] Significantly, Adler and Bobrow found among individuals with foreign policy influence a greater use of Congressional channels than of any other kind: 38% of their thirty-nine "foreign policy influentials" wrote to Congressmen and 33% talked to Congressmen; 15% wrote to, and 10% talked to, media executives; and 8% wrote to, and 10% talked to, people in the Executive Branch of the Government. [29]

Existing research tells us considerably less about the operations of foreign policy interest groups within the Executive branch than about attempts to influence Congress. The successful efforts of the West Coast fishing industry to place a responsible spokesman for the industry in an administrative position very close to the policy level in the State Department, [30] so that it could better influence the development of policy and negotiations on a fisheries settlement with Japan, are suggestive of a mode of political influence in the foreign policy field that may take place somewhat oftener than it is written about. At lower levels in the administrative hierarchy, we know that trade unions, trade associations, and other special interest groups are often used as advisors in foreign missions, or as advisors and delegates to international conferences on specialized subjects. Finally, a less common path of political influence runs through the political parties. This is uncommon because few interest groups can mobilize any important electoral power in the pursuit of specific foreign policy objectives. V. O. Key, Jr. writes of interest groups in general in this same sense: "A plausible tentative conclusion may be that one must look, in the main, to factors other than their power to punish at the polls to explain the influence of pressure groups. They gain power in some instances merely from having representatives on hand to

---

[28] V. O. Key, Jr., *Politics, Parties, and Pressure Groups*, 4th ed. (New York, 1948), p. 147.
[29] Adler and Bobrow, *op. cit.*, Table 2, p. 96.
[30] See Cohen, *op. cit.*, Chapter 12.

present their case to the legislature. In others their influence is founded on the simple fact that the legislator tends to go along with whatever interests are powerful in his district . . . In still others the legislators' convictions may happen to coincide with the interest of particular groups." [31] But once in a while electoral power can be brought to bear in an apparently successful way, especially when the interest groups involved are organizationally and/or numerically important elements in politically strategic constituencies. This has been true of the West Coast fishing industry on certain international fishing questions, as we shall see in a moment, and of most Jewish groups on the issue of Israel: "Jewish pressure, during the electoral campaign of 1948 in favor of American support of the new state of Israel, influenced both parties to adopt 'Zionist' planks in their party platforms." [32]

Obviously, then, one can find groups working through all the major points of access to the governmental process of foreign policy making: the Congress, the Executive and bureaucracy, and the political parties. Does it make any difference whether an organization chooses to work through one rather than another of these points? The answer is not clear-cut. Even with a poor record of cases on which to found our conclusions, it is readily apparent that there is no single point of access to influence in the process. They all work, and they all seem to work equally well or effectively. But we have to ask whether any particular group can function equally effectively anywhere in the process. I am inclined to believe that the answer is no; there seem to be regularities in the way groups approach the different elements in the process, making and utilizing contacts, and the conditions that determine what sets of relationships are effective are worth exploring in much greater detail than has been done heretofore.[33] For example, the West Coast fishing industry, all phases of which were organized into the Pacific Fisheries Conference, was effective in shaping the North Pacific Fisheries Convention by working at the start through their Congressmen. From this initial point of access all manner of influence flowed, including participation in policy formulation in the State Department. But all this was possible because the businesses and trade and labor associations which were represented in the Pacific Fisheries Conference were very important elements in the constituencies of a territorially compact group of Representatives and Senators who by virtue of geography and history were generally conceded a leading political interest in any settlement with Japan.[34] Had the fishing industry tried to work on the State Department directly, without the intercession of important members of Congress, its accomplishment would no doubt have been far less. But the course of action taken so

[31] V. O. Key, Jr., *op. cit.*, 2nd ed., p. 134.
[32] Gabriel Almond, *The American People and Foreign Policy* (New York, 1950), pp. 186–187.
[33] See, e.g., Cohen, *op. cit.*, esp. Chapter 5.
[34] *Ibid.*, Chapter 12.

effectively by the fishing groups is not open to all groups, since it is obviously dependent upon a particular arrangement or constellation of organizations, issues, and political positions.

Another dimension of the influence process that is worth further attention is what might be called the "ideological connection" between the would-be influential and the policy makers. It seems to be the case that policy makers are not often persuaded to act (or not act) in favor of persons or groups with whom they are in basic ideological or political conflict. Put more positively, there generally appears to be a close affinity between the policy maker and the individual or group whose position he is persuaded to support. John Masland noted this disposition in the pre-Pearl Harbor period: "The representatives of these various groups cultivated personal contact with members of Congress and of the Administration who were favorably inclined to their views. Fred Libby and Dorothy Detzer for many years worked closely with isolationists in Congress. General Wood moved into the office of Senator Wheeler for several days to assist in planning opposition strategy to revision of the Neutrality Act. Around the State Department Clark Eichelberger found doors open at all times, and consulted freely with officials, giving and receiving advice." [35] And the same thing can be discerned in much of the evidence dealing with contemporary policy issues. A fuller study of such varying susceptibilities of policy makers to influence would no doubt contribute a great deal to our better understanding of the whole influence process.

III. Ineffective Groups

In some respects the question of what groups are ineffective in shaping the form or substance of foreign policy is the other side of the coin we have just examined. But it is scarcely an adequate answer to say that all groups which have not been identified as effective are ineffective. By "ineffective" here is meant the exertion of a negligible amount of *direct* influence on policy; yet this should not be taken to mean that groups in this category have no influence of any kind on American policy. They might well have some indirect influence, for example, when they cluster in support of or in opposition to a broad course of policy.

No doubt most major interest groups in the United States think of themselves as influential with respect to public policy, including foreign policy; it would be natural for them to do so, and the public records of most associations indicate that they are quick to suggest, if not to claim, policy influence. Yet there is more evidence in the contemporary literature on the ineffectiveness of non-governmental groups in the field of foreign policy than there are signs of direct and positive influence. The evidence

[35] Masland, *op. cit.*, p. 121.

pointing to a lack of influence is sometimes explicit and sometimes implicit; we will be dealing with both varieties here.

The important point to make at the start is that, just as no one group is uniformly influential, at one time or another all groups that seek to influence foreign policy encounter the kind of failure that is evidence of political ineffectiveness. This is true even of business and commodity groups and trade associations, which we noted above were perhaps the most influential of all. In the case of the Japanese peace treaty, for example, business organizations were treated with cordiality and respect, but it is very doubtful whether they got on the whole any more satisfaction of their policy interests than Mr. Dulles was prepared in any case to give them.[36] Similarly, Administration bills to renew the Reciprocal Trade Agreements Act have gone through Congress relatively untouched year after year, despite the earnest efforts of commodity groups to influence it in their favor.[37]

But if all kinds of organizations are ineffective at one time or another, it still seems to be the case that some groups lack influence (in the direct sense, again) on foreign policy matters most of the time. This seems to be especially true of the large national organizations commonly placed in the categories of civic, professional, fraternal, women's, ideological, and even religious groups. These labels are ambiguous, to be sure, and generalizations made in their terms must be regarded as always subject to reformulation. Nevertheless, the presumption of ineffectiveness remains. Franklin Burdette makes the point indirectly, precisely by stressing the indirect effect of group support: "Support for post-war foreign policy has been forthcoming from such broad membership groups as the General Federation of Women's Clubs, the League of Women Voters, the United States Chamber of Commerce, the United States Junior Chamber of Commerce, the National Federation of Business and Professional Women's Clubs, the Foreign Policy Association, and many educational, civic, and fraternal bodies. The full power of these organizations has never been marshaled in peacetime in a unified effort for an objective in foreign policy, but their diversified strength is of enormous value in undergirding public support of American diplomacy." [38]

In a book entitled *The American Legion and American Foreign Policy*, Roscoe Baker has written a non-critical description of the Legion's position on virtually every matter relating to foreign policy in which the Legion has ever been interested. But the author carefully refrains from claiming influence for the Legion; and the net effect of reference after reference to the

---

[36] Cohen, *op. cit.*, pp. 217–218.

[37] See Carroll, *op. cit.*; also, J. Robert Barlow and Robert T. Holt, *The Reciprocal Trade Agreements Act of 1949: A Case Study*, Public Affairs 520-D, Woodrow Wilson School of Public and International Affairs, Princeton University, 1954, unpublished.)

[38] Burdette, *op. cit.*, p. 93.

enactment of legislation which had been opposed by the Legion is the firm impression that the Legion was in fact without much influence on matters of foreign policy. And with respect to women's groups, a typical appraisal is the following quotation from a staff member of the Senate Finance Committee: "Women's organizations have no significant influence on Congressmen on RTA [the Reciprocal Trade Act]. Their representatives appear at the hearings claiming to represent hundreds of thousands of women, who are actually unaware of the significance of RTA. These representatives often are simply sold a bill of goods by the State Department and by import interests, who also support lecturers and literature, and are very eloquent and persuasive. These women appear before the committees talking 'peace' and 'more world trade,' but the slightest questioning on economic issues can instantly embarrass them. Since the Congressmen are chivalrous, they don't press the lady, but let her go on her way." [39]

What can we say about the conditions that make for political ineffectiveness among interest groups? How do these groups differ from others that have a record of major influence on foreign policy? Many different reasons can be adduced to explain the failure of organizations to exert an influence on foreign policy; some of these reasons are institutional, others are situational. But in this as in other respects, it is hard to feel very confident that one has put one's finger on characteristics either of organization or of behavior that permanently or inflexibly distinguish the ineffective groups from the influential ones. As an example of the contradictory evidence that marks this aspect of the subject, Dexter quotes a Congressman as saying that in general, Congress hears from business groups too late: these organizations respond to the news, they write to protest a bill reported out of committee, but by then it is difficult to amend it.[40] But in the case of the Japanese peace settlement,[41] it was some of the business groups which were most alert to the treaty's impingement on their own interests and which moved both on Congress and on the Executive at an early stage, whereas the other more general interest organizations intervened much later, in response to news about the development of the issue.

By understanding some of the reasons for the general effectiveness of business groups, one can detect reasons why it may be much harder for other kinds of groups to influence the making of foreign policy. For one thing, there is the suggestion that a group can have little influence on policy unless its interest in the policy problem is recognized as legitimate by policy makers. This is no doubt one of the major factors that works to restrict the span of influence over policy of particular groups and thus to create the "division of influence" we took notice of earlier. With

[39] Holt and Barlow, *op. cit.*, p. 52.
[40] Lewis A. Dexter, "What do Congressmen Hear: The Mail," *Public Opinion Quarterly*, 20, 1 (Spring 1956), pp. 26–27.
[41] Cohen, *op. cit.*

respect to the tariff, for example, Frank Bonilla writes, on the basis of interviews with Congressmen and businessmen: "The consensus was that people with a legitimate interest in the controversy are primarily moved by economic considerations and that other motives or aims, while important, cannot be granted ascendance over the plea of economic injury." [42]

But there are other factors at work here, even in the context of a recognized legitimacy of interest in policy. Thus Bonilla writes that labor groups as well as business groups have a legitimate interest in the tariff, "but whereas *in no single case* did any of the legislators complain about pressures from industry, there were a number of remarks [made during interviews] describing the ineptness, boorishness, or lack of organization evident in labor pressure groups." [43] The implication here is not, fundamentally, an anti-labor attitude. Rather it seems to be a general, perhaps even a cultural, sympathy with business—a predisposition to regard its interests as legitimate; this is what Bonilla elsewhere calls a "congruence of opinion and sentiment." [44] It is in terms of such congruence that Bonilla distinguishes the psychological and subjective dimensions of pressure; it "helps explain the fact (sometimes puzzling to reformers) that demands from businessmen generated little resentment among legislators (even when they ran counter to the views of the Congressman concerned), while appeals from groups like the League of Women Voters provoked animosity in almost every case." [45] In this context, the remark of the staff member of the Senate Finance Committee which was quoted earlier takes on added meaning. The women talk "peace" and "more world trade," but the Congressmen apparently want to hear about the impact of policy on the personal and corporate lives of constituents.

Admittedly, it is difficult to distinguish between the legitimacy of business interest in economic policy and a general sentiment or bias in favor of the "practical businessman," particularly when most of the evidence to support such propositions is drawn from cases involving economic policy. Yet the notion that the businessman represents better than anyone else the kind of feet-on-the-ground practicality of which foreign policy is made is a recurring one. In his monograph for TNEC, Blaisdell wrote, "While important on occasion, the staying power, resources, and plausibility of program of these peace groups are hardly in the same class as those of the business groups with an economic stake in shipping policy. The peace groups by and large are considered either radical or unrealistic; the business groups, on the other hand, are generally regarded as 'sound'." [46] In the case of the Japanese peace treaty, the patent unreality of the policy proposals

---

[42] Bonilla, *op. cit.*, p. 45.
[43] *Ibid.*, p. 46; emphasis in original.
[44] *Ibid.*, p. 39.
[45] *Ibid.*, pp. 39–40.
[46] Donald Blaisdell, *Economic Power and Political Pressures*, p. 166.

advanced by the religious, pacifist, and ideological groups made them useless to the policy makers, and so they were dismissed more or less perfunc-
torily (Cohen, *op. cit.*, pp. 219–220).

One can find other evidence suggesting a not uncommon predilection
for the businessman's approach to foreign policy among American officials,
many of whom have had business experience themselves. For instance,
The James Forrestal Diaries contains numerous references to Forrestal's
belief that the businessman was the really indispensable element if the
United States was going to stand up successfully to the Soviet Union. On
March 3, 1947, for example, Forrestal wrote about a luncheon with Treasury
Secretary Snyder, at which they had discussed the rapidly maturing problem
of assistance for Greece and Turkey: "Talked to him about my beliefs
that if we are going to have a run for our side in the competition between
the Soviet system and our own, we shall have to harness all the talent and
brains in this country just as we had to do during the war. I said I felt
very strongly that the world could only be brought back to order by a
restoration of commerce, trade and business, and that would have to be
done by businessmen." [47] Senator Vandenberg had somewhat the same
notions with respect to the Marshall Plan. Writing to Under-secretary
Lovett, "he suggested as a practical matter the desirability of obtaining
'four or five top-level business executives of the country' as 'aggressive
witnesses' once the Committee hearings started on the Marshall Plan. This
was to be essentially a 'business' program." [48]

Another difference between business and non-business groups which may
affect their capacity to influence foreign policy is the degree of specificity
of the interest which they represent. Kensuke Yanagiya, in an unpublished
manuscript,[49] found some support both in the State Department and among
interest groups for the following views of a State Department official who
tried to explain why special-interest groups had more influence on policy
than large, national, general-interest organizations. "There are a number
of reasons for this: 1) their recommendations are specific, in contrast to
the necessarily general ideas of large groups; 2) they are far more interested and zealous; 3) counter-pressures usually do not exist either within or without their own group." [50]

But there are still other reasons why interest groups may be ineffective
in matters of foreign policy. One of these reasons must be the consonance

---

[47] Walter Millis, ed., *The James Forrestal Diaries* (New York: Viking, 1951), pp.
247–248; see also pp. 186–187, 251–252, 267–268.

[48] Arthur H. Vandenberg, Jr., ed., *The Private Papers of Senator Vandenberg* (Boston,
1952), p. 383; quoted in Handyside, *op. cit.*, p. 56.

[49] Kensuke Yanagiya, *The Renewal of ERP: A Case Study*. Public Affairs 520-D,
Woodrow Wilson School of Public and International Affairs (Princeton University,
1952), p. 37.

[50] See also Cohen, *op. cit.*, Chapter 5, for other differences in the behavior of
special-interest groups which might account for whatever differences in influence exist
between them and other interest groups.

of the policy being advocated by a group with the prevailing political temper of the times. No matter how reasonable a policy might once have been, if it is no longer regarded as reasonable or feasible because of the general tenor of developing opinion, the impact of its advocacy is likely to be small. An excellent illustration of this is provided by the America First Committee, which tried in the months before Pearl Harbor to reassert the validity of a foreign policy of utter neutrality and isolation but which failed so completely that it was "not even able to defeat any major administration 'short-of-war' proposal actually put to the test in Congress." [51]

Another reason why groups may lack a direct influence on policy may be found in the temporary existence of an approximate balance of opposing interests. By way of example, in an unpublished interview a former State Department official has described the problem of the recognition of the new Bolivian government after the 1952 coup as "a case where business pressure, usually very influential and articulate, cancelled itself out." Finally, another—and by no means unimportant—reason for the inability of groups to make much headway on foreign policy may be the conclusion of policy makers that the special treatment which they seek may be far too costly in terms of the public good. "The vain struggle of individuals and business enterprises to have private claims recognized in the [Japanese] peace treaty is evidence of the Department's firm interpretation of the greater good in this matter, even when the justice of the individual claims was beyond question." [52] Holbert Carroll similarly argues that the House Committee on Foreign Affairs resisted the particular pleas of all organized pressures with respect to the European Recovery Program, because to the Committee, as to the State Department, "the foreign policy objectives hold the highest priority." [53]

IV. Implications for World Affairs Organizations

In several important respects the picture drawn above is somewhat at odds with our expectations or, more accurately, our general impressions, of the influence of interest groups on American foreign policy. Indeed, the very nature of this inquiry suggests that the notion of the "group basis" of politics and policy making is as applicable in the foreign policy field as in the realm of domestic policy. The evidence that is currently available, however, cannot be said to support this notion. This may, of course, be a "research failure"—a consequence of the fact that academic specialists in this field have not been accustomed to ask the kind of questions which would illuminate the nature of direct influence on foreign

[51] Wayne S. Cole, *America First: The Battle Against Intervention 1940–1941* (Madison, Wisc., 1953), p. vii.

[52] Cohen, *op. cit.*, p. 218.

[53] Carroll, *op. cit.*, p. 127.

policy. Such a failure is understandable: we ought not to underestimate the very great difficulty in trying to identify and measure the impact of specific private individuals and groups within the tremendous flow of political impulses that shape public policy. As a research enterprise it may prove to be so very complex and indeterminate that it is scarcely worthwhile. But one might still expect, nevertheless, that a pattern of direct group influence, if it in fact existed, would show through, so to speak, even if one made only a casual rather than an especially detailed and sophisticated attempt to search it out. Yet, with the few exceptions noted in this paper, the influence of non-governmental groups on foreign policy seems as if it must be more indirect and diffuse than direct and specific.

Another aspect of our current picture of group influence which may be mildly disconcerting is its apparent (though small-scale) reversion to a "devil theory" of politics. By attributing major direct influence in foreign policy chiefly to business groups, it seems to suggest that there is an unseen hand of "big business" trying to use the means of foreign policy for its own private gain, no matter what the political costs or consequences. But such an implication is neither intended nor, all things considered, warranted; for, while business groups seem to be the most effective of the various types of interest groups, they are nevertheless only mildly influential and then only with respect to a rather narrow range of economic issues which comprise only a small proportion of the fundamental issues of American foreign policy.

Perhaps the most sensible interpretation is that our picture is much too fragmentary to warrant drawing many conclusions that purport to have some bearing on the operations of world affairs organizations. It is questionable, in fact, whether we are really entitled to talk about group influence on "foreign policy"; with very rare exceptions, the influence of non-governmental groups is on particular, discrete, rather highly specialized matters, which, even if they may be deemed to be within the foreign policy field, are very far from constituting or defining that field. Furthermore, most of our information focuses on the Congress, so that we really know rather little about the process or extent of group influence on the Executive branch, which is where the greater portion of the foreign policy power in the American government resides.

The Press
and Foreign Policy

Douglass Cater, Jr.

GOVERNMENT BY PUBLICITY

> The Nineteenth Century was the era of the novelist. The
> Twentieth is the era of the journalist. A distracted people, busy
> with the fierce competitions of modern life, must be addressed
> while they are paying attention, which is usually at the moment
> of some great national or international event.
>
> JAMES RESTON *

MORE than in any other capital in the world, or any other city in the
United States, there is prestige and privilege belonging to the lowly
reporter in Washington. Even those who have graduated to the higher
callings of columnist or bureau chief still take a modest pride in identifying
themselves by the lesser title. Within the press corps, faint derision attaches
to one who prefers anything more pretentious.

One aspect of this self-imposed humility—Washington reporters lay
great emphasis on the purely physical requirements of the craft. The good
reporter, it is said, can be judged by the condition of his legs. Success in
the field comes from a fortuitous combination of luck and shoe leather.
The business of getting the news is described in the metaphors of the
mine worker—pick and shovel, digging, a great deal of sweat. When Hugh
Gaitskell, leader of the Labour Party in the British House of Commons,
once complained to the erudite American columnist Joseph Alsop about
the sad condition of parliamentary reporting, Alsop replied: "My dear
fellow, the reason is quite simple. Your reporters just don't work as hard
as we do!" Alsop, like most columnists, would be mortally insulted to be
considered more pundit than reporter.

* Quoted by Joe Kraft in "Washington's Most Powerful Reporter," Esquire (November 1958).

The Washington correspondent has odd notions about himself. He clings to the image of the reporter as the supreme individual in the age of the organization man. He is the one standing up against the many. He denies stubbornly that the production of news can be likened to the mass production techniques of other large-scale industries. His prestige symbols encourage him in this notion. The Pulitzer Prizes, the Heywood Broun and Raymond Clapper Awards handed out each year go to the reporter who has beaten the system and gotten the "scoop"—to the one who has singlehandedly busted up the hidden enclave of intrigue and purified big government by the cleansing power of publicity.

The myth of the swashbuckling, free-wheeling, heavy drinking general reporter who pursues news with a hunch and a hangover dies hard. It is nourished in the literature of the profession and in the tall tales swapped around the National Press Club bar. But a look at the Press Club— principal gathering place for Washington reporters during off hours— soon dispels the myth. Except for the newspaper mats plastered along the entrance hall, it might be almost any big city eating club, its members as staid and undistinctive. Its consumption at the bar is certainly no heavier than most. If the conversation is a bit more lively, it is because the stock in trade of these merchants is words. Their trade routes often take them to where excitement lies.

The Washington correspondent is a member of a giant industry in the nation's capital, numbering upwards of twelve hundred. His business, like most big business, has become specialized, compartmentalized, channelized, even routinized to a degree that would shock his predecessor of a few decades ago. The growth of the news business has not been simply a stretching out to emcompass the broader sphere of government. It has been, in addition, an extension in time and space. News production for the hungry American public has become an instantaneous, continuous, many-faceted and layered operation.

Backbone of the industry and, to a certain extent, its central nervous system are the giant wire services with a labor force large enough to monitor every major news outlet in the capital and to maintain a steady outgoing flow of words. The wire-service employee scarcely conforms to old-fashioned notions of the reporter as one who each twenty-four hours dictates a first draft of history. He is rather the bucket boy for a never ceasing stream of news that may be scooped up at any hour of day or night and poured into print by the far-flung distributors. For him, the news is like fluid, to be portioned out in bulletins, and leads, and "takes." It is capable of being bottled in any quantity. Its production is more determined by the technical than by internal factors in the news itself. The great Associated Press "A" wire that binds the nation can carry an optimum sixty words a minute. News from Washington or London or Hong Kong moves onto it according to tightly scheduled "budgets," scarcely less methodically prepared than a big department store's allotment of display space to shoes and hats and women's lingerie.

Another sizable contingent of the Washington press corps is composed of the "localizers" of the news. They bear daily testament to the fact that the United States has become a world power whose interests are still heavily provincial. These reporters view Washington through the eyes of Dubuque, Iowa, or Kalamazoo, Michigan, or Nashville, Tennessee. They work as one-man vigilantes or as members of large bureaus specializing in perspectives from Maine to Texas. The good ones provide separate eyes and ears for their constituencies—a double check on the Congressmen. Unlike the Congressmen, they can carry even a picayune issue directly to the President with some hope of evoking a response.

There are the Washington bureaus of the big city dailies and the chain papers—highly varied operations ranging from the twenty-three-man princely state maintained by the *New York Times* to the one- and two-man outposts of the Denver *Post* and the Providence *Journal*. These reporters are the most direct spiritual heirs of the long tradition of the Washington correspondent. They, more than the rest, provide the warp and woof of reporting. They range widely in their purpose. For some it is an unending search for scandal and exposé. Some consider their function to be the more leisurely digestion of the raw meat of the headlines.

Other reporters view the Washington scene from other perspectives. Reporters for the news weeklies—artisans on a different type of assembly line from the wire services—dig out the primary components necessary to give a factual shape and color to the week's events. Other components— style, polish, "meaning"—are added further along the assembly line, in the skyscraper workshops of New York. Reporters for radio and television scan the horizon with restless radarscopes in search of news in shapes that can be heard and seen. Syndicated columnists, the most independent of the news merchants, batter the barricades for their "inside" news purveyed on a thrice or more weekly basis and ranging in content from foreign policy to freight rates. The foreign press corps works with varying success to chart America's course for their constituents.

A trade press in considerable numbers sifts the capital city for the particular nuggets that will be of value to the organized interest groups keeping a relentless vigil over the government. This is not to mention the the large group who pursue their living in the demi-world between journalism and out-and-out lobbying.

Within the larger Washington news bureau, government is a complex organization chart broken into sectors familiarly known as "beats." A recent assignment sheet of the Associated Press, for example, indicates the degree of compartmentalization:

Senate, 6 reporters; House of Representatives, 5; Supreme Court, 1; Pentagon and Atomic Energy Commission, 2; State Department, 3; White House, 1 or 2; Aviation, 1; Treasury, Federal Reserve and Commerce, 1; business news, 1; Justice and Transportation Commissions (ICC and FCC), 1; Labor, NLRB, and labor unions, 1; Interior, Welfare and outlying Agencies 1; regional staff, 20; world news, 7; and special features, 7.

Each beat has its prescribed routines. Within the government agencies, frequently within an agency's divisions and subdivisions, there are information offices to provide a point of contact for the reporter. The number of government information officers, who stand ready to "brief" him, totals close to three thousand, it has been estimated, or more than twice the number of the press corps itself. The reporter on the beat must devote a sizable amount of time to culling the massive documentary of "handouts" —i.e., mimeographed press releases—which represents the government's own idea of what the news should be.

But his work is by no means limited to this channelized intercourse with government. In Washington the reporter who limits his enterprise to use of the press agent and the handout is considered a slacker. He is expected to break through to other sources of information. He must "go upstairs" and query the policy makers in person. The reporter is outraged if he experiences difficulty in seeing Cabinet members or other political appointees. Even the career civil servant at the upper levels learns to be accessible to the press. Though it is not listed in his job specification, his career may well depend on his ability to feed information to reporters during critical policy struggles.

Reporting has grown complex and technical along with everything else. Take, for example, the shadings of attribution that can be given the source of a reporter's story—"high government officials," "informed circles," or simply "It was learned that . . ." The "leak" has become institutionalized. There is the background briefing, deep background, and off-the-record. Reporting has become ritualized. The open press conference has turned into a mass convocation, its usefulness often impeded by the hordes of reporters who feel duty-bent on being present to write down, to tape and to film all that occurs.

Reporting of government, like all big businesses, has its good points and its bad ones so far as the employee is concerned. The work habits are not so fixed as most, less adaptable to the time clock, more susceptible to peak and slack periods. The pay scale starts higher but advances more slowly than in comparable occupations. Those at the top—bureau chiefs, columnists, and certain well-known special correspondents—are paid very well, though not nearly so well as the elite in such roughly comparable activities as advertising and public relations. For the rank and file, the wage scale is by no means a major incentive.

The reporter in Washington finds in journalism a career that becomes no less physically demanding and little more remunerative as he reaches middle age. Each year's spill-over of weary correspondents into some form of public relations activities is high.

Other incentives hold the Washington correspondent to his trade. To judge by his own admission, they can be quite trivial. He finds the same thrill in chasing after the news event as the firehorse gets at the sound of the gong. There is ego satisfaction in seeing one's name at the head of a column of print. The reporter has an opportunity to associate on a fairly intimate basis with high officials and politicians.

But these, I submit, do not constitute the basic incentives of a substantial group of correspondents in Washington who show extraordinary devotion to the task of reporting government. They have done little to articulate for themselves or for others what is their motivation. It can only be discovered in their casual conversation.

They have an acute sense of involvement in the churning process that is government in America. The reporter is the recorder of government but he is also a participant. He operates in a system in which power is divided. He as much as anyone, and more than a great many, helps to shape the course of government. He is the indispensable broker and middleman among the subgovernments of Washington. He can choose from among the myriad events that seethe beneath the surface of government which to describe, which to ignore. He can illumine policy and notably assist in giving it sharpness and clarity; just as easily, he can prematurely expose policy and, as with an undeveloped film, cause its destruction. At his worst, operating with arbitrary and faulty standards, he can be an agent of disorder and confusion. At his best, he can exert a creative influence on Washington politics.

In no other major capital does the reporter have quite this political role. Patrick O'Donovan, correspondent for the London *Observer*, has commented:

Most strangers are astonished by the power of the American and, more particularly, the Washington press. It fulfills an almost constitutional function. And it works with a seriousness and responsibility which—even though it may lack the luxuries of style—cannot be matched in Britain today . . . The process has been many years in developing. It has produced a small group of writers who must be included in any outline of what constitutes "Washington" . . . They not only check and when necessary destroy individuals, they positively affect the course of policy. The inner group of them is privileged—a few by the Administration, most by the opposition that always exists even within the Civil Service and the Forces. They tend to be scholarly and are judged solely by their accuracy and the richness of their ideas. Without them, the idea of Washington could well be a dangerous one.

During the latter years of the Truman Administration the widely publicized challenge to presidential leadership arising in Congress aroused deep concern among those anxious about America's role in the free-world alliance. Yet, viewed with the hindsight of a very few years, it was a challenge that contained a curious contradiction. The President, even at the lowest ebb of his political fortunes, maintained a program and a budget that would have appeared grandiose to most earlier Presidents. The office of the President held a degree of paramountcy over legislative planning that never even existed before the time of Franklin D. Roosevelt. It is doubtful whether a single prerogative of the Presidency was actually diminished.

What had in fact happened was that the focus of public attention shifted from the White House to the committee rooms of Congress. Prior to 1950, the major events of government attracting the public attention included the Truman Doctrine, the Marshall Plan, Point Four, the Berlin Airlift, and the North Atlantic Treaty Organization with its accompanying Military Defense Assistance Program—all executive-inspired and carried out with the "advice and consent" of Congress. Then, in June 1950, there was the President's decision to send American troops to Korea.

But even before this display of presidential initiative, there had commenced on Capitol Hill a series of spectacles the effect of which was to make Congress, not the President, the principal source of news and explanation and opinion. In any newsman's book the major Washington stories from 1950 to 1953 would include the Tydings investigation of the Mc-Carthy charges, the MacArthur dismissal inquiry, the McCarran hearings, and Senator McCarthy's continuing warfare against the State Department. Even the news of a new President was almost obscured by the continued uproar from Capitol Hill. In all of this, of course, the Executive Branch of government played an active, if reluctant, role. But the staging, the judging, and the issuing of most pronouncements came from Congress or, more specifically, from certain members and groups in Congress.

It is important, I believe, to examine the consequences of this shift in public attention. The investigations themselves were singularly barren of conclusions. Despite all the furor, they did not result in drastic legislative reforms or even in substantial defeats to the Administration's foreign program. Yet, it would be idle to claim that this shift had not affected the balance of power in American government. It served to diminish the usefulness of a great many of the President's chief lieutenants and to elevate into positions of commanding importance hitherto obscure members of Congress. It enabled one comparatively junior Senator lacking the conventional trappings of seniority and prestige to sustain for a considerable time a threat to the President's control over the Executive Branch. It created serious doubts at home and abroad whether the President did in fact stand at the helm of government during a critical time in world affairs.

This era, in brief, illustrates that the way government is publicized can be of major importance. We have today what might be called government by publicity. It has grown with the growth of modern mass communications and public opinion polling—twin technologies that seek to revive the Aristotelian concept of the citizen as firsthand spectator and participant in the marketplace of government. Publicity is a force uniquely indispensable to the American system in which "public opinion" is called on daily to arbitrate between the two competing branches of government supposedly separate and coordinate according to what Woodrow Wilson called the "literary theory" of our Constitution.

In recent years the United States government has, in fact, experienced a curious turnabout in the exercise of powers from what was envisaged in constitutional doctrine. The President, aided by a growing staff of experts, has become the prime formulator of legislative program. Congress, on the other hand, with the proliferation of its investigative committees ever attempts to serve as board of review and veto over the ordinary administration of the Executive departments. Each, in testing the undefined limits of these new-claimed prerogatives, must resort unceasingly to public explanation to sustain the logic of its claims.

Within the Executive Branch itself, grown large and infinitely fragmented, the publicity competition frequently takes on the character of a life and death struggle. Inside the Pentagon, where a sizable chunk of the federal budget is divided up, the highest classifications of military secrecy often go out the window in the rivalry among the three services. When an Army Colonel was recently court-martialed for leaking to the press secret information about the Army missle Jupiter, Dr. Wernher von Braun, head of the Army Missile Program, testified in his defense, "The Jupiter involves . several million dollars of the taxpayers' money. One hundred per cent security would mean no information for the public, no money for the Army, no Jupiter . . . The Army has got to play the same game as the Air Force and the Navy." [1]

The competitive drive of men to attract public attention in order to attain political power is, of course, as old as politics itself. What is comparatively recent and, I believe, peculiar to the American system is the way in which publicity affects not only men and policies but the fundamental balances of government itself.

This analysis would have little point if the publicity system could be assumed to convey a precise image of government—if the shadows cast on the cave's wall for the citizen to see retained a rigid proportion to the reality they reflect. But this is by no means the case. As anyone who spends time in Washington surely comes to learn, the business of publicity is no more automatic nor free from artifice than the business of government

---

[1] *The New York Times,* June 27, 1957.

itself. Indeed, there are built-in biases that all too frequently make the images of government transmitted to the public take on strange and unnatural shapes. On occasion, publicity has been known to assume a generative spirit of its own—in turn re-creating the people and policies being publicized even as the Hollywood starlet is remade to fit the public stereotype.

The reporter in Washington has witnessed on numerous occasions the phenomenon described by the psychologist when the mask of the man takes possession of the true self. More than witness, he has helped to shape the mask which transforms the public figure. Many observed the phenomenal "growth" of Senator John McClellan, an obscure and occasionally demagogic politician until the time of the McCarthy extravaganzas. Undoubtedly McClellan in a time of challenge discovered hitherto unrealized sources of strength within himself. But close observers also noted a tendency in the Senator to live up to the heroic proportions attributed to him by certain prominent columnists.

A leading correspondent, who prefers to remain anonymous, has provided a revealing testament to this creative function in a letter to a friend:

> I have had one very important experience in this town. I knew Arthur Vandenberg when I thought he was the most pompous and prejudiced man in the United States Senate. I saw him change partly by the processes of mellowing old age, but mainly by accident and particularly as a result of public reaction to his famous speech of January 10, 1945. I happen to know that that speech, or rather the main parts of it, were largely accidental. I can say to you privately that I was, myself, quite by chance responsible for that change in the speech. But my point is that what changed Vandenberg was not the speech itself, but the press of public reaction to the speech, and from then on, as you know, he played an important and perhaps a decisive role in winning bipartisan support for the concept of collective security.

What the writer failed to add was that the "press of public reaction" was in large part stimulated by the tremendous fanfare given by leading newspapers to Vandenberg's speech, a build-up that took the Senator quite by surprise, as he confessed in his private papers, published posthumously. It was not the first time—or the last—that the Washington journalist has hailed the policy declaration which he himself had a hand in ghosting.

This creative power of publicity cannot be explained solely by the fact that in a democracy publicity influences public opinion, which in turn must ever be a determining influence on government. There are ways of short-cutting the classic workings of democracy. In an age of complex and fast-breaking events, the measurement of publicity comes to be taken as a cheap and convenient substitute for public opinion. For the politician and the bureaucrat the headline inch frequently serves as the day-to-day measure of public opinion on a great number of issues. By their responses to this synthetic public opinion they stimulate further publicity and so commences a reflexive cycle that has been known to move news stories from the inside to the front page and to reshape policies as surely as if public opinion had exerted its sovereign will.

To study the publicity process in government means to study the ways and means by which government explains itself to the people. It also means necessarily to study the news-forming habits and techniques of the press, radio, and television, which transmit most of the public explanation of government. It means to examine the definition of news itself. Just as individual man cannot communicate thoughts that lie beyond the limits of his vocabulary to express, so it might be said that the vocabulary of the press delimits the thinking of men in organized society, particularly on matters as remote to their daily experience as their national government.

It is strange that the political scientist has so long neglected the study of the interaction between government and the press. The American Fourth Estate operates as a *de facto,* quasiofficial fourth branch of government, its institutions no less important because they have been developed informally and, indeed, haphazardly. Twelve hundred or so members of the Washington press corps, bearing no authority other than accreditation by a newspaper, wire service, or network, are part of the privileged officialdom in the nation's capital. The senior among them claim a prestige commensurate with their continuing power. For Presidents come and go but press bureau chiefs are apt to remain a while.

The power they exercise is continuing and substantive. They are the articulators of those events of government which they and their bosses deem worthy of note. Their strength stems from their ability to select—to define what is news and what isn't. In Washington on an average day, a good many hundreds of thousands of words are spoken, tens of dozens of "events" occur. The press decides which of those words and events shall receive the prompt attention of millions and which, like timber falling in a deep and uninhabited forest, shall crash silently to the ground.

The reporter in Washington has prerogatives belonging to journalists in no other capital. He has access to the Chief Executive. At the White House press conference, he determines by his questions which matters shall be brought to the President's attention and in what way. The reporters, not the President, ultimately decide which of the President's utterances are headlined to the nation, which given lesser treatment, and which pretty well ignored.

The President, of course, gives the ritual of the press conference its basic content. But the reporters largely determine the form. It is a source of continual amazement to the uninitiated how loosely defined are the ground rules for interrogating our head of state.

The reporter serves as one systematic channel of communication between Congress and the Executive which continues to function when others have broken off. Through him the opposition as well as lesser members of the President's own party can bring their queries to the President's ear with some certainty of a response. Conversely, select reporters enjoy an intimacy with the congressional leaders that few members of the White House staff ever share.

In times of critical congressional debate, when the hour for voting draws near, the rooms outside the chambers become a beehive of whispered consultation between press and politician. News tickers in the Capitol and White House lobbies transmit the last-minute communiqués. The hastily torn off teletape rushed to the Senate floor is a familiar sight during the final frenzied assaults on the enemies' strongholds. As each congressional fight reaches its crisis, one is made sharply aware of the pervasive influence of news and newsmen.

No one who has been in on the development and growth of a major policy is likely to minimize the publicity consciousness which must guide its course every step of the way. At a gathering of newsmen to pay honor to him for his famous Plan, General George C. Marshall gave an unsolicited testimonial to this. "I found as in everything I touched almost, particularly in military operations, it is not so hard to make a general plan; the great problem is how to put that thing over; how you carry it through, and that was the case in this instance." Marshall went on to spell out those problems of putting across the Marshall Plan which have lingered in his memory. He told of his concern at the time of his speech at Harvard in June 1947, lest the conservative Middle West rise up to veto the Plan before it had got off the ground. What he had not anticipated and what proved to be a tremendous boon to the Plan was the immediate response of the European leaders to his speech. "The result of Messieurs Bevin and Bidault's anticipation of the Plan provoked so much reaction that the Middle West was forgotten for a month and a half," Marshall declared.

Of course, the Middle West was not forgotten at all, least of all by the people in the Middle West. But what really happened was that the great floodlights of the press were concentrated on the European news events rather than searching out, and perhaps stimulating, news events from Ohio.

This tendency for the development of news to influence reactively the development of the events on which it feeds should not be minimized. It is a force that cannot be precisely charted. It can be a result of pure chance. It can, as modern practitioners of the art of public relations appreciate, be made the object of manipulation. It can even be a product of conscious cooperation from the press. At the gathering in Marshall's honor, Paul Hoffman paid glowing tribute to certain members of the Washington press corps. "We would have never gotten the dollars," said Hoffman, "if it hadn't been for the support of the reporters of the Overseas Writers Club." The tribute was duly accepted by the members present, including representatives of the passionately objective wire services. There are many moments in a reporter's workday when he silently accepts the fact that the formulation of news is not exactly a scientific process foreign to the reporter's thoughts and feelings and ambitions.

The reporter works within limits. News is a vaguely definable commodity recognized more by instinct perhaps than by copybook maxims. One of the perennial sources of astonishment for the nonprofessional is to attend a congressional committee hearing and witness the row upon row of reporters seated at the press tables as they lift their pencils and lay them down with almost ballet corps precision while the flow of testimony moves along. The skilled reporter's measurement of "news" is not simply defined by what goes into the total story. It can be charted by which chunk goes into the "lead," which is buried in the tail, and which, with squirrel-like foresight, is tucked away for the "overnight." The dogmas of what is "news" help determine the priorities of what is communicated to the public about its government.

News standards go to the very core of policy formulation by officials. As a program moves from the tentative planning stage in the Executive department through the long wearisome process of legislative enactment, appropriation, further enactment, and still further appropriation, there is an inevitable tendency to accentuate those aspects which are newsworthy and to de-emphasize—sometimes causing atrophy—those aspects which are not newsworthy.

The competitive news advantage of one policy over another has great bearing on the comparative ease with which each survives the legislative process. Under the vast panoply of our foreign aid programs, military assistance with its newsworthy qualities—its marching troops, long lines of tanks, and low sweeping planes—has a publicity appeal which aids greatly its continuation. On the contrary, a worthy program like economic aid requires tremendous exertion to seek out its newsworthy traits, vast oversimplification, and the mammoth efforts of private groups who zealously exploit the small news potential in order to develop political support. Congressional ardor in approaching these two programs bears a direct relationship.

It is impossible to chart precisely the conforming influence of publicity upon policy. A few who were privy to the initial formulation of the Marshall Plan discovered that publicity requirements as much as anything else dictated its evolution from a program directed against "hunger and want" to one aimed more concretely at Communism. It was perhaps a subtle shift of emphasis but far-reaching in its effect.

It is useful to examine the basic conflict of interest that exists between government and the press. A more detailed inquiry into the nature of this conflict will be left to later chapters. Here I would simply point out that the official and the reporter are moved by fundamentally different compulsions. The official's first response to a newsworthy event is assimilative. He attempts to relate it to the broad body of record on which he precariously builds his policies. The reporter's first impulse, on the other hand, is distributive: he seeks to communicate the newsworthy event as speedily and widely as possible.

Inside the Executive Branch official cables, coded and decoded, lag by vital hours and sometimes days the dispatches of the press. On a weekend in 1955 the Undersecretary of State, acting in his superior's absence from the city, learns through a press report that Chinese Communist leader Chou En-lai has made a bid for negotiation on the Formosa Straits dispute. He knows, too, that the American public has been similarly informed. The press stands ready to take down, even insistent on receiving his response. The Undersecretary has not received an official report from the field evaluating the proposal, but he does not want to give the "publicity play" to the Communists over the weekend. He drafts a hurried reply summarily knocking down the Communist bid. It turns out that he has not had time to gauge the full import of Chou En-lai's proposal or to conceive a skillful answer. The Secretary, on his return, makes an effort to rectify the blunder. In this case, the priorities of the press have hustled the procedures of government.

The official must think in terms of finding the lowest common denominator of agreement. For him the business of policy making is a matter of accommodation. Particularly as it reaches the topmost levels of government, there is need to fuzz over disagreements in the quest for a sense of unanimity. Regular participants at meetings of the National Security Council, the nation's highest strategic body, testify that the problem frequently reduces itself to finding the phrase of appropriate subtlety to bridge unnecessary conflicts. The official, as Dean Acheson has remarked, remembers the words of Justice Holmes: "Some things have got to be stated obscurely before they can be stated clearly."

For the reporter, the basic quest is to discover and highlight traces of disunity. As a government official once complained, the reporter is Hegelian. He thinks in terms of thesis and antithesis. It is his premise that progress comes through controversy and that truth, as has been said, is generated by encounter as fire is made by rubbing together two sticks.

The official acts on the premise that premature publicity can be a destructive force if it undermines the effort to reconcile diverse interests and causes the hardening of fixed positions. The reporter believes in the purifying powers of publicity. He is the sworn enemy of secrecy. He holds firm in the faith that "public opinion" must have an opportunity to express itself while policy is still malleable and has not been molded into unchangeable dogma.

Arthur Krock, columnist of the *New York Times*, has summed up succinctly the conflicting mandates of newspaperman and official:

Our obligations are merely these in deciding whether to go into print with information: Is it true? Has it been legitimately acquired? Is it fit to print— public property or a private matter? These satisfactorily settled, the facts are ready for their bath of printer's ink.

But the statesman has other considerations. Is it premature? Will publication make the going more difficult? Will publication tend to confuse, rather than to clarify, the popular mind? These are some of the problems before him, particularly if he is President of the United States in a catastrophic hour, forcing the innermost fibers of his body and the full resources of his spirit into his colossal task.

It is interesting to note that in the Soviet Union there is no such dichotomy between the reporter and the commissar. By Communist definition, the press is an instrument of state and party for the "education" of the people. News can be held in a state of suspension for weeks or months without losing its newsworthiness when the decision to publish is finally made. Despite its lip service to a philosophy of dialectical materialism, the Soviet press has invented a whole new vocabulary to describe its government in nondialectical terms. Socialist progress as reported in *Pravda* is a straight-line proposition. The Soviet reporter will admit of no conflict of interest between government and the press.

But for American government, this conflict is very real. On Dean Acheson's last day in office as Secretary of State, he was paid a visit by James Reston, Washington correspondent for the *New York Times*. The purpose of Reston's call was to ask quite bluntly why the Secretary and he had not enjoyed better working relations. Underlying his question was the unhappy conviction that Acheson, who brought unusually high talents to the office, had been unwittingly caught in the riptides of publicity. The Secretary's effectiveness had been gradually eroded by failures of communication.

Secretary Acheson answered equally bluntly that what Reston suggested would have been impossible, since there was a basic conflict of purpose between the two of them. A Secretary of State, Acheson said, has to germinate new policies and to nurse them along until they have reached the stage of development when they can withstand the battering assaults of the political arena. The reporter's primary purpose, on the other hand, is to get news for his paper no matter what the effect on policy.

Reston stoutly denies that the conflict can be defined in quite these terms. He admits it is the duty of the reporter to get at the news while it is still news. In government today, when so many policy decisions are made in the closed precincts of the Executive departments, the press would be abdicating its function if it were to sit by until these decisions are formally announced. But Reston argues that Secretary Acheson failed to understand and make use of the creative power of the press to muster public support for sound policy and, alternatively, to gauge the full extent of public reaction to unsound or unrealistic policy.

This dialogue between the Secretary and the reporter—both able and earnest men, both anxious that democratic government should be effective government—reveals a dilemma of government and the press in a free society. It is a dilemma more recognizable in the United States than in the parliamentary democracies where the press does not play so intimate a role in the scheme of things. It afflicts Republican and Democratic administrations alike for it has nothing to do with partisan affiliations of government or the press.

There are other dilemmas. With the growth of big government and of modern mass techniques for communicating the news about government, there has been a parallel growth in the subtle art of manipulating the flow of information. To a remarkable extent, the public trust nowadays is afflicted with an acute public relations sense. The tendency to "manage the news" on the part of those having a particular interest in it disturbs and frequently confounds the best of reporters.

The following chapters describe in more detail our system of government by publicity and the challenge it poses for reporters and responsible public officials alike. I have tried to avoid harsh judgments or hasty panaceas. Certainly, the institutions of both government and the free press in America are equally ancient and inviolable. Much of the tension between the two is part of the healthy unrest of democracy.

Yet both need to be examined to discover how much or how little they contribute to a continuing disorder in democracy which results in weakness rather than strength. It is a failure for democracy when government fails to explain itself clearly and candidly to the citizens. It is equally a failure when the press fails to communicate intelligibly the news of government or when that news becomes a propaganda weapon employed by self-seeking interests to frustrate effective leadership in a democracy.

Bernard C. Cohen

FOREIGN POLICY-MAKERS
AND THE PRESS

THE most obvious external impingement on the governmental foreign policy making process is that of the press: Day after day, with great per-

Reprinted with permission of the publisher from *International Politics and Foreign Policy*, ed. James N. Rosenau. Copyright © 1961 by The Free Press of Glencoe, Inc.

sistence, the press invades the official circle of policy-makers, while other segments of the public try with indifferent success to get just an occasional hearing. But the newspaperman's access to the policy-makers is not like the access of other public spokesmen. His intrusion is welcomed; it is invited; it is sought after; which means that its significance and impact must be qualitatively different from that of other public groups whose access is occasional or incomplete. The nature of this relationship between the press and the foreign policy-maker is largely unexplored; whatever the reason, it is a strange lacuna in a field of so much general interest. The subject is much broader than the present compass; my intention here is to inquire into only one aspect of this relationship as it operates in the United States—viz., how does "the press" enter the world of foreign policy making? How do policy-makers perceive the significance of the press for their work? What do they take from it as a result? And what are the implications of this use of the press for the policy-making process? [1]

I

The most apparent way in which the press enters the policy-maker's world is by means of the daily newspaper. And the single most important newspaper is, of course, the *New York Times*. It is read by virtually everyone in the government who has an interest or responsibility in foreign affairs. A State Department official said, "The *New York Times* is read more generally than any other newspaper, owing to its more extensive coverage." A Senator's Legislative Assistant commented, "The *New York Times* is every man's CIA around here." One frequently runs across the familiar story: "It is often said that Foreign Service Officers get to their desks early in the morning to read the *New York Times*, so they can brief their bosses on what is going on." This canard is easily buried: The "bosses" are there early, too, reading the *New York Times* for themselves.

The *Times* has long been regarded as the American "prestige paper": ". . . the prestige paper has come to be an important and respected institu-

---

[1] This article is part of a more comprehensive study of the press and foreign policy making in the United States. I am grateful to the Center of International Studies, Princeton University, for its support of this study. The larger study is based in part on interviews conducted over several years with leading foreign affairs reporters and analysts for the major American newspapers and wire services; with officials in the Departments of State and Defense; and with Senators and Representatives and Congressional staff personnel who are especially interested in—and have important responsibilities in connection with—foreign affairs. The quotations in the present article are drawn from interviews with Executive and Legislative officials—about forty in number—which I conducted in the summer of 1960. The interviews themselves were arranged to provide direct evidence as to the way the press is perceived and utilized at all points and stages in the process of foreign policy making. Statistical treatment of this number of interviews is not proper. The portions of the interviews reproduced here were chosen to illustrate the nature and range—and also the flavor—of the evidence that this interview material provides.

tion. Governments, politicians, and businessmen depend upon it. One might ask what would happen in Washington if the New York Times stopped publication and no other paper took its place. There would certainly be a deterioration in American political intelligence." [2] But if a "prestige paper" is defined by its importance to the political and governmental elite, then the notion of *a* prestige paper has to yield, in the foreign policy field at least, to a plural concept.

There is no question that the New York Times is important. But it has distinguished company on the desks of the policy-makers: the *Washington Post*, the *New York Herald-Tribune*, the *Wall Street Journal*, the *Christian Science Monitor*, the *Baltimore Sun*, the *Washington Star*. Collectively, these form the prestige press in the foreign policy field. The relative importance of these papers varies, obviously, from individual to individual; but one can hardly avoid recognizing the significance, in Washington, of the *Washington Post*, and to a slightly lesser extent (perhaps because it is an evening paper) the *Washington Star*. The following quotes will illustrate. A Senator: "I read the *Post*, of course, and the *Star*, and the *New York Times*"; a State Department official: "I read the *New York Times*, of course, and the *Post*, and the *Star*"; a former State Department official: "Everyone in the State Department reads the *New York Times* and the *Washington Post*." [3] The *New York Times* is often the second newspaper to reach the foreign policy specialist in Washington; the *Post* is there first. In fact, for many of these people, the *Post* is the doorstep newspaper; they will pick up the *Times* on the way to the office, or it will be on their desk when they arrive. The *Times* is uniformly regarded as the authoritative paper in the foreign policy field. In the words of a State Department official in the public affairs field, "You can't work in the State Department without the *New York Times*. You can get along without the overnight telegrams sooner." But attitudes must be compared with actual practice, which puts the *New York Times* in the position of *primus inter pares*.[4]

The prestige press, then, does not consist simply of *one* newspaper whose publishers and editors have determined to make it qualitatively and quantitatively distinctive in the foreign affairs field—a "newspaper of record"; rather, it is an amalgam of the higher quality, better coverage

[2] Ithiel de Sola Pool, *The "Prestige Papers,"* Hoover Institute Studies, Series C.: Symbols, No. 2 (Palo Alto: Stanford University Press, January 1952), p. 8. See also Wilbur Schram's discussion of prestige papers in *One Day in the World's Press* (Palo Alto: Stanford University Press, 1959), p. 5.

[3] In May, 1953, the *Evening Star* reported that 95 Senators and 406 Representatives bought its weekday issues. Cited in Franklin L. Burdette, "The Influence of Noncongressional Pressures on Foreign Policy," *The Annals of the American Academy of Political and Social Science* (September 1953), p. 95.

[4] And sometimes it is not even *primus*. Each day the News Division of the State Department prepares a two-page survey of major foreign affairs news stories for the higher levels in the Department; these stories are culled from a number of the leading Eastern morning newspapers, and the *Times* is treated no differently from the others.

Eastern metropolitan newspapers which are available to the policy-makers on the day of issue. In other words, the prestige press is not a unique newspaper which policy-makers depend on for their political intelligence; rather, it is a larger network of communication, which helps to define for the policy-maker the current political universe. Washington survives when, from time to time, the *New York Times* is not published; it may be sorely missed, but there are a half-dozen other papers which, collectively, fill the gap. The larger network of communication is marginally, not centrally, affected.

A second way in which the press enters the foreign policy arena is via the wire-service tickers. For most newspapers in the country, the flow of national and international news from the tickers represents the well into which they must dip for their coverage of national and international affairs. Very few newspapers can afford the luxury of having their own foreign correspondents, and Washington itself is typically covered by only a one- or two-man bureau. Thus, wire-service coverage may be regarded as a vast, continuous, unedited newspaper—much more extensive in its coverage of foreign affairs than any single newspaper in the country, since no paper that relies on this source can publish all the information it produces. Moreover, not only do the wire services define the outer limits of foreign affairs coverage for most newspapers and for many policy-makers; they also may be regarded as "tomorrow's paper today," or "this afternoon's paper this morning." They give "the news" a number of hours before it could be obtained from ordinary newspaper sources.

For both of these reasons, the news tickers occupy a prominent place in the foreign policy makers' world. The State Department's News Division maintains Associated Press, United Press-International, and Reuters news tickers; the Agence France-Presse ticker in the State Department is located, for language reasons, in the Bureau of European Affairs. And there are also several tickers on the seventh floor, where the Secretary and Under Secretary have their offices. The tickers in the News Division are constantly monitored; eight copies come off each ticker, and additional copies are often duplicated in order to distribute the news items to all the relevant areas in the Department. There are AP and UPI teletype machines in the lobbies off the Senate and House floors. Here the copy is clipped and hung up, and is read continuously whenever the Congress is in session. According to one Member: "The tickers are used steadily; this is the first source of information—many hours before they read it in the press."

Considering the attention that is paid to the wire services by men of top political and governmental rank, one must include them as part of the "prestige press." Each of the news services has its own staff of correspondents, all over the world. Thus, each service represents an independent source of news of world affairs, roughly comparable in the extent of its coverage—and more rapid in its impact—to the best of the "prestige newspapers" which rely on their own staffs of correspondents abroad and in Washington. At first glance, it may seem to be a denial of the very concept to include the wire services in a "prestige press," but one should be guided here as much by the extent of coverage, and the uses to which it is put, as by presumptions about its quality. Even the Washington newspapers, one should add, having few foreign correspondents of their own, rely almost exclusively on the wires for their international news.

A third way in which the press enters the world of foreign policy making is through the personal relationships among policy-makers and the correspondents who gather and comment on foreign affairs news in Washington. Personal friendships among government officials and newsmen are common, and more-than-casual acquaintanceships are even more numerous, owing to the constant contact between officials and the reporters on a steady "beat." This informal interplay is valued by both—by the reporter, who must establish "contacts" to do his job well; and by the policy-maker, who wants to see the press do a good job, and who also knows that the good reporter has more ideas and information than he ordinarily uses in any one day. One State Department official, who remarked that he was not in direct contact with reporters very much because he sits in a protected position, nevertheless named about ten leading foreign affairs correspondents as personal friends; "I'm lunching today with a correspondent. . . . I do it often, with a number of them. I get ideas from ————, and he gets them from me. He knows all the top people here. We have a public duty to the press, to help them cover foreign affairs adequately." Another officer in the Department said that "about 80 per cent of my contacts with reporters are on a personal basis—reporters whom I know personally, some of them since we were in the 'field' together." This kind of contact with the press is much more specialized, intermittent, and unevenly distributed than are the other points of contact; its qualitative importance would be very difficult to measure, but it comes to the fore too often and too insistently to be overlooked.

Thus far, this discussion has been in terms of the newspaper press; however, one can define the press more broadly to include magazines (especially, in this context, weekly newsmagazines) and radio and television. All of these are important in the life of the policy-making official who is interested in the world around him. While the newsmagazines seem to be much less important than the newspapers mentioned above, they are regarded as an important channel for news to the interested public, and the correspondents for these newsmagazines are generally ranked with those of the leading newspapers and news services in terms of importance and competence. Radio and TV are somewhat different. There is a widespread pattern of morning listening to the network roundups of world news over these media; Secretary Dulles is reliably reported to have begun his day in this fashion. Even the reporters listen to "the news" each morning. If, therefore, I concentrate on the newspaper press here, it is not to underrate the significance of the electronic media. Rather, it represents a deliberate choice within an economy of means, a choice based on the different characteristics and functions of these media: radio and TV news is, by and large, spot news; it is very brief, and it is also ephemeral. It seems to serve the policy-maker, not as an alternative to the newspaper, but rather as a signal or an index: It tells him the "important" things to look for in the more detailed— and lasting—coverage provided in the newspaper (or, for the late-breaking items, the teletype machine). This does not refer at all to special features on radio and television. I would merely point out that there is no evidence whatever of a major, or even an important, reliance on these media for the kind of news that the "prestige press" supplies.

II

The fact that the press intrudes itself into the daily rounds of government officials is only the starting point for a study of its impact on policy-making. The real question is what happens to the press once it becomes part of the policy-maker's horizon. What do policy-makers get out of it that has a bearing on the policy environment?

Information. Although he is surrounded by official and unofficial networks of communication designed to keep him informed, the policy-maker still turns to the press for basic information about the international political world he lives in. Why should this be so? What can he learn from this source that he does not get from his established internal sources of information? Obviously, to a great extent the answer depends on how the internal network of communication serves different needs; and here one must make basic distinctions among the different kinds and levels of policy-making officials.

Except for the top foreign policy making officials, there is a specialization of area and/or function among the people in the State Department. The official network is designed to keep the specialists informed with respect to their own specialization; as a Department official pointed out, "The Embassies do not attempt to cover the news; they assume that people in the State Department read newspapers." A high-level view confirmed this attitude: "Most of the information you get, you get from the newspapers. . . . In the State Department the internal flow of communication is specialized; the broad scope of developments is found in the newspaper." For the few men at the top, the press also provides an independent report, outside of the diplomatic channel, on what is happening around the world. As one important official put it, "The *New York Times* and other newspapers with their own correspondents abroad have angles that you may not be aware of as a consequence of reading only the official reports."

Furthermore, they often get information sooner through the press than through official routes. Ultimately, for obvious reasons, they have to work with the information and analysis supplied by their own "reporters" abroad; but their contact with the rapidly changing contours of the international political world at any moment in time is as much through the press as through their own facilities—which in any case are not meant to compete with the press in the gathering of basic "news." Owing to the coding and decoding procedures, official reports generally run behind press reports. One observer said that, "In fast-breaking situations, the tickers beat cables by four or five hours—and in some cases by up to 24 hours." Another Department officer, who has the "news tickers clipped constantly and sent up to me all day long," concluded that "the State Department sources run about 24 hours behind the press." Under these circumstances, the press must have some impact on the way the men at the top initially define international situations. And because these officials are physically unable to read everything that comes into the Department through official channels, the press's definition of the structure of international affairs may become, by default, the "official" definition.

For the foreign policy specialists, the press also provides an independent, and somewhat more rapid, view of what is happening in their areas of interest. But since the flow of specialized material is great, the informational contribution of the press is proportionately less. One desk officer described it this way: "There will be a story in the *New York Times* from time to time which is *news* to us, and about which there is nothing on the cables from————. But it is usually the structural problem, not a particular event that gives rise to this story." The press supplies these people with other information, however: it tells them what is happening around the world in areas other than the one with which they are primarily concerned. Since they neither have access to, nor time to read, all the official reports from all over the world, these specialists—up to, and sometimes including, the Assistant Secretaries of State—depend upon the press for their broader knowledge of international developments. Clearly, however, the narrower the specialization, and the greater the distance between the specialist and the staff level in the State Department, the greater is this dependence.

The press also provides the specialist with information of a different kind. The specialist lives in a bureaucratic world, and he is familiar with the political struggles that accompany policy ideas and proposals along the route to decision. Of necessity, he acquires internal sources of information about relevant developments in proximate bureaucratic units, but here, too, his intelligence becomes more tenuous with increasing distance. And so he depends upon the press for information about things that are happening and proposals that are being made elsewhere in the foreign policy-making structure of the government. A Foreign Service Officer explained the situation tactfully: "You cannot divorce foreign policy from domestic political situations and political events. By and large the traditional departmental methods of informing departmental officers do not suffice; so the press plays an important role in factually informing officers."

As one might expect, the press is more important to Members of Congress, as a source of information on foreign policy, than to members of the Department of State, because the Congressman's alternative sources of information are not as extensive. The foreign affairs committees of the two houses do have alternative sources in their established links with the State Department; but the information that comes this way is not continuous, and is itself apt to be specialized. The legislative policy-maker who is interested in foreign affairs is no different from an ordinary citizen in his dependence upon the press: he reads the newspapers to find out what is going on. A member of the State Department with some legislative experience described it this way: "Senators read the press very carefully. They get ideas from it. They are asked to comment on events, so they have to be up on them. You go to the Senate lounges, you will see them reading their home press, the *New York Times*, the Washington press, the wire tickers. You will *always* see Senators reading them. They are well-posted on current problems. This is reflected in calls they make to the State Department asking, 'What about this problem I see in the paper?' " A Senator said, "Unless you are a member of the Foreign Relations Committee, who has access to classified sources of information, the newspapers and the commentators are the prime source of information. . . . I can't overemphasize the information function of the newspaper. We have to get our information just as the citizen gets his." And a member of the House Foreign Affairs Committee suggested that Executive sources of information are like frosting on the press cake: "The Committee, and the leadership on both sides, gets briefed by the Executive branch, so they get other information than what they get from the press."

The press, in this case, is still the "prestige press" as defined above, only slightly modified by the addition of constituency newspapers. For most Congressmen, constituency newspapers are not a source of foreign affairs news, either because their coverage is relatively skimpy, or because they arrive in Washington a day or two late. When they do arrive, they are used for different purposes; as a Democratic Senator's knowledgeable Legislative Counsel observed, "Local newspapers are read for their state political news, for their news about employment conditions, general or new business developments, and for what they say about the Senator."

Evaluation. Policy-makers turn to the press not only for information, but also for analysis and evaluation of developments and proposals, and sometimes even for new ideas on how to deal with the range of problems that confront them. It should be emphasized, however, that this is not one of the major uses of the press, if only because non-newspaper sources of foreign policy evaluation and analysis are better developed than are newspaper sources. In the press it is chiefly the columnists—e.g., Reston, Sulzberger, Lippmann, Alsop—who are regarded as useful for interpretation, or even for ideas. And while men who are professionally involved with foreign policy decisions are quick to acknowledge their constant readership of foreign affairs analysts in the press, some of them are reluctant to attach great importance to the evaluations of these columnists—as far as the development of their *own* thinking is concerned. There may be professional pride involved here, but there is something else besides: The able foreign policy people are capable of writing their own analyses, and may have even contributed on occasion to the very ideas and interpretations that end up in the news analysts' columns. As a result, they have a well-cultivated predisposition to wonder whether some vested interest is being served by the published interpretation or analysis.

But the press provides another kind of evaluation, which is no less important for its being less obvious. It is commonly understood that, in the political realm, what is *thought* to be true is often a more relevant source of political inspiration that what *is* true. A very close observer of foreign policy making put it this way: "The freedom of action of the diplomat is greatly limited; he has to work with the realities of the way people interpret events. The newspaperman is of the utmost importance in that field." The following sections will amplify this point by explaining how foreign policy makers extract from the press a sense of how reality is perceived—and, hence, a sense of political reality itself.

Importance. Policy-makers also draw from the press some measure of the "importance" of events. In their official capacities they are subject to varying flows of information from non-press sources, to which they must attach their own criteria of significance. They do this on the basis of the implicit or explicit theories they apply to that particular subject area; and they wish to check their "significance" with other people. This same problem exists with respect to the information they draw from the wire service tickers: Despite the processes of selection and editing to which wire service news is subjected, it comes out of the machine as a steady flow of raw material, and it has to be put into order—to have importance attached to it according to criteria that will "hold up" in the marketplace of ideas.

The newspaper supplies this independent ordering of the importance of events. As applied to a newspaper, the editorial process is basically an evaluative one: The editors, on the basis of their *own* theories of what constitutes "news," attach orders of priority to news items, which they make manifest by their location in the paper, the amount of space allocated to these items, and the size of the headlines that attract attention to them. In turning to the newspaper press, policy-makers are seeking a comparative evaluation of the importance of events; and in turning to particular newspapers, they are seeking the evaluation of editors in whose theories of what is "news" they have some tested faith.

One can distinguish two aspects of this search for comparative evaluation. The first is the rather obvious one of discovering how important the press thinks an event or situation is, in comparison with all the other events and situations that are occurring at the same time. A member of the State Department who was once a newspaperman stressed the meaning that this had, at least for him: "The press is more important here than the cables. There is a big difference in seeing a story on the front page, in comparison with all the other stories there, from St. Louis and everywhere else, and in the specialization of the cables. . . . The impact of the cables is not felt until it is seen in juxtaposition with other stories, on the front page of the *New York Times*."

The second aspect of this search may be put this way: Does the press attach such importance to a particular item that government officials *must* react to it in some way? In other words, under certain circumstances the order of priority which the press attaches to policy items may supersede the significance originally or ordinarily attached to them in the Department of State or elsewhere. This process may be discerned at the top levels in the Department in this description by someone close to it: "In the Executive Secretariat in the State Department the cables are screened for the top three officers in the Department. There is an editor—called just that—who determines which cables get summarized, which ones get shown in their entirety. He has different priorities from the newspaperman, but then he doesn't have to worry about 'news values.' Yet he has to think about 'news values' in case it breaks into print." And when it does break into print, there are individuals whose task it is to sift the stories and to bring up for discussion in the Executive staff meeting those items which "we may have to do something about." A Defense Department official phrased it in a way that applies equally to the State Department experience: "You know that a story that is scattered in newspapers across the country will stir up a certain reaction."

Thus, the press, by giving prominence to an issue, helps to nudge it somewhat higher on the list of items claiming the attention of policy-makers. We have already noted how this gets translated into one kind of pressure on the State Department, when Members of Congress call up and ask, "What about this problem I see in the paper?" And it may also have an impact on Congressional consideration of foreign policy; e.g., "Many Members [of the House Foreign Affairs Committee] bring cuts from newspapers to the Hearings, to ask witnesses specific questions."

There is, consequently, great incentive for policy-makers to turn to the newspaper, to make sure that they know what is about to become important because people elsewhere *think* it is important—after their newspaper implicitly told them it was.

Standards. The Eastern metropolitan newspapers, alone and also in conjunction with constituency newspapers, provide foreign policy makers in various parts of the government with standards by which to measure or judge what others involved in the political process are reading about foreign affairs. This is an important source of their insight into the way foreign policy issues are perceived and assimilated into political structures, foreign as well as domestic.

Congressmen, who are especially sensitive to the newspaper press as a source of information and political intelligence,[5] use the New York and Washington newspapers as a yardstick to measure what their constituents are—or are not—reading. This is not simply a way of comparing what they themselves are reading about the world around them with what their constituents are reading; in addition, they sometimes seem to accept the foreign affairs coverage in the leading Eastern papers as the benchmark of top quality, and use it to measure the inadequacies of local press coverage. Thus, a Senator commented: "I get an entirely different picture of priorities from my local newspapers than from the Washington papers. I want to know what the newspapers are telling *my* constituents about what is important in the world. I have to judge whether the emphases are accurate. . . ." And a Representative complained that "There is no rhyme or reason to foreign policy coverage in the . . . [constituency] papers. A story may get a big headline there, and just one inch of coverage in the *New York Times*. Some idiot of a night editor plays a story up out of all due proportion."

Congressmen also turn to the columnists who are syndicated in their constituency newspapers as another way of knowing what their constituents are reading in the foreign policy field. Franklin Burdette points out that the stories of syndicated columnists have an impact upon the mail that Congressmen receive from their districts, and hence they are "of marked effect in the political atmosphere of the capital."[6]

In the State Department, too, the New York and Washington newspapers provide a guide to what groups elsewhere are reading; this is an important way in which the State Department keeps track of new by-ways in the foreign policy "maps" of some of its most relevant "constituents." In the higher reaches of the Department, *Washington Post* editorials are read "because we know they are read on Capitol Hill." And at all levels in the Department—including the desk-level, where there is the most direct contact with specific country-problems—the *New York Times* is studied carefully because Department personnel are aware of the great attention accorded it by foreign Embassy personnel in Washington as the leading American newspaper, and the one which is reputed to have the closest

---

[5] Cf. Douglass Cater, *The Fourth Branch of Government* (Boston: Houghton Mifflin, 1959).

[6] Franklin L. Burdette, "The Influence of Noncongressional Pressures on Foreign Policy," *The Annals of the American Academy of Political and Social Science* (September 1953), p. 95.

connections with the State Department. A desk officer put it this way: "A *New York Times* editorial has more weight with us *because* it has more weight with our clients, the Embassies. This is why we have to read the *Times*. The Embassy people read it too, and it becomes a common point of departure for their reactions and for ours."

Opinions. Lastly, the press provides policy-makers with the ingredient which has long been assumed to be its chief contribution: a measure of "public opinion." Opinions in the press—especially editorial opinions, but also the views of "newsworthy" groups which are reported in news columns —are one of the leading channels by which foreign policy officials can regularly and continuously tap an informed and articulate segment of public opinion. To be sure, this is not the only way to gain an understanding of public responses to foreign policy, nor is it always the most relevant way; but lacking any other *daily* link to the outside, any other *daily* measure of how people are reacting to the ebb and flow of foreign policy developments, the policy-maker reaches for the newspaper as an important source of public opinion. The over-all political impact of the press in this respect was described by one man as follows: "The newspaper is a source of a daily 'feel' as to what is going on, and the public reaction to it. Your vision of the world comes at you from the paper, it hits you at breakfast."

That the press is used as a source of opinion is well understood. *How* it is used, however, is less clear. There are important variations, both in the way press opinion is perceived and in its political impact and utilization, and these merit brief exploration.

In the State Department, individual reactions to press opinion range from the extreme of total rejection (after careful reading) to the view that at times Department policy is determined in direct response to press opinion. The former is exemplified by the individual who, after identifying press opinion as "public opinion," argued vociferously that "Public opinion doesn't matter. . . . The official has set his goals, he believes in liberal trade, and all he wants is to get support for liberal trade, and he will not be influenced to believe the opposite. Protectionist newspapers do not influence us in the slightest degree." This man added: "Over the years I might be able to think of one case where the State Department changed its policy as a result of newspaper coverage, but I doubt it." The opposite position was well expressed by the observation that "State Department policy [toward Cuba in 1958–59] was dictated by the hue and cry in the press on the side of Castro."

The large middle ground between these points of view with respect to press opinion is occupied by two basic orientations, which we might call the political and the instrumental. The political orientation looks to press opinion for clues to the structure of political support for alternative policies. Where policy is relatively firm—as a desk officer put it—"the daily trend of editorial opinion is less significant." But where there is flux, "we are interested in seeing editorials, to see what is behind them, who wrote them, what weight they represent." Even those in the Department who regard themselves as free from the constraints of public opinion by virtue of their specialized responsibilities understand that political officers have to be more flexible and responsive to the possibilities of support for their ideals.

In the State Department the instrumental orientation seems to be at least as pervasive as the political orientation; it is certainly not limited to those officials whose primary responsibility is the Department's public relations. The instrumental orientation looks to the press for clues to the way policy is being received by the public, in order to determine whether such policy needs to be better justified or explained. An excellent statement of this outlook came not from a public opinion analyst, but from a member of the staff who has had an opportunity to observe the higher policy levels in the Department: "The main use of the press in making foreign policy decisions is alerting you to public reactions and to public interest—to the necessity for considering how policy decisions need to be interpreted when they are made public. You can only set forth the reasons [behind a policy] in an intelligent fashion if you know what the public is worried about. The press that we read here is the major source of our knowledge of public opinion." One might question whether this is in fact the "main use" of the press, even at levels in the Department where internal information flows abundantly—but the significance of this use is plain in any case.

As one would expect of elected representatives, Congressmen steep themselves in the public opinion that they find in the press. As a Senator described it, "Newspapers give us editorial reactions—personal reactions—of people who are informed—people whose reactions are an important gauge of the significance of developments abroad." But whereas Congressmen draw their foreign affairs information chiefly from the Eastern metropolitan press, they draw their views of public opinion from their constituency press too, since they are interested in the views of a particular public, as well as an especially informed one. Yet, Congressmen pay more attention to the editorials in the *New York Times* and *Washington Post* than one might expect of men from remote constituencies, according to common theories of electoral behavior. Since this is an unusual finding, we shall explore its possible sources.

One apparent reason for the relative downgrading of the local press is that many Congressmen feel that press editorials on foreign policy matters have no resonance in the local communities. While they are interested in "informed opinion," they want it to be the opinion of more than just one informed editorial writer; and where they suspect (rightly or wrongly) that the editor himself has no constituency, they are likely to rely more heavily on the Eastern newspapers for their foreign policy editorial opinion. A Midwestern Representative expressed this well when he said that "Reading the local paper doesn't give me any opinion information, because no matter how good the editorial columns are—and they are *the* foreign policy columns in the paper—I know that nobody reads them." Another Representative found most editorials worthless because they were "on the *obvious*, not the subtle, aspects of policy, and along the general thrust of attitudes. . . . Several of the great newspapers will discuss editorially the more important but less notorious aspects of foreign policy, but generally it is not done. The average citizen gets a very sketchy view of these problems."

Another possible reason for the editorial significance of the Eastern press did not emerge in interviews with Congressmen, but may be discerned in the circumstances of their political life: The longer a Congressman remains in Washington, the more attenuated become his ties with the district or state he "represents." He lives in a new community, an intensely political one, and if he is interested in foreign affairs he soon discovers that there is a lot of international politics in Washington, too. But his new foreign policy horizons are likely to have no counterpart in the editorial world of his constituency press; that may tell him a great deal, but it doesn't tell him how to respond to the stimuli that confront him in Washington. And so the Congressman turns to the editorial views that carry some weight in that community—thereby adding to their political importance.

III

Implications. One can hardly reach anything as definitive as "conclusions" about the relationship between the press and foreign policy after an examination of only one aspect of it. Yet, there are some implications in the analysis and findings set forth above which suggest new layers of meaning for some old observations and propositions.

The problem of policy coordination has absorbed the attention of many observers who have been aware of the growing complexity of foreign policy formulation and administration. In diverse ways, these analysts have sought to bring greater coherence and order to a decentralized policy-making process. When one ponders the utilization of the press in foreign policy making, however, one cannot help but be struck by how much real coordination of policy is provided by the institution of the press. Common exposure, on a continuous basis, to large amounts of information on foreign affairs, and common understandings of the relative "importance" of various issues, help to provide a common context for the individual and often specialized efforts of large numbers of participants in the enterprise of foreign policy making.

Without in the least depreciating the impact of the press upon even the specialists in the Executive branch, there is perhaps greater significance in the fact that Congressmen draw their understanding of the world of foreign affairs from a common pool than in the fact that this is also true of

Executive branch foreign policy officials. For one thing, the Executive official does not have the Congressman's constituency problem. The Congressman, as a political specialist, is constituency-oriented; and in the course of his ordinary local routine his exposure to foreign affairs information and salience would come to him in great measure through his constituency newspapers—or perhaps major regional newspapers. But living in Washington usually deprives a Congressman of ready access to his local newspaper on the day of issue; and it also provides him, as a part of the new community he lives in, with a new set of newspapers which reflect the dominant public interests of that community. The result is clear: Despite the wide range of individual backgrounds, despite the poor coverage of foreign affairs that would be found in most constituency papers, Congressmen in Washington are exposed in common to an abundant flow of information about the world of foreign affairs, and they are also exposed to uniform measures of salience, or importance. To be sure, these men bring diverse attitudes and policy orientations with them, which help to condition the way they seek and utilize information about foreign affairs; yet, one might speculate that Congressional consideration of foreign policy might be considerably more acrimonious and less consistent and relevant if its participants were differentially, rather than commonly, informed.

By giving policy-makers an insight into the political perceptions held at other points in the political process, the press helps to create common understandings or interpretations of political reality. There is thus some significance for the governmental—and hence public—debate on foreign policy in the fact that both Executive officials and Congressmen draw on approximately the same sources for their wider knowledge of "what is going on in the world," and how important it seems to be. Certain kinds of behavior can thus be reasonably predicted, and mutual expectation can become the basis for policy planning. Despite the specialized and confidential character of the State Department's diplomatic channels of information, continuous and meaningful discourse among foreign policy making officials in all parts of the government, at all times and at all levels, is possible within the bounds set by this independent source of information and intellectual structuring of policy.[7]

No matter what latitude a Congressman may have to vote according to his conscience or to go along with his party on a foreign policy issue, he still finds it necessary to "touch base" now and again with opinion in his constituency. But the parochialism that lurks in this necessity, and that is enforced on American politics by the electoral system, may be somewhat counterbalanced in the case of foreign policy, at least, by the continuous

---

[7] For a perceptive theoretical statement of the political communication function in a variety of political systems, including modern systems, see Gabriel A. Almond and James S. Coleman (eds.), *The Politics of the Developing Areas* (Princeton, N.J.: Princeton University Press, 1960), pp. 45–52.

tapping of a different stratum of opinion in the leading metropolitan newspapers that circulate in Washington. In this respect, the press may be helping to create for all Congressmen a common constituency, which is a little closer to the national constituency of the Executive branch and which is commensurate with the national responsibility inherent in the shaping of American foreign policy.

III

Congress
and Foreign Policy

INTRODUCTION

IN the essays and readings in Parts I and II of this volume we have attempted to set forth in broad outline the over-all context of American foreign policy and to examine the "environment" of foreign policy-making within the United States. We must now turn to an examination of the governmental structures and processes of policy-making. This section incorporates a series of essays on the role of Congress in the formulation and execution of American foreign policy and on the patterns of Congressional-Executive relations in this area of public affairs.

The first essay, by a senior member of the Senate Committee on Foreign Relations, provides us with an "insider's" view of the problem of developing foreign policy in the midst of what we have earlier described as an age of "concurrent revolutions." Although his primary focus is upon the Senate, as distinguished from the Congress as a whole, Senator Humphrey deals with the entire spectrum of legislative involvement in foreign policy and concludes with suggestions for modifying the machinery Congress has fashioned for the discharge of its responsibilities in this field. Although written several years ago, it points toward the kind of streamlining of the legislative branch that continues to be advocated by proponents of Congressional reform. The essay by H. Field Haviland further analyzes the structure and functioning of the legislative branch as it relates to foreign policy. Professor James H. Robinson, in the third essay in this section, explores the political aspects of Congressional participation in foreign-policy making in the framework of a functional analysis. Finally, this section includes Roger Hilsman's discussion of "Congressional-Executive Relations and the Foreign Policy Consensus." Dr. Hilsman, currently Assistant Secretary of State for Far Eastern Affairs, skillfully brings into focus the over-all pattern of conflict and consensus between Capitol Hill and the Executive establishment. He shows how, despite the disarray and problems that are encountered as a result of the separation of powers and the inherent conflict between the two political departments of the government, decisions are made and things "get done."

A word is in order to explain the rationale behind this particular selection of essays, and to relate this section to the discussions of the Executive establishment and the overseas administration of American foreign policy which will follow, as well as to the discussions of the policy-making "environment" in the preceding sections. What we are doing is moving from the periphery to the center of the policy-making process. Private groups and institutions, public opinion, and Congress are all involved in many ways in the shaping of American foreign policy. Congress is intimately involved, and its power and prerogatives are central to the form and substance of policy decisions, especially to *certain kinds* of decisions. It is indirectly involved, or informally involved, in many other decisions in which it does not immediately participate but in which executive officials make policy choices within the framework of certain expectations and beliefs—right or wrong—concerning what Congress will permit or tolerate, and what it will not allow. But the Executive is involved in *all* of these decisions, and that is why we have said that we see this book as progressing from the periphery to the center of decision-making.

This general scheme, the assumptions and hypotheses about foreign policy-making in the United States from which it is derived, and the immediate problem of the place of Congress in the determination of foreign policy, can all be illuminated if we think of foreign policy decisions as consisting of certain types of actions or choices. Roger Hilsman, in the essay reprinted in this section and in a subsequent article that appeared in the *Journal of Conflict Resolution*,[1] has suggested that a useful system for the classification of kinds of foreign policy decisions is a tripartite division into (1) declaratory or anticipatory policy decisions, (2) program policy decisions, and (3) crisis policy decisions. Declaratory and crisis policy are kinds of action in which the Executive clearly dominates. The power of Congress is most visibly present in those policy decisions which fall within the classification of program policy. Some discussion of each kind of policy will be useful as a prelude to the readings which follow.

Crisis policy is nowhere better represented than in the series of events leading to the "quarantine" of Cuba by the United States in October of 1962. During the summer and fall, the United States had maintained close aerial surveillance over Cuba, and photographic evidence obtained

1 "The Foreign-Policy Consensus: An Interim Research Report," *Journal of Conflict Resolution*, **III** (1959), pp. 361–382.

from high altitude flights on October 14 furnished "positive evidence" of the deployment of offensive Soviet missiles on the island.² On the basis of this evidence, the United States undertook an intensive military reconnaissance effort to determine the nature and extent of this ominous deployment of weapons. Then, on October 22, the President made public for the first time this series of events involving Cuba and announced the response of the United States Government. From the time of the evidence obtained on October 14 until the final resolution of the Cuban missile crisis, American policy hour-by-hour and day-by-day was in the hands of the President and his senior civilian and military advisers. Congressional leaders were consulted and informed of the progress of events, but they were in no position to shape the development of policy. Secrecy, speed, unity of action and purpose—all are prerequisites for coping with a crisis situation effectively. The very nature of Congress and the legislative process is antithetical, in a number of basic respects, to these prerequisites. It is the function of legislative deliberation to reflect upon courses of action, to articulate differences, to record the existence of these differences and, perhaps, to develop and weigh alternative courses of action—all of which are time-consuming activities. The demands of the Cuban crisis were inconsistent with the characteristic features of legislative policymaking.

Declaratory foreign policy further illustrates the difference in the functioning of Congress and the Executive, although the contrast is less sharp than in the case of crisis policy. Once again the Executive Branch is visibly in charge of events and Congress appears, if at all, only on the edge of the policy-making process. However, the area of discretion open to the Executive is likely to be restricted, and the possibility of Congressional dissent or insistence upon modification or change is more real. Congress is indirectly involved in the sense that its anticipated reactions may be very much in the minds of Executive officials.

An illustration of this relationship, and the kind of policy enunciation that could be classified as declaratory, is furnished by the decision in 1963 to establish a "NATO nuclear force." For several years the United States had been under varying degrees of pressure from several of its NATO allies to share with them control over the United States nuclear strike forces committed to the defense of Europe. The "NATO nuclear force" represents a response to this pressure. Actually, the United States component of the force consists of three Polaris submarines (each armed with sixteen Polaris missiles) assigned to the command of the Supreme Allied Commander in Europe, NATO's military chief. This officer is

---

² See the account in the testimony of Secretary of Defense McNamara and officials from the Defense Intelligence Agency in House, Subcommittee on the Committee on Appropriations, *Hearings, Department of Defense Appropriations for 1964* (88th Congress, 1st Session, 1963), Pt. 1, pp. 2–22.

presently General Lyman Lemnitzer of the United States, and the post has always been held by an American general. (The British made an assignment of RAF bombers.) In addition to these force assignments, the United States has also agreed with its allies in creating a post of deputy Supreme Commander responsible for nuclear affairs, who will be a European, and in bringing European officers into the development and coordination of operational planning for its Strategic Air Command.

This is a "declaratory policy" in the sense that it constitutes no basic change in the nature of the American obligations assumed under the NATO treaty. It is a modification of the implementation of that obligation, but within the framework of an existing consensus within the United States. No additional commitment of American resources was necessitated by this assignment of forces to a NATO command, and no change in the ultimate control of American nuclear weapons was required. By law, these weapons can be used only with the express authorization or order of the President, no matter to what command the forces are assigned. The United States was under pressure to share in some form its nuclear might. Seeking to provide its allies with a sense of joint partnership in the determination of the ultimate questions of policy and thereby to discourage them—hopefully—from developing other national nuclear forces, American leaders took this initiative.

It may be noted that, in instances where a firm national consensus about what policy is or ought to be is not so clearly in evidence as in the above example, the Executive may seek to associate Congress more closely with a given declaration of policy. The resolutions asked of Congress by the Eisenhower administration concerning the defense of Formosa, and in support of the Eisenhower doctrine for the Middle East, are cases in point. Congress, too, may issue a "declaratory policy" on occasion, usually for the edification of the American Executive rather than the chancelleries of the world. Usually these Congressional declarations take the form of a concurrent resolution, such as one expressing the "sense" of Congress that Communist China should not be admitted to the UN.

Program policy represents a different species of national policy decision. It does call for a change in the allocation of resources, for the creation of a new framework of consensus, or for both. The normal forms for this kind of policy decision are therefore appropriations, statutes, or treaties. Whatever the particular form, Congress—or at least the Senate—may have the decisive voice.

Let us assume, for instance, that the administration elects to do all that it can to go beyond the concept of the "NATO nuclear force" described above, and to bring into existence a multilateral nuclear force manned by mixed crews from participating NATO countries. This kind of force, as projected by some of its proponents, would entail the release of United States nuclear weapons to a new command outside the command and control system of the United States armed forces. Atomic energy legislation strictly forbids the transfer of United States nuclear weapons to any other nation or group of nations, and forbids their use by American forces save by presidential order. Obviously this legislation would have to be amended to create the multilateral, multinational nuclear force. A new consensus would have to be developed and ratified by Congress.

The concept of program policy can also be illustrated by certain kinds of on-going policies which appear to be supported by a national consensus in principle, but which require periodic reaffirmation and implementation in the form of funding or new legislation. The historic Marshall Plan for European economic recovery provides an example. Here there was a national decision, taken in 1948, that the United States should underwrite to some extent the recovery and rehabilitation of the war-torn economies of Western Europe, but within that framework of consensus additional resources had to be allocated each year of the Marshall Plan's operation through authorizing legislation and appropriations. All foreign-aid programs continue to require this annual action by the legislative branch.

In general, basic courses of national action must always find affirmation and implementation through programs of some nature, and this explains why the functions of Congress in foreign policy are so significant. It also explains the rather paradoxical fact that the importance of Congress' prerogatives in the conduct of American foreign policy has expanded so immensely, even though in a relative sense this century has seen a growth in the power of the Executive and a decline in the place of Congress in national affairs. As the essay by Professor Robinson shows, rarely does Congress assume the initiative in developing new programs or ideas in foreign policy. Its principal task is to act upon those which are put before it by the President. All of the great undertakings of American foreign policy for the last generation, however, have at some point received the stamp of some form of legislative action. This necessity for legislative action is not merely a constitutional or legal one, it should be noted explicitly, as our discussion has already implied.

Because of this compelling necessity for the participation of Congress in great national decisions about foreign policy, the emergence of the United States as the world's foremost power during the World War II raised serious questions about the compatibility of the responsibilities of world leadership with the danger of executive-legislative deadlock and impasse in the American governmental system. It is certainly no exaggeration to say that the ghosts of Woodrow Wilson and Henry Cabot Lodge haunted the White House, the Department of State, and the corridors of the Capitol during the early 1940's. American leaders of both branches of government, and of both parties, were acutely aware of the fact that the whole design and structure of American participation in world affairs after World War I had been wrecked by a clash between the executive and legislative branches.

To avoid a repetition of this tragedy became a central concern of President Roosevelt, Secretary of State Cordell Hull, and other major policy-makers during World War II. The vehicle selected to insure against such a recurrence was named "bipartisanship." Mr. Hull preferred the term "nonpartisan" foreign policy, which is in many ways more accurate, but the terminology is not important. Bipartisanship came to symbolize certain procedures, certain techniques, and a certain attitude, all of which were indispensable to what Professor William G. Carleton has called "the revolution in American Foreign policy" that occurred during and after World War II. When political power is dispersed, means must be found for it to be concerted if national aims are to be effectively pursued.

The procedures and techniques that bipartisanship involved consisted of joint sponsorship of foreign policy measures in both houses by Democratic and Republican legislators, the appointment of Republican leaders from outside of Congress (such as John Foster Dulles) to executive and administrative positions, and extensive consultations between the Executive and legislative leaders of both parties in the development and planning of important foreign policy undertakings. Given the nature of the American Congressional party system, it is obvious that bipartisanship encompasses something more than concerting the political parties and their leadership. It is also designed to concert Congressional power relative to the executive branch, a problem which in many respects transcends and subsumes party differences.

The need for this kind of an approach to the foreign policy sector of public affairs becomes evident when we reflect upon such United States commitments as are involved in the NATO treaty. To Europe, in 1949, weak and exhausted by the ordeal of World War II, denuded of military and economic strength and menaced by aggressive Soviet designs, a pledge of American power to its defense and recovery was vital. But such a commitment had to have the stamp of permanency if its purposes were to be achieved. If Europe had little reason to anticipate that NATO would endure beyond a single administration in Washington, the entire enterprise would have been undercut from the beginning.

The spirit of bipartisanship in foreign policy was indispensable to the success of the great undertakings of the United States in the immediate post-World War II years. The United Nations Charter received overwhelming Senate approval, in contrast to the melancholy fate of the League Covenant. The United Nations Participation Act passed with large majorities in both houses. When the winds of Cold War began to blow, and it became apparent that the design for a stable system of international order through the mechanism of the United Nations, and through other institutions for international cooperation, would not be immediately realized, and that effective measures had to be taken to contain the Soviets, the bipartisan approach again prevailed. The Congressional elections of 1946 had returned a Republican majority to both houses of Congress, and all of the pent-up emotions of partisanship and political strife that had lain dormant through the years of World War II and the first few months of President Truman's administration became painfully active in 1946 and early 1947. With rival parties in control of the two political departments of government, the times could hardly have appeared less propitious for the launching of an era of constructive and far-reaching foreign policy innovation. Nevertheless, a Democratic President and administration, and a Republican-controlled Congress, set in motion the Greek-Turkish aid program and the emergency economic aid for France and Italy, launched the Marshall Plan, agreed upon the new hemispheric system of the Organization of American States, ratified the Rio Treaty, and paved the way for the negotiation and ratification of the North Atlantic Treaty.

In view of these facts, the reader may be puzzled to note that the pages that follow do not include any sections dealing explicitly with bipartisanship as such, though all of them do deal with it in some way. The explanation is simple if one keeps in mind the distinction between the procedural and the substantive aspects of bipartisanship. The procedural aspects of bipartisanship are taken for granted by these writers. The techniques of bipartisanship that were important innovations in the era of Roosevelt, Hull, Truman, Byrnes, Connally, and Vandenberg are now established parts of the policy-making process.

On the substantive side, the bipartisanship of the earlier period provided a means of moving toward the resolution of the long-standing isolationist-internationalist conflict in American attitudes toward the rest of the world. The policy milestones of this period signified the end of the old isolationism that had wrecked the Wilsonian design for American foreign policy. The isolationist impulse is not dead, but the drive for a determined withdrawal from the course of world politics that the Neutrality Acts symbolized has disappeared except in the aspirations of various extremists outside the mainstream of American politics.

The *terms* of American participation in world affairs, however, cannot be settled once and for all. An array of second-level problems will continue to press upon policy-makers: What kind of a foreign aid program should the United States have? What type of leadership should it offer the free nations? What sorts of weapons systems should the nation invest in? On these issues, one should not desire nor expect bipartisan agreement. Foreign policy issues are no longer tangential to the main concerns of

American politics, they are central. One must expect vigorous debate and controversy about these issues in the same way that one expects it concerning taxes, labor-management relations, and farm policy.

In summary, then, we will expect to see the continued use of bipartisan procedural techniques in the sphere of foreign policy. We will expect to see a bipartisan approach to all problems of the first level of importance, such as the need of the United States to remain involved with the world, the need to resist Communist pressure, and the need to try to promote peace among nations. At the same time, we will also expect partisanship and interbranch rivalry in the secondary issues of foreign policy in the same way that we would expect it in the equivalent areas of domestic policy.

Hubert H. Humphrey

THE SENATE IN FOREIGN POLICY

WHAT is the role of a Senator in the formulation of United States foreign policy? The answer to this question depends upon the character of the times, the issues at hand, and the Senator himself. This essay is concerned with the continuing international crisis of our times, a period for which the term "total diplomacy" was appropriately invented. The issues at stake in the present crisis are almost beyond human calculation. Will a tension-ridden coexistence be catastrophically resolved in a nuclear war? Will Western culture and values be swept under by the rising tide of Communist imperialism?

The United States Senate today is a heterogeneous body reflecting the richness and diversity of the American people. It takes all types—conservatives, liberals, dreamers and practical men—to make a functioning Senate. There is no simple formula for taking its pulse or resolving its will. Its decisions emerge from a continuous process of criticism and analysis on the one hand and the necessity for action on the other. A great nation, like a man of action, cannot tarry for perfect answers. It always has to settle for the best it can get under less than optimum circumstances.

The Founding Fathers regarded the Senate as a council of elders which would deal largely with domestic political concerns. Its unique value, said Madison, is that it proceeds "with more coolness, with more system, and with more wisdom than the popular branch." Federalist Paper No. 64 said

FROM *Foreign Affairs,* **XXXVII** (July 1959). Copyright 1959 by the Council on Foreign Relations, Inc., New York.

"the Constitution provides that our negotiations for treaties shall have every advantage which can be derived from talents, information, integrity, and deliberate investigations, on the one hand, and from secrecy and dispatch on the other." Integrity and deliberation were virtues associated with the Senate while dispatch and secrecy were the qualities of the Executive Branch.

Foreign policy was an occasional and tangential function of the Senate in the eighteenth and nineteenth centuries. Today the mind and will of the Senate are never free from the burdens of the United States in the vast realm beyond the borders of its legal jurisdiction. The old distinction between *domestic* policies and *foreign* policies has given way to a new concept of *national* policies, each of which bears upon the course of events at home and abroad. The understanding of our national character and purposes abroad is deeply affected by laws dealing with immigration, civil rights, tariffs, subsidies and other "domestic" matters. Our capacity to lend substance to our stated goals is determined to no little extent by tax and budget laws.

The Breadth of Diplomatic Encounter

The interpenetration of the domestic and foreign realms in national policies today is only a reflection of the increasing degree and variety of interpenetration between all nations. Four or five centuries ago the peacetime contact between Western states was largely political in character. Mutual interests were affirmed and conflicting interests adjusted through classical diplomacy or, in the final resort, by war. The aims and policies of states were interpreted to one another by official emissaries. The commercial revolution of the fifteenth and sixteenth centuries provided an additional channel for nations to know one another through the face-to-face contacts of international trade.

Our Founding Fathers saw distant England and France almost exclusively through the eyes of diplomats and traders. In the nineteenth century a new pair of eyes was added, those of the missionary, upon whom we were largely dependent for our picture of the exotic lands of Asia and Africa.

The technological revolution of the twentieth century vastly increased the speed, volume and scope of the manner in which nations impinge on and interpenetrate each other. Today nations know one another not only through diplomats, traders and missionaries, but also through soldiers, correspondents, tourists, students, community leaders, intellectuals, artists and members of Congress. Among the Americans officially representing their Government abroad are agricultural experts, labor attachés, journalists and a great variety of other specialists. Direct contacts are supplemented by official and unofficial films, books, periodicals and short-wave broadcasts.

This is a far cry from the time when sovereigns, personally vested with full authority, commissioned ambassadors plenipotentiary to transact their business with other states. The autonomy of the classic diplomatic function has been broken down by the rapid communication and transportation provided by the technological revolution. The old diplomacy, indeed, is as obsolete today as the divine right of kings. And I have few regrets, although I do admit that we in the United States might well give more attention to the central virtue of the old diplomacy—the ability to conduct confidential negotiations confidentially.

The term total diplomacy refers to the new breadth of the diplomatic encounter, which reflects the diversity of interest of entire peoples, as well as to the inclusive nature of the struggle between the Communist world and the free world. In an era of total diplomacy there must be at least some understanding between the various cultures involved if international intercourse is to be fruitful. Cultural interpenetration will not by itself dispel the major political conflicts which divide nations, but it can help to clear the atmosphere of some basic misapprehensions and lower the level of hostility. It can help us define more accurately where our interests are mutual and where they are in conflict. Functional coöperation between American students, educators, scientists, doctors, civic leaders and legislators and their counterparts behind the iron and bamboo curtains can therefore have great political significance.

In a world of total diplomacy where every important political decision at home has an impact abroad and where the picture of our national will and purpose is transmitted to other peoples in a thousand ways, negotiation itself is broader than anything imagined under the classic rules and inescapably becomes involved in the interaction of national egos and purposes rooted deeply in national character and behavior.

Treaty-Making and Presidential Appointments

The advent of total diplomacy and the new position of the United States in the world have increased the Senate's role in the formation of foreign policy far beyond what had been envisioned by the framers of the Constitution, who regarded participation in treaty-making and consideration of Presidential appointments as its two chief functions. Although still crucial, these two responsibilities today constitute quantitatively only a small part of the Senate's foreign policy responsibilities.

The great increase in the Senate's work in the field of foreign policy is absolute rather than relative to that of the Executive Branch. If the Senate's responsibilities have increased ten-fold, the international responsibilities of the Executive Branch have increased a hundred-fold. The President's power inevitably increases in times of crisis, and we are living in a period of continuing crisis. Furthermore, history has thrust the United States into the forefront of a mighty struggle against a formidable adversary. A century ago it was said, "When Paris has a cold, Europe sneezes." Today Barbara Ward is not far wrong when she says, "America's foreign policy is everybody's destiny."

The power vested in the President to enter into legal contracts with other sovereign governments "with the advice and consent of the Senate" is one of the far-reaching prerogatives of his office. A treaty with another country takes precedence over domestic law if there is a conflict between the two. Under our system of checks and balances, the President shares this treaty-making power with the Senate. Sometimes the Senate has been called the "graveyard of treaties" because of its failure to give its consent to the Executive will or because it compromised the Executive will with restrictions and reservations. Since the Senate's rejection of the League of Nations, and especially since Pearl Harbor, our Presidents have attempted to keep Senate leaders fully informed on negotiations with other nations. In laying the groundwork for the United Nations, the Marshall Plan and NATO, the Executive Branch went beyond informing the Congress, and actually involved the leaders in both Houses and in both parties in extended consultations. These three historic developments gained the overwhelming acceptance of the American people in part because of the close partnership between the Executive and Legislative branches.

The power of the Senate to reject a Presidential appointment for ambassador has never been invoked, although on several occasions Senate opposition was sufficient to induce the President to withdraw his nominee. A growing awareness of the vital importance of our representation abroad, coupled recently with some unfortunate patronage appointments, has produced in the Senate a new interest in scrutinizing Presidential nominees. Many Senators were shocked when a candidate for a Latin American ambassadorial post gave as his chief qualification the fact that he spent his winters in Florida, and there was an outcry when another Presidential nominee could not name the Prime Minister of the country to which he had been assigned. Later it was learned that he did not even know what NATO was. Appointments of unqualified amateurs, which have been made by both Republican and Democratic Presidents as a reward for party contributions, reflect not only upon the President and his party, but also upon the Senate for its failure to establish and enforce minimum qualifications for confirmation.

An Embassy is fundamentally an executive office which coördinates the political, economic and military policies of the U. S. Government. We need ambassadors who combine administrative gifts with the capacity to understand the social and political forces of the area to which they are assigned. No member of the Foreign Relations Committee believes that a patronage appointment is automatically bad, or that the appointment of a career officer is always to be preferred. A list of our most effective ambassadors in recent years would include men from both categories. On balance, however, the trend toward more career appointments to top posts is to be commended. In 1924, career men headed only about one-third of the U. S. missions abroad; the ratio was 18 to 33. On April 1 of this year career appointees held almost 70 percent of the ambassadorships; the ratio was 51 to 23. But statistics do not tell the whole story. Of the 15 choice diplomatic posts in Western Europe, only six are now held by career officers—Athens, Lisbon, Luxembourg, Oslo, Stockholm and Vienna. One reason is that only men of independent means can afford to occupy posts where entertainment requirements exceed government appropriations for that purpose. In 1957 several of my colleagues and I urged Congress to double the $600,000 appropriated for representation allowances at American posts abroad.

It is not democratic, and it does not make for good morale and efficient performance, to bar qualified foreign service officers from the top posts in their profession by requiring that they have the private means to underwrite the necessary expenses of properly representing the United States in one of the large capitals of the world. No qualified American should be barred from serving in a top post abroad because he is rich; no qualified professional should be barred because he is not.

Under exceptional circumstances it is possible for the Senate to go beyond its "advice and consent" function in dealing with Presidential appointees. The recent confirmation of Secretary of State Christian A. Herter is a case in point. Moved by President Eisenhower's failure to say anything good about his nominee, the Senate Foreign Relations Committee took extraordinary measures to shore up his prestige on the eve of his critical talks with our allies on the Berlin crisis. Breaking precedent, the Committee unanimously voted to suspend its own six-day rule and then unanimously referred the nomination favorably to the Senate. In presenting Mr. Herter's name, Majority Leader Lyndon Johnson said: "I want the world to know that this nation is united behind the Secretary of State whose nomination is about to be confirmed."

A Senator and His Larger Constituency

In the twentieth century a Senator represents not only his state but also the nation, and under certain circumstances he operates directly in the international arena. If he loses contact with the interests, fears and hopes of the people from whom he draws his power he forfeits his moral and political right to represent them. This does not mean that he should be like a weathercock following the shifting winds of public passion. As Edmund Burke put it, "Your representative owes you, not his industry only, but his judgment; and he betrays instead of serving you, if he sacrifices it to your opinion." A Senator must at times lead, inform and even educate his constituents.

Informed public discussion is made difficult when the atmosphere is clouded either by cynical or optimistic illusions. When a Senator accuses his opponents of "twenty years of treason" or refers to the Korean conflict as a "Truman war," he poisons the channels of useful debate. On the other hand, if a Senator exaggerates the potential benefits of summit diplomacy (or any other single instrument of foreign policy) he makes the very difficult task of negotiating with the Russians even more difficult. Some of us who recalled the psychological backwash in the wake of the oversold summit conference of 1955 warned our people against expecting too much from new summit talks, at the same time insisting upon the importance of continuous negotiations.

The role of the Senate in dealing *directly* with international problems is severely and properly limited by the Constitution, which vests in the Executive Branch exclusive power to conduct foreign relations. Even in its restricted role of giving advice and consent to the President, it is limited by lack of adequate information and an understandable disposition to overlook what Charles Burton Marshall has called "the limits of foreign policy." [1] Some members of Congress, says Mr. Marshall, accustomed to dealing with domestic problems by passing laws, tend to forget that the "vast external realm" beyond the limits of our national jurisdiction is not subject to the parliamentary will or Executive fiat. In the international field a national policy objective often is highly restricted or may be entirely frustrated by external forces over which even the powerful United States has little or no control. The effectiveness of our foreign policy is limited by the power, purposes and unpredictability of other nations, whether hostile, allied or uncommitted; by the weight of tradition and precedent; by the facts of international economic life; and by the vicissitudes of history generally.

One of the best ways for a Senator to comprehend both the limits and possibilities of foreign policy is to have direct contact with the leaders and peoples of other nations. Since the end of World War II approximately half the members of Congress have had this opportunity. Well planned trips abroad have given our legislators a more profound and sympathetic understanding of the "vast external realm," and have helped the officials and people of other nations to get a more accurate picture of our national character and aspirations.

My own understanding of Middle East problems, for example, was greatly enhanced during an intensive 40-day study mission to that area several years ago. I talked with prime ministers and foreign ministers, and exchanged views with intellectual, business and labor leaders. Also invaluable to me was my tour of duty as a delegate to the United Nations and my trip last year to Western Europe and the Soviet Union. I believe such face-to-face contacts lead to mutual understanding, which always includes,

---

[1] *The Limits of Foreign Policy* (New York: Holt, 1954).

of course, a more precise awareness of the differences between the United States and the host country.

I benefited greatly by my visit with Premier Khrushchev, and I believe he gained a clearer understanding about the unity of the American people behind the essential elements of our foreign policy precisely because I was a politician and a member of the loyal opposition. A member of Congress is primarily a politician and not a diplomat; he sees things abroad through a different set of lenses and what he sees can make an important supplementary contribution to what an ambassador reports. Visits with foreign officials which do not confuse *contact* with *contract* do not presume upon the exclusive Presidential prerogative.

Foreign Relations Within the Senate

Since Hitler's march into Poland two decades ago, foreign policy has been the dominant concern within the Senate itself. The primacy of the Executive Branch in foreign affairs in no way lessens the moral and legal responsibility of the Congress to work for national policies which come to grips responsibly and realistically with urgent demands of the world crisis. In this connection the Senate's activities go far beyond scrutinizing treaties and Presidential appointments. Former Secretary of State Dean Acheson has correctly observed that in one "aspect of foreign affairs Congress is all-powerful. This is in the establishing and maintaining of those fundamental policies, with their supporting programs of action, which require legal authority, men and money. Without these foundations—solidly laid and kept in repair—even wise and skillful diplomacy cannot provide the power and develop the world environment indispensable to national independence and individual liberty for ourselves and others." [2] Parliamentary bodies cannot govern, and our Congress is no exception. But with its power of the purse, and through the right to investigate, to criticize and to advocate, the Congress does exert a significant influence on the quality and direction of United States foreign policy, and it usually does so without violating the integrity of the Executive Branch.

The body of fact and insight developed by a committee hearing or study can be drawn upon for informed criticism or for advocating new policies. A case in point was the careful study of the economic aid program conducted by a special Senate Committee two years ago, which helped to lay the foundation for our present more effective approach to the development needs of the politically unaligned nations of Asia and Africa. As chairman of the Subcommittee on Disarmament, I have often used information developed in hearings to raise questions with Administration spokesmen. Some of my questions about the relative position of the United States and

[2] *The New York Times Magazine* (January 6, 1957).

the U.S.S.R. in nuclear development and about the detection and identification of underground nuclear explosions proved to be of more than routine interest.

An individual Senator, apart from his committee work, can ask questions and advocate new ideas. The student exchange program is known by the name of its chief advocate, Senator Fulbright. Former Senator Bricker is known for his sustained but unsuccessful efforts to curb the treaty-making power of the President. In April of this year the Senate unanimously adopted a resolution which I introduced in support of our Government's efforts to negotiate an effective ban on nuclear weapons tests at the three-power Geneva talks then in progress.

Naturally Senators of the opposition party are more critical of the Administration than their colleagues on the other side of the aisle. This brings up the subject of "bipartisanship." Last April, Senator Fulbright insisted that "bipartisanship" is not a desirable objective in debate on foreign policy. He is right. What we need is genuine *non*partisan study and criticism, honest appraisal without reference to narrow partisan advantage. In recent years the slogan of "bipartisanship" has too often been invoked to muzzle criticism of Administration mistakes or to reduce the issue to the lowest common denominator to satisfy all but the extremists in both parties. The late Senator Arthur Vandenberg preferred the word non-partisanship, which he defined as "a mutual effort . . . to unite our official voice at the water's edge so that America speaks with maximum authority. . . . It does not involve the remotest surrender of free debate . . . and the 'loyal opposition' is under special obligation to see that this occurs."

Senator Vandenberg's insistence on free debate is correct, but debate cannot be arbitrarily stopped at "the water's edge." When a national consensus has been reached on a vital issue, and when policies appropriate to this consensus have been initiated, it is right that we close ranks to support them. But changing circumstances produce new problems which require new consideration. Responsible debate must never cease, even in wartime, but it must be carried on with restraint and with the national interest the objective rather than partisan advantage.

The Problem of Countervailing Expertise

If the "unique, deliberate—and, to me, agreeable—disarray of the American Government," to use William S. White's words, is to function properly, the foreign policy committees of Congress must have the resources to enable them to question, review, modify or reject the policies of the Executive Branch. The information, intelligence and insight available to the Executive Branch are vast and continue to expand. This is a natural development in an era of total diplomacy. But in contrast, says Myron M. Cowen in a recent letter to Senator Fulbright, there is "a concurrent scarcity of vigorous and continuing *countervailing expertise"* in Congress. Such independent expertise is absolutely necessary if the House and Senate are to fulfill their Constitutional responsibility of surveillance and initiative. Without competent independent sources of fact and wisdom they cannot make discriminating judgments between alternative programs and proposals. Faced with an impressive case by the Administration, and unarmed with counter facts and arguments, even a conscientious Senator sometimes vacillates between giving a grudging consent and opposing for the sake of opposing.

This imbalance constitutes a serious threat to the integrity of the Legislative Branch. The main answer is more adequate staffing, particularly for the Senate Foreign Relations Committee, the House Foreign Affairs Committee, and the Foreign Affairs Division of the Legislative Reference Service. At present there are eight foreign policy specialists on the Senate Committee staff, five on the House Committee staff, and 16 in the Legislative Reference Service—a total of only 29 experts directly in the service of Congress in the entire area of foreign relations. If one adds the professional staffs of the two Armed Services committees, the grand total is 35. Upon them falls much of the burden of examining the complex Defense, International Affairs and Mutual Security budgets totalling $48 billion a year. The size of this staff is out of all proportion to its enormous responsibility.

The Foreign Relations Committee needs a much larger and more specialized staff, loyal to the Legislative Branch, and equal in competence to the best talent in the State Department. My experience with the Disarmament Subcommittee convinces me that functional areas as well as geographic areas should be accorded subcommittee status, and that all subcommittees worth creating are worth an independent staff of experts. An adequate staff could perform many services now being performed poorly or not at all. It would have constant access to the facts and intelligence available from all branches of government, from organizations where independent research is carried on and from special Senate studies. Adequate staffing will alone enable Congress to escape from uniformed acquiescence on the one hand and irresponsible obstruction on the other.

The Problem of Fragmentation

The Founding Fathers bequeathed to us a government in which there is a separation of powers and a system of checks and balances. Some critics maintain that such a government is incapable of meeting the fast-moving demands of a technological age or of competing successfully with the dynamic, planned offensives of an expansionist totalitarian system. While I reject this view, I do acknowledge that "government as usual" is not good enough.

Our problem today does not seem to me to be primarily structural or bureaucratic so much as the lack of leadership at the top. Even a loose-fitting and overlapping governmental structure can be made to work if there is a sense of urgency and direction; and this only dynamic leadership can provide.

Even under present conditions there are some things in the area of structural manipulation which would enable us to deal more effectively than we do now with the challenges of the continuing crisis. The Executive Branch and the Congress are fragmented. There are a score of Executive agencies dealing with foreign policy in addition to the State Department and the Department of Defense. One sometimes gets the impression that the Bureau of the Budget is the most important of them all. Theoretically, the President with the aid of the National Security Council is supposed to sort out the priorities and coördinate a great variety of policies in the light of an agreed, long-range strategy. Unfortunately this rarely happens, first because the agreed strategy does not exist, second because the National Security Council is so preoccupied with day-by-day crises that it seldom has time for long-range planning.

The problem raised by the extent of governmental fragmentation is deep and pervasive and there are no easy answers. But I believe that the time has come to consider seriously the creation in the Executive Branch of a permanent research and policy-analyzing agency charged with the responsibility of thinking about comprehensive national strategy, embracing in that term all essential factors of domestic and foreign policy. This agency would relate the total capacities of the American people—military, economic, technical, intellectual and moral—to their responsibilities of international leadership. Without elaborating my proposal here, I want to make it clear that I do not regard such an agency as a substitute for politics—as an alternative to the present responsibilities of the Executive and Legislative Branches. I am not proposing that an intellectual élite be called in to decide our fate for us, but merely that an agency along the lines described could help our Government to develop a better sense of perspective and to integrate and coördinate the many agencies and programs which now often operate at cross-purposes.

Perhaps the Congress could prompt the Executive to put its house in order by itself creating a Joint Committee on National Strategy, to include the chairmen and ranking minority members of the major committees of the House and the Senate. I have recently proposed such a Committee. Its purpose would be to look at our total national strategy—military, political, economic and ideological. This Committee, a counterpart in the Congress of what I have proposed for the Executive Branch, would not usurp the functions of any of the present Committees, but supplement them by endowing their work with a larger frame of reference. The Chairmen of the Committees represented would come away from the meetings of the new Joint Committee with a greater appreciation, for instance, of the relationship between fiscal policy and national productivity and how both factors relate to our defense posture and our negotiating position. Responsible statesmanship consists precisely in the capacity to see complex relationships in a perspective as broad as the national purpose itself.

No amount of structural manipulation can make up for a lack of leadership that is politically wise and morally responsible. But if the essential idea underlying these twin proposals were adopted, I believe it would make a modest contribution toward creating a more integrated national policy; and in the face of the Communist challenge, even a modest contribution toward better strategic planning is not to be brushed aside.

Congress was not created to govern, and it should not attempt to do so. Yet this is no time for Congress to submit meekly to the Executive will. In fact, it could not submit even if it were so inclined, because there is not one Executive will, but a number of conflicting wills which have not yet surrendered to the authority of an over-riding national purpose.

H. Field Haviland
THE CONGRESS

THE dramatic rise of the United States to a role of world leadership has propelled the Congress to greater prominence in international affairs. The scope and costs of the new leadership responsibilities, the fading of the line between domestic and foreign policy, and the growing impact of international developments upon the domestic scene have been among the factors involving the Congress more intimately with foreign policy. More than half of the 36 standing committees now regularly deal with issues of international significance. This confronts the Congress with the same basic problem that faces the Government as a whole: the task of reconciling the competing concepts and requirements of a growing range of policies and organizational entities concerned with international affairs.

Relations With the Executive Branch

Before the Second World War, "foreign policy" was essentially what might be described as "political" foreign policy and the means and instruments to execute it. Issues like the tariff and immigration, and even the

FROM *The Formulation and Administration of United States Foreign Policy* by H. Field Haviland (Washington: The Brookings Institution, 1960). A study prepared at the request of the Committee on Foreign Relations, United States Senate. Reprinted by permission of the publisher.

state and use of military power, were considered essentially "domestic." Under the separation of powers, the division of labor resulted in Presidential preeminence in the shaping and execution of foreign policy, in special activity and concern by the Senate because of its powers regarding treaties and appointments and the prerogatives flowing from them, and an intermittent concern by the Congress centering around periodic legislative issues or in response to crises.

Today most important policies bear on foreign affairs. This has affected the balance between the Congress and the Executive. Because the increasing involvement of the United States in world affairs requires constant and substantial legislative support, the Congress has become a more active participant in the foreign policy process, concerned not only with broad goals but with such vital elements as economic development, farm surpluses, shipping subsidies, and cultural contacts. At the same time, there are major obstacles that tend to frustrate the legislative role, including the growing volume and complexity of international transactions, the speed and flexibility with which many foreign policy matters must be handled, the limiting effect of having to work in harness with other countries, and the secrecy that conceals many of these activities.

The adjustment of the Congress and the Executive to this new state of affairs has been pragmatic. Executive-legislative relations have come to involve hundreds of public and private contacts between the two branches at many levels. Agencies and processes to facilitate the achievement of cooperation, whether involving legislation or not, have multiplied. Consultative subcommittees, briefing sessions, participation by legislators in international meetings, joint executive-legislative commissions, strengthened staffs to maintain interbranch contact—all are efforts to bridge the gap.

The future promises to pose even more demanding tasks that will affect the division of responsibilities and the organization of relations between the two branches. Because the United States will be compelled to devote increasing attention and resources to foreign affairs, both sides will need to work together in a way that will enable them to deal adequately with the most fundamental issues without becoming bogged down in differences over detail. In order that the Congress as well as the Executive may act with the requisite speed, knowledge, and understanding, it will be desirable for increased time and energy to be devoted to strengthening the channels of information and consultation between the two branches on a basis that will discourage narrowly partisan distortion.

1. *Division of Responsibilities Between the Branches.* Against this background there is the persistent issue: How should the roles of the Congress and the Executive be defined? It is not easy to draw a clear boundary between the activities of the two branches for the simple reason that they overlap considerably. Nonetheless, it is both feasible and desirable to keep

in mind certain general distinctions between their roles based upon differences in their constitutional mandates and the functions and structures that have grown out of those mandates.

The essential role of the Congress is to provide a forum in which the representatives of hundreds of local constituencies may scrutinize and pass judgment on matters of national policy requiring legislative action. The individual Member of Congress is not simply a passive transmitter of the "public will" but a creative leader and interpreter as well. His main concern is to make certain that the interests he feels he represents are adequately protected and promoted. When those interests are not involved or are more or less evenly balanced, the Member is freer to act in accordance with his personal views, which is often the case with foreign policy. The general functions he has a responsibility to perform are to participate in enacting necessary legislative authorizations and appropriations and to inquire into policy problems and governmental actions related to those functions. While the Congress does not have the authority, staff, or time to oversee all of the details of day-to-day formulation and execution of foreign policy, it is, and and has a right to be, vitally interested in those details that affect its constituents' particular interests as well as broader policy objectives and programs.

The distinct nature of the Executive role flows from its basic responsibility to manage the multitudinous activities of the Federal Government within the limits of the laws and resources provided by the Congress. It follows that the Executive has no choice but to be concerned with all, rather than only some, of the details of daily policy. It must not only develop general directives into practical programs but, in turn, translate those programs into effective action. From these responsibilities flow the requirements for personnel and other resources that are capable of dealing with this vast range of affairs and at the same time are organized in such a way as to be responsible to a single, rather than multiple, source of authority representing the Nation as a whole.

Given this basic division of responsibilities, what specific functions should the Congress be expected to perform to carry out its role?

1. It has a responsibility to identify and inquire into problems that may call for legislative action.

2. It shares with the Executive the function of framing broad national objectives.

3. It can help to estimate the relative merits of alternative approaches to dealing with various problems.

4. It may give attention, on a selective basis, to questions of detail related to broader issues.

5. It has the exclusive responsibility for enacting authorization and appropriation legislation.

6. It can help, as part of its investigatory function, to evaluate the performance of the Executive, again on a selective basis.

The general conclusion that emerges from this discussion is that while both the President and the Congress have some exclusive prerogatives, the major portion of their functions are shared. The President alone is vested with "the executive power" to see "that the laws be faithfully executed." The Congress alone is endowed with "all legislative powers." But these mandates are interdependent and, therefore, call for a large area of interlocking powers which are the basis for legislative participation in the functions of inquiry, the formulation of general goals, the identification of major problems, the selective appraisal of alternative courses of action, and the evaluation of past policies and actions.

2. *Cooperation in Relation to Public Opinion.* A joint responsibility of the Congress and the Executive that deserves special emphasis is that of maintaining effective relations with the public which ultimately sets the limits of maneuver within which those who shape and execute policy must operate. The climate of opinion that emerges from the public is the product of many interacting factors—the impact of mass media, the activity of hundreds of interest groups, the initiatives of public leaders, the influence of foreign opinion, and the weighing of issues and individuals through the channels of party politics.

The anticipated course of future world developments promises to impose greater burdens than ever on the public in relation to foreign policy. At the same time, the obstacles to public understanding threaten to become even more severe. These include the secrecy that often shrouds official deliberations, the bewildering pace of change, and the intricacy of the issues. While this report cannot accommodate a detailed treatment of the role of public opinion, it is pertinent to consider briefly a few alternative approaches to thinking about the relationship between the Government, particularly the Congress, and the general public with respect to foreign policy.

One point of view would place minimal emphasis on governmental efforts to cultivate contacts with the public through informational activities. This attitude stems largely from the feeling that such efforts run the risk of putting the Government in the position of "selling" programs to the people, of manipulating them. There is also the concern that the general public cannot be expected to be well informed or active in relation to the daily flow of international affairs.

Another view is that the Congress and the executive branch should support a stronger foreign policy information program for the general public. The lives of all Americans are touched by the Nation's international policies; it is their survival which is at stake. The public's attitudes toward crucial foreign policies may be seriously distorted by the tendencies of some media toward sensationalism and superficiality.

A third view holds that a more systematic and energetic effort should be made to bring leaders of public opinion into closer touch with the officials and processes that shape U.S. foreign policy. These leaders are extremely important in informing and mobilizing the public and are most likely to make the best use of such an opportunity.

Many devices could be used to implement this third alternative. More high-level briefings might be conducted by the executive departments for selected groups. Some agencies, such as the Industrial College of the Armed Forces, have devised programs for Reserve officers and private citizens in various cities which could serve as models for the foreign affairs field. More opportunities might be given to leading individuals to take part in the policy process as consultants, temporary staff members, delegates, or visitors abroad. Arrangements to provide information and other services for groups conducting programs in world affairs could be strengthened. The Congress could contribute by reinforcing its relations with special groups and the media that reach those groups. Hearings could be held in various parts of the country, and Members of the Congress might more frequently form bipartisan teams to explain aspects of foreign policy and to sample attitudes. A few Members have already performed valuable services in this regard and have developed effective means of discussing the essence of policy with community audiences.

Of these three broad alternatives, the second and third are the most promising. If the Government is to move in the direction of bringing the public into closer touch with governmental policy, it will be necessary to have more adequate continuing collaboration between the two branches regarding both substantive and procedural aspects of the effort. The Congress should provide broad directives for this purpose and the necessary authority and funds to give life to the directives.

The factor of secrecy is of vital importance here. Some secrecy is necessary, but it can be used as a shield against legitimate criticism. As more governments impose restrictions on the flow of information, the public becomes increasingly dependent upon governmental releases. This can lead to serious distortion of public attitudes. Because there will always be justification for some measure of secrecy, especially in relation to matters close to the heart of national security, the solution must be one of degree. The direction should generally be toward a more permissive balance between concealment and disclosure that will provide the public with the basic information it needs to fulfill its responsibilities with regard to fundamental issues.

The politically responsible leaders of the executive and legislative branches play a primary role in this process of public enlightenment. It is their responsibility to interpret major policies to the people, to elevate their understanding, and to draw strength from them. The American statesman has also acquired—whether he fully realizes it or not—a constituency of hundreds of millions of people in other lands. He is part of the public image of America which is swiftly conveyed to the most remote parts of the world.

In summary, it would seem desirable that the Congress and the executive branch cooperate to establish more effective relations with the general public in the realm of foreign policy. Increased efforts should be made to maintain close contact with leadership groups and the communications media that serve those groups. To this end, the barrier of secrecy should be reduced to the lowest level consistent with the essential requirements of national security.

3. *Partisanship Versus Bipartisanship.* Given this allocation of roles and functions and the joint responsibilities of the two branches, there is the question: What should be the place of bipartisanship in the relations between the executive and legislative branches as well as within Congress itself? The roots of postwar bipartisanship may be traced to the two-party collaboration on the United Nations Charter during the Second World War, but its development as a continuing concept dates especially from the 80th Congress (1947–48).[1] According to its proponents, bipartisanship recognizes the necessity in foreign affairs of a high degree of responsibility and continuity in a hazardous world, and it represents an effort to overcome the dangers of disunity and delay to which a system of separation of powers is particularly susceptible. Those who resist bipartisan collaboration, or who would concede it only during periods of severe crisis, argue that bipartisanship clouds the issues, stifles useful criticism, dilutes the quality of policy in the search for agreement, and concedes excessive influence to the minority party and to the Congress. These critics claim that bipartisanship enables those in a majority to take disproportionate credit for successes and is a vehicle to diffuse responsibility in defeats and crises.

In practice, bipartisanship, or "nonpartisanship" as some have preferred to call it, has meant cooperation of many types and degrees between executive branch officials and coalitions of Republicans and Democrats in the Congress. Because of the unique qualities and responsibilities of the Senate and the leading roles of men like Senator Arthur H. Vandenberg, bipartisan arrangements involving the Senate have been more significant and more publicized than in the case of the House. The foreign policy committees have been main centers of bipartisanship, but the trend, in the past decade in particular, has been to draw party leaders and other influential members not assigned to the foreign policy committees into the process. Crisis situations have sometimes resulted in a formal display of bipartisan unity in the absence of significant advance

---

[1] Two recent studies of bipartisanship are Cecil V. Crabb, Jr., *Bipartisan Foreign Policy, Myth or Reality?* (Evanston, Ill.: Row, Peterson & Co., 1957); and H. Bradford Westerfield, *Foreign Policy and Party Politics, Pearl Harbor to Korea* (New Haven: Yale University Press, 1955).

consultation, as in the case of the movement to give aid to Greece and Turkey in 1947 and the Formosa resolution of early 1955. On the other hand, questions concerning the Middle East, the plight of Nationalist China beginning in 1948, and the conduct of the war in Korea have been seared by bitter partisanship.

Bipartisanship is a necessary means, in the U.S. system of government, of mobilizing strong and continuing political support for major policy positions. It does not require binding and unalterable commitments between the parties but an attitude that encourages objective, responsible action regarding issues of greatest significance to the national security. This concept would include a full sharing of the essential facts and honest negotiation on the basis of those facts, undistorted by extreme partisanship.

Because of the leading role of the President, the political party in charge of the executive branch must assume the major responsibility for taking the initiative in building coalitions of bipartisan support in the Congress. The minority party, or the majority party in a situation of divided party control, cannot be expected to abdicate its responsibility to explore policy alternatives and to vote its convictions when it cannot, after conscientious and thorough consultation, vote with the leadership of the other party.

Because the requirements of bipartisanship in terms of goals and procedures still remain somewhat nebulous, it would be helpful if the foreign policy committees of the House and the Senate would initiate a thorough review of bipartisanship. The purpose should be to gain a clearer and more widely shared understanding of the need for, and requirements of, bipartisanship.

This discussion leads to the conclusion that: The increasing importance of foreign policy to the security of the country calls for continuing bipartisan collaboration regarding the most critical issues. This does not require any inflexible commitment between the parties but calls for a voluntary understanding that they will conscientiously strive, through objective consultation and a candid sharing of essential data, to reach agreement on matters of major significance. To this end, it would be useful for the two foreign policy committees to undertake a review of the rationale and requirements of bipartisanship.

4. *Other Means of Strengthening Interbranch Cooperation.* Additional means of reinforcing interbranch collaboration have been suggested by the score. Except for a few proposals that would break too sharply with the Constitution and traditional practice, such as formal executive-legislative councils or proposals to import major segments of the parliamentary system, the Congress and the Executive have been willing to experiment. Without exaggeration, it can be said that the principal feasible means of facilitating responsible cooperation have been tried. The difficulties in exploiting these lie partly in the attitude of Members of Congress and

the executive branch regarding the allocation of time, attention, energy, and thought.

The main question to be considered here is: What steps might be taken to strengthen executive-legislative relations with regard to foreign policy?

One important channel for this purpose is the executive apparatus designed to maintain close relations with the Congress. Each department and agency concerned with foreign policy has a legislative staff to manage contacts with the Hill on a full-time basis, but they rely heavily on the substantive leadership for important testimony. The Department of State elevated its top legislative liaison officer to Assistant Secretary rank in 1949 and now has approximately six professional staff members to assist him. Several people in the White House office are also in close touch with the Congress. To keep these links strong, the executive leadership expends tremendous amounts of time and energy in preparing and delivering testimony, as well as in maintaining less formal relations. They know that they are dependent on congressional understanding and support, and that they must perform well to win the votes of those legislators who follow such matters conscientiously. One former Secretary of State has estimated that, during his years in Washington, he never devoted less than one-sixth of his time to dealing with the Congress, and for months at a time this function consumed most of his effort.[2] At the same time, executive personnel are wary about these relations because they know that the Congress has both a constitutional and a political incentive to find chinks in the executive armor and that, in irresponsible hands, the legislative power can be used destructively.

Although executive relations with the Congress have been strengthened, they could be further improved. An essential ingredient is an attitude on the part of executive personnel that understands the potential role of the Congress as an ally and appreciates the many able legislators who are prepared to deal fairly with the Executive. Another major need is a more continuous effort to consult with the relevant Members of Congress, not only when a crisis arises but on a regular basis, and the direction of more attention to committees other than the two foreign policy committees. Better means need to be devised to consult with a larger proportion of the membership of the Congress. Finally, it would be well to develop further the effort to achieve more regular contact between the top leadership of both branches. Problems of tradition, time, substance, partisanship, and personal idiosyncrasies have restricted such meetings, but they remain both desirable and feasible within limits.

On the legislative side, it is also important to foster a favorable climate of opinion—one that will encourage full, regular, and constructive consul-

[2] Dean Acheson, *A Citizen Looks at Congress* (New York: Harper & Row, 1957), pp. 64–70.

tation with appropriate representatives of the executive branch. In addition, there are organizational problems which are discussed further below. Suffice it to say here that arrangements such as the existing consultative sub-committees of the foreign relations committees should be supported so that full advantage may be taken of the opportunities for improved executive-legislative contact. This calls for staff, adequate in number and competence, to help maintain these relations.

This discussion points to the recommendation that: A major prerequisite for improved executive-legislative relations is a frame of mind on both sides that will encourage full and regular consultation with the object of striving to find mutually satisfactory bases for collaboration. This calls for organizational arrangements that will marshall the requisite time and energy to support these efforts.

Organization of the Congress

The Congress is characterized by wide dispersal of power, leadership, and authority which makes it difficult to develop a unified strategy and reconcile conflicting policies. While both branches of government are troubled by the pressures of friction and diffusion, the Congress finds it particularly difficult to create structures and processes that will foster unity because of the inherent partisan conflict, the division between the two Chambers, and the traditional reluctance to accept centralized leadership.

Each house displays distinctive characteristics that condition its response to foreign policy. The Senate's exclusive power to consent to treaties and to major Presidential appointments, coupled with the tradition that the President should consult it about foreign policy generally, have enhanced the prestige and influence of the Senate.

In the past, the House of Representatives occasionally exerted strong influence in foreign affairs in response to public moods, but its concern was episodic. Now the House is involved almost as deeply as the Senate. The powers it shares with the Senate, and its special custodianship of the Nation's purse, are major sources of support for the conduct of the Nation's business overseas.[3]

1. *Institutions and Processes to Deal with Foreign Affairs.* The com-mittees are the key to congressional behavior. Their decisions, more often than not, become the decisions of each house. The most important com-mittees on foreign policy are still the Senate Committee on Foreign Rela-tions and the House Committee on Foreign Affairs. Both are looked to by their respective Chambers for leadership regarding general foreign policy developments. The Senate Committee on Foreign Relations enjoys

---

[3] A recent study of the new importance of the House is Holbert N. Carroll, *The House of Representatives and Foreign Affairs* (Pittsburgh: University of Pittsburgh Press, 1958).

an especially favorable position in this respect, partly because of the special constitutional powers of the Senate and its tradition built up since the early history of the Republic. A particularly close relationship of confidence usually prevails between a few committee members and officials of the executive branch. This relationship provides a means for consultation about delicate foreign policy developments which it is deemed unwise to publicize and aids in building a bridge of understanding and support between the branches.

The consultative subcommittees established by each committee provide a more systematic means for continuing communication with the executive branch about particular geographic areas and other policy matters. A striking example of the value of this device was displayed in the intimate collaboration between the Far Eastern Affairs Subcommittee in the Senate and the Department of State in shaping the Japanese peace settlement in 1951 and 1952.[4] But a majority of the consultative subcommittees are inactive much of the time; even when they meet, it is difficult for members to devote much time to them. As a consequence of this inactivity and the tendency of the parent committees to concentrate on legislation, significant areas of foreign policy may be neglected until a crisis arises.

Other legislative committees of the House and Senate also deal with policies that bear upon international affairs. The committees on armed services have an especially crucial jurisdiction. While both committees on armed services have been compelled to air interservice disputes, and have probed from time to time into aspects of preparedness, the largest fraction of their time is consumed by legislation and problems concerned with such operational matters as military construction and personnel. Vital questions about broad military policy that bear importantly on the survival of the United States and its position in world affairs receive less attention. This choice in emphasis reflects in part the bewildering complexity of the issues raised by the revolution in military techniques and the reluctance to overrule the decisions of professional military experts.

The House Committee on Science and Astronautics and the Senate Committee on Aeronautical and Space Sciences have also acquired jurisdiction over matters of significant military and international concern. The Joint Committee on Atomic Energy has jurisdiction over the military applications of nuclear energy. The committees on government operations have an important voice concerning administrative aspects of foreign policy.

Virtually every other legislative committee conducts some business that may be classified as foreign policy. A dozen standing committees, in addition to the Committee on Foreign Affairs and the Committee on Foreign Relations, deal with aspects of foreign economic policy. These units are all

---

[4] See Bernard C. Cohen, *The Political Process and Foreign Policy: The Making of the Japanese Peace Settlement* (Princeton, N.J.: Princeton University Press, 1957).

deeply rooted in the domestic scene and vary widely in the extent to which they weigh the foreign policy implications of their decisions.

All foreign policy legislation approved by the Congress and the President is again reviewed, if money is involved, by the committees on appropriations. In theory, these committees are not concerned with the substance of policy, only the cost of what has already been authorized. In fact, they regularly make financial choices involving substantive judgments. In some policy areas for which the Congress grants long-term authority for appopriations, as in major areas of military policy, the money committees are the principal instruments of legislative control.

Each appropriations committee is a holding company for powerful subcommittees that dominate the financial decisions regarding their respective fields. Considerable influence is wielded by the chairmen of these subcommittees. The subcommittee decisions about their fractions of the budget are usually ratified without extensive deliberation by the full committees. The congressional judgment about the budget as a whole is the sum of its separate actions as compiled at the end of a legislative session.

The House subcommittees work much of the time in executive session, in virtual isolation from the substantive committees and from one another. The Senate group employs subcommittees for conducting most of its business, but, by contrast, the full committee considers foreign aid appropriations, and a larger proportion of its business is conducted in public. The rules of the Senate which provide for representation from the substantive committees to the appropriations subcommittees, and the fact that all committee members serve on another important committee, provide the basis for a blending of fiscal and substantive judgments by the Senate group.

When the activities of the committees on appropriations are added to the activities of the substantive committees, it is evident that at least half of the standing committees of Congress directly affect foreign policy. Occasionally committees cooperate closely, or special committees are devised to work in overlapping policy areas. An example is the Senate Special Committee to Study the Foreign Aid Program, which was active in 1956 and 1957 and which drew its membership from the Committees on Foreign Relations, Appropriations, and Armed Services. But most of the committees and their staffs work quite independently of one another. Each carefully guards its jurisdiction. In some instances, subcommittees have become quite independent entities, pursuing inquiries and engaging in other activities over which the parent committees exercise only nominal control. The directing influence of legislative and executive leadership, personal ties among members and staffs, and the fact that a Member of the Senate serves on two major committees modify these barriers but still leave much to be desired in the way of communication among these units.

The behavior of all committees, and thus of each House, is affected by the practice of awarding committee chairmanships according to seniority. Some members who rise to these posts have exceptional capacity and experience; others do not. While the seniority rule has been modified in practice on rare occasions, it is normally enforced because most Members prefer not to risk the controversy that would be involved in a more selective process.

The top party leaders rarely exert their influence at the level of committee activity. They are careful to respect the prerogatives of the chairmen and the ranking members of the committees. On the floor they usually support the bipartisan coalition in charge of a measure. When either House threatens to engage in what they consider to be a major aberration, or when the achievement of agreement is difficult, they employ their leadership resources more rigorously. Seldom do party meetings discuss foreign policy issues and relate these to party policy or to the broader picture of general legislative policy. The leaders are commonly drawn into executive-legislative consultations regarding foreign affairs and in unpublicized ways work to promote responsible agreement regarding foreign policy issues both within the Congress and between the branches. The President maintains continuing contact with his party leaders.

Except in times of grave crisis, broad foreign policy issues must contend with heavy competition in the allocation of a Member's time, attention, and thought. This generalization is less true for the members of the foreign policy committees, but even they are often so overwhelmed by other burdens that they find it difficult to give extended attention to general international developments. Most Members of the Congress feel that it is necessary to concentrate primarily on domestic issues that preoccupy most of their constituents.

Despite these difficulties, some Members have been sufficiently concerned with the critical importance of international issues to devote a major portion of their energies to foreign policy and, in some cases, they have acquired extraordinary expertise. Despite the generally domestic orientation of the public, there has been a trend toward greater interest in international affairs, especially as the result of two World Wars. In response to these changes, each political party has been gradually reorienting its consideration of foreign affairs toward a concept of national interest that is broader than the particulars of sectional demands.

James A. Robinson

CONGRESSIONAL INFLUENCE
AND INITIATIVE IN
FOREIGN POLICY-MAKING

Congress and the Total Policy Process

WEIGHT OF INFLUENCE

In considering Congress' participation in the total foreign policy-making process, it is useful to have in mind a model of policy processes. We shall adopt one which conceives of the decision process in terms of seven functions which are performed in the making of any decision.[1] These include the *intelligence* function, i.e., the gathering of information, which may include either information which suggests a problem for policy-makers' attention or information for the formulation of alternatives. A second function is the *recommendation* of one or more possible policy alternatives. A third is the *prescription* or enactment of one among several proposed alternative solutions. A fourth is the *invocation* of the adopted alternative, and a fifth is its *application* in specific situations by executive or enforcement officers. A sixth stage of the decision process is the *appraisal* of the effectiveness of the prescribed alternative, and the seventh is the *termination* of the original policy. The latter stages present the opportunity to gather new information, to evaluate the original policy, and to consider whether a new problem has arisen requiring new information, recommendations, or prescription. Then the decision process may begin again.

To consider the weight of influence which different roles and institutions within the total policy-making process exercise, it is useful to see which of these functions are primarily performed by legislatures as against executives. Although we lack the historical analysis, it would be interesting

---

[1] See Harold D. Lasswell, *The Decision Process: Seven Categories of Functional Analysis* (College Park, Maryland: Bureau of Governmental Research, University of Maryland, 1956). For applications of this schema in its author's research, see, e.g., Richard Arens and Harold D. Lasswell, *In Defense of Public Order: The Emerging Field of Sanction Law* (New York: Columbia University Press, 1961).

FROM *Congress and Foreign Policy-Making: A Study in Legislative Influence and Initiative* by James A. Robinson. Copyright 1962 by The Dorsey Press, Inc., Homewood, Ill. Reprinted by permission of the publisher.

to have data to indicate whether there have been shifts in the predominant participation of executives and legislatures in each of these seven functions. A judgment, not based upon as hard evidence as one would like to have, is that the legislative branch of the U.S. government is no more predominant in any one of these seven decision functions than it was, say, fifty years ago. For example, consider the intelligence function. It is not obvious what the primary sources of information were for Congress fifty years ago, but it does seem relatively clear that its primary source of information now is the executive branch. If one examines reports and studies of legislative committees, he will readily find that the data in them are from, and most of their bibliographic references are to, sources within the executive branch. It is customary that bills and resolutions referred to committees of Congress are almost invariably submitted to the executive for comment and analysis. Executive witnesses ordinarily open testimony in hearings on any bill or resolution. With respect to foreign relations, anyone who has observed hearings before either Foreign Affairs or Foreign Relations has noted the difference in attendance of Congressmen at a hearing on, say, the Mutual Security Bill when the Secretary of State or the Joint Chiefs of Staff testify and when private and nongovernmental groups testify.

Many people have commented on the "information revolution" of the 20th century.[2] The effect of the information revolution on executive-legislative relations is several-fold. First, it has increased by many times the amount of information which is available to policy-makers about the problems they confront. Although all decision-making has not been reduced to highly rational, computational techniques, rough observation indicates a great increase in the possibilities of comparing proposed means to given ends much more precisely than fifty or a hundred years ago. This fact probably has reduced the amount of guessing and judgment required when information about the problem is lacking. Second, the executive branches of government have learned to specialize more than legislatures, and in specializing have developed resources for the accumulation of large amounts of factual data about policy problems. It is not clear why Congress or other legislative bodies have not developed more bureaucratic and staff support, but it seems plausible that their failure to do so has put them at a disadvantage vis-à-vis the executive departments which have had the superior resources for handling the vast new amounts of information available to the total policy-making process.

This alteration in the intelligence function, which is a product of the 20th century and which is changing the role of information in policy-making year by year, has had substantial effect on other parts of the decision process. Consider the recommendation function. The executive branch,

---

[2] See, for example, Kenneth Boulding, "Decision-Making in the Modern World," in Lyman Bryson (ed.), *An Outline of Man's Knowledge of the Modern World* (New York: McGraw-Hill, 1960), pp. 418–42.

because of its superior information, is in a preferred position for identifying social and political problems. Thus, it can structure the agenda for the total decision process, including the agenda of the legislative branch. One notes, in this connection, the apparent increase in the tendency of Congress, including its leaders, to expect the executive to assume the initiative in identifying problems and proposing solutions for them. Thus, Democrats complained that Dwight D. Eisenhower was not a "strong President" who gave "leadership" to the legislative branch. What is a general tendency in policy-making is acute with respect to foreign affairs. In international relations the executive has always had an advantage constitutionally and the information revolution has accentuated it. In addition to possessing an advantage in the identification of problems, the executive has primacy in the formulation of alternatives. As a result there is an increasing inclination to rely on the executive for the presentation of proposals to deal with problems. Congress' role, then, becomes less and less one of the initiation of policy alternatives and more and more the modifier, negator, or legitimator of proposals which originate in the executive.

The work nearest to a historical survey of the relative importance of Congress and the Presidency in the initiation of legislation is Lawrence Chamberlain's study of 90 bills enacted between 1880 and 1945.[3] The 90, unfortunately, do not contain any foreign policy measures other than immigration and national defense bills. Unfortunately, also, the means by which the sample of 90 were chosen were unsystematic. They appear to be the author's conception of important legislation during that period. Nevertheless, one gets some very interesting relationships if he tries to graph the relative importance of Congress and the Presidency in initiating these 90 bills over time (see Figure). For example, Congress was the primary initiator prior to 1900 and then there was a sharp decline in its role concurrent with the Presidency of Theodore Roosevelt and then a slight increase again until 1925 when there is another peak of Congressional initiation almost as high as that of 1900. Then Congress' role drops off again and remains relatively low until the end of the survey in 1945. On the other hand, the Presidency, which was low as an initiator of legislation in 1900 and remains so through 1930 then takes an upturn through the 1930's before it begins to drop off. Corresponding with the decline of Congress and the increase of the Presidency in the initiation of legislation there is an overlapping trend which shows an increase in joint participation of Congress and the Presidency. Thus, a summary view of relative participation of Congress and the Presidency in the initiation of legislation in the 20th century looks like this: Congress declines as the Presidency participates jointly with Congress in the initiation of legislation. An ex-

[3] Lawrence Chamberlain, *The President, Congress, and Legislation* (New York: Columbia University Press, 1946).

Origins of Legislation—Congress or the Presidency

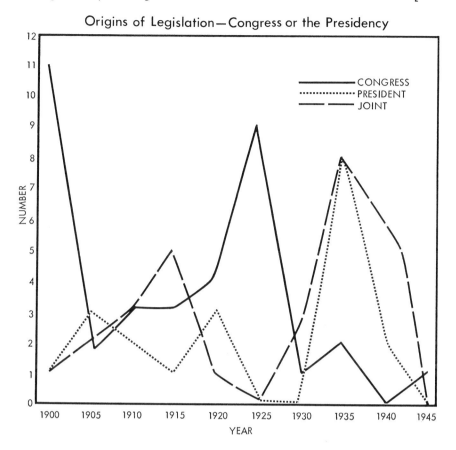

Source: Prepared from data in Lawrence Chamberlain, *The President, Congress, and Legislation* (New York: Columbia University Press, 1946).

tension of Chamberlain's study from 1945 to 1960 would be expected to show that joint collaboration has given way to virtually exclusive initiation by the executive.

SCOPE OF INFLUENCE

"Scope" refers to the number and kinds of issues, policies, or values affected by the holder of influence. In this case, the question is what foreign policy issues does Congress participate in deciding or affecting?

The Senate possesses a classic constitutional advantage over the House by virtue of the requirement that Presidential appointments of Ambassadors receive the advice and consent of the Senate. The Senate has never rejected a Presidential nomination for an ambassadorial post, "although," as Senator Humphrey has said, "on several occasions Senate opposition was sufficient to induce the President to withdraw his nominee.[4] On other occasions, a Senator's persistent opposition may lead a nominee to decline appointment, even when the Senate confirms him. This was the outcome of Wayne Morse's campaign against Clare Booth Luce, whom the President nominated as Ambassador to Brazil, in 1959. We have no way of knowing how the "rule of anticipated reaction"[5] has worked to cause the President to consider, before making a nomination, whether it would be acceptable to the Senate. On the whole, it seems fair to say, that the Senate has not actively used the confirmation of appointments as an opportunity to influence foreign policy. Senator William Fulbright has inquired into the diplomatic preparation and language competency of nominees, but in the one case in which he chose to oppose the nomination on grounds of competency, the Senate upheld the President.

On another occasion the Senate used the confirmation proceeding to give unprecedented support to a Presidential nominee who had been embarrassed by the President himself. In 1959, President Eisenhower chose Undersecretary of State Christian Herter to succeed John Foster Dulles as Secretary of State. However, Mr. Eisenhower and his press secretary, James Hagerty, created the impression that the appointment was made with reluctance and with reservations. Under the leadership of Chairman Fulbright and Majority Leader Lyndon Johnson, the Committee on Foreign Relations suspended its rule that nominations lay over six days before being acted on within the Committee. Instead, within four hours and thirteen minutes after receiving the nomination from the President, the Senate unanimously confirmed Mr. Herter, and Senate leaders publicly expressed their support and satisfaction with the nominee.[6] Nevertheless, this is an uncommon occurrence.

In addition to the authority to confirm certain Presidential nominees, the Senate also has the unique constitutional authority to give its advice and consent to treaties. This was once the primary opportunity for the Senate to participate in foreign policy,[7] although the initiative rested with the executive. Nevertheless, the mechanisms of foreign policy have been altered, especially in the last twenty-five years. The executive agreement,

[4] Hubert H. Humphrey, "The Senate in Foreign Policy," *Foreign Affairs*, **XXXVII** (1959), p. 528.

[5] This rule, given a name by Professor Carl J. Friedrich, refers to the phenomenon of one actor's modifying his behavior in anticipation of how another actor would respond if one's behavior were not modified. *Constitutional Government and Democracy* (Boston: Little, Brown, 1941), pp. 589–91.

[6] See the columns of Arthur Krock on the editorial page of the *The New York Times*, and Walter Lippmann, opposite the editorial page of the *Washington Post* and *Times-Herald*, April 23, 1959.

[7] For historical studies of the Senate's influence through its authority to give advice and consent to treaties, see George H. Haynes, *The Senate of the United States* (New York: Russell and Russell, 1960), Vol. II, pp. 569–720; Royden J. Dangerfield, *In Defense of the Senate* (Norman: University of Oklahoma Press, 1933); W. Stull Holt, *Treaties Defeated by the Senate* (Baltimore: Johns Hopkins Press, 1933).

introduced in quantity to handle tariff changes under the Reciprocal Trade Agreements Program, is much the more common form of internation activity. Further, foreign aid, in its many forms, has become a much more salient instrument of foreign policy than the treaty.

The scope of Congressional influence in foreign policy extends especially to appropriations, and in this field the House of Representatives is traditionally regarded as having the advantage over the Senate.[8] One of the most notable post-World War II changes in the foreign policy values affected by Congress is the appropriation of money. The major foreign policies since 1947 have been foreign aid, sometimes called European Recovery, Point IV, technical assistance, foreign economic operations, mutual security, and most recently AID (Act for International Development). These programs have cost vast amounts of money, second in size only to the outlay of sums for defense. The effect has been to enlarge the scope of the House's influence on foreign policy.[9] Former Speaker Martin recalls that in the 1920's foreign policy was a less expensive business. "For one week the House Foreign Affairs Committee debated to the exclusion of all other matters the question of authorizing a $20,000 appropriation for an international poultry show in Tulsa. This item, which we finally approved, was about the most important issue that came before the Committee in the whole session." [10]

The effect of Congressional influence on appropriations is consistently to reduce or maintain executive requests for foreign policy allotments. Rare is the occasion when Congress will enlarge an executive request for or initiate an expenditure for foreign policy.

One subject on which Congress has dominated the executive is immigration. Chamberlain's survey of the origins of legislation from 1880 to 1945 included nine immigration statutes.[11] In each case he assigned Congress the preponderant influence in determining the policy. Generally speaking, Congress has preferred a more restrictive immigration policy than the President, and Congress has ordinarily favored admitting new immigrants roughly in proportion to the distribution of foreign nationalities within the United States. Although Presidents have vetoed legislation affecting immigration, Congress has been united enough to override the veto, as in 1952, when the McCarran-Walter Act was adopted. The one occasion

[8] Robert Ash Wallace, *Congressional Control of Federal Spending* (Detroit: Wayne State University Press, 1960). Professor Richard Fenno of the University of Rochester is preparing a major study of the appropriations process. See his "The House Appropriations Committee as a Political System: The Problem of Integration," paper prepared for the annual meeting of the American Political Science Association (St. Louis, September 6–9, 1961).

[9] For a comprehensive study, see Holbert N. Carroll, *The House of Representatives and Foreign Affairs* (Pittsburgh: University of Pittsburgh Press, 1958).

[10] Joe Martin, *My First Fifty Years in Politics*, as told to Robert J. Donovan (New York: McGraw-Hill, 1960), p. 49.

[11] Chamberlain, *op. cit.*, p. 451.

when Congress took the initiative more "liberally" than the executive was in the repeal of the Chinese Exclusion Acts in 1943. In this case, the executive was reluctant to push the repeal, not for lack of sympathy for the objectives, but out of concern for whether there was sufficient support in Congress to complete repeal. Failure to succeed once the venture was undertaken, which would have been embarrassing for U.S. relations with China and the rest of Asia, was the concern of the executive.

The scope of Congressional influence also extends to the policy-making process within the executive. As we shall see in a later chapter much of Congress' foreign policy activity is in determining the organizational arrangements of the policy-making process, as distinguished from affecting substantive foreign policy by legislation. For example, during 1949–58, more than half the Senate bills and resolutions reported by the Foreign Relations Committee dealt with administrative and organizational machinery in the executive branch. This legislation included such issues as where the International Cooperation Administration should be located, in or out of the Department of State.

DOMAIN OF INFLUENCE

Measuring influence is a combination of gauging the degree of participation in making decisions, the scope or values affected by those decisions, and the extent of the consequences of and the number of persons affected by the decisions. Lasswell and Kaplan defined "domain" in terms of the number of persons affected.[12] It is useful to add something more in computing the importance of the decision. Only to consider the number affected is to ignore the consequences of the influence. Although this raises the difficult problems associated with ranking the intensity of preferences of people and ranking value consequences, one can state the problem even if he can not satisfactorily solve it.

Congressional influence in foreign policy tends to be influence "on the periphery," as Senator Fulbright is supposed to believe.[13] When House or Senate take the initiative, they do so on marginal and relatively unimportant matters. The scope of their influence may be broad in that it is related to several basic values—wealth, power, etc.—but the domain, the impact on those values, is much slighter than the executive's. Consider the most notable case of Congressional initiative in foreign policy in recent years, the Monroney Resolution.[14] The scope of the resolution's influence included the economies of underdeveloped countries, the more efficient use of surplus local currencies owned by the United States, and the possible

[12] Harold D. Laswell and Abraham Kaplan, *Power and Society: A Framework for Political Inquiry* (New Haven: Yale University Press, 1950), p. 73.

[13] E. W. Kenworthy, "The Fulbright Idea of Foreign Policy," *New York Times Magazine*, May 10, 1959, p. 74.

[14] James A. Robinson, *The Monroney Resolution: Congressional Initiative in Foreign Policy Making* (New York: Holt, 1959).

reduction of the amount of U.S. foreign aid. Yet the International Development Association, created as a result of the impetus of the resolution, was capitalized at only $1 billion and involved only a third that amount for the United States. Further, as we shall note below, one explanation for why this attempt at Congressional initiative succeeded was that it was a marginal issue to which little cost was attached.

On the other hand, the most famous unsuccessful attempt at Congressional initiative, the Bricker Amendment to the Constitution, was viewed by the executive as containing potentially threatening consequences. Had Senator Bricker's proposed amendment been ratified, its impact could hardly have been evaluated in terms of the number who would have been affected by it. Yet the alleged consequences of the Senator's designs for changing the treaty-making process were considerable, and the executive opposed it categorically.

The view that Congress originates marginal proposals is supported by comparing the content of bills initiated in Congress with those initiated by the executive. This is done in greater detail in a subsequent chapter. At this point it is worth noting that quantitatively Congress initiates more foreign policy proposals than the executive. In the period 1949–58, 80 per cent of the Senate bills and resolutions reported by the Committee on Foreign Relations originated with Senators and 20 per cent with the executive. In historical research of this kind it is difficult to identify all the executive-initiated bills and resolutions. We are confident that the 20 per cent is a minimum figure of executive measures, but a somewhat larger number may be more accurate, inasmuch as it is a common occurrence for a legislator to receive a suggestion from one of the departments and in turn seek its help in drafting his proposal. Nevertheless, the data would have to be very inaccurate to deny the proposition that many foreign policy proposals initiate in Congress. Yet none of the these are the measures which command the greatest amount of time of the Committee or occupy the attention of the "attentive publics." Foreign aid, fundamental international commitments, participation in international organizations—these bills with the greatest domain originate with the executive.

SUMMARY

To summarize, Congressional participation in foreign policy decisions is principally in the recommendation and prescription stages of the decision process. Recommendations of important measures frequently are initiated by the executive rather than the legislative branch. Thus, in the prescription stage Congress is legitimating, amending, or vetoing executive proposals. The scope of Congressional influence varies with the constitutional provisions governing the making and conduct of foreign relations. The Senate, with an advantage in confirming diplomatic appointments and approving treaties has not exploited the former and is finding the latter less and less an important instrument of policy. The House, with an advantage deriving from its constitutional position with respect to appropriations, awaits the executive budget and reacts to it by legitimating or cutting it, but rarely by raising it. In the initiation and determination of immigration policies Congress has consistently prevailed over the executive, and the scope of Congressional influence also extends to the organization of the executive for making and executing policy. Finally, the domain of Congressional influence, especially when it is initiative, tends to be on marginal and relatively less important matters.

Roger Hilsman

CONGRESSIONAL-EXECUTIVE RELATIONS
AND THE FOREIGN POLICY CONSENSUS

WHEN Woodrow Wilson, still in the early years of his academic career, studied the relations between Congress and the Executive, he focussed on organization and channels of leadership and responsibility.[1] He was distressed at the disorderliness of affairs in which Congress had a part, and he was convinced that its noisy and often undignified procedures were an impassable obstacle to good government. He pined for the logic and clearly fixed responsibilities of parliamentary government on the British model of that time, for its party discipline and for the clear-cut choices between alternative policies that it offered to the electorate.

For contemporary observers, Congressional-Executive relations still attract attention, particularly in the field of foreign affairs. But the factors which Wilson examined with the greatest care of all seem not to be less central than they were to him. Partly this is because the federal government itself has changed: it now has a vastly wider range of both responsibilities and control than it once had, and there have been shifts in the relative power of the different branches within the government, to which Wilson himself as President contributed much. But there are also other reasons. In an age of ideological extremes, a wider consent than a simple majority seems more desirable than it might have been in Wilson's day, and no one is certain that the parliamentary form is superior in providing

---

[1] Woodrow Wilson, *Congressional Government* (Boston: Houghton Mifflin, 1885).

FROM *The American Political Science Review*, **LLI**, No. 3 (September 1958). Reprinted by permission of the author and The American Political Science Association.

for this wider consent.[2] Then, too, as a result of the work of many men in the interval since Wilson wrote, we are probably sensitive to kinds of pressures on policy and to a range of functions that must be served in its development that were paid too little notice by Wilson or his contemporaries.[3]

I

One of the first points that today's observer of the Congressional scene might stress somewhat more than Wilson did is how well informed some members of Congress are. Among the more responsive and active members, there seem to be one or two for almost every major problem area who are just as knowledgeable as the specialists. Even the less responsive member can acquire a formidable knowledge of a subject during ten or fifteen years of service on a committee listening to expert briefings—perhaps even more knowledge, if the truth were known, than that of some Secretary or Assistant Secretary who has been on the job for only a year or two, as is more usual than not.

In this same connection, the contemporary observer might make a special point of how quickly information and ideas arrive on Capitol Hill in our day. The Congress, like the presidency or any locus of power, is a target center at which are aimed the activities of many groups with conflicting opinions, within the structure of government as well as outside it. To further its own ends, each of these groups utilizes every form of information and argument it can lay hands on. Thus each Congressman has at his disposal what is in effect a far-flung intelligence network numbering at least in the thousands. It is hardly surprising that an active Congressman is one of the first to learn of some new idea, discovery, or technique. As an example, he often learns of the results of university research just about as soon as people in other universities do—and sometimes sooner.

Another characteristic that impresses today's observer is the seriousness with which Congressmen take their jobs and their rather unusual sense of responsibility. Indeed, much of what appears to be irresponsibility to the casual observer probably stems from the kind of conceptual framework by which the individual Congressman interprets international events—the

[2] On this point, see Dean Acheson, *A Citizen Looks at Congress* (New York: Harper & Row, 1957).

[3] I have myself drawn most heavily on Robert A. Dahl, *Congress and Foreign Policy* (New York: Harcourt, Brace, 1950); and George B. Galloway, *The Legislative Process in Congress* (New York: Thomas Y. Crowell, 1953), who also read this manuscript and corrected a number of errors. Others among the more recent works are the following: Ernest S. Griffith, *Congress, Its Contemporary Role* (New York: New York University Press, 1956); H. Bradford Westerfield, *Foreign Policy and Party Politics* (New Haven: Yale University Press, 1955); and Roland Young, *The American Congress* (New York: Harper & Row, 1958).

pictures in his head, in Lippmann's phrase. A very high proportion of the Congress, for example, are lawyers—over half, it is said [4]—and it could be argued that in consequence of this there is among Congressmen a preoccupation with the legal aspects of international relations, with the wording of treaties and resolutions, with establishing which of the parties to a dispute are legally and morally "right" or "wrong." As with all men, others among Congressmen tend to personify relations between states and to project to international relations motives and behavior patterns generalized from their experience with individual persons. All of which is merely a roundabout way of saying that Congressmen have a wide variety of "pictures in their heads" and that their sense of responsibility is exercised in terms of these widely differing sets of assumptions. Apparent, as opposed to actual, responsibility would thus be increased, as would rationality, by improving Congressmen's understanding and the quality of assumptions by which they think about international relations. But this is equally true of all the rest of us, and Congress is nothing if not representative.

A more particular cause of apparent, as opposed to real, irresponsibility is the pressure on Congressmen and their busyness. The individual Congressman carries a formidable burden, and when one reflects on the nature and extent of this burden and on the seriousness and devotion that most Congressmen bring to their jobs, the irritation one feels at behavior that seems to fit the stereotype gives way to respect—and sometimes, for some of the outstanding members of the Congress, even a little awe. The Congressman, first, must handle a multitude of matters for individual constituents. He cannot avoid this, and clearly he should not. The individual citizen's access to his Congressman is a useful device by which to balance the necessarily impersonal procedures of bureaucracy. Also, it is through their work with constituents that Congressmen acquire much of the knowledge of values and preferences [5] that sets the limits on their voting behavior even if it does not always guide it. This is particularly true of knowledge of intensity of feeling about an issue, for which most other guides, such as public opinion polls, are of little use. And it takes only a short political experience to learn that a minority who hold a view with great intensity will have more political effect than a diffuse majority who believe the opposite, but not very forcefully.

A second element of the Congressman's busyness is the formal calendar. He must attend the floor for voting and do his homework on a variety of bills that run the whole gamut of our national life. Finally, he has committee work, with its endless hours of listening and mountains of materials for reading. As a result, the Congressman jumps from subject to subject with a tempo that approaches frenzy. His day begins early and ends late; his week lasts long. Nothing can be given sustained attention; nothing

---

[4] George B. Galloway, *op. cit.*, p. 373.
[5] The word is Dahl's, *op. cit.*

can be carried through to its completion; most projects are only half-done. The Congressional scene is, in a word, untidy. It is not surprising that Wilson's Calvinist soul was outraged. But here again what we have is the face of irresponsibility but not really the fact. The untidiness comes not from a lack of responsibility on the part of Congressmen but from the very extent of their responsibilities.

In reaction to the emphasis on pressure politics that followed the discovery of lobbyists and their activities, an observer today might also recognize that Congress has a greater freedom in the field of foreign policy than is ordinarily supposed. For one thing, there seem to be relatively few pressure groups at work on foreign policy, quite unlike the solid array that plead unceasingly for their points of view on domestic matters. The interest of producers' groups seems to be concentrated on protection, and with what is certainly notable success. But however important a liberal trade policy may be in the long run—in building, for example, a wider and more stable world system—it is doubtful if any country important in our foreign relations regards our tariffs as a major determinant of their immediate foreign policy in the present world situation. Japan is a case in point: it suffers as much from our tariff policies as any, yet power and political considerations keep it aligned with us on most matters.

Beyond their tariff demands, few producers' groups seem to be much concerned. Witness, for example, their rather half-hearted attempt to capitalize on the foreign aid program and the fact that their effect was confined principally to the clause reserving half the shipping business for American firms and the disposal of certain agricultural surpluses. The oil companies, with their interests in Latin America and the Middle East, seem to be the only important exception.

Apart from producers' groups, probably the national minorities are most prominent in the lobbies. These minority groups, of course, are very active, though not necessarily in any simple correspondence with the foreign policy of the homeland.[6] But for most minority groups—with the very notable exception of Zionist organizations—there is hardly any American foreign policy to work on at the moment except the same form of resistance to Soviet and Communist expansion that the whole nation is committed to. In some instances, as with the so-called China lobby, these pressures may keep our policy more inflexible than some might wish, but in general it seems to be only our policy toward the middle east that is subject to the kind of special interest pressures that are applied as a matter of course to domestic policy.

By and large, then, Congress seems to be somewhat freer from organized pressure when it comes to decide on an issue of foreign policy than it is on domestic policy. It also seems to be rather free from party control or

[6] D. W. Brogan, "Politics and United States Foreign Policy," *International Affairs*, Vol. 33 (April, 1957), pp. 166–167.

discipline. The national party dispenses only a very little patronage today, and what it does dispense seems to go more to the workers and contributors of the Presidential campaign than it does toward keeping Congress in line, especially in a day of rather full employment. The Congressional party dispenses even less patronage on Capitol Hill. In consequence, one would expect that the most important bait for party regularity that is controlled by the Congressional party would be committee assignments and chairmanships.

In assigning committee chairmanships party regularity has never been an important consideration, and it is doubtful if it ever will. If there were national party structures of the kind that would permit the national party effectively to deny to rebels the nomination under the party label, there might be some basis for the Congressional party using regularity as one of the criteria for assigning chairmanships. Until that time, however, the seniority rule provides a way of making the decision that is beyond bias or favoritism. Though the rule has been criticized because it does not award the chairmanships to the most capable except by accident, neither does it give affront, and this is a priceless quality in party structures so fragile as these.

In making committee assignments, as opposed to choosing chairmen, the party does apparently consider party regularity on occasion. But it is far down the list, and it seems to be invoked as a general rule only when two members in competition for the same post are nearly equal in other respects. Committee assignments seem to be used only rarely to punish transgressions of party discipline.[7] There are exceptions, however, as in the 69th Congress when two Wisconsin representatives were deprived of their committee chairmanships, and others were reduced in rank on their committees, for supporting the elder La Follette for the presidency in 1924. But a more typical as well as more recent example is that of Adam Clayton Powell. A Democrat from the Harlem district of New York City, he supported Eisenhower in the 1956 election, apparently as a protest against the opposition of Southern Democrats to civil rights legislation. The reaction among individual Democrats was sharp and included threats to retaliate by denying Powell his committee assignments. In the end, however, no such action was taken.[8] In any case, the violations in all these examples were of discipline in national elections and not on particular bills or items in the

[7] When a man changes parties completely, of course, he will ordinarily lose his privileges, as Wayne Morse did when he declared himself an independent in 1953. See Ralph K. Huitt, "The Morse Committee Assignment Controversy," *The American Political Science Review*, Vol. 41 (June 1957), p. 313.

[8] At about the same time, Powell also lost the chairmanship of a subcommittee he had previously held. This act, however, was not done by the party or even in the name of the party. Each committee has its own custom in regard to the establishment and staffing of subcommittees, but in general the power to establish subcommittees and appoint their chairmen lies completely with the chairman of the parent committee. See George B. Galloway, *op. cit.*, pp. 288–289.

party's program. On such matters, it seems clear, party pressure is exercised more subtly than by granting or withdrawing overt benefits. The important pressures seem to be more social and psychological: the good opinion of men one respects; the sense of belonging to the club; the fear of being isolated and alone.[9]

This general freedom of Congress to exercise its own discretion in foreign policy inevitably has its effects on relations with the Executive. For one thing, the individual Congressman is not so reluctant to disagree as he might be. Given his need for publicity and the obvious fact that in conflict lies news, the individual Congressman is sometimes tempted to disagree for disagreement's sake—or, more accurately, for publicity's.

But relations between Congress and the Executive are equally affected by other considerations. It is the Executive that controls the flow of information from overseas.[10] There need not be any conscious intent to suppress one kind of information and emphasize another to accomplish the same result as conscious suppression and emphasis. In such a massive flow the selection needed to make it physically possible for a single person merely to examine the information would be enough. In addition, there is the question of technical expertise and advice. It is the Executive that sets up the framework in which policies are discussed, that in a sense defines the problems for our foreign policy and the alternatives with which to meet them.

This power over information and this plethora of expertise give to the Executive what might be called the intellectual initiative in foreign policy. The Congress as a whole can criticize; it can add, amend, or block an action by the Executive; but it can only occasionally succeed in forcing the Executive's attention to the need for a change in policy, and hardly ever in developing and securing the adoption of an alternative policy of its own. The limits of Congressional power in developing policy independently of the Executive can be indicated by such examples as that of the loss of China to the Communists and, more recently, the response in the American aid program to the Soviet initiation of a foreign aid program of its own. There were members of Congress, as in all areas of American life including the Executive, who saw that China was being lost to the West and that a radically new policy was necessary. But the Executive's assumption that neither the Congress nor the people would support the kind of sacrifices which effective measures would require—even if the assumption was correct—still precluded a full exploration of those measures and in effect killed

[9] See Dahl, *op. cit.*, p. 50.

[10] Dahl had hoped that Congress might find an alternative source of information in the Central Intelligence Agency. But due to its unusual—even unique—relationship with the policy-making parts of government and its almost total isolation from Congress, the Central Intelligence Agency is in no position to help Congress break the Executive monopoly. See my *Strategic Intelligence and National Decisions* (Ill.: The Free Press of Glencoe, 1956).

any possibility of discovering that the assumption might be wrong. Since the Executive did not propose a bold program, Congress did not debate one. In the recent decisions on foreign aid following the Soviet entry into the field, however, the Congress went somewhat further. Disturbed in the spring of 1956 by what they apparently interpreted as an Executive decision to depend on an increase in funds for the old aid program to meet the new Soviet tactics rather than try to develop an entirely new program, the so-called liberal group in Congress that has always favored aid joined the long-time opponents of aid in forcing a review of the problem. In the end, the effort was not notably successful. The most that could have been expected is probably that Congress could have brought the Executive to look anew at the problem and not that it could have succeeded in forcing the Executive to carry out a program developed entirely on Capitol Hill.

Frequently, as actually happened in the above examples, there will be within the Executive minority groups of officials—or sometimes, indeed, virtually the whole of officialdom—who are personally opposed to the Administration's policy. Inevitably, this discontent becomes known, and between the pressure of Congress and the wheedling of the press much of both the information and the arguments on the other side soon becomes available. Congress, for example, not only knew of the existence of the Wedemeyer report on China, which in effect proposed a massive intervention in the civil war between Chiang Kai Shek and the Communists, but the nature of most of its contents.[11] With this kind of information, Congress can sometimes debate a policy that the Executive does not want debated and thereby test, or alter, or even nullify the policy. These are impressive powers, but still limited ones. Although Congress could almost always find a way of denying support to a particular policy and dictate policy in the sense of paralyzing it, one must doubt whether it can force the Executive to accept a positive alternative in foreign policy by the exercise of its formal powers. It has no way of making an Executive follow a different policy, and there are always tempting, if devious, routes by which the Executive can follow its own policy no matter how many obstacles Congress puts in the way. Congress cannot forget, to give only two very recent examples, that the Truman administration flatly refused to spend the funds Congress had added to the defense budget for a larger air force and that the Eisenhower administration merely put a similar appropriation aside to substitute for the appropriations of the subsequent year.

In addition to this intellectual initiative in foreign policy, the Executive also has what might be called an instrumental one. The right of negotiation belongs to the Executive, and he can in the exercise of this right make promises and commitments that put Congress in a position in which

11 See Westerfield, *op. cit.*, pp. 260–262.

failure to ratify his actions would impair not only the prestige of the United States abroad but faith in its ability to exercise its great power as well. Frequently, indeed, the Executive may proceed without any formal reference to Congress at all. Examples abound: the Yalta agreement, which so many Congressmen still resent; Roosevelt's destroyers-for-bases deal with Britain; Truman's decision to meet the blockade of Berlin with an airlift; his decision to resist the Communist aggression in Korea with troops as well as with material aid; and Eisenhower's intervention in Lebanon.

This power of the Executive to conduct the foreign policy of the nation without reference to Congress or even to evade the expressed desires of Congress is inevitably the cause of suspicion and distrust. The Congress, in consequence, is ever studious in trying to bind the Executive to its wishes and to guard its own powers and prerogatives. Though it is continually frustrated in its attempts to exercise detailed surveillance over the Executive's action in foreign policy, though it is constantly being circumvented, it cannot abdicate its responsibilities and it will undoubtedly continue trying to oversee the detailed operation of the foreign policy programs it authorizes and finances. It is here, in sum, that one finds the classic struggle of the separation of powers, foreseen and provided for by the founding fathers and remarked upon by every observer of American government since the time of De Tocqueville.

II

But the classic observations on the effects of the separation of powers are not completely satisfying. They explain the impasses in policy, perhaps, the arguments and rivalries, but not the achievements. Somehow, policies do get made. In spite of the public charges and countercharges, in spite of the demagoguery, the headlines, and the rivalry, many things do seem to get done. We know the formal powers of the different branches; we have the tests and precedents laid down by the courts. But it seems obvious that for decisions on major policies, those requiring sacrifices by the nation or the concentration on one set of objectives at the cost of neglecting others, a knowledge of formal powers and precedents is not enough. In both the development and ratification of these major policies, the process seems to be much more complex, involving a greater interaction between the different branches of government, than the formal powers and procedures would indicate.

We can, of course, be sure that this process by which decisions on major policies are reached is a political one, even when it takes place entirely within the government and screened from the public view. That is to say, first, that such decisions require the reconciliation of a diversity of goals and preferences as well as alternative means; second, that there are competing groups within the government as well as outside it who are identified with the alternative goals and policies; and, third, that the relative power of the participating groups is as relevant to the decision as the cogency and wisdom of their arguments. Keeping this in mind, we might then describe the process by an adaptation of the model used in public opinion analysis, the same model serving whether the action takes place in the public view or entirely inside the structure of government. By this simplified, almost schematic means, the public opinion process is dealt with as a competition of rival groups of advocates seeking approval for their policies not from the broad masses (since, as has been frequently demonstrated, about a third of the general population is apathetic toward any given issue, or at least willing to leave it to others) but from what Gabriel Almond has so aptly called the "attentive publics." [12] In this concept, issues are debated in front of particular audiences that are interested in the special field and to some extent informed about it. There is thus not one public, but many—a particular public for agricultural policy, another for fiscal policy, still another for foreign policy, or perhaps several according to the region or problem toward which the policy is directed. The size of the attentive publics varies with the topic and, over time, within one topic; and a member of one public may also be a member of another.

Applied to the policy-making process in government, the concept visualizes both the groups of advocates and the informed audiences as cutting across the formal boundaries of Executive, Congress, the press, or any other formal grouping. The emphasis is on the patterns of relationship in which consensus is developed, on the techniques of consensus-building, and on the different functions that the participating groups perform in the process—originating ideas, working out the requirements for their implementation, selling the proposal within the governmental structure, aggregating alternatives, modifying, vetoing, and enlisting public support where necessary. For it is consensus that is the object of the process, if not always the result.

If consensus is reached, and the weight of opinion in the particular audience settles on one or the other of the debated policies or on some adaptation of one of these, we have all the essentials for consistent, "bipartisan" policy over time. But notice that consensus of the informed is not always essential for all kinds of policy and that apathy in the general population may in some instances effectively substitute for it. The military policy of the first Eisenhower administration is an example. This policy rested on two major decisions. One was to concentrate on atomic air power at the expense of naval and especially ground power. The second was that the Strategic Air Command could safely be maintained at a constant level even though the Soviet Long Range Air Army seemed to be

[12] Gabriel A. Almond, *The American People and Foreign Policy* (New York: Harcourt, Brace, 1950).

growing so fast as to threaten to take the lead. (The assumptions behind this second decision were, that it would be wasteful to provide more H-bomb carriers than the minimum necessary to destroy the Soviet Union once and, second, that the number required for this task could be accurately determined in advance.) The informed and interested audiences for military policy, including a wide section of the armed services, the official bureaucracy, and Congress, split into two differing camps of opinion, both in opposition to the policy of the administration. One of these groups was uneasy about the decision to make no special effort to keep the Strategic Air Command ahead of its Soviet counterpart, and the other was perhaps even more uneasy about the failure to provide in our military preparations for a larger proportion of ground troops and in general a greater capability for fighting limited, local wars using conventional rather than atomic weapons. Top-level decision-makers in the Executive, however, were not in sympathy with either of these views around which at least a partial consensus formed, whether from a different assessment of the Soviet threat, a different assessment of the economic risks involved in high levels of defense spending, or simply from a conviction that the American people at large would not tolerate the sacrifices, in terms of a larger draft as well as increased taxes, that such policies would entail. Since the mass of the public combined an indifference to the details of military policy with a faith in the expertness of President Eisenhower as a general, the Executive had no need for the support of the rather small group that comprised either consensus and ignored them both at what appears to have been little or no political cost.

Notice also that the possibility of political cost in the direct sense of election returns exists only when the building of consensus takes place in terms of the wider publics. An important point in the consensus-building model is that the participating groups are not always part of the wider public but can exist at any one of many levels—entirely within the Executive branch; entirely within the "government" more broadly conceived as including Congress and the press (whose role is nonetheless an inherent part of the process for being an unofficial one); or a widespread, largely unofficial but still esoteric group having some special knowledge or expertise (as, for example, nuclear physicists). At some of these levels the political cost of ignoring the consensus might well be nil. On the other hand, political costs may still be high even when they are not direct. The cooperation and support of a group whose opinion has been completely ignored on one issue will not be readily given on others to which this support may be crucial. Then, again, the consensus of a small but unusually well qualified group may be very effective in bringing on a decision even though the group has no political power in the popular sense at all. The weight of responsibility a national leadership bears is alone sufficient to ensure that it will listen carefully to specialist opinion and go against the consensus of such opinion only with reluctance.

It is worth noting that when a "process" such as this development of consensus among informed participants does work, it may be rather efficient in the assessment of policy alternatives. Indeed, it could be argued that this process is responsible for whatever truth there is in the observation that however many mistakes of omission democracies make, they rarely make the great mistakes of commission that totalitarian regimes seem prone to—as for example Hitler's mistake of attacking the Soviet Union. When the subject under debate is one on which the competing groups of advocates are knowledgeable; the participating audiences are well informed; and the decision-making levels of government at least sensitive to the verdict (if not, as would be preferable, participating in the debate on both sides)— when all these conditions are fulfilled chances should be good that the resulting policy will be a wise one, at least providing that the circumstances make no demand for speed. An example of an occasion in which these conditions were largely fulfilled is the development of our policy toward Europe in the years following World War II. Here both the advocates and participating audiences were generally familiar with Europe and its problems and well supplied with a frame of knowledge against which to test proposed policies. The top-level decision-makers, finally, were completely sensitive to both the elements and the growth of the resulting consensus. In the problem presented by the disintegration of Nationalist China, on the other hand, and its progressive slide into the hands of the Chinese Communists, several of the basic requirements for exploring and producing consensus on an effective policy were lacking. There was pitifully little specialist knowledge on China in the United States and almost no familiarity, outside the ranks of specialists, with the elements bearing on the problem.

None of this, of course, is meant to suggest that every problem has a solution or that the "consensus-building" process is an automatic machine for grinding out these solutions. If pressed to the wall on the postwar China problem, for example, the dispassionate observer might well find himself ultimately standing on the proposition that this was one of several problems that were beyond the power of the United States to affect more than marginally, if at all. What is being suggested, on the contrary, is the notion that as a consequence of the dearth of specialist knowledge about China and the almost total ignorance of it among participants in the consensus-building process, all the possible policy alternatives may not have been spelled out; that those alternatives that were proposed—for example, those contained in the Wedemeyer report—may not have been adequately debated; and that, finally, the need for drastic measures may not have been understood widely enough to make politically acceptable the sacrifices necessary for these measures.

III

Viewed as part of a "consensus-building" process, aspects of Congressional behavior become understandable that seem nothing less than absurd when considered in the kind of "rational decision-making" context in which each part of government is responsible for a particular step in the making of a national decision. What otherwise appears as purposeless or even perverse behavior begins to acquire both reason and motive.

The Congressman's role, even in the field of foreign policy, is colored by his position as a maker of laws. When he acts as part of the participating audience, it is as that part which is to express the consensus directly, as law, resolution, or appropriation. And when he acts as a policy advocate, as the representative of a competing group of advocates, his aim may be as much to maneuver a certain point into law as it is to convince the participating audience that the point is a wise one.

But even with the qualifications implied in the Congressman's role as lawmaker, the consensus-building model still seems to be a useful way of looking at the role that Congressmen play in the making of foreign policy. The kinds of questions asked in hearings on a new proposal, for example, the kinds of amendments proposed to the bill implementing that proposal, all seem to be different from the kinds of questions a responsible executive might ask of subordinates who were presenting a new policy to him for consideration and approval. The questions asked by an executive, say the President or the Secretary of State, would be aimed at bringing out both the alternative means and the alternative goals, at making certain not only that this policy was the best for achieving the purposes sought, but also that some entirely different purposes might not be more desirable. The questions, if they meet the criteria of rationality, would also explore the subsidiary effects on other values, the political possibilities of putting each alternative into effect and the political consequences of doing so.

The questions asked by Congressmen, as is well known, are usually quite different from these. They seem to reflect a recognition that the questioner cannot force the Executive to adopt an alternative, or even to consider it, unless he can enlist wide public support and that there are only rare occasions on which there is sufficient reason, or a case with enough appeal, to bother to try. Except in unusual circumstances, when there is both reason and a case, Congressional questions therefore leave great areas untouched; they rarely explore alternatives, whether of means or goals, and they touch on the appropriateness of means to goals only sporadically.

Even when faced with a straightforward policy proposal from the Executive, as in the Middle East Resolution presented by the Eisenhower administration, for example, Congressmen can rarely give the alternatives, except for outright rejection, more than a glance. And this is often true even when they have doubts about the effectiveness of the proposal. If one can judge from an examination of the hearings and comments by Congressmen as quoted in the press, a rather wide feeling existed in Congress, on both sides of the aisle, that the Eisenhower doctrine on the Middle East, insofar as it meant that the United States was compelled to pick up responsibility there, was a necessary and sound policy. But many Congressmen also seemed to feel that it had not been thoroughly thought out—that it was a reaction rather than a developed policy. Many members seemed to suspect, first, that the doctrine was aimed at the least important of the dangers (*i.e.*, direct Communist aggression rather than the twin threats of subversion on the one hand, and, on the other, the possibility that third party wars, such as between the Arabs and Israel, would provide the Soviets with opportunities for easy victories). Second, they seemed to feel that the military requirements for implementing the resolution had been neither fully explored nor provided for. Third, they seemed to suspect that in the provision for aid the problem of where and how to spend the money, including the willingness of the Arabs to accept aid from the United States, had not been fully considered and might turn out to be somewhat different from what the Executive expected. Yet in spite of their doubts, a large majority voted for the resolution with only minor changes, and the questions they asked focussed mainly on the issue of whether or not the policy proposed was worthy of support substantially as proposed. Even when there is doubt about the wisdom or effectiveness of the policy, in sum, the questions aim not so much toward exploring the range of alternatives or presenting the arguments for a particular alternative as toward building the case against the policy proposal as it stands.

In the more usual form in which Congress is confronted with policy, its opportunity for examining alternatives is even less, and the individual Congressman's behavior is still more sharply at variance with what might be expected if his role were the taking of certain formal steps in a rational process by which the nation makes decisions. Look, for example, at defense appropriations. The questions Congress asks of Executive witnesses, the information they are given and demand, the time they spend at the job and the way they spend what time they have available, all seem to be different from what would be necessary to permit Congress to arrive at an independent, rational judgment on the level of defense expenditures necessary to achieve its foreign policy preferences or on the allocation of those funds among the services so as to maximize those preferences.[13] If, however, Congress as a practical matter is powerless to impose alternative policies

[13] For an analysis of the requirements for a rational determination of the level and allocation of defense expenditures, see Warner Schilling, "Fiscal '50," a case study being prepared for the Civil-Military Relations project of the Institute for War and Peace Studies, Columbia University. Also of interest in this connection is his "Civil-Naval Politics in World War I," *World Politics* (July 1955).

by its formal procedures and can effectively raise new problems and new policies for consideration only through the informal procedures of consensus-building, then the members' failure to examine basic strategic alternatives during budget hearings and their corresponding concentration on minutiae is understandable. A policy change that is beyond their reach except through the consensus-building process requires an entirely different approach. If the appeal is to be made to an esoteric public, almost entirely within the structure of government, hearings are hardly the vehicle. If the audience is the wider one, on the other hand, the appeal is not worth the effort unless it can be simplified and dramatized. If one conceives of the policy debate as an element in a very wide consensus-building process— as taking place, in other words, in front of an audience whose attention is easily diverted—then the alternatives under consideration must be very clear-cut and compelling. Most Congressmen might recognize, for example, that the size and composition of the armed forces have an infinite number of forms and that the worths of each of these forms in achieving foreign policy goals lie along a continuum. Yet for the purposes of building a wide consensus, the discussion must take place in much simpler and more dramatic terms—is a 70 group air force the one and only correct size, or is it 48? The Symington Subcommittee's hearings on Air Power, to give another example, were criticized by students of nuclear strategy, who were concerned about the possibilities of limited wars, on the grounds that they were addressed not only to a greatly oversimplified question but probably toward the wrong one. But if the only context in which Congress can raise policy alternatives effectively is the consensus-building one, then there is a great advantage in having an investigation of our military policy concentrate on the single question of who has the most airplanes, the Russians or ourselves. This is a question that anyone can understand, and if the answer is that it is the Russians, then the burden of proof lies on the Executive to justify itself and its policy. It may also be that this same question is the only one in the field of military policy with which a Congress of the opposition party could stand up to the enormous prestige of a President who is also a five-star general.

Faced, finally, with a massive and complex budget in which the policy choices are embedded in a tangle of established programs, the Congressman can only rarely find a policy alternative that has the characteristics that are essential if he is to have any success in pushing it. On an occasion when he has a proposal of this kind that he can call his own, his efforts can be focussed on winning enough support to force consideration of it. Without such an alternative, he tends to fall back on the device of sinking random holes on the off-chance that he might strike a pool of inefficiency, graft, or corruption—which has little to do with policy alternatives but which if successful may well attract the headlines. And he can console himself that the very least he has accomplished with these random probes is his duty toward the traditional watchdog function of helping to keep the Executive honest.

IV

Certain aspects of the behavior of officials in the Executive also seem more rational when viewed as part of a "consensus-building" process. The endless leaks of secret information are not really evidence of blabber-mouthed irresponsibility but attempts by one official or group of officials to force an issue or alternative up to the level of decision or to outflank the proponents of another view. One may also better understand the pop-ularity of the "background" press conference, which newspapermen resent as "self-plagiarism" because the source of the news must remain anonymous and the newspapermen themselves take the abuse no matter what kind of storm is raised. Here the function is not only the end-run around the opposition inside the Executive, but a launching pad for trial balloons that will test the possibility of creating a consensus without the penalty of making a genuine attempt and failing. The mechanics of this process of competition between groups of advocates also helps explain why it is so difficult to make a true decision-making body out of such interdepartmental committees as the National Security Council.[14] The principal reason, of course, is that the President, unlike the Prime Minister in a parliamentary system, is not directly dependent for his continuation in office on the sup-port of his ministers and fellow party members in the legislature. But beyond this, for many policies a wider consent seems to be needed than can be represented in a body like the National Security Council, and such a body is hardly suitable for making any of the bilateral arrangements that may be necessary in developing that wider consent, or for the weighing and balancing of power that a political process entails.

Neither is it just the separation of powers between Congress and the Executive that tends to turn the making of major policy decisions into a consensus-building process. The very size and complexity of the Execu-tive's task in modern times makes it difficult for a bureaucratic machinery to cope effectively with departures from the routine. Before a new problem or proposal can be raised to the level of decision, it must jostle out hundreds of others. Except for problems born of crisis, and sometimes even for these, this elbowing up through the echelons could be expected to require the approval and cooperation of a rather extensive range of people. And what might be called the "jurisdictional" effect of bureaucracy tends to increase the number of problems that must go the whole way up. The essence of bureaucracy is specialization of function and a division of labor and respon-

[14] See Sydney Hyman, "Cabinet's Job as Eisenhower Sees It," *New York Times Magazine*, July 20, 1958.

sibility accordingly. This device is indispensable in managing large-scale enterprises, but it presents peculiar difficulties when it comes time to fix responsibility for problems that cut across jurisdictional lines—which foreign policy problems tend to do in any age and especially so in a time of external threat when both military and economic instrumentalities are prominent. More often than not, complex problems arising out of interaction, as between military and political considerations, can be "recognized" in an official sense only at the top.

Most of the general implications of all this follow naturally without elaboration. A policy-making system that tends to depend heavily on developing a consensus among a rather wide range of participants puts a high premium on effective communication and an even higher penalty on a failure of communication. Achieving sophisticated policies is not just a problem of policy planning by an elite staff but also one of persuading, bargaining, and educating. What is more, there seems to be no one place where these tasks can be concentrated, since there are too many participants too widely scattered to be reached by the communications resources available to any one group of participants, including perhaps even the office of the President.

Paradoxically, the need for wide support also leads to overselling a policy proposal in the sense of claiming too much for it. In selling the foreign aid program, for example, there was a tendency to justify it on the grounds that economic development now would ensure democratic regimes in the underdeveloped countries ten years from now. This enormous oversimplification brings trouble both at home and abroad. At home, it not only creates false expectations and extreme reactions when the expectations are not fulfilled, but it also obscures the fact that power instrumentalities may be as important as "humanitarian" ones in maintaining democratic regimes. Abroad, it tends to defeat itself. Putting too high a value on economic development as opposed to the sanctity and dignity of the individual may give an impetus towards totalitarianism as the only form of government that can impose the sacrifices rapid development requires.

The effort that must go into "selling" a policy that requires wide support, the difficulty in a bureaucracy of getting some kinds of problems "recognized" except at the top, and the competition for the attention of these decision-making levels all combine to put obstacles in the way of any attempt at systematic policy making. Some issues or proposals, as for example the Marshall Plan, are the subject of massive concentration, while others are neglected almost entirely. There is a tendency to bounce from the crest of one crisis to the crest of another, and a bias toward postponing final choice among possible alternatives until the new crisis forces decisions that are mainly reactions, the children of events rather than their master. At the same time, there is also a tendency to decide as little as possible.

If wide consent is necessary, decisions will almost inevitably tend to deal with only one aspect of a problem, as the Eisenhower Doctrine dealt only with direct Communist aggression rather than with the whole complex of threats including subversion and third party wars. Similarly, a decision to make the intercontinental ballistic missile tends to be reached solely on technical grounds, without a full look at the political context or consequences. It is here, in what might be called the discontinuity of policy development, rather than in intelligence failures, that we are most likely to find the reason why America is so often surprised by the turn of international events. Most of our troubles in anticipating events in foreign affairs seem to derive not so much from a failure to foresee the consequences of policies adopted or alternatives considered and rejected, as from the problems we have never really faced as a nation even when individual citizens have raised them.

V

Among the implications of this pattern of policy making for the narrower subject of Congressional-Executive relations, probably the most important is that sales gimmicks are no final solution. There is, quite clearly, an important place for briefings for Congressmen, for prior consultation with key members, for the early breakfast call by the Secretary of State on the chairmen of the Congressional committees, and for all the varied arts of the Assistant Secretary of State for Congressional Relations. But there are very sharp and rather narrow limits on how far the Executive can go in bringing Congressmen into what Senator Vandenberg liked to call the take-off policy as well as the crash landing. The kinds of powers bestowed on Congress by the Constitution, the peculiar limitations on those powers, the individual Congressman's consequent need to rely on consensus-building as a tool, his independent source of political strength and the demands this makes on him—all these conspire to make it impossible for the Congressman to take a regular part in the actual formulation of policy with anything approaching consistent responsibility to Executive interests. As a man with long experience on Capitol Hill who later moved to the State Department once remarked, the Secretaries not only have to be willing to have Congressmen participate in the lengthy process of policy making, they have also to be grimly determined to hunt them down and drag them there. Without a studious attention to Congressional relations and a willingness to make some concessions to Congressional fears, an Administration may on some occasion be repudiated in spite of having what is actually a sound case. Woodrow Wilson's defeat on the League could probably serve as an example. But any attempt to go much further than this, to seek to avoid the obstacle course, say by trying to make key Congressmen into a sort of informal National Security Council with a specific role in the formulation of policy, seems unlikely to change the Washington scene very radically.

For what are essentially the same reasons, it would also seem that the Executive would be well advised not to go to Congress on the details of a policy or on secondary policies if it does not really need to. It was apparently on this count that President Truman decided not to go to Congress for an endorsement of the general statement of the Truman Doctrine but only for the specific grant of funds to implement it. The same thing could be said of his action in meeting the Berlin blockade and in deciding to fight in Korea. Congress had supported our participation in the occupation of Berlin by its appropriations, and our endorsement of the collective security provisions of the UN charter by its passage of the United Nations Participation Act. Both were clearly being challenged by the Communists; and the situation in each instance was one of crisis, demanding speed above all. Few administrations will make this mistake of seeking Congressional advice on the minutiae of policy more than once. But in choosing which policies need Congressional support and which do not it is essential to avoid giving the impression that the intention is merely to evade. President Roosevelt, for example, apparently felt that defeat and repudiation were the only possible results of a request to Congress on the destroyers-for-bases deal; but the cost of his independent action in terms of Congressional resentment was very high and unusually persistent.

When the Executive does go to Congress, the manner and timing are vital. Here the most important point revolves around the Executive's monopoly of initiative. The fact of the matter seems to be, as so many observers have remarked, that the system itself is so constituted that policy and the nation flounder if the Executive does not exercise his initiative by anticipating problems and engaging himself in the process of building a consensus among the wider publics early enough for an informed opinion to develop. If he does not do this, there may not be enough general support to overcome resistance to objections to secondary points or to force agreement on an acceptable compromise. Even more frequently, however, the result of a failure to anticipate problems and lay a groundwork in public opinion is that decisive alternatives are killed within the Executive itself on the paradoxical ground that Congress would never support them. Many a military budget, for example, has been fixed at a level far below what Congress could have been brought to support simply because the need for a larger budget was not recognized in time to permit sufficient discussion of the reasons for the need. Another example, of a different kind, was the decision not to intervene in Indochina at the time of Dienbienphu. The decision may well have been entirely sound, but one cannot help suspecting that it went the way it did not on rational grounds, but simply because the very idea of intervention in Indochina was brought up so late and was so new to so many people, within the Executive as well as in Congress, that the initial resistance was too great to overcome in the time available.[15]

The danger of drift, of course, derives as much from the massive power of Congress for obstructing policy, in spite of the weight of advantage on the side of the Executive, as it does from the nature of the consensus-building process. Thus a revolution in the process might be worked if another succession of strong Presidents develops new and better techniques for either evading Congress or manipulating it. Yet the completely nominal role for Congress that would remain at the end of such a revolution could hardly be desirable. In spite of the cynicism of our age it still seems a desirable goal for democracy that the policies of the government be designed to realize the values of the maximum number of people, that those policies work toward the kind of world the maximum number wants. The President, as the representative of all the people, is able to accomplish a great deal towards identifying these preferences, but he is also limited. When he goes to the country in an election, the whole spectrum of government policy is under scrutiny, and his mandate is much too vague to serve as an adequate guide on specific issues. When he goes to the country in a less formal sense, his limited sample of opinion is not likely to capture any more than the grossest outlines of sentiment. Quite clearly, the President's role in this identification of preferences is foremost, but he cannot personally weigh the conflicting desires and their varying intensities in a nation of opinion, and without some other device than the presidency to accomplish an aggregation of views, the preferences served in national policy would probably correspond to those of the mass of the people only intermittently.

The task in adapting democracy to a mass age is also not just the simple one of identifying and expressing the preferences of the bulk of the people. Indeed, the most important function is probably one of interpretation—of identifying achievable goals in foreign policy, say, and relating these in the minds of the mass publics to the basic values of the society. Here, too, the President's role is foremost, especially the act of leadership that shows the different bodies of opinion where in the jumble of events their true interests lie. But he cannot hope to accomplish these purposes of representation and interpretation alone, and some additional device seems mandatory. Traditionally in democracies the device to that end has been the parliament or Congress, and it seems clear that it still has its uses today. Diminishing the role that Congress plays in foreign affairs, in sum, would be more likely to set us back in the task of adapting democracy to our mass age than to further it.

Second to the danger of drift in this peculiar relationship of Congress and the Executive is that of stalemate. If the Executive fails to face up to

[15] See Robert J. Donovan, *Eisenhower: The Inside Story* (New York: Harper & Row, 1956), Ch. 19, *passim;* and Marquis Childs, *Eisenhower: Captive Hero* (New York: Harcourt, Brace, 1958), pp. 201–203.

an issue, he can go on failing to face up to it without anyone being able to do very much to change matters. If he weds himself to a short-sighted or even wrong-headed policy, the only formal power that Congress has any chance of exercising is that of stalling policy entirely.

There are, of course, procedures within the executive branch by which established policies are challenged and alternatives put forward, including the consensus-building process. There are also ways in this process by which outside groups may inject ideas into the system. But is this machinery adequate to the burdens likely to be placed upon it? Foreign policy in our day must meet a staccato series of new problems and issues. On the one hand are the rapid shifts in political context likely to result from both Communist aggressiveness and the rise of the Afro-asians. On the other hand, there are the effects on both the modes and structure of international relations of technological change and the nuclear revolution in military strategy. Considering the requirements these developments will place on the policy-making machinery, one cannot help being uneasy at the thought that alternative policies can be considered only by the grace of executive officials or only as a result of indirect pressures on them through the consensus-building process.

If Congress is handicapped in terms of information, time and staff, in developing alternative policies as well as in the power to enforce them, is not the one method that Congress does have for raising new problems and for presenting the case for alternative policies—the consensus-building process itself—in danger? Without Congress playing a more positive role in debating the complex problems of foreign and military policy, will the attentive and participating audiences outside the Executive have any opportunity to know, much less to understand the alternatives, or, indeed, any choice at all other than accepting or rejecting a single proposal? What also happens to the traditional role of expressing the people's preferences and of interpreting policies to the people in terms of their preferences? Can representative democracy really be adapted to a mass, technological society if Congress does not have the necessary machinery and means for exploring alternative policies and introducing them into the process more decisively than it now does?

One may doubt that it can, but at the same time providing Congress with any formal machinery for developing policy would be a formidable task. Indeed, after reflection on the lack of party discipline in the American system, the nature of Congressional responsibilities, and other aspects of Congressional method and structure, the conclusion may well be that it is an impossible one. As a basic proposition, in other words, it seems wise to assume that no radical change in either the form of our government or in the powers of the different branches is practicable. Even if we could be sure the proposed reform was desirable, the suspicion and distrust an attempt to rearrange things would generate, the uncertainties of the period of adjustment in which each side tested its new authorities, would all be much too disruptive to tolerate for a nation facing external threats. The only way of meeting the evolutionary changes in the situation, in sum, would seem to be with an evolutionary counter, developed within the present framework.

The heart of the difficulty probably lies in the technicality of foreign and military policy today and the limited knowledge about its problems, as well as in the difficulty of bringing research and new additions to knowledge into the policy-making process.[16] When knowledge, the ability to predict the consequences of action, is inadequate, intelligent choice will necessarily turn on the weighting to be given the different possible effects of means— means that are highly technical and as yet only partly understood. Even in an ideal society without barriers to full discussion, debates on foreign policy today would probably center more on disagreements among specialists about the suitability of means for accomplishing goals than on competition between mass publics about the goals themselves. Indeed, when goals are the subject of discussion the question would normally be whether the instrumentalities available were sufficient to accomplish a certain goal, and, if not, whether we would not be wiser to content ourselves with a more modest goal. The likely alternatives would be, on the one hand, a policy that had an uncertain chance of accomplishing a very desirable goal, and, on the other, a policy that would more surely accomplish one that is some-what less desirable. The choice would present itself in terms of the degree of risk to be shouldered, and would depend on a rather intimate understanding of the technical problems that define and clarify that risk.

If it is correct to say that much of the debate on foreign and military policy must necessarily concern technical problems, then one possible approach would seem to lie in providing Congressmen with greater access to specialist assistance. This might make the Congressman's task easier, but probably only modest improvement in the quality of foreign policy could be expected from it. Too much of the difficulty does not lie in Congress at all.

The same technicality of foreign policy today also raises doubts about the wisdom of some efforts in citizen education [17] and of the long-standing advocacy by some political scientists of a greater party responsibility, and other reforms inspired by the parliamentary system that would help give the electorate a clear choice between alternative policies. The electorate might go right on behaving as it does now and policy making might then continue to be much the same, in some circumstances a monopoly to the

---

[16] For an attempt to examine the role that research might play in the making of foreign policy decisions, see Ch. 8, "Knowledge and Action," of my *Strategic Intelligence and National Decisions,* already cited.

[17] The phrase is Bernard C. Cohen's; see his *Citizen Education in World Affairs* (Princeton, 1953).

President and his immediate entourage, and in others permitting the participation of attentive audiences in something similar to the process of consensus-building. If so, the goals of democracy might be better served by improving the consensus building process itself, both in its accessibility to potential participants and in the means and procedures by which the participants communicate.

For this we need more details on how the process works. What kinds of people participate in what kinds of foreign policy decisions? What are the different ways of becoming a participant? Is there a small core—a super-elite—that participates in all types of decisions? If not, who coordinates the policies in different fields, or is there no significant coordination? What functions do the different groups of participants perform? Who originates ideas; who vetoes, who aggregates alternatives? Which kinds of policies require a wide consensus and which a very narrow one, and what implications do these differences hold for traditional democratic theory?

With a greater knowledge of how the system really works, we might be in a better position to reconcile the classic goals of democratic thought to conditions in a mass age. The most promising course, in sum, may lie neither in tinkering with structure and organization nor in developing an elite of philosopher-politicians from which to draw candidates for Congress, but at this entirely different level of attempting to understand the subtleties of the system in which national policy is made and of accommodating ourselves to the opportunities it presents.

IV

The Executive Establishment

INTRODUCTION

IN introducing the collection of essays on Congress we observed that Congress' involvement in the formulation of foreign policy varied with the kind of policy decision appropriate to a particular situation, and that, indeed, in some kinds of policy decisions it was hardly involved at all in the sense of determining policy choices. Accordingly, we noted that our progression from "public opinion," to "nongovernmental groups," to "the press," and then to Congress and executive-legislative relations was, in a sense, a movement from the periphery to the center of policy-making. The "center" is the "Executive Establishment."

If Congress and other groups and institutions are involved in different ways with different kinds of decisions, the involvement and participation of the Executive is ubiquitous. More than any area of governmental action, foreign policy is within the peculiar province of the Executive branch.

There are many reasons—technical and political—for this Executive ascendancy. Many of these have been explored in the preceding section on Congress, so there is no need to repeat them here. However, while recognizing the fact of Executive primacy, let us also recognize some limitations on the imagery this implies about the nature of the Executive and Executive power. For in articulating the inherent weaknesses of the legislative branch in this field, specifying its diffuse power structure and its slow, deliberative, ponderous processes of making up its mind, we tend simultaneously to think of *the* Executive as highly structured, hierarchical, endowed with a great capacity to act and to decide. But *the Executive* is an extraordinarily complex arrangement of departments, agencies, bureaus, commissions, committees, and other groups. The President is only *one* man and the Executive Branch is too large, too complex, and is composed of too many complementary and competing sources of influence for it to be under his effective supervision in all instances.

Nevertheless, as provided in Article II of the Constitution, the executive power is formally invested in one man, the President, and this is a vital difference. It is not easily done, but if the President has the necessary drive, skill, and imagination he can imprint his own style upon the Executive machinery and invest it with an over-all sense of purpose and direction.

The problem of orchestrating so many instruments into a coherent, efficiently operating system is not peculiar to the foreign policy sector of the spectrum of public policy. It cuts across all policy sectors. It is not even unique to the present era. It has become so critical in the complex and chaotic environment of the post-World War I era, however, that extensive structural changes have occurred in the Executive branch directed toward infusing a greater degree of rationality and system into the tasks of policy planning, coordination and execution. This rationalization and systematization had a significant beginning with the passage of the Budget and Accounting Act of 1921, but it took on new emphasis in the depression years of the 1930's as government responsibilities and agencies multiplied. It was summed up in the words of the Brownlow Committee (the President's Committee on Administrative Management) in 1937: "The President needs help."

But the activity of the 1930's in providing the President with help, in the White House Office, the Executive Office of the President, and in organizational changes in the Executive Branch itself, was primarily oriented toward domestic policy. As the United States moved closer to world-wide involvement in the global conflict that began in September 1939, and then went to war in December 1941, changes in the policy-making process were chiefly on the basis of improvisation. There was a State-War-Navy Committee, made up of the secretaries of those departments, and there was a War Resources Board. But these groups had little to do, as such, and were not really working bodies for the planning and coordination of policy. Indeed, there were sharp differences about the entire orientation of policy within these groups, and within other executive agencies.

From the summer of 1940 until Pearl Harbor, for example, one of the most critical problems persistently before American officialdom was that of providing military and economic aid to Britain and her allies. Initially this was a task largely in the hands of the Secretary of the Treasury, Henry Morgenthau, and his aides. Treasury, not State, drafted the Lend-Lease Bill, which pledged all-out U.S. assistance to Britain, and the direction of that vital program was first turned over to a Division of Defense Aid Reports in the Office of Emergency Management in the Executive Office. During 1941, and then during the war years, the principal civilian aid to the President, in Lend-Lease and all other matters central to the war effort, and his most important emissary and most influential adviser, was Harry

Hopkins. Hopkins held no Cabinet rank—he was an "Assistant to the President." Military matters were in the hands of the Joint Chiefs of Staff, a body which did not then even have statutory existence but which was called into being by virtue of necessity.

It must be pointed out that the structure and processes of policy-making which developed during the World War II era were in part the product of the kinds of internal political constraints under which the President and his closest advisers worked, especially before Pearl Harbor, and in part of the personal preferences and "style" of the President. Even when these considerations are accounted for, however, it remains a fact that the American Government was not "organized" for the demands that world leadership imposed upon it, and that it was compelled to improvise and to create an *ad hoc* system to operate in such a situation.

Long before the end of the war, it was recognized that the United States would necessarily play a much larger "peacetime" role in world affairs, and that it could never again retire into an isolationist corner and watch the rest of the world go by. If there had been any serious doubts about this, the dawn of the nuclear age in the closing days of the war ended them. So far as strengthening the organization of the government for more effective operations in this larger world role, however, the activity of the war years was almost exclusively directed toward reorganization of the military services—specifically, toward the "unification" of the armed forces. Planning for organizational change in the area of foreign affairs was directed toward international institutions in which the United States would participate—the United Nations, the "specialized agencies," and the Hemispheric organizations. Two lines of development gave both these ventures new emphases and direction in the immediate postwar environment.

The first development was the onset of cold war, instead of a hoped-for era of international cooperation and stability in which the Grand Alliance would continue to function through new, more elaborate, and more comprehensive institutional arrangements. The "concurrent revolutions" sketched earlier began to be perceived—not by any means fully, for they are only imperfectly perceived even now. Nevertheless, there was a recognition that instability and conflict, and new threats to American and Western security, were pressing issues and challenges which had to be faced.

The second development was the expansion of the debate over the "unification" of the armed forces to include considerations broader than the military aspects of national security. This was partially an unintended result of the Navy Department's resistance to the unifications plans of the Army and the Army Air Force (already virtually autonomous), which left the Navy in the position of needing to put forward alternative proposals of its own. But beyond this, Secretary of the Navy Forrestal, many of his advisers, and other officials who remembered the war experiences, believed strongly that the problem of "getting organized" was a question that went beyond service unification. The upshot was a report which laid the basis for the National Security Act of 1947. This statute provided for unification of the services (in name, at least), created the Central Intelligence Agency, established an agency for economic mobilization (initially, the National Security Resources Board), and provided other new arrangements. For our purposes here, its most important sections were those creating the National Security Council, charging it with the responsibility of "effectively coordinating the policies and functions of the departments and agencies of the Government relating to the national security," as directed by the President.[1] NSC was provided with a staff, though it was not a staff agency as such. It was—and is—an interdepartmental committee of the operating heads of line departments, for the most part, whose functions relate most immediately to questions of foreign policy and national security.

NSC has many defects and failings. As a committee, it has inherent weaknesses. Critics can easily say that a committee does not offer a creative environment, and that one so composed as NSC will tend to compromise departmental differences. Further, it has been pointed out that NSC was modeled after the British War Cabinet in some vital respects, and that this institution, while very effective in the British system, is not compatible with a presidential system. All of these observations are true, as far as they go. Nevertheless, NSC provides that capability for coordination—for orchestrating the various elements of policy at the highest levels—which is essential when a nation's affairs throughout the world are as complex and involved as are those of the United States. Perhaps even more important, however, has been the symbolic significance of the NSC. However effective or ineffective in practice, it represents a clear beginning to the American effort to organize its government for meeting the demands of world leadership.

As this process of reorganization has proceeded, one further trend should be noted as a prelude to the essays which follow on the "Executive Establishment." That is the sustained effort to strengthen the Department of State and to restore the Secretary of State to a position of primacy as foreign policy adviser to the President.

Certainly the State Department approached the nadir of its fortunes in the World War II era. For many reasons, the President did not utilize State as the key agency of foreign policy, except in the planning and negotiation of postwar international organizations, and its position worsened through the war years. It was not prepared for the demands of war and world leadership, and both the Department and the Foreign

---

1 See below for a fuller statement of the Council's responsibilities.

Service have been extensively "overhauled" since 1945. Moreover, the position of the Secretary of State has come very far indeed from its low estate in 1941–45. The role of an Acheson or a Dulles contrasts vividly with that of Hull.

The Department of State has long been a favorite target of political criticism, and it has never had the kind of domestic political support that the Department of Defense has, for example. Despite this, practitioners and academicians in international affairs have insisted upon its central role in foreign policy, next to the President, and in the main that viewpoint has prevailed. A president must be left with freedom to organize his administration in ways appropriate to his preferences and policy priorities, but strengthening State and the Executive machinery is not really antithetical to that need for flexibility. The President may need his "Hopkins" from time to time, but a nation with great international obligations and responsibilities needs a central office for direction of its external affairs. State is that office. Only such a central office provides the institutional expertise, experience, and continuity that is required.

Our approach, in selecting the essays that follow, has not been predicated on describing the institutional complex of foreign policy-making in any detailed way. Instead we have focused upon certain key officials and institutions, their interrelationships, and the general nature of the structure within which they work. In addition, we have extracted three functional areas that are of particular significance, for consideration in this examination of the process of policy-making: the policy planning function, the budgetary element, and the new role of science and research in policy-making. This approach, the editors hope, will provide a generalized description of the policy process not related to the specifics of departmental and agency structure and organization, for these are always subject to change. Our aim has been to depict a process, as it has developed within a structure now deeply embedded in the American political system.

The President and the Secretary of State

ADMINISTRATION OF NATIONAL SECURITY: BASIC ISSUES

I. The President's Problem

> The other point is something that President Eisenhower said to me on January 19, 1961. He said, "There are no easy matters that will ever come to you as President. If they are easy, they will be settled at a lower level." So that the matters that come to you as President are always the difficult matters, and matters that carry with them large implications.
>
> PRESIDENT JOHN F. KENNEDY, telecast interview, December 17, 1962

BY law and practice the President is the chief maker of national security policy. He conducts foreign affairs. He is Commander in Chief of the Armed Forces. He makes the crucial decisions on the budget he submits to Congress. He is the Nation's Chief Executive, responsible under the Constitution for taking care that the laws are faithfully executed. As such, he supervises the departments and agencies. Although he is not in any simple sense their manager—for their responsibilities run not only to him but also to Congress—he is the only coordinator our constitutional system provides.

The new complexities of national security make the task of a President more difficult today than ever before.

The boundary between foreign and domestic policy has almost been erased. Foreign policy, military policy, and economic policy are now intimately linked. The United States has relations with over 100 countries, mutual defense treaties with over 40, and participates in scores of regional and international organizations. Policy must be made and executed in the context of fast-moving and world-shaking events—the deadly contest with, and perhaps within, the Communist world, the building of new structures in the free world, the emergence into statehood of new nations with great

FROM the staff report submitted by the Subcommittee on National Security Staffing and Operations to the Senate Committee on Government Operations, January 18, 1963.

expectations and greater problems, and advancing technologies that may upset the balances of power.

A President must look to the national security departments and agencies for help in initiating and carrying out national policy. The Departments of State and Defense, the military services, and related agencies at home and in the field are for the most part staffed with experienced, capable, and dedicated people. They are a vast storehouse of information, historical perspective, skills, and resources.

But these assets are not automatically available to a President. He must know how to put them to work in planning and executing national security operations—how to make them serve his needs while they carry on the important tasks that cannot receive his attention. The art of administration is to staff and organize for this purpose.

The very size of the national security organization is one of the problems. It is too big for any one man to know all about it. It is so big that unusual astuteness and knowledge are required to draw on it.

Congress, of course, influences national policy and sets limits within which a President can act. It creates departments and agencies; it authorizes programs; it influences the size and composition of the Armed Forces and the nature of aid and information and related policies; it appropriates funds for the conduct of national security policies; the laws it passes affect the Government's ability to hire and hold good people; its attitudes reflect the American people's understanding of national security problems and their willingness to support national security programs.

On the whole, the United States has adjusted quickly to the shifting demands of a world in change. But the process of adjustment has only begun and success is not assured. Many emotionally charged areas must be realistically examined and calmly appraised.

If the Nation is to pass the tests that lie ahead, the Presidency and State and Defense and the other national security agencies must handle their jobs with new excellence. And Congress, too.

II. Dilemmas of Administration

> . . . it is at this point that we run head first into the system of "checks and balances" as it applies to the executive departments.
> . . . This is really a method of requiring power to be shared—even though responsibility may not be—and of introducing rival claimants from another department with a different mission into the policymaking or decision-taking process.
> This is the "foulup factor" in our methods . . .
> Whether or not this itch to get in the act is a form of status seeking, the idea seems to have got around that just because some decision may affect your activities, you automatically have a right to take part in making it . . . there is some reason to feel that the doctrine may be getting out of hand and that what was designed to act as a policeman may, in fact, become a jailer.
>
> ROBERT A. LOVETT, statement before the Senate Subcommittee on National Policy Machinery, February 23, 1960

Argument between conflicting interests and views is healthy—indeed indispensable—if kept within reasonable bounds. But it may be carried too far and create what Robert Lovett has called the "foulup factor."

A continuing Presidential dilemma is whom to listen to, and how much, before he moves.

One can appreciate a President's desire to let advisers have their say, and to hear as much as possible before committing himself. Yet it may be best to err on the side of small groups of responsible officers and to avoid large free-for-all sessions which are as likely to confuse as to clarify the choices he faces.

The President and the National Security Organization

The needs of a President and the needs of the departments and agencies are not identical—and herein lies a source of administrative difficulties and misunderstanding.

What does a President need to do his job?

Essentially he wants to keep control of the situation—to get early warning of items for his agenda before his options are foreclosed, to pick his issues and lift these out of normal channels, to obtain priority attention from key officials on the issues he pulls to his desk, to get prompt support for his initiatives, and to keep other matters on a smooth course, with his lines of information open, so that he can intervene if a need arises.

As top officials meet the President's urgent requirements, their other duties necessarily receive lower priority. Their regular meetings are canceled. They become less accessible to their subordinates. Ad hoc procedures are devised. Much is done verbally that would normally be put in writing. This all becomes exceedingly hard on subordinate officials, for it interferes with their handling of the usual run of business.

What do the officials of our vast departments and agencies need to do their job?

Essentially they want orderly, deliberate, familiar procedures—accustomed forums in which to air their interests, a top-level umpire to blow the whistle when the time has come to end debate, and written records of the decisions by which they should be governed.

It is no secret that the abolition of the Operations Coordinating Board came as a disappointment to many at the middle levels of government, who found in it a way of getting within hailing distance of the center of power. Vocal status seeking is one of the curses of government and increases the "foulup factor." But middle-level yearnings for some equivalent of the OCB involve more than status only. They have their origin in the desire to have one's views heard through some set, certain, reliable procedure which binds the highest levels as well as other agencies.

It is worth recalling that the National Security Council was chiefly the inspiration of James Forrestal, who wanted to enhance the defense role in peacetime policymaking and especially to insure regular consultation by future Presidents with their principal civilian and military advisers. The purpose was at least as much to make the Presidency serve the needs of the departments as to make the latter serve the former.

It is not surprising that the departments often find a President's way of doing business unsettling—or that Presidents sometimes view the departments almost as adversaries.

A continuing dilemma, demanding a subtle appreciation on all sides of the needs of a President and the departments, is how to manage the Government so that Presidential business is transacted to his satisfaction, and so that the normal run of business, also vital to the national interest, can be transacted in a fashion suited to the needs of large scale organization.

Decision at the Center and Delegation

A President can make only the smallest fraction of the total number of decisions relating to national security. His are the guiding or directional decisions, but millions of supporting operational decisions, and associated actions, must be taken by men in the long lines radiating from the White House through the headquarters of the national security agencies to officers in posts throughout the Nation and the world.

Delegation is therefore not merely desirable; it is unavoidable. It is the way an organization gets the day's work done.

Clearly, however, there are powerful forces which push and pull issues to the President's desk and make decentralization difficult.

First, Washington is the center of power and the center has a strong magnetic attraction, especially in a period remarkable for its ease of travel and communication. Because issues can be referred to Washington by radio, cable, and airmail, they are. Because embassy officials can travel to Washington and Washington officials can travel to the field, they do. Foreigners are also attracted, and visits to Washington by heads of state, prime ministers, foreign ministers, and others are increasingly popular. The visitors tend to bring issues with them for decision—because they want to take home some good news.

Second, issues seldom present themselves nowadays as one-department or one-country problems. But Washington is organized into departments and the field into country missions and this pushes decision-making and operations coordination toward the White House. Only the President stands above all departments and agencies and only he and his principal lieutenants can see the problems of a country or a region in the perspective of national policy as a whole.

Third, history records a number of instances in which delegated authority was used unwisely, sometimes with serious consequences.

Fourth, the higher that issues are pulled for decision, the greater the chance that the pressure of special interests can be resisted, that irrelevant considerations will be screened out, and that material considerations will be properly weighed.

Fifth, and perhaps most important, in a period when war or peace may hinge on the way in which a quarantine of Cuba is handled, there is a strong tendency for a President to exert control from the center, because of the risks of leaving delicate matters to subordinates. It scarcely is an accident that one characteristic of the second Cuban crisis, perhaps in response to lessons learned from the first, was tight, detailed control from the Cabinet room over a host of subordinate operations.

Yet delegation of the right issues with appropriate guidance to able subordinates is of critical importance. The Nation's security depends not only on a President's skill in handling crises and major issues but also on the steady and competent handling of less vital matters by the department chiefs and the national security organization as a whole.

Without successful delegation, problems will pile up on the President's desk and the talents of key officials in Washington and the field will be underemployed. More important, too much of a President's time and energy will be dissipated on matters of less than first priority.

The key to delegation is a clear and reasoned basic policy line authoritatively stated to department and agency heads—and defining as part of the decision itself the priority the policy is to receive. Understanding, more than command, is the secret of successful teamwork.

In our system, two men have the chief responsibility for providing this guidance—the President and his first adviser, the Secretary of State. And to get the job done, the relation of the President and the Secretary of State has to be close, marked by solid mutual respect.

But even with ideal relations between these two, the objective of clear and reasoned policy guidance will be hard to reach and hold. For the nature of concrete policy issues and the character of governmental action processes push for a pragmatic one-thing-at-a-time-on-its-own-terms approach.

Planning and Action

A President is concerned with fires and firefighting, and as with fire chiefs everywhere, firefighting has to have priority.

In many ways it is easier, though more nerve racking, to fight fires than to take steps to prevent them. The Government functions best under pressure. When the alarm bell rings, its ponderous machinery begins to move. A task force can be assembled and used to mobilize the resources of the departments and agencies for the job at hand.

But planning in order to stop trouble before it starts is more difficult, in part because it is hard for top officers to give it their attention and in part because of confusion about the nature and purpose of planning. It is not an ivory tower activity, which can be carried on, as some have proposed, far from the hurly-burly of Washington, although it may draw on the ideas of men working at the frontiers of knowledge.

Planning is critically dependent on the unplannable flashes of insight which are usually sparked by worrying and wrestling with actual problems.

The European Recovery Program was not dreamed up on a campus, though it was announced on one. It was the product of the interplay of minds between Marshall, Lovett, Clayton, Acheson, and President Truman, who saw what was happening in Europe and were searching for ways to reverse the trend of events.

The object of planning is not to blueprint future actions—although there may be a limited utility in so-called contingency planning, or thinking of the "what-would-we-do-if" variety.

The object is to decide what should be done now in light of the best present estimate of how the future will look. Planners think about the future in order to act wisely in the present.

Seen in this way, every action is explicitly or implicitly the fruit of planning. One move is chosen in preference to another because its anticipated consequences are preferred. The distinction between the planner and the operator has been overdrawn. If there is one, it is less in the time span with which each is concerned than with the narrowness or breadth of their perspectives. The Air Force or the Navy or the Army looks to the future when it advises on weapons systems, but its perspective is narrower, more nearly that of a special pleader, than the perspective of the President, the Secretary of State, and the Secretary of Defense when they, also looking ahead, consider one weapons system in relation to a total defense system and the latter in turn as one component of a total strategy for the defense and advancement of national interests.

It is because of the need for wide perspectives and for fitting the part into the whole that a President and his key advisers have essential roles to play in long-term planning. But this activity competes for their time—on unfavorable terms—with planning and action to meet the crises of the day. Who could concentrate on Laos and Cambodia in relation to South Vietnam, or on the Common Market in relation to NATO, when Cuba threatened to engulf the world in flames?

A continuing administrative problem, which every administration has had to face and none has wholly solved, is how to fit what might be called trouble-avoidance planning into days crowded with crisis-coping plans and operations. There has been a tendency to think that the first could be entrusted to planning councils or boards of one kind or another or perhaps even to "think groups"—and such organizations may make useful contributions. But not the whole contribution, for in the final analysis, a top executive must do his own planning. Otherwise, he will not be truly committed in his own mind to plans that may bear his signature.

One is reminded that the National Security Council study known as NSC 68 was little more than a paper plan until it was ratified in the President's mind by the movement of North Korean troops across the 38th parallel.

III. The President, the Secretary of State, and the Problem of Coordination

> President Kennedy "has made it very clear that he does not want a large separate organization between him and his Secretary of State. Neither does he wish any question to arise as to the clear authority and responsibility of the Secretary of State, not only in his own Department, and not only in such large-scale related areas as foreign aid and information policy, but also as the agent of coordination in all our major policies toward other nations."
>
> McGeorge Bundy, Special Assistant to the President for National Security Affairs, letter to Senator Henry M. Jackson, September 4, 1961

The Office of the Presidency is the only place in which departmental lines of decision and action converge. As a result a President can rarely look to one man or one department for advice and assistance on any major matter and must act as his own Secretary for National Security Affairs. But he cannot do the job alone.

In this fact lies the problem of coordinating national security policy and operations. The budgetary process offers the President unique assistance in controlling the size and composition of the armed services and the size and nature of aid and related programs, and in assigning priorities in the use of resources. But the budgetary process is of little relevance to the day-to-day coordination of national security operations. The President's Special Assistant for National Security Affairs can help to keep the President informed about matters that may require his attention and see that he is staffed on issues that he takes into his own hands. With the help of his Office, therefore, the President can coordinate policy and operations—to the extent that he can take command. But when, considering the wise use of his time, he cannot perform the coordinating role or chooses not to do it, who can? The answer is that no one can but someone must.

The Secretary of State's Coordinating Role

A key question is the proper role of the Secretary of State.

Subject to a President's direction, his Secretary of State is charged with responsibility for overseeing the conduct of all aspects of the Nation's relations with other states. In this broad area his interests, though not his authority, are coextensive with the President's.

The Secretary is the President's principal adviser with respect to economic and military aid, cultural and information programs, and policies for the reduction and control of arms, as well as diplomacy, and the President's agent for coordinating all these elements of foreign policy.

But he is not the President's principal adviser on defense policy, and it is the skillful merger of defense and foreign policies that one has particularly in mind when speaking of national security policy.

Yet if planning and operations are to be coordinated, they must be coordinated by someone. And someone is a singular word.

The logical choice for this well-nigh impossible task is the Secretary of State. Of the Cabinet, only a Secretary of State is primarily charged with looking at the Nation as a whole in relation to the world. The nature of his post leads him, more than any other Cabinet officer, to have a perspective closely approximating the President's.

But to have a fighting chance of success, a Secretary will have to command unusual confidence and support of a President. Indeed, the attitude of a President toward his Secretary of State can determine whether he will be a great Secretary. When a President is close to him, confides in him, and relies on him, the Secretary has a chance. A President will have to be reluctant to intervene in those matters he has put into his Secretary's hands, for if another Cabinet officer can frequently obtain Presidential satisfaction when he is disappointed, the Secretary will not be able to do the job a President needs done.

By the same token, a Secretary must be willing to assert his own position and exercise his proper influence across the whole front of national security matters, as they relate to foreign policy. He should also, of course, be quick to refer matters to the President when his decision is needed.

All this depends therefore on a special relationship of trust and easy understanding between a President and his Secretary of State. Given this, a Secretary will seldom have difficulty in working with a Secretary of Defense and will be able to assist his chief in coordinating plans and operations for national security.

A question of importance is whether the Department of State, and particularly the Office of the Secretary, is staffed and organized to support the Secretary in exercising this responsibility. A complicating factor is that the responsibilities of the Secretary are wider than those of his Department.

One hears a good deal these days about organizing the Secretary's office around action-forcing processes. Much of the talk, however, centers on analogies that are not necessarily apt.

The foreign affairs budget, for example, does not provide the same leverage for the coordination of foreign policies that the defense budget provides the Secretary of Defense. Although a Comptroller for Foreign Affairs would therefore not be able to serve the Secretary of State as the Comptroller of Defense serves the Secretary of Defense, the possibility of using budgetary control as a coordinating device might well be studied.

Some have drawn an analogy to the Joint Chiefs of Staff. But although the Secretary of State, the Administrator of AID, the Director of USIA, and the Director of the Arms Control and Disarmament Agency might coordinate foreign policies as the JCS coordinates military policies, they could not integrate defense and foreign policies.

What are the action-forcing processes that might be more effectively employed? Two suggest themselves: the preparation of recommendations for the President on national security policies and the sending of instructions to U.S. missions and military commanders overseas.

In the early days of the National Security Council the Secretary of State acted as chairman whenever the President did not take the chair, and was responsible for preparing recommendations to the President. One proposal is that this arrangement might be reestablished—and applied also in any Executive Committee of the NSC.

Another proposal relates directly to the coordination of defense and foreign policy. It is that better means should be found to insure that instructions to U.S. missions and military commanders overseas are consistent, are issued in such a way as to have the authority of the President behind them, and are known to, and binding upon, all departments and agencies concerned. This might call for a review of all outgoing messages by an appropriate staff.

A third proposal is that the Secretary of State should play the key role in the management of interagency task forces which are not led by the President himself, and that his office should be staffed to handle their management.

The Interagency Task Force

The present administration has made much use of the interagency task force as a device for the day-to-day handling of complex and critical operations.

The Berlin task force is an interagency group whose members have major responsibilities in their departments for the kinds of operations which might be used to meet the crisis. It is chaired by State (originally by Defense) and reports to the President through the Secretary of State. It is concerned with ongoing planning and operations for the maintenance of the Western position in Berlin, including the coordination of American policy and action with the major European allies and with NATO.

The Counterinsurgency task force is chaired by State (originally by the President's military representative) and reports to the President through the Secretary of State. It is concerned with planning and operations to prepare the United States for intensified warfare where conventional military forces and operations are not the full answer.

Recently the Executive Committee of the NSC, with the President himself in active command of planning and operations, was in effect a task force for the Cuban crisis.

An interagency task force is therefore an interdepartmental coordinating committee. It is a flexible device, participation in which can be adjusted to the needs of the situation. It may bring together the highest officers of the Government or officers at the second or third level in the departments involved. For the time being they give overriding or even exclusive priority to the task at hand.

At the same time, every improvisation, such as the creation of a Berlin task force or an executive committee of the NSC, is an acknowledgment that existing ways of doing business have proved inadequate, and that the President has had to spend time devising ad hoc methods of making and executing policy.

The task force differs from the usual interdepartmental committee in that it has a specific, limited job of great interest to the President and goes out of active existence when the job is done, is action-oriented, and puts a strong chairman—in some cases the President himself—over strong members who can get things done in their departments.

Superficially the interagency task force seems to provide the answer to the problem of coordination, at least for critical issues. But the experience—touched on here—has been mixed. Some have been successful; others have been disappointing. The record is extensive enough so that it should be possible to find out why one works but not another.

It may be worth asking how a task force can be prevented from becoming just another interdepartmental committee, with a production of paper inversely proportional to its influence. Is one requirement that there be strong Presidential interest in its work? Should a place at the table go only to responsible officers of departments and agencies which have genuine authority and responsibility for executive operations? Should the task force chairman be an Assistant Secretary of State or higher ranking officer who enjoys the confident trust of the Secretary of State and the President and has access to them? At what point does the membership of a task force grow too large?

Also, it is worth asking what would have happened if the Executive Committee of the NSC had had to maintain the pace of the Cuban crisis for 2 or 3 more weeks, with other important issues piling up, and a whole new system of Executive Committee subcommittees beginning to blanket the executive branch.

It would be folly to conceive a government in which every interagency task was assigned to a special force. On the other hand, a satisfactory scheme of organization will surely provide something like task forces to deal with certain problems that do not fit tidily within departmental jurisdictions.

Dean Acheson

THE PRESIDENT AND THE SECRETARY OF STATE

I<small>F</small>, as Justice Holmes has said, in the life of the law a page of history is worth a volume of logic, it seems likely that in what is called political science these pages of history may be worth as many volumes of theory. At least it gives us a fairly solid point from which to start our discussion of the desirable relations between the President and his senior Secretary.

That point might be put this way: it is highly desirable that from first to last both parties to the relationship understand which is the President. Without this mutual understanding a successful relationship is most unlikely.

This does not mean subserviency on the part of the Secretary. In a much more hazardous age Lord Burghley saw and did his duty of standing squarely up to the great Queen when her interests and those of the realm required it. Much else, as we shall see, should rest upon this cornerstone of the relationship, the recognition of primacy. It is enough here to mention two mutual obligations. One, of course, is the Secretary's duty to see that the President is kept fully and timely informed so that he may perform his constitutional duty of conducting the nation's foreign relations with all the freedom of decision which each situation permits. The correlative obligation is that the President should perform his function of decision so clearly, and support his decisions so strongly, that action may flow from them. . . .

The Nature of Foreign Relations

The nature of an undertaking must obviously have a great bearing on the desirable relations between those who are directing it. Running a battleship is different from running a bank and calls for differences in the relations between the top men. Two factors make the nature of the problems of our

F R O M *The Secretary of State,* ed. Don. K. Price. © 1960, by the American Assembly, Columbia University, N.Y. By permission of Prentice-Hall, Inc., Englewood Cliffs, New Jersey.

foreign relations quite different from those existing, say, in agriculture, finance, or the administration of justice.

First of all, we are dealing with people and with geographical areas which are beyond our jurisdiction and control. Within our borders our government may command. Beyond them it cannot. In the second place, what is occurring in what the Supreme Court has called "that vast external realm," is so complex, so complicated, and so voluminous that we cannot currently comprehend it; nor, until too much time has elapsed, grasp its full significance. This is not wholly, or even principally, because of man-made impediments to knowledge—iron curtains, censorship, etc.—but because of the obscurity and complexity of the molecular changes which combine to bring about the growth or decay of power, will, and purpose in foreign lands. While it was reasonable to suppose that changes in the relative power of European states had occurred in the four or five decades before Sarajevo, not even the First World War wholly revealed how great they were. The façades of vanished power, including our own, still deceive us. Even yet our understanding of this changing world is far behind the fact.

This means that the basic problems of our foreign relations are those of understanding the true nature, dimensions, and immediacy of the problems which confront us from abroad and of putting in train the measures with which to meet them. These problems are particularly hard for Americans to keep in focus. Townsend Hoopes writes: [1]

> Our difficulty is that, as a nation of short-term pragmatists accustomed to dealing with the future only when it has become the present, we find it hard to regard future trends as serious realities. We have not achieved the capacity to treat as real and urgent—as demanding action today—problems which appear in critical dimension only at some future date. Yet failure to achieve this new habit of mind is likely to prove fatal.

Years ago, when I was about to assume sobering responsibilities, an old lady expressed the short-term pragmatic view when she said to me, "Always remember that the future comes one day at a time." This was heartening and wise advice. At times one must live by this faith with thanksgiving. But, like most wise sayings, it is not the totality of wisdom. While it is true that the problems of the voyage come to the mariner day by day, it is essential to his success, and perhaps survival, that he knows where he is going, keep on course, and also use all the knowledge at his disposal to learn what forces are building up around him and to prepare, as best he may, for what lies ahead.

Foreign policy is not a book of answers. Our foreign policies—for many are needed—should be inter-connected courses of action adopted and followed to meet external conditions confronting us. The action of others

[1] Quoted by permission. *Yale Review*, Spring 1960. Copyright Yale University Press.

beyond our borders can rarely be exactly predicted, and may take us by surprise. But these actions may be modified greatly in our interest if our courses of action have been founded on correct analyses of conditions and have been vigorously followed. Should we still be surprised by acts hostile to us, we can act more effectively to counter them if our policies have given us the capability of doing so.

At the heart, therefore, of the conduct of our foreign relations, a task confided to the President, lies this primary task of understanding the forces at work abroad, and devising, adopting, and energetically following courses of action to affect or meet these forces. Important as other essential tasks may be, it is this one which should most color the relations between the two men principally involved with it, and hence the President's judgment in choosing his foreign secretary.

One can see at a glance that if these two men are going to do their work properly they have got to spend a lot of time together, much of which may not be pleasant. The problems are frustrating. They are sure to provoke controversy in many quarters. Most of the desirable measures are distasteful to accept. All of the decisions are hard. So the Secretary of State has the makings of an unwelcome visitor. But for the President to delegate the functions of understanding and deciding is to delegate his office. The worst of all courses would be for the President to delegate the function of understanding to some super staff officer and retain the function of deciding, or apparently deciding, for himself.

So, to get the job done and to have the relationship successful needs solid mutual respect, based upon conviction by each that the other is wholly straightforward, loyal, and living up to his full obligation. It helps enormously to maintain mutual confidence if there is a strong admixture of affection between them; for in Washington they are working in an environment where some of the methods would have aroused the envy of the Borgias. . . .

The Secretary's Working Relations with the President

Here, again, everything depends on the temperament and character of the men involved. But one can note certain recurring circumstances. President-elect Harrison wrote, and then struck out, in his letter to Mr. Blaine a reference to "my lack of study and experience in foreign affairs." He was a perceptive and truthful man; but the presidential instinct prevailed. In 1960 an unusual number of the aspirants to the White House have had some exposure to foreign affairs through study and travel. This will doubtless fortify a conviction of competence in foreign affairs which soon comes to a President and to his personal staff, often outrunning the fact.

This is not peculiar to Presidents. To columnists, correspondents, legislators, some academicians, and most New York lawyers over forty, foreign affairs are an open book, though they often differ on the meaning of the text. Their opinions are available to the President directly, through the press, and through reports of various groups, more or less devoted to the study of our foreign relations. These opinions usually call for a change from conventional, unimaginative, and outmoded policies—i.e., those currently being followed—in favor of flexible, dynamic, and forward-looking policies, governed by faith and hope in the future rather than by fear and distrust.

From these groups comes a great deal of advice which reaches the President through the White House staff. To this staff foreign affairs present the ideal subject for a speech by the President. By "ideal" is meant a speech which will attract not merely national but worldwide attention and comment; a speech which will display "world leadership" on a "high level"; and which will not produce disagreement within the party, such as might come from a speech on tax revision or on the issues presented by school or farm problems. The State Department is apt to be terror-stricken by these suggestions with very considerable justification. But to oppose is a losing gambit.

Since the Secretary cannot, and perhaps should not, stop these initiatives, he had better join them. And he must do it himself. No one down the line—least of all a speech writer—can control the White House composers gathered around the Cabinet table, with a draft of a foreign policy speech before them and the bit in their teeth. The Secretary, if he is wise, will join the fray himself, with his own draft, and try to guide and direct it. He can carry more weight than any of his associates, particularly in the final stages when the President himself, as I knew the procedure, joins the group and makes the final decisions.

It may seem absurd—and doubtless is—for a Secretary of State to be spending his time as a member of a Presidential speech-writing group.[2] But this is often where policy is made, regardless of where it is supposed to be made. The despised speech, often agreed to be made months beforehand without thought of subject, a nuisance to prepare and an annoyance to deliver, has often proved the vehicle for statements of far-reaching effect for good or ill. As both a junior and a senior official, I have fought this guerrilla warfare; sometimes to get things done which would otherwise be stopped, and sometimes to prevent others from doing the same thing. The Point Four proposal contained in the Inaugural Address of January 20, 1949—in which I was not involved—can be used to illustrate many points made here.

•   •   •

[2] My former colleagues tell me that I exaggerate my participation in Presidential speech-writing. They are doubtless right. Messrs. Philip Jessup, Paul Nitze, Marshal Shulman, and others, all did much of the work which I have described here.

Returning from this digression to the working relations between the Secretary and the President, there were times when I would see the President, on business almost every day, and rarely less than four times a week. Every Monday and Thursday we met alone for a half an hour to an hour; or two other days in the Cabinet and in the National Security Council. Special meetings prepared him for foreign visitors, to deal with a variety of emergencies, great and small, to confer with groups of Senators and Congressmen, and so on. Finally, we talked frequently on the White House telephone.

The private meetings began by disposing of his and my agenda of specific matters, such as appointments, troubles (foreign and domestic), legislative goals and obstacles. The great utility and importance of these meetings lay in the opportunity for talk, talk in which I could learn from the President his thoughts of all sorts; what portended in the domestic field or in defense matters and their probable effects on foreign policy; how he was appraising the consequences of various actions of ours abroad; whether our conduct had or lacked Congressional or popular support and what should be done. Then, again, these talks gave me an important opportunity to prepare him for developments which were foreseen by my colleagues and to discuss courses of action before crises burst upon us. In short, over the years these talks enabled us not only to keep one another informed but to see events and choices each from the other's point of view. This, I venture to suggest, can play a more effective part in developing a coherent national policy than the multiplication of staff and what is called "coordination."

SUPER-CABINET OFFICERS
AND SUPERSTAFFS

THIS is the first of a series of staff reports to be issued by the Subcommittee on National Policy Machinery during the next few months. Drawing upon testimony and counsel given the subcommittee during this past year, the reports will make detailed recommendations for improving the national security policymaking process.

These studies will be appearing at a time when a new President is preparing to take over the reins of our Government. There is widespread agreement that the executive branch of our Government is not now giving the President all the support he needs in meeting his responsibilities in

F R O M the staff report submitted by the Subcommittee on National Policy Machinery to the Senate Committee on Government Operations, November 16, 1960.

foreign and defense affairs. This unsatisfactory situation has been clearly brought out in the testimony given the subcommittee and in comments by other competent authorities.

The magnitude and the apparent intractability of many of these difficulties have led some to believe that the problems can be solved only by radical organizational changes. The changes proposed would tend to shift the center of gravity in policy development and coordination away from the great departments of the Government and closer toward the Presidential level. The proposals have in common the creation of "super-Cabinet" officers or "super-Cabinet" staffs.

This first report has a limited aim. Its purpose is to examine the merit of these proposals and to provide a background for the detailed suggestions for improving policy machinery which will be contained in forthcoming reports.

The Besetting Problem

By law and practice the President is responsible for the conduct of foreign relations. He is Commander in Chief of the Armed Forces. He directs the departments and agencies. He makes the key decisions on the executive budget. He cannot delegate these great tasks to any council or committee. The responsibility is his, and his alone.

New dimensions of national security make the proper exercise of the President's responsibility more difficult than ever before in our history.

The line between foreign and domestic policy, never clear to begin with, has now almost been erased. Foreign policy and military policy have become more inseparable than ever. The tools of foreign policy have multiplied to include economic aid, information, technical assistance, scientific help, educational and cultural exchange, and foreign military assistance.

Historically, a President has looked to the Department of State for his principal help in developing and executing foreign policy. But today the sphere of the Department of State is far narrower than the full range of contemporary foreign relations. As an organization, the Department of State can now claim no greater concern in certain aspects of foreign policy than the Department of Defense. The interest of Treasury and Agriculture in some areas of international affairs is almost equal to that of State.

Indeed, today, almost every department of our Government, and some 18 independent agencies also, are involved with national security policy. Four Government agencies and six international financial organizations work in the field of foreign economic aid alone.

The net result is this: The planning and execution of national security policy cut across the jurisdiction of many departments and agencies. This situation imposes upon the President a heavy burden. A host of responsible protagonists urge divergent advice upon him. He must resolve these conflicting approaches, select his own course of action, and see to its faithful and efficient execution by the very officials whose advice he may have rejected.

Presidents have in the past employed the budgetary process as an instrument for policy and program review and coordination. The budgetary process, in other words, has been traditionally much more than an exercise in accountancy, in the sense of merely keeping ledgers on the cost of ongoing and contemplated programs. Recent years, however, have seen a decline in the use of the budgetary process as a prime tool of the President in program evaluation and integration. The process has become more and more limited to an overly narrow concern for the fiscal aspects of foreign policy and defense programs.

Throughout the past decade, increasingly elaborate and complicated interdepartmental mechanisms have been created to assist the President in policy development, coordination, and execution. The best known of these bodies is the National Security Council and its subordinate organs, the Planning Board and the Operations Coordinating Board. At last count, there were some 160 other formal interdepartmental and interagency committees in the field of international affairs alone.

This interdepartmental machinery has certain inherent limitations in assisting the President.

Committees, including the National Security Council, are primarily coordinating mechanisms. But they can coordinate and integrate only what their members bring to them; they cannot originate national security policy. The role of a committee in policy formulation is essentially critical and cautionary, not creative. The prime source of policy innovations is the contribution of a responsible individual who wrestles day in and day out with the problems of national security. Given imaginative proposals from such individuals, a committee may be helpful in criticizing, countering, or embroidering them.

If interdepartmental committees have limitations in policy initiation, they also have inherent shortcomings in policy coordination. The heads of the great departments and major agencies have been unwilling for the most part to concede to interagency committees the authority in policy development and execution which they regard as their right or the President's.

When policy stakes are high and differences in outlook sharp, department heads traditionally have sought to bypass coordinating committees while keeping them busy with secondary matters. Where this has not been possible, department heads have traditionally tried to keep the product of coordination from binding them tightly or specifically to undesired courses of action. The net result has tended to be "coordination" on the lowest common denominator of agreement, which is often tantamount to no coordination at all.

The President has been left in an unenviable position. He has found it necessary to undertake an endless round of negotiations with his own department heads or else he has been confronted at a very late date by crisis situations resulting from the lack of adequate coordination at an earlier stage. The burdens of the President have been increased correspondingly, and after-the-fact improvisation has too often substituted for forward planning.

A First Secretary of the Government?

Contemplating the problems now faced by a President, some have concluded that he requires the assistance of a new "super-Cabinet" official who would deal across the board with national security problems. The idea is not new. In 1955 former President Hoover suggested creating two appointive Vice Presidents, one responsible for foreign and the other for domestic affairs. More recently, President Eisenhower's Advisory Committee on Government Organization has studied variants of the concept of a "super-Cabinet" official.

In July of this year, Gov. Nelson Rockefeller, former Chairman of the Advisory Committee, appeared before the Subcommittee on National Policy Machinery and made a specific proposal for statutory creation of a "First Secretary" of the Government.

This officer would be appointed by the President subject to Senate confirmation. In Governor Rockefeller's words, he would be "above the Cabinet" and exercise Presidential authority by delegation in all areas "of national security and international affairs." The First Secretary would be authorized "to act for the President . . . at the Prime Ministerial level." He would have statutory designation as "Executive Chairman of NSC" and would have statutory authority by delegation from the President to appoint the heads of subordinate and related interdepartmental committees. The First Secretary would have a staff of his own, and would supervise the personnel of the National Security Council and the Operations Coordinating Board. He would also be "empowered to use and reorganize all of the interdepartmental planning machinery . . . in the area of national security and foreign affairs."

At first glance, the proposal may appear an answer to current difficulties in the operation of policy machinery. The First Secretary's perspective would be expected to encompass the whole range of national security problems. He would be charged with giving committee coordinating mechanisms the stiffening of authoritative direction. Theoretically, he would be no mere White House staff assistant but a super-Cabinet member, thus able to direct fellow Cabinet members in a way that ordinary Presidential aides cannot. Theoretically again, he could relieve a President of many burdens both within the Government and in negotiations with other chiefs of Government. Finally, he could act as a first adviser to the President on foreign policy in its full modern context.

Careful analysis of the First Secretary proposal, however, reveals serious shortcomings and limitations. The proposal would fail to solve the problems it is meant to meet, and would also introduce grave new difficulties into the working of our national policy machinery.

This proposal raises two problems. One concerns a First Secretary's relationship with department heads.

Giving a man the title of "First Secretary" does not thereby give him power. Under this proposal, the Secretaries of State and Defense and other Cabinet officers would retain their present statutory functions and authority. These officials would continue to be accountable to the Congress for the proper performance of their statutory duties. They would equally continue to be responsible to the President.

Being responsible to the President, the Secretaries of State and Defense and other Cabinet officers would report directly to him. They would be bound to question the decisions of a First Secretary; his placement between them and the President would inevitably generate friction and resentment. The First Secretary could gain the power he needed only if the President consistently accepted the First Secretary's judgment over that of his department heads.

But if the President were consistently so deferential to his First Secretary, who then would be President?

And who would then be willing to be Cabinet officers? The primacy of the First Secretary could conceivably be established by filling Cabinet offices with relatively submissive men who lack strong convictions or much will of their own. But this is a period of history when our Government needs more—not less—vigor and drive in high positions. This end would not be served by choosing for Cabinet positions men who could acquiesce to the downgrading of the historic posts that they are asked to occupy.

A second problem raised by this proposal involves the relations of the First Secretary to the President.

The historical record shows that Presidential assistants draw effective power from their demonstrated intimacy with the President. On numerous occasions in the past, a President has deputized an intimate adviser to take charge of certain plans or operations and to act for him in dealing with department heads. In varying degree, such men as House, Hopkins, Byrnes, and Adams have served effectively as Presidential deputies. But the positions of such men were always very different from that proposed for the First Secretary. Past deputyships have been ad hoc assignments given temporarily at the President's own pleasure to persons in his confidence whose intimacy with him was matched by their complete dependence on him. At the height of their effectiveness in Government, a Hopkins or an Adams drew power, not from statutes, titles, staffs, or paper prerogatives of any sort, but solely from the President's evident confidence in them and reliance on them.

Yet the proposed First Secretary would be in a very poor position to sustain that intimate relationship even if he had it at the outset. His statutory position, his formal status in the Government, his supervision of assorted staffs, his chairmanship of manifold committees, his attraction for the press, and his accountability to the Senate which confirmed him—all would mitigate against the maintenance of his close, confidential, personal relationship with the President.

It is most unlikely that a President would in fact give a First Secretary the consistent backing and support he would require to maintain his primacy over other Cabinet members. To do so would run the risk that the First Secretary would become an independent force, politically capable of rivaling the President himself. It would run the further risk of rousing combined opposition from departmental and congressional sources and from affected interest groups.

The likelihood of congressional opposition to domination of departments by a "super-Cabinet" officer rests on the fact that Congress is constitutionally the creator of departments, the source of their statutory mandates, and the steward of their operations. Congressional committees long associated with particular governmental agencies could be expected to side with those agencies in their efforts to assert independence of the First Secretary. He would enjoy no counterpart of the solicitude which congressional committees often show to the heads of departments and agencies within their jurisdiction.

It is essential that a President have full, frank, and frequent discussions with his departmental and agency chiefs. To fully understand the meaning and consequences of alternative courses of action, he must expose himself directly to the clash of argument and counter-argument between advocates of different policy courses. Papers, no matter how carefully staffed, can never convey the full meaning of the issues in question. To the degree a First Secretary insulated the President from day-to-day contact with key Cabinet officers, he would leave his chief less knowledgeable than ever about matters he alone had to decide.

Even if the President were to give the First Secretary substantial backing, this official would still be unable to do the job expected of him. For the critical budgetary decisions on the allocation of resources between national security needs and other national needs would still be outside his jurisdiction.

Only the President's responsibility is as wide as the Nation's affairs. Only he can balance domestic, economic, and defense needs—and if anyone else were to be given the job the President would become a kind of constitutional figurehead.

In summary: Our governmental system has no place for a First Secretary.

He is thought of as a mediator and a judge of the conflicting national security policies advocated by the major departments, the Congress and its committees, and private groups. But in the American system only one official has the constitutional and political power required to assume that role and to maintain it. That official is the President of the United States. He cannot be relieved of his burdens by supplying him with a "deputy" to do what only he can do.

The Vice President and National Security Affairs

A variation of the First Secretary plan would assign to the Vice President continuing duties in the national security area as a matter of discretionary delegation from the President. One proposal recommends that the President authorize the Vice President to "coordinate and direct the Secretary of State, the Secretary of the Treasury, and all of the other instruments of Government" in the general area of national security, excluding defense matters.

Such plans originate in the same dissatisfaction which gives rise to the First Secretary proposal. Yet assigning the Vice President this responsibility would not only create the same problems associated with a First Secretary —it would also produce still other problems.

The specific proposal in question would exclude defense problems from the surveillance of the Vice President. This means that his jurisdiction would end precisely at the wrong point—the point of coordination between diplomatic, economic, and information programs on the one hand and military programs on the other.

A "super-Cabinet" officer whose jurisdiction was confined to that of the most tradition-bound Secretaries of State could do little to integrate foreign and military policy. If anything, the plan would make integration more difficult than it now is. It would reduce the Secretary of State to the level of Vice President's Assistant, and add one more set of relationships which can only be adjusted by the President himself.

A deputyship of this kind for an elected Vice President creates still another difficulty for the President. A modern Vice President is likely to be a person of importance in the President's own party. A broad grant of executive authority to the Vice President could invite eventual misunderstandings and embarrassments between the two highest officials of our Government. The President, it must be remembered, has no control over the Vice President's tenure of office.

The role of the Vice President need not, of course, be limited to his constitutional obligation to preside over the Senate. Many ways of helping the President can be worked out by mutual agreement. When proper occasions arise, these can include tasks in the field of foreign policy. For example, a Vice President can relieve the President of part of the protocol burden; he can undertake special missions abroad; he can from time to time make special studies. He may, of course, play a role of great importance in the relations between the legislative and executive branches.

But any attempt to make the Vice President a kind of Deputy President for Foreign Affairs would be to give the wrong man the wrong job. It would impair the effectiveness of the responsible Cabinet officers, the Vice President, and the President himself.

There have been still more drastic proposals regarding the Vice President which would make him not merely the repository of delegated authority from the President but a full-fledged deputy in the executive branch, charged by statute with authority for direction and coordination.

But the Vice President is constitutionally the presiding officer of the senior body in the legislative branch. The executive power is constitutionally vested in the President who heads another branch. At a minimum, any proposal to vest executive authority in an officer of the legislative branch by statute would raise serious questions involving both the spirit and letter of the Constitution.

A Superstaff for National Security?

A "super-Cabinet" official charged with broad responsibilities for national security would, of course, require major staff assistance. Indeed, most proposals for a First Secretary assume he will have the help of a sizable staff.

Some who would stop short of the First Secretary concept would nonetheless establish major White House or Executive Office staffs for national security planning and coordination. A representative proposal of this type would replace the present National Security Council staff, the Planning Board, and the Operations Coordinating Board with a Presidential Staff Agency for National Security Affairs.

The appeal of such an above-the-department staff agency is readily apparent. Those associated with this Agency could presumably view national security problems "in the round"; their horizons would not be limited to the more parochial perspectives of the departments. And not being burdened with day-to-day operating responsibilities, they could presumably do a better job of long-term planning than their harassed counterparts within the departments.

But how much assistance would such an agency give the President? Its plans would lack the coloration, the perspectives, and the realism which come from actual involvement in operating problems. It would be hard to avoid ivory tower thinking. Beyond this, the Agency would create a new layer of planning between the President and the departments and thus insulate and shield him from the full flavor of the planning of responsible operating officials.

Such an agency would, of course, be a bureaucratic rival of the historic departments. It seems safe to say the rivalry would be one sided. The Staff Agency would confront the traditional unwillingness of the departments to surrender their own responsibility for policy development and execution. Lacking the autonomy and fixed entrenchments of a departmental base, such an agency could not compete for long, on favorable terms, with State, Defense, or Treasury.

The end result, in fact, might be the worst of two possible worlds, with the Staff Agency lacking enough power to give the President effective assistance, but sufficiently powerful nonetheless to meddle in the affairs of the great departments.

A President will, of course, need some assistants who concern themselves primarily with national security policy. But such assistants would act as extensions of the President's eyes and ears in a confidential relationship, not as members of a large and highly institutionalized "superstaff."

Conclusion

This study has argued that "super-Cabinet" officers or above-the-department "superstaffs" would not ease the problems now faced by the President in setting and maintaining our national course. In fact, such additions to the policy process would make his burdens heavier.

Reforms, to be effective, must be made in terms of the real requirements and possibilities of the American governmental system.

That system provides no alternative to relying upon the President as the judge and arbiter of the forward course of policy for his administration.

It provides no good alternative to reliance upon the great departments for the conduct of executive operations and for the initiation of most policy proposals relating to these operations. Departments possess the statutory authority, the knowledge and experience and the technical staffs needed to advise the President, and the line administrators who alone can implement executive decisions. They will always be the main wellsprings of policy ideas and innovations.

Finally, the American system provides no good alternative to reliance on the budget process as a means of reviewing the ongoing activities of the departments and raising periodically for Presidential decision issues of effectiveness in actual performance.

But to reject the radical solutions is not at the same time to dismiss the besetting problems in which they have their origin. The problems remain. They cannot be solved by maintaining the status quo.

Forthcoming staff reports will make wide-ranging recommendations for changes in the policy process. The promising paths to reform lead in these general directions:

First: There are better ways for the President to delegate more authority for decisionmaking to individual heads of departments and agencies. There has been too much emphasis on coordination and too little on delegation. Policymaking has tended to be reduced to a group effort where no single person has real authority to act and where no one individual can be rewarded for success or penalized for failure. In the words of Mr. Robert Lovett:

> . . . The authority of the individual executive must be restored: The derogation of the authority of the individual in government, and the exaltation of the anonymous mass, has resulted in a noticeable lack of decisiveness. Committees cannot effectively replace the decisionmaking power of the individual who takes the oath of office; nor can committees provide the essential qualities of leadership . . .

Second: There are better ways to make the National Security Council a forum for more meaningful debate on issues which the President alone can decide. One should not ask the National Security Council to do what it is not really capable of doing. The Council is an interagency committee: It can inform, debate, review, adjust, and validate. But, as a collective body, the Council cannot develop bold new ideas or translate them into effective action.

Yet the Council can still be a highly useful advisory mechanism to a President. The evidence strongly suggests that this role can best be discharged by a Council which has fewer rather than more participants in its meetings; which concerns itself only with issues of central importance for Presidential decision; which works through less, rather than more, institutionalized procedures; which relates its activities more closely to the budgetary process; and which gives the Secretary of State a greater role in the development of broad policy initiatives.

Third: There are better ways to enable the Secretary of State to serve the President as first adviser in national security problems. The Secretary of State *is* the First Secretary of the Government. He should be able to advise the President on the full range of national security matters, from the point of view of their relation to foreign problems and policies.

The Secretary of State need not and should not have any legal or supervisory authority over other Cabinet officers. Any moves in this direction would have many of the disadvantages of the "super-Cabinet" officer proposal. The goal is not to give the Secretary of State greater command authority: it is to enlarge the scope of his guidance and influence.

If the President is to ask more, and to get more, from the Secretary of State, the Secretary must be better staffed to offer policy guidance and initiatives across the whole span of national security problems. This does not mean a larger Department of State; it may well mean a smaller one. But it does mean a Department competently staffed with generalists, economists, and military and scientific experts to support the Secretary in understanding and following all fields falling within his broad concern.

Fourth: There are better ways to relate military power more closely to foreign policy requirements. The Secretary of Defense shares with the Secretary of State the main burden of advising the President on national security problems. A full and welcome partnership of the Departments of State and Defense is the prerequisite of coherent political-strategic counsel for the President.

In viewing the Pentagon, one must guard against seeking organizational solutions for problems which are not really organizational in origin. Yet there are reforms which are promising of results. They point in the direction of more vigorous employment of the broad authority already invested in the Secretary of Defense; more active participation of the Secretary of Defense in the deliberations of the Joint Chiefs of Staff; increased reliance upon the Joint Staff for planning; an acceleration of existing trends toward functional commands; a budgetary process more consonant with the requirements of modern weapons technology; a promotion system which encourages officers to become versed in the broad problems of national security; a Pentagon career service which does more to develop outstanding civilian officials; and selecting for top policy positions only candidates willing to remain in their posts well beyond the period of apprenticeship on their jobs.

Fifth: There are better ways to make the budgetary process a more effective instrument for reviewing and integrating programs and performance in the area of national security. There is need to return to the earlier tradition which regarded the budgetary process as a key program management tool of the President.

Budget targets should be regarded not primarily as fiscal instruments but as policy instruments. The investigative analyses needed to achieve and adjust these targets must begin and end with substantive concerns and not simply considerations of administrative organization and financial management.

Sixth: There are better ways to organize the Presidency to intervene flexibly, imaginatively, and fast where gaps in policy development or execution threaten to upset the President's cardinal objectives. This does not require new and elaborate staff offices or highly institutionalized interdepartmental committees. It calls rather for more discriminating use of able staff assistants right in the immediate office of the President himself who are alert to trouble spots and sensitive to the President's own information needs.

Seventh: There are better ways to attract and retain outstanding officials for both appointive and career posts in the national security departments and agencies. Poor decisions often result less from poor organization than from poor policymakers. The one thing which could do the most to improve national security policy would be to raise the standards of excellence among career and appointive officials.

The Nation should be grateful for the skill and dedication of those who now man the posts of responsibility in the area of foreign and defense policy. But there is still room for vast improvement in developing and using the rich resources of talent now found among our career officials.

There is room for equally great improvement in eliminating the legal and financial problems which now discourage highly qualified private citizens from serving governmental tours of duty.

And, above all, there is need to abandon the outmoded conventions which have often deprived an administration of the service of members of the opposite political party. The yardstick for making appointments to key national security posts must be ability to do the job, regardless of party.

Specific recommendations for speeding progress in these seven areas, together with suggestions for other reforms of the policy process, will be contained in succeeding staff reports.

STATEMENT OF RICHARD E. NEUSTADT

THANK you, Mr. Chairman and Senator Javits.

It is a privilege to appear before you. This subcommittee and its predecessor have contributed a great deal to the fund of information on which we in universities depend for the enlightenment of those we teach. If I can be of use to you today, please take it with my thanks as a return for benefits received.

You have asked me to comment on basic issues in national security staffing and operations. This is a vast field and a very complex one, where troubles are hard to track down and "solutions" come harder still. The field is full of genuine dilemmas, many of them quite new to our governmental system but all of them quite likely to endure as far ahead as one can see. Durability is a common characteristic. So is difficulty.

Perhaps the chief of these dilemmas is the one placed first in the subcommittee's recent, cogent staff report on "Basic Issues." To quote from that report:

> The needs of a President and the needs of the departments and agencies are not identical. . . .

Presented before the Subcommittee on National Security Staffing and Operations of the Senate Committee on Government Operations, March 25, 1963.

What does a President need to do his job?

Essentially . . . to keep control . . . to get early warning of items for his agenda before his options are foreclosed, to pick his issues and lift these out of normal channels, to obtain priority attention from key officials on the issues he pulls to his desk, to get prompt support for his initiatives, and to keep other matters on a smooth course, with his lines of information open, so that he can intervene if need arises. . . .

What do the officials of our vast departments and agencies need to do their jobs?

Essentially . . . orderly, deliberate, familiar procedures—accustomed forms in which to air their interests, a top-level umpire to blow the whistle . . . written records of the decisions by which they should be governed.

. . . middle-level yearnings for some equivalent of the OCB [originate] in the desire to have one's views heard through some set, certain, reliable procedure which binds the highest levels as well as other agencies.

A President needs flexibility, freedom to improvise, in dealing with those below. Officialdom needs stability, assurance of regularity, in dealing with those above. To a degree these needs are incompatible; hence the dilemma. As your staff report notes: "It is not surprising that the departments often find a President's way of doing business unsettling—or that Presidents sometimes view the departments almost as adversaries."

In considering the problems now before you, I find it the beginning of wisdom to face this dilemma candidly. That is what I hope to do today.

The President versus Officialdom

So much of our literature and everyday discussion treats the executive branch as though it were an entity that effort is required to visualize the President apart from the departments, in effect a separate "branch," with needs and interests differing from those of "his" officialdom. Yet constitutional prescription, political tradition, governmental practice, and democratic theory all unite to make this so. In all these terms the separateness of presidential need and interest are inevitable—and legitimate.

The man in the White House is constitutional commander of our military forces, conductor of foreign relations, selector of department heads, custodian of the "take care clause" and of the veto power. No other person in our system has so massive a responsibility for national security. At the same time he is the one executive official holding office on popular election, and save for the Vice President he is our only public officer accountable directly to a national electorate. He is, besides, a relative short-timer in our Government. Members of Congress and career officials often hold high places for a generation. He, at most, holds his for just 8 years. The first year is a learning time, the last year usually a stalemate. Whatever personal imprint he can hope to make it usually reserved to the short span between. Yet his name becomes the label for an "era" in the history books; his accountability widens as time goes on. Schoolchildren yet unborn may hold him personally responsible for everything that happens to the country in "his" years.

The constitutional responsibility, the political accountability, the time perspective, the judgment of history: all these adhere to the President himself, not as an "institution" but as a human being. In this combination his situation is unique. No one else in the executive branch—or for that matter in the Government—shares equally in his responsibility or feels an equal heat from his electorate and history. It is no wonder that his needs can be distinguished from, and actually are different from, the needs of most officials in executive departments.

Cold war and nuclear weapons make the difference greater. A new dimension of risk has come upon American decisionmaking. Its effect has been to magnify the President's responsibility, and to intensify his needs for flexibility, for information, for control. This new dimension first began to manifest itself in President Eisenhower's second term. Mr. Kennedy is the first President to live with it from the outset of his administration.

The President As Risktaker

What a President now lives with is the consequence of a substantial nuclear delivery capability acquired by the Soviet Union as well as the United States. It is the mutual capability which pushes our decisionmaking —and theirs, too, of course—into a new dimension of risk. In an article included in your volume of selected papers, I have termed this the risk of "irreversibility," the risk that either bureaucratic momentum in a large-scale undertaking or mutual miscalculation by atomic adversaries, or both combined, may make it infeasible to call back, or play over, or revise, an action taken in our foreign relations, at least within the range of the cold war. But the term "irreversibility," standing alone, does not really suffice to convey what is new in this dimension. Bureaucratic momentum and multiple miscalculations made a German emperor's snap reaction after Sarajevo "irreversible" as long ago as July 1914. Therefore, to amend the term: what is new since the Soviets acquired their ICBM's is the risk of irreversibility become irremediable. Unlike the problems facing Kaiser Wilhelm 50 years ago—or those of President Roosevelt in World War II, or even those of President Truman in Korea—a possible result of present action is that nothing one does later can ward off, reduce, repair, or compensate for costs to one's society.

Let me underscore this point; it goes to the heart of my presentation today. Last October we all glimpsed the new dimension in a President's risk-taking. But the Cuban confrontation seems to me a relatively simplified affair: geographically, in the issue raised, in the number of contestants, and in duration. What if there were two or three such issues simultaneously, or stretched over 2 months instead of 2 weeks? What if there were—as Mr. Kennedy told us last week there may be 10 years hence—a multiplicity of nuclear powers, a multiplicity of possible miscalculators, each capable of setting off irreparable consequences? Consider the next President's risk-taking, let alone Mr. Kennedy's. This new dimension deepens year by year.

The consequences for the Presidency are profound.

One consequence is that the sitting President lives daily with the knowledge that at any time he, personally, may have to make a human judgment —or may fail to control someone else's judgment—which puts half the world in jeopardy and cannot be called back. You and I will recognize his burden intellectually; he actually experiences it emotionally. It cannot help but set him—and his needs—sharply apart from all the rest of us, not least from the officials who have only to advise him. As Mr. Kennedy remarked in his December television interview: "The President bears the burden of the responsibility. The advisers may move on to new advice."

A second related consequence is that now more than ever before his mind becomes the only source available from which to draw politically legitimated judgments on what, broadly speaking, can be termed the political feasibilities of contemplated action vis-à-vis our world antagonists: judgments on where history is tending, what opponents can stand, what friends will take, what officials will enforce, what "men in the street" will tolerate; judgments on the balance of support, opposition, indifference at home and abroad. Our Constitution contemplated that such judgments should emanate from President and Congress, from a combination of the men who owed their places to electorates, who had themselves experienced the hazards of nomination and election. The democratic element in our system consists, essentially, of reserving these judgments to men with that experience. But when it comes to action risking war, technology has modified the Constitution: the President, perforce, becomes the only such man in the system capable of exercising judgment under the extraordinary limits now imposed by secrecy, complexity, and time.

Therefore as a matter not alone of securing his own peace of mind, but also of preserving the essentials in our democratic order, a President, these days, is virtually compelled to reach for information and to seek control over details of operation deep inside executive departments. For it is at the level of detail, of concrete plans, of actual performance, on "small" operations, to say nothing of large ones, that there often is a fleeting chance—sometimes the only chance—to interject effective judgment. And it is at this level that risks of the gravest sort are often run. "Irreversibility becomes irremediable" is not to be considered something separate from details of operation. If, as reported, Mr. Kennedy kept track of every movement of blockading warships during the Cuban crisis of October 1962, this is but a natural and necessary corollary of the new dimension of risk shadowing us all, but most of all a President.

The net effect is to restrict, if not repeal, a hallowed aspect of American military doctrine, the autonomy of field commanders, which as recently as Mr. Truman's time, as recently as the Korean war, was thought to set sharp limits upon White House intervention in details of operation. The conduct of diplomacy is comparably affected. So, I presume, is the conduct of intelligence. Also, we now rediscover that age-old problem for the rulers of States: timely and secure communications. The complications here are mind stretching.

The only persons qualified to give you a full appreciation of the President's felt needs in such a situation are Mr. Eisenhower, keeping his last years in view, and Mr. Kennedy. Mr. Khrushchev might now be equipped to offer some contributory evidence. The situation is so new and so unprecedented that outside the narrow circle of these men and their immediate associates one cannot look with confidence for understanding of their prospects or requirements as these appear to them. I do not advance this caution out of modesty—though my competence suffers along with the rest of the outsiders—but to suggest that there remains, at least for the time being, a further source of differences between the President and most executive officials: the former cannot fail for long to see what he is up against; the latter have not seen enough of men so placed to have much sympathy or a sure sense for how it feels these days, in these conditions, to be President. What they see with assurance is what they in their jobs want of him in his, a very different matter. Such differing perceptions of the Presidential task are bound to widen differences of perceived need between the White House where responsibility is focused and officialdom where it is not.

The same phenomenon of differing perceptions seems to play a part in other Presidential relationships. No doubt it has some bearing on the current difficulties of relationship between the White House and its counterparts in certain allied capitals where political leaders, in their own capacities, have not experienced the risk to which our President is heir because they lack the power which produced it. Presumably some of the sore spots in congressional relations have a comparable source. Certainly this is the case with some of the complaints voiced against Messrs. Eisenhower and Kennedy, in turn, by private groups intent upon particular action programs.

The lack of common outlook increases the Presidency's isolation and thus reinforces the dictates of common prudence for a man who bears the burden of that office in our time, namely, to stretch his personal control, his human judgment, as wide and deep as he can make them reach. Your staff report is quite right in its catalog of Presidential needs.

Officialdom versus the President

The cold war, however, and the pace of technology have not affected only Presidential needs. They also have affected departmental needs, and in a very different way.

Well before the Soviets achieved ICBM's the pace of change in our own weaponry combined with our wide-ranging economic and political endeavors overseas were mixing up the jurisdictions of all agencies with roles to play, or claim, in national security: mingling operations along programmatic lines, cutting across vertical lines of authority, breaching the neat boxes on organizational charts. Defense, State, CIA, AID, Treasury, together with the President's Executive Office staffs, now form a single complex—a national security complex, if you will—tied together by an intricate network of program and staff interrelationships in Washington and in the field. AEC, ACDA, USIA are also in the complex; others lurk nearby, tied in to a degree, as for example Commerce.

As early as the National Security Act of 1947 we formally acknowledged the close ties of foreign, military, economic policy; these ties had been rendered very plain by World War II experience. But in the pre-Korean years when ECA was on its own, when CIA was new, when MAAG's were hardly heard of, while atom bombs were ours alone and military budgets stood at under $15 billion, a Secretary of Defense could forbid contacts between Pentagon and State at any level lower than his own, and within limits could enforce his ban. That happened only 14 years ago. In bureaucratic terms it is as remote as the stone age.

While operations now have been entangled inextricably, our formal organizations and their statutory powers and the jurisdictions of congressional committees remain much as ever: distinct, disparate, dispersed. Our personnel systems are equally dispersed. In the national security complex alone, I count at least seven separate professional career systems—military included—along with the general civil service which to most intents and purposes is departmentalized.

These days few staffs in any agency can do their work alone without active support or at least passive acquiescence from staffs outside, in other agencies—often many others. Yet no one agency, no personnel system is the effective boss of any other; no one staff owes effective loyalty to the others. By and large the stakes which move men's loyalties—whether purpose, prestige, power, or promotion—run to one's own program, one's own career system, along agency lines not across them.

These developments place premiums on interstaff negotiation, compromise, agreement in the course of everybody's action. This subcommittee has deplored the horrors of committee work: the wastes of time, the earstrain—and the eyestrain—the "papering over" of differences, the search for lowest common denominators of agreement. I deplore these horrors, too, and freely advocate "committee killing," periodically, to keep them within bounds. But given the realities of programing and operations, interagency negotiation cannot be avoided. To "kill" committees is, at most, to drive them underground. Officials have to find at least an informal equivalent. What else are they to do?

One other thing they can do is push their pet issues up for argument and settlement at higher levels. Once started on this course, there is no very satisfactory place to stop short of the White House. In logic and in law only the Presidency stands somewhat above all agencies, all personnel systems, all staffs. Here one can hope to gain decisions as definitive as our system permits; congressional committees may be able to supplant them, special pleaders may be able to reverse them, foot-draggers may be able to subvert them—even so, they are the surest thing obtainable.

Accordingly officials urged to show initiative, to quit logrolling in committee, to be vigorous in advocacy, firm in execution, turn toward the White House seeking from it regular, reliable, consistent service as a fixed and constant court of arbitration for the national security complex. This means, of course, a court which knows how courts behave and does not enter cases prematurely. Your staff report rightly describes the sort of service wanted; in the circumstances of officials they do well to want it.

Their need for such a service is unquestionable, and legitimate. To flounder through the mush of "iffy" answers, or evasions; to struggle through the murk of many voices, few directives; to fight without assurance of a referee; to face the Hill without assurance of a buffer; or on the other hand, to clean up after eager amateurs, to repair damage done by ex parte proceedings; to cope with happy thoughts in highest places—these are what officialdom complains of, and with reason. For the work of large-scale enterprises tends to be disrupted by such breaches of "good order" and routine. Not bureaucrats alone but also Presidents have stakes in the effectiveness of the Executive bureaucracy. From any point of view, officials surely are entitled to want White House service in support of their performance.

But if a President should give this service to their satisfaction, what becomes of him? While he sits as the judge of issues brought by others—keeping order, following procedure, filing decisions, clearing dockets—what happens to his personal initiative, his search for information, his reach for control, his mastery of detail? What happens to his own concerns outside the sphere of national security? In short, where is his flexibility? The answers I think are plain. Thus the dilemma with which I began: to a degree—a large degree—his needs and theirs are incompatible.

Help from the Secretary of State?

It is tempting to assert that this dilemma could be resolved at a stroke by the appointment of a "czar," a Presidential deputy, to serve as court-of-first-resort for all disputes within the national security complex except the ones the President preempted out of interest to himself or to the Nation. The "solution" is tempting but I find it quite unreal. I do not see how this role can be built into our system. I share the reservations put on record by the reports of your predecessor subcommittee.

Setting aside grandiose solutions, what might be done to ease the tension between presidential and official needs, to keep the pains of this dilemma within bounds? The answer I believe—insofar as one exists—lies in careful and selective augmentation of the Presidency's staff resources. A President may not need deputies, writ large, to keep decisions from him but he certainly needs ready and responsive staff work in the preparatory phases of decisionmaking and followup. The better he is served thereby, the better will officialdom be served as well. In this their needs run parallel: effective staff work for him cannot help but put some firm procedure under foot for them; such staff work promises that bases will be touched, standpoints explored—with rocks turned over and the worms revealed—positions traced, appeals arranged, compromises tested. When this prospect is seen ahead official hearts are glad.

In the nature of the case, a President's assistants at the White House cannot do that sort of staff work by themselves except—they hope and so does he—on issues having top priority for him in his own mind and schedule, day-to-day. Preparatory work on issues not yet in that class and followup on issues which have left it must be done, if done at all, at one remove through staff facilities less dominated by the President's immediate requirements. Hence the distinction introduced a quarter-century ago between personal staff at the White House and institutional staff, mainly career staff, in the executive offices across the street, of which the longest-lived example is the Bureau of the Budget.

But in the sphere of national security there is no Budget Bureau. Its nearest counterpart remains the Office of the Secretary of State. This is the traditional source of "institutional" assistance for a President in what was once the peacetime sum of foreign relations: diplomacy. And while the Office has not kept pace with the meaning of that term, no full-scale substitute has been built in its stead. I hope none will be. I hope, rather, that the Secretary's Office can be rebuilt on a scale commensurate with the contemporary reach of foreign relations.

Reliance on the Secretary's Office as an institutional staff resource seems to have been envisaged at the start of Mr. Kennedy's administration. On the White House side Mr. Bundy was named to the necessary personal assistantship, filling a post established in the previous administration:

"Special Assistant for National Security Affairs." But formalized committee structures and secretariats built up around his post during the 1950's were scaled down or disestablished by the new administration. This was done with the expressed intent of improving staff performance by transferring staff functions to the Office of the Secretary of State. OCB is a case in point. As Mr. Bundy wrote your chairman on September 4, 1961:

> It was and is our belief that there is much to be done that the OCB could not do, and that the things it did do can be done as well or better in other ways.
> The most important of these other ways is an increased reliance on the leadership of the Department of State . . . the President has made it very clear that he does not want a large separate organization between him and his Secretary of State. Neither does he wish any question to arise as to the clear authority and responsibility of the Secretary of State, not only in his own Department, and not only in such large-scale related areas as foreign aid and information policy, but also as the agent of coordination in all our major policies toward other nations.

For a variety of reasons, some of them beyond my range of observation, this staffing patterns has not been set firmly up to now: the White House side, the "personal" side, seems firm enough but not the other side, the "institutional" side. So far as I can judge, the State Department has not yet found means to take the proffered role and play it vigorously across the board of national security affairs. The difficulties here may be endemic; the role may ask too much of one department among others. But I think it is decidedly too soon to tell. State, I conceive, should have the benefit of every doubt and more time for experiment.

This seems to be the view of the administration. It is striking that in all these months the White House staff has set up no procedures or "machinery" which would interfere in any way with building up the Secretary's Office as a Presidential "agent of coordination." It is striking also that the Secretary has moved toward enhancement of his Office by equipping it with a strong No. 3 position in the person of Mr. Harriman, who preceded me at your hearings. The burdens of advice-giving and of negotiation weigh heavily these days not only on the Secretary but also on the Under Secretary. This position thus comes into play as in effect their common deputyship. Mr. Harriman, I take it, with his new authority as second Under Secretary has more opportunity than they to be a source of guidance and of stiffening—and interference-running—for careerists in the State Department, as they deal with one another and with staffs outside. If he actually can do this, if he too is not weighed down by other duties, then the ground may be prepared now for substantial further movement toward development of central staff work in the national security sphere.

Until now, I gather, no one has had time to make himself consistently an energizer, catalyst, connective for the several sorts of planners, secretariats, task forces, and action officers now scattered through the upper floors of our vast new State building. The Secretary may sit at the center of this vastness, but his Office has almost no staff which he can call his own. To weld together such a staff out of these scattered pieces, to imbue it with cohesion and a government-wide outlook, to implant it as a Presidential agent of coordination for the sweep of national security affairs: all this is far from done. I need not tell you why I think the doing will take time.

The Secretary versus the Others

But I must not mislead you. What I offer here is "conventional wisdom," my hopes are conventional hopes. To call for augmentation of the Presidency's staff resources is to echo what has been prescribed for almost every governmental ailment these past 30 years. To fasten on the Secretary's Office as the means is to follow the footsteps of innumerable study groups intent upon improving something in particular within the range of foreign operations. The Herter Committee very recently, concerned for personnel in Foreign Service, charged the Secretary's Office with coordination of civilian career systems. Now I come along to charge the Office with coordinative staff work in the realm of policy. Such unanimity is dangerous.

The danger is that as we try to make the Secretary's Office serve the needs of personnel directors, or of action officers, or White House aides, or Presidents, we may forget the Secretary's needs. The danger is that as we try to make him a strong instrument for other people's purposes we may forget that he will have some purpose of his own. The modern secretaryship of state is not merely a Presidential staff resource—or a personnel agency for that matter—nor can it be used simply to bridge differences between the President and officialdom. This Office has its own compelling and divergent needs apart from theirs; it has its own dilemma differing from theirs. To seek the best of both worlds from the Secretary's Office, to intend effective staff work for both President and Secretary, is to present as delicate a task of institution building as the Executive has faced in modern times. Because it is so delicate the outcome is uncertain. The danger is that in our advocacy we forget the delicacy, the uncertainty, or both.

Consider for a moment the responsibility of any modern Secretary of State. Always in form, usually in fact, the man becomes a very senior personal adviser to the President, a source of brainpower and judgment for him both as one man to another and at working sessions of his chosen inner circle—currently the executive committee of the National Security Council. Perhaps this was not Mr. Bryan's role—to reach far back—or Mr. Hull's, but certainly it was the role of Messrs. Marshall, Acheson, and Dulles, among others. Under conditions of cold war, this role is sharpened, rendered more intense by emergence of the Secretary of Defense, an officer with roughly equal claim but necessarily different focus, as a source of judgment in the foreign relations sphere. Balance of advice becomes important on each issue every day.

The Secretary of State is much more than a personal adviser. He also is our ranking diplomat at large for sensitive negotiations just short of the summit. Furthermore, he serves as an administration voice to Congress, to the country, and abroad whose public word is weighty in proportion to his rank. At the same time he is actively in charge of a complex administrative entity. He is "Mr. State Department" and "Mr. Foreign Service," leader of officials, spokesman for their causes, guardian of their interests, judge of their disputes, superintendent of their work, master of their careers.

The Secretary of State has a dilemma all his own. These roles are mutually reinforcing: his advice gains weight because he represents the whole Department, his public statements and internal orders gain in potency because he is so often at the White House. But these roles are also mutually antagonistic: fronting for officials strains his credit as an adviser, advising keeps his mind off management, negotiating preempts energy and time. No modern Secretary has performed the miracle of playing all these roles at once so skillfully and carefully that he obtains the benefits of all and pays no penalties. Presumably there is no way to do it.

A Secretary cannot wriggle out of this dilemma by ditching his department and retreating to the White House, although at least one Secretary may have wished he could. His job cannot be done from there, nor is he needed there. Another man can serve, and does, as White House aide for national security affairs; like others of his kind the aide stays close at hand to deal with action issues on the President's agenda when and how the President's own mind, interests, and work habits require as he meets his own time pressures and priorities. No doubt this personal assistantship includes a role as personal adviser. The Secretary also is a personal adviser. But this coincidence does not make them the same, nor would it help the President to have two such assistants and no Secretary.

The Secretary's usefulness as an adviser lies precisely in the fact that he is more than just another aide whose work is tied entirely to the President's. The Secretary has work of his own, resources of his own, vistas of his own. He is in business under his own name and in his name powers are exercised, decisions taken. Therefore he can press his personal authority, his own opinion, his adviser's role, wherever he sees fit across the whole contemporary reach of foreign relations, never mind the organization charts. He cannot hope to win all arguments in such a sphere, nor is he in position to contest them indiscriminately. But his status and the tasks of his Department give him every right to raise his voice where, when and as he chooses. To abandon his Department in an effort to escape its burdens and distractions is to cloud his title as adviser.

Yet to concentrate on running his department—combating weaknesses, asserting jurisdictions, adjudicating feuds—is no better solution for a Secretary's problem. With a President absorbed, as Presidents must be, in foreign operations, in diplomacy, defense, no Secretary worth his salt would spend much time on management while others drafted cables in the Cabinet room. And if he did he would not long remain effective as a personal adviser.

The modern Secretary of State, whoever he may be, deserves more sympathy than most receive. He lives with his dilemma but he cannot take the comfort which officials, facing theirs, draw from longevity: "This too shall pass." Nor can he take the comfort which a President derives from being, for a fixed term, No. 1. The Secretary's only consolation is to share with Gilbert's Gondoliers "the satisfying feeling that our duty has been done." But "duty" is exceedingly ambiguous for him. What about the duties he has slighted?

Two Notes of Caution

Under these circumstances it would add insult to injury if this man were asked to serve in any simple sense as the Director of a Presidential staff facility on the model of the Bureau of the Budget. For self-protection he would have to shirk the task if it were his. Otherwise he would be kept so busy checking on the work of his resentful Cabinet colleagues that every present role might suffer more than it does now. What is the gain from that? But if we simply move the upper reaches of the State Department out from under him and tie them to the Presidency apart from him, where does he get his staff work done, who bulwarks his initiatives, supports his roles? Yet if we leave his departmental aides to serve him only and turn elsewhere for the Presidency's service—if, as some have urged, we simply set up a new "Office of National Security Affairs" in the Executive Offices beside the Budget Bureau—what happens to the Secretary's status and utility in doing what he now does for our Government?

I pose these questions to be cautious, not equivocal. I hope that through the Secretary's Office we can build an institution serving both the Presidency and the Secretary himself. I hope thereby that we can ease the tension between President and officialdom, and at the same time ease the Secretary's own dilemma. In my opinion we should try to realize these hopes. But I would not pretend to you that such a course is either safe or certain. And assuredly it is not simple.

In closing let me add a second caution: even with time, even with good use of it, even if we master complex institution building, we can expect no miracles from policy. Even if the Secretary's Office should become a partner with the White House in the Presidency's business while the Secretary's business is protected and enhanced, even then both sorts of business would be botched on numerous occasions. For methods and procedures at their best cannot abolish the deep difficulties of perception, of analysis, of judgment, of persuasion which confront our policymakers now and in the future. Organizational arrangements at their most ingenious cannot rub out the underlying differences of duty, interest, role, perspective, separating Presidency from officialdom—and separating both from Congress, for that matter.

These difficulties, differences, lie at the root of most "botched business" we have witnessed in the past and will experience in future. Machinery may confine the damage, or enlarge it, but to see the source of damage as the vehicle in use is to ignore the driver, and his passengers, and road conditions, and the other drivers. To claim that it could be made damage-proof by redesign is to divert attention from the human condition. I would make no such claim. Machinery is important; our President and our executive officials need the most effective mechanisms they can get. Still, this remains emphatically a government of men who face in national security affairs unprecedented problems mostly not of their own making.

They dare not hope for too much from machinery, nor should we. To do so is to court unnecessary disappointment. As the world goes these days I see no need for that. There seems to be quite enough necessary disappointment.

•   •   •

SENATOR JACKSON. Senator Miller?

SENATOR MILLER. Thank you, Mr. Chairman.

Professor Neustadt, I want you to know first that I very much enjoyed being here to hear your presentation. I apologize that I was detained and unable to hear all of it.

I began to get some hopes when you reached the point in your testimony that, in connection with the solutions, the answer would be to augment the President's staff resources. You indicated that, insofar as a solution existed, this would be the approach. Immediately I conjured up in my mind the thought that you were going to get to the Office of National Security Affairs which, I might say, was one solution that had appealed to me heretofore. Then a little later on you dashed my hopes by saying that you thought that the solution should come within the Office of the Secretary of State. Then a little later on you pointed out that balance of advice is very important.

I must confess that I find it difficult to appreciate how the balance that you refer to can be obtained if you go to the Office of the Secretary of State or to the Office of the Secretary of Defense, or to any of the other Cabinet officers. It seems to me that if we are going to, indeed, augment the President's own staff, we should do so within the framework of the White House, and that the Office of National Security Affairs, if properly staffed, would provide us with the balance which we could not find in any of the Cabinet officers.

Let me give you an example of where I think we would fail to find that balance if, indeed, it were sought in the Office of the Secretary of State. I think when we talk about national security affairs, there is a tendency, too often, to think in terms of the military or in terms of foreign relations. On the other hand one of the most vital and fundamental features of our entire system is our economic system, economic planning, long-range economic planning, based upon a thorough inventory of our economic resources, with a view to programing these resources in the areas of domestic and social programs, military programs, space programs, and commerce and foreign aid.

These are areas, particularly vis-à-vis the Soviets, that are not yet covered properly. I cannot understand how these can be covered properly in the Office of the Secretary of State. But I could understand how they could be covered properly in an Office of National Security Affairs operating somewhat as the Bureau of the Budget operates.

Let me point out to you that your reservation with respect to the Office of National Security Affairs expressed in the question: "What happens to the Secretary of State's status and utility?" could be answered by saying that that would depend upon the Secretary of State. If he is a strong Secretary of State, I am not worried about his status or his utility. If he a weak one, then, of course, I would worry—for other reasons.

But I think that this is a problem you are going to find regardless of where you go for your solution.

Mr. Neustadt. I agree, sir. And if you feel that I kept shifting from foot to foot in the last half of my statement, you are absolutely right. Let me put it as candidly as possible: I don't like the thought that we may have to come to another fairly large-scale institutionalized office in the President's own neighborhood. I think we ought to avoid it if we can. I am not, as you can see, prepared to come here as a student and say to you, "It can be avoided." I don't know if it can be. You have suggested reasons why it is going to be extremely difficult to do it.

Let me simply say that staff facilities around the Presidency are not an unmixed blessing for the President. The man needs the kind of flexibility, the kind of reach, that staff is supposed to give him, the kind of balanced advice that staff is supposed to be able to procure for him by careful watching and airing of difficulties and differences and grievances and information which may not appear upon the surface of advice from the departments.

But staff itself can become, all too quickly, another "department," another complicating echelon in a very complex system. There are two ways one could build up the staff now in the President's neighborhood; both ways have disadvantages. The first way is to markedly enlarge the Bundy office. But the more one does that, the more one threatens Mr. Bundy's utility as a personal aide. He is pushed toward the troubles that your predecessor subcommittee treated in its staff report on super-Cabinet officers and superstaffs, the troubles Mr. Rockefeller evidently found himself in 8 years ago, or Mr. Stassen and others, when their personal service, their ability to be personal agents, to move quickly, to keep abreast of the President's mind—in short, their intimacy—was compromised by all the second-level work their staffs were doing, all the fights their staffs were getting into. The personal assistant begins to bog down as a personal watchdog and intimate servant, once he starts presiding over 50, 80, or 100 subordinates.

A second way of building staff is to create an Office of National Security Affairs detached from the Bundy office, manned by careerists across the street, like the Budget Bureau. We may come to this in time. But, in doing so, we must remember that we are adding another echelon, another level for clearances, another level for negotiations, another set of career officials who have to relate every day with Pentagon and State and the domestic economic agencies; thus, to a degree, we are throwing more pressure on the White House for personal staff work to protect the President's interest in these new interagency interrelationships. My feeling is we should resist this as long as we can.

.   .   .

Mr. Neustadt. There is one other difficulty, Senator, and without spending a lot of time on it, let me put it before you. It underlies my caution and it complicates your hopes, I think.

In my experience, the most effective kind of staff organization is an organization built around what I would call an action-forcing process, by which I mean a steady stream of actionable issues, concrete issues, that have to be attended to, issues where something has to be done, a decision has to be reached.

In this national security area, you have a number of these processes: the budget process with its statutory deadline is one of these; action cables coming in from Embassies abroad requesting answers and instructions, are another; requests for instructions from military assistance groups, the flow through ISA is another. In wartime, the conduct of hostilities creates still others.

Wherever you build staff, you ought to try to build it around one or another of these streams of action, issues that have to be attended to. Otherwise, you just get planners floating in a void, as you suggest. Now, most of these action streams do flow through the departments. The action cables come through the State Department or, if the military are involved, through the Pentagon.

One reason why the Bureau of the Budget, as an institution, is stronger and has lasted longer than others at the Presidential level, is that it is built around just such a stream of actions, budget deadlines, apportionment deadlines, which belong to no department but are imposed routinely and directly on the President himself. If you compare the strength of this entity with the strength of the Council of Economic Advisers, which has much less of an action orientation, I think you will see the difference.

One of the reasons why I keep backing away from an Office of National Security Affairs is that if the staff work there were to be effective, it seems to me you would have to lift up to the President's level, on a routine basis, a great part of the action issues and the action officers now located in Pentagon and State. Otherwise, the Office of National Security Affairs would be a kibitzer, another echelon of planner-kibitzers, on the business, the day-by-day business, of the two Secretaries and their subordinates.

So if we build the new office and then try to insure its success, we tend to pull away from the two Secretaries a lot of relatively routine action-taking, decision-taking before we are done. If we don't pull it away, we run the risk that we just have this other layer, this waffle layer of planners and kibitzers operating in a void. If we do pull it away what have we done to the President?

This is very tricky, in my opinion, and it is the underlying reason why I would like to see the preparatory staff work and the followup on everything the White House now can't handle kept down as close to the present operators as possible.

I grant you that if we took the new Office of Science and Technology, instead of the Budget Bureau, as a model for staff up above the Departments, the case for an Office of National Security Affairs might look a lot better, at least on the surface. Mr. Wiesner and PSAC and OST, taken together, have made quite an impact even though they aren't organized around an action-forcing process they can call their own. But I think this is partly because their full-time staff is still rather small. I don't think I would want to be in Mr. Wiesner's shoes when his staff gets big as it will surely tend to do. More importantly, he and his associates have been able, up to now, to reach out and hook onto action-issues in other people's bailiwicks for a rather special reason: his office has been able to do this with others because it can claim special expertise, because it can lay hands on technical resources, judgments, better or more readily or more confidently than they can. An Office of National Security could never hope to be in such a good position vis-à-vis the expert claims and confidence of others, especially not others like the Pentagon, or CIA, or State—or Treasury, the Fed, and even Commerce, for that matter, if you want to talk about economics. This is part of the problem of the Council of Economic Advisers.

SENATOR MILLER. Let's say we have an Office of National Security Planning set up. Would you prefer to see it set up along the lines of the Council of Economic Advisers, or would you prefer to set it up along—let's talk about action.

Would you prefer to see it confined to actions of the type, if you want to call them that, the Council of Economic Advisers performs, or such as the Bureau of the Budget performs?

MR. NEUSTADT. If you are going to have a strong staff office, you have to build it around actions. You have to build it around the process of receiving and answering requests for instructions from diplomatic and military missions abroad. There is something solid, a solid core of work to build a staff around. If you build it around that, what have you done to the work of the Office of the Secretary of Defense and the Office of the Secretary of State?

SENATOR MILLER. Then I am very happy that I asked you this question and have received your answer.

Let me point out to you that I do not have, in my own mind, any idea of doing that. I think that that is a type of action that ought to be left to the Cabinet office. I do have in mind a planning function which is now being handled, but the way it is being handled is pretty much dependent on the desire and ability to coordinate properly between agencies, and I would certainly not favor having an Office of National Security Planning established that would get into the action level, to which you refer.

I grant that it is difficult to draw the line between policy and action, but I do think that the line should be drawn at the level that you pointed out. I would not be concerned with that. I would envision more difficulty in drawing the line at a higher level. But I think once policy is properly developed, wherever it is developed, that the action will follow. If policy is not properly developed, we are going to have difficulty with our actions.

The Secretary and the Department of State

THE SECRETARY OF STATE

Foreword

The Subcommittee on National Security Staffing and Operations has been making a nonpartisan and professional study of the administration of national security at home and in the field. This is the second in a series of staff reports being issued by the subcommittee.

In the American system of government, the Secretary of State occupies a position of central importance. He is the President's principal adviser on foreign affairs; he often serves as Presidential agent in dealing with other governments; he speaks with authority in declaring and explaining American foreign policy at home and abroad; he has heavy responsibility for coordinating the many elements of policy; and he directs the worldwide activities of the Department of State. As Congress fully appreciates, there is no substitute for a Secretary who is willing and able to exercise leadership in all our major policies toward other nations. The role of the Secretary of State, and the support given him by his Department, have therefore been at the heart of the subcommittee's inquiry.

In approaching its task the subcommittee has built on the work of its predecessor, the Subcommittee on National Policy Machinery.

The present subcommittee has released testimony on the State Department by Secretary of State Rusk, Under Secretary of State Harriman, Deputy Under Secretary of State Crockett, and a number of eminent retired and active ambassadors who have combined work abroad with service in top State Department posts. In addition, it has secured the views of other distinguished present and former Government officials and students of the State Department and the policy process. An initial staff report on the basic issues of the inquiry has been published, together with several background studies.

This staff report, drawing upon the experience of recent years, makes

A Study submitted by the Subcommittee on National Security Staffing and Operations to the Committee on Government Operations, United States Senate, January 20, 1964.

certain suggestions about the role of the Secretary of State and his Department in the administration of the Nation's foreign affairs.

Henry M. Jackson, *Chairman,*
Subcommittee on National Security
Staffing and Operations.

I. Introduction

It is not surprising that the departments often find a President's way of doing business unsettling—or that Presidents sometimes view the departments almost as adversaries.

A continuing dilemma, demanding a subtle appreciation on all sides of the needs of a President and the departments, is how to manage the Government so that Presidential business is transacted to his satisfaction, and so that the normal run of business, also vital to the national interest, can be transacted in a fashion suited to the needs of large scale organization.

Initial staff report, *Basic Issues,* Subcommittee on National Security Staffing and Operations, January 18, 1963

THE administration of national security is a vast and complex undertaking, full of enduring dilemmas which manifest themselves differently in every administration, depending on the operating style of the President and his key associates.

The predecessor Subcommittee on National Policy Machinery concentrated on the problems at the end of the Eisenhower Administration when its patterns of staffing and operations had given rise to certain characteristic difficulties. The Kennedy Administration tried to avoid highly institutionalized procedures, preferring a flexible, informal approach that fitted President Kennedy's way of working. Like all administrations it took some time for its mode of operation to become set. Now the Nation has entered a new transition period with the Johnson Administration.

The tragedy of November 22, 1963, emphasized the importance of continuity. The new President made clear that he would carry on the broad lines of national policy inherited from his predecessor. He showed that he would rely heavily on the staffs already brought together. The Government carried on well.

But when a new President takes charge, many things have to change. We cannot expect the Johnson Administration to continue meeting substantive problems in exactly the same fashion as the Kennedy Administration, or to handle emerging administrative problems in the way the Kennedy Administration might have done, or to maintain the same officials indefinitely in their places.

President Johnson was right and needed to emphasize continuity—especially in policy—during the early days of the transition. But the President—and his Secretary of State—should be free to adopt their own work methods and to select their own subordinates in order to meet their own

Organization of the Department of State

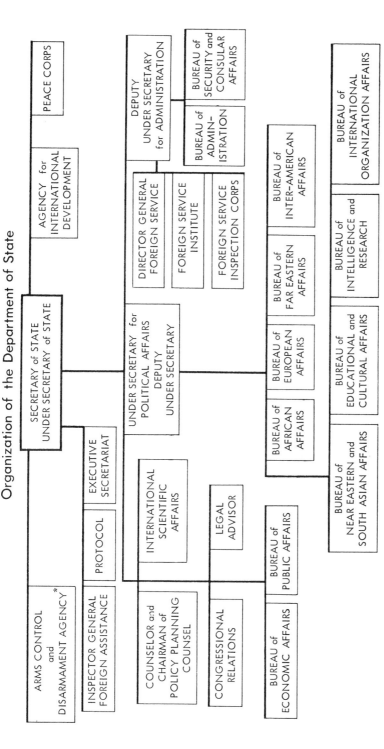

*A separate agency with the Director reporting directly to the Secretary and serving as principal advisor to the Secretary and the President on arms control and disarmament.

needs and their own styles of decision and action. Inevitably, they will
want to employ some new assistants and some new methods. This is as it
should be.

While this is taking place, it seems timely to look at a question which
each new administration has to answer: How can a Secretary of State and
his Department best help the President?

II. The Dilemma of the Secretary of State

> For I want you to know that I look upon the Department of
> State, under the President, as the central force in the framing
> and execution of the foreign policy of this country. . . . I shall
> look to this Department for initiative in proposal, energy in
> action, and frankness in advice.
>
> PRESIDENT LYNDON B. JOHNSON, remarks to officers of the
> Department of State, December 5, 1963

A Secretary of State's duties are extremely heavy.

He is a senior personal adviser to the President, both in private talks
and at working sessions of the President's inner councils. The importance
of this role has increased greatly with the new position of the United States
in world affairs and the coming of the cold war; the role has been complicated by the large place of military factors in the conduct of American
foreign policy and the emergence of the Secretary of Defense as an important adviser on national security affairs—but with a necessarily different
focus and responsibility. The Secretary of State is the only Cabinet officer
primarily charged with looking at our nation as a whole in its relations to
the outside world, and his perspective is needed in all major decisions of
national security planning and policy.

The Secretary of State is also our ranking diplomat in dealing with
foreign governments. As such, he stands at the intersection of affairs: advocate of American policies to other governments, and official channel
of suggestions and protests about American policies from other governments—the hurricane over cancellation of SKYBOLT, the feathers that flew
in the "chicken war" of 1963, and so on. Thus a Secretary is put in the awkward position of transmitting bad news and interpreting "the foreign point
of view" to the President, to other agencies and to the Congress. A Secretary
of State must often feel that he has the makings of an unwelcome visitor.

At the same time, a Secretary serves as an administration spokesman on
American foreign policy to the Congress, to the country, and abroad.
Furthermore, he is chief of the State Department and of the Foreign
Service, and like other department heads, he is responsible to the President
and accountable to the Congress. Finally, he is "Mr. Coordinator"—the
superintendent, for the President, of most major activities affecting our
relations with other countries.

These roles can reinforce each other. At the White House his advice and counsel gain weight because he speaks for his Department, bringing its knowledge, experience, and expertise to bear on questions of concern to the President. His public statements and guidance to the Department and other agencies carry force because he is so often with the President.

The Secretary's roles can also be antagonistic. If he becomes too much a spokesman for the Department and the President comes to feel that he has been "captured" by the bureaucrats, the Secretary's credit as a Presidential adviser may be strained. But if the Secretary spends too much time at the White House—or on the road as negotiator for the President— his direction of the Department may be impaired.

A Secretary cannot escape his dilemma.

To abandon his Department in order to spend time in the White House—an idea once seriously entertained by a recent Secretary—would cloud his title as adviser to the President. The Secretary's comparative advantage as an adviser lies in the fact that he is much more than just another White House assistant. He is the head of a great department with a history and traditions stretching back almost 175 years. In the councils of the President a Secretary ought to be the Department.

However, to absorb himself in running the Department is no solution. No Secretary could afford to spend most of his time on departmental management while others advise the President on the critical issues of the cold war. And if he did, he would soon lose his effectiveness as personal adviser —as well as his real authority in the Department and his influence on Capitol Hill.

The modern Secretary of State is thus adviser, negotiator, reporter of trouble, spokesman, manager, and coordinator. This is all too much. Yet somehow he must handle it. He cannot just take any one piece of his job. He has to do the best he can with all his several duties. None can be sacrificed—or wholly delegated to others. As a result some duties are bound to be shortchanged. Some things that need doing, by him, will be left to others—or left undone, for they will not have sufficient priority to crowd other things off his schedule.

A Secretary of State lives with his dilemma, performing his multiple duties as skillfully and as wisely as he can. But the dimensions of the job are becoming more than man-sized, and ways to ease his burdens are badly needed for the country's sake as well as his own.

To fortify a Secretary in the discharge of his duties, three conditions seem to be of cardinal importance:

One: He needs to enjoy the unusual respect and support of the President.

Two: He needs to have the assistance of a strong, well-staffed, well-run Department.

Three: He needs to have relations with Congress which reinforce him as foreign policy leader.

III. The President and the Secretary

A President may, and will, listen to whom he wishes. But his relationship with the Secretary of State will not prosper if the latter is not accepted as his principal adviser and executive agent in foreign affairs, and the trusted confidant of all his thoughts and plans relating to them.

DEAN ACHESON in *The Secretary of State,* issued by
The American Assembly (1960)

The attitude of a President toward his Secretary of State determines whether he can do the job a President needs done. A Secretary's subordinates within the Department, his Cabinet colleagues, Congress, and the officials of other governments soon discern the true relationship between him and the President. If a President is close to his Secretary, confides in him, and relies heavily on him, a Secretary has a chance to be a great Secretary.

In our system, the President and the Secretary have mutual obligations.

One, clearly, is a Secretary's duty to keep the President promptly and fully informed so that he can handle major issues and crises in the nation's foreign relations with as much freedom of Presidential choice as each situation allows. The President's corresponding obligation is to make his decisions in a clear and reasoned way—providing as part of the decision itself the priority it is to receive—so the Secretary can carry on from where the President leaves off. A President should, of course, support his own decisions so strongly that action can follow from them.

Another obligation is scarcely less important. It is a Secretary's duty to assert his own position and exercise his proper interest across the whole contemporary front of foreign relations. The shoes are big: it is his duty to fill them if he can. The correlative obligation is that the President should be careful not to ask other officers to handle independently tasks which fall within the jurisdiction of the Secretary of State. And he should be cautious about overruling the Secretary on matters that have been entrusted to him, for if other Cabinet officers find that they habitually can get satisfaction at the White House when they have lost out with the Secretary, the Secretary will not long be able to fulfill his responsibilities.

A Secretary's role requires that he be able to see the President whenever he believes he needs to—and see him alone when he wants to. The Secretary and the President need unhurried private occasions for frank talk about the more puzzling problems of foreign policy.

All of this depends on a President's confidence in his Secretary and a conviction that the Secretary can help him more than others in contending with the issues he sees ahead.

IV. The Secretary and the Department

> This device of inviting argument between conflicting interests
> —which we can call the "foulup factor" in our equation of per-
> formance . . . needs some careful examination because there is,
> I think, a discernible and constantly increasing tendency to try
> to expand the intent of the system to the point where mere
> curiosity on the part of someone or some agency, and not a
> "need to know" can be used as a ticket of admission to the merry-
> go-round of "concurrences." This doctrine, unless carefully and
> boldly policed, can become so fertile a spawner of committees
> as to blanket the whole executive branch with an embalmed
> atmosphere.
>
> ROBERT A. LOVETT, Statement before the Senate Subcommittee
> on National Policy Machinery, February 23, 1960

At the heart of a Secretary of State's dilemma is his Department.

The Department's growth would dismay even Mr. Parkinson. On the eve of our entry into World War II the Department employed less than 6,200 at home and overseas. Today, over 24,000 are on the rolls (roughly 7,000 serving in the United States, and 17,000 abroad—including about 10,000 foreign nationals recruited locally).

The Department's burden of business is enormous. It operates some 274 posts abroad—embassies, legations, special missions, and consular offices. Its daily volume of telegraphic traffic includes about 1,500 incoming and 1,500 outgoing cables, carrying more than 400,000 words.

In the vast new State building a Secretary sits amidst 2 Under Secretaries and 2 Deputy Under Secretaries, 13 Assistant Secretaries or their equivalent in charge of 13 Bureaus, over 30 Deputy Assistant Secretaries, more than 60 area and other Office Directors, and over 90 Country Desk Officers, together with assorted advisers and special assistants, counselors and inspector generals, and emissaries from the agencies that lie only partly within the Secretary's jurisdiction.

As things are, the Country Desk Officer stands 7 or 8 levels down in the Department. Above him are:

Deputy Office Director
Office Director
Deputy Assistant Secretary
Assistant Secretary
Deputy Under Secretary for Political Affairs
Under Secretary for Political Affairs
Under Secretary
The Secretary

In practice, no doubt, most business does not have to run the entire gauntlet. But, Secretary Rusk told the subcommittee: "I would say . . . that inside of the Department our principal problem is layering." To illustrate his point Secretary Rusk gave this example:

. . . when I read a telegram coming in in the morning, it poses a very specific question, and the moment I read it I know myself what the answer must be. But that telegram goes on its appointed course into the Bureau, and through the office and down to the desk. If it doesn't go down there, somebody feels that he is being deprived of his participation in a matter of his responsibility.

Then it goes from the action officer back up through the Department to me a week or 10 days later, and if it isn't the answer that I knew had to be the answer, then I change it at that point, having taken into account the advice that came from below. But usually it is the answer that everybody would know has to be the answer.

To tie this unwieldy organization together, and relate it to AID, USIA, Defense, CIA, to the rest of the Government and to other governments, there are committees, boards, commissions and task forces—permanent, ad hoc, large, small, formal, informal, high-level, working level, intra-agency, inter-agency, and now inter-governmental. As Ambassador David Bruce told the subcommittee: "If you want to see anybody in Defense or State, or any other department I know of, they seem to be perpetually off in committee meetings."

In the cold war the ability to act and react quickly is one of our most powerful weapons. A prompt move can dispose of a crisis right off the bat. But if officials are occupied in following routines, respecting petty procedures, chasing around for one "concurrence" after another, and spending hours in committee meetings until every last voice is heard, then the opportunity to act in time is lost. A stale product is the natural offspring of bureaucracy.

The objective is clear and hard-hitting policies—but, as the old proverb goes, "the more cooks the worse pottage."

The Department is at once a burden and a source of strength to the Secretary. How can he turn it into less of a burden and more of an asset? How can the Department be made more manageable and therefore more of a help to the Secretary and to the President?

Robert Lovett, in his testimony to the predecessor subcommittee in 1960, put his finger on the problem:

. . . the position of the individual in Government is being constantly downgraded. . . . Committees cannot effectively replace the decisionmaking power of the individual who takes the oath of office; nor can committees provide the essential qualities of leadership. . . . The authority of the individual executive must be restored . . .

A Secretary could obtain more help from his Department by applying the Lovett philosophy—placing responsibility and authority in the hands of individuals, expecting them to use it, and holding them accountable for their use of it.

The need is for a determined effort in State to consolidate overlapping functions, reduce layering, trim unnecessary staff, kill committees, and make clear assignments of responsibility.

In his testimony to the subcommittee, Secretary Rusk was stimulating on this point. Referring to the regional bureaus, he spoke of the possibility of an experiment to eliminate the Office level, upgrade the Desk Officer, and strengthen the position of the Assistant Secretary.

If the regional Office level could be abolished, a major layer in the Department hierarchy would be excised. This step would enable Desk Officers to report directly to regional Assistant Secretaries. A Desk Officer could be given greater responsibility for handling country problems, on the basis of general guidance. In this event, a Desk Officer should be the equal of an Ambassador in experience and judgment. As Secretary Rusk said: "It seems to me that the man in Washington who spends all of his time brooding about a country like Brazil ought to be a man comparable in competence to the man who is Ambassador to Brazil."

If this were the situation, Assistant Secretaries could be freed to become what they were intended to be—assistants to the Secretary. They could take on more of the cross-cutting, ad hoc, and crisis problems within their sphere of responsibility. It should be possible to eliminate excessive layering above the level of Assistant Secretary by appropriate understandings of the division of work among the top officers.

If results of this sort should flow from the Secretary's suggestions, these would help materially to meet Robert Lovett's standard—giving responsibility to individuals who are able, willing and expected to decide and act.

One looks forward to an elaboration of Secretary Rusk's ideas. Results, of course, will take time to show themselves, and experiments will take time to prove themselves.

A further point: Progress in giving more authority for decision and action to individuals in the State Department sharpens the need for a free interplay of ideas—a lively give-and-take—between a Secretary and officers of the Department, so that they will know how their chief sees things and what he wants. Mutual understanding is the secret of effective teamwork.

V. The Secretary and Interdepartmental Coordination

> . . . the coordination of policy . . . requires not only some understanding of the main substantive aspects of the policy, but also an appreciation of the subtle interconnections of various parts of the government that can come only from years of experience. More than that, it calls for a professional sympathy, a bond of mutual trust based on a common corporate loyalty, between those working in the several departments concerned. This is why we often make no progress toward coordination either by giving additional authority to a political executive or by legislating elaborate structures of interdepartmental coordination.
>
> DON K. PRICE, "Administrative Leadership,"
> *Daedalus* (Fall 1961)

A President, with the help of his own Office, can coordinate national security policy and operations—to the extent he takes command. The President's own Special Assistant for National Security Affairs is indispensable in keeping the President informed about matters that may require his attention and in seeing that he is staffed on issues that he takes into his own hands.

But the Secretary of State is a natural candidate for the coordinating role, when the President cannot perform it or does not choose to. The nature of the Secretary's post leads him more than any other Cabinet officer to have a perspective closely approximating the President's; moreover, for most of the things the Secretary wants to accomplish he must seek help from other agencies and departments—from Defense, Treasury, Agriculture, Commerce, and the like; also, a Secretary has the job of conveying to other parts of the government foreign complaints about American policies and, if necessary, getting something done about them.

A Secretary's authority to command is confined to his own Department. In dealing with others, he can only request, or guide and influence. But given the full confidence and backing of the President, and given sturdy support by his Department, a Secretary will be able to assist his chief in the tasks of coordination.

This role is complicated, of course, by the jungle of interagency committees—the accustomed ground of bureaucratic warfare.

A President and a Secretary, in coordinating national security planning and action, are critically dependent upon strong officers in the State Department who can get things done there, working with strong officers in the other departments and agencies. Interdepartmental coordination calls for individuals in the several agencies who have real authority and responsibility for executive operations, who know and trust each other, and who are in a position to staff out a problem in their own shop and get an answer, without having to go to one more committee. Coordination of policy is not readily achieved where one committee has to consult another.

Delegation of Responsibility

A Secretary of State, like a President, can give his personal attention to only a small number of the problems requiring coordinated interagency decisions and action. For the others—in quantity, the great majority—a Secretary's responsibilities must be delegated.

Deputy Under Secretary of State Crockett spoke to this problem before the subcommittee: "Within the Department itself, we have not yet found satisfactory methods of delegating the Secretary's coordinating responsibilities to officials farther down the chain of command.

In this connection, the Deputy Under Secretary told of certain steps being taken: A start has been made in establishing Desk Officers as the pivot for country working groups; experiments are being tried to designate regional Assistant Secretaries as chairmen of regional interagency policy committees.

If Desk Officers were given authority and responsibility as chairmen of "country teams" in Washington, they would be able to respond to an Ambassador on his level concerning country problems. This would go far to meet a common complaint by American Ambassadors, namely that Washington takes too much time in answering their requests for instructions. Also, the Desk Officer could take the lead in forward country planning in collaboration with the Department's Policy Planning Council, and increasingly with the Ambassador in the field.

Assistant Secretaries, of course, have to earn the position of coordinators. They have to become men whose support is as valuable as their opposition is formidable, and if they do, officers in other parts of the government could be expected to turn increasingly to them for guidance when difficult issues arise. To succeed, Assistant Secretaries need easy access to the Secretary, so that they can speak for him with confidence. They also need to cultivate the kind of rapport with their opposite numbers in the Defense Department and other national security agencies on which a common understanding of policy can be built.

In developing the authority of Assistant Secretaries, the hand of the Secretary of State should be strengthened—not weakened. This requires that Assistant Secretaries should be considered assistants to the Secretary, and not additions to the White House staff. It also requires that any Presidential charge of authority should stipulate that the coordinating responsibility of an Assistant Secretary is exercised on behalf of the Secretary.

Task Forces

In the nature of things special problems and emergency situations call for ad hoc arrangements. The task force has been a natural response. As Secretary Rusk told the subcommittee: "If we were to decide as a matter of theory that task forces are not the right answer, we would still have them because any President or Secretary of State is going to pull together people that he wants to have with him in advising him about what ought to be done in a given situation."

A task force is an interdepartmental committe with extra "oomph." Some task forces have had it; some have not.

Experience to date suggests that a task force can be useful when the following conditions are satisfied:

First: The task force should know for whom it is working and should have a clear assignment—often difficult to achieve in Washington.

Second: A task force must have a chairman—usually an Assistant Secretary or higher officer of the State Department—who will assume personal responsibility for the results.

Third: A task force chairman needs access to the President and the Secretary of State in order to make the work operationally significant.

Fourth: A task force should be quickly and definitively disbanded when the conditions which prompted its establishment have lost their urgency.

Access to Information

If the Secretary of State and his principal assistants are to perform main coordinating roles, they need the fullest possible access to the flow of messages relating to national security. Information is a major source of power. As things now stand, a Secretary of State may not hear of important developments until sometime after a number of other top military and civilian officials have been informed. This state of affairs is not consistent with the responsibilities of the Secretary of State.

The Department of State lacks adequate communications with many countries of the world. This situation is incompatible with the national interest. The cost of fully modern communications is moderate (in comparison with the cost of even a minor military operation in which we might become engaged as a result of poor communications), and the investment is one that should be made.

Also, plans now being developed in the Executive Branch for a National Communications System should ensure that the needs of the Secretary of State are fully met, and that the system, whatever the technical arrangements may be, is operated to his satisfaction.

VI. The Secretary and Senior Officers

> I think we can still say in these days, as in the past, that a good man is hard to find.
>
> I think when we find one who has has judgment and courage and intellect and intuitiveness that we should do everything we can to bring him along fast. We have to put him in situations where he can be subjected to real pressure, where he has to take a position, where he can add not only to his knowledge and experience but to his character at the same time . . . You have to give responsibility . . . you have to force the growth.
>
> GENERAL LAURIS NORSTAD, Statement before the Senate Subcommittee on National Security Staffing and Operations, March 11, 1963

A President and a Secretary of State require more officers in key national security jobs who have diversified experience and a wide perspective on policy.

Today, the State Department at home and abroad needs a corps of 400 to 500 men and women, all of whom are qualified for posts equivalent to that of Career Minister or higher. Some will be citizens drawn from private life; there is a place for non-career appointees who have unusual qualifications and who are called upon to serve one or more tours of duty. Most, however, should and will come from the Foreign Service.

The personal qualifications required for top national security jobs are easy to state and hard to find. Among the main ones are: mature judgment that comes with long and varied experience and a good understanding and sense of history; the ability to lead and inspire subordinates; a "feel" for what is operationally significant in a situation; and a shrewdness in collecting and evaluating evidence.

Officials who have long service but who do not measure up to the high standard demanded at the level of Desk Officer and above, should not be permitted to block the way up for those who do. In a Government as large as ours it usually should be possible to find posts where their experience will enable them to be useful, but in no case should mere seniority serve as a claim to a post exceeding a man's abilities.

Specialist vs. Generalist

For some years there has been a rather sterile controversy over the relative merits in positions of high responsibility of the so-called specialist and the so-called generalist. The State Department and other national security agencies need both specialists and generalists—specialists in economics, law, science, communications, and so forth, and generalists—men and women with good judgment.

A generalist is a specialist who has widened his interests and sacrificed extreme specialization, with its rewards, for assignments presenting broader challenges, and the rewards associated with work covering much or all of the range of foreign policy. But a generalist needs a solid foundation in some specialty. Without it he will be all breadth and no depth and will lack the confidence that comes from mastery of a particular field—a confidence, by the way, that springs from an understanding that specialization seldom justifies a claim to speak with authority on complex issues.

In the past, many of the most outstanding career officers of the State Department have been men who had made top-rank reputations in international law, trade and finance, Soviet affairs, and so on. Today, the Department should have more officers who have made names for themselves in their own specialties and who are accepted as authorities by fellow workers in their own fields. But they cannot be recruited at the beginning rung of the Foreign Service ladder. If one is to earn a reputation of this kind he must complete a full program of graduate work, or its equivalent in terms of practical experience, and spend some time practicing his specialty before entering the Foreign Service. Ambassador Bruce addressed himself to this problem in his testimony to the subcommittee:

> I think it would be helpful if everyone in the Foreign Service started out by doing something else, and had some practical experience in business, and, if it were possible, in a profession—in both, or in one or the other.
>
> For example, if it were not for the pressure of wanting to get in at an early age, it certainly would be a good thing if one who is going into the Foreign Service had practiced law for 5 years—I found it enormously useful myself.

The Foreign Service of course offers unique opportunities to develop certain specialties. But too few of the able young Foreign Service officers are allowed to spend enough time in one place or one line of work to become genuine specialists on the affairs of a country or region or subject, even though such specialization may provide a better foundation for high-level posts than a series of assignments designed to "broaden" a man's experience.

In short, "specialization," properly understood, is not in conflict with the development of generalists, but one way of training people for broad responsibility.

As Ambassador Samuel Berger correctly said to the subcommittee:

> . . . the great need in the Foreign Service is for more officers at the top —whether they are generalists or specialists—who have drive and the kind of experience that enables them to relate one field to another. The Foreign Service has many bright and hard-working specialists and generalists: what it needs is to select, encourage, guide, and train the most promising for appointment to the senior positions.

Training vs. Experience

The Government may be suffering currently from overconfidence in formal educative processes and an overestimation of the benefits of formal training. For the Foreign Service officer, and the officers of most other national security agencies, assuming a good educational background, experience is almost always the best teacher.

Comparisons of time spent in training military officers can be quite misleading. In times of peace the military establishment is in being but not in full operation, while the Foreign Service is wholly engaged, and it can scarcely spare good people for formal education when it does not have enough good people to fill all the critical posts around the world. It does not follow, therefore, that the Foreign Service should have its own educational institutions, just because the military have theirs.

On the job training and experience are likely to be more "educational" for Foreign Service officers than a year at an educational institution. Officers unable to derive wisdom from responsibility for real problems are not likely to grow while sitting in the classroom or in the library.

This is not to say that formal educational opportunities have no place in the training of Foreign Service officers, but to put the utility of such opportunities in proportion to the benefits that can reasonably be expected.

For some officers a chance to catch up with the advances in their fields of specialization or become acquainted with thinking and research in a field new to them may be useful. For this purpose, major reliance should be placed on existing universities and research centers because the instruction is likely to be better than can be provided by a government institution with its special limitations. It is probable, furthermore, that such a use of existing universities and centers will cost the government less than an effort to create and maintain a high quality graduate school under federal auspices.

For training related to government requirements, better use can be made of interagency job exchanges, like the State-Defense Officer Exchange Program. It is also possible that the mid-career and senior officer programs of the Foreign Service Institute could be strengthened as a way of introducing officers to new and urgent government problems.

Finally, the Service War Colleges, the Industrial College of the Armed Forces, the National War College, and such comparable programs as the NATO Defense College now provide opportunities for a number of Foreign Service officers and officers from other agencies to study foreign affairs from a new perspective and in association with colleagues from the military services. Foreign Service officers who have had this experience are unanimous in their judgment that it was valuable. At small cost a few additional officers could be enrolled in these institutions.

These suggested steps are modest. But they are practicable, and they are realistic in that they recognize that the most important education a Foreign Service officer obtains is on the job—working, in effect, as an apprentice to the top men in his field.

VII. The Secretary and the Congress

> For methods and procedures at their best cannot abolish the deep difficulties of perception, of analysis, of judgment, of persuasion which confront our policymakers now and in the future. Organizational arrangements at their most ingenious cannot rub out the underlying differences of duty, interest, role, perspective, separating Presidency from officialdom—and separating both from Congress, for that matter.
>
> RICHARD E. NEUSTADT, Statement before the Senate Subcommittee on National Security Staffing and Operations, March 25, 1963

In the American system, two men have the chief responsibility for the making and execution of foreign policy—the President and the Secretary of State. But Congress, too, has its responsibilities.

Congress is constitutionally the creator of executive departments, the source of their statutory mandates, and the monitor of their operations; it authorizes programs; it appropriates funds; it investigates the executive agencies; the laws it passes can help or hinder the government in recruiting and retaining good people; the Senate advises and consents to treaties, and to appointments of Cabinet members, Ambassadors, and other top officials.

In our governmental system the Secretaries of State and Defense and other department heads are not only responsible to the President, but they are also accountable to the Congress for the proper performance of their statutory duties—and for the very good reason that in our system we do not place unlimited confidence or authority in any one man.

An illustration of how things can go wrong in the absence of executive accountability is provided by Hitler's Germany. Robert Lovett, on a post-war inspection trip to Germany, was told by a leading industrialist:

> . . . one of the reasons that the German economy collapsed and that the Wehrmacht was left inadequately supplied in the latter days was because under a dictatorship, once a department head got the nod from Hitler, he went ahead as a little dictator and rode his particular hobby without criticism. There was no performance audit run on him as his program continued.

Robert Lovett added this comment in his 1960 testimony:

> . . . if I had to choose between having a congressional committee breathe on the back of my neck as a form of performance audit and getting in the position as a department executive of riding some particular conviction or belief to the point of defeat I would choose a congressional hearing. And I still feel that way about it. Appearing before committees is time consuming, it is exhausting, sometimes terribly irritating, but on the whole, as long as we have our form of governmental system, I think it is a necessary part of it.

Our system of government is a system of checks and balances, and despite occasional proposals, usually of academic origin, that we should trade it in on a parliamentary model nothing of the kind is going to happen. The problem is to make our system work better.

It is obvious, as it long has been, that checking and balancing can produce controversy, and sometimes a bruising battle. What is less obvious, perhaps, is that such a condition may reflect real differences of view about national policy—differences that need to be taken seriously. The 1963 Congressional debate over the foreign aid program provides a contemporary case in point.

By the nature of his post, a Secretary of State bears heavy responsibility for developing the support in Congress to sustain public policy. But this task is not without its special problems.

For one, neither the Executive nor the Congress are fully unified. Various executive departments and bureaus may act quite independently in dealing with the Congress. At the same time, the responsibilities of Congress are exercised to a large degree by individual committees in both Houses—for many purposes there is a multitude of little Congresses with which the executive agencies deal. This situation creates hazards for a Secretary of State, who is trying to take the most general view of the national interest.

Then, too, a Secretary of State's duties put him in a world of knowledge different from the world the Congress inhabits. Members of Congress know a lot about what is happening abroad, but they know it differently from the Secretary and the State Department, at a different time, and they see it first from their own perspective.

In addition, a Secretary of State is the bearer of bad tidings to Congress. He interprets complaints of foreign governments to its committees, and he often presses the case of a foreign government because he thinks it has a case and that Congress has in fact acted unwisely. A Secretary and his Department, thus, come to Capitol Hill as a kind of counsel for "the vast external realm" beyond our borders. There they confront members of Congress who are, in effect, counsels for the "folks back home" with the duty to represent them and to take care of their interests.

The differences of concern and perspective separating Congress and the State Department lie at the root of many past difficulties. They will remain a source of trouble. Fortunately, most members of Congress agree with Edmund Burke's counsel to his Bristol constituents: "Your representative owes you, not his industry only, but his judgment"; furthermore, there are a great many Senators and Representatives with long experience and good sense in national security matters; and, traditionally, Congress has handled vital defense and foreign policy issues in terms of our national interests. Fortunately, also, some officials in State—though too few—understand not only foreign policy, but Congress.

Other things can be done.

For example, the State Department can do more to inform members of Congress in advance of a crisis condition. There is always a tendency in the Executive Branch to let matters slide until trouble occurs. It is then too late, more often than not, to build the understanding needed in support of a line of policy. In a crisis the appeal is for unity, and the appeal is almost always answered, but the consequences may be undesirable in terms of long-run cooperation, for Congress should not be put under the gun as a normal routine of Executive-Legislative relationships.

Better use can be made of informal meetings for full, frank, and frequent exchanges. Some Secretaries and Under Secretaries of State in the recent past have been skillful and effective in building an understanding of national security policies through informal consultations with key members of Congress, especially in connection with matters too delicate for public discussion. Legislative liaison staffs cannot do this job.

Better opportunities should be created for Congress to see national security issues "in the round." As things now stand, defense and foreign policies are cut into jigsaw-puzzle pieces which are never put together.

Except in the general terms of the State of the Union message and the Budget, national security information and program requests are presented to Congress in fragments. Congressional procedures compound the problem. The authorization process separates things that are, or should be, indivisible. At least five major Senate committees handle pieces of national security policy. If the domestic economic implications of national security are taken into account, as they should be, at least seven major Senate committees are involved. A similar situation exists in the House.

To help meet this situation, Congress might create suitable occasions for the Secretaries of State and Defense and other high officials to make over-all presentations of national security policies and programs, and to respond to questions. One good time for such a joint appearance would be early in each session. An effort should be made to avoid imposing on Cabinet officials repeated presentations of the same material.

Other useful steps could be taken to meet the problem of fragmentation. Main committees can undertake to obtain more comprehensive testimony on policies and programs before they are divided up among subcommittees for detailed analysis. Closer working relationships between revenue and expenditure committees can be encouraged. In some cases, committees may need additional competent help from staff and consultants.

But procedural improvements cannot solve the basic problem of Executive-Legislative relationships in national security affairs. For genuine differences of perspective stem from differences of responsibility. It is incumbent on members of Congress to recognize that these differences do exist and that both perspectives are legitimate. One cannot and should not ask Congressmen to ignore their own responsibilities, but one can ask that in this twentieth year since the onset of the cold war, members of Congress take pains to see the Secretary of State's situation, his dilemmas and his legitimate concerns and to respect his perspective, even though often it will and must differ from theirs.

And vice versa.

Robert Ellsworth Elder

COUNTRY DESK OFFICER:
LOW MAN ON THE TOTEM POLE

A country desk officer in one of the regional bureaus of the Department of State may be low man on the totem pole so far as seniority in policy-making is concerned, yet he wields significant power in the formulation of American foreign policy. With a considerable degree of truth, it may be said of him that he is both wheelhorse and sparkplug of the decision-making process.

Policy-making in the Department of State is centered in five regional bureaus, which in turn are composed of sub-regional offices. The five regional bureaus cover (1) European Affairs, (2) Far Eastern Affairs, (3) Near Eastern and South Asian Affairs, (4) Inter-American Affairs, and (5) African Affairs. (The Bureau of International Organization Affairs is often considered a sixth regional bureau because it is responsible for Department relations with the American mission to the United Nations. It assumes action responsibility for items on the United Nation's agenda, in the same fashion that the five reorganized regional bureaus are responsible for relations with their assigned areas.)

The bureaus maintain close contact with American embassies in their respective continental areas of responsibility, receiving despatches from abroad and sending out policy instructions. An Assistant Secretary of State heads each regional bureau. He serves in somewhat the same capacity as an operating vice president in the business world. Below him in the hierarchy are his Office Directors, each responsible for operations in a small group of countries. The country desk officer is at the bottom of this heap. He usually concerns himself, subject to supervision and review from above, with policy toward a single foreign nation.

In the comfortable, pre-World War II days, when the Department still had less than 1,000 employees, policy-making was the responsibility of small regional divisions which dealt through desk officers with American embassies and legations overseas. Desk officers were in close contact with the single Assistant Secretary of State who headed the regional divisions,

FROM *The Policy Machine* by Robert Ellsworth Elder. Copyright 1960 by Syracuse University Press, Syracuse, New York. Reprinted by permission of the publisher. All and often consulted directly with the Secretary of State. The growing workload of the Department during and after World War II, with a concurrent increase in personnel and almost continuous reorganization, changed the divisions to offices and then to bureaus. The country desk officer worked at the same old last, but the hierarchy above him became more complex. The Office Director separated him from regular contact with his Assistant Secretary, now one among five Assistant Secretaries heading regional bureaus. An Under Secretary for Political Affairs lessened the need for consultation with the Secretary of State, who had become much too busy to see desk officers anyway.

In spite of these changes, the Department's 114 country desk officers remain the eyes and ears, the brain and voice, of America in a troubled world. They keep daily watch over events in 179 political entities from Aden through Zanzibar. Almost every scrap of information which government agencies collect on an area and many policy papers from other agencies proposing action in an area cross the country desk, at a rate of 250 to 350 documents per day. (The desk man learns to get the gist of a document in ten seconds, to know whether he must read it in detail or not.) The desk remains the real contact point in the Department for the diplomatic post abroad and the foreign embassy in Washington.

As the drafting officer who usually is first to put policy ideas on paper, the desk man is in a sense the initiator of American policy toward his assigned country. He writes telegrams, memoranda, and even more formal policy papers. His drafts, perhaps modified by a superior but many times not touched at all, often reach an Assistant Secretary of State, may go in revised form before the National Security Council for consideration and final decision by the President. In whatever form his broad policy paper may at last be adopted by the NSC, he is likely to be consulted in the drafting of the Operations Coordinating Board's more specific paper on how the NSC policy shall be implemented. Later, he will draft OCB progress reports on actual implementation, how policy operations are progressing in the field, subject to the opinion and attitudes of others in an OCB working group.

The desk man's influence at all levels in the decision-making process stems from his detailed knowledge of an area and his role as a drafting officer. Unless he is really out of step, it is easier for his bosses to concur or make minor revisions than to disagree and upset his apple cart. The "tyranny of the written word" works in his favor. On day-to-day routine matters, the desk officer is cock of the walk. He may have considerable influence upon policy decisions at higher levels. However, his room for maneuver in the formulation of policy is not too great. He is quite conscious of the views of his superiors. He does not make policy in a vacuum.

The basic assumptions and broad goals of American policy already considered by the National Security Council and approved by the President, as well as implementing policies previously formulated by the Operations Coordinating Board, quickly become an inherent part of his thinking. These are likely to be of a relatively stable and continuing nature, predating his coming to the desk. They tend to set the limits within which he will operate on policy matters, for agonizing reappraisals are more likely to come from above than from below. The desk man has an opportunity to know public, legislative, and executive opinion in America and abroad. This knowledge limits the practical alternatives open to his consideration. His recommendations on unusual or controversial questions are thoroughly reviewed. After all, he is low man on the foreign policy-making totem pole. There is no question of the right of those above him to disapprove policies he proposes or to force revision of his proposals. This authority is often used. Members of the Department of State Policy Planning Staff, as well as regional and functional planners, have as one of their major functions the development of policy statements which may be approved by top Department officials. True, the desk officer is likely to be consulted as work progresses if the policy involves his country directly, but broader regional and functional considerations may minimize the effectiveness of his argument. The desk officer must fall in line.

When the chips are down and an international crisis flares, the desk officer may take part with his Office Director and Assistant Secretary in "telecon" conferences with posts overseas. He may work round the clock drafting instructions to the American embassy in his country. But these are subject to review by the Assistant Secretary. If it is a question of peace or war, the decision is made at an even higher level. At such a time, the Secretary, Under Secretary, and Under Secretary for Political Affairs may consider the Department's recommendations with the Deputy Under Secretary for Administration and the Assistant Secretaries. The final executive decision may be taken by the President, probably after informal consultation with several trusted members of the National Security Council. The narrower country interests of the desk officer are buried under this parade of high brass. It is just as well. There is no time for paperwork. The discussions are face to face. The decisions must be immediate, the considerations global.

The Foreign Service Type

There is probably no such thing as a typical desk officer, but there have been those who once served at the desk level who could be defined as the "desk officer type," in the same way that William S. White defines the "senate type" in *Citadel*, "a man for whom the Institution is a career in itself, a life in itself and an end in itself." [1] In the good old days (at least

---

[1] William Smith White, *Citadel* (New York: Harper & Row, 1957).

a decade ago), before Wristonization [2] with its integration of Department personnel into the Foreign Service, during the mid-1950's, the desk officer type—though certainly always in a minority among the Department's desk officers—must have existed and even flourished. Indeed, he was often viewed with alarm by young Foreign Service officers in the field. They knew him neither by sight nor sound but doubted that he understood their areas, their recommendations, or the necessity of ever taking prompt action. They did know he had a veritable worship of forms and red tape and found reporting officers at posts abroad wretched creatures of incomparable imperfection.

The situation of endless tenure on the desk, coupled with a condition of permanent servitude in the field, which led to so many misunderstandings in the past, no longer abounds. By and large, the desk officer type either has gone to his reward, been retired, transferred to another agency, or—worst of all—been sent to the field. His replacement is usually a "Foreign Service type," younger, more flexible, easier to get along with, certainly much better fitted in many ways for the rough-and-tumble exigencies of policy-making in the hydrogen missile and earth satellite age. This new type comes from the field, often with several years of specialized training and experience before assignment, works the desk for no more than four years, and returns to the field.

One speaks of the "Foreign Service type" without derogation; the appellation can be viewed only as a symbol of forthright flattery by anyone who knows the modern country desk officer. College-trained and usually in his late thirties or early forties, the Foreign Service type desk officer is personable and intelligent, possessing some verbal skill, considerable initiative, and a sense of responsibility. It is expected of this modern Foreign Service type desk officer that he be as American as Hoosier fried chicken, as moral as the man who sits next to you in church on Sunday, and as mature and agile of mind as a senior member of a university faculty. He must possess a cosmopolitan urbanity which provides him with an ability to be at home with people, either at a hot dog roast in suburbia or a caviar and cocktail affair on embassy row. The latter he counts as business rather than pleasure. Not all desk officers measure up equally well to every one of these

[2] The term "Wristonization" is derived from the fact that Henry M. Wriston, while still President of Brown University, served as chairman of the committee which recommended the integration of Departmental and Foreign Service personnel. The purpose was to better acquaint Foreign Service officers with the problems at home, and the Department staff members with the situation in the field. "Wristonees" are the Department officers, formerly in the Civil Service and subject only to assignment in Washington, who were accepted into the Foreign Service and became subject to assignment overseas. As a result of the implementation of the Wriston Committee's recommendations, additional positions were opened to Foreign Service officers in the Department—including many at desk officer level. Conversely, many "Wristonees"—including a number of former desk officers—were sent abroad for service at American embassies or legations. If this new flexibility of assignment solved some problems, it created others.

demanding specifications, but the Foreign Service type—with his enthusiasm, tolerance, and sense of humor—will have a good try at meeting these requirements. Failure to achieve perfection does not particularly bother him. The Foreign Service type, in contrast with the desk officer type, readily confesses that he is occasionally fallible, that to err is human. This modest admission is one of his most engaging traits.

Since Wristonization, the dream of every real Foreign Service type is to hold down a country desk in the Department of State at one point in his career; the enchanting vision is before him always, once he passes his written and oral examinations and is inducted into the Foreign Service of the United States. Such a coveted assignment will be ample compensation for years at lonely outposts overseas. Not that he necessarily wants a Washington tour. Living conditions are expensive, adequate housing difficult to find, servants out of the question; all this is quite upsetting to Foreign Service wives, if an Americanizing influence upon their children. But if the Foreign Service type goes to Washington at all, he hopes it will be to the desk. He views the desk not only as an end in itself but as a steppingstone toward further preferment in the Foreign Service.

Policy-making and political operations are the primary functions for which the Department of State is in business, but the successful carrying on of line tasks requires adequate supplemental staffing. In the interest of building a well-balanced Foreign Service, many young officers are assigned Departmental tours of duty in the fields of intelligence, administration, and public affairs—possibly as economic or political analysts in functional bureaus. The true Foreign Service type serves faithfully but rather unhappily when assigned Department duty outside the regional bureaus. Almost always, he continues to cast a wistful eye toward the desk. There the responsibility appears to be more directly related to policy formulation and operations. These are the functions he considers to be the essence of his life's work.

Even if the desk has lost some of its direct personal relationship with the Secretary of State, as the Department has grown in response to American assumption of leadership in an increasingly complex world, the desk has lost little of its attraction or glamour. It is true that the desk officer no longer serves as a "little despot," making policy on the cables. More and more consideration must be given to the wishes of other areas and bureaus within the Department, to the conflicting interests of other departments, and to the coordinating agencies like the National Security Council and the Operations Coordinating Board. American policy-makers face the necessity of developing some consistency between policies toward individual states, for entire regions, and of a global nature. Today, country policy is a small cog which must mesh in several larger wheels. Even so, with the increasing stature of the United States in world politics and the positive rather than the passive role now played by America overseas, the Foreign

Service type may have a greater net influence upon international affairs than did his desk officer type predecessor (in spite of a loss of power in relationship to other groups in the Department or outside it).

Let us make a necessary but small point. The Department of State distinguishes between the terms "desk officer" and "officer in charge." There is, for example, an Officer in Charge of France-Iberia Affairs. There is also a French desk officer. There is presumably a single desk officer for Spain and Portugal. The desk officers, in this case, are guided to some extent in their operations by their officer in charge. In most bureaus, an officer in charge can initiate and send a telegram of routine instructions to the field over the Secretary of State's signature without clearing with a superior officer. A desk officer may draft such a telegram, but the authority for sending it would rest with the officer in charge.

For present purposes, both officers in charge and desk officers fall loosely under our working phrase, desk officer. "Officer in charge" sounds more pretentious and may be best suited to the desk officer type of recent memory, but the modest title of "desk officer" well befits all the hardworking, quick-witted young men who today fill these closely related posts.

Enough has been said of the function and nature of the desk officer in the regional bureaus of the Department of State to indicate the degree of his importance to an understanding of the foreign policy decision-making process. A more detailed look at how he performs his duties is desirable.

Sources of Information

Without a constant flow of information, the Department of State might just as well shut up shop. Furthermore, the right facts must reach the right people at the right time. In most instances, sufficient facts—and a great many more—are available at the proper time for the performance of the desk officer's policy-making operations. The success of the efficient flow of information and policy papers through the Department must be attributed in some measure to the Executive Secretariat, which monitors the process from on high, as an adjunct to the Office of the Secretary.

The desk man's most important source of information is the American Foreign Service post abroad. Embassies send daily telegrams on questions requiring immediate action. Despatches via diplomatic courier or air mail pouch include additional detail. Each week the post forwards a broad report covering political, economic, and military developments, the so-called "weeka." It includes information on cultural, psychological, agricultural, and other aspects of national life. Conditions are viewed with more perspective in quarterly, semi-annual, and annual reports from the post. At some posts, in addition, eager beaver Foreign Service type officers prepare a thorough round-up despatch a year after being assigned to a country, and another when they finish their tour of duty. This is a valuable training device and also yields useful information for the desk officer in the Department.

Daily political, economic, and military intelligence reports are available to desk officers. These are of value in day-to-day operations. By the time the Central Intelligence Agency's weekly summary reaches the desk, its information may be old stuff, but its evaluative comment is appreciated. Information copies of detailed reports by our embassy attachés to the departments of Defense, Commerce, Treasury, Agriculture, Labor, the International Cooperation Administration, and the United States Information Agency also pass across the desk. They are useful as background but not for daily operations.

News stories and editorial comment from leading foreign newspapers are wired daily from some embassies to the desk. Press clippings air mailed from the post are a more common practice. Foreign language newspapers and periodicals published in the United States are also received. Desk officers interested in our good neighbors to the South read *Diario Las Americas* and the Latin American edition of *Time*. Press reports are not official, but Department news tickers sometimes carry information before it comes from the post. Associated Press, United Press International, and Reuters ticker reports from the Office of News are fanned out to the desks every hour. Press clippings from twenty-eight American papers are distributed daily.

Summaries of editorial comment in the American press are circulated each day to many desks by the Department's Public Opinion Studies Staff. A monthly summary sets public opinion in a broader context. Special studies give more detailed analyses of American attitudes toward policy in specific areas. The desk officer is less interested in this material than higher-ranking officers in the Department who must wrestle more directly with the question of political feasibility.

The *New York Times* is the desk officer's favorite newspaper. At the office, in most bureaus, he reads a marked copy which indicates articles or comments related to his country. More leisurely reading at home may fill him in on other world developments. Contact with scholarly publications may be maintained by regular routing of periodicals from the Library Division or by personal subscription. One desk man in the Bureau of Far Eastern Affairs, for example, reads the *Far Eastern Quarterly*, *Foreign Affairs*, and the *Annals of the American Academy of Political and Social Sciences*. Interest of desk officers in this type of publication is quite uneven.

The desk officer does little of his own research. Some pertinent research information appears in studies prepared for the Senate Foreign Relations and House Foreign Affairs Committees by the Legislative Reference Service or on contract by outside consultants. Within the Department, the desk obtains specialized research studies from the Bureau of Intelligence and Research, the Historical Office, the Legal Adviser, and the Bureau of Economic Affairs.

Embassies of foreign nations in Washington often have less basic data available on their countries than the desk officer. Informal and formal relations between the desk and embassy are primarily of use in providing operational information.

The Daily Routine

Since no desk officer can ever count ahead of time upon a routine day, a single day's schedule of one desk officer's activities may not be typical of all desk men's routines, but it is revealing:

8:45–9:15 A.M.   Reads incoming correspondence and telegrams from the field. (Actually, he often arrives at 8:00 A.M. to do this.) Takes action as necessary. Reads newspaper.

9:15–10:00 A.M.   Daily staff conference with other desk officers, chaired by his Office Director. (The Office Director has just come from the Assistant Secretary's staff conference.)

10:00–11:45 A.M.   Conference with representatives from State, Agriculture, and the International Cooperation Administration to agree on text of a grant to his country under Public Law 480 dealing with the disposal of surplus agricultural commodities.

11:45–12:45 P.M.   Drafts telegram to American embassy overseas, informing it of present stage of developments on grant. Carries telegram by hand around Department for clearance.

12:45–1:45 P.M.   Drafts tentative copy of formal *Department Instructions* which will go to American embassy overseas to accompany text of proposed grant.

1:45–2:15 P.M.   Lunch.

2:15–3:00 P.M.   Writes a personal and informal letter to the Chargé d'Affaires in the American embassy overseas to explain the proposed grant.

3:00–4:00 P.M.   Attends special conference to brief the Under Secretary of Commerce who is going to a trade fair in his country as the President's representative. The desk officer details political and economic conditions in the country and explains cultural differences.

4:00–4:30 P.M.   Briefs a teacher who is going to his country on an exchange program. Discusses housing problems, the country's educational system, research facilities, as well as political, economic and social conditions.

4:30–5:30 P.M.   Reads memoranda and telegrams which have come to his desk during day for clearance. Writes comments or recommendations.

5:30–6:00 P.M.   (He's working overtime again.) Reads reports from field and other sources of information which have come to his desk during the day.

In addition to these formally recorded events, there were a number of phone calls, both in and out—for example, one from a member of Congress, another from a businessman with interests in the desk man's country, one to the country's embassy in Washington, another from it. Also, he checked several matters with desk officers in neighboring offices and, on one occasion, sought the advice of his Office Director. There happened to be no face-to-face relations with any representative of his country's embassy during this particular day.

Relations of the desk and embassy may be either business or social, official functions or informal gatherings. Minor business is discussed by telephone or by a visit of someone from the embassy to the desk. The range of problems arising in embassy-desk relations is great and may include matters of either private or public concern. The parents of a child stricken by polio in a foreign land appeal through their embassy in Washington for special treatment available only in the United States. The embassy arranges for free care by a private agency. When the mother arrives in America with her child, there is a misunderstanding about arrangements with the agency. To whom does the embassy turn for advice and assistance? Several phone calls by the desk officer resolve the difficulty. A husband whose nationality is that of the desk officer's country unthoughtfully murders his wife, a former United States citizen. Her brother is an American citizen. The husband is put in jail. The brother gains custody of the children and brings them to the United States. The husband's wealthy family in the desk officer's country seeks through the embassy in Washington to gain custody of the children. Who is right in the middle of the tugging and hauling? The desk officer, of course.

The ambassador may call at the Department in person if his government's interests are directly involved. When he talks with an appropriate Assistant Secretary or the Under Secretary, the desk officer is usually present. The ambassador may present a "note" or leave an *aide memoire*. If the ambassador informs the Department ahead of time as to the subject of his visit, the desk officer draws up a "briefing memorandum" for the Assistant Secretary, including background information and a recommended American position. If the subject is not known, the memorandum covers several possible topics. Immediately after the meeting, the desk officer prepares a "memorandum of conversation" for the Assistant Secretary. He also writes the first draft of any reply necessitated by the discussion. Information copies of both go in final form to interested posts overseas and government agencies in Washington.

An agreement may have been reached between the foreign embassy and the Department for the transfer of surplus equipment at an airfield abroad.

The desk officer drafts a third person note to the foreign embassy expressing the Department's pleasure at agreement. "The Department will arrange for the details of transfer." He sends a telegram advising the American post overseas of the agreement. If he has intimate knowledge which will be useful to the post in making the transfer, he writes a personal letter to some member of the staff. He also draws up detailed formal instructions to the American embassy, outlining the transfer process: documents involved, who must sign, number and routing of copies.

From time to time the desk officer is drawn into the process of drafting position papers to guide American negotiators at the United Nations or attending special international conferences. Papers of this type require coordination with other regional or functional bureaus and cooperation with the Bureau of International Organization Affairs. The position paper (with background, discussion, and recommendations) can be a challenging task to the desk officer. He must set in historical context the position which states have previously taken on the problem, anticipate the maximum and minimum demands of those likely to oppose the American position, suggest maximum and minimum positions for the United States. Then he must discuss this variety of possible positions, presenting the arguments for each. Finally, he sums up and justifies a set of policy recommendations.

No less a challenge is the desk officer's role in congressional relations. If legislation which is to be proposed to Congress by the Department may affect his country, an officer is drawn into discusions within the Department during the legislative drafting sessions. He may participate later in conferences with other agencies and with representatives of the Bureau of the Budget in getting clearance for such legislative measures within the executive branch. When the bill has been introduced and reaches a congressional committee for hearings, the desk man is likely to testify before an executive session of the committee.

He is also drawn into the answering of Department mail from a congressional source. Such letters are routed into the Department by the Bureau of Congressional Relations and must be answered within three days. If an official policy statement cannot be cleared within that time, the desk officer must notify the Congressman by phone or letter why an answer is not immediately forthcoming, and approximately when an answer can be given. Even questions posed to the Department by a Congressman on behalf of his constituents are sometimes forwarded to the desk officer for a reply.

Not all of the desk officer's daily routine is paperwork. He has many visitors, most not connected with embassies. They must be interspersed with drafting, clearances, conferences, staff meetings, and telephone calls. He talks with researchers or social workers going out to his area, to business men with interests abroad, and to ordinary citizens with family problems in a foreign country. The telephone is indispensable to the desk officer. As the center of information in the Department on a certain country, all sorts of queries are directed to him. If he doesn't know the answer, he has to know where to get it. He has information contacts throughout the Department and in many other government agencies. Without the telephone, the desk officer could not gather spot information from his colleagues nor get rapid and informal clearance of notes to embassies, telegrams and instructions to the field, or policy papers (not to mention letters to Congressmen).

Clearance and Coordination

Many desk officers prefer to keep paperwork at a minimum and consult or exchange information in person with fellow desk officers or their immediate superior, the Office Director. Others are confirmed "paper pushers," memorandum writers who send most information up the line or to other desks in typed form. Information in a despatch reaching the desk from the field may be important enough to demand consideration at higher levels. The desk officer summarizes the despatch, makes a recommendation, and forwards the memorandum to his Office Director. The despatch, with important sections underlined, goes along as an attachment.

Normally, a memorandum is drafted on any question to be considered by an Assistant Secretary. Memoranda are factual, usually a page in length, and hardly ever more than three. Over a third conclude with a policy recommendation. New desk officers send more problems to the office of their Assistant Secretary for review than do experienced desk men. If the question is controversial, like East-West relations or Tunisian-French relations, the desk seeks guidance. The Office Director forwards memoranda on matters of sufficient importance—approved or disapproved—to the Assistant Secretary.

Failure by the desk officer to obtain clearance from other bureaus in the Department or from other government agencies with a direct interest in a note, telegram, or policy paper means that agreement must be sought at a higher level or the matter dropped. An attempt is made to solve a problem at as low a level as possible. The purpose is not to arrogate power but to reduce the burden on the Assistant Secretary and those above him. The policy-making pyramid narrows rapidly, with fewer decision-makers and broader areas of authority at the top. Department leaders must be protected from being literally smothered in their offices by the flow of paper. Even with efficient screening of materials which reach them, these men work under constant pressure.

A single problem concerning Near Eastern oil may involve the country desk officer for Iran and desk officers for the USSR, Great Britain, the United Arab Republic, Jordan, and Saudi Arabia; representatives of the Bureaus of Intelligence and Research, Economic Affairs, International Organization Affairs, and Congressional Relations; plus desk officers or specialists from the Central Intelligence Agency, the Departments of Defense and Commerce, the International Cooperation Administration, and the United States Information Agency.

When a policy statement prepared by the desk officer for Iran runs into trouble in the clearance process—and how can it avoid being tempest-tossed with such a variety of interests to be accommodated—a conference of interested bureaus and agencies is held at the desk level to attempt a resolution of differences. If this fails, the question may go up to the Office Director, with a recommendation from the desk. The Office Director checks with others at his level in the Department and other agencies. If speed is of the essence and problems continue to separate the interested parties, the question must be forwarded to the Assistant Secretary and arrangements made for an inter-agency conference at this relatively high level. If this meeting does not produce agreement, the Under Secretary for Political Affairs or perhaps his deputy will take a crack at resolving differences with his peers in other departments and agencies. (By this time, at least, the Department itself must be pretty much united on the issue.) The search for a solution may require direct intervention by the Under Secretary or the Secretary of State himself. When the question is of such national importance that differences must be resolved and action taken, disagreement among departments at the Under Secretary or Secretary level sends the problem to the National Security Council, after as thorough staff preparation as time will allow, for a final decision by the President. As the sign said on President Harry Truman's desk when he was in the White House, "The buck stops here."

Charlton Ogburn, Jr.

THE FLOW OF POLICY-MAKING IN THE DEPARTMENT OF STATE

THE Department of State is an organism that is constantly responding to a vast assortment of stimuli. A new Soviet threat to Berlin, a forthcoming conference of Foreign Ministers of the Organization of American States, a request from Poland for credit, a solicitation for support of a candidacy for the Presidency of the United Nations General Assembly, a plea from an ambassador that the head of the government to which he is accredited be

FROM *The Formulation and Administration of United States Foreign Policy,* H. Field Haviland, ed. (Washington: The Brookings Institution, 1960). Reprinted by permission of the publisher.

invited to visit the United States officially, a refusal by another government to permit the duty-free importation of some official supplies for a U.S. consulate, a request from the White House for comment on the foreign affairs section of a major presidential address, an earthquake in the Aegean creating hardships which it appears the U.S. Navy might be able to alleviate, a request for a speaker from a foreign policy association in California, a transmittal slip from a Member of Congress asking for information with which to reply to a letter from a constituent protesting discriminatory actions against his business by a foreign government, letters from citizens both supporting and deploring the policy of nonrecognition of Communist China, a continuing inquiry by a press correspondent who has got wind of a top secret telegram from Embassy Bonn on the subject of German rearmament and is determined to find out what is in it, a demand by a Protestant church group that the Department take steps to prevent harassment of their coreligionists in a foreign country, a request by a delegation of a federation of women's clubs for a briefing on southeast Asia and suggestions as to how its members might be useful in their planned tour of the area, a request from Consulate General Brazzaville for a revision of cost-of-living allowances, a visit by a commission of inquiry into the operations of U.S. foreign aid programs, a notification from the staff of the National Security Council that a revision of the National Security Council paper on dependent areas is due, a telegram from a U.S. embassy in the Near East declaring that last night's flareups make a visit by the Assistant Secretary for Near Eastern and South Asian Affairs, now in mid-Atlantic, inopportune at the moment, a warning by a European Foreign Minister of the consequences should the United States fail to support his nation's position in the Security Council, and a counterwarning by an African representative at the United Nations of the consequences should the United States do so— this is a sample of the requirements made of the Department of State in a typical day. Of course it does not include the oceans of informational reports that come into the Department by telegram and air pouch or the countless periodicals from all parts of the world that arrive by sea.

What is required to begin with is that the flow be routed into the right channels. This does not apply to press correspondents and foreign embassy officials; they usually know where to go without being directed. For the rest, almost every piece of business—every requirement or opportunity for action—comes within the Department's ken first as a piece of paper. These pieces of paper—telegrams, dispatches (or "despatches," as the Department prefers to call them), letters—must be gotten as speedily as possible into the hands of the officers who will have to do something about them or whose jobs require that they know about them.

The telegram and mail branches of the Division of Communication Services, a part of the Bureau of Administration, receive the incoming material and, after decoding and reproducing the telegrams, indicate on each communication the distribution it should receive among the bureaus or equivalent components of the Department. If, in the case of a letter or a dispatch, there are not enough copies to go around, the recipients are listed one after another and receive it consecutively, the original going first to the bureau responsible for taking whatever action the document requires. With telegrams, the deliveries are simultaneous. Several score copies of a telegram may be run off. A yellow copy, called the action copy, like the original of a dispatch or letter, goes to the bureau responsible for taking any necessary action; white copies go to all others interested.

A telegram (No. 1029, let us say) from a major U.S. embassy in Western Europe reports the warning of the Foreign Minister of X country that a grave strain would be imposed on relations between X and the United States should the latter fail to vote with X on a sensitive colonial issue in the United Nations General Assembly. Such a telegram would have a wide distribution. The action copy would go to the Bureau of European Affairs. The action copy of a telegram to the same purpose from the U.S. delegation to the United Nations in New York, quoting the X delegation, would go to the Bureau of International Organization Affairs. This is a matter of convention.

Information copies of a telegram of such importance would go to all officers in the higher echelons—the Secretary of State (via the executive secretariat), the Under Secretaries, the Deputy Under Secretaries, the counselor. They would also go to the Policy Planning Staff, to the Bureau of African Affairs because of the involvement of certain territories within its jurisdiction, to the Bureau of Far Eastern Affairs and the Bureau of Near Eastern and South Asian Affairs because the telegram concerns the incendiary question of European peoples' ruling non-European peoples, and of course to the Bureau of Intelligence and Research. Other copies would go to the Department of Defense and the Central Intelligence Agency. The executive secretariat would doubtless make certain that the Secretary would see the telegram. In addition, its staff would include a condensation in the secret daily summary, a slim compendium distributed in the Department on a need-to-know basis. If classified top secret, it would be included in the top secret daily staff summary, or black book, which goes only to Assistant Secretary-level officials and higher.

In the bureaus, incoming material is received by the message centers. There a further and more refined distribution would be made of telegram 1029. Copies would go to the Office of the Assistant Secretary (the so-called front office), to the United Nations adviser, to the public affairs adviser (since the United States is going to be in for trouble with public opinion in either one part of the world or the other), and to whatever geographic office or offices may seem to have the major interest. In the Bureau of International Organization Affairs, this would be the Office of United

Nations Political and Security Affairs. Another copy, however, might go to the Office of Dependent Area Affairs.

In the Bureau of European Affairs, the yellow action copy of the telegram goes to the Office of Western European Affairs and thence to the X country desk, where it is the first thing to greet the desk officer's eye in the morning. As it happens, the desk officer was out the evening before at an official function where he discussed at length with the first secretary of the X embassy the desirability of avoiding any extremes of action in the United Nations over the territory in question. In the front office of the Bureau, the staff assistant has entered in his records the salient details of the problem the Bureau is charged with and has passed the telegram on to the Assistant Secretary.

The following scenes are now enacted:

The X country desk officer crosses the hall to the office of his superior, the officer-in-charge, and the two together repair to the office of the Director of the Office of Western European Affairs. The three officers put in a call to the Assistant Secretary for European Affairs and tell his secretary that they would like as early an appointment as possible.

The Director of the Office of United Nations Political and Security Affairs (UNP) telephones the Director of the Office of Western European Affairs (WE). He says he assumes WE will be drafting an instruction to the U.S. embassy in X to try to dissuade the Foreign Office from its course, and that UNP would like to be in on it. He adds that they had thought of getting the U.S. delegation to the United Nations (US Del) to present this view to the X mission in New York but that there seemed to be no point in doing so since the latter would already be advising its government to take account of world opinion.

After the Secretary's morning staff conference, where the matter is discussed briefly, a conference is held in the Office of the Assistant Secretary for European Affairs to decide on a line to take with the X government. The X desk officer is designated to prepare the first draft of a telegram embodying it. The draft is reviewed and modified by his officer-in-charge and the Office Director for Western European Affairs.

The telegram instructs the U.S. embassy in X to make clear to the X government our fear that its projected course of action "will only play into hands extremists and dishearten and undermine position elements friendly to West" and suggests that the X government emphasize its policy to take account of the legitimate aspirations of the indigenous population of the territory in order to improve the atmosphere for consideration of the problem by the General Assembly. The Assistant Secretary, after scrutinizing and approving the telegram, finds it necessary only to add the Bureau of Near Eastern and South Asian Affairs to the clearances. Those already listed for clearance are the Deputy Under Secretary for Political Affairs, the Bureau of International Organization Affairs, and the Bureau of African Affairs. He says it can be left to the Deputy Under Secretary for Political Affairs to sign the telegram; he does not see that the telegram need go higher.

It remains for the drafting officer to circulate the telegram for approval by those marked for clearance. In the Bureau of African Affairs the telegram is termed extremely gentle to the X government but is initialed as it stands. The Office of United Nations Political and Security Affairs (UNP) wishes to remind X that the United States, setting an example of its adherence to the principle of affording the widest latitude to the General Assembly, had even accepted on occasion the inscription of an item on the agenda accusing the United States of aggression. The X desk officer states, however, that WE would not favor such an addition, which might only further antagonize the X government. Thereupon, UNP, yielding on this point, requests deletion of a phrase in the telegram seeming to place the United States behind the X contention that the question is not appropriate for discussion in the United Nations. The drafter of the telegram telephones the Director of the Office of Western European Affairs who authorizes the deletion, having decided that he can do so on his own without referring the question to his superior, the Assistant Secretary.

With that, the Director of the Office of United Nations Political and Security Affairs initials the telegram for his Bureau, and the X desk officer "hand carries" the telegram (in the departmental phrase), with telegram 1029 attached, to the Office of the Deputy Under Secretary for Political Affairs and leaves it with his secretary. At 6 o'clock he is informed by telephone that the Deputy Under Secretary has signed the telegram (that is, signed the Secretary's name with his own initials beneath) without comment. The desk officer goes to the fifth floor, retrieves it, and takes it to the correspondence review staff of the executive secretariat, where the telegram is examined for intelligibility, completion of clearances, conformity with departmental practices, etc., before being sped to the Telegram Branch for enciphering and transmission.

The next morning, all offices of the Department participating in the framing of the telegram receive copies of it hectographed on pink outgoing telegram forms. The telegram, bearing the transmission time of 8:16 p.m., has entered history as the Department's No. 736 to the embassy in X. The X desk officer writes "telegram sent," with the date, in the space indicated by a rubber stamp on the yellow copy of the original telegram 1029, and the staff assistant in the front office makes an equivalent notation in his records. The yellow copy is then sent on to the central files, whence in time it will probably be consigned to the National Archives. Only the white copies may be kept in the Bureau's files.

In this case, however, no one is under any illusion that the matter has been disposed of. Scarcely 24 hours later comes a new telegram 1035 from the embassy in X reporting that, while the X government may possibly make some concessions, it will certainly wage an all-out fight against inscription of the item and will expect the United States to exert itself to marshal all the negative votes possible. The question is, what position will the United States in fact take and how much effort will it make to win adherents for its position? No one supposes for a moment that this explosive question can be decided on the bureau level. Only the Secretary can do so— as the Secretary himself unhappily realizes.

At the end of a staff meeting on Berlin, the Secretary turns to the Assistant Secretary for Policy Planning and asks him to give some thought within the next few days to the alternatives open on the question. The official addressed sets the wheels in motion at once. A meeting is called for the next morning. Attending are: the Assistant Secretary for Policy Planning himself and several members of his staff (including the European and African specialists), the Director of the Office of United Nations Political and Security Affairs, the Western European officer-in-charge, the X desk officer, a member of the policy guidance and coordination staff of the Bureau of Public Affairs, and two intelligence specialists, namely, the Director of the Office of Research and Analysis for Western Europe and the Director of the Office of Research and Analysis for the Near East, South Asia, and Africa.

The discussion explores all ramifications of the issues involved and is generally detached and dispassionate. The object of the meeting is to help clarify the issues so that the Policy Planning Staff may be sure all relevant considerations are taken into account in the staff paper it will prepare for the Secretary.

The Secretary is in a difficult position. The President's views on what course of action to take are somewhat different from his. The Congress is also of divided view, with some Members impressed by the irresistible force of nationalism among dependent peoples, others by the essential role of X in NATO and European defense. The ambassadors of some countries pull him one way, others another. One of the Nation's leading newspapers editorially counsels "restraint, understanding and vision." At the staff meeting he calls to arrive at a decision, the Secretary perceives that his subordinates are as deeply divided as he feared. He takes counsel with each— the Assistant Secretaries for Policy Planning, European Affairs, African Affairs, and Near Eastern and South Asian Affairs. At the end he sums up and announces his decision. Thereupon the following things happen:

The Assistant Secretaries take the news back to their bureaus.

An urgent telegram is sent to the U.S. Embassy in X reporting the decision.

Telegrams are sent to embassies in important capitals around the world instructing the ambassador to go to the Foreign Office and present the U.S. case in persuasive terms.

A similar telegram is sent to the U.S. delegation in New York for its use in talks with the delegations of other United Nations members.

Conferences attended by representatives of the geographic bureaus concerned, of the Bureau of Public Affairs, and of the U.S. Information Agency, are held. Afterward, the representatives of the U.S. Information Agency return to their headquarters to draft guidances to the U.S. Information Service establishments all over the world. Such guidances tell how news of the U.S. decision is to be played when it breaks.

The more important the problem, the more the upper levels of the Department become involved. In a crisis—one brought about, say, by the overthrow of A, a Western-oriented government in the Middle East—the Secretary himself will take over. However, the bulk of the Department's business is carried on, of necessity, by the lower ranking officers. Even when a crisis receives the Secretary's personal, day-to-day direction, the desk officer and the officer-in-charge are always at hand to provide the detailed information only specialists possess, while in the intelligence bureau, country analysts and branch chiefs will be putting in 10-hour days and 6- or 7-day weeks. Generally, moreover, the crisis will have been preceded by a good deal of work on the part of lower level officials.

In the case suggested, it was apparent for some time that all was not well in A. The U.S. Embassy in A was aware of growing discontent with the regime through its indirect contacts with opposition political elements, from information from Cairo, from evidences of tension, from clandestine publications. Additional straws in the wind were supplied by the public affairs officer in A both to the embassy and to the U.S. Information Agency because of his special contacts among professional groups. On the strength of these reports and of dispatches from American foreign correspondents in the area, and equipped with analyses from the Bureau of Intelligence and Research, all pointing in the same direction, the desk officer at a staff meeting of the Office of Near Eastern Affairs imparts his disquiet. He is directed to prepare a memorandum which, if convincing in its presentation, the Office Director undertakes to put before the Assistant Secretary.

What the desk officer has in mind will require national action, so what he drafts takes the form of a memorandum to the Secretary. It embodies a statement of the problem, the actions recommended, a review of the facts bearing upon the problem, and a conclusion. At the end are listed the symbols of the offices of the Department from which concurrences must be sought. Backing up the memorandum will be supporting documents, especially telegrams from the embassy, each identified by a tab. The mass fills a third of an in-box.

The problem is defined as that of strengthening the present pro-Western regime of A. By way of recommendation, the desk officer is especially sensitive to the problems and needs of the country for which he is responsible. He calls for more detachment of the United States from A's rival, B, expediting U.S. arms deliveries to A and the supply of certain recoiless rifles and jet fighter planes the A government has been requesting, support for A's membership in various United Nations agencies, a Presidential invitation to the Prime Minister of A to visit the United States. Much of what the memorandum recommends has to be fought out in the Bureau and even in the Office since it conflicts with the claims of countries (and the desk officers responsible for them) in the same jurisdiction. While neither the Office Director nor the Assistant Secretary doubts that support of B is a handicap in the region, they consider that a proposal for a radical departure would simply doom the memorandum by preventing anyone from taking it seriously.

As it finally leaves the Bureau with the Assistant Secretary's signature, the memorandum is considerably revised, and further change awaits it. The Department of Defense cannot provide the desired recoiless rifles and jet fighters. The Bureau of International Organization Affairs cannot offer any undertakings at this stage with respect to the question of membership in United Nations agencies. The Deputy Under Secretary for Political Affairs rules out a request of the President to invite the A Prime Minister for an official visit because the number of those invited is already too large.

Among recommendations in memorandums to the Secretary, as among salmon battling their way upstream to the spawning grounds, mortality is heavy. Almost everywhere in the world, things are far from satisfactory, but the United States cannot be doing everything everywhere at the same time. And A, far from seeming to cry out for attention, looks like the one Middle Eastern country about which it is not necessary to worry.

Then the uprising occurs in A. Early in the morning, the officer-in-charge of A and one other country is awakened by the ringing of the telephone. In a flash, before his feet have touched the floor, he has visualized every conceivable disaster that could have befallen his area and has picked the overthrow of the monarchy in C as the most likely. Or did the security people find a top secret document under his desk?

On the telephone, the watch officer at the Department tells him that a "Niact" (a night action telegram, which means "Get this one read immediately even if you have to rout someone out of bed") is coming off the machine and it looks serious—he had better come down. En route, the officer-in-charge turns on his car radio and picks up a news broadcast, but nothing is said about A. Uncle Sam has beaten the press agencies.

At the Department, he finds the telegram wholly decoded and reads the hectograph master. There is revolution in A. The top leadership has been either murdered or banished. The officer in charge could legitimately awaken the Assistant Secretary, but for the moment it seems there is nothing that can be done, so he decides to hold off until 6 a.m. and then call the Office Director and put it up to him. He does, however, call the A desk officer and tell him to get on his way. To share his vigil beside the watch officer's window there is a representative of the executive secretariat, who will have the telegram ready for the Secretary to read immediately on his arrival. In the Bureau of Intelligence and Research—it being now after 4 o'clock—the morning briefers have arrived to go over the night's take and write up items of importance, with analyses, for the Director's use in briefing the Secretary's morning staff conference. The briefer for the Office of Research and Analysis for the Near East, South Asia and Africa—a GS–11 specialist on India—takes one look at the Niact on A and gets on the telephone to the A analyst.

By the time the Secretary has stepped from his black limousine and headed for the private elevator a good deal has happened. In the Bureau of Near Eastern and South Asian Affairs, everyone concerned with A from the Assistant Secretary down, and including the officer-in-charge of Baghdad Pact and Southeast Asia Treaty Organization affairs and the special assistant who serves as a policy and planning adviser, has been in conference for an hour laying out the tasks requiring immediate attention. Two more Niacts have come in from A, one reporting that so far no Americans are known to have been injured but offering little assurance with respect to the future. The Assistant Secretary has already put in a call to the Director of Intelligence Research to ask that all possible information on the new leader of A and his connections be marshaled and that the Central Intelligence Agency be informed of the need. For the rest, the following represent the Assistant Secretary's conception of what should be done first:

1. The Department of Defense must be apprised of the Department of State's anxiety and be requested to have transport planes in readiness at nearby fields for the evacuation of Americans if necessary in accordance with prearranged plans. There must be consultation on what instruments are available if American lives have to be protected by force.

2. The U.S. embassy in C, a friendly neighbor of A's to which the Niacts have been repeated, will be heard from at any moment, and the Special Assistant for Mutual Security Coordination in the Office of the Under Secretary for Economic Affairs and, also, the Office of International Security Affairs in the Department of Defense will have to be alerted to the possibility of emergency military assistance for C.

3. Anything in the pipeline for A should be held up. The Special Assistant for Mutual Security Coordination must be advised of this.

4. The possibility of a demonstration by the U.S. 6th Fleet in support of C's independence and integrity will have to be discussed with the Department of Defense.

5. A crash national intelligence estimate will be requested of the Central Intelligence Agency, provided the Agency does not consider the situation too fluid for a formal estimate to be useful.

6. The public affairs adviser will get in touch with the Bureau of Public

Affairs, the departmental spokesman and the U.S. Information Agency to agree on the kind of face the United States will put on the affair.

7. The B Ambassador will probably have to be called in and apprised of the critical need for his government's acquiescence in overflights of B for the purpose of getting supplies to C. The B and C desk officers had better get busy immediately on a draft telegram to embassy B (repeat to C) setting forth the case the ambassador should make urgently to the B Foreign Office.

At 9:12, anticipating that he will be called to accompany the Secretary to the White House, the Assistant Secretary instructs his secretary to cancel all his appointments for the day, including one with the dentist but excepting his appointment with the C ambassador. ("Mr. Ambassador, you may assure His Majesty that my Government remains fully determined to support the sovereignty and territorial integrity of his nation.")

At 9:14, 1 minute before the scheduled commencement of the staff meeting, the Assistant Secretary joins his colleagues in the Secretary's anteroom, prepared to hear the estimate of the Director of Intelligence and Research and to give his own appraisal and submit his plan of action.

The Policy Planning Process

Dean Acheson

THOUGHTS ABOUT THOUGHT
IN HIGH PLACES

LAST June, President Eisenhower made the commencement speech to the first graduating class of the Senior Foreign Officers School.

"In the years that Secretary Dulles and I served together," he said, "he often spoke about the lack of opportunity of high officers of Government, and indeed of high officers of any profession, for contemplation. He felt so strongly about this that he believed that there should be some reorganization in the very highest echelons of the executive departments so that there could be more time to think about the job."

When I read this my mind flew to the signs which, for a time, hung on the walls of some offices, urging "THINK"—and the addendum written in pencil on one of them, "OR THWIM." For this pungent alternative seemed to me to go to the heart of the problem of contemplation in the executive departments.

These departments are meant to be what they are called—"executive" departments, that is, agencies of action. Contemplation, in these departments, is not an end in itself; it is a means to action—the wisest action under the circumstances, to be sure, but action. What is needed is not, as the President said, "to think about the job"—that is for professors and columnists—but to think about what to do and how to do it. In the executive departments salvation lies only in works.

Now it happens that Secretary Dulles also talked with me on this subject. He had come to the department in response to my invitation to arrange an orderly transfer of responsibility. He told me that he was not going to work as I had done, but would free himself from involvement with what he referred to as personnel and administrative problems, in order to have more time to think.

I did not comment, but was much struck by the conjunction of ideas. I

FROM *The New York Times Magazine,* October 11, 1959. © 1959 by the New York Times Company. Reprinted by permission.

wondered how it would turn out. For it had been my experience that thought was not of much use without knowledge and guidance, and that who should give me both and how competent they would be must depend on who chose, dealt with, assigned and promoted these people and established the forms of organization within which they worked. All this seemed a precondition of thinking which I could not ignore if my thoughts were going to amount to anything.

So the President's commencement speech has nagged at me. This absorption with the Executive as Emerson's "Man Thinking," surrounded by a Cabinet of Rodin statues, bound in an oblivion of thought, chin on fist, elbow on knee, seemed to me unnatural and unnecessary. Surely thinking is not so difficult, so hard to come by, so solemn as all this.

Isn't the problem, I have wondered, a little different? Doesn't it involve a choice of what the "very highest echelons," the President and the Cabinet, spend their time on, and of finding ways of making available to them the right information to think with and about? Executives should not be encouraged to spin thoughts and policies out of their own viscera as spiders spin their webs.

It is hard to get reliable data on the matters which now occupy the time of "the very highest echelons." Of course, they vary with the men involved, their physical and mental vitality, their powers of concentration, their resources of knowledge, experience, and wisdom. Their tasks are difficult ones. This cannot be altered. Our present question is: Is their time well spent? If not, is the remedy "reorganization in the very highest echelons?"

The most available data we have, skimpy and inadequate as it is, is the daily announcement of the President's appointments. For the first and last weeks of July, typical weeks, ...

No one knows better than I that the published appointment list of the President or a Cabinet officer is only that one-tenth of the iceberg which appears above water. But even a short study of the sample given makes two points clear: First, at least half the appointments are wholly unnecessary; and, second, those which are necessary are neither very time-consuming nor exhausting.

One other matter needs to be stressed in any consideration of time for contemplation—the long weekends in Maryland and Pennsylvania in carefully preserved seclusion from run-of-the-mill concerns. This is wise and proper. All through the war, President Roosevelt, as those who have read William Hassett's delightful "Off the Record With F.D.R." know, sought refuge at Hyde Park from the insistent pressures of Washington and there achieved the essential prerequisite of contemplation, relaxation. One can think under pressure, but not contemplate. Ruminants lie down to ruminate.

So I suggest again that perhaps the problem is both not so great and greater than has been imagined. Not so great, in that there is time enough both to think and to contemplate if the highest echelons do not give in to the human desire, shared by the lower echelons, to avoid the pain of thought by escape to something less exacting, like routine or going somewhere. And the problem is greater because the world's and the Nation's problems today are so complex, tough, and recalcitrant as to blunt the sharpest thought. This means that they are not likely to yield to any amount of reorganization of the thinkers.

The military substitute for thought at the top is staff. Staff is of great importance. It performs the indispensable function of collecting the food for thought, appraising and preparing it. It is the means of carrying out decisions made. But, when it also performs the function of final thought, judgment, and decision, then there is no top—only the appearance of one. This can happen in a number of ways, but the most insidious, because it seems so highly efficient, is the "agreed" staff paper sent up for "action," a euphemism for "approval."

"One can always," I have said elsewhere, "get an agreed paper by increasing the vagueness and generality of its statements. The staff of any interdepartmental committee has a fatal weakness for this type of agreement by exhaustion." But a chief who wants to perform his function of knowing the issues, the factors involved and their magnitudes, and of deciding, needs, where there is any doubt at all, not agreed papers, but disagreed papers.

Original thought on the frontiers of knowledge is, as Prof. Percy Bridgman has pointed out, a lonely and individual process. But the thought of a chief of a Governmental department or of a Government itself does and should involve others. I have already suggested part of the reason why, but only part. Popular conceptions about government are in large part interesting folklore; and the instinct of the bureaucracy for self-preservation and the egotism of the chiefs perpetuate it. One of these concepts is that "policy" originates at the top and is passed down.

To be sure, great decisions are, for the most part, made at the top, when they are not made by events. But, as for policy—the sum total of many decisions—it must be said; as it has been said of sovereignty, that its real sources are undiscoverable. One fact, however, is clear to anyone with experience in government: The springs of policy bubble up; they do not trickle down.

When this upsurgence of information, ideas, and suggestions is vigorous, appreciated, and encouraged, strong, imaginative, and effective policies are most apt to result. When the whole function of determining what is what, and what to do about it, is gathered into one hand, or into a small group at the top, the resulting action may or may not be strong, but it is likely to be ill-adapted to reality and self-defeating.

What has just been said underlines the judicial element in the function of headship and the great importance of interplay between head and staff at all stages in the development of decisions. By this I mean that the chief must from time to time familiarize himself with the whole record; he must consider opposing views, put forward as ably as possible. He must examine the proponents vigorously and convince them that he knows the record, is intolerant of superficiality or of favor-seeking, and not only welcomes but demands criticism.

As General Marshall said at the beginning of his Secretaryship, when I asked what he expected of me as what he called his Chief of Staff, "First, the most unvarnished truth, particularly about myself. I have no feelings" —then added—"except those which I reserve for Mrs. Marshall." And he never faltered in this attitude.

Through this judicial function, through pondering what has been read and heard, and a suggestion or decision that one of several lines is the one to be pursued, the chief makes his most valuable contribution to thought and policy. It takes work and it takes time.

It also requires orderly procedure. Meetings should be as small as possible. Anyone who needs or permits platoons of aides to accompany him brands himself as incompetent. All parties in interest should be present at the same time, should have their say and hear what is said by all others. They should also hear the decision, which should be in writing or recorded. This, I am sure, seems disappointingly simple. But it is disappointingly rare.

All readers of Sir Arthur Bryant's "The Turn of the Tide" (based on the war diaries of Lord Alanbrooke, Chief of the British Imperial General Staff) will recall their amazement at the time and energy which Prime Minister Churchill devoted to this procedure at all stages in the development of war policy. "On Active Service in Peace and War" shows Secretary of War Stimson doing the same.

President Roosevelt found the practice difficult, and a good many of his troubles came from this. Decisions made, or which seemed to have been made, on incomplete investigation or ex parte hearings, had to be modified or reversed, sometimes without everyone knowing that this had occurred. (Sir Winston tells us, in "The Gathering Storm," that his initial order on becoming the King's First Minister was that all decisions be put in writing. To many of us this innovation ranks in importance with the discovery of the wheel.)

The method and procedures I have mentioned are of the greatest help to the chief and to the staff, keeping in mind that Cabinet members are both chiefs in their departments and staff officers to the Chief of Government. They provide a chief who can learn with the best means of doing so—information, carefully prepared; then a discussion of its meaning, conducted with spirit, criticism, and relevance; and an indication of the course of action. They also give the chief timely opportunities to guide and stimulate the development of thought and action.

To the staff this practice is a constant demonstration both that their contribution is important and that it is fairly heard and considered. It is a stimulus to their best effort, a devastating arena for the poorly prepared or pedestrian mind, which soon disappears, and a method by which specialized experience and outlook, which must sacrifice breadth to depth, can adjust to the larger problem and purpose.

Even being present to see and hear the chief give his decisions meets a fundamental, almost primitive, need of the staff. Confidence in leadership, loyalty to the processes of government, require first of all belief that commands put out in the name of the chief not only are, but authentically appear to be, his.

The curse of leadership has always been the major-domo, the chamberlain, the chief secretary, the favorite—usually envied and disliked—who emerged from the Presence with the Word. But whose word was it? Did it have that authority behind it which demanded obedience, or would a plot or a protest, a discreet leak by "unimpeachable" sources to the press or to the Hill—if that is not tautological—upset it? In a city where since the "Gettysburg Address," few public men have written their own utterances, one should not underestimate the importance of the chief's announcing, explaining, and, on occasion, discussing his decisions in the presence of his staff.

One may predict with some assurance that any attempt to reorganize the highest echelons to give them more time for thought will inevitably have two characteristics. It will cut the chief off from his principal officers, and, in accordance with Parkinson's law, it will interpose new personnel, or "coordinating" staff, between the chief and his principal officers.

The result will be that he will have to see just as many people, but they will be the wrong people. His reading may be reduced, but it will be predigested, and both the protein of fact and the fermenting bacteria of conflict and criticism will be minimized in the bland passage through an insulating special staff.

This has been the experience with the National Security Council. The NSC in essence, is merely the means for orderly and prepared meetings between the President and a restricted group of his principal assistants charged with protecting the Nation against danger from abroad.

The problems which they can profitably discuss are far easier to identify than to resolve. Cabinet officers and military officers prodded by their own assistants and by the President can identify them. To resolve them requires work within the departments, and between them, by the responsible officers at what is happily called the working level, with constant reference to their chiefs and often discussion between them. If serious differences arise, as they often should, these are the stuff for Presidential thought and decision after argument and submission.

To interject into this refreshingly simple situation a new and separate staff for the NSC itself, as has been done, only complicates without improving. A few recordkeepers, agenda makers, prodders, or gadflies, yes. But a separate staff cannot add knowledge, which remains in the departments; or responsible advice to the President, which is the duty and right of his Cabinet Secretaries. More bodies only clutter up a meeting and strain a flow of communication.

Organization—or reorganization in government—can often be a trap for the unwary. The relationships involved in the division of labor and responsibility as well as the channeling of communication and decision in any activity is far more subtle and complex than the little boxes which the graph drawers put on paper with their perpendicular and horizontal connecting lines. A good many years ago Chief Justice Taft said to a friend, "I have just been talking with So-and-So (using an eminent name) about what he calls the machinery of government"—then added, chuckling, "and, you know, he thinks it really is machinery."

Well, it is not that. The nature of an organization and the relationships within it depend wholly upon what the people organized are supposed to do. I have a suspicion that the need for complexity in organization goes hand in hand with the extent to which those organized are dealing with physical things. In the field of thought, as such, its importance decreases, though no one would be foolish enough to suggest that it can be dispensed with. But where people are organized for thought, the simpler arrangements are kept, the better.

How, then, can the highest echelons increase their time for contemplation? There is only one answer. One cannot "make" more time—despite the colloquial phrase. One should not delegate contemplation. There remains discipline and intelligent choice of how time is used.

Demands crowd insistently on a chief. Far more of them seem important than can be met. To weed out the timewasters involves ruthlessness and some hurt feelings. It also involves some self-discipline. The importance of relaxation and quiet as inducements to contemplation has already been stressed. I would also stress that the use of all a chief's private time for competitive games, indoor and out, does not make for contemplation. A vast amount of reading is essential. So is relaxed, unhurried talk. So is quiet.

Obviously, ceremonies and the ceremonial side of politics—the endless palaver about the nonessential—offer fertile fields in which to harvest time. One could begin on Washington and Embassy society which, despite Allen Drury's entertaining novel of capital life, contribute nothing whatever in return for the time they take. The same is true of the public dinners—allegedly humorous, testimonial, or celebrant—put on by a hundred organizations, perennial or episodic. To put all of these invitations courteously to one side requires an appointments secretary with a southern accent, a heart of ice, and a will of iron.

Then there is travel. Before the second World War, tradition had it that the President never left the country. The occasion on which President Wilson broke the tradition did not encourage emulation. The same rule, though not so absolute, kept Secretaries of State and other Cabinet officers for the most part directing their departments.

Then, during and since the war, came the swing—and a most unfortunate one it was—to the opposite extreme. This is not the place for a review of conferences or meetings at the summit. I have done that elsewhere and concluded that there were only two successful ones in over 300 years—the Congresses of Muenster and Osnabrueck, which ended the Thirty Years War, and the Congress of Vienna, which brought peace after the Napoleonic wars.

Foreign Ministers' meetings have also become a menace. Former Secretary Byrnes tells us that, of his 562 days' tenure in the State Department, 350 were spent at international meetings. Secretary Herter, as I write, has already clocked up 80 days out of 115 in office away from Washington. In large part this time is wasted, and that it would be was clearly foreseen.

Personal diplomacy at the top has largely become the substitution of improvisation for the sound and difficult domestic and foreign policies which would prevent us from getting into weak and exposed positions. Improvisation will not work, and all this traveling around depreciates the standing of those who, in any sensible system, should be the representatives of the Republic in communicating with foreign states. We are in a vicious circle in which the idea that only chiefs can talk to other chiefs keeps them rushing about so much that they do not have the time to devise and execute the policies which would make these frantic and repeated journeys unnecessary.

The time which the highest echelons need to think is not for brooding in isolated detachment, it is needed to devise the action to meet the exigencies of our times, to bring conviction of the need of that action to the Congress and people of the United States, and to explain it to the world. The hours which can be used for this lie all around them. At present, they are not being frugally used.

W. W. Rostow

THE FALLACY OF THE FERTILE GONDOLAS

. . . The story of the gondolas was told me by Alvin Johnson, who applied it to the disappointed hopes of those who aspired to some unification of thought in the Social Science Encyclopedia.

FROM *The Harvard Alumni Bulletin* (May 25, 1957). Reprinted by permission.

When the Chicago World's Fair of 1893 was planned it was built around a Venice motif: with lagoons, Italian folk songs, and, even, gondolas. The issue of gondolas arose before the board of aldermen, and it was suggested that 12 be purchased. At this stage a rather sleepy alderman, concerned for the budget, objected: "Why buy 12? We have plenty of time. Why not buy a male and a female and let nature take its course?"

My theme is, simply, that we go about making national policy and we go about training our professionals in graduate schools on different versions of the same fallacy. We assume that unified courses of national action and unified conceptions of the world of things and of human beings will somehow emerge by rattling around in high-level committees a collection of special problems, or by laying together, side by side, narrow fields of specialized knowledge. If my view is right it applies in roughly equal measure to the National Security Council and the distinguished graduate schools of Cambridge. But before making some specific observations on the consequences of these ways of doing business I should like to look back for a moment at the sources of the problem, in our national style.

Our operating style in matters of both high policy and advanced education derive from the Nation's philosophical cast of mind; and I should like to begin with a few observations on how we, as a nation and a culture, have come to look at the world and to solve the problems we confronted in it.

It is, of course, a cliché to assert that America developed, from at least the 1830's, a cast of mind empirical in method, pragmatic in solutions. But men have a need and instinct to generalize their experience, to organize, somehow, the chaos around them; and, when Americans busy with limited practical chores reached out for larger abstractions, they tended to balloon out concepts derived from personal, practical experience. They generalized what they intimately knew.

The American mind came to be one devoted to arduous practical tasks, but filled also with an arsenal of general concepts—often legitimate but partial insights—not rigorously related to each other or to the bodies of fact they were meant to illuminate. There was little in American life—its content and its values—that encouraged the care and contemplation required to array the intermediate structure of abstractions, test them for internal consistency, and to make orderly patterns of thought.

From the beginning American popular education reflected a bias towards practical, usable thought, embedded in living experience. In James and Dewey we produced expositors of the case for it. When American institutions of higher learning moved towards maturity at the close of the 19th century, they came to incorporate a version of this philosophic style; and the new graduate schools reinforced it powerfully, notably in the study of human affairs. Americans were instinctively drawn to German university

models, and strongly influenced by them. The Germans placed a high premium on facts and their ordering by precise rules of evidence. Their concept
of professional hard-working scholarship harmonized with the instincts
of a nation of empiricists, entering into an age of industrialism and specialization. The Germans, too, when they came to generalize, were prone to
broad concepts, only loosely linked to the bodies of fact they so painstak-
ingly compiled. On the whole Americans pulled up short of the cosmic
level of German abstractions, mainly steering clear of universal systems;
but a family resemblance remains. Modern American historiography, for
example, has been built up by the loose interweaving of schools of specialized research, each inspired by a simple, broad concept derived, in turn,
from a legitimate but partial insight into the facts of American experience:
the frontier concept; the determining influence of special economic interests;
the rise of the city; the influence of the immigrant; and so on. As De
Tocqueville noted, we have continued, in a substantial part of the Nation's
intellectual life, "to explain a mass of facts by a single cause." This mixture
of specialized empiricism, yielding conclusions of a modest order of abstraction, bound into rough unity by vague high-order generalizations, remains
the dominant mode of American advanced education, although subject to
significant change in recent decades. It has produced many knowledgeable
men; a number of creative insights; and, at its best, figures of wisdom, with
great sensibility about how human life is really conducted. But it has
yielded few general theoretical formulations of distinction.

In both its dimensions—a devotion to the ordering of fact in terms of
low-order abstraction and a certain vague disorder at high levels of abstraction—the American intellectual style has reflected the operator's biases and
fitted his needs. Committed to do the best he can in terms of goals defined
by the institutions of which he is a part, the operator desires to know in
detail his field of action but wishes to be as eclectic as he need be—and as
unhampered as possible by considerations outside those implicit in his
operations.

This style has, by and large, worked well for us because of the remarkably
continuous character of our national experience. Within the context of
the high-value goals of the Declaration of Independence and the disabused
political shrewdness of the Constitution we have evolved immensely subtle
political and social processes that—except for the Civil War—have kept
unity in a continental nation marked by powerful regional interests, and
kept unity in local communities marked by acute individualism and by
strong class, racial, and religious differences. With the frontier available
to 1890 and the enormous industrial potential of the Nation, we evolved
a progressively richer and more successful economy. And we managed,
within its orbit, to maintain a workable and acceptable balance between
the requirements of private capitalism and the requirements of individual
opportunity and human dignity by a dialectical process that has worked

from Jefferson's acceptance of the essence of the Hamiltonian institution in 1800 to Eisenhower's acceptance of the essence of the New Deal and Fair Deal in the past 4 years.

Men successfully operate processes by accumulating experience, feel, judgment, by sensing recurrent patterns rather than isolating clean-cut logical connections of cause and effect. This is how good captains of sailing vessels have worked, good politicians, good businessmen. This has been the typical American style in operating and developing the Nation's society. Its success, however, is dependent on two conditions which are, to a degree, alternatives: first, that the problems confronted be, in their essence, relatively familiar, capable of solution by only moderately radical innovation, on the basis of existing principles or institutions; second, that time be allowed for the experimental exploration of possible solutions, and the osmotic process of accepting change. The more the time permitted, the greater the workability of a technique of problem solving by empirical experiment and institutional change inertia.

It is thus, in the less radical orders of innovation—in science, industry, and politics—that the Nation has excelled. Or, put another way, the American style is least effective when it confronts issues which require radical innovation promptly.

It is precisely here that we are in trouble. We live in a world of extremely rapid change, where the survival of our society hinges on prompt innovation, while our intellectual style and our national institutions are accommodated to the slow and carefully balanced modifications of a successful ongoing process.

Let me be a bit more precise. We now have in Washington two institutions designed to assess the overall position of the Nation in the world and to prescribe unified policies to guarantee our survival: The Joint Chiefs of Staff and the National Security Council. Each has access to enormous staff structures, filled with experts on every region of the world, every sort of weapon, every sort of expertise from Leontief input-output tables to a Russian research center model of mutual role expectations in Soviet society. At first glance it would appear that we have accepted our permanent burden as a world power; staffed Washington with the best products of our graduate schools, each in a specialized section fitting his doctoral working papers; and crowned the structure with unifying institutions to formulate neatly and cleanly the choices open to the Commander in Chief.

But it doesn't work; or at least it works quite badly. And the reason is this: Successful policymaking in a world where weapons systems are outdated in (say) 4 years, a world caught up in revolutionary change, depends on a series of major innovations; that is, on major new ideas, quite discontinuous with past experience. The change of weapons models from year to year cannot be conducted by enlarging the fins or changing the color combinations; one cannot deal with Nasser, or with the disintegration of Indonesia, or with the current mood of Western Europe by formulae relevant even to such recent experiences as the Korean war or the Marshall plan.

Now ideas—major innovations—do not emerge from a hierarchical bureaucratic process; they emerge in the heads of lonely individual men, or from small likeminded groups, thrashing freely about for the answer to a problem that fits no particular section or division of the bureaucracy, neatly delimited by professional administrators, no highly specialized department of a graduate school.

And when ideas do work their way up—for, blessedly, the American bureaucrat has thus far not wholly accepted the world of Kafka and remains a bit of a buccaneer—what is there at the top? The JCS and the NSC are committees of operators, bureaucratic departmental chieftains, each freighted with large vested interests to protect, each biased heavily toward the *status quo*, as, indeed, operators must be. They cannot, under these circumstances, survey in a systematic way the horizons of our national position and formulate policies which effectively unify day-to-day operations.

High-level policy tends to emerge in one of two forms: Either as general statements so broad that operators can go on doing what they are doing, interpreting policy statements as they will; or as tough, practical compromises, allocating money or other scarce resources, in which the pattern of policy is much less important to the outcome than the bargaining weight of the negotiators. First-class ideas cannot emerge from a committee of hardpressed bureaucrats any more than a first-class book can be written by a committee of professors.

What is the result? American policymaking consists in a series of reactions to major crises. Having failed to define, to anticipate, and to deal with forces loose in the world, having tried merely to keep the great machine of government ticking over from day to day, at last the problems never recognized or swept under the rug come ticking in over the incoming cables. Then, as a nation of operators, we respect the reality of the matter, and—in the past at least—we have turned to with vigor. We rig up an ad hoc effort—often bypassing all the bureaucratic machinery created to deal with our affairs, launch hastily some new courses of action; and these become the working norms of policy until the next crisis comes along. As a first approximation it is quite accurate to say, of any moment over the past 15 years, that current policy has been a bureaucratized version of that created ad hoc to deal with the last crisis.

We are, thus, applying an empirical, pragmatic style, created out of a remarkably continuous national experience, to a world where it is altogether possible that crises take the form of situations where even the most vigorous ad hoc effort by the Nation would come too late to retrieve our abiding interests.

What shall we conclude? Instinctively—as good Americans—we think first of institutional change; and indeed, the NSC would be vastly improved if it had an independent staff of first-rate men, freed of ties to particular bureaucracies, paid to think in terms of the totality of our policy problem, empowered to lay proposals on the table. Indeed, the three military services need badly to be unified and the Pentagon provided with a top-level staff of men paid to think only about the character of our military problem, with the present services interwoven in task force units, each task force stemming from a central conception of the rapidly changing security problem.

But more is involved here than the restructuring of institutions. In the end national policy and university life are linked by the fact that they are high exercises in the world of ideas. As Santayana said:

> Practical men may not notice it, but in fact human discourse is intrinsically addressed not to natural existing things but to ideal essences, poetic or logical terms which thought may define and play with. When fortune or necessity diverts our attention from this congenial ideal sport to crude facts and pressing issues, we turn our frail poetic ideas into symbols for those terrible irruptive things. In that paper money of our own stamping, the legal tender of the mind, we are obliged to reckon all the movements and values of the world.

And the two realms of thought—in government and university life—are linked in a quite particular way. When a decision of high national policy is taken it cannot be based on an assessment of economic factors alone, on social factors, on political factors, on military factors. Policy must be based on an assessment which achieves a unified view of the field of action and a unified view of the possible impact of American instruments of politics, economics, and force. Ideally the synthesis in the President's head—as he looks out on the changes in Soviet society or the forces at work in Egyptian politics—should bear a close relation to the synthesis achieved by our scholars. But, generally speaking, our scholars back away from the task of synthesis; and our politicians do the best they can with highly simplified models of the world they face, based on concepts absorbed in their youth, ratified by successful use within the confines of American life. I can attest that there is an enormous gap between the best level of university thought—and, even between the best level of thought in the working levels of our bureaucracies—and the thought ultimately brought to bear on high policy decisions. And the gap is not to be blamed wholly on the politicians. It stems from the fallacy of fertile gondolas—yielding unmanageable bureaucratic techniques for securing synthesis in our Government.

If our universities are to make the contribution they should in an age requiring radical innovation, they must look beyond Ranke's rule of sources and develop more unified concepts of man and the world. It is out of the intermediate and higher ranges of abstraction that new ways of looking at things emerge which embrace but transcend what we know from our own lives; and it is from new ways of looking at things that new paths for action emerge. Without losing our grip on facts and our respect for their hard reality, we must begin to transcend the pre-1914 German patterns on which our intellectual trade schools are based. With all due respect for James and Dewey it takes more than a common sense instinctive to the round of American life to deal with the age of guided missiles; the age of revolution in Asia, the Middle East, and Africa; and with that exciting but dangerous passage of history in which communism as we have known it discovers that it is not historically viable. To bring to bear what understanding the human mind can generate demands more than shelves of specialized monographs. We must come to give as much systematic thought to the problem of unifying knowledge as we now give to extending its factual range.

And this must be reflected, somehow, in Washington, gripped in dangerous inhibitions since, roughly, the summer of 1951. The individual human beings in the great bureaucracies must be encouraged to think, to throw up new ideas, openly to debate. The illusion that our affairs can successfully be handled by negotiating minimum consensus, in layer after layer of interdepartmental committees, must be broken. The Government must recapture a sense that creation is something we badly need; and that creation is a job of lonely individuals, backing their play with integrity; and this spirit must suffuse the whole apparatus from the Office of the President to the lowest GS–5—the President above all, for our Constitution gives him among many other burdens the unavoidable, personal responsibility for innovation in military and foreign policy. Yes, of course, the interdepartmental machinery of negotiation and consensus will continue to grind along. Bureaucracy will not end. But its processes must be made to grind on something other than departmental vested interests and the pre-compromised views of men anxious, above all, to avoid controversy or trouble.

The tombstone of most nations which held and lost greatness could bear the inscription:

They preferred to go down in the style to which they had become accustomed.

I do not for one moment believe that the processes of our Government, the intellectual heritage of our universities, or the quality and vigor of our society as a whole have already decreed our fall. On the other hand, the challenge is real for us all—and it is urgent.

Dean Rusk

A FRESH LOOK AT THE FORMULATION
OF FOREIGN POLICY

I am happy to have a chance to talk with my new colleagues here in the Department about some of the things that are on my mind as well as some of the things which may be on your mind early in the new administration. I suppose you are wondering what the significance of a new administration is. You haven't experienced a change of party administration since 1952, and before that not since 1932. . . .

Foreign Policy in Its Total Context

With this enlarged role in mind, I should like to make a few suggestions: What we in the United States do or do not do will make a very large difference in what happens in the rest of the world. We in this Department must think about foreign policy in its total context. We cannot regard foreign policy as something left over after defense policy or trade policy or fiscal policy has been extracted. Foreign policy is the total involvement of the American people with peoples and governments abroad. That means that, if we are to achieve a new standard of leadership, we must think in terms of the total context of our situation. It is the concern of the Department of State that the American people are safe and secure—defense is not a monopoly concern of the Department of Defense. It is also the concern of the Department of State that our trading relationships with the rest of the world are vigorous, profitable, and active—this is not just a passing interest or a matter of concern only to the Department of Commerce. We can no longer rely on interdepartmental machinery "somewhere upstairs" to resolve differences between this and other departments. Assistant Secretaries of State will now carry an increased burden of active formulation and coordination of policies. Means must be found to enable us to keep in touch as regularly and as efficiently as possible with our colleagues in other departments concerned with foreign policy.

I think we need to concern ourselves also with the timeliness of action. Every policy officer cannot help but be a planning officer. Unless we keep our eyes on the horizon ahead, we shall fail to bring ourselves on target with the present. The movement of events is so fast, the pace so severe,

F R O M *The Department of State Bulletin,* March 20, 1961.

that an attempt to peer into the future is essential if we are to think accurately about the present. If there is anything which we can do in the executive branch of the Government to speed up the processes by which we come to decisions on matters on which we must act promptly, that in itself would be a major contribution to the conduct of our affairs. Action taken today is often far more valuable than action taken several months later in response to a situation then out of control.

There will of course be times for delay and inaction. What I am suggesting is that when we delay, or when we fail to act, we do so intentionally and not through inadvertence or through bureaucratic or procedural difficulties.

I also hope that we can do something about reducing the infant mortality rate of ideas—an affliction of all bureaucracies. We want to stimulate ideas from the bottom to the top of the Department. We want to make sure that our junior colleagues realize that ideas are welcome, that initiative goes right down to the bottom and goes all the way to the top. I hope no one expects that only Presidential appointees are looked upon as sources of ideas. The responsibility for taking the initiative in generating ideas is that of every officer in the Department who has a policy function, regardless of rank.

Further, I would hope that we could pay attention to little things. While observing the operations of our Government in various parts of the world, I have felt that in many situations where our policies were good we have tended to ignore minor problems which spoiled our main effort. To cite only a few examples: The wrong man in the wrong position, perhaps even in a junior position abroad, can be a source of great harm to our policy; the attitudes of a U.N. delegate who experiences difficulty in finding adequate housing in New York City, or of a foreign diplomat in similar circumstances in our Capital, can easily be directed against the United States and all that it stands for. Dozens of seemingly small matters go wrong all over the world. Sometimes those who know about them are too far down the line to be able to do anything about them. I would hope that we could create the recognition in the Department and overseas that those who come across little things going wrong have the responsibility for bringing these to the attention of those who can do something about them.

If the Department of State is to take primary responsibility for foreign policy in Washington, it follows that the Ambassador is expected to take charge overseas. This does not mean in a purely bureaucratic sense but in an active, operational, interested, responsible fashion. He is expected to know about what is going on among the representatives of other agencies who are stationed in his country. He is expected to supervise, to encourage, to direct, to assist in any way he can. If any official operation abroad begins to go wrong, we shall look to the Ambassador to find out why and to get suggestions for remedial action.

The Problems of a Policy Officer

It occurred to me that you might be interested in some thoughts which I expressed privately in recent years, in the hope of clearing up a certain confusion in the public mind about what foreign policy is all about and what it means, and of developing a certain compassion for those who are carrying such responsibilities inside Government. I tried to do so by calling to their attention some of the problems that a senior departmental policy officer faces. This means practically everybody in this room. Whether it will strike home for you or not will be for you to determine.

The senior policy officer may be moved to think hard about a problem by any of an infinite variety of stimuli: an idea in his own head, the suggestions of a colleague, a question from the Secretary or the President, a proposal by another department, a communication from a foreign government or an American ambassador abroad, the filing of an item for the agenda of the United Nations or of any other of dozens of international bodies, a news item read at the breakfast table, a question to the President or the Secretary at a news conference, a speech by a Senator or Congressman, an article in a periodical, a resolution from a national organization, a request for assistance from some private American interests abroad, et cetera, ad infinitum. The policy officer lives with his antennae alerted for the questions which fall within his range of responsibility.

His first thought is about the question itself: Is there a question here for American foreign policy, and, if so, what is it? For he knows that the first and sometimes most difficult job is to know what the question is—that when it is accurately identified it sometimes answers itself, and that the way in which it is posed frequently shapes the answer.

Chewing it over with his colleagues and in his own mind, he reaches a tentative identification of the question—tentative because it may change as he explores it further and because, if no tolerable answer can be found, it may have to be changed into one which can be answered.

Meanwhile he has been thinking about the facts surrounding the problem, facts which he knows can never be complete, and the general background, much of which has already been lost to history. He is appreciative of the expert help available to him and draws these resources into play, taking care to examine at least some of the raw material which underlies their frequently policy-oriented conclusions. He knows that he must give the expert his place, but he knows that he must also keep him in it.

He is already beginning to box the compass of alternative lines of action, including doing nothing. He knows that he is thinking about action in relation to a future which can be perceived but dimly through a merciful fog. But he takes his bearings from the great guidelines of policy, well-established precedents, the commitments of the United States under international charters and treaties, basic statutes, and well-understood notions of the American people about how we are to conduct ourselves, in policy literature such as country papers and National Security Council papers accumulated in the Department.

He will not be surprised to find that general principles produce conflicting results in the factual situation with which he is confronted. He must think about which of these principles must take precedence. He will know that general policy papers written months before may not fit his problem because of crucial changes in circumstance. He is aware that every moderately important problem merges imperceptibly into every other problem. He must deal with the question of how to manage a part when it cannot be handled without relation to the whole—when the whole is too large to grasp.

He must think of others who have a stake in the question and in its answer. Who should be consulted among his colleagues in the Department or other departments and agencies of the Government? Which American ambassadors could provide helpful advice? Are private interests sufficiently involved to be consulted? What is the probable attitude of other governments, including those less directly involved? How and at what stage and in what sequence are other governments to be consulted?

If action is indicated, what kind of action is relevant to the problem? The selection of the wrong tools can mean waste, at best, and at worst an unwanted inflammation of the problem itself. Can the President or the Secretary act under existing authority, or will new legislation and new money be required? Should the action be unilateral or multilateral? Is the matter one for the United Nations or some other international body? For, if so, the path leads through a complex process of parliamentary diplomacy which adds still another dimension to the problem.

Respect for the Opinions of Mankind

What type of action can hope to win public support, first in this country and then abroad? For the policy officer will know that action can almost never be secret and that in general the effectiveness of policy will be conditioned by the readiness of the country to sustain it. He is interested in public opinion for two reasons: first, because it is important in itself, and, second, because he knows that the American public cares about a decent respect for the opinions of mankind. And, given probable public attitudes —about which reasonably good estimates can be made—what action is called for to insure necessary support?

May I add a caution on this particular point? We do not want policy officers below the level of Presidential appointees to concern themselves too much with problems of domestic politics in recommending foreign policy action. In the first place our business is foreign policy, and it is the business of the Presidential leadership and his appointees in the Department to consider the domestic political aspects of a problem. Mr. Truman emphasized this point by saying, "You fellows in the Department of State don't know much about domestic politics."

This is an important consideration. If we sit here reading editorials and looking at public-opinion polls and other reports that cross our desks, we should realize that this is raw, undigested opinion expressed in the absence of leadership. What the American people will do turns in large degree on their leadership. We cannot test public opinion until the President and the leaders of the country have gone to the public to explain what is required and have asked them for support for the necessary action. I doubt, for example, that, 3 months before the leadership began to talk about what came to be the Marshall plan, any public-opinion expert would have said that the country would have accepted such proposals.

The problem in the policy officer's mind thus begins to take shape as a galaxy of utterly complicated factors—political, military, economic, financial, legal, legislative, procedural, administrative—to be sorted out and handled within a political system which moves by consent in relation to an external environment which cannot be under control.

And the policy officer has the hounds of time snapping at his heels. He knows that there is a time to act and a time to wait. But which is it in this instance? Today is not yesterday and tomorrow will be something else, and his problem is changing while he and his colleagues are working on it. He may labor prodigiously to produce an answer to a question which no longer exists.

In any event he knows that an idea is not a policy and that the transformation of an idea into a policy is frequently an exhausting and frustrating process. He is aware of the difference between a conclusion and a decision. The professor, the commentator, the lecturer may indulge in conclusions, may defer them until all the evidence is in, may change them when facts so compel. But the policy officer must move from conclusion to decision and must be prepared to live with the results, for he does not have a chance to do it again. If he waits, he has already made a decision, sometimes the right one, but the white heat of responsibility is upon him and he cannot escape it, however strenuously he tries.

There is one type of study which I have not seen, which I hope we can do something about in the months ahead. The pilot of a jet aircraft has a check list of many dozen questions which he must answer satisfactorily before he takes off his plane on a flight. Would it not be interesting and revealing if we had a check list of questions which we should answer systematically before we take off on a policy?

Perhaps this is a point at which to inject another passing comment. The processes of government have sometimes been described as a struggle for power among those holding public office. I am convinced that this is true only in a certain formal and bureaucratic sense, having to do with appropriations, job descriptions, trappings of prestige, water bottles, and things of that sort. There is another struggle of far more consequence, the effort to diffuse or avoid responsibility. Power gravitates to those who are willing to make decisions and live with the results, simply because there are so many who readily yield to the intrepid few who take their duties seriously.

On this particular point the Department of State is entering, I think, something of a new phase in its existence. We are expected to take charge. We shall be supported in taking charge, but it throws upon us an enormous responsibility to think broadly and deeply and in a timely fashion about how the United States shall conduct itself in this tumultuous world in which we live.

I want to transmit to you not only my own complete confidence but the confidence of the President in our determination to back you in one of the most onerous responsibilities in the country, and indeed in the world today, and ask you for your maximum help as we try to get on with this job in the months ahead.

I hope to be seeing you from time to time in your own offices. Both Mr. Bowles and I will try to visit different sections of the Department in the weeks ahead. In the meantime you may be sure that we shall be vitally interested in how you see this job and how you think the United States should move to take charge of its future, to do its part to shape the course of events—to make history, which will cause those after us to call us "blessed."

Thank you very much.

STATEMENT OF PAUL H. NITZE

Mr. Chairman, any person attentive to the wide ranging and perceptive testimony already given before this distinguished subcommittee must wonder just how to add anything of value on his own. My ideas, far from being original contributions, can only serve to underscore points brought out by preceding witnesses.

The topic is the problem of gearing up the Government for effective foreign policy and defense policy. It is always with us—a problem never solved with finality.

These realms of policy do not differ from purely domestic policy in

Presented before the Subcommittee on National Policy Machinery of the Senate Committee on Government Operations, June 17, 1960.

respect to purpose and controlling principles. All policies of this Government are supposed to be informed by the great purposes of the state laid down in the preamble of the Constitution. What distinguishes foreign policy and defense policy—the specific concern to this subcommittee—from the domestic policy is a matter of jurisdiction. Foreign policy and defense policy are directed toward the world environment. They reflect the national will toward matters lying beyond our jurisdiction. In that realm the Government does not exercise ruling authority. It cannot quite lay down the law. It can at best only influence events and circumstances, not ordain them. Other wills are at work. They stem from premises and focus on purposes often different from our own and quite often not merely different but inimical.

This basic, simple characteristic makes foreign and defense policy more chancy and speculative and sometimes more exasperating than domestic affairs. While the inherent character of these realms of policy sets limits on what can be accomplished by planning, it also makes important and essential that we muster all the foresight, intellectual rigor, and circumspection that we can.

It is for this reason that I, among many, welcome the efforts of this subcommittee in developing a greater consciousness of the nature of policy in these fields and the problem of so organizing as to make possible our best performance.

There are dangers of oversimplification in any discussion of this subject. Analysis inevitably produces some distortion. One makes nice distinctions between policy formulation and operations or between command and staff functions. One draws neat charts dividing responsibilities into geometrically precise compartments. One speaks of levels of authority as if government could be arranged with the measured symmetry of a staircase. For analysis we divide things up; in practice they are all of a piece together.

Another set of difficulties arises. The precepts of sound policy and sound policymaking boil down to a set of maxims of copybook clarity—concepts indisputable and obvious. One is likely to say of them that the principles are mere matters of commonsense, that everybody knows them. In a way this is true. Yet I think also that something which Clausewitz said of warfare is applicable here. He said that the important things were all simple and that the simple things were most difficult. I am sure that there is nothing recondite about sound policymaking. On the other hand, putting the simple precepts into practice in a government is an enormously exacting task. It requires sustained and rigorous application and unremitting exercise of authority and intellect. Discipline and order within a governing apparatus have to be created anew continuously.

My own way of getting at the problem is to divide the field of policy according to the breadth and the duration of the ideas involved.

I would begin with the enduring end of U.S. policy toward the world external to our fiat. It is to maintain and to enhance conditions in the world environment favorable to the survival, as political realities within our domain, of the precepts and values chosen and asserted in the foundation of our Nation. This is the constant purpose. What it entails varies from one historic phase to another.

What it entails in any one phase might be called our national strategy. This strategy must be recast from epoch to epoch. To do this requires encompassing judgments and broad decisions which set the tone and establish the general premises of our undertakings in world affairs.

You may ask for examples. I suppose the first one in our national history was the decision to venture into independence, the decision that the Americans would constitute themselves as a nation, work out their own history, and deal with the external world in their own right. A second, surely, was the early decision to establish a base of continental scope. A third was the great decision asserting the inviolability of the American Hemisphere.

More recent decades give us other instances: The decision recognizing the threat to us explicit in the ambitions of the Axis and determining to counter that threat; the decision to bring on and to relate ourselves to an organized pattern of international responsibility in the sequel to World War II; the decision recognizing the true nature of the threat inherent in the power and thrust of communism and of the necessity of countervailing action.

How are such decisions arrived at? One may often pinpoint their emergence in some specific pronouncement such as Washington's Farewell Message, President Monroe's message which marked the origin of what has come to be known as the Monroe Doctrine, or, to take a recent instance, the Truman doctrine. These specific, clear acts are certainly great sources of policy. They are also, however, results of policymaking. They were not struck off as sudden, original acts without antecedents. They emerged from great interplay of forces and ideas and hard consideration within administrations, between administrations and the Congress, and between governing institutions and the public. I know no way of reducing to a graph or to any neat formula the complexities that go to make up the great decisions of policy which in turn serve as the bedrock on which still further structures of policy are erected.

Take one decision which is rarely commented on: The decision which grew out of the experience of the Korean war to involve ourselves specifically and concretely by the continuing commitment of U.S. military forces to positions on other continents.

Parenthetically, it is noteworthy how often this aspect of the Korean struggle is overlooked. The tactical frustrations of the fighting on the Korean peninsula are dwelt upon almost to the exclusion of consideration of the great strategic decisions of global importance accompanying that struggle and essentially related to it.

What I wish to emphasize here is merely the elusiveness and complexity of these great decisions. They were of historic import. Yet, from what I know about the processes producing them, I should find it most difficult to identify the moment when it will become resolved, or when multifarious forces converged to produce one clear stream of action, or to say that this or that was the procedure by which it was accomplished.

What I would stress here is the fallacy of the idea—however much I find implicit in much that is said and written about policy—that the great decisions are matters requiring only periodic attention.

Decision in this field is not like buying a new car. It is not a case of giving heed to the requirements at stated intervals—making up one's mind on what model to get and then putting the matter out of mind until the thing becomes worn out or outdated by changes in style. The requirement is for unremitting hard work. The great decisions can be made adequately only in consequence of a great many contributory determinations.

The articulation of our national strategy by no means exhausts the formulation of policy. The attitudes, appreciations, and the will to act reflected in the major strategic determinations must take form in wide arrays of policy undertakings. Auxiliary actions to give effect to our main intentions must be determined upon. Particular situations making demands upon our capabilities arise, and old exigencies decline—often in consequence of actions we ourselves have taken.

The allocation of resources among our purposes must be continuously reappraised and modified to suit circumstance. Specific policies must be refreshed in response to surges of change in an everfluctuating environment. Demands arise from political changes within and among other political entities, from shifts in their economies, and from the dynamic of invention. New means have to be devised for emerging situations. Our own schedule of priorities for action must undergo continuous reexamination so as to make the best use we can of what resources we can bring to bear.

So, to recapitulate, our policies have an enduring end. What this enjoins upon us, phase by phase, must be decided on in major strategic determinations. In keeping with these, a host of lesser and more particular decisions have to be made and actions taken—narrowing down to matters of mere detail and matters of limited and passing significance. Yet I would warn against any attempt to classify decisions according to any fixed scale of importance. There are great fluctuations in importance and difficulty among particular facets of policy from one phase to another. Problems have a way of blowing hot and cold—rising and falling in their criticalness, passing along on the escalator of importance both upward and downward. What are marginal problems in one phase may become central problems in another and vice versa.

Obviously, one characteristic of a properly functioning Government is that problems should always get to the proper level of authority for decision

—proper according to a sensible notion of who should be deciding what and of the criteria for decision. This is something so easy to say and so very difficult to insure. Things go wrong when the level of the deciding authority fails to match the intrinsic importance of the things decided or when the criteria by which decisions are resolved are too narrow.

Obviously a proper economy of authority requires not only that decisions be recognized for their inherent significance, passed to a sufficiently high level of responsibility, and decided according to the fitting criteria, but also that the time of those in the high places of authority should not be squandered on questions of inferior importance. This is elementary.

Now there is no final formula for determining the ratios of importance among problems and assigning them to various levels in the hierarchy of authority—the question can be worked out only through constant superintendence.

The other main principles of sound policymaking can be reduced to similar simple statements of the obvious. The strategic concepts should be in focus with the actualities of the exterior world and represent an adequate correspondence to the enduring purpose of our policies. Our broad undertakings should be commensurate with the strategic appreciation. The particular actions giving effect to these undertakings should be up to the mark—that is, adequate with respect to the intentions they are supposed to effectuate. Our means should be allocated among these intentions in accordance with some rational and realistic conception of the hierarchy of our interests and the range of our capabilities. All of it sounds so simple, and all of it is so endlessly exacting in practice.

If our problem were one of mechanics, we could devise our answers on charts, settle our difficulties by procedure, and keep things from getting out of hand by rigging up devices for balance and coordination. The trouble is, however, that our problems are not of this order. They involve another dimension—the factor of will. Empirical processes can tell us much about the nature of the world exterior to our jurisdiction and the forces operating in it, but they never complete for us the image of what these things are or the understanding of what we must do. What we must do flows, in part, from what we are. A study of the environment tells us the problems but never the answer for which we must strive. This must come from some inner dictate—from values inherent in our nationhood and in our concept of human dignity. The whole society is custodian of these values. The defining of what they impose on us in relation to our environment falls, above all and essentially, to the President.

The task of seeing that the major policies are all of a piece and that, taken together, they are congruent with the strategic concept determined upon requires continuous superintendence which only the powers of the Presidential office can supply.

I do not mean just an office. I mean also a man and his full attention.

The appreciations necessary to the strategic conception which is the basic element of our policy cannot be achieved by intermittent attention. They cannot emerge from briefings designed to reduce all complexities to a nutshell. They cannot be arrived at through policy papers designed to cover up dilemmas and smooth over the points of crux. The job cannot merely be distributed among subordinates.

If this central requirement of Presidential leadership and executive energy is not fulfilled, it is difficult to the point of impossibility to redress the lack at other points. A thousand committees may deliberate, 10,000 position papers may issue, and the bureaucratic mills may whir to unprecedented levels of output in memorandums, estimates, and joint reports—but little will come of it all if the exercise of the central authority vested in the President is faltering, intermittent, or ambiguous.

What I point out here is a consequence of the way our system is geared up. This subcommittee, the Congress as a whole, or any number of people however concerned they may feel, cannot provide substitute answers.

The task of seeing that the major policies form a consistent whole, congruent with the strategic concept determined upon, requires continuous superintendence that again must fall mainly to the President's responsibility. I would not, however, expect any President to do this alone. He will certainly require a vicar, a general manager, a chief of staff, for the foreign policy-defense fields. I believe that vicar should be the Secretary of State. No committee can perform this function for the President. No council can do it. The role must be assigned to an individual—authorized, deputized, and recognized for that purpose. I believe he should have the backing of one of the line departments of the executive branch.

I know that it is a common practice to invoke the magic term "coordination." It is assumed that all that is required is to divide up the pie of responsibilities between the departments and agencies of Government and then to direct that lateral coordination between them shall take place. I doubt that the problem is that simple.

The policy framework within which coordination is to take place is all important. Unless that framework is filled in first, coordination in foreign and defense policy become meaningless, even mischievous.

In this connection I shall quote from my colleague, Charles Burton Marshall:

> My ears pick up on hearing some new plan for coordination among, say, the political, military, and economic aspects of policy. What shall one call the preeminent function, the engrossing principle—as to which the elements of policy are to be coordinated and to which they are to be subordinated—if not some political function or principle?
>
> States relate to each other in many ways—the intimidatory or reassuring effect, one to another, of their capabilities for force; the interplay of their capacities to help or hinder or excel each other in production of goods and

income; their influence on one another regarding the arts and training; the interchange among them, or the withholding, of organized knowledge about natural phenomena; and direct touch between governments through official channels and through the organizations created to facilitate interchange and collaboration. That list—military, economic, cultural, scientific, diplomatic, and organizational—is representative but not exhaustive. My question is: What is the political function if not that which encompasses, transcends, and interrelates all the other aspects? The political is the coordinating function, not a function to be coordinated.

A source of feebleness in our making of policy is that we have forgotten the preeminently and essentially political character of the state and have vainly expected coordination of policy to materialize without any sufficient political principle around which to coordinate its elements.

I do not mean to rule out committees and councils and the like. They are unequivocally necessary in running a government. Moreover, I am sure that the National Security Council as conceived in the National Defense Act of 1947 is an adjunct of high utility to any President who uses it rightly —that is, as a forum of decision and not just as a papermill grinding through the motions of action without really acting or formulating apparent decisions that often do not decide anything.

I do not intend to dismiss the staff function either. Ideas must flow in both directions—up as well as down—in the channels of policy. The President, his Secretary of State, and all the chiefs of the organs of policy concerned must always have the candid counsel and steadfast assistance of the best brains they can get.

This brings us to an old point of discussion: Whether organizations or individuals count for most in this respect. It is a futile argument. I cannot imagine any organization functioning in the abstract without people to fill the slots. I cannot imagine individuals at work in this field without some understood and rational relationship among them. You must have good organization to get good use out of the right people. You have to have the right people to make even the conceptually best organization work. Good men will demand good organization or else leave. Good organization makes it possible to get and to hold onto the talents of good people.

It is well to remember that we are speaking of functions of government, and that that word comes from a Greek verb for operating a ship. That requires a man at the bridge with a destination in mind and a sense of direction. It requires a first officer who accurately reflects the master's intentions and estimates. Beyond that, the ship must be well organized and well manned. These are not two different things. It is not a question of which at the expense of the other. The two are mutually dependent.

The continuous reappraisal, the sensing of the exterior situation, the sensing of opportunities for action, the sorting out between the feasible and the infeasible in the realms of action, the anticipating of problems even before they emerge, and the recognition of those which have emerged for what they are—all these tasks integral to policymaking require mental exercise as exacting as any in human affairs.

It sometimes seems to me that the human attributes for this are the rarest and most highly required of all our needs. Yet in retrospect I often wonder at the richness of the talents available to the Government. Whatever may be wrong with the situation in which we find ourselves, I am sure that the deficiency is not in respect to the spirit and skills of the people available.

Yet we should not take the attributes of the right human resources for granted. The component elements—here I draw on my own recollections of the public servants of true creative value I have known in the Government —include, first of all, energy; sheer capacity to get hard work done. Second is acumen; the capacity to engage the mind with reality. Third is intellectual honesty. That is a moral quality involving a sense of devotion to truth, however painful and however at odds with what a superior may wish to hear. I recall a Secretary of State who in a salutory address to the Department, laid stress on what he called positive loyalty. I think something should be said for the importance of negative loyalty also—a faculty for shaking the head and saying no when that is what the situation demands.

These are the qualities to be sought, cultivated, and preserved in the channels of policymaking. Good organization is that which attracts individuals with such attributes and makes good use of them by giving them scope and opportunity to be heard. There are no formulas for this in terms of structure and procedures. It is mainly and essentially a question of the spirit which informs policy from the center of authority.

In conclusion I offer a few tentative ideas on organization for policymaking in this complex and difficult field.

(*a*) The organizational arrangements must be responsive to the President's will. He alone can know his own requirements and how they can best be met.

(*b*) It would seem to me to be normal and sensible if the President were to turn to his Secretary of State to act as his general manager in the foreign field where diplomatic, military, economic, and psychological aspects need to be pulled together under a basically political concept. In this general manager capacity the Secretary of State would have the responsibility of seeing to it that the significant questions and data were brought to the President's attention and that he was spared the necessity of squandering his time on the less significant issues.

(*c*) If the Secretary of State has, or is given, this general manager responsibility, he will need a staff recruited, trained, and organized to help him in this policy development and coordination function. This function is quite different from that of diplomacy for which most of the Foreign Service is now trained.

(*d*) The National Security Council, the Secretary of Defense's Office, perhaps the Joint Chiefs of Staff, and the Bureau of the Budget, under this organizational concept, would require staff people having general training and a point of view similar to that of the Secretary of State's staff for policy development and coordination.

Thank you, Mr. Chairman.

Henry A. Kissinger
THE POLICYMAKER AND
THE INTELLECTUAL

ANY observer of the American scene must be struck by the tentative quality of our policy both foreign and domestic. Major parts of the world are undergoing revolutionary upheaval; but we seem hardly aware that peoples abroad find increasingly little in America with which to identify themselves. Beyond any disagreement or dissatisfaction over specific policies there exists an ever-growing distrust or at least incomprehension of America's purposes.

It would be comforting to believe that this state of affairs is due to particular mistakes of policy that can be reversed more or less easily. Unfortunately the problem is more deep-seated. Our policymakers' lack of vigor is matched by that of many of their critics. It has been a long time since there has been a real debate on policy issues beyond a bland competition for slogans such as coexistence or flexibility.

This stagnation is often ascribed to the fact that our best people are not attracted into government service. But it may be pertinent to inquire how qualified our eminent men are for the task of policymaking in a revolutionary period. Others trace the cause of our difficulties to the lack of respect shown the intellectual by our society. However, a case could be made for the proposition that in some respects the intellectual has never been more in demand; that he makes such a relatively small contribution not because he is rejected but because his function is misunderstood. He is sought after enthusiastically but for the wrong reasons and in pursuit of the wrong purposes.

One of the paradoxes of an increasingly specialized, bureaucratized society is that the qualities rewarded in the rise to eminence are less and less the qualities required once eminence is reached. Specialization encourages

FROM *The Reporter* (March 5, 1959). Reprinted by permission of the author and the publisher.

administrative and technical skills, which are not necessarily related to the vision and creativity needed for leadership. The essence of good administration is co-ordination among the specialized functions of a bureaucracy. The task of the executive is to infuse and occasionally to transcend routine with purpose.

Yet while the head of an organization requires a different outlook from that of his administrative subordinates, he must generally be recruited from their ranks. Eminence thus is often reached for reasons and according to criteria which are irrelevant to the tasks which must be performed in the highest positions. Despite all personnel procedures and perhaps because of them, superior performance at the apex of an organization is frequently in the deepest sense accidental.

This problem, serious enough in the private sector, is even more complicated in government. In a society that has prided itself on its free-enterprise character, it is inevitable that the qualities which are most esteemed in civilian pursuits should also be generally rewarded by high public office. But very little in the experience that forms American leadership groups produces the combination of political acumen, conceptual skill, persuasive power, and administrative ability required for the highest positions of government.

Our executives are shaped by a style of life that inhibits reflectiveness. For one of the characteristics of a society based on specialization is the enormous work load of its top personnel. The smooth functioning of the administrative apparatus absorbs more energies than the definition of criteria on which decision is to be based. Issues are reduced to their simplest terms. Decision making is increasingly turned into a group effort. The executive's task is conceived as choosing among administrative proposals in the formulation of which he has no part and with the substance of which he is often unfamiliar. A premium is placed on "presentations" which take the least effort to grasp and which in practice usually mean oral "briefing." (This accounts for the emergence of the specialist in "briefings" who prepares charts, one-page summaries, etc.) In our society the policymaker is dependent to an increasing extent on his subordinates' conception of the essential elements of a problem.

The bureaucratization of our society reflects not only its inevitable specialization but also certain deep-seated philosophical attitudes all the more pervasive for rarely being made explicit. Two generations of Americans have been shaped by the pragmatic conviction that inadequate performance is somehow the result of a failure to properly understand an "objective" environment and that group effort is valuable in itself. The interaction of several minds is supposed to broaden the range of "experience," and "experience" is believed to be the ultimate source of knowledge.

Pragmatism, at least in its generally accepted forms, produces a tendency to identify a policy issue with the search for empirical data. It sees in consensus a test of validity; it distrusts individual effort or at least individual certitude and it tends to suppress personal judgment as "subjective."

The low valuation of personal views produces a greater concern with the collection of facts than with an interpretation of their significance; therefore the myth in our government that intelligence does not advise, it only reports. It leads to a multiplication of advisory staffs and a great reliance on study groups of all types. Each difficulty calls into being new panels which frequently act as if nothing had ever been done before, partly, at least, because the very existence of a problem is taken as an indication of the inadequacy of the previous advice.

The situation is compounded by the personal humility that is one of the most attractive American traits. Most Americans are convinced that no one is ever entirely "right," or, as the saying goes, that if there is disagreement each party is probably a little in error. The fear of dogmatism pervades the American scene. But the corollary of the tentativeness of most views is an incurable inward insecurity. Even very eminent people are reluctant to stand alone, and they see in concurrence one of their chief tests of validity.

Philosophical conviction and psychological bias thus combine to produce in and out of government a penchant for policymaking by committee. The obvious insurance against the possibility of error is to obtain as many opinions as possible. An unanimity is important, in that its absence is a standing reminder of the tentativeness of the course adopted. The committee approach to decision making is often less an organizational device than a spiritual necessity.

In this manner, policy is fragmented into a series of *ad hoc* decisions which make it difficult to achieve a sense of direction or even to profit from experience. Substantive problems are transformed into administrative ones. Innovation is subjected to "objective" tests which deprive it of spontaneity. "Policy planning" becomes the projection of familiar problems into the future. Momentum is confused with purpose. There is greater concern with how things are than with which things matter. The illusion is created that we can avoid recourse to personal judgment and responsibility as the final determinant of policy.

The debilitating tendency of this approach is often obscured in the private sector of our society because the goals of our economic effort are relatively limited. They involve less the creation of a policy framework than successfully operating within one—itself a conciliatory procedure. But when the same method is applied to national policy, its limitations become dramatically apparent. Many of our policymakers begin their governmental careers with only superficial acquaintance with the problems of their office. This is partly because the rise to eminence has often absorbed most of their energies, partly because civic consciousness, where it exists, most often finds its outlet on the local level. Whatever the reason, few of our executives (or lawyers with business background) can benefit in government from the strong will which is often their outstanding trait and which gained them success. Consciously or not, our top policymakers often lack the assurance and the conceptual framework to impose a pattern on events or to impart a sense of direction to their administrative staffs. Their unfamiliarity with their subject matter reinforces their already strong tendency to identify a policy problem with an administrative breakdown and a policy solution with an aggregate of administrative proposals.

The impact on national policy is pernicious. Even our highest policy bodies, such as the National Security Council, are less concerned with developing over-all measures in terms of a well-understood national purpose than with adjusting the varying approaches of semi-autonomous departments. The elaborateness of the process is compounded by the tendency of advisers to advise; for silence may be taken to mean not that the idea under discussion is good but that the adviser is inadequate. The committee system is more concerned with co-ordination and adjustment than with purpose.

A policy dilemma is produced because the advantages and disadvantages of alternative measures appear fairly evenly balanced; otherwise there would be no need for discussion. (This leaves aside the question to what extent the committee procedure encourages a neutral personality to which the pros and cons of almost any course of action always seem fairly even and which therefore creates artificial dilemmas.) But in assessing these alternatives the risks always seem more certain than the opportunities. No one can ever prove that an opportunity existed, but failure to foresee a danger involves swift retribution. As a result, much of the committee procedure is designed to permit each participant or agency to register objections, and the system stresses avoidance of risk rather than boldness of conception.

Our method of arriving at decisions and the attitudes of our officials distort the essence of policy. Effective policy depends not only on the skill of individual moves but even more importantly on their relationship to each other. It requires a sense of proportion; a sense of style provides it with inner discipline. All these intangibles are negated where problems become isolated cases each of which is disposed of on its merits by experts in the special difficulties it involves. It is as if in commissioning a painting, a patron would ask one artist to draw the face, another the body, another the hands, and still another the feet, simply because each artist is particularly good in one category. Such a procedure in stressing the components would lose the meaning of the whole.

The result is a paradox: the more intense the search for certainty by means of administrative devices, the greater is the inward insecurity of the participants. The more they seek "objectivity," the more diffuse their efforts become. The insecurity of many of our policymakers sometimes leads to almost compulsive traits. Officials—and other executives as well—tend to work to the point of exhaustion as one indication that they have done all that could be asked. The insecurity of many of our policymakers sometimes is also shown by the fact that almost in direct proportion as advisory staffs multiply they are distrusted by those at the top. Officials increasingly feel the need for "outside"—and therefore unbiased—advice. Memoranda that are produced within the bureaucracy are taken less seriously than similar papers that are available to the general public. Crucial policy advice is increasingly requested from *ad hoc* committees of outside experts. (See, e.g., the Gaither Committee on national defense or the Draper Committee on economic assistance.)

These committees are often extraordinarily useful. They provide a fresh point of view. They can focus public discussion. They make possible the tapping of talent that would otherwise be unavailable, particularly in the scientific field. (A good case in point is James Killian's method of operation as science adviser to the President.) They may even galvanize the bureaucracy. Nevertheless they suffer from serious drawbacks. Whatever the previous experience of the members, they require extensive "briefing." This places an additional strain on the bureaucracy, while the members of the committee are frequently ready to make their best contribution at the point when the group is disbanded. Then again, the committee is inevitably drawn from the same segment of society as the top officials. Its members have therefore also been victims of the prevailing administrative pace. And the committee process, with its trend toward the fragmentation of policy and its bias toward simplified approaches, is almost as pervasive in *ad hoc* groups as in regular governmental committees.

In some respects *ad hoc* groups can even be said to represent an important diversion of talent. The number of outstanding individuals with experience in a given field is severely limited. As a result the same group is called again and again on related tasks. Its discussions soon become predictable and sometimes even stereotyped. The ideal situation would be a "leap-frogging" process in which the current high officials expend their intellectual capital while others, usually outside government, develop new concepts and approaches. But constant membership on committees causes many of their members to stagnate and freezes them at the level of the experience or effort that gained them their reputation.

Moreover, outside groups are handicapped by the fact that unless they constitute themselves into a pressure group seeking to mold public opinion —a function beyond their scope and usually contrary to their purpose—they can be effective only if they convince the bureaucracy. If they are too far in advance of existing thinking, they are ignored. If they only confirm what has already been considered within the government, they are unnecessary. *Ad hoc* committees generally can be effective only in a narrowly circumscribed area which may be somewhat ahead of official views but which rarely touches the essence of the problem: to challenge the existing assumptions or to define a new sense of direction.

The committee system not only has a tendency to ask the wrong questions, it also puts a premium on the wrong qualities. The committee process is geared to the pace of conversation. Even where the agenda is composed of memoranda, these are prepared primarily as a background for discussion, and they stand and fall on the skill with which they are presented. Hence quickness of comprehension is more important than reflectiveness, fluency more useful than creativeness. The ideal "committee man" does not make his associates uncomfortable; he does not operate with ideas too far outside of what is generally accepted. Thus the thrust of committees is toward a standard of average performance. Since a complicated idea cannot be easily absorbed by ear—particularly when it is new—committees lean toward what fits in with the most familiar experience of their members. They therefore produce great pressure in favor of the *status quo*. Committees are consumers and sometimes sterilizers of ideas, rarely creators of them.

For all their cumbersome procedure and their striving for "objectivity," there is something approaching frivolity about many committees. Ideas are accepted because no one can think of an objection fast enough; or they are rejected because they cannot readily be grasped. Unfortunately, not everything that sounds plausible is important and many important ideas do not seem plausible—at least at first glance, the only glance permitted by most committees. Rapidity of comprehension is not always equivalent to responsible assessment; it may even be contrary to it. The result is a vicious circle: in the absence of well-understood goals each problem becomes a special case. But the more fragmented our approach to policy, the more difficult it becomes to act consistently and purposefully. The typical pattern of our governmental process is therefore endless debate about whether a given set of circumstances is in fact a problem, until a crisis removes all doubts but also the possibility of effective action. The committee system, which is an attempt to reduce the inward insecurity of our top personnel, leads to the paradoxical consequence of institutionalizing it.

The result is that American policy displays a combination of abstractness and rigidity. Our method of arriving at decisions and the qualities it reflects and rewards place a greater premium on form than on substance. Thus on any given issue some paper will be produced for almost any eventuality. But because policy results from what are in effect adversary proceedings, proposals by the various departments or agencies are often overstated to permit compromise, or phrased vaguely to allow freedom of interpretation. In any case, what is considered policy is usually the embodiment of a consensus in a paper. The very qualities which make the consensus possible tend to inhibit sustained and subtle effort: for the statement is frequently so general that it must be renegotiated when the situation to which it applies arises.

The rigidity of American policy is therefore a symptom of the psychological burden placed on our policymakers. Policies developed with great inward doubt become almost sacrosanct as soon as they are finally officially adopted. The reason is psychological. The *status quo* has at least the advantage of familiarity. An attempt to change course involves the prospect that the whole searing process of arriving at a decision will have to be repeated. By the same token, most of our initiatives tend to occur during crisis periods. When frustration becomes too great or a crisis brooks no further evasion, there arises the demand for innovation almost for its own sake. Yet innovation cannot be achieved by fiat. Crisis conditions do not encourage calm consideration; they rarely permit anything except defensive moves.

The combination of unreflectiveness produced by the style of life of our most eminent people in and out of government, faith in administrative processes, and the conversational approach to policy accounts for much of the uncertainty of our policy. It leads to an enormous waste of intellectual resources. The price we pay for the absence of a sense of direction is that we appear to the rest of the world as vacillating, confused, and, what is most worrisome, increasingly irrelevant.

The Demand for Intellectuals

In a revolutionary period, then, it is precisely the practical man who is most apt to become a prisoner of events. It is most frequently the administrator who is unable to transcend the requirements of the moment. Are there any groups in our society who can overcome this impasse? How about those who are not engaged in administrative tasks nor part of large organizations; the individuals who devote themselves to furthering or disseminating knowledge—the intellectuals?

Any survey of the contemporary American scene reveals, however, that the problem is more complicated than our refusal or inability to utilize this source of talent. Many organizations, governmental or private, rely on panels of experts. Political leaders have intellectuals as advisers. Throughout our society, policy-planning bodies proliferate. Research organizations multiply. The need for talent is a theme of countless reports. What then is the difficulty?

One problem is the demand for expertise itself. Every problem which our society becomes concerned about—leaving aside the question whether these are always the most significant—calls into being panels, committees, or study groups supported by either private or governmental funds. Many organizations constantly call on intellectuals. As a result, intellectuals with a reputation soon find themselves so burdened that their pace of life hardly differs from that of the executives whom they advise. They cannot supply perspective because they are as harassed as the policymakers. In his desire to be helpful, the intellectual is too frequently compelled to sacrifice what should be his greatest contribution to society: his creativity.

Moreover, the pressure is not only produced by the organizations that ask for advice: some of it is generated by the self-image of the intellectual. In a pragmatic society, it is almost inevitable not only that the pursuit of knowledge for its own sake should be lightly regarded by the community but also that it should engender feelings of insecurity or even guilt among some of those who have dedicated themselves to it. There are many who believe that their ultimate contribution as intellectuals depends on the degree of their participation in what is considered the active life. It is not a long step from the willingness to give advice to having one's self-esteem gratified by a consulting relationship with a large organization. And since individuals who challenge the presuppositions of the bureaucracy, governmental or private, rarely can keep their positions as advisers, great pressures are created to elaborate on familiar themes rather than risk new departures that may both fail and prove unacceptable.

The great valuation our society places on expertise may be even more inimical to innovation than indifference. Since the American intellectual is so strongly committed to the same pragmatic values as the rest of society, it produces a tremendous overspecialization. This in turn makes it difficult for the intellectual to introduce a general perspective even from the vantage point of his own calling. Panels of experts are deliberately assembled to contain representatives of particular approaches: a committee on military policy will have spokesmen for the "all-out war" as well as for the "limited war" concept. A committee on foreign policy will have proponents for the "uncommitted areas" as well as specialists for Europe. These are then expected to adjust their differences by analogy with the committee procedure of the bureaucracy. Not surprisingly, the result is more often a common denominator than a well-rounded point of view.

This tendency is compounded by the conception of the intellectual held by the officials or organizations that call on him. The specialization of functions of a bureaucratized society delimits tasks and establishes categories of expectations. A person is considered suitable for assignments within certain classifications. But the classification of the intellectual is determined by the premium our society places on administrative skill. The intellectual is rarely found at the level where decisions are made; his role is commonly advisory. He is called in as a "specialist" in ideas whose advice is compounded with that of others from different fields of endeavor on the assumption that the policymaker is able to choose the correct amalgam between "theoretical" and "practical" advice. And even in this capacity the intellectual is not a free agent. It is the executive who determines in the first place whether he needs advice. He and the bureaucracy frame the question to be answered. The policymaker determines the standard of relevance. He decides who is consulted and thereby the definition of "expertness."

The fact that the need for excellence is constantly invoked is no guarantee that its nature will be understood. Excellence is more often thought to consist in the ability to perform the familiar as well as possible than in pushing back the frontiers of knowledge or insight. The search for talent consists more frequently in seeking personnel for well-understood tasks than in an effort to bring about an environment that constantly produces new and not yet imagined types of performance. The "expert" not uncommonly is the person who elaborates the existing framework most ably, rather than the individual charting new paths.

The contribution of the intellectual to policy is therefore in terms of criteria that he has played a minor role in establishing. He is rarely given the opportunity to point out that a query delimits a range of possible solutions or that an issue is posed in irrelevant terms. He is asked to solve problems, not to contribute to the definition of goals. Where decisions are arrived at by negotiation, the intellectual—particularly if he is not himself part of the bureaucracy—is a useful weight in the scale. He can serve as a means to filter ideas to the top outside of organization channels or as a legitimizer for the viewpoint of contending factions within and among departments. This is why many organizations build up batteries of outside experts or create semi-independent research groups, and why articles or books become tools in the bureaucratic struggle. In short, all too often what the policymaker wants from the intellectual is not ideas but endorsement.

This is not to say that the motivation of the policymaker toward the intellectual is cynical. The policymaker sincerely wants help. His problem is that he does not know the nature of the help he requires. And he generally does not become aware of a need until the problem is already critical. He is subject to the misconception that he can make an effective choice among conflicting advisers on the basis of administrative rules of thumb and without being fully familiar with the subject matter. Of necessity the bureaucracy gears the intellectual effort to its own requirements and its own pace: the deadlines are inevitably those of the policymaker, and all too often they demand a premature disclosure of ideas which are then dissected before they are fully developed. The administrative approach to intellectual effort tends to destroy the environment from which innovation grows. Its insistence on "results" discourages the intellectual climate that might produce important ideas whether or not the bureaucracy feels it needs them.

For these reasons, research institutes set up by governmental agencies have sometimes reflected the views of their sponsor even when they were financially independent. As long as the sponsoring agency retains the right to define the tasks of its research agency—or even the majority of these tasks—it will also determine the point of view of the product. The uniformity of the administrative approach is after all primarily the result less of fiscal control than of all the intangibles of fellowship and concern produced by association with a particular group and constant concentration on the same range of issues. It is not overcome if the "outside" research institute has no greater possibility for applying a wider perspective than its sponsoring agency has.

Thus though the intellectual participates in policymaking to an almost unprecedented degree, the result has not necessarily been salutary for him or of full benefit for the organization using him. In fact, the two have sometimes compounded each other's weaknesses. Nor has the present manner of utilizing outside experts and research institutes done more than reduce somewhat the dilemmas of the policymakers. The production of so much research often simply adds another burden to already overworked officials. It tends to divert attention from the act of judgment on which policy ultimately depends to the assembly of facts—which is relatively the easiest step in policy formation. Few if any of the recent crises of U.S. policy have been caused by the unavailability of data. Our policymakers do not lack advice; they are in many respects overwhelmed by it. They do lack criteria on which to base judgments. In the absence of commonly understood and meaningful standards, all advice tends to become equivalent. In seeking to help the bureaucracy out of this maze, the intellectual too frequently becomes an extension of the administrative machine, accepting its criteria and elaborating its problems. While this too is a necessary task and sometimes even an important one, it does not touch the heart of the problem: that purpose must dominate the mechanism if we are to avoid disaster. The dilemma of our policy is not so much that it cannot act on what it has defined as useful—though this too happens occasionally —but that the standards of utility are in need of redefinition. Neither the intellectual nor the policymaker performs his full responsibility if he shies away from this essential task.

Recharging the Batteries

This is not a call for the intellectual to remain aloof from policymaking. Nor have intellectuals who have chosen withdrawal necessarily helped the situation. There are intellectuals outside the bureaucracy who are not part of the maelstrom of committees and study groups but who have nevertheless contributed to the existing stagnation through a perfectionism that paralyzes action by posing unreal alternatives. (If we have the choice between rebuilding our cities or launching a satellite, we must choose the former.) There are intellectuals within the bureaucracy who have avoided the administrative approach but who must share the responsibility for the prevailing confusion because they refuse to recognize the inevitable element of conjecture in policymaking. (How can we be *sure* about Soviet motives? How can we be *certain* that in say thirty years the Soviet system will not be like ours?) The intellectuals of other countries in the free world where the influence of pragmatism is less pronounced and the demands of the bureaucracies less insatiable have not made a more significant contribution. The spiritual malaise described here may have other symptoms elsewhere. The fact remains that the entire free world suffers not only from administrative myopia but also from self-righteousness and the lack of a sense of direction.

One reason why intellectuals outside the administrative machines have not made a greater contribution is that for them protest has too often become an end in itself. Whether they have withdrawn by choice or because of the nature of their society, many intellectuals have confused the issues by simplifying them too greatly. They have refused to recognize that policymaking involves not only the clear conception of ideas but also the management of men. In the process analysis has been too often identified with policymaking.

But the equivalence is not absolute, particularly if analysis is conceived too rigidly. Effective policy fits its measures to circumstances. Analysis strives to eliminate the accidental; it seeks principles of general validity. The policymaker is faced with situations where at some point discussion will be overtaken by events, where to delay for the sake of refinement of thought may invite disaster. Analysis, by contrast, can and must always sacrifice time to clarity; it is not completed until all avenues of research have been explored. The difference between the mode of policy and the mode of analysis is therefore one of perspective. Policy looks toward the future; its pace is dictated by the need for decision in a finite time. Analysis assumes an accomplished act or a given set of factors; its pace is the pace of reflection.

The difficulty arises not from the analytic method but from the failure to relate it to the problems of the policymaker. The quest for certainty, essential for analysis, may be paralyzing when pushed to extremes with respect to policy. The search for universality, which has produced so much of the greatest intellectual effort, may lead to something close to dogmatism in national affairs. The result can be a tendency to recoil before the act of choosing among alternatives which is inseparable from policymaking, and to ignore the tragic aspect of policymaking which lies precisely in its unavoidable component of conjecture. There can come about a temptation to seek to combine the advantage of every course of action; to delay commitment until "all the facts are in," until, that is, the future has been reduced to an aspect of the past.

As a consequence, on many issues the short-run and manipulative approach of the bureaucracy and its adjuncts is opposed, if at all, by an abstract, dogmatic moralism that all too often cannot be related to the problem at hand. The technicians who act as if the cold war were its own purpose are confronted by others who sometimes talk as if the cold war could be ended by redefining the term. The Machiavellianism of short-term expedients much too frequently has as its sole antagonist a Utopianism that seems more concerned with registering a dissent than with contributing a sense of direction. The self-righteousness that sees in conscientious co-ordinating procedures a sufficient gauge of valid policy is little affected by a perfectionism that segments policy into cycles of domestic and foreign concerns (do we have the moral right to act abroad as long as there is a Little Rock?); or by a fastidiousness that spends more energy on establishing a moral equivalence between our attitudes and those of Communism than on defining the moral content of what we stand for. (Since we and the Communists distrust each other, an attempt on our part to claim superior morality is the most certain means to prevent a lasting peace.)

Thus if the intellectual is to deepen national policy he faces a delicate task. He must steer between the Scylla of letting the bureaucracy prescribe what is relevant or useful and the Charybdis of defining these criteria too abstractly. If he inclines too much toward the former, he will turn into a promoter of technical remedies; if he chooses the latter, he will run the risks of confusing dogmatism with morality and of courting martyrdom—of becoming, in short, as wrapped up in a cult of rejection as the activist is in a cult of success.

Where to draw the line between excessive commitment to the bureaucracy and paralyzing aloofness depends on so many intangibles of circumstance and personality that it is difficult to generalize. Perhaps the matter can be stated as follows: one of the challenges of the contemporary situation is to demonstrate the overwhelming importance of purpose over technique. The intellectual should therefore not refuse to participate in policymaking, for to do so would confirm the administrative stagnation. But in co-operating, the intellectual has two loyalties: to the organization that employs him as well as to values which transcend the bureaucratic framework and which provide his basic motivation. It is important for him to remember that one of his contributions to the administrative process is his independence, and that one of his tasks is to seek to prevent unthinking routine from becoming an end in itself.

The intellectual must therefore decide not only whether to participate in the administrative process but also in what capacity: whether as an intellectual or as an administrator. If he assumes the former role, it is essential for him to retain the freedom to deal with the policymaker from a position of independence, and to reserve the right to assess the policymaker's demands in terms of his own standards. Paradoxically, this may turn out to be also most helpful to the policymaker. For the greater the bureaucratization and the more eminent the policymaker, the more difficult it is to obtain advice in which substantive considerations are not submerged by or at least identified with organizational requirements.

Such an attitude requires an occasional separation from administration. In all humility, the intellectual must guard his distinctive and in this particular context most crucial qualities: the pursuit of knowledge rather than of administrative ends, the perspective supplied by a nontechnical vantage point. It is therefore essential for him to return from time to time to his library or his laboratory to "recharge his batteries." If he fails to do this he will turn into an administrator, distinguished from some of his colleagues only by having been recruited from the intellectual community. Such a relationship does not preclude a major contribution. But it will then have to be in terms of the organization's criteria, which can be changed from within only by those in the most pre-eminent positions.

The Highest of Stakes

Ultimately the problem is not the intellectual's alone or even primarily. There is no substitute for greater insight on the part of our executives, in or out of government. Advice cannot replace knowledge. Neither Churchill nor Lincoln nor Roosevelt was the product of a staff. As long as our executives conceive their special skill to be a kind of intuitive ability to choose among conflicting advice and as long as they see this skill largely in administrative or psychological but not substantive terms, their relationship with the intellectual will produce frustration as often as mutual support. The executive, while making a ritual of consulting the intellectual, will consider him hopelessly abstract or judge him by his suitability in achieving short-term ends. And the intellectual, while participating in the policymaking process, will always have the feeling that he never had a chance to present the most important considerations. The executives' lack of understanding of the process of reflection and the fragmented nature of their approach to policy causes them to place a premium on qualities in intellectuals which they can most easily duplicate in their own organization. It leads them to apply administrative criteria to the problems of creativity, thereby making it difficult to transcend the standards of the moment. The intellectuals' unfamiliarity with the management of men makes them overlook the difficulty in the application of their maxims.

The solution is not to turn philosophers into kings or kings into philosophers. But it is essential that our leadership groups overcome the approach to national issues as an extracurricular activity that does not touch the core of their concerns. The future course of our society is not a matter to be charted administratively. The specialization of functions turns into a caricature when decision making and the pursuit of knowledge on which it is based are treated as completely separate activities, by either executives or intellectuals. Our society requires above all to overcome its current lassitude, to risk itself on new approaches in a situation different from our historical expectation. This sense of purpose cannot come from a bureaucracy, and it will not come from our present leadership groups if they continue to see the challenge primarily as a succession of technical problems.

It is true that many of the difficulties described here are due to qualities which also account for the strength and vitality of our society. Against the background of our sudden projection into world affairs we have undoubtedly performed creditably. Unfortunately, our period offers no prizes for having done reasonably well; it does not permit us to rest on historical comparison. Our sole measure is our ability to contribute a sense of direction in a world in turmoil.

The stakes could hardly be higher. The deepest cause of the inhumanity of our time is probably the pedantic application of administrative norms. Its symbol may well be the "commissar," the ideal type of bureaucrat, who condemns thousands without love and without hatred simply in pursuance of an abstract duty. But we would do ourselves an injustice if we ignored that the commissar is not just a Soviet but a universal phenomenon—the Soviet system has simply encouraged it in its most extreme form. He is the administrator whose world is defined by regulations in whose making he had no part, and whose substance does not concern him, to whom reality is exhausted by the organization in which he finds himself. Our challenge is to rescue the individual from this process; to escape from the pretentiousness and stultifying quality of an atmosphere in which all sense of reverence for the unique is lost in the quest for reducing everything to manipulable quantities. The way we face this challenge will be the ultimate test of our long-proclaimed belief in the dignity of the individual.

The National Security Council

COMPOSITION AND ACTIVITIES OF THE NATIONAL SECURITY COUNCIL

Creation and Purposes. The National Security Council was established by the National Security Act of 1947 (61 Stat. 496; U.S.C. 402), amended by the National Security Act Amendments of 1949 (63 Stat. 579; 50 U.S.C. 401 et seq.). Its function is to advise the President with respect to the integration of domestic, foreign, and military policies relating to the national security so as to enable the military services and the other departments and agencies of the Government to cooperate more effectively in matters involving the national security. The Council was formally located within the Executive Office of the President by Reorganization Plan 4 of 1949.

Organization. The Council is composed of the President, the Secretary of State, the Secretary of Defense, and the Director of the Office of Emergency Planning. The act provides that the Secretaries and Under Secretaries of other executive departments and of the military departments may serve as members of the Council, when appointed by the President by and with the advice and consent of the Senate. Under the direction of the Council is a Central Intelligence Agency, headed by a Director of Central Intelligence. The Council staff is headed by a civilian executive secretary, appointed by the President.

Activities. The duties of the Council are to assess and appraise the objectives, commitments, and risks of the United States in relation to its actual and potential military power, in the interest of national security, for the purpose of making recommendations to the President; and to consider policies on matters of common interest to the departments and agencies of the Government concerned with the national security, and to make recommendations to the President.

APPROVED

BROMLEY SMITH
Executive Secretary

THE NATIONAL SECURITY COUNCIL

THIS is the second of a series of staff reports being issued by the Subcommittee on National Policy Machinery. These studies, which draw upon the large body of testimony and counsel given the subcommittee since it was established over a year ago, make suggestions for improving the national security policymaking process.

By law and practice, the President has the prime role in guarding the Nation's safety. He is responsible for the conduct of foreign relations. He commands the Armed Forces. He has the initiative in budgetmaking. He, and he alone, must finally weigh all the factors—domestic, foreign, military—which affect our position in the world and by which we seek to influence the world environment.

The National Security Council was created by statute in 1947 to assist the President in fulfilling his responsibilities. The Council is charged with advising the President—"with respect to the integration of domestic, foreign, and military policies relating to the national security so as to enable the military services and the other departments and agencies of the Government to cooperate more effectively in matters involving the national security."

The NSC was one of the answers to the frustrations met by World War II policymakers in trying to coordinate military and foreign policy. It is a descendant of such wartime groups as the State-War-Navy Coordinating Committee (SWNCC).

The Council is not a decisionmaking body; it does not itself make policy. It serves only in an *advisory* capacity to the President, helping him arrive at decisions which he alone can make.

Although the NSC was created by statute, each successive President has great latitude in deciding how he will employ the Council to meet his particular needs. He can use the Council as little, or as much, as he wishes. He is solely responsible for determining what policy matters will be handled within the Council framework, and how they will be handled.

An important question facing the new President, therefore, is how he will use the Council to suit his own style of decision and action.

This study, drawing upon the experience of the past 13 years, places at the service of the incoming administration certain observations concerning the role of the Council in the formulation and execution of national security policy.

A staff paper issued by the Subcommittee on National Policy Machinery of the Senate Committee on Government Operations, December 12, 1960.

The Council and the System

When he takes office in January, the new President will find in being a *National Security Council* and an *NSC system.*

The Council itself is a forum where the President and his chief lieutenants can discuss and resolve problems of national security. It brings together as statutory members the President, the Vice President, the Secretaries of State and Defense, the Director of the Office of Civil and Defense Mobilization, and as statutory advisers the Director of Central Intelligence and the Chairman of the Joint Chiefs of Staff. The President can also ask other key aides to take part in Council deliberations. The Secretary of the Treasury, for example, has attended regularly by Presidential invitation.

But there is also in being today an NSC system, which has evolved since 1947. This system consists of highly institutionalized procedures and staff arrangements, and a complex interdepartmental committee substructure. These are intended to undergird the activities of the Council. Two interagency committees—the Planning Board and the Operations Coordinating Board—comprise the major pieces of this substructure. The former prepares so-called "policy papers" for consideration by the Council; the latter is expected to help follow through on the execution of presidentially approved NSC papers.

The new President will have to decide how he wishes to use the Council and the NSC system. His approach to the first meetings of the Council under his administration will be important. These early sessions will set precedents. Action taken or not taken, assignments given or not given, invitations to attend extended or not extended, will make it subsequently easier or harder for the President to shape the Council and the system to his needs and habits of work.

He faces questions like these: What principals and advisers should be invited to attend the first Council meetings? What part should Presidential staff assistants play? What should the participants be told about the planned role and use of the NSC system? Who will prepare the agenda? What items will be placed on the agenda? Should the Council meet regularly or as need arises?

The New President's Choice

The new President has two broad choices in his approach to the National Security Council.

First: He can use the Council as an intimate forum where he joins with his chief advisers in searching discussion and debate of a limited number of critical problems involving major long-term strategic choices or demanding immediate action.

Mr. Robert Lovett has described this concept of the Council in terms of "a kind of 'Court of Domestic and Foreign Relations' ":

> The National Security Council process, as originally envisaged—perhaps "dreamed of" is more accurate—contemplated the devotion of whatever number of hours were necessary in order to exhaust a subject and not just exhaust the listeners.
>
> . . . The purpose was to insure that the President was in possession of all the available facts, that he got firsthand a chance to evaluate an alternative course of action disclosed by the dissenting views, and that all implications in either course of action were explored before he was asked to take the heavy responsibility of the final decision.

Second: The President can look upon the Council differently. He can view it as the apex of a comprehensive and highly institutionalized system for generating policy proposals and following through on presidentially approved decisions.

Seen in this light, the Council itself sits at the top of what has been called "policy hill." Policy papers are supposed to travel through interdepartmental committees up one side of the hill. They are considered in the Council. If approved by the President, they travel down the opposite side of the hill, through other interdepartmental mechanisms, to the operating departments and agencies.

The Council's Span of Concern

The voluminous record of meetings held, and papers produced, makes it clear that the Council and its subordinate machinery are now very busy and active. A long list of questions always awaits entry on the NSC agenda.

Presidential orders now in force provide that all decisions on national security policy, except for special emergencies, will be made within the Council framework. In theory, the embrace of the NSC over such matters is total.

Yet many of the most critical questions affecting national security are not really handled within the NSC framework.

The main work of the NSC has centered largely around the consideration of *foreign policy* questions, rather than *national security* problems in their full contemporary sense. A high proportion of the Council's time has been devoted to the production and study of so-called "country papers"—statements of our national position toward this or that foreign nation.

The Council, indeed, appears to be only marginally involved in helping resolve many of the most important problems which affect the future course of national security policy. For example, the Council seems to have only a peripheral or *pro forma* concern with such matters as the key decisions on the size and composition of the total national security budget, the strength and makeup of the armed services, the scale and scope of many major agency programs in such fields as foreign economic policy and atomic energy, the translation of policy goals into concrete plans and programs through the budgetary process, and many critical operational decisions with great long-term policy consequences.

The fact is that the departments and agencies often work actively and successfully to keep critical policy issues outside the NSC system. When policy stakes are high and departmental differences deep, agency heads are loath to submit problems to the scrutiny of coordinating committees or councils. They aim in such cases to bypass the committees while keeping them occupied with less important matters. They try to settle important questions in dispute through "out of court" informal interagency negotiations, when they are doubtful of the President's position. Or else they try "end runs" to the President himself when they think this might be advantageous.

Despite the vigorous activity of the NSC system, it is not at all clear that the system now concerns itself with many of the most important questions determining our long-term national strategy or with many of the critical operational decisions which have fateful and enduring impact on future policy.

The Planning Board

As the NSC system operates today, most of the matters which appear on the Council agenda are the product of a highly formalized and complex "policy paper production" system. The heart of this system is the NSC Planning Board, an interagency committee whose membership parallels that of the Council at the Assistant Secretary level. The initial drafts of policy papers are normally written by the departments and agencies, acting individually or in concert. But the Planning Board is responsible for the final content and language of most papers which reach the Council table. As Governor Rockefeller told the subcommittee: "I think the public does not recognize the degree to which the Planning Board really does 95 percent of the work, and it is not very often that a paper is changed by the Security Council."

The Planning Board is an interdepartmental committee, chaired by the Special Assistant to the President for National Security Affairs. Although formally appointed by the President, who has admonished them to act in their individual capacities in seeking "statesmanlike" solutions, the departmental members are oriented to the problems and perspectives of their own agencies. They can be expected to try to guard departmental interests.

From the outset, the drafting of a Planning Board paper is an involved process of negotiation, barter, offer, and counteroffer among the many departments involved. Governor Rockefeller has described the Planning Board process in these words:

> A major question is presented to the Planning Board and the various parties at interest, namely, the departments, each with its own role in relation to the area under discussion, work pretty carefully with highly skilled representatives to get language into the position paper which, while it does not violate the objective, protects their own position and their own special— I don't say interest—responsibility in this field. . . . So you get a watered-down version before it comes to the NSC and . . . permissive language which is not too obvious in the phraseology. This is quite an art, this business.

Many papers going from the Planning Board to the Council do indeed contain "splits"—statements of different departmental viewpoints.

But it is not at all clear that the "splits" actually help the Council understand the real policy alternatives and the true policy options available on some issue under debate. They may crystallize minor points of difference between competing agency views. The alternatives the "splits" normally reflect, in any case, represent differences in departmental or agency viewpoint. Such differences do not necessarily define or illuminate the real policy choices available. Moreover, "splits" are themselves a product of interagency bargaining. Their phrasing is adjusted to what the traffic can bear and shaped in the interest of winning allies for particular points of view.

Furthermore, the Planning Board papers are not "costed" except in the most general way. The budgetary consequences of proposed courses of action are set forth only in order of magnitude terms. As a result, Council members are little assisted in weighing the benefits of alternative policy courses against the costs.

Finally, the Planning Board, by its very nature, is not a creative instrument for developing and bringing forward imaginative and sharply defined choices, particularly in uncharted areas of policy. Interagency committees of this kind have a built-in drive toward lowest common denominator solutions. They can comment, review, and adjust. But they are not good instruments of innovation.

The limitation of the Planning Board itself in developing new responses to new problems is in part demonstrated by the employment for this purpose of outside consultants and "distinguished citizens committees," such as the Killian and Gaither Committees on defense and the Draper Committee on military and economic assistance.

The main source of policy innovations is the contribution of an individual. He may be found outside, or anywhere within, the Government. But normally he will be found working in a department or agency, grappling day in and day out with some pressing national security problem.

Given imaginative proposals from such individuals, interagency committees like the Planning Board can be helpful in criticizing and commenting. But if, in the interest of "agreed solutions," such committees blur the edges and destroy the coherence of these proposals, they do the President a disservice. There is strong reason to believe this is now the case.

The Council Itself

The National Security Council now holds regular weekly meetings. The meetings vary in size. Sometimes the President meets with only a handful of principals in conducting important business. On other occasions, 30 or 40 people may attend. A typical session, however, may have two dozen people present. Some 15 people may sit at the Council table, with perhaps another 10 looking on as observers and aides.

Mr. James Perkins has made this comment on the size of Council meetings: ". . . I think that the more one uses the NSC as a system of interagency coordination and the legitimatizing of decisions already arrived at, the growth in numbers is inevitable, because people left out of it and not at the meetings whose concurrence is required have a prima facie case for attending."

But if one views the Council primarily as a Presidential advisory body, the point quickly comes when the sheer numbers of participants and observers at a meeting limits the depth and dilutes the quality of the discussion. The present size of most Council meetings appears to have reached and passed this point.

There are different kinds of Council meetings. Some are briefing sessions designed to acquaint the participants with, for example, an important advance in weapons technology. Other meetings center around so-called "discussion papers," which aim not at proposing a solution to some policy problem but at clarifying its nature and outlining possible alternative courses of action.

The more typical Council session, however, follows a precise agenda and focuses upon the consideration of Planning Board policy papers. These papers have a routine format. As Robert Cutler has described them:

> For convenience, a routine format for policy statements was developed. Thus, the busy reader would always know where to find the covering letter, the general considerations, the objectives, the courses of action to carry out the objectives, the financial appendixes, the supporting staff study; for they invariably appeared in this sequence in the final document.
> . . . The standardization of these techniques made it possible for the Council to transact, week in and week out, an enormously heavy load of work.

The main work of the Council, thus, now consists of discussion and a search for consensus, centering around Planning Board papers.

The normal end product of Council discussion is a presidentially approved paper setting forth the recommendations of the Planning Board paper, with such amendments, if any, as are adopted after Council deliberations. This paper is transmitted through the Operations Coordinating Board to the operating departments and agencies.

But one point is fundamental: Policy *papers* and actual *policy* are not necessarily the same.

Pieces of paper are important only as steps in a process leading to action —as minutes of decisions to do or not to do certain things.

Papers which do not affect the course of governmental action are not policy: they are mere statements of aspiration. NSC papers are policy only if they result in *action*. They are policy only if they cause the Government to adopt one course of conduct and to reject another, with one group of advocates "winning" and the other "losing."

It appears that many of the papers now emerging from the Council do not meet the test of policy in this sense.

The Operations Coordinating Board

The job of helping follow through on policies emerging from the Council and approved by the President is entrusted to the Council's Operations Coordinating Board. In terms of the NSC system, the OCB is to policy followup what the Planning Board is to policy development. It is an interdepartmental committee on the Under Secretary level, chaired, like the Planning Board, by the Special Assistant to the President for National Security Affairs.

The OCB, assisted by an elaborate system of interagency working groups, prepares plans for carrying out the intent of NSC policies, transmits them to the departments and agencies, secures information on the status of programs under way, and reports back through the NSC to the President on progress.

In theory, the OCB does not *make* policy. Its mandate extends only to helping *carry out* policy. But this limitation is not and cannot be observed in practice.

When it receives an NSC policy paper, the initial job of the OCB is to determine the real meaning of the document in hand. It must often translate general statements, susceptible of varying interpretations, into tangible objectives together with plans for achieving them.

Departmental aims and interests are at stake in this determination. The process of translating an NSC paper into an action-oriented program therefore involves the same kind of interagency bartering and negotiating which takes place earlier in the Planning Board.

The OCB is an interagency committee which lacks command authority. It can advise, but not direct, the operating agencies.

Many of the most important decisions affecting the course of programs under OCB surveillance are made outside the framework of the Board. Programmatic budgetary decisions are a notable example. Also, the departments often bypass the OCB, pursuing their own interpretations of policy or engaging in "bootleg" coordination through extramural means.

The formal machinery of the OCB includes a large number of working groups which turn out detailed followup studies and papers. The significance of much of this work has been strongly questioned. Secretary of State Herter made this comment before the subcommittee:

> I was Chairman of OCB for 2 years. The feeling of utility varied an awful lot. At times you felt that you were being very useful. At other times you felt you were fanning the air or spending a lot of time reviewing minutiae. . . . When you get into the formal sessions, you again apply yourself to paperwork. Sometimes you get yourself so bogged down in the editing of a word or a sentence that you say, "My God, why am I spending so much time on this?"

The nature of the danger seems clear. Actually, the OCB has little impact on the real coordination of policy execution. Yet, at the same time, the existence of this elaborate machinery creates a false sense of security by inviting the conclusion that the problem of teamwork in the execution of policy is well in hand.

Recently, the Board has abandoned or relaxed many of the rigid reporting requirements which governed its work when it was established, and has focused its attention upon a smaller number of important problems rather than spreading its efforts across the board. These steps have reportedly been helpful.

But there is a more fundamental question at issue: Can an interdepartmental committee, like the OCB, be counted on to discharge effectively major responsibilities for followthrough? The evidence points to the contrary.

New Directions

Two main conclusions about the National Security Council emerge:

First: The real worth of the Council to a President lies in being an accustomed forum where he and a small number of his top advisers can gain that intellectual intimacy and mutual understanding on which true coordination depends. Viewed thus, the Council is a place where the President can receive from his department and agency heads a full exposition of policy alternatives available to him, and, in turn, give them clear-cut guidance for action.

Second: The effectiveness of the Council in this primary role has been diminished by the working of the NSC system. The root causes of difficulty are found in overly crowded agenda, overly elaborate and stylized procedures, excessive reliance on subordinate interdepartmental mechanisms, and the use of the NSC system for comprehensive coordinating and follow-through responsibilities it is ill suited to discharge.

The philosophy of the suggestions which follow can be summed up in this way—to "deinstitutionalize" and to "humanize" the NSC process.

The President's Instrument. The Council exists only to serve the President. It should meet when he wishes advice on some matter, or when his chief foreign and defense policy advisers require Presidential guidance on an issue which cannot be resolved without his intervention.

There are disadvantages in regularly scheduled meetings. The necessity of having to present and to discuss something at such meetings may generate business not really demanding Presidential consideration. Council meetings and the Council agenda should never become ritualistic.

The Purpose of Council Discussion. The true goal of "completed staff work" is not to spare the President the necessity of choice. It it to make his choices more meaningful by defining the essential issues which he alone must decide and by sharpening the precise positions on the opposing sides.

Meetings of the Council should be regarded as vehicles for clarifying differences of view on major policy departures or new courses of action advocated by department heads or contemplated by the President himself.

The aim of the discussion should be a full airing of divergent views, so that all implications of possible courses of action stand out in bold relief. Even a major issue may not belong on the Council agenda if not yet ripe for sharp and informed discussion.

Attendance at Council Meetings. The Secretaries of State and Defense share the main responsibility of advising the President on national security problems. They are the key members of the Council. Whom the President invites to Council sessions will, of course, depend on the issue under discussion. However, mere "need to know," or marginal involvement with the matter at hand, should not justify attendance.

Council meetings should be kept small. When the President turns for advice to his top foreign policy and defense officials, he is concerned with what *they themselves* think.

The meetings should, therefore, be considered gatherings of principals, not staff aides. Staff attendance should be tightly controlled.

As a corollary to the strict limitation of attendance, a written record of decisions should be maintained and given necessary distribution.

The Planning Board. The NSC Planning Board now tends to overshadow in importance, though not in prestige, the Council itself. However, some group akin to the present Board, playing a rather different role than it now does, can be of continuing help to the Council in the future.

Such a Board would be used mainly to criticize and comment upon policy initiatives developed by the departments or stimulated by the

President. It would not be used as an instrument for negotiating "agreed positions" and securing departmental concurrences.

More reliance could also be placed on informal working groups. They could be profitably employed both to prepare matters for Council discussion and to study problems which the Council decides need further examination. The make-up and life of these groups would depend on the problem involved.

So, too, intermittent outside consultants or "distinguished citizens committees," such as the Gaither Committee, could on occasion be highly useful in introducing fresh perspectives on critical problems.

The Role of the Secretary of State. The Secretary of State is crucial to the successful operation of the Council. Other officials, particularly the Secretary of Defense, play important parts. But the President must rely mainly upon the Secretary of State for the initial synthesis of the political, military, economic, and other elements which go into the making of a coherent national strategy. He must also be mainly responsible for bringing to the President proposals for major new departures in national policy.

To do his job properly the Secretary must draw upon the resources of a Department of State staffed broadly and competently enough with generalists, economists, and military and scientific experts to assist him in all areas falling within his full concern. He and the President need unhurried opportunities to consider the basic directions of American policy.

The Operations Coordinating Board. The case for abolishing the OCB is strong. An interdepartmental committee like the OCB has inherent limitations as an instrument for assisting with the problem of policy followthrough. If formal interagency machinery is subsequently found to be needed, it can be established later.

Responsibility for implementation of policies cutting across departmental lines should, wherever possible, be assigned to a particular department or to a particular action officer, possibly assisted by an informal interdepartmental group.

In addition, the President must continue to rely heavily on the budgetary process, and on his own personal assistants in performance auditing.

Problems of Staff. The President should at all times have the help and protection of a small personal staff whose members work "outside the system," who are sensitive to the President's own information needs, and who can assist him in asking relevant questions of his departmental chiefs, in making suggestions for policy initiatives not emerging from the operating departments and agencies, and in spotting gaps in policy execution.

The Council will continue to require a staff of its own, including a key official in charge. This staff should consist of a limited number of highly able aides who can help prepare the work of the Council, record its decisions, and troubleshoot on spot assignments.

The NSC system now contains several staff components. These might well be more closely integrated. Also, various special project staffs on foreign policy matters have been established in recent years at the White House. Consideration could be given to bringing them within the NSC framework.

A Special Problem. The National Security Act intended that one Council member regularly bring to the NSC perspectives on our domestic economy and domestic resources.

The Director of the Office of Civil and Defense Mobilization is the present heir of that role. But the concern of the OCDM focuses upon civil defense and mobilization problems of wartime emergencies. The Council of Economic Advisers, among other agencies, is now much more concerned than the OCDM with the kind of domestic perspectives relevant to the problems of a protracted conflict which stops short of major war.

The new President and the Congress may therefore wish to ask whether the Director of OCDM should have continued statutory membership on the Council.

The NSC and the Budgetary Process. Today, there is often little resemblance between a policy statement emerging from the NSC and programs finally carried out by the operating departments and agencies. The actual scale and scope of these programs is determined largely by budgetary decisions made outside the Council.

An attempt to use the Council for the details of resource allocation would be no more feasible than trying to use the Cabinet for this purpose. Yet the search for ways and means of relating the Council's advice more closely to the budget process must be pursued.

The problem is not to make the Council manager or czar of budget preparation. Rather it is to insure that the perspectives of the Secretaries of State and Defense are brought to bear on an ordering of national priorities at the target-setting stage of the annual budget preparation.

The National Security Council is the appropriate body for helping the President define such priorities.

EXCHANGE OF LETTERS BETWEEN
SENATOR HENRY M. JACKSON AND
McGEORGE BUNDY

U.S. SENATE,
SUBCOMMITTEE ON NATIONAL POLICY MACHINERY,
July 13, 1961.

MR. McGEORGE BUNDY,
Special Assistant to the President for National Security Affairs,
The White House, Washington, D.C.

DEAR MR. BUNDY: As you know, our subcommittee will shortly hold hearings bringing to a close its nonpartisan study of how our Government can best staff and organize itself to develop and carry out the kind of national security policies required to meet the challenge of world communism.

As you also know, we have been deeply concerned from the outset with the organization and procedures of the National Security Council, its subordinate organs, and related planning and followthrough mechanisms in the area of national security.

Early in our study, the previous administration was kind enough to make available to the subcommittee a series of official memorandums describing the functions, organization, and procedures of the National Security Council and its supporting mechanisms. These memorandums, which were printed by the subcommittee in our Selected Materials, proved of great interest and value to our members, to students and interpreters of the policy process, and to the wide general audience which has been following our inquiry.

The purpose of this letter is to ask whether the present administration could now furnish us with official memorandums which would be the current equivalent of the above documents given us by the Eisenhower administration.

I presume that this material is readily at hand, and that it could be made available to us by August 4, so that we could profit from its study during the final phase of our hearings and make it a part of our permanent record.

Sincerely yours,

HENRY M. JACKSON,
Chairman, Subcommittee on National Policy Machinery.

———

THE WHITE HOUSE,
Washington, September 4, 1961.

HON. HENRY M. JACKSON,
U.S. Senate, Washington, D.C.

DEAR SENATOR JACKSON: I have thought hard about your letter of July 13, which asks for official memorandums that would be the current equivalent of memorandums submitted by the previous administration. I find that this is not easy to do, but let me try. The previous administration wrote out of many years of experience in which it had gradually developed a large and complex series of processes. This administration has been revising these arrangements to fit the needs of a new President, but the work of revision is far from done, and it is too soon for me to report with any finality upon the matters about which you ask. It seems to me preferable, at this early stage in our work, to give you an informal interim account in this letter.

Much of what you have been told in the reports of the previous administration about the legal framework and concept of the Council remains true today. There has been no recent change in the National Security Act of 1947. Nor has there been any change in the basic and decisive fact that the Council is advisory only. Decisions are made by the President. Finally, there has been no change in the basic proposition that, in the language of Robert Cutler, "the Council is a vehicle for a President to use in accordance with its suitability to his plans for conducting his great office." As Mr. Cutler further remarked, "a peculiar virtue of the National Security Act is its flexibility," and "each President may use the Council as he finds most suitable at a given time." [1] It is within the spirit of this doctrine that a new process of using the NSC is developing.

The specific changes which have occurred are three. First, the NSC meets less often than it did. There were 16 meetings in the first 6 months of the Kennedy administration. Much that used to flow routinely to the weekly meetings of the Council is now settled in other ways—by separate meetings with the President, by letters, by written memorandums, and at levels below that of the President. President Kennedy has preferred to call meetings of the NSC only after determining that a particular issue is ready for discussion in this particular forum.

I know you share my understanding that the National Security Council has never been and should never become the only instrument of counsel and decision available to the President in dealing with the problems of our national security. I believe this fact cannot be overemphasized. It is not easy for me to be sure of the procedures of earlier administrations, but I have the impression that many of the great episodes of the Truman and Eisenhower administrations were not dealt with, in their most vital aspects, through the machinery of the NSC. It was not in an NSC meeting that we got into the Korean war, or made the Korean truce. The NSC was not, characteristically, the place of decision on specific major budgetary issues, which so often affect both policy and strategy. It was not the usual forum of diplomatic decision; it was not, for example, a major center of work on Berlin at any time before 1961. The National Security Council is one instrument among many; it must never be made an end in itself.

But for certain issues of great moment, the NSC is indeed valuable. President Kennedy has used it for discussion of basic national policy toward a number of countries. He has used it both for advice on particular pressing decisions and for recommendations on long-term policy. As new attitudes develop within the administration, and as new issues arise in the world, the NSC is likely to continue as a major channel through which broad

[1] Robert Cutler, "The Development of the National Security Council," *Foreign Affairs* (April 1956). "Organizing for National Security," reprinted in "Selected Materials," committee print of the Committee on Government Operations of the Senate (GPO, 1960).

issues of national security policy come forward for Presidential decision.

Meanwhile, the President continues to meet at very frequent intervals with the Secretary of State, the Secretary of Defense, and other officials closely concerned with problems of national security. Such meetings may be as large as an NSC meeting or as small as a face-to-face discussion with a single Cabinet officer. What they have in common is that a careful record is kept, in the appropriate way, whenever a decision is reached. Where primary responsibility falls clearly to a single Department, the primary record of such decisions will usually be made through the Department. Where the issue is broader, or where the action requires continued White House attention, the decision will be recorded through the process of the National Security Council. Thus the business of the National Security staff goes well beyond what is treated in formal meetings of the National Security Council. It is our purpose, in cooperation with other Presidential staff officers, to meet the President's staff needs throughout the national security area.

The second and more significant change in the administration of the National Security Council and its subordinate agencies is the abolition by Executive Order 10920 of the Operations Coordinating Board. This change needs to be understood both for what it is and for what it is not. It is not in any sense a downgrading of the tasks of coordination and followup; neither is it an abandonment of Presidential responsibility for these tasks. It is rather a move to eliminate an instrument that does not match the style of operation and coordination of the current administration.

From the point of view of the new administration, the decisive difficulty in the OCB was that without unanimity it had no authority. No one of its eight members had authority over any other. It was never a truly Presidential instrument, and its practices were those of a group of able men attempting, at the second and third levels of Government, to keep large departments in reasonable harmony with each other. Because of good will among its members, and unusual administrative skill in its secretariat, it did much useful work; it also had weaknesses. But its most serious weakness, for the new administration, was simply that neither the President himself nor the present administration as a whole conceives of operational coordination as a task for a large committee in which no one man has authority. It was and is our belief that there is much to be done that the OCB could not do, and that the things it did do can be done as well or better in other ways.

The most important of these other ways is an increased reliance on the leadership of the Department of State. It would not be appropriate for me to describe in detail the changes which the Department of State has begun to execute in meeting the large responsibilities which fall to it under this concept of administration. It is enough if I say that the President has made it very clear that he does not want a large separate organization between him and his Secretary of State. Neither does he wish any question to arise as to the clear authority and responsibility of the Secretary of State, not only in his own Department, and not only in such large-scale related areas as foreign aid and information policy, but also as the agent of coordination in all our major policies toward other nations.

The third change in the affairs of the NSC grows out of the first two and has a similar purpose. We have deliberately rubbed out the distinction between planning and operation which governed the administrative structure of the NSC staff in the last administration. This distinction, real enough at the extremes of the daily cable traffic and long-range assessment of future possibilities, breaks down in most of the business of decision and action. This is especially true at the level of Presidential action. Thus it seems to us best that the NSC staff, which is essentially a Presidential instrument, should be composed of men who can serve equally well in the process of planning and in that of operational followup. Already it has been made plain, in a number of cases, that the President's interests and purposes can be better served if the staff officer who keeps in daily touch with operations in a given area is also the officer who acts for the White House staff in related planning activities.

Let me turn briefly, in closing, to the role of the Presidential staff as a whole, in national security affairs. This staff is smaller than it was in the last administration, and it is more closely knit. The President uses in these areas a number of officers holding White House appointments, and a number of others holding appointments in the National Security Council staff. He also uses extensively the staff of the Bureau of the Budget. These men are all staff officers. Their job is to help the President, not to supersede or supplement any of the high officials who hold line responsibilities in the executive departments and agencies. Their task is that of all staff officers: to extend the range and enlarge the direct effectiveness of the man they serve. Heavy responsibilities for operation, for coordination, and for diplomatic relations can be and are delegated to the Department of State. Full use of all the powers of leadership can be and is expected in other departments and agencies. There remains a crushing burden of responsibility, and of sheer work, on the President himself; there remains also the steady flow of questions, of ideas, of executive energy which a strong President will give off like sparks. If his Cabinet officers are to be free to do their own work, the President's work must be done—to the extent that he cannot do it himself—by staff officers under his direct oversight. But this is, I repeat, something entirely different from the interposition of such a staff between the President and his Cabinet officers.

I hope this rather general exposition may be helpful to you. I have been conscious, in writing it, of the limits which are imposed upon me by the need to avoid classified questions, and still more by the requirement that the President's own business be treated in confidence. Within those limits I have tried to tell you clearly how we are trying to do our job.

Sincerely,

McGeorge Bundy.

Paul Y. Hammond

THE NATIONAL SECURITY COUNCIL AS A DEVICE FOR INTERDEPARTMENTAL COORDINATION: AN INTERPRETATION AND APPRAISAL

The National Security Council constitutes the most ambitious effort yet made to coordinate policy on the cabinet level in the American federal government. An examination of the experience of the NSC, together with the assumptions and expectations that went into proposing, establishing, and developing it, should help to clarify the problem of policy coordination under the President.

I. Origins in American Naval and British Cabinet Traditions

Various proposals for a special war cabinet in the United States, usually called a Council of National Defense, date back as far as 1911. The National Defense Act of 1916 established a body by such a name, headed by the Secretary of War. The statute was so watered down from the original proposals, however, that its uses were negligible, except later as a convenient peg for the National Defense Advisory Council (NDAC) and its subsidiaries that Roosevelt called into being in 1940. After World War I, both armed services revived the idea of a more powerful Council in an effort to find some base of support for their military policies, and as a counter to proposals for unification, proposals which they both opposed because these were founded on unrealistic expectations about the sums of money that could be saved through reorganization of the service departments.

When, at the close of World War II unification threatened again, the Navy Department turned back to that earlier defense against it, proposing,

from *The American Political Science Review*, LIV, No. 4 (December 1960). Reprinted by permission of the author and the American Political Science Association.

instead of a single department, secretary, and military chief, several interdepartmental committees capped by a National Security Council which
would coordinate the services with each other and with the civil departments and agencies which played important roles in our external relations.
The basis of the Navy proposals for postwar reorganization was the
Eberstadt Report, a series of studies and a set of proposals commissioned in
the summer of 1945 by the Secretary of the Navy, James Forrestal, and
prepared under the direction of Ferdinand Eberstadt. The Eberstadt Report assumed that the proposed National Security Council could be a kind
of war cabinet in which the responsibilities of the President could be vested.
This assumption was not immediately apparent from a reading of the
record, for the premise arose not out of any lack of awareness of the Constitutional power of the President, but out of an inclination to modify the
Presidency as an institution. The National Security Council (NSC), the
report noted, would be only advisory to the President, for it was also an
accepted premise of the Eberstadt group, as well as of Forrestal and the
Navy protagonists in the unification controversy, that the President could
not be forced to share the Constitutional responsibilities of his office.[1]
Their failure to understand the Presidency lay in assuming that the President could choose to share those responsibilities without incurring substantial losses to his status as President.[2]

Eberstadt's proposals actually included both a National Security Council
for national strategic planning and a National Security Resources Board
for national mobilization planning, and both are involved in this misconception of the Presidency. The misconception began with its British origins.
"In the opinion of the many qualified British authorities," Myron P.
Gilmore concluded in his study of foreign and military policies for the
Eberstadt Report, "it has been proven once more that the peace-time
machinery of the Committee of Imperial Defense," which had been transformed in both World Wars into a War Cabinet, "could be well adapted
to the conduct of a major war." Ignoring the difference between cabinet
and presidential government, Gilmore went on to recommend a national
security council, the duties of which "would be formally described as
advisory." He made clear that only in a formal sense would it be advisory:
"The fact that the President himself heads the Council would for all
practical purposes insure that the advice it offered would be accepted."[3]

---

[1] Senate Naval Affairs Committee, *Unification of the War and Navy Departments
and Postwar Organization for National Security, Report to Hon. James Forrestal,
Secretary of the Navy*, Committee Print, 79th Cong., 1st sess. (1945), [hereafter cited
as *Eberstadt Report*], p. 55. See also, e.g., Forrestal's testimony, Senate Armed Services
Committee, *National Defense Establishment*, Hearings, 80th Cong., 1st sess., p. 53.

[2] Forrestal, for instance, could assert without qualification that the President has a
right to choose his Cabinet members, at the same time that he was supporting a statutory determination of the membership of the NSC which he conceived to be a war
cabinet. *Ibid.*, pp. 40, 53.

[3] *Eberstadt Report*, pp. 50, 55.

The Council would, moreover, supersede the Bureau of the Budget, for it would be the final reviewer of the State Department and military budgets prior to their submittal to Congress, and would advise the President "in writing" regarding them—"in writing" being specified presumably in order to make formal and final the NSC decision, and also make it available to Congress.

In his own report, Eberstadt followed the same lines laid out by Gilmore. The NSC should make annual reports to the President, which should be published when secrecy considerations permitted,[4] as would undoubtedly be the case with most budget matters. Someone more concerned with Presidential prerogatives, or willing to recognize that an NSC decision was in fact confidential executive branch advice to the President, would never have suggested publication as a general rule on any grounds. If, as Eberstadt asserted, the NSC was to be advisory to the President, then he was in effect proposing to waive the Constitutional tenet that advice to the President is privileged, and to confine the claim for executive secrecy to matters classified in the interest of national security. Such a change was not the intention: Eberstadt evidently did not think of NSC decisions as advice, or of the NSC as advisory, but as a war cabinet which carried a kind of collective responsibility.

The position of the Navy Department on the status of the NSC, as presented to Congress in 1945, differed somewhat from the Gilmore study and from Eberstadt's recommendations. In the Navy presentation, the NSC was not intended to replace the Bureau of the Budget. Rather, it was to correlate the service budgets and integrate them prior to their submittal to the President *via* the Bureau of the Budget. Gilmore had the NSC superseding the Bureau of the Budget, and to the extent that publication of its reports would give it direct access to Congress, superseding the President himself. In the Navy's modified plan, the NSC was to perform the functions of an executive department secretary. Although, later, the National Security Act of 1947 was to provide for a Secretary of Defense, this Navy conception of the role of the NSC as a kind of substitute Secretary of Defense also carried over into the statute.[5]

Furthermore, within an essentially British conception of cabinet government other persistent problems of Executive Branch relationships were apparently expected to dissolve. The confusion of the President's relationship to the NSC was never clarified. Similarly, although Eberstadt argued for "an intimate, active, and continuous relationship between those respon-

[4] *Ibid.*, pp. 7–8.
[5] The clearest statement of this conception of the NSC as a substitute Secretary of Defense was provided by Rear Admiral Thomas Robbins, the chief witness on the Navy's reorganization plan. See Senate Military Affairs Committee, *Department of the Armed Services, Department of Military Security*, Hearings, 79th Cong., 1st Sess. (1945), pp. 588–89, 596.

sible for our foreign and our military policies" through the NSC,[6] he did not examine whether such a relationship was possible with the closed staff system of the Joint Chiefs of Staff (JCS). Indeed, even the Chief Executive's relations with Congress were to be dealt with by diffusion rather than definition: following an approach to Congressional relations stylish in the early post-World War II period—not to speak of other times—Congress was to be kept in line by the participation of key Congressmen in the handling of national security matters in the Executive Branch rather than by the more formal relations with Congressional committees (although he did not specify that they would participate in the deliberations of the NSC). This short-circuit approach to Congressional relations, along with the council idea, was strikingly parallel to the early Council of National Defense proposals—which, in fact, Gilmore described in his study.[7]

In both Eberstadt's and the Navy proposals, the image of the President as Chief Executive was blurred. Irrespective of any connections with British or Navy Department traditions, an imperfect vision of the Presidency was a necessary outcome of attempting to cope with the dilemma in which Eberstadt and Forrestal were caught of their own choice. At once they wished to assert that the problem of coordinating national security policy was very broad, and to deny the necessity for the executive power to coordinate. So long as they were concerned with the government as a whole, their dilemma was not too uncomfortable; but when it came to dealing with the military establishment, the discomfort grew. It is easy to state their problem in retrospect, or in contrast with the Army proposals: they accepted as necessary a single military establishment, but denied that there had to be a Secretary of Defense. The duties which would normally be performed by the head of a major executive department they expected to be discharged collectively by the National Security Council.

The NSC, the most remarkable and enduring element in the Eberstadt Report, was to become the king-pin of Forrestal's hopes, and only a little less important in the reorganization legislation of 1947. Yet it was thus based on a misconception about the Executive Branch in the American government. Whether the NSC "germinated" out of the British Committee of Imperial Defense, as Forrestal told Churchill, and as the Eberstadt

---

[6] *Ibid.*, p. 37.

[7] *Eberstadt Report*, pp. 51–52. Eberstadt recommended that the participation of key Congressmen was preferable to formal committee reorganization. This would have left a Military Affairs and a Naval Affairs Committee in each house of Congress to consider the substantive legislation concerned with national security. Beyond the advantages to the Navy in this approach (particularly since the Eberstadt Report recommended the establishment of a separate Air Force Department), the weak position in which each of these committees would be placed when attempting to deal with "coordinated" military policies should be obvious. For comparison, see D. S. Cheever and H. F. Haviland, *American Foreign Policy and the Separation of Powers* (Cambridge: Harvard University Press, 1952).

Report indicates,[8] or was derived from long-standing Navy views about a Council of National Defense, makes little difference because both were inappropriate. Cabinet solidarity may be the cement of the British government, and interdepartmental committees may have certain uses, but the American Executive Branch is held together, if at all, by the authority of the President. The Eberstadt Report treated the powers of the President as something which could be embodied in a committee.

Viewed in terms of Navy traditions, the NSC represented two important characteristics, the Navy perception of its role in national policy-making, as expressed in its Council of National Defense proposals in the Wilson era, and the reliance on horizontal organizational structure—on voluntary coordination, so to speak. The latter was the major characteristic of the old Navy Department organization that had miraculously worked in World War I, but required substantial reconstruction in World War II; it was the assumption that people responsible only for segments could nevertheless produce a whole—a whole military policy in this case, a coordinated naval policy in the earlier one. In contradiction to the traditions of War Department administration, it asserted that a policy program could be achieved by an organization without a unified command structure at the center.

II. Early Practice and Appraisal

Once the NSC was established, the divergent purposes which had brought it into being all yielded, of necessity, to one: the Presidential purpose. For while the NSC could be less, it could be no more than what the President wanted it to be, if he knew his mind. No doubt some of its supporters had wanted to devise an arrangement which would prevent a President from running things in the disorderly fashion that seemed to characterize Franklin D. Roosevelt's performance in the White House as an administrator. In this sense, it was supposed to mold Presidential behavior. President Truman answered a fundamental question of defense policy-making concerning the NSC by making it a practice not to sit with the NSC during its first three years, until the Korean War began. Forrestal had anticipated that he would not attend simply because the burdens of the Presidency made the delegation of his responsibilities necessary. Yet, that was not the reason. Rather, it was because Truman felt his presence on the NSC might imply a delegation of authority which he did not intend.[9]

---

[8] Walter Millis (ed.), *The Forrestal Diaries* (New York, 1951), p. 145; *Eberstadt Report*, pp. 47–50.

[9] The reason has been explained variously: He did not want to stifle free discussion in the NSC; he wanted to be free to accept or reject the outcome of its deliberations; or more generally, he was concerned that the NSC might encroach upon Presidential powers, and this was a device to keep it from doing so. Truman mentions in his *Memoirs*, Vol. 2, *Years of Trial and Hope 1946–1952* (Garden City, 1956), p. 60, with disapproval that "there were times during the early days of the National Security

The first appraisal of the newly instituted NSC was conducted a year after its establishment. The Hoover Commission Task Force on National Security Organization, chaired by Ferdinand Eberstadt, reported in November, 1948. Its proposals promised considerable invigoration of the Secretary of Defense and the JCS as centers of initiative in the military establishment, not so much because of proposed changes in formal powers as by virtue of the fact—or was it only a dubious premise?—that more adequate staff arrangements would allow them both to get away from the excessive details with which they were overburdened.

These recommendations, however, or even those of Forrestal himself, could not surmount the difficulties the committee revealed by its own exposition. The National Security Act of 1947 had arranged the military establishment to work properly only if it had adequate policy guidance flowing from the NSC, which was to be, to modify Elihu Root's phrase, the "source of politico-military energy." However, the NSC did not prove to be such a source before the Korean War (or, indeed, after it). As will be explained later, there were fundamental reasons why it was not likely to be.

The committee acknowledged the fact that the flow had not occurred, and that it was needed. It called for a fuller utilization of the NSC to provide the necessary guide-lines for defense policies. Yet it tended to overlook both the need for these guide-lines for a proper functioning of the organization and the difficulties involved in obtaining them. In effect, therefore, it went on to hedge against the possibility that the NSC would continue to prove disappointing. In two major areas, budget integration and economizing, and strategic planning by the JCS, what the committee recommended amounted to going on without NSC guidance. In both cases the implications of such a course of action, as well as the way the role of NSC guide-lines was minimized, are worth noting.

The Task Force had reported that

> The President's directive of July 26, 1948, placing a ceiling of $15 billion on the National Military Establishment budget for fiscal year 1950 was apparently issued without the formal advice either of the Joint Chiefs of Staff (his "principal military advisers") or of the National Security Council, whose statutory function it is "to advise the President" in regard to foreign and military policies.[10]

This account misses the point concerning the Joint Chiefs. The ceiling had been set at least a month before the President's directive was issued, which

---

Council when one or two of its members tried to change it into an operating super-cabinet on the British model . . . [by assuming] the authority of supervising other agencies of the government and seeing that the approved decisions of the Council were carried out."

[10] The Commission on Organization of the Executive Branch of the Government, *Task Force Report on National Security Organization* (Washington: Government Printing Office, 1949), p. 38.

in turn was only a matter of weeks after the JCS had asked for $9 billion as a supplement to an $11 billion fiscal 1949 budget. They had accepted Forrestal's cut on economic grounds. Later, in their fiscal 1950 estimates, they could not bring themselves under $30 billions, or at least $23.5 billions if the McNarney Committee's figures are taken into account. Under these circumstances, which the Task Force committee acknowledged, the fact that the President had not obtained their "formal advice" on a defense budget ceiling is meaningless. In the first place, he knew quite well how much they wanted; and in the second, their figures were so far from what was possible (as the Truman Administration then saw it) that they were practically irrelevant. That the Task Force committee ignored these difficulties was an indication of its tendency to overlook the problems and limitations of political leadership in defense policy-making.

Furthermore, because it overlooked them, it went on to compound those difficulties. Since the agencies concerned with national security "are not performing their respective functions adequately, either individually or in sound relation to each other," the committee observed,

> . . . national policy is not emanating, clearly and firmly, from above and descending effectively through the chain of agencies for translation into an efficient and economical military establishment measured against our national needs. As a result, the military have picked up the ball of national policy and are starting down the field with it. Justly concerned about our national security—but at the same time with an eye to individual service ambitions—they have sometimes made their own assessments and appraisals of our "objectives, commitments, and risks" and have translated them into their own ideas of our proper military strength.[11]

The Task Force Committee's solution, however, encouraged the procedures it condemned by making the operation of the military establishment easier in the absence of NSC guidance. Undoubtedly the solution was a responsible one. Making defense policy *more* dependent on a source of guidance which had thus far proven disappointing, in the hope that greater dependence would force improvements, could hardly have been considered seriously. Nevertheless, accommodating the military establishment to the absence of policy guidance was bound to encourage the dominance of military operational—or business management—imperatives over strategy and, ultimately, over policy.

III. NSC Structure and Operations: A Recent View

Organization. Because of the limited amount of information available about the National Security Council, it is all the more important to keep

[11] *Ibid.*, pp. 37, 38, 42.

the objectives of our inquiry in mind. Our concern is with the NSC as a source of coordinated policy guidance. It should be apparent, however, that this is a particular case of a more general problem, the relationship of policy planning to executive leadership—for evidence on which we need not be restricted entirely to the sparse data on the record about the operations of the NSC itself. Since the evidence suggests that Truman was sensitive to the possible effects which this legislation might have on the powers of his office, and would certainly not have convened and used the NSC simply because Congress had told him to, one might well wonder whether the statutory basis for the NSC had any significance whatsoever. While it would be easy to exaggerate that significance, the long-run value of the statute is quite clear. As Ernest R. May has suggested, it stood as evidence of Congressional approval for the idea that the President should obtain guidance from a secret council regarding national security matters.[12]

The statutory membership of the National Security Council consists of the President and Vice President, the Secretaries of State and Defense, and the Director of the Office of Civil and Defense Mobilization. The Chairman of the Joint Chiefs of Staff and the Director of Central Intelligence are statutory *advisors* to the Council. Since the President may choose his own counsellors, however, this number has normally been augmented during the Eisenhower Administration by three principal officials and several lesser ones. The principal ones are the Secretary of the Treasury, the Director of the Bureau of the Budget, and the Chairman of the Atomic Energy Commission. The others include four special assistants to the President—for National Security Affairs, Security Operations Coordination, Foreign Economic Policy, and Science and Technology; the Assistant to the President—the "chief" of his White House staff—and the White House staff secretary; the Under Secretary of State and the Director of the United States Information Agency; and the two ranking officials of the NSC Staff, the Executive Secretary and the Deputy Secretary. In addition, the President from time to time invites other officials to participate on an *ad hoc* basis.

The principal subsidiary organs of the Council are the Planning Board, the NSC Staff, and the Operations Coordination Board (OCB). The NSC Staff remains essentially a secretariat. The OCB is a follow-up mechanism to see that NSC decisions are executed. Since it is an interdepartmental committee, it is largely a reporting and monitoring device. (Technically, it is not a part of the NSC structure.) The Planning Board consists of representatives of assistant secretary rank for the statutory members of the NSC, plus the Bureau of the Budget. "Observers" from other agencies may attend as their interests require. The Central Intelligence Agency and the Joint Chiefs of Staff regularly provide advisors. The President's Special Assistant for National Security Affairs chairs the Board. Its function is to

---

[12] Ernest R. May, "The Development of Political-Military Consultation in the United States," *Political Science Quarterly*, 70 (June 1955), p. 180.

conduct a thorough preliminary examination of all subjects before they are considered by the Council. Sometimes knowledgeable private citizens are appointed as informal advisors, called Consultants, who may, individually, work with the Planning Board, or, as a committee, present their views directly to the Council.[13]

The most crucial question about the National Security Council is bound to be what kinds of decisions it is capable of making—not in the sense of what subjects it deals with, but as an appraisal of what it accomplishes. At the outset we should distinguish between two elements here: the quality of the decision as a rational process and its practical effects. One could conceive, for instance, of a brilliant exposition of the preventive war thesis, based on a devastating logic, which is never refuted, yet which has negligible effect because it cannot be the policy of the American government. Of course, rationality and practicality are really related to each other. The hypothetical preventive war plan could probably be shown to be either rationally unsound because it ran counter to the values of the state and society which was supposed to support it, or impractical because it could never command the necessary support to make it effective. But the distinction between rationality and practicality will be useful for analytical purposes, providing its limitations are kept in mind.

Two sides have become distinguishable in appraising the practicality and rationality of NSC decisions. The supporters of NSC are best represented by two of the men who have served as President Eisenhower's Special Assistant for National Security Affairs, Robert Cutler and Dillon Anderson,[14] both of whom have published accounts of NSC operations.

Between them, Cutler and Anderson have indicated that the sources for subjects and proposals in the NSC are many and varied enough so that we might be assured that important matters are not overlooked.[15] The working committee for the NSC is the Planning Board. It is the function of the Planning Board, we are told, to reconcile differences when possible, to find the common ground of agreement, and to put its finger on illusory disagreements. Then, "when an irreconcilable disagreement arises between the de-

---

[13] Most of the foregoing description is based upon a paper prepared for delivery at the 1959 Annual Meeting of the American Political Science Association by Gordon Gray, entitled "Role of the National Security Council in the Formulation of National Policy" (mimeo.), now published in Senate Government Operations Committee, *Organizing for National Security: Selected Materials*, 86th Cong., 2d sess., pp. 62–71.

[14] Cutler held the position from 1953 until 1955, and from January, 1957 to July, 1958. Anderson held it from 1955 until September, 1956. From September, 1956 until January, 1957, William H. Jackson occupied it. Since Cutler's second resignation, Gordon Gray has held it.

[15] Dillon Anderson, "The President and National Security," *Atlantic Monthly*, CXCVII (January 1956), 2–3; Robert Cutler, "The Seamless Web," *Harvard Alumni Bulletin*, LVII, 16 (June 4, 1955), 449–451. More recent (though no more revealing) statements by Cutler and Anderson appear in Senate Committee on Government Operations, *Organizing for National Security*, Hearings, Pt. IV, *op. cit.*, pp. 577–603 and 608–618, respectively.

partments represented, the Planning Board must identify clearly the elements of the disagreement and spell out the alternative policy courses and reasons therefor so that they may be presented fully to the National Security Council." [16] "In the acid bath of the Planning Board," Cutler has written, "all points of view are represented, heard, explored and contested. There is in this process a guarantee against *ex parte* judgments, against imprecise guidance to the Chief Executive and against suppression of conflicting views." [17]

The picture we are given of NSC deliberations themselves is also of a searching examination of issues:

> When he became President, General Eisenhower transformed the Council into a forum for vigorous discussion against a background of painstakingly prepared and carefully studied papers. He likes nothing better than the flashing interchange of views among his principal advisers. Out of the grinding of these minds comes a refinement of the raw material into valuable metal; out of the frank assertion of differing views, backed up by preparation that searches every nook and cranny, emerges a resolution that reasonable men can support. Differences of views which have developed at lower levels are not swept under the rug, but exposed.[18]

The Cabinet Status Problem. What Anderson and Cutler have said about the NSC is reassuring. The other side in the appraisal, however, is not. From a variety of sources, some of which obviously have access to members of the Planning Board and the NSC itself, have come the same criticisms: that the Planning Board, in its pursuit of "common grounds," is inclined to "plaster over" significant issues and differences with carefully chosen ambiguities, or language plagued with equivocations expressive of the lowest common denominator of agreement. In the NSC itself as well, it is claimed, there is a reluctance to exacerbate differences of view and opinion, with the result that discussion is inclined to be more courteous than probing. Finally, it is sometimes claimed that agencies are reluctant to bring issues before the NSC, that they even try to keep some important matters out of it. Franklin Lindsay of the Hoover Commission's Procurement Task Force staff observed in June, 1955, that "in recent months there have been situations reported in which policy formulation in vital and urgent issues has been seriously hampered by a lack of free exchange among the Departments represented on the Council." [19]

[16] Anderson, *op. cit.*, p. 3.
[17] Cutler, *op. cit.*, p. 444.
[18] *Ibid.*, p. 443.
[19] Task Force on Procurement, *Defense Procurement: The Vital Roles of the National Security Council and the Joint Chiefs of Staff* (mimeo., 1955), p. A-13. This and several other criticisms of NSC operations have been dealt with in Gray, *op. cit.* The larger setting of the problem as part of the policy-making process, which lends greatest credence to the criticism of the NSC, is given only passing consideration in this paper.

Undoubtedly there is some substance to these complaints. Among other things, they fit the larger pattern of behavior of the President's cabinet over the years. It is a well documented fact that cabinet meetings have seldom amounted to much because cabinet officers prefer to transact their business with the President without the interference of other executive department heads.[20] The more a President actually refuses to discuss and decide anything that does not go through his cabinet system, the more likely it is that the real issues will come up there. No doubt the determination and professional inclinations of President Eisenhower have stood him well in his resolve to strengthen the performance of his cabinet and of the NSC.[21] Yet it seems unlikely that he has stopped off all channels for maneuver. To begin with, the existence of two different "cabinets," the traditional one which is intended to deal primarily with domestic affairs and the NSC, which is supposed to specialize in national security, or foreign, affairs, with dual membership for some, has left an obvious means of maneuver—the choice of the most favorable forum—with results about which we can at least speculate. Furthermore, there are disadvantages as well as advantages to choking off the individual contacts which weaken the cabinet system: independent and timely information, and informal and candid advice, to name only some. No Presidential prerogative is defended with greater consistency by *all* Presidents than the right to secret counsel. If the right has any validity *vis-à-vis* Congress, the press, or the public in general, it must also be valid within the executive branch. Yet any exercise of it there undermines the cabinet system by allowing individual officials the alternative of by-passing the Cabinet or the NSC and transacting business directly with the President.

While it is clear that President Eisenhower has taken seriously the implications of his staff procedures, it is equally clear that he has continued to allow a number of administration officials direct access to him. Indeed, it may be that the preeminent influence in their time of the former Secretary of the Treasury, George F. Humphrey, and the late Secretary of State, John Foster Dulles, within the Eisenhower Administration, was due in part to their special privilege of access to President Eisenhower; as the converse was certainly the case. Even if that is true, however—if the President has been willing to talk business with a certain few of his cabinet

[20] Much of the documentation is summarized in Richard J. Fenno's study of the cabinet since Taft: *The President's Cabinet* (Cambridge: Harvard University Press, 1959). For a summary analysis in a similar vein see Arthur M. Schlesinger, Jr., *The Coming of the New Deal*, Vol. II of *The Age of Roosevelt* (Boston, 1959), pp. 518–20 and 522ff.

[21] So, "The President has determined that he will not assign an area of national security policy formulation permanently as the responsibility of a department, agency, or individual outside the NSC mechanism or make decisions on national security policy—except in special cases or urgency—outside the framework of the Council." Gray, *op. cit.* (mimeo.), p. 4.

members, but, quite consistently, not with the rest—that situation would not assure that those who were not intimates of the President would be forced to submit their problems to the cabinet process; for, as an alternative, they could make their arrangement with those who were.

Furthermore, the required access need not be given a literal interpretation. President Eisenhower may have been remarkably effective in avoiding *ex parte* presentations and decisions outside of his established staff procedures, yet have allowed that same thing to have resulted from his following those procedures. If Humphrey and Dulles, or anyone else, were the dominant forces in the NSC meetings, it could not matter whether they in fact saw the President privately very much or not. Their special "access" to the President in those meetings would provide, as an alternative to drag-out debates in the NSC, another way for agency heads to advance their interests with the President. The crucial act for them would then be the persuasion of Humphrey or Dulles, rather than an effective presentation in the Planning Board or the Thursday morning White House meetings of the NSC.

This analysis is not intended as a harsh judgment of public officials. We are not entitled to treat lightly the particular perspectives of public officials which derive from the responsibilities of their positions. President Eisenhower has directed that the members of the NSC and the Planning Board should forsake their agency perspectives and advise him from a government-wide viewpoint. It is doubtful, however, that he has been successful in wiping out by directive the agency perspectives of his cabinet or council members. If the NSC operates as has been described, it does so not because of the bad faith or scheming nature of its members, but despite their best efforts, and because of the very forces which have made the NSC seem necessary. The heavy responsibilities and work loads of conscientious men determine in some degree what they will know and think about issues and proposals related to their duties. Moreover, whatever the value of NSC work, the statutory responsibility of each member of it is for the proper operation of his department. His first loyalty may be to the President, but he is responsible to the President for administering an agency in a way that he is never responsible for NSC actions.

Concern with the protection of the agency program or viewpoint does not end with the success or failure of the effort to gain access to the forum most favorable to the agency. Once the forum is chosen, the agency will wish to maximize the achievement of its interests there, an objective which may not be identical with the systematic exposure and preliminary exploration of all issues and problems on their merits in the Planning Board, or the free and frank discussion before the President in the NSC of issues and problems not resolvable on their merits in the Planning Board. Indeed, expediency could dictate the withholding of pertinent information which might weigh against the agency's interest or established position, the avoidance of some issues and the suppression of others in the Planning Board, and finally, the settlement for some kind of half-of-a-loaf in the Planning Board because of an estimation that a better bargain can be struck there than in the Council. And the same kinds of considerations could inhibit debate in the Council itself. Always the alternative may be available of assuring that in fact no decision is really made in either the Planning Board or the NSC by settling for language in the staff paper which is sufficiently ambiguous so that in effect it preserves the latitude of choice desired by one's agency.

The President's Special Assistant has attempted to enforce standards of precision in the drafting of NSC papers,[22] which seems to suggest that he would oppose any such efforts to "plaster over" issues with the language of the draft. But an ambiguous draft agreement is only one of several tactics available for avoiding decisions by committee. Representative councils must depend to a large degree upon their members for access to, and even the interpretation of, the relevant facts, while the ability to eliminate ambiguity will depend upon a mastery of the facts. Those upon whom the Planning Board and the NSC depend for information are therefore in a position to influence, and in some cases to control, the degree of precision with which a problem is presented, discussed, and settled, despite the best efforts of the President's Special Assistant, or of anyone else, to achieve precision in the settlement.

Moreover, the Special Assistant is himself likely to contribute unintentionally to the ambiguity which he seeks to avoid. He is responsible for expediting the work of the Planning Board and the NSC. In carrying out the two functions of the Planning Board, to identify the area of agreement, and to explore the area of disagreement on any matter to be considered by the NSC, his objectives of precision and expeditiousness may conflict. We are assured that the Special Assistant does not desire to suppress disagreements, and we may take that assurance on its face. Yet, unavoidably, he must expedite the processes which distinguish between real and superficial disagreement and between ambiguous and clear language. In deciding when a draft is sufficiently precise, and when the differences it covers are "illusory" or non-existent, he cannot resolve all doubts against precision and illusion. And when he does not, like the department which seeks to avoid an NSC decision, he may be condoning ambiguity and the suppression of important issues.

There can be, finally, the problem of third parties. The subjects of NSC deliberations involve some departments more than others, and sometimes one of them most of all. At any rate, the questions of jurisdiction, expertise, and authority are not likely to be absent from the deliberations of the Council. The President's directive referred to above was probably intended to encourage "third-parties"—that is, departmental representatives in the

[22] Anthony J. Leviero, "Untouchable and Unquotable," *New York Times Sunday Magazine*, January 30, 1955, p. 62.

Planning Board or the Council—to voice their opinions on questions before them even when their particular agency provides them with no special knowledge or expert judgment, and has no special concern about the question at hand. Surely the implications of the staff work done in connection with NSC operations suggest this interpretation of the President's directive if there is any room for doubt as to its meaning. It appears, however, that under the pressure to accomplish its work, the Planning Board has been quite resentful of "third party" contributions, and that in fact it has operated with unwritten rules of jurisdiction on this score which, when violated, have caused considerable friction.

There is no reason to doubt that the same pressures have operated to some degree in the Council. One reason for the effectiveness of this kind of inhibition upon frank discussion, it should be noted, is that it may appear as only the desire of modest men not to sound foolish, or to interfere with matters which would suggest a lack of confidence in their colleagues. Once the third party is eliminated from the discussion in this manner, however, and the field is left to the agencies most directly involved, they will be the ones which are, by definition, working most closely together anyway on the matter, and will have every advantage in cooperating to bring the problems to the NSC when and how they, by agreement, want to.[23]

While some of the foregoing analysis has been speculative in the sense that it has not been based upon knowledge of specific events, it is nevertheless based upon assumptions about loyalty and perspectives which are well established, and which have, for instance, long been evident in the operation, or lack of operation, of the President's cabinet and in the JCS. They are intended to suggest that there are some inherent difficulties in the operation of the NSC—particularly in the making of clear-cut decisions, which lend credence to the continuing criticisms of the NSC on that score.

The Democratic Policy-Making Problem: The Required Range of Consensus. The dimensions of consensus and commitment necessary for policy-making in a democracy constitute a further limitation on the value of NSC "decisions" for the administration of the military establishment. The neo-

[23] With this in mind it may be worth speculating about the way the NSC deals with foreign aid matters. The State Department's dominance in the making of policy has statutory origins. Its relations with its major potential rival in policy-making are of a particular character. The office of the Assistant Secretary of Defense for International Security Affairs (ISA) is in this area something of a State Department outpost in the Defense Department. ISA also happens to represent the Defense Department on the Planning Board. It is doubtful that in the Planning Board either the State or the Defense Department is much interested in exploring in front of other officials, in particular normally hostile ones like the Bureau of the Budget or the Treasury Department, the merits of the foreign aid programs in anything like a candid or searching way. If this is true, then consideration of foreign aid matters in the Council itself would be severely limited in its value by the inadequacy of the staff work upon which the Council undoubtedly relies so heavily.

realism in American foreign relations of the post-World War II period showed how artificial was the American propensity to consider official pronouncements to be foreign policy. Policy, it was asserted, is more than words: it is also the power and determination to achieve one's objectives.[24] The extraordinary faith in secret plans involved in the higher evaluations of the NSC may be another version of that "legalistic" or "moralistic" fallacy in American foreign relations which the neo-realists seemed to have destroyed so effectively.

The President's setting his signature to an NSC document does not make it policy. What does is his will and capability to get it executed, coupled with effective support from Congress. How much of the last is necessary, of course, may vary, and in any case is not precise. Yet the requisite support is not likely to be obtained for any but the most exceptional cases through, for instance, the secret briefing of a handful of Congressmen. The members of the two houses are inclined to be suspicious of the judgment of their own kind when the latter appear to have been "captured" by the executive branch. Even if that were not so, the necessity for Congressmen to come to terms with their constituencies would still limit strictly the usefulness of such devices as secret briefings and special liaison arrangements. Unless an NSC "policy" happens to coincide with a general public viewpoint, sooner or later it must run the gamut of public discussion. In this respect, the NSC got off to a bad start. The first general policy statement attributed (somewhat inaccurately) to it, NSC-68, which was completed in April, 1950, advocated substantial increases in expenditures in a variety of programs connected with national security, a policy which was clearly at variance with prevailing conceptions of public opinion held contemporaneously in Congress and in the Administration. As to what the Administration might have done to bring the secret policy paper and the public consensus closer together had the Korean War not occurred, we can only speculate. As it was, the war made them converge. Once the war started it was necessary only to make general references to the larger picture of the Soviet threat and to a consequent need for a build-up of a far more general character than the Korean War required, and, privately, to read the document in the light of the entirely new situation, in order to close the gap completely. Even if it were a reasonable expectation, one should not hope that history would again solve in this manner the problem of translating a secret "policy" into a national commitment.

The problem, it should be emphasized, is not properly seen in the terms by which early advocates of a Council of National Defense, and, later, the NSC visualized it: how to gain wide support, through the "non-rational"

[24] Hans J. Morgenthau, *In Defense of the National Interest: A Critical Examination of American Foreign Policy* (New York, 1951), pp. 22–39, 91–112; George F. Kennan, *American Diplomacy 1900–1950* (Chicago: University of Chicago Press, 1951), pp. 95–103.

channels of politics, for "rational" defense policies constructed by a few men privately where they are free from political pressures. If it were indeed possible to construct a security council for the nation which was free from political pressures yet powerful enough to be useful, the NSC is not it. Nor have we evidence that it has always had the edge in rationality. The political vacuum in which the NSC operates is not caused by a total lack of politics in its atmosphere, but only by barriers which prevent the continuing readjustment of atmospheric pressures within the NSC to those outside it. The Eisenhower Administration's commitment through NSC procedures to the massive retaliation doctrine announced by Secretary of State Dulles on January 12, 1954, in a widely publicized (and criticized) speech was evidently the acceptance of a favorite and long-held notion of Mr. Dulles (which he had shared with other Administration officials). Its acceptance was a device for reconciling both the somber security perspectives of NSC-162, the annual survey of American strategy which had been approved the previous October, and the disappointing failure of the new JCS team to cut the defense budget, with demands to cut the federal budget substantially, pressed by Budget Director Joseph Dodge, and the Secretary of the Treasury, George Humphrey.

In the face of powerful and numerous criticisms of the massive retaliation doctrine, including, we may presume, the private counsel received at a foreign ministers' conference in Berlin that winter,[25] Dulles' further "clarifications" of the meaning of his original speech in fact substantially modified it. One of the most important "clarifications" of it was published in *Foreign Affairs* in April, 1954, just as the Administration was learning the inadequacy of the massive retaliation doctrine in the hard test posed by Dienbienphu. On the one hand, the publication of the doctrine by Dulles had exposed it to critical comment sufficiently persuasive so that Dulles chose to modify his public statements rather than defend it publicly, although the military posture the Administration continued to maintain was substantially that of reliance upon a massive retaliation capability.[26] On the other

[25] *Cf.* Anthony Eden, *Full Circle* (Boston: Houghton Mifflin Co., 1960), pp. 72–80, 98, 99.

[26] The speech was printed in *The New York Times*, January 13, 1954. The article revising the massive retaliation doctrine is John Foster Dulles, "Policy for Security and Peace," *Foreign Affairs*, **XXXII** (April 1954), 353–64. Other Dulles pronouncements during this period bearing on massive retaliation are summarized and criticized in William W. Kaufmann, "The Requirements of Deterrence," published as ch. I in *Military Policy and National Security* (Princeton: Princeton University Press, 1956), which he edited; and in Bernard Brodie, *Strategy in the Missile Age* (Princeton: Princeton University Press, 1959), pp. 248–63. Robert E. Osgood, *Limited War: The Challenge to American Strategy* (Chicago: University of Chicago Press, 1957), pp. 201–33, is a summary and appraisal set in a broader context. The literature of criticism of reliance on massive retaliation is itself massive. In addition to the foregoing, the most prominent are Henry A. Kissinger, "Military Policy and Defense of the 'Grey Areas,' " *Foreign Affairs* **XXXIII** (April 1955), 416–28; and Kissinger, *Nuclear Weapons and Foreign Policy* (New York, 1957), pp. 86–136. For background on Dulles' views on

hand in the clutch of the crisis in Indo-China, the Administration had shown itself not strongly enough committed to its newly adopted strategic concept to attempt the rescue of Dienbienphu. It had flinched in two most significant respects. First, apparently the President in the NSC rejected Admiral Radford's proposal to break the siege of the doomed fortress with massive air strikes, being persuaded by General Ridgway that American military commitments could not stop there. Eisenhower was evidently convinced that ground forces would be needed, and that supplying them would be extremely difficult. At least, it appears, he was so far convinced as to insist on encumbering his commitment to Radford's proposal with heavy qualifications: the United States would assist the French in Indo-China provided we could gain the support of allies in this undertaking.

At the same time, the Administration was evidently willing to carry out its NSC "policy" towards Indo-China if it could gain privately the support of powerful members of Congress, but it was unwilling to do so if it had to make the strong public commitments which would be required to obtain formal Congressional support,[27] a condition the subtleties of which undoubtedly were missed in the phraseology of the NSC paper. Thus what was perhaps the most important decision made through the NSC machinery during the first term of the Eisenhower Administration did not stand the test of either its first public exposition or its first application. Each test, it should be noted, assayed some aspect of its rationality as well as probed the depths of the Administration's commitment. The least we can conclude from what is known about the NSC's role in the Indo-China crisis and the formulation of the massive retaliation doctrine of the Eisenhower Administration is that in this case its freedom from partisan political considerations did not assure it a greater rationality than the more public channels of government decision-making would permit it.

Furthermore, this account is illustrative of the fact that there can be no entirely workable separation between the planning and the operational stages of national security policy, for in politics ends and means must be tested against each other: it is in the interaction of that testing that consensus becomes wide enough and commitments strong enough for policy to become a reality. Put more prosaically, defenders of the NSC are on sound enough ground when asserting the President's right to confidential counsel from his appointees, for it is the only way he can be sure of getting frank advice. They are also reasonable in insisting that the NSC, as they conceive it, must operate in secret for security reasons as well. But they

strategy, on NSC and on JCS action see Glenn H. Snyder, *The Military "New Look" of 1953* (mimeo., Institute of War and Peace Studies, Columbia University, 1958), pp. 8–43 and *passim*.

[27] Chalmers M. Roberts, "The Day We Didn't Go To War," *The Reporter,* **XI** (September 14, 1954), 31–35. The NSC deliberations are described in Marquis Childs, *The Ragged Edge: The Diary of a Crisis* (Garden City, N.Y.: Doubleday, 1955), pp. 153–58.

are misled if they believe that the result is the government's policy. It may be the President's policy, although that it doubtful: What President is so infallible that he can predict in the political isolation of the NSC what will be politically possible in the future, or so rigid that he will never change when he is wrong? The give and take of the NSC chamber, in which, so we are told, all the issues are brought out and tested, the advantages and disadvantages weighed—including the fiscal and the program viewpoints—must be repeated for the interested public in the Congressional-Executive dialogue and the other forums of our public life. The quality of the public performance may be considerably inferior to the Thursday morning meetings in the White House. Undoubtedly public discussions must be carried on without the benefit of access to a considerable amount of relevant information because of security reasons, although they in turn will make use of information which was not available or considered in the privy councils of the White House. But the relative quality of the public and the secret debates over foreign policy have nothing to do with whether the latter will or ought to occur, for they are a political necessity.

Despite these obstacles to effective NSC operation it would be unwise to conclude that the NSC is inoperable, or that its acts must be insignificant. Departmental heads are not simply prisoners of their situations. Indeed, their status within their own agency can be enhanced by their participation in the NSC. The fact that the department head has demands placed upon him in the NSC to rise above departmental viewpoints can be a part of that enhanced status, for all the more must he be reckoned with as the President's spokesman within his own agency. Furthermore, the staff mechanisms of the NSC can make substantial inroads upon the obstacles to effective NSC operation described above. The momentum of staff work, by having available facts and arguments from the previous consideration of the same or similar subjects, can the more effectively evoke current information from the departments and evaluate current departmental judgments and arguments. For instance, simply to record and keep the positions of an agency on file, together with the evidence it provides on a particular subject over time, can build up a record which would at least limit its freedom of maneuver and might force it, increasingly, to discuss the subject on its merits. At the same time, the determination of the Chief Executive to make use of the NSC can in some cases force his agency heads to make use of it also. Finally, there is a *prima facie* argument that the greater the speed and flexibility which the NSC and its staff mechanisms develop—specifically, the more continuous their review of established policies becomes—the more the gap between secret plans and political realities is likely to be closed.[28]

[28] "Before the end of President Eisenhower's first administration, virtually every policy of the previous administration had been reviewed and revised by the new members of the Council, in some cases by developing substantially new policies. Since that

But all of these prospects for overcoming difficulties in the operation of the NSC are substantially limited in what they can accomplish. While it would be unwise to overlook the potentialities of the NSC, or of a cabinet, it would be foolish to ignore their limitations. Like any balance, this one cannot provide the assurance of stability.

Those who praise the NSC are likely to underrate its limitations, even while paying deference to the notion that it is imperfect and can be improved.[29] On the other hand, those who find it wanting conclude too readily that it is dispensable.[30] As real as are the inherent limitations on the effective operations of the NSC which have been mentioned above, the need for it, or for something very much like it, is equally unavoidable. While the mind of one man may be the most effective instrument for devising diplomatic moves and strategic maneuvers, and for infusing staff work with creative purpose, its product is bound to be insufficient to meet the needs of the vast organizational structures and the military, economic, and diplomatic programs which are the instruments of foreign policy. The most sensitive and subtle mechanism is ineffective when overloaded. And as ponderous in comparison with a single mind as are the actions of a large-scale organization, or even a committee, nevertheless coming to terms with the requirements of the bureaucracy is as much a necessity as is flexibility and speed in foreign policy-making.

Since this accommodation to the operational aspects of national security is unavoidable, it only remains to determine the means for accomplishing it. Aside from trivial variations of either, there is only one real alternative to the NSC type of coordinative machinery, a Presidential staff in the Executive Office of the President with no operating responsibilities. While it would avoid the loyalty conflicts (and their many ramifications) of a council of responsible operators such as the NSC, a Presidential staff would have its own inherent difficulties: It would be outweighed in any serious dispute with a department, unless it destroyed the President's confidence in his department head. Its "plans" would lack the sense of reality and the prestige which comes with responsibility. It would have information-gathering problems of its own. It would not necessarily identify itself with the President's viewpoint. And it could become as much or more isolated from political realities than the NSC.

In the end, the question of how best to achieve interdepartmental coordination of national security policy must be answered by weighing these

---

time, most of the policy statements approved by the President during his first term have undergone at least one revision and, in many cases, more than two." Gray, *op. cit.* (mimeo.), p. 10.

[29] *E.g.*, Anderson, *op. cit.*; Cutler, *op. cit.*

[30] *E.g.*, Hans J. Morgenthau, "Can We Entrust Defense to a Committee?," *New York Times Magazine*, June 7, 1959, pp. 9, 62ff. Morgenthau did not specifically suggest its abolition, but, instead, that some one other than the President be made responsible for what the NSC is now supposed to accomplish.

two major alternatives against each other, or by finding the optimum mixture of them. As the query can be put in the more practical terms of increments, should the NSC staff be strengthened with a view to its becoming an independent force in NSC deliberations? Or should civilians without administrative responsibilities be added to the Council? Put in this form the problem is one of the most persistent and universal questions posed in administrative organization: Is coordination to be achieved through lateral clearance or line command? The disadvantages and impossibilities of line-command solutions are usually more visible than the obstacles to effective lateral accommodation. The Eisenhower administration can be credited with having developed the capabilities of both methods by improving the staff mechanisms of the NSC along with its increasing use of the Council. Yet it seems to have been much more aware of the limitations of staff agents than of advisory councils to a presidential executive.

Samuel P. Huntington
STRATEGIC PLANNING AND THE POLITICAL PROCESS

III

STRATEGIC programs are thus decided upon in the Executive rather than in Congress. The process of decision within the Executive, however, bears many striking resemblances to the process of decision in Congress. It retains a peculiarly legislative flavor. Legislative and executive *processes* of policy-making do not necessarily correspond to the legislative and executive *branches* of government. A policy-making process is legislative in character to the extent that (1) the units participating in the process are relatively equal in power (and consequently must bargain with each other), (2) important disagreements exist concerning the goals of policy, and (3) there are many possible alternatives. A process is executive in character to the extent that (1) the participating units differ in power (*i.e.* are hierarchically arranged), (2) fundamental goals and values are not at issue, and (3) the range of possible choice is limited.

Strategic programs, like other major policies, are not the product of expert planners rationally determining the actions necessary to achieve desired goals. Rather, they are the product of controversy, negotiation and

FROM *Foreign Affairs*, **XXXVIII** (1960). Copyright 1960 by the Council on Foreign Relations, Inc., New York. Reprinted by permission of the author.

bargaining among different groups with different interests and perspectives. The conflicts between budgeteers and security spokesmen, between the defenders of military and non-military programs, among the four services, and among the partisans of massive retaliation, continental defense and limited war, are as real and as sharp as most conflicts of group interests in Congress. The location of the groups within the executive branch makes their differences no less difficult to resolve. The variety and importance of the interests, the intensity of the conflicting claims, the significance of the values at stake, all compel recourse to the complex processes of legislation. The inability of Congress to legislate strategic programs does not eliminate the necessity to proceed through a legislative process. It simply concentrates it in the executive branch.

To be sure, the specific techniques for innovating proposals, mobilizing support, distracting and dissuading opponents, and timing decisions may differ in the executive "legislative" process from those in the congressional "legislative" process. None the less, in its broad outlines the development of a major strategic program, such as continental air defense, lacks none of the phases involved in the passage of a major piece of domestic legislation through Congress. The need for the program is recognized by an executive agency or some skill group (nuclear physicists) or consulting group close to the executive branch. The agency or group develops policy proposals to deal with the problem and arouses support for them among other executive agencies, congressional committees and, possibly, some non-governmental groups. Opposition develops. Alternative solutions to the problem are proposed. Coalitions pro and con are organized. The proposals are referred from committee to committee. Consultants and advisory groups lend their prestige to one side or another. The policies are bargained over and compromised. Eventually a decision or, more accurately, an agreement is hammered out among the interested agencies, probably through the mechanisms of the Joint Chiefs of Staff and the National Security Council, and is approved by the President. The locus of decision is executive; the process of decision is primarily legislative.

The building of a consensus for a particular strategic program is as complex and subtle as it is for either domestic policy or foreign policy. At a minimum, within the Executive, it involves complicated interlocking patterns of vertical bargaining along the executive hierarchy and horizontal bargaining through a conciliar structure. In almost no executive hierarchy is the exercise of power all in one direction: the actual authority—even the influence—of administrative superiors over their subordinates is hedged around by a variety of inhibiting considerations. Underlying the hierarchy is a set of bargaining relationships, explicit or implicit. The dispersion of power in American society and the separation of powers in government tend to reinforce this tendency. Agencies and officials in subordinate positions often are substantially independent of their administrative superiors. At best the superior may be able to persuade; at worst he may be openly defied.

Vertical bargaining is exemplified in the efforts of the Administration to secure the concurrence of the Joint Chiefs of Staff, individually and collectively, in its budgetary and force-level decisions. On the one hand, each Chief presses for what he believes is essential for his service; on the other, the Administration attempts to cut back and fit service demands into its strategic plan and budgetary goals. Each side has to balance the risks involved in alienating the other against the benefits gained in shaping the final decision. The interlarding of hierarchical and bargaining roles inevitably enhances the possibilities for ambiguity and confusion. As subordinates the Chiefs would be expected to accept but not necessarily to approve decisions made by their administrative superiors. "I'd be worried," Secretary Wilson once declared, "if Ridgway didn't believe in the good old Army." [1] On the other hand, the semi-autonomous position of the Chiefs enhances the value of their approval to their superiors. An administrative decision derives legitimacy (as well as effectiveness) in part from its acceptance and support by the subordinate officials and agencies affected by it. Consequently, great efforts are made to secure the Chiefs' concurrence. "The pressure brought on me to make my military judgment conform to the views of higher authority," General Ridgway declared, "was sometimes subtly, sometimes crudely, applied." [2] The intensity of the pressure applied was tribute to the value of the approval sought.

While vertical bargaining plays a crucial role in strategic decision-making, horizontal bargaining is probably even more widespread and important. Theoretically, of course, authority to determine strategic programs rests with the President and the Secretary of Defense. Actually, the compromising and balancing of interests tends to focus about the two most important committees in the executive branch of the national government: the J.C.S. and the N.S.C. On the surface, it seems strange that two committees should play such important roles in the formulation of military policy and national security. These are areas where one might expect clear-cut lines of authority and executive decision-making. Within the executive branch, few committees of comparable stature exist in domestic areas of policy-making. The J.C.S. and the N.S.C. are significant, however, precisely because they do perform essentially legislative rather than executive functions. They have what Congress lacks: the political capability to legislate strategy. Just as agricultural policy is the product of conflict, bargaining and compromise among the interested groups represented in Congress, military strategy is the product of conflict, bargaining and compromise among the interested

[1] Duncan Norton-Taylor, "The Wilson Pentagon," *Fortune* (December 1954), p. 94.
[2] General Matthew B. Ridgway, "My Battles in War and Peace," *The Saturday Evening Post* (January 21, 1956), p. 46.

groups represented in the J.C.S. and the N.S.C. Hence, the same criticisms are now leveled at these committees which have long been leveled at Congress: logrolling prevails; over-all objectives get lost in the mechanism; a premium is put upon agreement rather than decision. Just as Congress often wrote tariff legislation by giving each industry the protection it wanted, the N.S.C. and the Joint Chiefs make decisions on weapons by giving each service what it desires. The individual members of these bodies suffer the classic conflict known to members of all legislatures: on the one hand, they must represent the interests of their departments or constituencies; on the other, their decisions are expected to be in the national interest.

IV

In strategy, as elsewhere, effective policy requires some measure of both content and consensus. Strategic programs, like statutes or treaties, are both prescriptions for future action and ratifications of existing power relationships. A strategy which is so vague or contradictory that it provides no prescription for action is no strategy. So too, a strategy whose prescriptions are so unacceptable that they are ignored is no strategy. Consensus is a cost to each participant but a prerequisite of effective policy.

In strategy-making, as in congressional legislating, one means of avoiding disagreement is to postpone decision. The proliferation of committees serves the useful political end of facilitating and, in some cases, legitimizing the avoidance of decision. Issues can be referred from committee to committee, up and down the hierarchy. Normally the same service and departmental interests are represented on all the committees; agreement in one is just as unlikely as agreement in any other. Controversial decisions may also be removed entirely from the jurisdiction of the N.S.C. or the Joint Chiefs and devolved back upon the interested agencies; the "decision" is that each will pursue its own policy. Disagreement on major issues also may be avoided simply by devoting more time to minor ones. The J.C.S. "dips into matters it should avoid," Vannevar Bush complained in 1952, "it fails to bring well considered resolution to our most important military problems, and it fritters away its energy on minutiae." [3] The Joint Chiefs, however, were treading a classic legislative path. In almost identical terms, political scientists for years have accused Congress of refusing to grapple with major issues of public policy and of wasting time and energy on minor matters of administrative detail.

Where stringent limits are imposed from the outside, the decision-makers are especially prone to compromise. As the $14 and $13 billion ceilings firmly succeeded each other in the late 1940s, the tendency to divide the funds equally among the three services became more and more pronounced.

[3] "Planning," speech at Mayo Clinic Auditorium, Rochester, Minnesota, September 26, 1952, p. 8.

On the other hand, if the limits permitted by superior executive authority are relatively undefined or broad, logrolling enables each agency to obtain what it considers most important. The result is "Operation Paperclip," in which Army, Navy and Air Force proposals are added together and called a joint plan. Duplication in weapons systems—Thor and Jupiter, Nike and Bomarc—is simply the price of harmony. It is hardly surprising that the J.C.S. should be referred to as "a trading post." This, after all, is the traditional legislative means of achieving agreement among conflicting interests. As one Congressman remarked to his colleagues:

> If you are concerned, you politicians, with getting unanimity of action, I refer you to the Joint Chiefs of Staff. There is a classic example of unanimity of action on anything: You scratch my back and I will scratch yours. "Give me atomic carriers," says the Navy, "and you can have your B-52s in the Air Force." I do not know why General Taylor is going along, because I have never been able to find anything that the Army is getting out of the deal.[4]

The political and legislative character of the strategy-making process also casts a different light on the argument that the N.S.C. and J.C.S. have failed to initiate new policy proposals. As many observers of the domestic legislative process have pointed out, relatively few statutes actually originate within a legislative assembly. They are first developed by interest groups or executive agencies. It is therefore not surprising that relatively few strategic programs originally come to life in the committees or staffs of the N.S.C. or J.C.S. The latter necessarily serve as negotiating bodies; the responsibility for innovation lies with the participating agencies.

Just as much of the early criticism of Congress stemmed from a failure to appreciate the political roles of that body, so much of the criticism of the N.S.C. and J.C.S. stems from the application to these bodies of non-political standards. At times in the past, it has been assumed that through investigation and debate all members of a legislative body should arrive at similar conclusions as to where the public interest lay. More recently, conflict within a legislature has been viewed as normal, and policy thought of as the result, not of a collective process of rational inquiry, but of a mutual process of political give and take. Congress is seldom criticized today because of conflicts and disagreements among its members. To a considerable extent, however, the J.C.S. and the N.S.C. are judged by the former theory: in them disagreement is still considered inherently evil. As one naval officer wryly commented: "How curious it is that the Congress *debates*, the Supreme Court *deliberates*, but for some reason or other the Joint Chiefs of Staff just *bicker!*" [5]

[4] Rep. Daniel J. Flood, *Congressional Record* (85th Congress, 1st Session), May 27, 1957, p. 7733.
[5] Vice Admiral H. E. Orem, "Shall We Junk the Joint Chiefs of Staff?" *U.S. Naval Institute Proceedings* (February 1958), p. 57.

Significantly, the Joint Chiefs have also been criticized for employing precisely those mechanisms designed for reaching agreement: delay, devolution, referral, platitudinous policies, compromise, logrolling. On the one hand, the Chiefs are criticized because they cannot resolve major issues; on the other hand, they are criticized because they do resolve them through the classic means of politics.

Much criticism of strategic decision-making has failed to appreciate the tenuous and limited character of hierarchical authority in American government. Reacting against the prevalence of horizontal bargaining, the critics have advocated the abolition of committees and the strengthening of executive controls. In brief periods of emergency, presidential coördination may partially replace the normal bargaining processes. But no presidential laying on of hands can accomplish this on a permanent basis. Decisions on strategic programs are simply too important to be fitted into a symmetrical and immaculate model of executive decision-making. Clarifications of the chain of command and legal assertions of formal authority may reduce bargaining, but they can never eliminate it. Each of the three reorganizations of the military establishment since 1947 has purported to give the Secretary of Defense full legal authority to control his department and yet each succeeding Secretary found his control circumscribed if not frustrated. The existence of counterparts to the N.S.C. and J.C.S. in virtually every other modern state suggests that the causes which have brought them into existence may be pervasive and inherent in the problems with which they deal.

The problem of legislating strategic programs is thus the dual one of producing both content and consensus. On the one hand, little is gained by assuming that effective policy can be achieved without compromise, or that the political problems of strategy-making can be eliminated by strengthening the executive chain of command. On the other hand, it is also impossible to accept what emerges from the bargaining processes as ipso facto in the national interest. Too often, this has blatantly not been the case, and national purposes have been lost in bureaucratic feuding and compromise. The road to reform begins with recognition of the inherently complex political and legislative character of strategic decision-making. The need is for methods which will, at best, contribute both to the substance and the acceptance of policy, or, failing that, at least contribute more to the improvement of one than to the impairment of the other.

v

When the strategy-making process is viewed as essentially legislative in nature, the critical points appear to be not the prevalence of bargaining but rather the weakness of legislative leadership and the limited scope of the strategic consensus.

In the traditional legislative process, interest groups and executive agencies originate proposals, the President integrates them into a coherent legislative program, Congress debates, amends and decides. In the strategy-making process, executive agencies and related groups originate proposals, the N.S.C., the J.C.S., the President and Secretary of Defense debate, amend and decide upon them. But who plays the role of the legislative leader? Who winnows out the various ideas in the light of an over-all set of priorities or grand strategy and integrates these proposals into general programs which can then be discussed, amended and ratified? In the decade after World War II no clear concept developed as to which official or agency had the responsibility for leading the J.C.S. and the N.S.C. in their deliberations. In actual practice, leadership tended to rest with the Chairman in the J.C.S. and with the Department of State in the N.S.C. However, the case was frequently made for expanding the N.S.C. staff in the Executive Office of the President and for strengthening the Special Assistant for National Security Affairs. Similarly, it was often urged that the Secretary of Defense be provided with a mixed civilian-military policy staff which would, at the least, give him an independent source of advice, and, at most, enable him to play a stronger role in making strategic decisions. Other suggestions [6] include the creation outside the executive hierarchy of a council of elder statesmen, a "supreme court" for foreign and military policy, or an "academy of political affairs" (modeled on the National Academy of Sciences) which could study national security problems, issue reports and advise the President directly.

It seems likely that either the leadership functions of the Secretary of State and the Chairman of the Joint Chiefs will become more fully recognized and clarified, or the Special Assistant and Secretary of Defense will develop the staff facilities necessary to perform these functions, or new organs of policy recommendation will come into existence. Such developments would not only facilitate consensus but also would probably improve the content of strategic decisions. The form in which issues are presented for decision often drastically affects the nature of the decision. The problem in the Executive today resides not in the presence of bargaining but rather at the point at which bargaining begins. The development of more effective leadership organs in the N.S.C. and J.C.S. would permit bargaining to be more limited and focused. The starting point would become not three separate proposals advanced by three separate departments but rather one set of proposals advanced by the legislative leader. The requirements of consensus might still cause those proposals to be torn apart tooth and limb, but, at the very least, the clear visibility of the mutilation would have certain restraining effects. It has had them in Congress.

A related and perhaps more important problem concerns the relatively

[6] See Walter Millis, "The Constitution and the Common Defense" (New York: The Fund for the Republic, 1959), pp. 36–46.

limited scope of the strategic consensus. The strategy-making process goes on largely within the Executive, and the consensus arrived at, if any, is primarily an executive one. As a result, it tends to be both tenuous and tentative. Although the effective power of decision rests with the executive branch, the possibility always exists that it may be upset by forces from the outside. Consequently the activity of the Administration is largely devoted to defending a policy which has been decided upon rather than advocating a policy which has yet to be adopted.

In the traditional legislative process, an issue is debated first within the Executive and then publicly within and about Congress. All the debate, however, contributes directly or indirectly to shaping the final product: to pushing the legislation through without change, amending it in one direction or another, or defeating it entirely. When the President signs the bill, the policy-making process is over, and the debate stops—or at least lessens—for a while. In strategy-making, debate among the various executive agencies and related groups also contributes directly to shaping the measure. Once the decision is made, this debate subsides, but as soon as the decision becomes known to non-executive agencies and groups, the public debate begins. The likelihood of such debate may have had its effects upon the executive policy-makers before the decision was reached, but their anticipation of public reaction to policy often is, at best, an informed hunch and, at worst, a rationalization that the public will not accept policies which they do not accept themselves. Public debate of a strategic decision may also affect its implementation and may influence subsequent decisions. Coming after the initial decision, however, the debate necessarily loses much of its force and value.

It is striking that both the Truman and Eisenhower Administrations, different as they are otherwise, have been regularly criticized for not exercising "leadership" in national security policy. In each case, it is alleged, the President has failed to take the initiative in bringing strategic issues to the people, in arousing support for foreign and military policy proposals, and in educating the public to its responsibilities in the nuclear age. Such criticism assumes that the President should play the same leadership role in strategic matters that he does in domestic legislation. In the latter, the President must be the source of energy for his program, and it is normally in his interest to dramatize the issue and to broaden the public concern with it. The concept of presidential leadership is that of Theodore Roosevelt, Wilson, F.D.R. rallying support for a legislative program which he is urging upon a recalcitrant Congress.

In the strategy process, however, the President's role is very different, and the domestic model is inapplicable. Here, the President and his Administration have little reason to desire public debate and many reasons to fear it. The decision has been made; the policy is being implemented. The extension of the public concerned with the policy can only lead to pressure to change it in one respect or another and to the exploitation of the issues by the opposition. The primary role of the Administration has to be defensive: to protect the balance of interests, the policy equilibrium which has been laboriously reached within the Executive, against the impact of profane forces and interests outside the Executive. Mr. Cutler put the matter bluntly when he declared:

> There is another seamlessness in our complex world: the fabric of our national defense. Perhaps the most potent argument against public disclosure of secret projects or of short-falls (which inevitably always exist) in any one aspect of our national defense is that such disclosure builds up a Potomac propaganda war to rectify that defect or over-finance that project. But if you devote larger resources to one area of national defense, you are apt to imbalance the rest.[7]

Given the nature of the decision-making process, this concern is a natural one. The cold-war Presidents have evolved a variety of means to limit public interest in strategy, to minimize the concern of external groups with force levels and weapons, and, most particularly, to insulate and protect the executive balance from the disruption of outside interests. Hence the tendency of both Presidents and their Administrations to reassure the public, to pour on the "soothing syrup" which has so exasperated the Alsops and others, to limit the information available on American deficiencies and Soviet achievements, to discount these achievements and to minimize their significance, to preserve discipline and to suppress leaks, to discourage dissenting and disquieting testimony before congressional committees, and in general to maintain an air of calm assurance, an imperturbable façade. All these actions stem from a fear of the fragility of the executive consensus and of the irrationality and uncontrollability of the external political forces. These are the new "defensive" weapons of presidential leadership, as important to an Administration in the formulation of strategy as the old "offensive" techniques are in the promotion of domestic legislation in Congress.

A striking feature of the past dozen years has been the extent to which expressions of alarm at the decline of presidential leadership have occurred simultaneously with expressions of alarm at the growth of executive power. This apparent paradox simply reflects the fact that the increasing responsibility of the executive branch in making crucial decisions on strategic programs has undermined the ability of the President to lead. The more the President becomes, at least in theory, the judge, the less he can be the advocate. Yet, in practice, even his power to decide strategic issues is difficult to exercise. To be sure, the N.S.C. and the J.S.C. are theoretically only his advisors: no policy exists until he has approved it. But in part this

---

[7] "The Seamless Web," *Harvard Alumni Bulletin* (June 4, 1955), p. 665.

is a myth to preserve the appearance of presidential decision-making. Surely the President does not over-ride united opinion among his top advisors much more often than he vetoes acts of Congress. The theory that the President makes the decisions, in short, serves as a cloak to shield the elaborate processes of executive legislation and bargaining through which the policies are actually hammered out. Consequently, the President may be less influential as a decision-maker than he is as a legislative leader. The latter function is personal to him. The former is one which he shares with a variety of other groups in the executive branch.

Whatever defects may exist in this situation cannot be removed by shifting the point of decision away from the executive branch. The tenuous character of the decisions and the defensive role of the Administration could be modified only by broadening the scope of discussion and concern in the early stages of the policy process—*before* key decisions are made. Once adequate legislative leadership emerges in the executive branch, the debate could focus on the proposals of this leadership, provided they were made public to the fullest extent possible. Greater publicity for and public participation in strategy-making at an earlier stage would tend to restrain some of the more gross forms of "horse trading" in the Executive, and should enhance the President's actual power of decision. At present, one way in which issues are brought to the top and forced upon the President for decision is through the lobbying activities of congressional committees. Broader and earlier public discussion of strategic programs would in all probability have a similar effect, and instead of interested guesses we would be provided with concrete evidence of what "the public will support." Certainly, discussion is more useful before decisions are made than afterwards. Broadening the scope of the policy consensus could well go hand in hand with improving the quality of the policy content.

The Budgetary Process

THE BUREAU OF THE BUDGET AND THE BUDGETARY PROCESS

The Problem

THE struggle with world communism is broadening, deepening, and quickening.

Our rivals are pledged to see their system triumph over the free way of life. They think, plan, and act in terms of the long haul.

The task confronting us is harshly plain—to outthink, outplan, outperform, and outlast our foes.

Our answer to the challenge cannot consist of mere responses to Communist thrusts and probes. A policy of simply reacting to the initiatives of Moscow and Peiping can lead only to the eventual defeat of freedom.

We need a forward and affirmative national strategy—a clear and widely shared understanding of where we aim to go in the world, and how we purpose to get there. The key problem of the President is to create such a strategy and to establish an order of national priorities on its behalf. His task is to map a course of action which puts first things first, which separates the necessary from the merely desirable, and which distinguishes between what must be done today and what can wait until tomorrow.

The President must grapple with formidable questions: How much of our national substance should be devoted to the requirements of national security? What is the right level of foreign aid? What is the best division between military and economic aid? What is the proper balance between conventional and nuclear military forces? What should be the relative emphasis on offensive and defensive armaments? Will prospective revenues cover the cost of needed programs? If not, how should we meet the bill?

In answering these questions, a President requires and seeks help from many quarters. He turns to the National Security Council, State and Defense, his own staff aides, the score of other departments and agencies concerned with national security matters, and to interagency committees and task forces.

A staff report issued by the Subcommittee on National Policy Machinery of the Senate Committee on Government Operations, October 16, 1961.

In addition, a President can secure major help from the Bureau of the Budget and the budgetary process.

The need is this: To make sure that the Bureau of the Budget and our Government's use of the budgetary process keep pace with the spiraling complexity of foreign and defense policy, toward the end of giving the President and the Congress maximum assistance in a world of Berlin and the ballistic missile.

The Bureau of the Budget and National Security

The Budget Bureau will never win a bureaucratic popularity contest. The total program requests of the operating departments always far exceed any budget a President can prudently approve. The Bureau must often be a no-sayer and help the Chief Executive trim agency programs to fit the Presidential cloth. Hence its reputation, even if undeserved, as the villain of the executive branch.

Each President must decide how he wants to use the Bureau.

A President can employ the Bureau mainly to keep a lid on expenditures. The Bureau, in such cases, is told to "hold the line"—but may be given little guidance concerning the Chief Executive's priorities and program goals. In coordinating and auditing executive branch performance, less reliance is placed on the Bureau and more on interdepartmental coordinating mechanisms or White House aides.

Used thus, the Bureau becomes a kind of "Certified Presidential Accounting" office.

A President, however, can employ the Bureau differently. He can use it as his "lengthened shadow" across the whole front of fiscal policy and program management. The Director of this kind of Budget Bureau sits in the innermost policy councils of the Presidency. Program planning and budgeting are seen as but different aspects of one process, which starts with the formulation of policy objectives and ends with costed and time-phased programs for action. The President regards the Bureau as his strong right arm in executive management.

A President will do well to use the Bureau of the Budget in this way.

The budgetary process can be the President's most powerful instrument for establishing a scale of national priorities and marshalling, through the Congress, the resources required on their behalf.

The budget pulls together, into one comprehensive reckoning, information on all the competing claims of national policy, foreign and domestic. It offers the President unique help in ranking rival claims on the basis of a system of priorities, and allocating resources accordingly. Mr. David Bell, the Director of the Bureau of the Budget, put it this way to the subcommittee: "The budget operates as an extremely effective element of discipline on the President and the executive branch because it requires that each proposed use of resources—for defense, science, national resources, or whatever—be tested against others and against the total size of the budget."

Employed with sophistication, the budgetary process can also be the President's most discriminating and effective tool in controlling the executive branch. It reaches deep into the activities of the great departments; it is the one Presidential management device common to all of them; it works on that most sensitive pressure point—the pocketbook nerve.

The Bureau of the Budget helps the President in other major ways. On his behalf, it reviews all legislative proposals originating in the departments or agencies or the Congress to see whether they conform to the program of the Chief Executive. The Bureau also assists the President by continually reviewing the organization of the Federal establishment, and making recommendations for improving its effectiveness.

The Bureau is uniquely equipped to serve the President well. Aside from the President himself, the Budget Director has the most comprehensive view of the policies and programs of the Government. As an "above-the-department" Presidential staff unit in the Executive Office, the Bureau is exempt from the shortcomings of interdepartmental committees. The Bureau's permanent professional staff of almost 300 members dwarfs any other found at the Presidential level and is seasoned and outstandingly able.

Certain things follow if the Bureau is to be the President's true "lengthened shadow."

The Budget Director and his colleagues should never be left in the dark about the President's scale of priorities and his policy aims. The Director should not only be privy to the inner councils of the Chief Executive, but the Presidential "word" must get down the line to the junior officials of the Bureau. Unless the Bureau, from top to bottom, has a clear and current understanding of the President's aims, its predilections may come to substitute for the President's pleasure. The Bureau then becomes an independent agency, a rival both of the departments and of its chief. The stronger the Bureau the more the need for clear Presidential direction and strong Presidential control.

The Bureau should preserve an arm's-length relationship with the departments and agencies. In working with agency program and budgetary officers, the danger is always present that Bureau members may themselves become committed to particular agency budgets, and end as departmental protagonists. The Bureau members must remain the President's men.

The Bureau should on occasion be a prodder and a yea-sayer. New programs important for the President's goals may lack a natural departmental home—an effective lobby. Or programs with low agency priority may have high Presidential priority. The Bureau should then be prepared to recommend that we do more and go faster.

One point above all. The Bureau ought to be staffed more broadly and richly with officials who have a substantive understanding of the issues crossing their desks. The Bureau need not have a stable of technical experts in every specialized field. But its members should be able to comprehend the significance of programs in terms of the President's overall policy objectives. Nowhere is this more important than in the area of national security, where the price paid for poor counsel is highest.

Modernizing Budget Making

Over the past 40 years, each administration has made improvements in the budgetary process. Distinguished private citizens, like the members of the Brownlow Committee and the First and Second Hoover Commissions, have helped in this task.

But budgetary reform, particularly in the area of national security, has not kept pace with the changing and growing challenges to our Nation.

The budget sent to the Congress last January retains the essential format of the first budget President Harding submitted to the Congress. To too great a degree, its appropriations categories, its emphases, its balance of information detail between programs, remain unchanged.

Over the years the budget has increased in size and complexity. It is now a massive document about the size of a big-city telephone directory. It takes over 2 years to prepare. The budget has developed its own vocabulary, comprehensible in large measure only to budgetary specialists. It distinguishes, for example, between "direct obligations," "new obligational authority," "reimbursable obligations," "obligations incurred," "recoveries of prior year obligations," and "total obligations." The budget, moreover, carries a heavy overburden of legacies from the past. Matters of little contemporary importance are treated in exhaustive, and exhausting, detail—while information on far more important programs is meager or nonexistent.

A President, a top agency official, a Senator, or a Congressman must now run an obstacle course of obscure funding concepts, archaic appropriations categories, and fiscal jargon in using the budget to help make policy and program decisions.

The time is at hand for a determined effort to make the budget shorter, simpler, and easier to read and understand.

The main problem, however, goes deeper. Despite substantial progress in budgetary reform, our Government has been slow to take full advantage of the contributions which the budget process can make to planning and executive management.

Federal budgetmaking, in the main, has concentrated on developing information useful for day-to-day administration of the departments and agencies. Not nearly as much attention has been paid to preparing budgets in such a way as to make them most useful in establishing priorities, in forward planning, in choosing between programs, and in measuring expenditures against meaningful performance yardsticks.

This is in strong contrast to the contemporary budgetary practices of progressive private organizations—business firms, banks, and universities. A modern corporation uses the budgetary process for much more than checking costs and controlling expenditures. It employs it as a main tool in planning its corporate future. Budgeting is used to help decide upon capital expenditures and establish product lines, to spot management weaknesses, and, most important, as an early warning system of problems and opportunities coming up on the corporate horizon. Programs and budgets extending several years into the future have become the rule.

The job of making the budgetary process a more versatile and useful tool of the President badly needs doing.

Two problems rang highest: How to make the budget more helpful in forward planning. And how to make it more useful in illuminating program choices and measuring program performance.

Extending the Budgetary Time Horizon

Particularly in the area of national security, our Government needs to extend its budgetary time horizons farther into the future. We need to know where the cost of present plans and activities may take us, not simply through the next fiscal year, but for several years ahead.

A 12-month budget reveals only the tip of the fiscal iceberg. The initial outlays for the man to the moon program will result in billions of dollars being spent during the remainder of this decade. The development of major weapons systems and foreign aid programs are other obvious cases in point. Cost estimates, to be meaningful, must be based on the full expected lifetime of programs.

Longer term budgetary projections do not imply a change in the present system of presenting a budget to the Congress each year, and voting appropriations on an annual basis. Nor is the aim to make in 1962 decisions that can only be made in 1966. It is to take greater account of the consequences in 1966 of the budgetary decisions which must be made in 1962.

Mr. Maurice Stans, who served as President Eisenhower's last Budget Director, made this comment before the subcommittee: "I would not agree that we should appropriate for defense purposes for more than 1 year in advance, but I think it is very important that the Congress and all concerned know the implications of the beginning of a program in 1 year on the budget requirements of future years."

Forward budgetary projections, of course, grow less accurate as they extend into the future. It is easier, also, to project spending for military hardware than for foreign policy, where the unpredictable and the uncontrollable loom so great. Alternative projections, based on different assumptions about the future, may be necessary. In any event, the projections must be revised as necessary and kept up to date.

The previous administration published in its final days a pioneering 10-year projection of the Federal budget for the period 1960–70—with high, medium, and low estimates of Federal expenditures.

The Bureau of the Budget, under the new administration, is now testing the feasibility of developing comprehensive 5-year program and budgetary projections. It is at the same time encouraging the departments and agencies to plan, program, and budget on a longer time scale. Last spring, a set of alternative forward projections compiled by the Bureau were considered by the President in establishing guidelines for the 1963 Federal budget.

The Department of Defense has been in the vanguard of this effort. It aims, beginning in fiscal year 1963, to have available at all times a projection of requirements and tentatively approved programs with dollar signs attached, extending at least 5 years into the future. As Secretary of Defense McNamara told the subcommittee: "We . . . propose to maintain that plan or budget up to date with monthly revisions to it so that at any particular time when a budget for a special period, such as the fiscal year, is required, it can be abstracted from the continually modified and continually adjusted military program."

Forward budgeting can be no better than the forward planning which underlies it. Many departments and agencies have had little experience with long-range programing—and relating such planning to budgeting. Departmental planning staffs, traditionally, have only occasionally viewed themselves as coworkers of budgetary officers. The problem of developing the necessary planning skills and of creating a productive partnership between the planner and the budget officer is a vexing one. Its solution deserves, and will require, sustained effort.

This applies particularly to the Department of State. The concern of the Secretary of State, like that of the President, is political-strategic. The Secretary speaks for the primacy of national policy over lesser aims. A President can find no effective substitute for the Secretary and his Department in helping him define the basic direction and broad priorities of national security policy. The Department of State should be staffed to do more forward planning—and asked to do more.

FORWARD ECONOMIC PROJECTIONS

The relationship between the budget, on the one hand, and the economy and the Government's tax receipts, on the other, is critical. Can program costs in prospect over the next several years be met within the present tax structure? Or will they require deficit financing, new taxes, or other measures to stimulate Federal revenues?

Revenue estimates for the current fiscal year are of only limited help in answering this question. Treasury receipts may be abnormally high or unusually low—depending on the stage of the business cycle.

In making program and budgetary decisions, a President should therefore have available to him projections of national income and associated tax receipts for several years ahead, based on differing assumptions about the factors which will influence the level of economic activity.

The Bureau of the Budget, the Treasury, and the Council of Economic Advisers are now cooperating in preparing longer term economic projections.

Projections of economic activity and tax revenues for a particular future year are subject to notoriously large margins of error. Projections can, however, shed helpful light on broad trends. They should be regarded as helpful informational aids—not as predictions or forecasts of future economic performance.

Better Ways of Federal Budgeting

No one form of budget preparation and presentation is the best for all purposes. Modern corporations know this. A progressive company may work with three or four budgets at the same time, each serving a different purpose—checking plant efficiency, planning capital expenditures, measuring the contributions of different products to the profits of the enterprise.

The appropriations categories of today's Federal budget, oriented as they are toward the administrative surveillance of department and agency programs, serve one useful purpose. But the budgetary process can also provide other ways of "walking around the elephant." Different ways of packaging and presenting budgetary information lead to insights not otherwise obtainable.

The new administration, building upon the efforts of its predecessors to present budgetary information in more useful forms, is moving along three fronts.

Program Packaging. In its traditional form, the Defense budget has been prepared and presented in terms of the requirements of the individual services and certain expenditure categories like "military personnel," "operation and maintenance," and "procurement." While useful for many purposes, this way of presenting budgetary information does not relate defense spending to military missions or tasks—defending the North American Continent against attack, or moving troops to crisis areas, and the like.

It is important that the Defense budget be made a more useful informational tool for comparing the cost and worth of alternative programs in terms of functions or missions to be performed. Although it has been possible to assemble such information for special requirements, the financial management system in the past has not been designed to do this on a continuing basis.

The Department of Defense is now undertaking a systematic and comprehensive effort to relate military spending to missions. It plans to supplement the traditional form of budget presentation with a series of program packages which will cut across the lines both of the services and the traditional expenditure categories. Some examples of these packages are "central war offensive forces," "central war defensive forces," and "sealift and airlift." These packages will try to project the costs of such end programs 5 or 6 years into the future.

By relating costs to jobs to be done, and by doing this on a longer time scale than has heretofore been the case, the program package approach should contribute to a better appraisal of program alternatives.

Country Development Programing. It is important that our aid to foreign governments be closely related to a nation's self-help development programs and to assistance forthcoming from international agencies or other outside sources. Moreover, each part of the United States effort—economic or military aid, loans or grants, or food for peace sales—ought to be seen in the light of an overall program.

In preparing our foreign aid budgets, the administration is now trying to relate our own assistance more closely to country development programs which look several years into the future. This step should help in deciding upon appropriate forms and levels of United States aid, and in making sure that all types of aid that we give to a country make a maximum contribution to our true national interest there.

Coordinated Forward Budgets. Particularly in research and development, many important national security programs are widely dispersed between departments and agencies. This year a coordinated oceanographic research program involving seven different agencies was sent to the Congress. Coordinated forward budgets make sense in numerous other areas. They pull related activities together; they make it easier for each agency to do its own planning in relationship to the plans of others; and they help the President and the Congress see programs "in the round."

The law of diminishing returns places obvious limitations on the number of ways in which budgetary information can usefully be pulled together. As Mr. Wilfred McNeil, the former Comptroller of the Department of Defense, warned the subcommittee: "An effort to be too accurate or too precise can get the real objective lost in the details."

The budgetmakers' task, however, has been made much easier by the development of computers and coding devices. Ideally, the financial management system should eventually be able to produce information on costs in terms of whatever program groupings are helpful to the President, his key lieutenants, and the Congress.

PERFORMANCE MEASUREMENT

Business has a yardstick for judging its effectiveness—profit and loss statements. Efficiently run private enterprises also hold their managers strictly accountable for results.

It is necessarily more difficult for our Government to determine how well its national security programs are faring. By what criteria do we measure the success or failure of some assistance programs? How do we judge whether we are getting the most for our money?

Granted the difficulties, our Government pays insufficient attention to this problem of performance measurement. The whole field is almost unexplored.

We cannot learn from our successes or our mistakes unless we can identify them.

The Bureau of the Budget, working with the departments and agencies, ought to take the lead in developing better ways of measuring performance.

STATEMENT OF MAURICE H. STANS

MR. Chairman and members of the committee, I very much appreciate the invitation to meet with you today and to discuss some of the problems related to organizing our Government for national security. Certainly this subject is one which is vital to our future as a nation, and the committee is to be commended for the serious attention which it has focused on it.

The committee's careful and judicious consideration of the points of view offered in these hearings can lead to valuable conclusions that will strengthen the national capacity for survival. This will be true even if the committee concludes that in many areas past and present procedures are not susceptible to significant improvement—since the endorsements of the committee, where appropriate, will strengthen the confidence of our citizens in the management of our affairs in these times of stress and tension.

Although the responsibilities of a Director of the Budget are manifold, it seems to me that there are two areas which are of particular interest to this committee: (1) the assistance given to the President in respect to the Federal budget; and (2) the aid provided to the President in regard

Presented before the Subcommittee on National Policy Machinery of the Senate Committee on Government Operations, July 31, 1961.

to the organization and management of the Federal Government. Within this compass I thought it might be helpful if I were to devote some time in these initial remarks to two separate areas in which in one way or another I carried responsibilities: (1) the budgetary process; and (2) the organization of the Executive Office of the President. These two subjects, of course, relate to the efficiency of the staff assistance available to the President.

The Budget Process

For perspective, I would like to touch first on a few elementary facts about the budget process:

1. The Bureau of the Budget is a statutory arm of the President. In budgetary matters it does not operate in a vacuum. It undertakes to carry out the express or implied policies of the President. It acts as it believes the President would act if time permitted him to deal with each particular situation in the light of all the known facts.

2. The annual budget is the President's budget. The decisions which it reflects are his—not only as to programs and activities but as to fiscal policy.

In other words, the major budgetary function of the Bureau is to evaluate priorities and issues for the President and to advise him of their relationship to his policies. All of the Bureau's activities in the budget process are directed to the end of preparing a document which represents the President's concept of national needs and priorities. From this the Congress exercises its judgment in making appropriations.

One even more elementary fact: Budgeting is choosing among spending alternatives. If there is enough money to meet all demands, and no choices are necessary, then the plans are no longer a budget but a spending list. Actually, there is never enough to go around—which means that it is necessary to fix the priority of claims on resources. Priority may be recognized by inclusion of a request in whole or in part, or by rejection.

It is natural then that there may be dissatisfaction with this process by those dedicated, determined people in the Government agencies who seek more funds than they receive. They sometimes fail to see that their own budget requests are based on subjective, provincial points of view. Only the President sees the overall measures of the Nation's needs and can keep them in proportion. (If I may be permitted a less serious note, I think the matter is summed up in a phrase which I used some time ago and which has since been publicly referred to as "Stans' Law": "Effective budgeting is the uniform distribution of dissatisfaction.")

Thus it is also natural in budgeting for an organization as large as the Government of the United States that there be misunderstandings. These misunderstandings result in various accusations, some of which have crept into these hearings: The Bureau of the Budget is "arbitrary and capricious." It "fixes ceilings." It is "preoccupied with balancing." It "controls our defense policies"; and so on.

My first and perhaps major point here today is a defense of the budget process and of the Bureau of the Budget as essential to the Nation's organization of its activities. If there were not a budget process basically similar to that which we have there would be fiscal chaos. If there were not a Bureau of the Budget there would have to be another agency under another name performing the same functions.

With all this as background, I come now to the matter of how the process works and how it can be improved, to the advantage of the President, of Congress, of the national security and of the taxpaying public.

In this regard, it has seemed to me that perhaps it would be most useful if I were to discuss seriatim some of the principal questions raised about the budget process during the past year—both before this committee and elsewhere. I am sure there are other questions to which you would like me to respond and I should, of course, be happy to do so later.

The question which appears to have been raised most frequently is whether our national security processes and our budget processes have been closely enough related. During my term of service as Director of the Budget, I was quite convinced that they were.

This is not intended to mean that there are no opportunities for betterment in the mechanics of budget analysis and presentation. Some notable improvements were made in the last few years, other changes are now being planned, and as time goes on there will surely be found many ways of making more clear the significance of budget proposals. But I do mean that there has been, I believe, every reasonable opportunity for the exposure, communication, advocacy and evaluation of program ideas advanced by all agencies, including Defense, and that the President formulated his budgets under these conditions.

Perhaps the second most frequently raised question has been whether the budget process, over the past few years, has permitted the Budget Director to impose ceilings on the Department of Defense.

Over 2 years ago I testified under oath on this question before the Preparedness Investigating Subcommittee of the Committee on Armed Services of the Senate. For your own records I should like to repeat again what I said at that time in response to the question: "Have you fixed a ceiling or formulated a target for the 1961 budget?"

My reply was:

Well, I want to answer that carefully because the choice of words is very important. I have not fixed a ceiling this year and did not fix one last year.

I do think that it is important, in considering a budget of this size, to take a look at it at various levels. By that I mean I think the Department of Defense should determine what kind of defense it can provide for $40 billion.

If this is done and everything is given its proper ranking in priority, then it can be determined whether or not it provides an adequate program, which items are next in rank of priority that should be considered, and which items are marginal or least essential. This does not mean I think that the defense of the country can unquestionably be satisfied for $40 billion. It means that as a matter of method I think the Department should start with a figure of that general magnitude and see what kind of a budget it can prepare at that level, and what, if anything, is then left out that is still sufficiently important that it has to be added.

That, in my opinion, is not a ceiling at all and it is not a target either. It is a method of procedure that I think is a desirable one to follow. I think all agencies of the Government should use a similar approach.

In the context of today's hearing, with the committee looking for constructive ways of improving the budget process, I would like not only to reiterate this view but to express a related thought. There is a tendency at budget time for both defense and nondefense agencies and subordinate units to look at a budget for one year as a "floor" for the next year, with new programs and other growth entirely additive. To accept this would be to ignore the responsibility to require the older items to compete properly with the new in priorities. Every item in a budget request should be severely tested, and this cannot be done unless some flotation process is found to bring to the top the lesser or marginal items of the previous budget. This is why I believe so strongly that a budget based for one year should start at a point significantly less in total than the previous year, and that items proposed for addition to that base should be evaluated in relative importance and need, whether old or new. Only by this means will less important going programs ever be retired or reduced.

This leads to a question, raised in one of this committee's early reports, of whether there might be advance preparation of alternate budgets for major national security programs. The report noted:

> Some wish to see one proposed budget at X dollars; another at perhaps 10 percent below this level; and still another at perhaps 10 percent above. Such a procedure, they hold, will permit policymakers to see more clearly, and sooner, what is sacrificed and what is gained at various expenditure levels. Can and should this be done?

In actuality, in the development of the Defense budget the past several years, this is substantially what was done. Since we had to take some common starting point, we selected the total expenditure figure for the current year and asked the Department of Defense what the adequacy would be for the next year of a budget which provided either the same amount of money, or 10 percent less, or 10 percent more. The Secretary of Defense used this formula, but with other percentages.

Pursuing the matter a step further, however, it has also been suggested that the budget document itself might well reproduce these alternative possibilities. I have considerable doubt whether this would be feasible. The budget must necessarily reflect decision rather than indecision, and in any event the budget message itself can and should provide in regard to certain major programs some explanation of why a particular course of action was selected. It is the responsibility of the President to recommend, and it is not conceivable to me that any purpose would be served by parading anywhere in the budget some or all of the items that he does not recommend.

Another question which frequently arises is whether or not we would profit from budgeting for longer periods of time—say for 5 years. Here I believe we should distinguish carefully between planning and budgeting. There is no question but that *planning* for years ahead is desirable. However, *budgeting*, in the sense of seeking appropriations for such periods of time, could create several types of serious problems.

The net effect of a multiyear budget for any period for any program is to give that program an absolute priority over all other programs which do not enjoy such an automatic availability of funds. In other words, in the preparation of each year's budget, it would be necessary to allocate to such a program whatever amount had previously been appropriated in advance, regardless of the requirements of other programs. Assuming that funds are not unlimited, and since the controllable portion of the annual budget is relatively small, this could effectively destroy budgetary management.

Depending on the year in which it was approved, a 5-year program budget could deny to one or even two succeeding Congresses any control over that program through the appropriations process.

Inflexibility

One of the most serious objections to any 5-year budget lies in the fact that it is almost impossible to project requirements so far ahead, even if one pays no attention to the priorities of competing programs or the projected availability of funds. The 5-year projection may turn out to represent more than is actually required, so that adherence to the plan would represent a waste of funds. If the projection turns out to represent less than is required the result is to place completely undesirable restraints on the program.

A fair question is whether what is really intended in discussions of multiyear budgets is the provision of some minimum amount for a 3- or 5-year period, with these amounts augmented each year to meet presumably new and pressing requirements. In such case, of course, it is no longer a 3- or 5-year budget.

None of these objections applies to long-range planning, and that is certainly to be encouraged. As you know, it is relatively easy for the Government to start an activity with a small amount of money, with clear knowledge that subsequent expenditures will be much greater. Unless the full implications of ongoing programs are projected well into the future, the aggregate significance of enacted commitments may not be recognized, and this can have a disastrous effect on future fiscal management of the Government.

For some years, the Bureau of the Budget has required most of the agencies to develop 3-year estimates of requirements, and these have entered to some extent into the President's consideration of new proposals. Without doubt this procedure can be improved and extended, but I would express the caution that any public use of future projections should be clearly labeled as tentative and for planning purposes only, so as not to imply any commitment of future resources.

The committee will undoubtedly be interested in knowing that in January of this year I delivered to the President a 10-year projection of future Government spending. Although this is a public document, it does not seem to have received the attention it deserves. As a guide to future planning, it provides a projection of amounts of spending by 1970 at three levels: one somewhat austere, one which carries on the trend (and the commitments) of the last decade or so, and one in between these extremes. Further study and work along this line should be encouraged.

Organization

Perhaps the most important question which can be raised with respect to organization for national security is to ask what process can best assure that the total intellectual resources of the Government are made available to assist the President in making crucial policy decisions.

Several points are critical here. First, that in making such policy decisions the President have available the advice of all those counselors whose responsibilities bear on the matter at hand; there is no substitute in the making of policy for the participation of those who will be charged with carrying out that policy. Secondly, and equally important, is the matter of confrontation—of assuring that proponents of alternative courses of action, or of modifications of proposals—debate each other before the President; no other procedure will as rapidly expose the totality of facts bearing on the problem. Thirdly, and also very important, that communication of policy factors and decisions be precise; this means that oral reports of considerations and policy conclusions will not do, because they are too often incomplete and inaccurate, or become so as they pass through agency networks. Carefully written and debated policy statements, approved by the President, are essential to avoid confusion and worse.

Just how a President assures that these concepts are achieved is, of course, a matter for his own determination. Personally, however, I thought the national security policy process as it has evolved over the last decade, and as I participated in it, met these requirements well.

A second question which might properly be raised is how the Executive Office of the President might be better organized to meet the President's requirements. In this connection I would like very much to recall to you certain points which President Eisenhower made in his last budget message.

He wrote:

> The duties placed on the President by the Constitution and the statutes demand the most careful attention to the staffing and organization of the President's office. While the present organization of the Executive Office of the President reflects many constructive steps taken over a period of years, much remains to be done to improve the facilities available to the President. The first requirement for improvement is for the Congress to give the President greater flexibility in organizing his own office to meet his great responsibilities.
>
> Specifically, the Congress should enact legislation authorizing the President to reorganize the Executive Office of the President, including the authority to redistribute statutory functions among the units of the Office; to change the names of units and titles of officers within the Office; to make changes in the membership of the statutory bodies in the Office; and, within the limits of existing laws and available appropriations, to establish new units in the Executive Office and fix the compensation of officers. Such action would insure that future Presidents will possess the latitude to design the working structure of the Presidential Office as they deem necessary for the effective conduct of their duties under the Constitution and the laws. Enactment of such legislation would be a major step forward in strengthening the Office of the President for the critical test that will surely continue to face our Nation in the years to come. These matters are obviously devoid of partisan considerations.
>
> My experience leads me to suggest the establishment of an Office of Executive Management in the Executive Office of the President in which would be grouped the staff functions necessary to assist the President in the discharge of his managerial responsibilities. In an enterprise as large and as diversified as the executive branch of the Government, there is an imperative need for effective and imaginative central management to strengthen program planning and evaluation, promote efficiency, identify and eliminate waste and duplication, and coordinate numerous interagency operations within approved policy and statutory objectives. The establishment of an Office of Executive Management is highly desirable to help the President achieve the high standards of effective management that the Congress and the people rightfully expect.
>
> I have given much personal study to the assistance the President needs in meeting the multitude of demands placed upon him in conducting and

correlating all aspects of foreign political, economic, social, and military affairs. I have reached the conclusion that serious attention should be given to providing in the President's Office an official ranking higher than Cabinet members, possibly with the title of First Secretary of the Government, to assist the President in consulting with the departments on the formulation of national security objectives, in coordinating international programs, and in representing the President at meetings with foreign officials above the rank of Foreign Minister and below the rank of head of state.

I would urge that this legacy of thought by an outgoing President, after 8 years of experience with the burdens of office, be seriously considered by this committee.

Conclusion

Now, in conclusion, I would like to recall one other paragraph from his fiscal year 1962 budget message, in which President Eisenhower said:

The budget process is a means of establishing Government policies, improving the management of Government operations, and planning and conducting the Government's fiscal role in the life of the Nation. Whether that role is increasing, decreasing, or remaining unchanged, the budget process is perhaps our most significant device for planning, controlling, and coordinating our programs and policies as well as our finances. Thus the President and the Congress will always need to give attention to the improvement and full utilization of the budget system.

As to ways and means for improving the overall budget process, I would have two suggestions.

First, although the President presents one budget for the entire Government to the Congress each year, the Congress considers the budget in a multitude of pieces rather than as a whole. Financing methods outside the regular appropriation process (so-called back-door spending) are one phase of the problem. The complete separation of the handling of tax legislation from the consideration of appropriations and expenditures adds to the total difficulty. There would be marked gains if the Congress could find a mechanism by which total receipts, total appropriations, and total expenditures could be considered in relation to each other.

Secondly, I believe that future Presidents ought to have the authority to veto items of appropriation measures without the necessity of disapproving an entire appropriation bill. Many Presidents have recommended that this authority be given our Chief Executive and more than 80 percent of the States have given it to their Governors. It is a necessary procedure for strengthening fiscal responsibility, and a proper way by which the President can, in effect, ask the Congress to reconsider an item. As in the case of other vetoes, the Congress would have the authority to override an item veto.

I would not be wholly in character if I did not end with one plea. The protection of the Nation's security requires that we be economically strong as well as militarily strong. We could lose the cold war as easily by the pursuit of unsound fiscal policies that resulted in impairment of our money and our economic strength as we could by neglect of our military resources. In times of tension such as the present, the budgetary flexibility we need to meet emergencies can be provided only if all Americans exercise restraint in their demands for more nonmilitary domestic spending programs. I hope the committee, in whatever conclusions it reaches, will emphasize this point.

Henry A. Kissinger
STRATEGY AND ORGANIZATION

. . . ANOTHER factor which inhibits the development of strategic doctrine is the predominance of fiscal considerations in our defense planning. This is not even always a question of deliberate choice. One of the reasons for the emphasis on fiscal policy and technology has been that the former has been explicit and the latter impressively demanding. In the process of coördinating diverse policies, which is the primary function of the National Security Council, there always exists a clear fiscal policy, largely because governmental economy is the *raison d'être* of the Bureau of the Budget and because only one agency—the Treasury Department—is responsible for setting objectives in the fiscal field. But there is rarely, if ever, a clear National Security policy to oppose it. On the contrary, the contending services have been tempted to enlist the backing of the Treasury Department and the Bureau of the Budget by advocating their particular strategy as contributing to governmental economy. The fiscal viewpoint, therefore, often comes to predominate by default; in a conceptual vacuum the side with the clearest and most consistent position will gain ascendancy.

Whatever the reason, every administration since World War II has at some time held the view that this country could not afford more than a certain sum for military appropriations, overriding the question of whether we could afford to be without an adequate military establishment.

F R O M *Foreign Affairs,* **XXV**, No. 3 (April 1957). Copyright 1957 by The Council on Foreign Relations, Inc., New York. Reprinted by permission of the author.

Now the imposition of a budgetary ceiling is not inevitably pernicious; a removal of all budgetary restrictions would inhibit doctrine even more, because it would lead each service to hoard weapons for every eventuality —as occurred to some extent during the Korean War. And the proliferation of weapons systems unrelated to doctrine will cause strategic decisions —which always involve choices—to be made in the confusion of battle. The difficulty with our present budgetary process is that by giving priority to cost over requirement its subordinates doctrine to technology. Budgetary requests are not formulated in the light of strategic doctrine; rather doctrine is tailored and if necessary invented to fit budgetary requests.

The predominance of fiscal considerations makes for doctrinal rigidity because it causes each service to be afraid that a change in doctrine will lead to a cut in appropriations. This is illustrated by a violent dispute in 1950 between advocates of strategic air power and a group of scientists at the Lincoln Laboratory of the Massachusetts Institute of Technology, who were accused of advocating a cut in our retaliatory force in order to build up air defense. The remarkable thing about this dispute was that the M.I.T. group explicitly denied underrating the importance of strategic air power; they insisted that their recommendations had been solely concerned with building up our air defense. Yet the partisans of strategic air power had psychology, if not logic, on their side. With a fixed ceiling on defense expenditures it was clear that any new appropriation was bound to lead to the reduction of existing forces; a new capability could in practice be developed only at the expense of an existing one.

As a result, budgetary pressures compound the inherent conservatism of the military and end in subordinating doctrine to the battle for appropriations. Each service pushes weapons development in every category without sufficient regard for the program of other services, and each service seeks to obtain control over as many different weapons as possible as a form of insurance against drastic budgetary cuts in the future. The predominance of fiscal considerations in our defense planning actually encourages a subtle form of waste: in the absence of an agreed strategic doctrine, it leads to the proliferation of partially overlapping, partially inconsistent weapons systems. Because to relinquish a weapons system may mean to relinquish the appropriations that go with it, every service has a powerful incentive to hold on to every weapon even after it has outlived its usefulness.

The doctrinal handicap imposed by the predominance of fiscal considerations is not compensated for by an increase in civilian control either within the Executive Branch or by Congress. The difficulty of effective control over military programs is due to two factors: the fiction of the yearly review of programs and their technical complexity. The yearly review is increasingly inconsistent with the realities of defense planning. The hiatus between development and procurement is several years in the case of most weapons; the introduction of a new weapon into a unit implies that all units will be so equipped over a period of time. Thus the first order for B-52s logically carried with it the obligation to continue procurement until all heavy bomber wings of the Strategic Air Command were composed of jet planes. Similarly, the beginning of construction of an aircraft carrier makes almost inescapable future appropriations to complete its construction.

In these circumstances, a yearly review does not bring about effective control; it does ensure, however, that no dispute is ever finally resolved. Each year the same arguments about the efficacy of limited war, airlift and the relative merits of carrier and strategic aviation are repeated, and they are not settled until some technical development outstrips the dispute or an administrative decision allocates rôles and missions which the losing service accepts only because it has every prospect of reopening the issue in the following year. In the absence of doctrinal agreement, inter-service disputes can be resolved only by compromises which may define merely the least unacceptable strategy or by adding to the number of missions and weapons systems.

The technical complexity of most disputes complicates civilian control and particularly Congressional control even further. Within the Department of Defense the multiplication of civilian officials, often in office for only a year or two, causes the Secretaries and Assistant Secretaries to become less agents of control than a device to legitimize inter-service disputes. Their short term in office makes it difficult if not impossible for them to become familiar with the subtleties of the strategic problems. Instead of being able to establish a unified concept, they become spokesmen for the professional staff on whose advice they are dependent.

As for Congressional control, the only forum where the over-all defense program can be considered is in the Appropriations Committee. A meaningful judgment by the Congress on the defense budget would presuppose an assessment of the military strength achieved by a given expenditure and the relationship of this strength to a set of national security objectives. Neither condition is met by current practice. To be sure, the budget is introduced by testimony of the service chiefs and their civilian superiors regarding the gravity of the international situation. But no attempt is made to show the relationship of strategy to events abroad beyond the general implication that the proposed program would ensure the security of the United States. In turn, the Congressional Committees can make their judgments only in terms of a vague assessment of the international situation: they will be hesitant to reduce the budget if they feel the situation too grave and they will be disposed to pare requests drastically when they think the situation is not as serious as represented.

Such Congressional consideration of strategic concepts as does take place is usually produced by the dissatisfaction of some service with its budgetary allocations. Thus the B-36 hearings in 1949 resulted from the cancellation by Secretary Johnson of the Navy's giant carrier and the Symington Committee hearings on air power were the consequence of the budgetary ceiling imposed on the Air Force (and other services too) by Secretary Wilson. This procedure has the disadvantage of emphasizing the problems of one particular service and of obscuring the real difficulties which occur in the area of overlapping strategies. Moreover, even the hearings explicitly addressed to the problems of the rôles and missions of the services tend to be conducted in the familiar technical categories. Thus during the Symington hearings on American air power in 1956, relatively little attention was paid to the strategic concepts of the services; on the whole, the Committee was content to take the services at their own valuations. But a great deal of time was spent on the relative numbers of the Soviet and United States heavy bomber forces and the relative thrust of jet engines. These figures are important, to be sure, but their meaning derives from strategic doctrine. Without a concept of war—or at least of air war—comparative numbers mean little and the relative thrust of jet engines means less. The quest for numbers is a symptom of the abdication of doctrine.

In order to create a favorable climate for their budgetary requests, the services tend to emphasize the most ominous aspects of the United States security problem. Because of their awareness that there exists a greater receptiveness for programs which seem to offer total solutions, each service is encouraged to stress the part of its mission which poses the most absolute sanctions. Thus in 1951 the Army produced the "atomic cannon," a cumbersome, hybrid and already obsolescent weapon, in part to obtain access to the nuclear stockpile. Similarly, after the B-36 hearings, the Navy ceased to oppose the identification of deterrence with maximum retaliatory power; in fact, it adopted the theory as its own and in its budgetary presentations, at least, it has emphasized its contribution to the strategic striking force more than its less dramatic task of anti-submarine warfare. And Congressional hearings leave little doubt that even within the Air Force, the Strategic Air Command has the most prestige value.

Thus the budgetary process places a premium on the weapons systems which fit best with the traditional preconceptions of American strategic thought. It is not that the belief in the importance of strategic striking forces is wrong in itself; indeed, the Strategic Air Command must continue to have the first claim on our defense budget. It is simply that the overemphasis on total solutions reinforces the already powerful tendency against supplementing our retaliatory force with subtler military capabilities that address themselves to the likelier dangers and involve a less destructive strategy. A vicious circle is thereby set up: the more terrible we paint Soviet capabilities, the more we confirm our predilection for an all-out strategy. But the more fearful the consequences of our strategy, the more reluctant will the political leadership be to invoke it. In every crisis, we are obliged to gear our measures to the availability of forces instead of having in advance geared our forces to the most likely danger. And even with respect to the forces which we have available our hesitations are multiplied because the services do not agree among themselves about strategy either for limited or for total war, but particularly for the former.

The Military Instrument and Foreign Policy

Samuel P. Huntington

STRATEGIC PLANNING AND THE POLITICAL PROCESS

For a decade or more statesmen and scholars have been unhappy about American methods of making decisions on strategic programs—that is, decisions on the over-all size of the military effort, the scope and character of military programs (continental defense, anti-submarine warfare), the composition of the military forces (force levels), and the number and nature of their weapons. The most common criticisms have been:

1. National security policy lacks unity and coherence. Decisions are made on an ad hoc basis, unguided by an over-all purpose.
2. National security policies are stated largely in terms of compromises and generalities. The real issues are not brought to the highest level for decision.
3. Delay and slowness characterize the policy-making process.
4. The principal organs of policy-making, particularly the National Security Council, are ineffective vehicles for the development of new ideas and approaches. They tend to routinize the old rather than stimulate the new.
5. Policy-making procedures tend to magnify the obstacles and difficulties facing any proposed course of action.
6. These deficiences are primarily the product of government by committee, especially when the committee members must represent the interests of particular departments and services.

Few persons familiar with the processes by which strategic programs are determined would challenge the general accuracy of these allegations. The

FROM *Foreign Affairs*, **XXXVIII** (January 1960). Copyright 1960 by the Council on Foreign Relations, Inc., New York. Reprinted by permission of the author.

persistence of the criticism since World War II, moreover, suggests that the defects are not incidental phenomena easily remedied by exhortations to high-mindedness, assertions of executive authority, or changes in personnel or Administration. Instead, it suggests the necessity of viewing the defects in the context of the political system of which they are a part, and of analyzing the functions which they serve in that system and the underlying causes which have brought them into existence.

II

In domestic legislation, it is often said, the Exective proposes and Congress disposes. Except when a presidential veto seems likely to be involved, the political processes of arousing support or opposition for bills are directed toward the Congress. In determining strategic programs, on the other hand, the effective power of decision rests not with Congress and its committees but with the President and his advisors.

Congressional incapacity to determine force levels and strategic programs is often attributed to the lack of proper information and technical competence. This is indeed a factor, but it is only a contributory one. Congressmen often tend to consider broad questions of general military policy as technical while at the same time they do not hesitate to probe thoroughly and to render judgments about highly specialized and detailed questions of military administration. The inability of Congress to act effectively on strategic programs derives primarily not from its technical failings but from its political ones.

The initiation and elimination of programs and the apportionment of resources among them are highly political decisions involving conflicting interests and groups. They can be made only by bodies in which all the conflicting interests can be brought in focus. The principal groups concerned with the determination of strategic programs are the armed services, the Office of the Secretary of Defense, the State Department, the Treasury, the Budget Bureau, plus a few other governmental departments. The military programs have to be weighed against each other, against conflicting interpretations of the security threats and military requirements, against domestic needs and non-military foreign policy programs, and against probable tax revenues and the demands of fiscal policy. No congressional committee is competent to do this, not because it lacks the technical knowledge, but because it lacks the legal authority and political capability to bring together all these conflicting interests, balance off one against another, and arrive at some sort of compromise or decision. Congress cannot effectively determine strategic programs because the interests which are primarily concerned with those programs are not adequately represented in any single congressional body. The armed services, appropriations, finance, foreign relations, space and atomic energy committees are all, in one way or another, involved in the process. No one of them can have more than a partial view of the interests involved in the determination of any single major strategic program. Every congressional action in military affairs is to some extent *ex parte.*

Congressional bodies may become advocates of particular programs, but they lack sufficient political competence to determine an over-all program. After World War II, except when confronted by similar competing programs, Congress *never* vetoed directly a major strategic program, a force-level recommendation or a major weapons system proposed by the Administration in power. Nor did Congress ever achieve this result, with one partial exception (the Navy's second nuclear carrier), through the failure to appropriate funds recommended by the Executive. The relative inviolability of the military requests was striking when compared with those for domestic or foreign-aid appropriations. Almost regularly, of course, Congress reduced the *total* military request, but it virtually never did this in a manner which seriously affected a major strategic program. Quite properly, Congressmen generally feel that they are ill-equipped to be responsible for the security of the country, and they have, by and large, recognized and accepted the decisive role of the Executive in formulating strategic programs. "God help the American people," Senator Russell once remarked, "if Congress starts legislating military strategy."

The inability and unwillingness of Congress to choose and decide does not mean that congressional groups play no role in the formulation of strategic programs. On the contrary, with respect to strategy, Congress has, like Bagehot's queen, "the right to be consulted, the right to encourage, the right to warn." The most prominent congressional role is that of prodder or goad of the Executive on behalf of specific programs or activities. With the Executive as the decision-maker, Congress has become the lobbyist. Congressional groups engage in sustained campaigns of pressure and persuasion to produce the desired strategic decisions on the part of the Executive, just as in other areas the Administration uses pressure and persuasion to move its legislation through Congress.

In lobbying with the Executive, Congress employs three major techniques. First, congressional groups may attempt, through letters, speeches, investigations and threats of retaliation in other fields, to bring continuing pressure upon the Administration to construct certain types of weapons. The Joint Committee on Atomic Energy, for instance, has been an active lobby on behalf of nuclear weapons: its members played important roles in prompting executive decisions on the hydrogen bomb, the nuclear powered submarine, the intermediate-range ballistic missiles. On the other hand, no lobby ever scores 100 percent, and the Committee was somewhat less successful with the Polaris speed-up and the nuclear-powered airplane.

Second, congressional groups may establish force-level minimums for their favored services or appropriate more money for the services than the Administration requested. In these cases, Congress attempts to use its ancient powers of authorization and appropriation for the positive purpose of establishing *floors*, whereas these powers were designed originally for the negative purpose of establishing *ceilings* to prevent a tyrannical executive from maintaining military forces without the consent of the people. Such actions undoubtedly influence the Administration in planning future force levels, and in two cases involving the National Guard and the Marine Corps, the Administration formally complied with congressional wishes. In the final analysis, however, no way has yet been evolved of compelling an Administration to maintain forces it does not wish to maintain or to spend money it does not wish to spend.

Third, Congress can bring pressure upon the Executive through investigation and debate. Although it is generally held that Congress' power to investigate rests upon its power to legislate, in actual fact Congress investigates, in the grand manner, matters which it cannot legislate. The activities of Senators McCarthy and Kefauver are obvious examples, but more reputable and worthwhile ones are furnished by the great investigations of strategy: the 1949 inquiry into "Unification and Strategy," the 1951 MacArthur investigation, the 1956 Symington airpower hearings, and the Johnson missile investigation of 1957–1958. None of these directly produced legislation but they did compel the Administration to make a public defense of its policies, enabled Congress to bring pressure to bear on the Executive and helped to educate the attentive public on strategic issues.

Robert A. Lovett

ROLE OF THE MILITARY SERVICES IN GOVERNMENT

A N Y examination of the appropriate role of the military in our Government must conclude, I believe, that the separation of the military and civilian functions is not only well established by custom and implicit in our Constitution itself but also that the subordination of the military to civilian authority is specifically established by the provision of the Constitution which makes the President the Chief Executive and the Commander in Chief of the Armed Forces.

From this separation has grown one of our great national military tradi-

---

F R O M "Memorandum for Special Preparedness Subcommittee of the Senate Committee on Armed Forces," dated January 16, 1962, in *Administration of National Security—Selected Papers* (Washington: GPO, 1962).

tions: that the military should be nonpolitical and that career military officers should stick to their demanding profession and take no part in partisan activities or become involved in discussions of our political issues. This well-established tradition, which has grown more important in this century, should, in my opinion, apply equally to the civilian heads of these departments while in office for many of the same reasons which apply to the military personnel.

But, since World War II, there is a particular and an additional reason for observance of this tradition and it is of great importance. I refer to authorization by the Congress of the continued use of the absentee ballot for military personnel in reliance on the good faith of military and civilian superiors that the votes will not be influenced from Washington or by commanders in the field. I shall later refer to this quasi-trustee relationship in more detail.

One of the great virtues of the removal of our professional military services from partisan politics is that it permits the President and the Senate, representing the country as a whole, to appoint professionally trained officers based solely on judgment as to what the man can do professionally rather than on what he has done politically. As a consequence, in time of war or of great national emergencies, both the Congress and the people have found it possible to trust our military implicitly and to turn to the military services for men who are above party and who, as professional military officers, serve no faction and no special cause and seek no political advantage.

From the days of Cromwell, some of whose officers not only sat in Parliament but also dissolved it when Parliament failed to do their bidding, peoples whose form of government is based on Anglo-Saxon traditions and institutions have wisely insisted on separating the military and civilian arms of government. Although the lines between the military and civilian functions today are increasingly blurred and overlap because of new weapons of appalling destructiveness, the emergence of a new, competitive world power and disappearance of "splendid isolation," it seems important to retain the separation and to recall Professor Santayana's great warning, "Those who cannot remember the past are condemned to repeat it."

Functions of the Military Services in National Policymaking

The primary function of career military officers in national policymaking, apart from their obvious administrative, staff and command responsibilities, is that of advising on military policies and of preparing detailed, strategic plans as part of the complex of specialized advice from which an overall national policy can be evolved. Their activities in their own professional field take place under the direction and control of the civilian head responsible for the Military Establishment and in accordance with instructions from the President. Therefore, when the governmental policy has been decided on, the President is entitled to expect from them more than the mere virtue of minding their own business. He is entitled to receive instant obedience and the loyalty which makes it their duty to avoid any activities which would tend to undermine the policies established by the Government of which the President is the head.

There are appropriate places for debating the merits of a course of action before a decision is reached. Differences in points of view can be vigorously pressed at several levels—sometimes even to the point of causing exasperation. But these debates customarily take place on a confidential basis and differences are not to be aired in public while policy is being hammered out.

As is known, the Constitution places a duty on the Congress "to raise and support" military forces and "to provide for the common defense," thereby imposing an obligation on the military establishments to respond to requests from the appropriate committees of Congress for such information as is necessary to enable the Congress to discharge its constitutional responsibility.

The decisionmaking process was complicated beyond belief in World War II. It was frequently necessary for General Marshall to disagree strongly with courses of action advanced by foreign and domestic military and civilian officials with powerful political backing. These differences in points-of-view were aggravated by the fact that the war was global in character and that our allies were numerous and vocal.

In these trying circumstances, General Marshall had a simple rule which earned him the admiration of his colleagues at home and abroad and the gratitude of his Commander in Chief as well. He felt that it was of cardinal importance that the Chief of Staff state his plans strongly, make his arguments as forcefully and persuasively as possible (but never in the form of "posterity papers") and that, if he was overruled and then felt that he could not loyally and in good conscience carry out the policy, he should resign.

He said, "I think . . . what we suffer at times . . . is the unwillingness of the individual to take issue on a confidential basis with his Commander in Chief. That is pretty hard to get people to do. There is where you state your case and put your own commission, or command, or position in peril . . . ." But, when the policymaking discussions had been completed and the decision had been reached, General Marshall, having had his say, gave and required the most complete loyalty in carrying out the policy which had been established. He said "when the Chief of Staff of the Army sets an example to the whole Army by disloyalty to his Chief and superior, who is the Secretary of the Army, he has just about ruined the Army, in my opinion." He pointed out "you (as a general) preach loyalty all the time. You are dealing with an organization where a man receives an order, from even a captain, which leads to his death or his wound and he has to obey that order. He doesn't debate it. He obeys it and that has to be instinctive. Now, if the example at the top is contrary to that, then you have got a very serious situation."

When entering the armed services, military officers voluntarily forego certain privileges retained by civilians who are not members of a disciplined arm of government, and I cannot see how there can be any reasonable justification for the career officer attempting to influence elections or taking part in political activities, either domestic or foreign. These seem properly to be the sole responsibility of governmental officials of the legislative, executive, or judicial branches, who are specifically chosen by the people and put into office as their representatives. In this connection, it is worth remembering that the military officer holds his commission by selection and not by election.

New Responsibilities of the Military Services

I have mentioned above in earlier paragraphs the conviction that military professionals should be contributors to and not deciders of final national policies and have tried to emphasize that they are trained to carry out such political policy but not expected to originate it.

It is appropriate now to consider certain enlarged responsibilities placed on the military by force of circumstances, including technological advances, vastly improved communications and annihilation of distance, and the emergence of a formidable, aggressive-minded world power to threaten us with premature burial, over which it hopes to preside. All of these matters have a direct and potent effect on the major responsibility of the military in connection with raising, training and putting into the field combat-worthy fighting men.

A new and increasing emphasis is placed on the necessity for proper education and indoctrination of military personnel, both active and reserve, bearing most directly on the performance of troops in the field and on occupational duty. Thus, a heavy and continuing duty is laid upon military officers to discuss with troops under their command not only the use of increasingly complicated weapon systems but also certain forms of psychological warfare, brain washing techniques, etc., and the characteristics, tactics and wholly different philosophy of communism and of our potential enemy. This has become an important part of protection of troops from insidious methods of modern warfare.

Admittedly, the problem is complicated by the fact that there can be questions of judgment as to what is both effective and appropriate in exposing the communist devices—particularly, their use of deceit and perfidy as part of their normal foreign policy. It is hard to do this job of exposure by use of the easily available incidents and at the same time avoid completely the rocks and shoals of comment on political beliefs which may be held by some groups in this country. But I think it can be done. It will probably require the use of carefully worked-out programs, outlining a series of curriculums suitable for all units of the military establishments, and prepared with the approval of the responsible military officers in command of the troops and public officials of the military departments. It does not seem to me to be either necessary or feasible to draw too sharp a line in such cases but, with appropriate forewarning and reasonable guidelines, it would appear possible to set standards which will permit the avoidance of pitfalls.

Troop training and indoctrination is, however, a far simpler subject to deal with than your question of "what is the proper function of the military in public indoctrination in the cold war field. . . ." As a general rule, it seems to me that both the military and civilian personnel of the Department of Defense should hold their public speeches to a minimum and in them deal largely with facts in the area of their direct responsibility. I cannot escape the feeling that, as a government, we tend to talk too much. To be sure, we are an open society but we give the impression of being unbuttoned. Military officers on active duty in particular should, in my opinion, restrict themselves to informing the public on matters for which responsibility is placed on them by the Department of Defense and should, as indicated in earlier paragraphs, exercise care not to express partisan views or take positions contrary to the approved national political policy.

I have mentioned what seems to me to be the necessity for some system of overall review by the responsible top level departmental officials because the military clearly face a considerable problem in walking the thin line between obvious military matters and those having important bearing on the conduct of troops on foreign duty which would appear to involve, to some extent at least, discussion of relations with the foreign country acting as host or under occupation. Correct conduct of our troops, for example, in West Berlin, or West Germany, becomes of the greatest importance if serious incidents arising out of carelessness or ignorance are to be avoided. The troops are, therefore, necessarily forewarned of the customs, habits, and sensitivity of the country involved, as well as the provocations, incitements, and similar traps which the enemy may be expected to spring in order to cause dissension and unrest.

At this point we enter the sensitive area of "review," "clearance," "evaluation," et cetera, which have always been a red rag to a bull. It has usually seemed to me that the rag looked redder to the bulls outside the services than to those in them. If we are not to have four military services going their divergent ways and adding to public confusion concerning our foreign policy or some pending domestic matter, it seems entirely reasonable to me to require some form of higher level clearance applicable to military officers and civilian officials alike. The crux of handling the problem, in my opinion, lies in the quality, proven judgment, and attitude of the individual who must do the reviewing. I believe the checking should be done at the highest and most experienced level available. If the clearance or evaluation is done routinely, or at some relatively low level, or by someone or a group who gives the impression of being unsympathetic, arbitrary, or power-proud, cries of "censorship" will be deafening.

I do not propose to add to the scar tissue I have acquired in former jousts in this field by now venturing to discuss the limits of "free speech" by those in national service. I certainly cannot state them or precisely define them. But most people will admit that some limit must exist. I merely point out now that I believe that, in the military services, duty and loyalty impose one such limit even if self-restraint and good taste did not.

Practical Reasons for Restraint on Certain Subjects

There are at least two reasons, as mentioned earlier in this memorandum, why partisan views on political issues have, in the past, been considered improper subjects for education of troops. The first of these is one mentioned earlier: the fact that the Congress and the Defense Department have continued the use of the absentee ballot by soldiers on active service abroad, relying on and trusting in the traditional attitude of the professional military and particularly of the commanding officers that the services will take no part in partisan politics and will do nothing to influence the vote one way or the other.

Secretary Stimson during World War II, drawing on his knowledge of the Army gained from his tenure of the Secretary of War position under President Taft and his knowledge of foreign policy gained as President Hoover's Secretary of State, said in September 1943, in speaking of the War Department's reaction against political activities of Army officers:

"That policy is founded upon the fundamental concept that it would undermine the sound theories of democracy to permit military personnel to take advantage of their service by appealing for election to civil office, and that it would be plainly incompatible with the effective fighting of the war to allow members of the Armed Forces to divide their energies between military duty and any outside interest, whether political, business, or professional.

.   .   .

"The existence of the prohibition against political activities by military personnel is not new to the Military Establishment. The policy of the War Department for a century and a half has been constantly adverse to the participation by members of the Armed Forces on active duty in political affairs. The present Army regulation is nothing more than a mere collation of the various directives pertaining to this matter.

"The War Department considers the existing policy to be wholly consonant with democratic principles and procedures. Nothing could more directly expose a poiltical system to improper intrusions by the military than to allow military personnel to exercise their civil and military offices contemporaneously. The War Department firmly believes that the present policy is essential to the maintenance of the tradition of the American people that the military and civilian branches of Government remain separated."

The American soldier is allowed freely to read the news columns and editorials in a free press. He is subject to the normal channels of information from his parents, his friends, his neighbors, and the civilian candidates for office soliciting his vote. In these circumstances, there would appear to be little excuse for the military officer to inject himself into partisan discussion on political matters. One of the most dangerous things which can happen to a government is to permit the establishment of a political party line by officers on duty.

The great tradition of the proper role of the career officer is exemplified in the conduct and record of Pershing, Marshall, Eisenhower, Bradley and, indeed, most of the great leaders of World War I and II, who took the view that the military should speak publicly only on military matters and that they should leave the public statement of foreign policy and national policy to the elected head of the State. Any other course, they believed, brought divided counsels and weakened the authority both of the Chief Executive and the military commanders.

A second practical and fundamental reason for avoiding any form of electioneering or partisan political discussion by the military on active duty is the invitation such acts would extend to politicians to enter the control of, say, the Army. If certain generals are identified with one party or one faction, each new administration will have to seek men who will execute its particular policy. It is difficult to imagine a more dangerous situation for the military or the country. If you have doubts on this, look at unhappy France.

Civil-Military Relations

Your request that I comment on any general impressions that I may have as to "Civil-Military Relations" is a very difficult one since I have been remote from specific problems in this field for some time. I will, therefore, with your permission limit my reply to comments on an evolutionary development apparent from newspaper accounts and possible problems arising from it.

One predictable result of the extraordinary scientific breakthroughs translated into military uses by new technologies and the simultaneous emergence of a new and aggressive world power, one of whose goals is our destruction, is the increasing intermingling of military and civilian personnel and the blurring of lines between civil and military activities. A group of many skills is now needed in most of our national security activities and the difference in organization, wages, discipline, et cetera, inevitably cause some irritation. It has existed in the past where the military felt that civilian agencies were poaching on their preserves. We have seen this in the missile field a little while ago. But I think that such disputes over who does what are a common occupational disease in government and becomes more virulent at budget time. They are certainly not, in my opinion, evidence of anything sinister. This civil-military intermingling could, in fact, be very helpful to each if they can succeed in exchanging something other than their bad habits.

Official and personal relations between the military and civilians—looked at from the outside—seem good, judging by the moderate number of times one reads that tired old story about "restoring civilian control." Alarmist cries about the lack of civilian control over the military, in our Nation, deal with a strawman issue. They are concerned with a problem that does not really exist, and they are divisive and damaging by falsely implying that the military does not accept our historic tradition of civilian supremacy. Nothing could be more wrong. I have been with the military in three wars and have worked with them in other governmental capacities and I have never heard any military commander raise the slightest question at any time as to their subordination to civilian control. The only real occasion when civilian control is in doubt is when the civilian officials themselves fail to exercise it, or neglect to use the powers legally vested in them. In my opinion, there will be no such problem under the competent direction and control by the unusually able present Secretary and Deputy Secretary of Defense.

As a final observation, I must say that after many years of direct experience with the military services in a variety of capacities, I have the greatest admiration for our dedicated and skilled career officers and I know of no country more fortunate than we in having military services with the traditions and loyalties that ours possess. I have seen our career officers in competition with those of other countries in the ultimate arenas of war, as administrators of conquered or occupied countries, and as participants in the councils of peace and I have been proud to have them compared with the men of any other country in the world.

Gene M. Lyons
THE NEW CIVIL-MILITARY RELATIONS

HISTORICALLY the character of civil-military relations in the United States has been dominated by the concept of civilian control of the military. This has largely been a response to the fear of praetorianism. As recently as 1949, for example, the first Hoover Commission asserted that one of the major reasons for strengthening the "means of exercising civilian control" over the defense establishment was to "safeguard our democratic traditions against militarism." [1] This same warning was raised in the report of the Rockefeller Committee on defense organization in 1953. While the overriding purpose of the committee's recommendations was to provide "the Nation with maximum security at minimum cost," the report made it clear that this had to be achieved "without danger to our free institutions, based on the fundamental principle of civilian control of the Military Establishment." [2] Finally, during the debate on the reorganization proposals of 1958, senators and congressmen used the theme of a "Prussianized" military staff to attempt to slow down the trend towards centralization in the military establishment.[3]

Despite this imposing support, the concept of civilian control of the military has little significance for contemporary problems of national security in the United States. In the first place, military leaders are divided among themselves, although their differences cannot be reduced to a crass contrast between dichomatic doctrines. Air Force leaders who are gravely concerned over the need to maintain a decisive nuclear retaliatory force are by now acknowledging the need to develop a limited war capability. At the same time, Army leaders are quite frank to admit that "flexible response" requires both strategic and tactical power of sizable strength, although they are particularly committed to developing a large tactical force. If these differences appear to be only differences in emphasis, they are nonetheless crucial in a political process within which priorities must be established

---

[1] Commission on Organization of the Executive Branch of the Government, *The National Security Organization*, A Report to the Congress, February 1949, pp. 2–3.
[2] *Report of the Rockefeller Committee on Department of Defense Organization*, Committee Print, Senate Committee on Armed Services, 83d Cong., 1st sess. 1953, p. 1.
[3] See, e.g., Rept. No. 1765, *Department of Defense Reorganization Act of 1958*, House Committee on Armed Services, 85th Cong., 2d sess., esp. pp. 24–33.

FROM *The American Political Science Review*, LV, 1 (March 1961). Reprinted by permission of the author and The American Political Science Association.

and choices must be made. Without firm agreement on priorities, there is little reason to expect that the military can control government policy even if civilian authorities abdicate responsibility for basic decisions. The most that can result is a compromise between different military positions. Commonly, military disagreement, if exposed, is an invitation for civilian intervention.

Secondly, the concept of civilian control of the military ignores two other factors that complicate civil-military relations. On the one hand, the military themselves accept the principle of civilian supremacy; on the other, they have been thrown into a political role in the formation of policy. The resignation of General Gavin over the budgetary restrictions of the "New Look" strategy is a case in point. The General disagreed with the judgment of his civilian superiors but, like General Ridgway before him and General Taylor after him, held his most violent fire until he was out of uniform and freed from the limits of professional restrictions.[4] His case dramatically illustrates the dilemma of the military as they move into the center of defense policy-making. Here they have to struggle between the non-partisan tenets of their creed and the requirements of effective participation in the political process. Their advice as experts is not only used by the Executive to bolster its case, but is eagerly courted by Congress and the public as a basis for testing the caliber of executive action. In one respect the political role of the military tends to dilute their own professionalism. But in another, it affords them more than one opportunity to maintain a balance between their professional code and the individual conscience. The nature of the American political system thus provides an outlet for frustration which, in other settings, has been the catalyst to set off an outburst of militarism.

In its broadest sense, the concept of civilian control of the military means military responsiveness to the policies of politically responsible government. But this too needs to be reinterpreted in the light of revolutionary changes that have greatly complicated the formation of defense policy. Preparedness is as much the product of civilian expertise in science and engineering and of civilian decisions on the allocation of national resources as it is of military planning. At the same time, it is very often the military who put defense policy to the test of political accountability by exposing the bases for decisions to congressional and public inquiry. As a result, there is a constant reversal of traditional roles, a situation that has brought civilians and military into a new set of relationships. These relationships have been reflected only in a limited way in recent organizational changes that have strengthened the central agencies of the defense establishment. To appreciate their

---

[4] The views of all three Generals have been documented in books they published shortly after they retired: James M. Gavin, *War and Peace in the Space Age* (New York, 1958), Matthew Ridgway, *Soldier* (New York, 1956); and Maxwell D. Taylor, *The Uncertain Trumpet* (New York, 1959).

full significance, it is also necessary to understand changes in the character of both civilian and military leadership in defense affairs. Civilians are becoming "militarized" and the military "civilianized" and it is these changes that reflect more clearly than organization alone, a fundamental break with tradition in the evolution of civil-military relations.[5]

The Evolution of Defense Organization

Like many institutions in American political life, a highly centralized, civilian-dominated Pentagon has developed in response to changing forces and conditions. Had the Joint Chiefs of Staff been able to function as a collegial unit rather than as a divided group of service representatives, it is possible that reorganization trends might have taken different directions. Centralization, however, was probably inevitable in one form or another. Increasing defense costs made centralized budgeting and programming a necessity. The bite of military expenditures in the total federal budget makes it impossible to ignore the impact of defense on the national economy, the government's tax program and the whole range of complex problems of resources allocation. The impact of technology has also been a centralizing factor. Indeed, work on the military applications of atomic energy had already been centralized in the Atomic Energy Commission. But work on missiles had been left in the separate services and the duplication of effort in three competitive programs brought on demands for greater coordination in propulsion programs in the late 1950's. Finally, both these areas of financial management and of research and development require skills that are "civilian," in essence, and are not yet possessed by many high ranking military officers. Thus it might be argued that "civilianization," as well as centralization, was inevitable given the nature of the problems that needed to be solved.

The growth of central civilian authority has nevertheless come in stages. The first Secretary of Defense, James Forrestal, had been opposed to the development of a large central staff even after he had come around to accept the concept of an overall defense chief. As a former Navy Secretary he was committed to the retention of strong civilian leadership in the individual services, first, to avoid a situation that might lead to the domination of a single strategic doctrine and, second, to keep civilian authority lodged at the operating levels of the military departments. He insisted that the Secretary "must be free to concentrate his efforts on the establishment of broad policy" and in so doing "must look to the secretaries of the military departments for the information and data upon which his policy is to be based

[5] For a theoretical statement of the concept of civilian control of the military, together with references to other major analyses of the subject, see Samuel P. Huntington, "Civilian Control of the Military: a Theoretical Statement," in Eulau, Eldersveld and Janowitz (ed.), *Political Behavior* (Glencoe, Ill., 1956), pp. 380ff.

and then look again to them for the execution of these policies." [6] Within these guidelines, he was reported to want only a "a very small executive force for the single Secretary to consist of [a total of] 15 to 25 '$10,000-a-year men' and officers." [7]

The National Security Act of 1947, highly influenced by Forrestal's views, thus created a federation of military departments with little authority in the office of the Secretary of National Defense. In little more than a year, however, Forrestal himself recommended a number of statutory changes that mark the second step in the strengthening of centralized civilian authority. The critical problem he had faced was the absence of any military consensus upon which to develop strategic programs. He therefore sought to develop independent staff at the Defense Department level, including an Undersecretary of Defense, a Chairman for the Joint Chiefs of Staff and a larger Joint Staff. He also called for greatly clarified responsibility over the military departments to enable the Secretary to settle controversies over the roles and missions of the separate services and the allocation of budgtary resources.[8]

Forrestal's recommendations, largely reinforced by the report of the first Hoover Commission a year later, were the basis for the National Security Act Amendments of 1949 which created a Department of Defense where only a coordinating mechanism had hitherto existed. The Secretary, however strengthened his position became, was nonetheless still forbidden, by law, to encroach upon the "combatant functions assigned to the military services." Congress deliberately used this basic prohibition to maintain the essential identity of the individual services, a tactic that has been retained in subsequent major reorganizations in 1953 and 1958. Nevertheless, this restriction has become less limiting on the authority of the Secretary of Defense as major strategic decisions have turned on problems of weapons development and financial management rather than directly on the controversy over roles and missions.

The reorganization plan of 1953 went another step in centralizing authority in the civilian leadership by creating assistant secretaries of defense with responsibilities in functional areas, such as supply and logistics, and manpower and personnel. These posts were established with the understanding that "they should not be in the direct line of administrative

---

[6] See his letter to Chairman Chan Gurney of the Senate Armed Services Committee, reprinted in that Committee's Hearings, 80th Cong., 1st sess., *National Defense Establishment*, Pt. 1, p. 185. More generally, see Paul Y. Hammond, "The National Security Council as a Device for Interdepartmental Coordination," this REVIEW, Vol. 54 (Dec. 1960), pp. 899–910, and his forthcoming book, *Organizing for Defense* (Princeton University Press, 1961).

[7] Testimony of Admiral Sherman, *ibid.*, p. 155.

[8] *First Report of the Secretary of Defense*, National Defense Eestablishment, 1948, pp. 2–4.

authority between [the Secretary] and the three military departments, but instead should assist in developing policies, prescribing standards, and bringing to the Secretary of Defense information on which he may base his decisions." [9] Under these terms, the authority of the assistant secretaries was ambiguous. Administration witnesses were always cautious to assure congressional committees that the assistant secretaries of defense had no operating authority and were exclusively advisory to the Secretary. While this was theoretically so, actual practice was often to the contrary since they were frequently in a strong position to recommend that service positions be over-ruled.[10] And the authority of the Secretary of Defense to delegate powers to his assistant secretaries was confirmed under the 1958 Act, apparently clearing away the ambiguity.

The growth of centralized civilian authority has thus been related to the decline in the authority of the service secretaries. Forrestal himself had found at an early stage that the service secretaries could not administer the individual departments and still act as his deputies in the formation and execution of overall policy. As service heads they were obliged to support major positions developed by their military chiefs or risk losing the main leverage they had to be effective in their jobs. The policy process is largely a process of bargaining and persuasion. Without the confidence of the military leaders, a civilian secretary cannot hope to persuade them to alter their views. At the same time, he has little chance to gain their confidence unless he largely supports the positions they have developed. He thus plays a dual role, representing the Defense Department at the Service level and the military department at the Defense level. Under the pressures of inter-service competition for limited resources and the development of a large secretariat in the Department of Defense, the service secretary has become more and more a spokesman for his service's position and less and less a positive instrument in the formation of policy by the Secretary of Defense.

But by far the greatest part of the increase of authority gained by the civilian leadership in the Defense Department has accrued because of the inability of the Joint Chiefs of Staff to come to agreed positions on the military requirements of national security. The far-reaching provisions of the 1958 Act were largely in direct response to the wide range of problems raised by service disagreement. Under the Act, the Secretary of Defense can exercise direct authority over unified commands, transfer weapons systems from one service to another and maintain centralized direction of all military research and development through the Director of Research and Engi-

---

[9] *Report of the Rockefeller Committee on Department of Defense Organization, op. cit.*, p. 11.

[10] See, for example, the dialogue between Senator Symington and the Assistant Secretary of Defense (Logistics and Supply) in Hearings, Senate Committee on Armed Services, 85th Cong., 1st sess., *Nominations*, pp. 12–14.

neering. The practical impact of these powers is to give the Secretary considerable influence over the roles and missions of the services which are still prescribed by law within the broad and flexible categories of land, air, and sea forces. The concept of unified commands and the sweeping authority over weapons development now enable the Secretary to bring about *de facto* unification of the armed services even within the framework of a three-departmental system.[11] But to accomplish this, he has a total civilian staff of almost 2,000—a far cry from the "15 to 25 '$10,000-a-year men' and officers" that Forrestal had wanted less than 15 years ago.[12] . . .

The Changing Character of Military Leadership

The significance of the professionalization of civilian leadership cannot be judged without some consideration of the changing character of military leadership. When General Maxwell Taylor retired in mid-1959, a veteran Washington reporter commented that this marked "the point at which the Old Army is drawing to the end of its mission—and even of its relevance." He called Taylor "the last great captain of the old hunters . . ." and his successor, General Lyman Lemnitzer, "an intellectual, a staff officer of vast experience, a kind of professor of the new kind of war." [13] The contrast is perhaps over-drawn, for it is difficult to think of the military— without its "heroic leaders," left to the impersonal calculations of the

[11] Almost two years after the passage of the Reorganization Act of 1958, the *Army, Navy, Air Force Journal* (May 28, 1960) summed up some of the ways Secretary of Defense Gates "is using the full powers of his office . . . to achieve increased unification within the terms of existing legislation." These included centralization of missile test ranges, centralization of toxicological research, and establishment of an All-Service Defense Communications Agency. In addition, early in 1960, Secretary Gates sent a memorandum to the Chairman of the JCS, stating: "It is requested that I be promptly informed regarding any issue on which a difference of opinion is developing within the Joint Chiefs of Staff. I intend that either the Secretary of Defense and/or the Deputy Secretary of Defense will promptly meet with the Joint Chiefs at such times as they consider the issue in question . . ." (reprinted in *Army, Navy, Air Force Journal*, January 16, 1960).

[12] This contrast has risen to plague subsequent Secretaries of Defense. Secretary McElroy facing questions on it during the reorganization hearings in 1958, offered the following. "I have heard others report to me about the expressions by Jim Forrestal about getting along with 100 people, and that kind of thing. I have also heard that after he got into the job, he found that he needed a great many more. The history is nothing that I am prepared to support because I don't know precisely what did go on there. But I honestly—while I agree with you fully that numbers are not a measure of the importance or efficiency of an organization, I mean large numbers, I wouldn't know how anybody could operate a department of this size and complexity with 100 people." Hearings, House Committee on Armed Services, 85th Cong., 2d sess., *Reorganization of the Department of Defense*, p. 6072.

[13] William S. White, "The End of the Old Army," *Harper's* (June 1959), pp. 82–85. The contrast might have been more apt had Lemnitzer been compared with General Ridgway who was wholly a soldier's soldier while Taylor has certain professorial features of his own.

"military managers." [14] It nevertheless catches the essence of a fundamental change in the character of military leadership.

Military leadership is changing under the impact of two forces: the revolutionary developments in weapons technology; and the close relationship between military programs and foreign and economic policies. The management of a missile program or a test range, the constabulary duties of an overseas assignment, the pseudo-diplomatic function of a military assistance advisory group, the planning involved in a Pentagon or a NATO slot—these are the tasks for which the military must prepare the officers of the future. At the same time, the threat of war, total, nuclear, limited or conventional, and the demands that open hostilities make on military leadership, are ever present. Thus the old attributes of "heroic leaders," the qualities of discipline, courage and command ability, cannot be forgotten. In this respect, the new responsibilities of military leaders have not so much altered their fundamental make-up as they have added new dimensions to their character and made them more complex human beings. This new complexity is being reflected in a number of changes in the military profession. Three of these are particularly important: the broadening base for officer recruitment; the development of higher military education; and new policies for selection and promotion to higher rank.

To a large extent, the broadening base for officer recruitment is a matter of arithmetic. In recent years the services have had to draw in more than 40,000 new officers every year, with a good percentage of these needed on a career basis. At the same time, the service academies graduate only about 1,500 new lieutenants and ensigns. As a result, the services have had to look to other sources for career officers, particularly civilian colleges and universities. This development has more than quantitative significance, however. It is also qualitative. The broadening recruitment base for young officers is bringing into the services men with new outlooks and new areas of technical competence that serve to meet the widening range of military responsibilities.[15]

The elaborate structure of higher military education is also responding to the broadening character of military responsibility. Curriculum changes in undergraduate programs at the service academies and in military programs in civilian colleges and universities are moving in two directions: first, they are incorporating new material to expose the students to the expanding technology that is making such an impact on military life; and, second, undergraduate courses are becoming less vocationalized and are taking the form of preprofessional education to lay a solid intellectual base

---

[14] The terms in quotations are borrowed (as is much that follows) from Morris Janowitz, *The Professional Soldier* (Glencoe, Ill., 1960).

[15] Gene M. Lyons and John W. Masland, *Education and Military Leadership* (Princeton, 1959), esp. Ch. I.

for future career development.[16] At the post-commissioning schools—from the command and staff colleges through the service war colleges to the Industrial College of the Armed Forces and the National War College— there is an increased emphasis on the problems of international politics, the dilemmas of war and peace brought on by nuclear weapons, the impact of defense on the national economy and the complexities of life in a world of allies, international organizations and uncommitted nations. There are still weaknesses in military education: there is a tendency to be highly technical and vocational, even in dealing with social science material; service-organized programs also tend to be parochial, emphasizing the narrow views of the service itself; and the image of the world scene that is projected in military teaching is static and over-simplified. The advancements in the last fifteen years have nevertheless been striking and have taken military education far beyond the traditional emphasis on "loyalty, precedent, specific technical skill, and a gentlemanly code of conduct." [17]

Traditions, however, die hard. In the transition from one generation of military leaders to another, the qualities of the "heroic leader" continue to have primary importance and significance for those older officers who grew up in the "old Army," in the "black-shoe Navy" or even in the "propeller-driven Air Force." These are the officers, moreover, who control the machinery for selection and promotion. Here the struggle between the old and the new takes place. While assignments to the war colleges and long tours of duty in technical posts seem to be good preparation for the new roles military men are undertaking, they are not always the best routes to higher rank. Loyalty, length of service and the number of tours on sea and command duty are very often the qualifications that members of a military selection board look for. A few years ago, the Secretary of the Navy, in an attempt to break down these traditional barriers to advancement, instructed the selection board to accelerate the promotions of officers who were "head and shoulders" above their colleagues. The reverberations of these orders are still shaking the Navy's high command.[18] Accelerating promotion means advancing officers in grade because of "potential" rather than actual performance. It thus involves an exercise of judgment about human behavior, as well as future military requirements, that is, at best, difficult to make. It is more difficult during a transition period when the old consensus on military qualities is breaking down and a new concept of military leadership is evolving.

16 *Ibid.*, Chs. VI and VII.

17 John W. Masland and Laurence I. Radway, *Soldiers and Scholars* (Princeton, 1957), p. 5. This work is a study of the response of military education to the widening policy role of military leadership.

18 See Vice Admiral L. S. Sabin, "Deep Selections," United States Naval Institute *Proceedings*, 86 (March 1960), pp. 46 ff; also the large number of comments on Admiral Sabin's article in the June 1960 issue of the *Proceedings* (86, No. 6), especially Admiral Carney's letter, pp. 104–106.

More recently, the Secretary of Defense, in December 1959, issued a directive that "all officers . . . will serve a normal tour of duty with a Joint, Combined, Allied or OSD [Office of Secretary of Defense] Staff before being considered qualified for promotion to general or flag officer rank." Significantly, the directive makes an exception of Army and Air Force officers "whose proposed advancement and qualifications for promotion are based primarily upon their scientific and technical achievement and proposed utilization in that specialty." [19] This emphasis on planning and technical experience and the de-emphasis on parochial views were also underscored in the instructions of the Secretary of the Navy to the Flag Selection Board in 1960. Acknowledging the traditional concern for "a thorough seagoing background in the Line of the Navy," the Secretary brought the Board's attention to the need for "high performance on the planning level and a keen discernment of future operational requirements." He then went on, at some length, to explain that "the explosive technology of our modern weapons systems requires a high degree of concentration and knowledge in particular areas and precludes, to a great degree, the rapid rotation from job to job of many of our most outstanding officers for the purpose of qualifying them in all phases of naval warfare in the pattern of the past." [20]

Both these actions reflect the concern of civilian leaders with the new dimensions of military leadership. Nevertheless, however "civilianized" military officers may become, the profession itself will continue to be anchored in the distinct nature of its trade, the process that has so succinctly and meaningfully been called the "management of violence" by Harold Lasswell. And, in the fulfillment of their mission, the military will continue to be highly influenced by the particular tools of their craft. Indeed, without this distinction what is the meaning of the military profession as a separate group in society? And what do military leaders have to offer that physicists, engineers, diplomats and economists cannot do to meet the requirements of national security? The answer, obviously, is nothing. At the same time, within the framework of its primary and unique contribution, the military profession is dramatically changing. At the moment, it is in a state of transition from the old to the new with the dimensions of the new still unformed, still taking shape, still resembling the contours of an earlier day.

[19] Department of Defense Directive 1320.5, reprinted in *Army, Navy, Air Force Journal*, December 19, 1959. For a summary of the reaction of the services to this directive, see the article (p. 1) entitled "Pentagon Orders New Barriers to General and Flag Ranks," in the same issue.

[20] Dispatch from Secretary of the Navy William B. Franke to Admiral Herbert G. Hopwood, President of the Flag Selection Board, reprinted in the *Army, Navy, Air Force Journal*, July 16, 1960.

Toward a New Concept of Civil-Military Relations

The nature of civil-military relations is thus being changed through the strengthening of central organization in the Department of Defense, through the professionalization of civilian leadership and through the broadening character of the military profession. These trends might also be expressed as the "militarization" of civilians and the "civilianization" of the military. When extended to their logical conclusion, they suggest new relationships between civilians and military based on a more complex division of labor than has heretofore existed. These relationships, however, are responsive to the new shape of national security in which military affairs are no longer a monopoly of the military and a clean-cut division between matters of war and peace, between foreign and military policies, is a false and misleading notion.

It is nevertheless as essential as ever that defense planning be attuned to the broader perspectives of national policy. This is a problem which can no longer be met through civilian control of the military, however. We need to be concerned with the whole complex of professional direction in defense planning and the dilemma of relating the problems of security to the goals and values of national policy. In this task there are limits to what organizational techniques can accomplish. The spectrum is too broad. There is also the danger of accepting institutional devices as a solution without pressing forward along other lines as well. These include arousing enthusiasm for public service in the leading professions in our society, developing a sense of the stakes involved in national security among the general public, encouraging the study of foreign and military policy in educational programs, strengthening the civil service, urging new re-cruitment and educational standards for military careers and continuing innovation in government administration. In this context the purpose of organization is not so much to control as it is to create the machinery through which to bring the full force of our intellectual resources to bear on the complex issues we have to meet.

Jerry Greene
CIVILIAN ON HORSEBACK?

THE explosive uproar over the TFX fighter plane contract was, in final analysis, an angry and noisy reflection of Congressional indigestion resulting

F R O M *Army* (July 1963). Reprinted by permission.

from having to swallow what the Congress itself had cooked. After more than 15 years of struggle, trial and error costing billions in waste, the Congress was finding that it was possible to manage the unified armed services and to some of the legislators, the dish was far from tasty.

In 1958 they had put the stamp of approval for a strong, centralized civilian control of the military by passing the Defense Reorganization Act. This was the last action in a series of steps taken over the years. The approach had been gingerly because of fears of the General on Horseback. Now a potent segment of the Congress was sounding alarms, contending that a civilian named Robert S. McNamara had mounted the horse from the offside while they had their eyes on the near.

Hints of discontent over President Kennedy's Secretary of Defense had been seeping from congressional committee rooms long before Senator John McClellan and his Permanent Investigations subcommittee tore into the TFX complexities—and personalities.

Chairman Carl Vinson (D-Ga.) of the House Armed Services Committee, where the issue of secretarial power was raised during the annual military posture hearings, told protesting colleagues: "The Congress in creating the Department of Defense set up the guidelines of its operations. And we deliberately said the Secretary of Defense should have the right to make decisions, giving him the authority, direction and control of the Department of Defense in that area.

"If you read this record, it shows the Secretary of Defense has lived up to his responsibilities and has made his decisions. . . . I don't know whether we should have given that authority. But as long as you give it and he has the authority, why you give something to him to prove whether his judgment is right, and time will determine that. . . ."

The mellowed Vinson observations did not preclude the venerable chairman from leading his group to add several hundred millions of dollars, unwanted by the administration, to the military authorization bill for more nuclear attack submarines and for two more RS-70 bombers, which he knew would not be built.

Nor did his view serve in the slightest to deter the McClellan subcommittee from plunging into a semipublic probe which raised hackles and blood pressure to an extent not seen in the capital since the McCarthy-Army hearings a decade past. The TFX inquiry could have been a mild and routine political accommodation. It got out of hand, awkwardly, and turned into a test of strength, a challenge of McNamara's judgment, and his stewardship of national security. Among other things it made the nation conscious of the fact that many leaders in uniform were unhappy over the growing centralization of authority in the Office of the Secretary of Defense.

Because of the spectacular name-calling which cropped out during the investigation, not too much attention was paid to the really grave fact that the subcommittee was hearing challenges of the Secretary's judgment and centralization of authority. Both the Air Force and Navy witnesses were able to get across the idea that McNamara was wrong.

The whole investigation turned into a somewhat bitter demonstration of the very factors which led Congress toward and into the controversial area of service unification after World War II.

Efforts of civilian leaders to obtain agreement among the military men of the Army, Navy and Air Force as to which systems and techniques might be needed for maintenance of peace or the prosecution of another war, how and where a war might be fought, who would do what, have been marked with trouble since the end of the last one. The efforts, with sincere military men both supporting and opposing, led to passage of the National Defense Act of 1947. This "unification" measure created the separate Air Force and the Defense Department.

Two years later, Congress stripped the service secretaries of cabinet rank and strengthened the hand of the Secretary of Defense. The bickering continued. Partisan maneuvers to oversell one role, one technique, to gain a bigger piece of the defense dollar, bred more confusion, uncertainty and waste. In one three-year period, the Pentagon cancelled more than $3 billion in "absolutely essential" defense projects—an aircraft, a missle, a revolutionary type engine, an exotic fuel development.

Congress Opens the Door

An unhappy Congress, mindful of this continuing state of affairs, decided in a series of amendments to the Defense Act in 1958, to put the responsibility for orderliness in national security affairs squarely upon one man, a Secretary of Defense who would be responsible only to the President.

That action opened the current phase of the struggle to find a suitable system of military security in this swift new age of space, missiles and the incomprehensible destructive power of nuclear weapons systems.

Former Defense Secretary Thomas S. Gates began the obviously ordained shakeup at the Pentagon. He created a single Defense Communications Agency and began moves for further consolidations of common activities. He said his greatest achievement—and it took him a year—was creation of a Joint Strategic Targeting Committee which for the first time really fused war plans of the three services on the strategic level.

When President Kennedy plucked McNamara from the presidency of the Ford Motor Company to become, at 44, Secretary of Defense, he passed along a simple directive: Provide the U. S. with the armed forces necessary for national security, and do the job at the lowest possible cost. There was no ceiling on either requirement.

McNamara Walks In

McNamara felt there weren't many problems around that hard management measures couldn't improve, if not solve. Other successful executives had preceded him, seven of them in 14 years, but there was a difference. He was young and he planned to stay.

There are a few other factors involved in what has happened, and will continue to happen, that have not received proper consideration, certainly by McNamara's opponents and perhaps by the general public. For the first time since the death of the late FDR, the nation has a President who has a deep personal interest in Pentagon details and operations. For the first time ever, the Joint Chiefs of Staff have a chairman in General Maxwell D. Taylor who has been a confidant and personal military adviser to the President in the White House, and who has a firm and intimate working relationship with the Secretary of Defense.

This makes for effectiveness of centralization, it might be said.

Mr. Kennedy had made an issue of national defense during the 1960 campaign. It was good, he said, but it ought to be much better and certainly this attitude foretold a change of policy, beyond purely management. He had grown weary of the old John Foster Dulles theory of massive retaliation, a theory which had been misinterpreted in the first place and outmoded from the day Russia got The Bomb, and he was intrigued with the ideas of Taylor about maintenance of balanced forces with a little less total reliance on a nuclear offensive. Taylor had retired as chief of staff of the Army after failing to sell his ideas either to the JCS or the Congress during the mid-1950's.

Thus McNamara had a dual task: To implement a policy switch and to install a system to manage it.

"The basic policy that we have established is a policy that shifts from a a reliance on massive retaliation to the option response," McNamara told the House Armed Services Committee this spring.

"It is a shift, however, that requires a complete rebalancing of the military forces of this nation, and it is not something, therefore, that could simply be turned over to the Services for them to decide unilaterally how they should proceed.

"We must insure that the Army is balanced to the Air Force, that the Navy is balanced to the requirements of the Army, that the financial budget is balanced to the military force structure required as a foundation for our foreign policy."

Beef-up of the Army

So far as policy change was concerned, this wasn't as great an operation as might be contended, this balancing of the forces. To achieve the aims, what was required principally was a beefing up of the Army, a wholesale modernization.

Such improvements were urged fervently in a Rockefeller Brothers Fund study in 1957–58. Former President Eisenhower had demonstrated emphatically that less than massive retaliation was the order of the day when he sent troops into Lebanon; ground forces held lines in Europe and Korea.

What was required was much more money, and management which would insure application of the funds in the proper places. This, McNamara held, called for installation of a system. The feeling was that time permitted no evolution, there must be revolution under the authority granted the Secretary by Congress in 1958. Even today, as McNamara told the House Armed Services Committee, he considers the Pentagon in a state of transition from the old to the new way of doing things. During this transition period, until he can build "a decision pyramid and a system of administration in which all possible decisions are pushed to the bottom of that pyramid" the basic decisions must be made at the top. Once the pyramid is built, the system working, he told Congress, any competent executive can run the show, and much of the responsibility, most of the decisions can be returned to JCS and the Services.

"I don't believe we will be passing through such a period of transition continuously or permanently," McNamara told the Committee.

Cost Effectiveness Appears

The creed of the new regime can be found in a document written long after it was chalked up as a determined Pentagon guideline. It took only two sentences:

"In order to achieve the greatest overall military effectiveness from the large but not unlimited resources available for defense purposes, each activity within the Department of Defense must provide a benefit justified by its cost. This requires that a methodical examination be made of alternative ways of accomplishing desirable military missions in order to select those weapons and forces which provide the greatest return for the defense dollar."

McNamara handpicked the civilian team he wanted to help in the tasks ahead, working from a card file made up from a list of recommendations and applications.

McNamara had never met any of his top aides before he hired them except Secretary of Air Eugene Zuckert.

Much nonsense has been spread across the country about McNamara's "Whiz Kids" and their supposed free wheeling activities, much of them presumably devoted to overriding military men in decisions on military matters.

The four most powerful men in the Pentagon, after McNamara, on the civilian side, are Roswell Gilpatric, 56-year-old New York lawyer; Dr. Charles Hitch, 53, an economist; Paul Nitze, 56, a New York investment banker; and Dr. Harold Brown, 35, a nuclear physicist.

Gilpatric, as Deputy Secretary, has been McNamara's alter ego and has shared with the Secretary the job of making 500 to 600 final decisions on issues of sufficient importance to reach the top level. (On the big, critical issues, such as the RS-70 bomber, McNamara has carried a recommendation to the White House where the President himself has made the final judgment.)

Gilpatric ("I don't consider myself a whiz and I'm certainly no kid") was no stranger to national security. He had served as Assistant Secretary, then Under Secretary of the Air Force in 1951–53; he had played a major part in drafting the Rockefeller Studies Project Report on National Security in 1956–57. This was the survey which urged great increase in defense expenditures, with many structural changes within the department. Not unsurprisingly, most of the recommendations were adopted in the first two years of the McNamara-Gilpatric regime.

Nitze had long government service as a State Department planner. As Assistant Secretary for International Affairs, he has directed the mutual aid programs and has served as the principal link between the Defense and State Departments.

Dr. Brown, a controversial character whose age and self-assurance have drawn fire in Congress and, in largely muttered form, from older professional military men in the Pentagon, is a closer than first generation descendant of the fathers of the atomic bomb. He has been closely associated with the Department since 1956 and with nuclear research since 1950. He had been director of the Lawrence Radiation Laboratory at Livermore, Calif. and had served the Air Force, the Navy and the Secretary of Defense as a scientific adviser. Brown is Director of Defense Research and Engineering.

The New Breed Moves In

There aren't very many elderly atomic scientists.

Dr. Hitch, Assistant Secretary of Defense (Comptroller), is high priest of the New Order. He represents the acceptance, formally, of the civilian economist as a military strategist, a new breed of cats developed to fill a planning vacuum growing from the maturity of strategic bombardment concepts and production of nuclear weapons.

Hitch, as an analyzing economist, had been studying war, and the insides of the Defense Department since 1948. A native of Boonville, Mo., graduate of the University of Arizona, who became a Rhodes Scholar after a year at Harvard, Hitch served on Averell Harriman's first lend-lease mission in London in 1941–42, moved to the War Production Board, thence into the Army for an assignment with the Office of Strategic Services. He was discharged a first lieutenant in 1945 to become chief of the stabilization controls division of the Office of War Mobilization and Reconversion.

Hitch went to the Rand Corporation in 1948. A non-profit brain trust, Rand was formed to do research for the Department of Defense, principally the Air Force, the Atomic Energy Commission and now the National Space Agency. The researchers deal in a wide range of classified projects.

It was in this area, through Rand and several similar non-profit organizations formed to make available to the Pentagon the best brains of the nation's laboratories and universities, that the economists moved into military planning.

"The application of quantitative analysis in relating weapons systems to national security objectives," says one of the economists, "is a new problem grown in the last 20 years. And you don't become an expert in solving it by the conduct of military operations."

Here, and in the research and development field, is where younger men have made their appearance in the Pentagon. This has caused resentment in the military services. But there has been resentment before as new generations of youngsters moved in on their elders.

Budget Is the Master Tool

With or without ceilings, the defense budget remains the heart of Pentagon operations, disputes, weakness and strength. Here was where Mc-Namara would begin, for this was one quick place where a 1960 campaign pledge "to do more" could be fulfilled. Former President Eisenhower, in his waning days in office, had submitted a military budget of $44.9 billion for fiscal 1962; it would be increased almost immediately to $51 billion.

To find what was needed, McNamara directed Hitch to study the strategic weapons field. Nitze was assigned the study of limited and sub-limited warfare, and Brown was told off for research and development requirements.

Movement toward a division of the defense budget by function, rather than by allocation to the military departments, had been simmering on a back burner long before McNamara and Hitch reached the Pentagon. Under such a system, decisions on amounts to be spent for weapons systems and force structures would cut across departmental lines. Duplication of forces could be avoided. The House Appropriations Committee's Defense Subcommittee had been pressing for such cost estimates for years. In the mid-1950's, General Taylor, then Army Chief of Staff, was among the first to give public advocacy to the functional system.

Hitch had developed the idea. In the book which he and Roland N. McKean wrote in 1960, *The Economics of Defense in the Nuclear Age*, he added suggestions on how to make the system work.

The new comptroller told McNamara that when his temporary job on force and money requirements was done, he had an idea about fixing up the whole budget along functional lines, using what was called "Program Packages."

The Packages Give Control

Hitch said he thought he might be able to get his plans in order to make a test run by the following year.

"Fine," McNamara said. "Except that we'll do it this year, not next."

This was in the early spring of 1961. This was the decision that truly implemented unification. The shock waves still roll between the Capitol and the Pentagon.

In years past, the Secretary of Defense gave the Services budget ceilings, plus a few guidelines, during the summer. The Services submitted their individual budgets in October, the Bureau of the Budget took a whack at them and after White House consultation, the Secretary made decisions on unresolved issues.

The McNamara-Hitch plan hit the Pentagon with a paperwork cyclone. In May 1961, the Services were asked to submit the force structures needed to carry out their missions, with all financial requirements necessary to support them—for the next five years.

"First," says Hitch, "we had a complete laying out of the elements of the program, such as combat units, weapon systems, development projects, and so on. When the layout was completed, the elements were put together in program packages."

The Big Economy Eight

Originally, there were seven "Program Packages": Strategic Retaliatory Forces, Continental Air and Missile Defense Forces, General Purpose Forces, Sealift and Airlift, Reserve Forces, Research and Development and General Support. Civil Defense was added as the eighth when this function was transferred to the Pentagon.

Weapon systems were assigned to a package according to a primary role. An aircraft carrier, for example, would be justified before Congress for use in both general and limited war, but its basic role would be for limited war and it would thus go into the General Purpose Forces package.

This gigantic planning switch was made in time to accommodate the fiscal 1963 military budget, which became effective July 1, 1962, with some of the final decisions having to be made during the pressure of the Berlin crisis. When the document was completed, the Congress, for the first time— and the White House and the Pentagon as well—had a reasonably solid idea of what the armed forces would look like for the foreseeable future. Importantly, the total cost of a weapon system could be seen, not merely the iceberg portion visible at the time a program was inaugurated.

Under the system, development of subsequent budgets would become a relatively simple matter. There would be a new five-year plan each year, extending the status forecast accordingly. Alterations, new ideas, new systems, would come through the submission during the year of proposed "Program Changes." Generally, such changes would be submitted by the military departments but they might come from any source. Several proposals during the last year were submitted directly by the Joint Chiefs of Staff.

A new watchword swept through the Pentagon—"cost effectiveness." This became the measure: Justify. Will this idea, this weapon, deliver the greatest effectiveness for the money spent or will something else do the job better?

Computers Price the Packages

Proposed Program Changes must withstand the cost-effectiveness scrutiny and test to stand a chance of final approval and inclusion in a subsequent budget.

That's the judgment that caught up with the RS-70, and Skybolt, and which is now being applied in studies of the Navy's carrier task forces which served so well in World War II. The system is the surest producer of a battle with Congress the Pentagon has ever found; the young scientists and economists are used in the cost-effectiveness studies—along with an increasing number of military professionals. They prepare reports.

One such economist, 33-year-old Dr. Alain C. Enthoven, deputy comptroller for systems analysis, drew personal attention from an inquiring subcommittee of the House Armed Services Committee. Rep. Porter Hardy, the chairman, and his subcommittee learned that Dr. Enthoven had been put in charge of the review of proposed Program Changes for eight of 24 major items. His list includes such significant matters as the Minuteman missile force level, increased funding for the Navy's Polaris system, the Nike Zeus antiaircraft missile, shipbuilding and conversion, the tactical force level, and Navy and Marine tactical aircraft.

The personable Dr. Enthoven, former Rhodes scholar and economics instructor at MIT, had worked with his boss Hitch at the Rand Corporation.

McNamara explained to the subcommittee that Enthoven had been assigned responsibility for consolidating various papers on the projects and preparing briefs on them for the Secretary's personal review, "since I propose to personally review all of the recommendations prepared by the

Secretaries, the Chiefs of Staff, and the Chairman of the Joint Chiefs, on those very important projects."

"Do you have any idea of his age, military experience and background?" McNamara was asked.

"No," the Secretary replied, "I don't have any idea as to his age but I have the highest opinion of his intelligence."

"How much military experience does he have?"

"I can't speak to that. He is not rendering a military judgment here, as I mentioned to you."

What Enthoven, and others like him, does is to apply the quantitative analysis technique to the military proposals and to seek out for McNamara's consideration alternatives, if the military men have presented an all-or-nothing choice. In one instance examination indicated that the nation was buying 40 per cent of one program which costed out at an eventual total of $100 billion. An alternative which seemed attractive and more "effective" was to buy 100 per cent of a $50 billion program—certainly in the time span. The time span has become increasingly important, for in this new technological age if weapons can't be delivered as planned they may be obsolete at the hour of first production.

There was the question whether it would be preferable to have 1,500 SAC bombers vulnerably crowded on 60 bases, or to keep 800 bombers more safely dispersed on 200 bases, not forgetting the cost, the political and economic impact of land acquisition and new construction, with the whole checked off against megatonnage of destruction delivered on target plus the proposition of maintaining X proportion of the bombers on airborne alert, figuring in the problem of keeping crews available and not forgetting engine depreciation and metal fatigue in aircraft frames.

It would be difficult to see why anybody but an economist would want to spend his days in a mess like this. But word goes around among the civilians in the Pentagon that the military men are catching onto the system and are coming along strong. With such acceptance, the lower echelon civilians will tend to be absorbed along with the military in the system itself.

There has been, and there is, a strong feeling among many military leaders, including some of highest rank, against the centralization of authority now brought into the office of the Secretary of Defense.

There exists a belief that McNamara and his civilians don't understand people, that the peculiar personal relationships to be found in military life, military operations, remain a disregarded unknown.

General Lauris Norstad told a Senate Committee after his retirement from NATO as Supreme Commander: "Too much attention tends to be paid to *system* and perhaps too little to men and their relationships."

Battle Is the Final Test

One top officer said: "There is only one accurate cost-effectiveness test, the one we hope will never be made, and that's on the battlefield."

A case can be made for the complainants, for mistakes have been made, a notable instance being a failure to realize the local impact of calling up some of the reserves in 1961.

But there are wide and deep differences between some of the professional military people over more than one key issue, the matter of close support for ground troops and the role of Army aviation being fair samples.

The functional budget and the Program Package system may point the way out; it comes closer with a guiding lantern than anything seen around Washington yet.

It is to be remembered that McNamara has added $24 billion to the defense budgets above the originally proposed 1962 level—in just 18 months. And despite this, he had to lop off $13 billion in Package Change proposals from the Military Departments in the new 1964 budget alone.

It's prices like these which caused Congress in 1958 to saddle up the horse. Somebody had to ride it. Robert S. McNamara sits a firm saddle and holds a tight rein. He will not be unseated easily.

The Intelligence Community

Roberta Wohlstetter

INTELLIGENCE AND DECISION-MAKING

IF our intelligence system and all our other channels of information failed to produce an accurate image of Japanese intentions and capabilities, it was not for want of the relevant materials. Never before have we had so complete an intelligence picture of the enemy. And perhaps never again will we have such a magnificent collection of sources at our disposal.

RETROSPECT

To review these sources briefly, an American cryptanalyst, Col. William F. Friedman, had broken the top-priority Japanese diplomatic code, which enabled us to listen to a large proportion of the privileged communications between Tokyo and the major Japanese embassies throughout the world. Not only did we know in advance how the Japanese ambassadors in Washington were advised, and how much they were instructed to say, but we also were listening to top-secret messages on the Tokyo-Berlin and Tokyo-Rome circuits, which gave us information vital for conduct of the war in the Atlantic and Europe. In the Far East this source provided minute details on movements connected with the Japanese program of expansion into Southeast Asia.

Besides the strictly diplomatic codes, our cryptanalysts also had some success in reading codes used by Japanese agents in major American and foreign ports. Those who were on the distribution list for MAGIC had access to much of what these agents were reporting to Tokyo and what Tokyo was demanding of them in the Panama Canal Zone, in cities along the east and west coasts of the Americas from northern Canada as far south as Brazil, and in ports throughout the Far East, including the Philippines and the Hawaiian Islands. They could determine what installations, what troop and ship movements, and what alert and defense measures were of

FROM *Pearl Harbor: Warning and Decision* by Roberta Wohlstetter. Reprinted with the permission of the publishers, Stanford University Press. © 1962 by the Board of Trustees of the Leland Stanford Junior University.

interest to Tokyo at these points on the globe, as well as approximately how much correct information her agents were sending her.

Our naval leaders also had at their disposal the results of radio traffic analysis. While before the war our naval radio experts could not read the content of any Japanese naval or military coded messages, they were able to deduce from a study of intercepted ship call signs the composition and location of the Japanese Fleet units. After a change in call signs, they might lose sight of some units, and units that went into port in home waters were also lost because the ships in port used frequencies that our radios were unable to intercept. Most of the time, however, our traffic analysts had the various Japanese Fleet units accurately pinpointed on our naval maps.

Extremely competent on-the-spot economic and political analysis was furnished by Ambassador Grew and his staff in Tokyo. Ambassador Grew was himself a most sensitive and accurate observer, as evidenced by his dispatches to the State Department. His observations were supported and supplemented with military detail by frequent reports from American naval attachés and observers in key Far Eastern ports. Navy Intelligence had men with radio equipment located along the coast of China, for example, who reported the convoy movements toward Indochina. There were also naval observers stationed in various high-tension areas in Thailand and Indochina who could fill in the local outlines of Japanese political intrigue and military planning. In Tokyo and other Japanese cities, it is true, Japanese censorship grew more and more rigid during 1941, until Ambassador Grew felt it necessary to disclaim any responsibility for noting or reporting overt military evidence of an imminent outbreak of war. This careful Japanese censorship naturally cut down visual confirmation of the decoded information but very probably never achieved the opaqueness of Russia's Iron Curtain.

During this period the data and interpretations of British intelligence were also available to American officers in Washington and the Far East, though the British and Americans tended to distrust each other's privileged information.

In addition to secret sources, there were some excellent public ones. Foreign correspondents for *The New York Times*, *The Herald Tribune*, and *The Washington Post* were stationed in Tokyo and Shanghai and in Canberra, Australia. Their reporting as well as their predictions on the Japanese political scene were on a very high level. Frequently their access to news was more rapid and their judgment of its significance as reliable as that of our Intelligence officers. This was certainly the case for 1940 and most of 1941. For the last few weeks before the Pearl Harbor strike, however, the public newspaper accounts were not very useful. It was necessary to have secret information in order to know what was happening. Both Tokyo and Washington exercised very tight control over leaks during this crucial period, and the newsmen accordingly had to limit their accounts to speculation and notices of diplomatic meetings with no exact indication of the content of the diplomatic exchanges.

The Japanese press was another important public source. During 1941 it proclaimed with increasing shrillness the Japanese government's determination to pursue its program of expansion into Southeast Asia and the desire of the military to clear the Far East of British and American colonial exploitation. This particular source was rife with explicit signals of aggressive intent.

Finally, an essential part of the intelligence picture for 1941 was both public and privileged information on American policy and activities in the Far East. During the year the pattern of action and interaction between the Japanese and American governments grew more and more complex. At the last, it became especially important for anyone charged with the responsibility of ordering an alert to know what moves the American government was going to make with respect to Japan, as well as to try to guess what Japan's next move would be, since Japan's next move would respond in part to ours. Unfortunately our military leaders, and especially our Intelligence officers, were sometimes as surprised as the Japanese at the moves of the White House and the State Department. They usually had more orderly anticipations about Japanese policy and conduct than they had about America's. On the other hand, it was also true that State Department and White House officials were handicapped in judging Japanese intentions and estimates of risk by an inadequate picture of our own military vulnerability.

All of the public and private sources of information mentioned were available to America's political and military leaders in 1941. It is only fair to remark, however, that no single person or agency ever had at any given moment all the signals existing in this vast information network. The signals lay scattered in a number of different agencies; some were decoded, some were not; some traveled through rapid channels of communication, some were blocked by technical or procedural delays; some never reached a center of decision. But it is legitimate to review again the general sort of picture that emerged during the first week of December from the signals readily at hand. Anyone close to President Roosevelt was likely to have before him the following significant fragments.

There was first of all a picture of gathering troop and ship movements down the China coast and into Indochina. The large dimensions of this movement to the south were established publicly and visually as well as by analysis of ship call signs. Two changes in Japanese naval call signs— one on November 1 and another on December 1—had also been evaluated by Naval Intelligence as extremely unusual and as signs of major preparations for some sort of Japanese offensive. The two changes had interfered with the speed of American radio traffic analysis. Thousands of interceptions after December 1 were necessary before the new call signs could be read. Partly for this reason American radio analysts disagreed about the locations of the Japanese carriers. One group held that all the carriers were near Japan because they had not been able to identify a carrier call sign since the middle of November. Another group believed that they had located one carrier division in the Marshalls. The probability seemed to be that the carriers, wherever they were, had gone into radio silence; and past experience led the analysts to believe that they were therefore in waters near the Japanese homeland, where they could communicate with each other on wavelengths that we could not intercept. However, our inability to locate the carriers exactly, combined with the two changes in call signs, was itself a danger signal.

Our best secret source, MAGIC, was confirming the aggressive intention of the new military cabinet in Tokyo, which had replaced the last moderate cabinet on October 17. In particular, MAGIC provided details of some of the preparations for the move into Southeast Asia. Running counter to this were increased troop shipments to the Manchurian border in October. (The intelligence picture is never clear-cut.) But withdrawals had begun toward the end of that month. MAGIC also carried explicit instructions to the Japanese ambassadors in Washington to pursue diplomatic negotiations with the United States with increasing energy, but at the same time it announced a deadline for the favorable conclusion of the negotiations, first for November 25, later postponed until November 29. In case of diplomatic failure by that date, the Japanese ambassadors were told, Japanese patience would be exhausted, Japan was determined to pursue her Greater East Asia policy, and on November 29 "things" would automatically begin to happen.

On November 26 Secretary Hull rejected Japan's latest bid for American approval of her policies in China and Indochina. MAGIC had repeatedly characterized this Japanese overture as the "last," and it now revealed the ambassadors' reaction of consternation and despair over the American refusal and also their country's characterization of the American Ten Point Note as an "ultimatum."

On the basis of this collection of signals, Army and Navy Intelligence experts in Washington tentatively placed D-day *for the Japanese Southeastern campaign* during the week end of November 30, and when this failed to materialize, during the week end of December 7. They also compiled an accurate list of probable British and Dutch targets and included the Philippines and Guam as possible American targets.

Also available in this mass of information, but long forgotten, was a rumor reported by Ambassador Grew in January, 1941. It came from what was regarded as a not-very-reliable source, the Peruvian embassy, and stated that the Japanese were preparing a surprise air attack on Pearl Harbor. Curiously the date of the report is coincident roughly with what we now know to have been the date of inception of Yamamoto's plan; but the rumor was labeled by everyone, including Ambassador Grew, as quite fantastic and the plan as absurdly impossible. American judgment was consistent with Japanese judgment at this time, since Yamamoto's plan was in direct contradiction to Japanese naval tactical doctrine.

PERSPECTIVE

On the basis of this rapid recapitulation of the highlights in the signal picture, it is apparent that our decisionmakers had at hand an impressive amount of information on the enemy. They did not have the complete list of targets, since none of the last-minute estimates included Pearl Harbor. They did not know the exact hour and date for opening the attack. They did not have an accurate knowledge of Japanese capabilities or of Japanese ability to accept very high risks. The crucial question then, we repeat, is, If we could enumerate accurately the British and Dutch targets and give credence to a Japanese attack against them either on November 30 or December 7, why were we not expecting a specific danger to *ourselves?* And by the word "expecting," we mean expecting in the sense of taking specific alert actions to meet the contingencies of attack by land, sea, or air.

There are several answers to this question that have become apparent in the course of this study. First of all, it is much easier *after* the event to sort the relevant from the irrelevant signals. After the event, of course, a signal is always crystal clear; we can now see what disaster it was signaling, since the disaster has occurred. But before the event it is obscure and pregnant with conflicting meanings. It comes to the observer embedded in an atmosphere of "noise," i.e., in the company of all sorts of information that is useless and irrelevant for predicting the particular disaster. For example, in Washington, Pearl Harbor signals were competing with a vast number of signals from the European theater. These European signals announced danger more frequently and more specifically than any coming from the Far East. The Far Eastern signals were also arriving at a center of decision where they had to compete with the prevailing belief that an unprotected offensive force acts as a deterrent rather than a target. In Honolulu they were competing *not* with signals from the European theater, but rather with a large number of signals announcing Japanese intentions and preparations to attack Soviet Russia rather than to move southward; here they were also competing with expectations of local sabotage prepared by previous alert situations.

In short, we failed to anticipate Pearl Harbor not for want of the relevant materials, but because of a plethora of irrelevant ones. Much of the appearance of wanton neglect that emerged in various investigations of the disaster resulted from the unconscious suppression of vast congeries of signs pointing in every direction except Pearl Harbor. It was difficult later to recall these signs since they had led nowhere. Signals that are characterized today as absolutely unequivocal warnings of surprise air attack on Pearl Harbor become, on analysis in the context of December, 1941, not merely ambiguous but occasionally inconsistent with such an attack. To recall one of the most controversial and publicized examples, the winds code, both General Short and Admiral Kimmel testified that if they had had this information, they would have been prepared on the morning of December 7 for an air attack from without. The messages establishing the winds code are often described in the Pearl Harbor literature as Tokyo's declaration of war against America. If they indeed amounted to such a declaration, obviously the failure to inform Honolulu of this vital news would have been criminal negligence. On examination, however, the messages proved to be instructions for code communication after normal commercial channels had been cut. In one message the recipient was instructed on receipt of an execute to destroy all remaining codes in his possession. In another version the recipient was warned that the execute would be sent out "when relations are becoming dangerous" between Japan and three other countries. There was a different code term for each country: England, America, and the Soviet Union.

There is no evidence that an authentic execute of either message was ever intercepted by the United States before December 7. The message ordering code destruction was in any case superseded by a much more explicit code-destruction order from Tokyo that was intercepted on December 2 and translated on December 3. After December 2, the receipt of a winds-code execute for code destruction would therefore have added nothing new to our information, and code destruction in itself cannot be taken as an unambiguous substitute for a formal declaration of war. During the first week of December the United States ordered all American consulates in the Far East to destroy all American codes, yet no one has attempted to prove that this order was equivalent to an American declaration of war against Japan. As for the other winds-code message, provided an execute had been received warning that relations were dangerous between Japan and the United States, there would still have been no way on the basis of this signal alone to determine whether Tokyo was signaling Japanese intent to attack the United States or Japanese fear of an American surprise attack (in reprisal for Japanese aggressive moves against American allies in the Far East). It was only after the event that "dangerous relations" could be interpreted as "surprise air attack on Pearl Harbor."

There is a difference, then, between having a signal available somewhere in the heap of irrelevancies, and perceiving it as a warning; and there is also a difference between perceiving it as a warning, and acting or getting action on it. These distinctions, simple as they are, illuminate the obscurity shrouding this moment in history.

Many instances of these distinctions have been examined in the course of this study. We shall recall a few of the most dramatic now. To illustrate the difference between having and perceiving a signal, let us return to Colonel Fielder, whom we met in Chapter 1. Though he was an untrained and inexperienced Intelligence officer, he headed Army Intelligence at Pearl Harbor at the time of the attack. He had been on the job for only four months, and he regarded as quite satisfactory his sources of information and his contacts with the Navy locally and with Army Intelligence in Washington. Evidently he was unaware that Army Intelligence in Washington was not allowed to send him any "action" or policy information, and he was therefore not especially concerned about trying to read beyond the obvious meaning of any given communication that came under his eyes. Colonel Bratton, head of Army Far Eastern Intelligence in Washington, however, had a somewhat more realistic view of the extent of Colonel Fielder's knowledge. At the end of November, Colonel Bratton had learned about the winds-code setup and was also apprised that the naval traffic analysis unit under Commander Rochefort in Honolulu was monitoring 24 hours a day for an execute. He was understandably worried about the lack of communication between this unit and Colonel Fielder's office, and by December 5 he finally felt that the matter was urgent enough to warrant sending a message directly to Colonel Fielder about the winds code. Now any information on the winds code, since it belonged to the highest classification of secret information, and since it was therefore automatically evaluated as "action" information, could not be sent through normal G-2 channels. Colonel Bratton had to figure out another way to get the information to Colonel Fielder. He sent this message: "Contact Commander Rochefort immediately thru Commandant Fourteenth Naval District regarding broadcasts from Tokyo reference weather." Signal Corps records establish that Colonel Fielder received this message. How did he react to it? He filed it. According to his testimony in 1945, it made no impression on him and he did not attempt to see Rochefort. He could not sense any urgency behind the lines because he was not expecting immediate trouble, and his expectations determined what he read. A warning signal was available to him, but he did not perceive it.

Colonel Fielder's lack of experience may make this example seem to be an exception. So let us recall the performance of Captain Wilkinson, the naval officer who headed the Office of Naval Intelligence in Washington in the fall of 1941 and who is unanimously acclaimed for a distinguished and brilliant career. His treatment of a now-famous Pearl Harbor signal does not sound much different in the telling. After the event, the signal in question was labeled "the bomb-plot message." It originated in Tokyo on September 24 and was sent to an agent in Honolulu. It requested the agent to divide Pearl Harbor into five areas and to make his future reports on ships in harbor with reference to those areas. Tokyo was especially interested in the locations of battleships, destroyers, and carriers, and also in any information on the anchoring of more than one ship at a single dock.

This message was decoded and translated on October 9 and shortly thereafter distributed to Army, Navy, and State Department recipients of MAGIC. Commander Kramer, a naval expert on MAGIC, had marked the message with an asterisk, signifying that he thought it to be of particular interest. But what was its interest? Both he and Wilkinson agreed that it illustrated the "nicety" of Japanese intelligence, the incredible zeal and efficiency with which they collected detail. The division into areas was interpreted as a device for shortening the reports. Admiral Stark was similarly impressed with Japanese efficiency, and no one felt it necessary to forward the message to Admiral Kimmel. No one read into it a specific danger to ships anchored at Pearl Harbor. At the time, this was a reasonable estimate, since somewhat similar requests for information were going to Japanese agents in Panama, Vancouver, Portland, San Diego, San Francisco, and other places. It should be observed, however, that the estimate was reasonable only on the basis of a very rough check on the quantity of espionage messages passing between Tokyo and these American ports. No one in Far Eastern Intelligence had subjected the messages to any more refined analysis. An observer assigned to such a job would have been able to record an increase in the frequency and specificity of Tokyo's requests concerning Manila and Pearl Harbor in the last weeks before the outbreak of war, and he would have noted that Tokyo was not displaying the same interest in other American ports. These observations, while not significant in isolation, might have been useful in the general signal picture.

There is no need, however, to confine our examples to Intelligence personnel. Indeed, the crucial areas where the signals failed to communicate a warning were in the operational branches of the armed services. Let us take Admiral Kimmel and his reaction to the information that the Japanese were destroying most of their codes in major Far Eastern consulates and also in London and Washington. Since the Pearl Harbor attack, this information has frequently been characterized by military experts who were not stationed in Honolulu as an "unmistakable tip-off." As Admiral Ingersoll explained at the congressional hearings, with the lucidity characteristic of statements after the event:

> If you rupture diplomatic negotiations you do not necessarily have to burn your codes. The diplomats go home and they can pack up their codes with their dolls and take them home. Also, when you rupture diplomatic negotiations, you do not rupture consular relations. The consuls stay on.
>
> Now, in this particular set of dispatches that did not mean a rupture of diplomatic negotiations, it meant war, and that information was sent out to the fleets as soon as we got it. . . .[1]

[1] *Hearings*, Part 9, p. 4226.

The phrase "it meant war" was, of course, pretty vague; war in Manila, Hong Kong, Singapore, and Batavia is not war 5000 miles away in Pearl Harbor. Before the event, for Admiral Kimmel, code burning in major Japanese consulates in the Far East may have "meant war," but it did not signal danger of an air attack on Pearl Harbor. In the first place, the information that he received was not the original MAGIC. He learned from Washington that Japanese consulates were burning "almost all" of their codes, not all of them, and Honolulu was not included on the list. He knew from a local source that the Japanese consulate in Honolulu was burning secret papers (not necessarily codes), and this back yard burning had happened three or four times during the year. In July, 1941, Kimmel had been informed that the Japanese consulates in lands neighboring Indo-china had destroyed codes, and he interpreted the code burning in December as a similar attempt to protect codes in case the Americans or their British and Dutch allies tried to seize the consulates in reprisal for the southern advance. This also was a reasonable interpretation at the time, though not an especially keen one.

Indeed, at the time there was a good deal of evidence available to support all the wrong interpretations of last-minute signals, and the interpretations appeared wrong only *after* the event. There was, for example, a good deal of evidence to support the hypothesis that Japan would attack the Soviet Union from the east while the Russian Army was heavily engaged in the west. Admiral Turner, head of Navy War Plans in Washington, was an enthusiastic adherent of this view and argued the high probability of a Japanese attack on Russia up until the last week in November, when he had to concede that most of Japan's men and supplies were moving south. Richard Sorge, the expert Soviet spy who had direct access to the Japanese Cabinet, had correctly predicted the southern move as early as July, 1941, but even he was deeply alarmed during September and early October by the large number of troop movements to the Manchurian border. He feared that his July advice to the Soviet Union had been in error, and his alarm ultimately led to his capture on October 14. For at this time he increased his radio messages to Moscow to the point where it was possible for the Japanese police to pinpoint the source of the broadcasts.

It is important to emphasize here that most of the men that we have cited in our examples, such as Captain Wilkinson and Admirals Turner and Kimmel—these men and their colleagues who were involved in the Pearl Harbor disaster—were as efficient and loyal a group of men as one could find. Some of them were exceptionally able and dedicated. The fact of surprise at Pearl Harbor has never been persuasively explained by accusing the participants, individually or in groups, of conspiracy or negligence or stupidity. What these examples illustrate is rather the very human tendency to pay attention to the signals that support current expectations about enemy behavior. If no one is listening for signals of an attack against a highly improbable target, then it is very difficult for the signals to be heard.

For every signal that came into the information net in 1941 there were usually several plausible alternative explanations, and it is not surprising that our observers and analysts were inclined to select the explanations that fitted the popular hypotheses. They sometimes set down new contradictory evidence side by side with existing hypotheses, and they also sometimes held two contradictory beliefs at the same time. We have seen this happen in G-2 estimates for the fall of 1941. Apparently human beings have a stubborn attachment to old beliefs and an equally stubborn resistance to new material that will upset them.

Besides the tendency to select whatever was in accord with one's expectations, there were many other blocks to perception that prevented our analysts from making the correct interpretation. We have just mentioned the masses of conflicting evidence that supported alternative and equally reasonable hypotheses. This is the phenomenon of noise in which a signal is embedded. Even at its normal level, noise presents problems in distraction; but in addition to the natural clatter of useless information and competing signals, in 1941 a number of factors combined to raise the usual noise level. First of all, it had been raised, especially in Honolulu, by the background of previous alert situations and false alarms. Earlier alerts, as we have seen, had centered attention on local sabotage and on signals supporting the hypothesis of a probable Japanese attack on Russia. Second, in both Honolulu and Washington, individual reactions to danger had been numbered, or at least dulled, by the continuous international tension.

A third factor that served to increase the natural noise level was the positive effort made by the enemy to keep the relevant signals quiet. The Japanese security system was an important and successful block to perception. It was able to keep the strictest cloak of secrecy around the Pearl Harbor attack and to limit knowledge only to those closely associated with the details of military and naval planning. In the Japanese Cabinet only the Navy Minister and the Army Minister (who was also Prime Minister) knew of the plan before the task force left its final port of departure.

In addition to keeping certain signals quiet, the enemy tried to create noise, and sent false signals into our information system by carrying on elaborate "spoofs." False radio traffic made us believe that certain ships were maneuvering near the mainland of Japan. The Japanese also sent to individual commanders false war plans for Chinese targets, which were changed only at the last moment to bring them into line with the Southeastern movement.

A fifth barrier to accurate perception was the fact that the relevant signals were subject to change, often very sudden change. This was true even of the so-called static intelligence, which included data on capabilities and the composition of military forces. In the case of our 1941 estimates of the infeasibility of torpedo attacks in the shallow waters of Pearl Harbor, or the underestimation of the range and performance of the Japanese Zero, the changes happened too quickly to appear in an intelligence estimate.

Sixth, our own security system sometimes prevented the communication of signals. It confronted our officers with the problem of trying to keep information from the enemy without keeping it from each other, and, as in the case of MAGIC, they were not always successful. As we have seen, only a very few key individuals saw these secret messages, and they saw them only briefly. They had no opportunity or time to make a critical review of the material, and each one assumed that others who had seen it would arrive at identical interpretations. Exactly who those "others" were was not quite clear to any recipient. Admiral Stark, for example, thought Admiral Kimmel was reading all of MAGIC. Those who were not on the list of recipients, but who had learned somehow of the existence of the decodes, were sure that they contained military as well as diplomatic information and believed that the contents were much fuller and more precise than they actually were. The effect of carefully limiting the reading and discussion of MAGIC, which was certainly necessary to safeguard the secret of our knowledge of the code, was thus to reduce this group of signals to the point where they were scarcely heard.

To these barriers of noise and security we must add the fact that the necessarily precarious character of intelligence information and predictions was reflected in the wording of instructions to take action. The warning messages were somewhat vague and ambiguous. Enemy moves are often subject to reversal on short notice, and this was true for the Japanese. They had plans for canceling their attacks on American possessions in the Pacific up to 24 hours before the time set for attack. A full alert in the Hawaiian Islands, for example, was one condition that might have caused the Pearl Harbor task force to return to Japan on December 5 or 6. The fact that intelligence predictions must be based on moves that are almost always reversible makes understandable the reluctance of the intelligence analyst to make bold assertions. Even if he is willing to risk his reputation on a firm prediction of attack at a definite time and place, no commander will in turn lightly risk the penalties and costs of a full alert. In December, 1941, a full alert required shooting down any unidentified aircraft sighted over the Hawaiian Islands. Yet this might have been interpreted by Japan as the first overt act. At least that was one consideration that influenced General Short to order his lowest degree of alert. While the cautious phrasing in the messages to the theater is certainly understandable, it nevertheless constituted another block on the road to perception. The sentences in the final theater warnings—"A surprise aggressive move in any direction is a possibility" and "Japanese future action unpredictable but hostile action possible at any moment"—could scarcely have been expected to inform the theater commanders of any change in their strategic situation.

Last but not least we must also mention the blocks to perception and communication inherent in any large bureaucratic organization, and those that stemmed from intraservice and interservice rivalries. The most glaring example of rivalry in the Pearl Harbor case was that between Naval War Plans and Naval Intelligence. A general prejudice against intellectuals and specialists, not confined to the military but unfortunately widely held in America, also made it difficult for intelligence experts to be heard. McCollum, Bratton, Sadtler, and a few others who felt that the signal picture was ominous enough to warrant more urgent warnings had no power to influence decision. The Far Eastern code analysts, for example, were believed to be too immersed in the "Oriental point of view." Low budgets for American Intelligence departments reflected the low prestige of this activity, whereas in England, Germany, and Japan, 1941 budgets reached a height that was regarded by the American Congress as quite beyond reason.

In view of all these limitations to perception and communication, is the fact of surprise at Pearl Harbor, then, really so surprising? Even with these limitations explicitly recognized, there remains the step between perception and action. Let us assume that the first hurdle has been crossed: An available signal has been perceived as an indication of imminent danger. Then how do we resolve the next questions: What specific danger is the signal trying to communicate, and what specific action or preparation should follow?

On November 27, General MacArthur had received a war warning very similar to the one received by General Short in Honolulu. MacArthur's response had been promptly translated into orders designed to protect his bombers from possible air attack from Formosan land bases. But the orders were carried out very slowly. By December 8, Philippine time, only half of the bombers ordered to the south had left the Manila area, and reconnaissance over Formosa had not been undertaken. There was no sense of urgency in preparing for a Japanese air attack, partly because our intelligence estimates had calculated that the Japanese aircraft did not have sufficient range to bomb Manila from Formosa.

The information that Pearl Harbor had been attacked arrived at Manila early in the morning of December 8, giving the Philippine forces some 9 or 10 hours to prepare for an attack. But did an air attack on Pearl Harbor necessarily mean that the Japanese would strike from the air at the Philippines? Did they have enough equipment to mount both air attacks successfully? Would they come from Formosa or from carriers? Intelligence had indicated that they would have to come from carriers, yet the carriers were evidently off Hawaii. MacArthur's headquarters also pointed out that there had been no formal declaration of war against Japan by the

United States. Therefore approval could not be granted for a counterattack on Formosan bases. Furthermore there were technical disagreements among airmen as to whether a counterattack should be mounted without advance photographic reconnaissance. While Brereton was arranging permission to undertake photographic reconnaissance, there was further disagreement about what to do with the aircraft in the meantime. Should they be sent aloft or should they be dispersed to avoid destruction in case the Japanese reached the airfields? When the Japanese bombers arrived shortly after noon, they found all the American aircraft wingtip to wingtip on the ground. Even the signal of an actual attack on Pearl Harbor was not an unambiguous signal of an attack on the Philippines, and it did not make clear what response was best.

PROSPECT

The history of Pearl Harbor has an interest exceeding by far any tale of an isolated catastrophe that might have been the result of negligence or stupidity or treachery, however lurid. For we have found the roots of this surprise in circumstances that affected honest, dedicated, and intelligent men. The possibility of such surprise at any time lies in the conditions of human perception and stems from uncertainties so basic that they are not likely to be eliminated, though they might be reduced.

It is only to be expected that the relevant signals, so clearly audible after an event, will be partially obscured before the event by surrounding noise. Even past diligence constructs its own background of noise, in the form of false alarms, which make less likely an alarm when the real thing arrives: the old story of "cry wolf" has a permanent relevance. A totalitarian aggressor can draw a tight curtain of secrecy about his actions and thus muffle the signals of attack. The Western democracies must interpret such signals responsibly and cautiously, for the process of commitment to war, except *in extremis*, is hedged about by the requirements of consultation. The precautions of secrecy, which are necessary even in a democracy to keep open privileged sources of information, may hamper the use of that information or may slow its transmission to those who have the power of decision. Moreover, human attention is directed by beliefs as to what is likely to occur, and one cannot always listen for the right sounds. An all-out thermonuclear attack on a Western power would be an unprecedented event, and some little time (which might be vital) would surely have to pass before the power's allies could understand the nature of the event and take appropriate action.

There is a good deal of evidence, some of it quantitative, that in conditions of great uncertainty people tend to predict that events that they want to happen actually will happen. Wishfulness in conditions of uncertainty is natural and is hard to banish simply by exhortation—or by wishing. Further, the uncertainty of strategic warning is intrinsic, since an enemy decision to attack might be reversed or the direction of the attack changed; and a defensive action can be taken only at some cost. (For example, at Pearl Harbor, flying a 360-degree reconnaissance would have meant sacrificing training, would have interrupted the high-priority shipment program to the Philippines, and would have exhausted crews and worn out equipment within a few weeks.) In general, an extraordinary state of alert that brings about a peak in readiness must be followed by a trough at a later date. In some cases the cost of the defensive actions is hard to estimate and their relevance is uncertain. Therefore the choice of action in response to strategic warning must also be uncertain. Finally, the balance of technical and military factors that might make an attack infeasible at one time can change swiftly and without notice to make it feasible at another. In our day such balances are changing with unprecedented speed.

Pearl Harbor is not an isolated catastrophe. It can be matched by many examples of effective surprise attack. The German attack on Russia in the summer of 1941 was preceded by a flood of signals, the massing of troops, and even direct warnings to Russia by the governments of the United States and the United Kingdom, both of whom had been correctly informed about the imminence of the onslaught. Yet it achieved total surprise.[2] Soviet arguments current today that Stalin and Marshal Zhukov, his Chief of the General Staff, knew and failed to act have obvious parallels with the accusations about President Roosevelt's conspiracy of silence. The Soviet reinterpretations of history aim not only to downgrade Stalin, but also to establish that Soviet leaders were not *really* surprised in 1941, and the Soviet Union can therefore count on adequate warning in any future conflict.[3] But the difficulties of discerning a surprise attack on oneself apply equally to totalitarian and democratic states.

The stunning tactical success of the Japanese attack on the British at Singapore was made possible by the deeply held British faith in the impregnability of that fortress. As Captain Grenfell put it, newspapers and statesmen like their fortresses to be impregnable. "Every fortress," he wrote, "that has come into the news in my lifetime—Port Arthur, Tsing Tao, the great French defensive system of the Maginot Line—has been popularly described as impregnable before it had been attacked. . . . One way or another it became a virtually accepted fact in Britain and the Dominions that

[2] I am grateful to William W. Kaufmann of the M.I.T. Center for International Studies for permission to read his unpublished paper, "Operation Barbarossa," which deals with the background of the German surprise attack.

[3] For a recent Russian view of the Pearl Harbor attack and its lessons on the "launching of aggression by imperialist states," see Maj. Gen. N. Pavlenko, "Documents on Pearl Harbor," *Voenno-Istoricheskii Zhurnal* (*Military-Historical Journal*), No. 1, January, 1961, pp. 85–105. I am indebted for this reference to John Thomas of the Institute of Defense Analysis and to Arnold Horelick, Soviet analyst of The RAND Corporation.

Singapore was an impregnable bastion of Imperial security." [4] Yet the defenses of Singapore were rendered useless by military surprise in the form of an attack from an unexpected, northerly direction.

More recently, the Korean War provided some striking examples of surprise. The original North Korean attack was preceded by almost weekly maneuvers probing the border. These regular week-end penetrations built up so high a level of noise that on June 25, 1950, the actual initiation of hostilities was not distinguished from the preceding tests and false alarms. The intervention of the Chinese, at a later stage of the Korean War, was preceded by mass movements of Chinese troops and explicit warnings by the Chinese government to our own, by way of India, that this was precisely what they would do if we crossed the 38th parallel. Nonetheless, in important respects, we were surprised by the Chinese Communist forces in November, 1950. [5]

How do matters stand with reference to a future thermonuclear aggression by a totalitarian power? Would such an attack be harder or easier to conceal than the Japanese aggression against Pearl Harbor? There have been many attempts in recent years to cheer us with the thought that the H-bomb has so outmoded general war that this question may appear unimportant. However, such attempts to comfort ourselves really beg the question. The question is, Will it be possible in the future for a totalitarian power so to conceal an impending attack on the forces that we have disposed for retaliation as to have a high probability of virtually eliminating them before they receive warning or have time to respond to it? In this connection it is important to observe that there is no cause for complacency. In spite of the vast increase in expenditures for collecting and analyzing intelligence data and in spite of advances in the art of machine decoding and machine translation, the balance of advantage seems clearly to have shifted since Pearl Harbor in favor of a surprise attacker. The benefits to be expected from achieving surprise have increased enormously and the penalties for losing the initiative in an all-out war have grown correspondingly. In fact, since only by an all-out surprise attack could an attacker hope to prevent retaliation, anything less would be suicidal, assuming that some form of attack is contemplated by one major power against another.

In such a surprise attack a major power today would have advantages exceeding those enjoyed by the Japanese in 1941. It is a familiar fact that with the ever-increasing readiness of bomber and missile forces, strategic warning becomes harder and harder to obtain; and with the decrease in

[4] Russell Grenfell, *Main Fleet to Singapore* (New York: The Macmillan Co., 1952), p. 64.

[5] For a succinct and lucid account, see "Strategic Surprise in the Korean War," an unpublished paper by Harvey DeWeerd of The RAND Corporation and the National Security Studies Program, University of California at Los Angeles.

the flight time for delivery of massive weapons of destruction, tactical warning times have contracted from weeks to minutes. It is no longer necessary for the aggressor to undertake huge movements of troops and ships in the weeks immediately preceding an all-out war, such as we described in our account of the Japanese war plan. Manned bombers capable of delivering a blow many times more devastating than anything dreamed of by the Japanese might be on their way from bases deep inside their homeland without yielding any substantial intelligence warning; they might conceivably follow routes that, by avoiding detection or at least identification among the friendly and unknown traffic appearing on radars, would be unlikely to give even any considerable tactical warning. Submarines might be kept on station several hundred miles off our coast during years of peace and might launch ballistic missiles on the receipt of a prearranged signal. Finally, intercontinental ballistic missiles might be kept for years at a high degree of readiness, and, if there were enough of them, they might be launched after simply being "counted down," with no further visible preparation. Total flight time for such rockets between continents might be less than fifteen minutes and radar warning less than that. Most important, such blows, unlike those leveled by the Japanese at Pearl Harbor, might determine the outcome not merely of a battle, but of the war itself. In short, the subject of surprise attack continues to be of vital concern. This fact has been suggested by the great debate among the powers on arms control and on the possibilities of using limitation and inspection arrangements to guard against surprise attack. The very little we have said suggests that such arrangements present formidable difficulties.

This study has not been intended as a "how-to-do-it" manual on intelligence, but perhaps one major practical lesson emerges from it. We cannot *count* on strategic warning. We *might* get it, and we might be able to take useful preparatory actions that would be impossible without it. We certainly ought to plan to exploit such a possibility should it occur. However, since we cannot rely on strategic warning, our defenses, if we are to have confidence in them, must be designed to function without it. If we accept the fact that the signal picture for impending attacks is almost sure to be ambiguous, we shall prearrange actions that are right and feasible in response to ambiguous signals, including signs of an attack that might be false. We must be capable of reacting repeatedly to false alarms without committing ourselves or the enemy to wage thermonuclear war.

It is only human to want some unique and univocal signal, to want a guarantee from intelligence, an unambiguous substitute for a formal declaration of war. This is surely the unconscious motivation of all the rewriting of Pearl Harbor history, which sees in such wavering and uncertain sources of information as the winds code and all of the various and much-argued MAGIC texts a clear statement of Japanese intent. But we have seen how drastically such an interpretation oversimplifies the task of the analyst and decisionmaker. If the study of Pearl Harbor has anything to offer for the future, it is this: We have to accept the fact of uncertainty and learn to live with it. No magic, in code or otherwise, will provide certainty. Our plans must work without it.

Roger Hilsman

INTELLIGENCE AND POLICY-MAKING IN FOREIGN AFFAIRS

The Validity of Current Doctrine

WHAT now of the soundness of current doctrine? Let us consider first the warning role. The reader will recall that in the intelligence brotherhood the definition of warning is broad: to foresee problems of every sort, to call attention to the need for policy wherever need arises. Now in our working model, the decision-maker's first step in recognizing a problem is to predict the outcome if events are allowed to go unmolested. By doing this he hopes to make out what impact the problem will have on his values. In other words, he performs, for himself, a warning function. In our frame of reference, "warning" is merely the act of recognizing a problem and making a preliminary analysis of it. Under the present division of labor, then, the steps in solving a problem are: (1) intelligence sets out to acquire a knowledge of American values, or is given such knowledge by the operating divisions; (2) intelligence next recognizes that a problem exists, makes a preliminary analysis of it, and informs the operating divisions of the probable outcome and the effect on American values if nothing is done to influence the course events will take; (3) the operating divisions then analyze the problem to determine the alternatives open and the gains and costs of each. Both organizations thus do the same kind of work, and need the same information, knowledge, method, and skills. In a number of ways, in fact, this division of labor seems to be both arbitrary and awkward. Although we have broken the process of decision-making into a series of steps for the purposes of analysis, there is no reason to suppose that the solution of real problems falls into this ideal pattern. We can therefore expect that it will be difficult to evolve a rule defining the line between preliminary and detailed analysis that will be workable in a practical, bureaucratic sense. Since the organization responsible for the detailed analysis can make another preliminary analysis in passing (as it does its

FROM *World Politics,* **V** (October 1962), pp. 33–45. Reprinted by permission.

detailed analysis), there is also no guarantee either that this division of labor will save time and effort or that it will even be respected.[1]

However, it is obviously possible to let both organizations give "warning" —to let both do a preliminary analysis so that the one will check the work of the other. This would be a clear-cut case of that bugaboo, "duplication," but it could be argued that if there are enough of the kind of expert who is qualified to do this sort of thing to staff both organizations, the government could afford the luxury. Notice, however, that if both organizations do this analysis, the "warning" role will tend to become a kind of critical role as well. One kind of warning, for example, could be given when a threat is not foreseen because no one ever suspects that there may be a problem. In the past such a complete failure to recognize a problem has usually occurred when the necessary conceptual tools simply did not exist. The Great Plague is a case in point. Without knowledge of the cause and means of transmittal of disease, the filth and increase in rats which made the plague possible had no significance. Obviously, in such circumstances it would be unreasonable to expect much from intelligence.[2] Another kind of warning could be given when the operators have recognized the existence of a problem, but have decided after analysis that it will work itself out without harmful effects. If intelligence warns that there is a threat after all, it is in effect criticizing the analysis of the people who decided otherwise, and saying that the present policy of taking no action to meet the threat is wrong. A third type of warning could be given when a threat has already been recognized, and a decision to employ a certain means already made. In these circumstances, a warning that the threat will materialize after all implies that the chosen means is ineffective, or that it will bring new threats—again, that the policy is wrong. And notice that an intelligence unit could not justify a statement that the present course was not the proper one unless it had made a detailed analysis as well as a preliminary one. The "warning" role, in sum, will usually become a "warning-critic" one.

The only objection to this role for intelligence is that it means repeating work already done in the operating divisions. It does, that is, if we can assume that those divisions have both the time and skills necessary for

---

[1] Insofar as the complaints of intelligence people that no one ever pays attention to their "warnings" are correct, this—the ease with which the operating divisions can make another preliminary analysis in passing—may be an explanation. Another may be that the operating divisions, having better information sooner, may have made their preliminary analysis first. Still another may be that although the operating divisions have not made their analysis first, they will have to do it eventually, and are too busy to bother with the intelligence version.

[2] The only hope in circumstances such as these is that the kind of people who forge new and world-shaking conceptual tools are alive at the time, that those minds are focused on the area of the unrecognized problem before the catastrophe and not after, that the groundwork for an advance in that field is already laid, and that people with the power to take action to meet the problem will listen to the man with the new idea.

systematic analysis. Still proceeding on this assumption, we can also say that there is not much to commend the role. A check on the operating divisions might occasionally be helpful, but this same "warning-critic" role is performed with varying thoroughness by a number of individuals and groups outside the government—scholars in the universities, newspaper editorialists and columnists, foreign policy associations, special interest groups, or any person who thinks and talks about foreign policy problems. The question really is: is it worth while to have an organization performing the role within the structure of government in addition to those performing it outside? To an important extent, the answer depends on whether or not our assumption is met—whether or not, that is, the people in the operating divisions have the time and skills necessary for rational analysis. If the operators meet these prerequisites adequately, a "warning-critic" intelligence unit will be of little benefit. However, for each unit of measurement by which the operators fall short there will be a corresponding increase in the value of a "warning-critic" organization that really criticizes. But this is true only if the members of that organization have the time and skills the operators lack. And it is difficult to believe at present either that lack of time is decisive or that the skills of the operator and those of the intelligence man differ significantly.

The second basic role assigned to intelligence is that of furnishing the information on which policy is based. The reader will recall that this work is usually described as fitting together bits and pieces of information, like working a jigsaw puzzle, until a balanced "picture" of a foreign situation is built up. But if an intelligence unit goes through this process without any knowledge of the problems facing the operators, its work will often be irrelevant. Most people, however, recognize at least this minimum need for "coordination" or "guidance." [3] One could, of course, reverse one of the arguments for a separate intelligence unit—that the operators do not have time for research and analysis [4]—and say that there also may not be time for the necessary "guidance." Let us assume, however, that the policy people do succeed in giving intelligence a general kind of guidance —information on what the operating divisions have decided are the objectives, their general foreign policies and plans, and a list of the problems they are currently facing. The question is: would the information furnished by intelligence with this sort of guidance be that which is needed in each of the steps of decision-making outlined in the working model given above and would it come out in a usable form?

We saw above that the number of facts which could be amassed about the elements and persons involved in even a simple problem in international

[3] Sherman Kent, *Strategic Intelligence for American World Policy* (Princeton: Princeton University Press, 1949), pp. 81–82; and George S. Pettee, *The Future of American Secret Intelligence* (Washington, D.C.: Infantry Journal Press, 1946), p. 104.
[4] Kent, *op. cit.*, p. 114.

relations becomes impossible to conceive; that even the "practical" man
has a number of notions which make him feel that when certain things
take place, certain results follow; and that it is this "theory," these assumptions, expectations, or hypotheses which help him to select the facts he
believes are pertinent. Thus the decision-maker's procedure is, first, to ask
a question (what will be the effects of such and such a course of action?);
secondly, to identify a theory with the question; and, finally, to look for the
information indicated by the theory in order to answer the question.[5]
For instance, if appeasement, a concession to the demand of some nation,
is under scrutiny as an alternative course of action, and the "theory"
accepted by the decision-maker indicates that certain political and psychological conditions will determine whether or not a concession will accomplish the desired result, the decision-maker goes to current information
looking for these particular points. He looks for information with both
the theory and the specific question in mind, and he must know both before he can proceed rationally and economically. The work done in making
a decision, in other words, is itself a form of research in which the decision-
maker brings these two things to a body of data. He does not receive
the data he wants in a vacuum, but seeks it out specifically, following
the signposts erected by his theory. And he could not have been able to
choose this theory if he had not known the specific question. The data, in
sum, is not integrated into a "picture" and brought to the problem, but
the problem is brought to the data.

A study prepared by an intelligence unit with only general "guidance,"
then, would have to be a sort of one-volume encyclopedia. To serve its
purpose, the study would have to cover all the information which might be
pertinent to some unknown alternative course of action, and, to be safe,
pertinent to some unknown or dimly guessed theory or assumption as well.
Considerable effort would go into its preparation, and yet much of the
information contained in it would be irrelevant to the courses of action
actually weighed and the theories actually used. Even so, since it would
be prepared in relative isolation, such a study might well omit some
significant bit of information made relevant by some unknown theory to
some unknown course of action. In view of all this, it is not surprising
that the operators do not seem to find the time to read very much of
the product of intelligence units, and continue, consciously or uncon-
sciously, to collect and use, with or without adequate analysis, their own

---

[5] If, in the process of analysis, the decision-maker uncovers facts which in the framework of his thought seem to indicate that existing theory is inadequate or fallacious, he
may have to modify it or develop new theory as he goes along. The course of action
under consideration is also an hypothesis; it may be modified to fit facts which are
uncovered during investigation, or a course of action previously unrecognized may be
evolved.

data.[6] If the existing intelligence units must furnish information with only the more or less general guidance assumed here, there seems little reason to believe that their efforts either significantly improve the quality of decisions on foreign policy, or noticeably reduce the burden on the operating divisions and the top command.[7]

Since "guidance" which is merely general is not satisfactory, let us assume that intelligence is given a specific "guidance" that will enable it to furnish all the information required for a problem and only the information required. However, it is obvious from the preceding paragraphs that this would necessarily be the list of alternatives under study. No other "guidance" except this list could give intelligence all that it would need to decide what information was pertinent. Having received this list, intelligence could select the appropriate theory and seek out the data pointed to by that theory. Since the information needed is indicated both by the original question and theory and by the hypotheses and conclusions reached in the earlier phases of the analysis, intelligence would have to go through many of the same steps and would frequently complete the whole analytical process. If the goal of intelligence is to furnish exactly the information needed, the procedure seems to become a senseless one in which intelligence, in order to assemble that information, goes through much of the same analysis that the operating divisions are to make after they receive it.

[6] Probably the tendency also is to continue to do the job of inferring, correctly or incorrectly, the "facts" which are needed from facts which are available. Since it is the policy man who is analyzing the alternative courses of action, it is he and only he who can know what data are needed. If the policy man is actually going through a disciplined analysis, he will sometimes be grateful to have an intelligence unit dig up a particular bit of information for him, but there will be many times when he will not have the time to stop his work while the "liaison" machinery grinds away. If, as many do, the operator works partly according to intuition, even he will not know which facts are needed. The intelligence man, however, is lost in either case. If he is not asked a specific question, he will not know which facts are needed, and he will find himself doing nothing at all, amassing material of doubtful relevance, or spending a lot of time and energy in a mild form of interorganizational espionage, trying to find out what is going on so he can "anticipate" the needs of the policy people.

[7] It is frequently argued by supporters of "current" intelligence that the role of a newspaper is to furnish information without knowing the specific purpose for which it is to be used, and that intelligence is a kind of governmental newspaper, specializing in secret information, for the private use of policy people. It seems obvious, however, that even the best of newspapers could not furnish all the information wanted by a number of people who have different "theories." Even the most "objective" of newspapers, furthermore, must select the information it presents in terms of the expectations and assumptions of its reporters and editors. If it did not, and merely furnished information in the abstract, its stories would be a jumble of incoherency. An "objective" newspaper is not one which attempts the impossible task of giving *all* the facts, but one which gives all the facts, both for and against its own stand, *that its editors and reporters think are important*. And the facts its editors and reporters think are important are determined by their "theories." Presumably the editors of a conscientious newspaper would also try to add whatever information they think is relevant to the "theories" they suppose their readers hold. But more than this they cannot hope to do.

And frequently the operating divisions could not give the "guidance" required—the list of alternatives—until after they had made this same analysis.

If our reasoning is correct, there seems to be very little gain in having a large research and analysis unit, staffed with scarce and expensive people, engaged in "furnishing" information to the operating divisions. Insofar as it is necessary to have an organization to "furnish" information, a library and reference service could probably provide all that would be desired. Utilizing normal commercial and embassy facilities, with the addition of only a tiny field force of its own, this service could collect published, or "overt," materials of general interest on its own initiative, and materials of particular interest by special request. It could index, classify, and catalogue all this information and also the secret information accumulated by the espionage services. Much of the information needed by the analyst of a foreign policy problem would thus be available in a central location, properly filed and indexed. If the analyst could also directly and quickly call on both the State Department missions overseas and the espionage branches to seek out specific data, his position would be ideal—if only in the limited sense that whatever information was available to his government would also be available to him.[8]

There is, however, one other possible division of labor. Let us suppose that intelligence is given the list of alternatives, and then told to do the whole analysis, draw the conclusions, and estimate the probable gains and costs for each alternative furnished. This means that the one organization will do the preliminary analysis, including the work of selecting tentative objectives and of laying out alternative courses of action, and the other the detailed. In other words, this division of labor is a reversal, in all but minor points, of one of our earlier cases in which we had the intelligence people do the preliminary analysis (in order to give "warning"), and the operators the detailed. Similar objections apply: (1) both organizations would be doing the same kind of work, and both would need the same information, knowledge, method, and skills; (2) in real problems, the process of decision-making will not necessarily fall into the same pattern of sequential steps, and a workable rule defining the line between the two kinds of analysis would therefore be difficult to evolve; (3) there is no reason to believe that there would be a saving in time or effort since the people responsible for the detailed analysis would be able to do their own preliminary analysis in passing.

The end point of our reasoning is simply that the most satisfactory "guidance" is that of values. The relationship becomes, in other words, the familiar one of the layman and the expert. The layman tells the expert his desires; the expert, as completely as knowledge will permit, replies with

---

[8] From all accounts, neither the operator nor the intelligence analyst can now direct the secret agent to get specific data. See Willmoore Kendall, "The Function of Intelligence," *World Politics*, I (July 1949), p. 545, and Kent, *op. cit.*, pp. 167–68.

the courses of action that are open, stating the probable gains and costs of each, and pointing to the values, if any, that are mutually exclusive. With this advice the layman weighs his values—and makes his choice.

The relationship between the elected officials of government on the one hand, and the bureaucrats in the State Department on the other, is presumably the same one of the layman and the expert. It is the President, his directly appointed representatives, and the members of Congress who express desires and make the final choice; it is the policy and operating officials in the State Department who are the government employees formally responsible for analyzing problems and offering technical advice on the probable gains and costs of each alternative. In this present arrangement, the relationship of intelligence is not primarily with the layman, although intelligence may sometimes "furnish" him information, but with the policy and operating "expert" in the State or Defense Department.

Suppose, however, that intelligence is given the responsibility for analyzing, planning, and recommending policy for the laymen, and the operating divisions are confined—with leeway for decisions on timing and for weighting factors on the spot—to carrying out policy.[9] The only arguments that will support such a division of labor are the same ones used for the "warning-critic" role. These are either that the operating divisions lack the skills for the necessary research and analysis, or that they lack the time. And, as we said before, it is difficult to believe that the skills of the two groups are not roughly equal. Intelligence, furthermore, falls short of what an organization supposedly devoted to analysis and research should be. In the first place, there is much room for improvement in the quality and composition of its staff; although there are able people in intelligence, more are needed. Also, there should be both a higher proportion of social scientists, and an on-the-job training program to help bring the rest up to a minimum standard. Then, too, the composition of the group of social scientists should be altered—at present, there is an unduly large group of historians in relation to men from the other disciplines.[10]

There is thus little reason to expect that there will be a noticeable improvement if intelligence is given sole responsibility for analyzing and re-

[9] Presumably the present division of labor between the Policy Planning Staff and the operating divisions is basically different from this, since the Staff is supposed to be a kind of committee concerned with long-range planning and not with analyzing and recommending policy on current problems. In practice, however, and in spite of periodic attempts to extricate itself, the Staff seems to have entered more deeply into current problems than was ever intended (see the *New York Times*, April 14, 1950, pp. 1 and 3; and the Hoover Commission's Report on Foreign Affairs, U.S. Govt. Printing Office). Perhaps it could therefore be argued that the Policy Planning Staff is in fact already performing the role contemplated here, even if it is not explicitly charged with it.

[10] Emphasizing history to the point of neglecting the other disciplines is probably due to the influence of the doctrines. The result is primarily to make a break with those doctrines even more difficult, but there are also other undesirable effects. See Kendall, *op. cit.*, pp. 550–51.

commending policy. However, the argument that lack of time is significant may have some validity. Of course, many of the decisions in foreign affairs are taken in haste by necessity. When South Korea was invaded, there was no time for leisurely analysis and research. A decision had to be made even though its implications could be only dimly seen. Nevertheless, the possibility of an attack had been recognized, and an organization with more time than was available to the operating divisions might have been able to have looked more deeply.

However, any benefits from this division of labor may be overbalanced by the drawbacks. In the first place, if the danger now is that there is too little of disciplined analysis, the danger of a sharp distinction between analysis and implementation is that analysis would be out of touch with reality—that action would be either completely isolated from knowledge, or forced into an arbitrary and rigid mold. If our working model has a point, it is that the need is not for a separation of knowledge and action, but for an integration of the two. In rationally conducted foreign affairs, the relationship of knowledge and action should be one of continuous interplay; knowledge and action should interact, should condition and control each other at every point. From the time that a problem is recognized the two should proceed in unison. Knowledge for these purposes must be adapted to the uses of action, shaped to the task of best utilizing the means for action that are at hand. From beginning to end, knowledge should be recipient as well as provider; it should be cast in the frame which action presents, nurtured by the information uncovered as action is carried out, and tested in the laboratory that action provides. Action in turn should not only be planned by knowledge, but guided by it at every stage—in the pause, perhaps, between question and reply in some vital negotiation. Action must be carried out with full understanding of alternatives and implications; the actor knowledgeably alert to new aspects, to the need for modification of assumptions and hypotheses, and to the new problem that arises or is created as the action goes forward. In the ideal diplomacy, the bringer of knowledge should work in a context of policy and action; the implementer should act in a framework of knowledge. The need is for a union, an amalgamation of knowledge and action; and until this condition is met, this integration achieved, it is not likely that a real and effective division of labor can be worked out.

In the second place, setting up an organization responsible for policy analysis does not guarantee that the analysis will be the systematic, disciplined, and rational kind that is needed. The policy and operating divisions are today responsible for analyzing policy problems, yet in spite of much good work there apparently remains a greater need for rational analysis than is justified by the argument that their staff is overworked. Although the operators recognize the importance of analysis and sober thought, they do not seem to understand the disciplined procedures of scientific research or the role of theory and conceptual tools in thinking. From all accounts, their thought-tools are often an ill-assorted collection of unrecognized or partly conscious cultural attitudes and prejudices; of logically inconsistent generalizations made from the haphazard samplings of reality that personal experience must ever be; of hypotheses fashioned from shibboleths, the imperfectly understood theories of others, and casually selected, partial information.[11] Too frequently, it seems, their decisions are jerry-built of these materials, slapped together with defective logic, and placed on a narrow and shaky foundation of facts. And, amazingly, these criticisms made of the operators are also applicable to many of the intelligence people—the researchers supposedly hired for their analytical skills.

Thus no clever organizational scheme or gadget, no ingenious division of labor is likely to solve the problem. By a painful process akin to self-analysis, both the operators and the researchers must dredge out and make explicit their hidden but nonetheless powerful attitudes and predispositions. These must then be coldly scrutinized to see which are unfit as a base for understanding reality, and therefore useless in the tasks that lie ahead. Both operators and researchers must overcome their tendencies to make off-the-cuff decisions in terms of these unexamined and only partly conscious assumptions, and train themselves for systematic, rational thought. They must rid themselves of attitudes which formed mental blocks to a conscious use of knowledge, and then set to work to build a well-stocked kit of carefully inspected intellectual tools and to acquire a professional skill and facility in their use.

At the same time the researchers must become policy-oriented. An analysis of a problem in foreign affairs will rarely be of much practical use if it is not pitched to the needs of purposive action. No sort of analysis, in other words, that does not approach a problem in terms of the factors bearing upon it, and of the ways in which those factors can be influenced, will be as meaningful for the purpose of taking action as one that does. If the function of research and analysis is to be useful and significant, it should be frankly and consciously concerned with policy.

The first step in orienting intelligence toward policy is to free it from some of its unremunerative tasks. If it is wasteful and somewhat pointless to furnish information in the abstract rather than in terms of specific problems and the possible alternatives to meet those problems, the effort now spent in writing the numerous encyclopedic country surveys could

---

[11] See, for example, Frederick S. Dunn, "Education and Foreign Affairs: A Challenge for the Universities," *The Public Service and University Education*, ed. Joseph E. McLean (Princeton: Princeton University Press, 1949); Alexander H. Leighton, *Human Relations in a Changing World* (New York: E. P. Dutton, 1949); Gabriel Almond, *The American People and Foreign Policy* (New York: Harcourt, Brace, 1950). Stephen Kemp Bailey, *Congress Makes a Law: The Story Behind the Employment Act of 1946* (New York, 1950).

be better applied elsewhere. The daily summary and comment could also be abandoned. If the present library and reference services are centralized and expanded, as suggested above, intelligence could also turn over to them the responsibility for furnishing spot information—for answering the telephone request for a name or date. "Backstopping," on the other hand, would more properly be the function, no matter whether the analyst is a member of the operating or the intelligence divisions, of the analyst's research assistant. Intelligence, finally, should dispense with its formal periodic "estimate" of the "capabilities and intentions" of each nation. There is no point in continuing to use it as a vehicle either to "furnish" information or to give "warning"; and, for the rest, an analyst could certainly determine the "capabilities and intentions" of a nation more realistically and accurately if he calculated them not in isolation, but in the study of specific alternatives to deal with an actual problem.

But however helpful getting rid of these tasks might be, the important step for intelligence is an intellectual reorientation designed to create a new set of attitudes—a frame of mind which is manipulative, instrumental, action-conscious, policy-oriented. The major task before the researchers is one of recasting their thought to the context of action, and adapting their tools to the needs of policy.

Ultimately, both operators and researchers must move from hunch and intuition to an improved capacity for explicit and disciplined policy analysis. If at the same time the researchers become policy-oriented, there may develop a more effective integration of knowledge and action. A situation may thus be created in which a useful and practical division of labor between research and operations can be worked out. The problem, in sum, is only secondarily an organizational one. The first problem is one of attitudes and skills.

Roger Hilsman
THE INTELLIGENCE PROCESS

In their comments on the different intelligence vehicles, the operators seemed to put rather small value on the work of the intelligence agencies, or at least on the work of research and analysis branches of those agencies. Some officials felt that the periodic intelligence summary and comment— the daily, weekly, or monthly intelligence "newspaper" which reports and

Reprinted with permission of the publisher from *Strategic Intelligence and National Decisions* by Roger Hilsman. Copyright 1956 by The Free Press, A Corporation.

comments on "significant" events—was useful as a check to see if they were getting full information through their own channels or as an aid in keeping up with events in countries outside their own areas of responsibility. But others said that it was simply a waste of time, complaining that the "newspapers" were too long, that there were too many of them, that they contained too much irrelevant material, and that for one or another of these reasons one could not even manage to read what was offered, much less absorb it. The encyclopedic country survey was not so widely known among the operators as the "newspaper," but it did have some supporters.[1] One official, for example, was most pleased with the survey made on a country in his area; he said that it had performed a useful service by bringing together widely scattered information, and that it gave one a good background for dealing with day-to-day problems. The long-range research project, on the other hand, seemed to have the fewest supporters of all. The feeling seemed to be that these studies usually turned out to be "academic tomes" that had little in common with practical problems.[2] The formal intelligence estimate of capabilities, intentions, and future developments, finally, was not only well known but it also seemed to be thoroughly accepted as a permanent feature. Not that its permanence placed it above criticism; although none of the policy-makers argued that the estimate should be abolished, many felt that it was usually so cautious, so thoroughly surrounded with caveats and qualifications, that the man who reads one is none the wiser for having done so. As a story recently circulating in the government puts it, if the intelligence men ever got into the weather bureau, forecasts would start reading that tomorrow's weather would be fine, if it did not rain, if it did not snow.

To avoid getting a false impression, which these generalizations might create, the interviewer asked each official if he could recall a specific example of something intelligence had done that was especially useful. One official said that he had just recently been involved in a problem that was an excellent example of good research intelligence work. A spokesman for a foreign government had charged American officials with failing to keep a long list of promises they were supposed to have made in public speeches, and his office in the State Department was faced with the problem of deciding whether or not to answer the charges. Of course, the

---

[1] The country survey is a continuously revised report containing voluminous political, economic, military, and sociological "background" information on each country in the world. . . .

[2] The members of the Task Force of the Hoover Commission on Foreign Affairs found similar views, and they, themselves, concluded that intelligence organizations tended to be too "academic." See *Task Force Report on Foreign Affairs* (Appendix H) prepared for the Commission on Organization of the Executive Branch of the Government, January, 1949 (U.S. Government Printing Office), p. 95. See also The Commission on Organization of the Executive Branch of the Government, *Foreign Affairs, A Report to the Congress*, February, 1949 (U.S. Government Printing Office), pp. 15, 16, 56, and 57.

official continued, there had been so many people going around making speeches since the war that no one could be expected to remember everything that had been said. But before his office could make a decision, it needed to know for sure if any American officials had really said what the foreign spokesman had charged them with saying. The intelligence research units had come to the rescue with a paper containing everything American officials had ever said about policy toward that country, and "it took them only twenty-four hours to do it, too!"

The same official mentioned one other example. He said that some time ago the "powers that be" had decided to take another look at American policy toward the problem of the postwar boundaries of a state in his area of responsibility. The steps in evolving the new policy had been as follows: (1) a review of past American statements on the boundary, (2) a factual review of international developments connected with the boundary, and (3) a decision on the new policy. It had been the job of the intelligence division of the Department to produce a paper dealing with the first two steps, and with this information in front of them the policy bureaus had then dealt with the third.

Another official also gave two examples of useful intelligence products. He said that some time ago his office had discovered that there was some doubt about title to the Coronados Islands, a very small group off the coast of California. His office decided that for political reasons the United States should renounce any claims it might have, and they needed something to support this recommendation. By going over old deeds, maps, diaries, and so on, intelligence was able to show that throughout history American officials had always assumed that these islands were not possessions of the United States, and, supported by this historical background, his office was able to recommend the official renunciation of American rights, exactly as they had wanted.

The official said that his second example was connected with the problem of enforcing the migratory labor treaty between Mexico and the United States. In this case, the job for intelligence had been to furnish a history of the problem which the policy bureaus could use in making their own study and in deriving policy recommendations. Although the history intelligence finally submitted had covered a lot of familiar ground, there was also a great deal of material in it that was new to him and very useful.

A third official gave as an example the case of an old quarrel that had finally found its way to the agenda of the United Nations. Intelligence did a historical study on the case at the request of the policy officials, who were not as intimately familiar with the problem as they wanted to be, and this study had turned up some new and useful background information which showed that, contrary to what the policy officials had always thought, there was something to be said on both sides. In this case the job of the American representatives in the UN had been to act as judges, and this paper had helped him, at least, get a clear picture of what it was that he was judging. The official then went on to say that he thought this was an ideal example of the function of intelligence. Since policy people did not have time for such things, and since they were generalists—experts in political relations rather than in a particular area—they needed background, history, and a description of the general situation to help them in making policy. The function of intelligence was to fill this need by preparing factual statements without prejudice.

"Backstopping"

It is important to notice that the intelligence product described in most of these examples, the intelligence product that the operators found useful, stems from a single kind of research intelligence work—the function intelligence officials call "backstopping." By this term research intelligence men mean either a chronological history of events leading up to a problem or a mechanical search for facts tending to support a policy decision that has already been made. The word implies that one is backing the operator up with facts, protecting him by supplying him with facts to defend his position. The connotations are similar to those of the word *rationalizing*, in the sense of searching for good reasons to support doing what one is going to do anyway. Thus in the first of these examples the intelligence officials had to dig up copies of old speeches; in the second they searched for information that would support an *a priori* conclusion (to renounce title to the Coronados); and in each of the others they compiled a general factual history of the problem being considered. The point is that in such work there is no elements of analysis; it is nothing more than grubbing through mountains of material in a routine search for facts. . . .

By way of conclusion to this subject of the operators' opinion of the different intelligence products, it should be said in defense of the officials quoted here that their tendency not to value the work of the research and analysis branches of intelligence very highly does not necessarily mean that they are uninformed, for in no sense are the operators forced to rely solely on the research intelligence organizations for information. They get the same United Press and Associated Press dispatches that the research men do, and they also get the same espionage reports. More than this, the reports the operators get from the embassies and missions abroad and from foreign representatives in Washington almost always contain, for obvious reasons, more pertinent, more timely, and fuller information than either the press services or the espionage reports could ever hope to supply. Thus what the research agencies can give the operators in the way of new information, as opposed to older, already available but widely scattered information that they can gather together in one paper, is likely to be of only marginal importance. Still, to assume that the operators make no more use of the product of the research and analysis branches of intelligence than this interview material indicates would probably be quite wrong. . . .

The Warning and Estimating Function

Most popular writers on the subject of intelligence assume that the warning function is a basic role of intelligence; an efficient intelligence service, they seem to believe, would have warned us of the Pearl Harbor attack, the Berlin blockade, the victory of the Chinese Communists, the attack on South Korea, the Chinese intervention in Korea, and of each of the long list of events that have surprised and dismayed us through the years. If one is talking about the kind of warning a secret agent would give, spying out some dramatic bit of information that has obvious and immediate significance, the operators would almost unanimously agree. But if one is talking about the kind of warning a research and analysis unit would give, the kind of warning that comes from estimating trends, analyzing capabilities, and deducing intentions, their opinions would tend to vary.

When asked specifically about this kind of warning, many officials said that they approved of it, but they often went on to say that they thought other functions were more important. One official, for example, said that intelligence should be encouraged to sound a warning if, after going over the information, it felt that something unpleasant was going to happen or that some new problem was coming up. Nevertheless, he still felt the major function of intelligence should be to see that policy people had all the facts—those that supported the policy of the moment, and especially those that didn't. This was the reason that intelligence should be separate: so that it would be sure to get the facts that didn't support prevailing policy. After all, policy people were human, too. Like everyone else they tended to overlook facts that were inconvenient. You had a better chance of getting the whole picture if you kept intelligence separate so it could get *all* the facts.

It was a good idea, another official said, to have some organization, like intelligence, responsible for giving warnings and making estimates. He pointed out, however, that even though intelligence was responsible for giving warning, this should not mean that everyone else should be muzzled. It would do no harm if some of the policy people, as they usually would, saw the threat at the same time.

A few officials were willing to approve the function, but doubted that anything would ever come of it. One official said that the warning and estimating function was logically valid, but that so far he had not seen it in practice—he had never personally received a warning from intelligence. Another official said that the warning function was fine, if intelligence could really do it. He said that he had yet to see them give a clear-cut warning, one that you could recognize as a warning, one that wasn't hedged around with ifs. And speaking realistically, he felt it would be very difficult. Only an unusual person could avoid theoretical discussions; the result could too easily come out an atomic war on the one hand or perpetual peace on the other.

. . .

Thus the pattern of similarity in the reasoning of the operators interviewed seems to have a variety of sources, ranging from common power interests to limitations on what the research intelligence agencies are able to offer. Yet it should not be assumed that these are cynical men who think only of their own narrow interest. On the contrary, the impression received by an outsider is that they are conscientious and sometimes almost naively sincere. In addition, it must be remembered that the operators offer a positive role for the research intelligence organizations, a role which they clearly believe is meaningful and which must be taken seriously, not as the nakedly cynical defense of power-seekers acting in collusion, but as the considered opinion of responsible men. Accordingly, there seems reason to believe that in addition to common power interests and limitations on what the intelligence agencies can offer, other factors are also at work. As a hypothesis, which on the evidence available can be nothing more than tentative, it is suggested that one of these other factors might be a set of shared assumptions and attitudes—assumptions about the role of facts and of theory, attitudes toward experience, feelings of anti-intellectualism, inclinations toward activism and simplism—that have channeled the thinking of these officials and shaped the solution they advocate. The hypothesis is, first, that most of these officials share a common outlook and set of basic assumptions about causal relationships, about what makes things tick; and, secondly, that this set of attitudes and assumptions has both directly and indirectly shaped the thinking of these officials on this problem of a role for intelligence.[3]

Intelligence and Policy

Since so many of the operators are somewhat suspicious of the warning and estimating function, which is popularly assumed to be a typical intelligence job, it is not surprising to find still more of them objecting even

[3] The concept that people from the same cultural group share a way of looking at things by means of which they interpret events and in terms of which they choose courses of action is, of course, well established in the field of cultural anthropology. See, for example, the works of Ruth Benedict, Abram Kardiner, Clyde Kluckhohn, Cora Du Bois, Ralph Linton, Margaret Mead, and Geoffrey Gorer. Interesting applications of this concept in the field of political science include Gabriel A. Almond, *The American People and Foreign Policy* (New York: Harcourt, Brace, 1950); and Nathan Leites, *A Study of Bolshevism* (Glencoe, Ill.: The Free Press, 1953).

more strongly to any suggestion that intelligence should be allowed to come any closer to policy—that intelligence should either explore policy alternatives open to the United States in a certain area or examine the validity of premises on which a certain policy is based. When one official was asked what he thought intelligence could do to help in predicting the effects of the alternative policies open to the United States, he said that if the political officer asked intelligence to explore alternatives he was dodging his responsibility. Even if the political officer did not have the facts on a problem, he should still make the decisions. Actually, the Department should see that he was furnished the facts, which was why there were such things as intelligence units. Intelligence, the official firmly concluded, should furnish information and nothing more.

Another official said that this kind of work would go beyond the functions of intelligence as he saw it. Intelligence ought to collect facts, organize them, and assign weight to the body of facts collected and organized. If intelligence did this, they would be doing a worth-while job—other parts of the Department would then have an independent check on their own work. What to do about a problem, however, was a function of the policy people, who had had practical experience with this sort of thing.

In a discussion about an intelligence study on the Far East, a third official was asked what conclusions the study had come to. The official echoed the word *conclusions* with a tone of irritated disbelief. He said that intelligence was not supposed to come to conclusions. They should see that a report contained all the facts available. Their job was background, and background was essential. When pressed, the official admitted that under many circumstances intelligence could not avoid coming to some kind of conclusions, but he said that when they did this sort of thing they tended to get away from both the necessary facts and the realities of what could be done. They tended to be "ivory-towerish," and consequently any conclusions they offered should be gone over very carefully by people who dealt with a country on a day-to-day basis. The official said that of course you needed a "long-range" view as well as a "practical" one. You needed both. The danger was in letting one or the other become too powerful. Something like finding out whether the Voice of America was having any effect was a good function for intelligence. Intelligence should be building up bits and pieces about something, like the Voice, in which the policy people were interested.

The reasoning implicit in these arguments comes up again and again when the operators are asked to justify their position about the role of intelligence. These officials, first, put extreme emphasis on the importance of having "all" the facts. They also fear that the man who is attempting to solve a problem, the man who is thinking of policy, will become an unreasoning advocate of some pet solution. They feel that if this man also collects facts on the problem, he will tend to select facts that support his policy and therefore will not find the true answer. And there is also a distrust of the research man. Since this attitude seems to extend only partly to the economist and hardly at all the physical scientist, it may stem, at least in part, from the incomplete development of the social sciences themselves. But in any event, to the operator, who must feel like the Sorcerer's Apprentice as he tries to keep up with the flood of immediate problems demanding action, the researcher is something of a dreamer, a man who spends his life poring over dusty books in musty libraries far removed from the realities of life. At the same time, the operators tend to believe that practical experience, rather than scholarly academic training, is the true and perhaps the only path to the kind of knowledge and judgment needed in dealing with problems that arise in the real world, in the rough and tumble of the market place. They apparently believe that out of practical experience a man develops a "feel" for a problem, a talent for accurate hunches, and that only this sort of sixth sense can sweep away the tangle of doubt and complexity surrounding problems in foreign affairs and seize the one effective course of action. . . .

The Intelligence Man and the Operator

In any event, among the majority of the intelligence officials interviewed there seemed to be much the same complex of assumptions, traits, and attitudes as there was among the operators. This is not to say, however, that the two groups are therefore in perfect accord. There is obviously some bickering—and bitterness—between them. As I have said, although both the intelligence men and the operators stressed the importance of practical experience, they found it hard to agree on just what kind of experience is practical. The loose definitions of the words *policy* and *fact*, like that of *experience*, also make for trouble. An intelligence man who says that the German people are inherently militaristic, for example, may often regard his statement as an unvarnished fact, and not as a conclusion. But to the policy official, who often seems to feel that an ally who is realistically necessary must also be morally good, the statement that this ally is "undemocratic" is neither a fact nor a conclusion, but an implied recommendation of policy.

1. *Frustration and Isolation.* Although there are also other differences between the intelligence men and the operators, there is only one of these that seems to be very important. This is the doubt many of the intelligence officials seemed to have about their very reason for existing. One official, for example, said that in his opinion intelligence was isolated—there was not even a forum at which it could be heard. On one problem, about which the intelligence people had felt strongly, they had submitted their estimate in a special paper. But the paper was not even challenged; it was just ignored. The issue intelligence had pointed out was never tackled. Another

said that one of the big questions in his mind was the contribution of intelligence. He often wondered if it was an important one. In a sense, he said, this was a practical, bureaucratic question, i.e., how did one find a criterion of the value of an intelligence outfit? Certainly not by counting the number of books produced. The policy official could measure the success or failure of his policy, but the intelligence officer could never tell what his influence had been. There were no objective criteria; the intelligence officer couldn't tell if he was doing a good job. In business it was different. If the businessman couldn't sell his product, he knew that something was wrong with his organization so he looked and tried to find out what it was. The intelligence man didn't know if he was doing any good except in rare and usually dramatic circumstances. Therefore, the official continued, to get reassurance the intelligence man had to circle back to the theory of why intelligence was necessary. Generally speaking, intelligence people thought they knew what the intelligence function should be, but there was never any payoff. So they always had to fall back on the theory. If an intelligence man predicted something and it happened, everything was fine. But he never knew how many off-the-cuff forecasters had seen the same thing, and he didn't know if any of the geographic desk people had read his prediction. To get a commendation is helpful bureaucratically, but the Secretary didn't say how the work that had been commended changed his thinking, so the intelligence man never knew. A man on one of the geographic desks might have done the same thing in five minutes. The test of intelligence was the influence it had on the thinking of the operating people. Intelligence people could get a check on where their reports were sent, and on how accurate their predictions had been, but not on how influential their product had been on policy. This was not exactly frustrating, but it was part of the psychology of a human being to want to know if he was effective. The official being interviewed said that Thursday he had had an argument with a policy man. Saturday the man took a neutral view. The official said that he had probably been responsible for the change, but that he was sure the man he had argued with didn't give him the credit.

As these two officials imply, it is to most people a humiliating experience to feel useless and unimportant. But when a man believes, as many intelligence officials apparently do, that correct policy springs full-blown from the facts, he cannot help being both bewildered and indignant if he decides that policy is usually made without facts, or at least without those facts furnished by intelligence, who have the formal responsibility for furnishing them. One official, for example, said that what struck him was that there were two categories of "intelligence." One was the sheer process of gathering information, evaluating, and estimating. This was done by everyone, policy people and intelligence people. In this sense "intelligence" was at the base of all action. Then, secondly, there was formal "intelligence"—the collection, evaluation, and estimating done by people formally responsible for intelligence. This intelligence played a damned small role. Even in the Army, the G-3 (plans and operations) paid no attention to the G-2—and neither did the Commanding General, except in rare cases where the G-2 was outstanding in every way. Perhaps there was something basically wrong with American intelligence, but the planners didn't encourage intelligence, so there was no incentive for improvement. The best people didn't go into intelligence work.

The official went on to say that the State Department didn't pay a lot of attention to the intelligence organizations either. Intelligence people had to do long background papers, but they weren't let into the highest councils. Intelligence people just didn't get in on things. They didn't even know what was needed. How could they work if they didn't know what was going on? He supposed that the State Department desk people were more able than intelligence people and made their own estimates. If they were more able than intelligence people, and got more information, which they did, then there was no need for intelligence at all. The official said that he did think that *logically* there was a need—a need for a group who, independently of the policy-makers, could make estimates in terms of the facts. The role of intelligence should be to evaluate, estimate, and collate information to give a picture of the situation. But in practice, policy was made and intelligence was then asked for the information to support it.

Another official said that intelligence should come first, and then policy. In reality, however, policy was made, and then intelligence was expected to rationalize it. Take the Military Aid Program. The policy people decided on the program, and then asked intelligence for an estimate of European willingness to fight. The policy was formed in an absence of intelligence and intelligence appraisal.

Another official said that "the whole damned thing" was wrong. Before they did anything else, policy people should call on intelligence for the information and an estimate. Then they should make their policy. In reality, however, policy was made without intelligence or was only supplemented by intelligence. Intelligence people always had to analyze what had already happened, or had to give support for policy decisions that were already made. The policy people wanted from intelligence nothing more than supporting material for already decided policy and already decided propaganda. Intelligence did nothing but hack work and research. In practice everything was all backwards.

2. *Conclusion.* If an intelligence official believes that in practice everything is all backwards, that the logical and ordained sequence of events is violated, his unhappiness is understandable. It comes from the humiliation of feeling useless, impotent, and ignored, of feeling that no matter how hard one works or how good one's work really is, the policy-maker will never look at it, or look at it only after its real usefulness is past, when the policy decision has already been made. Although there does seem to be a rather

high turnover in the research intelligence organizations (intelligence, like the Communist Party, seems to have more ex-members than members), the number of intelligence officials who really doubt their reason for existing is probably very small. The important point, however, is what makes it possible for these doubts to arise in the first place—the suspicion that something is wrong, that things are not going as they should.

Science, Research, and Foreign Policy

Warner R. Schilling

SCIENTISTS, FOREIGN POLICY, AND POLITICS

> . . . we must take, so far as we can, a picture of the world into our minds. Is it not a startling circumstance for one thing that the great discoveries of science, that the quiet study of men in laboratories, that the thoughtful developments which have taken place in quiet lecture rooms, have now been turned to the destruction of civilization? . . . The enemy whom we have just overcome had at its seats of learning some of the principal centres of scientific study and discovery, and used them in order to make destruction sudden and complete; and only the watchful, continuous cooperation of men can see to it that science, as well as armed men, is kept within the harness of civilization.[1]

I

THESE words were spoken in Paris in January 1919 by Woodrow Wilson, addressing the second Plenary Session of the Peace Conference. Wilson believed he had found a watchdog for civilization in the League of Nations. In this he was sadly mistaken. Science and armed men have indeed been harnessed, but in order to promote and maintain the goals of conflicting polities. Whether in the pursuit of these ends the cause of civilization will yet be served remains, we may hope, an open question.

The cooperation of scientists and armed men was not a new relationship, even in Wilson's day. In the United States, for example, the president of the American Association for the Advancement of Science had declared in 1861:

[1] U.S. Department of State, *Papers Relating to the Foreign Relations of the United States, The Peace Conference*, 13 vols. (Washington, 1942–1947), vol. 3, p. 179.

FROM *The American Political Science Review*, **LVI**, 2 (June 1962). Reprinted by permission of the author and The American Political Science Association.

. . . it is easy to see that there are few applications of science which do not bear on the interests of commerce and navigation, naval or military concerns, the customs, the lighthouses, the public lands, post offices or post roads, either directly or remotely. If all examination is refused . . . the Government may lose a most important advantage.[2]

As a result of the interest of a number of American scientists and government officials, the National Academy of Sciences was established in 1863 for the purpose of providing scientific advice to the United States Government. The use made of this Academy by the War Department between 1863 and 1913 bespeaks a bygone era. During those years the Department requested the Academy to constitute scientific committees on exactly five matters:

On the Question of Tests for the Purity of Whiskey; On the Preservation of Paint on Army Knapsacks; On Galvanic Action from Association of Zinc and Iron; On the Exploration of the Yellowstone; On questions of Meteorological Science and its Applications.[3]

It would be unfair to presume from this list that the War Department was uninterested in new weapons systems. Until about the turn of the century, military technology, like industrial technology, generally developed independently of advances in basic scientific knowledge. Thus, in 1915, when Wilson's Secretary of the Navy decided to establish a "Department of Invention and Development" in the hope of securing effective weapons with which to combat that "new and terrible engine of warfare . . . the submarine," it was the inventor, Thomas Edison, who was asked to head the new organization.[4] Although the contributions of university and industrial scientists to the fighting of World War I were marked enough to have caught Wilson's imagination, it was not until a generation later, with the advent of World War II, that the mobilization of scientists brought military results which were of great and in some instances decisive importance to the course of combat.

What has transformed the relationship between science and war has been the fact that in the twentieth century the development of technology has become increasingly dependent upon advances in basic knowledge about the physical world. Moreover, in the technically advanced nations, both the rate of technological innovation and the growth of new scientific knowledge have been increasing exponentially. As crudely measured by the volume of scientific publication, scientific knowledge has been doubling

---

[2] Quoted in *Science and Technology Act of 1958*, Staff Study of the Senate Committee on Government Operations, 85th Cong., 2d sess., Washington, 1958, p. 110.

[3] *Ibid.*, p. 115.

[4] See Daniels' letter to Edison, in Josephus Daniels, *The Wilson Era: Years of Peace, 1910–1917* (Chapel Hill: The University of North Carolina Press, 1944), p. 491.

every ten to fifteen years.[5] In a non-Wilsonian world, the consequences of these conditions for national security policy have been as necessary as they are obvious. As the United States and the Soviet Union throw one weapons system after another into the effort to maintain at least a balance of terror, neither dares fall behind in either the discovery of new physical relationships or in the application of scientific knowledge to military hardware and political-military strategy. Thus, by the end of the first decade of the Cold War, about 50 per cent of the engineers in the United States and 25 per cent of the scientists were employed by the Federal government, either directly or on contract, and about 65 per cent of the scientific research in universities and 57 per cent of that in private industry was government-financed.[6]

Indicative of the new relationship between science and war, figures and graphs comparing the Great Powers in numbers of scientists and engineers have become as familiar as those in the 1930s which compared the Powers in their output of steel, coal, and oil. Nor is it only in the military field that science and technology have become vital to the course of foreign policy. Science has been harnessed to the advancement of foreign policy goals in such diverse fields as the exploration of space, birth and disease control, weather modification, economic development, and global communications.[7]

Present, prospective, and future developments in science and technology are certain to bring a host of problems and opportunities to those responsible for the conduct of foreign policy. In recognition of this fact, the governments of the major Powers have endeavored to find ways to make themselves more alert to such developments and more active in determining the course of science and technology. The United States and the Soviet Union are the most extensively engaged in this effort, but it should not be forgotten that the nations of Western and Central Europe were among the pioneers in cultivating the relationship between science and government. The three elements that have revolutionized current military technology and strategy (electronics, missiles, and nuclear weapons) had their harbingers in the World War II development of British radar, the German V-2, and the American A-bomb, and it is noteworthy that the two European developments were conceived, initiated, and directed by officials and employees of established government organizations. In contrast, the American

[5] Ellis A. Johnson, "The Crisis in Science and Technology and its Effect on Military Development," *Operations Research* (January-February 1958), pp. 14–15.

[6] See Lee A. DuBridge, "The American Scientist: 1955," *Yale Review* (Spring 1955), p. 13, and the *Bulletin of the Atomic Scientists*, March 1957, p. 82, and May-June 1961, p. 254. The figure for private industry is for the year 1959; the others are for the year 1955.

[7] For a more detailed treatment of some of the points in the preceding paragraphs and a general discussion of the effect of science on international relations, see the present writer's "Science, Technology, and Foreign Policy," *Journal of International Affairs* (Fall 1959), pp. 7–18.

A-bomb was the result of conceptions and initiatives that came from outside the government—and primarily from exiled Europeans at that.

As an integral part of the efforts of governments to become both more responsive to and responsible for the development of science and technology, scientists have been invited into the highest councils of government, and it is with some of the problems occasioned by the presence of these "new" participants in the making of national policy that the remainder of this article will be concerned. Although some illustrative material will be drawn from the experience of other governments, the paper focuses on problems associated with the participation of scientists in the American policy process.

Needless to say, the problems in policy-making that may arise will vary greatly with the kind of scientist participating (oceanographer, theoretical physicist, specialist in space medicine, industrial chemist), with the nature of the policy issue at stake (weapons development, science education, public health, the exploration of space, the allocation of funds for basic research), and with the manner in which the scientist is involved in the policy process (member of the attentive public, adviser to the President, worker in a government laboratory, official in an executive department or agency). This article will make no attempt to deal systematically with the combinations possible among these three variables (profession, issue, and involvement). The discussion will be confined to a few of the central problems that the layman and the scientist are likely to encounter in working together on national security issues; and the treatment, as will become evident, will be of a very general and suggestive order.

In their general character, the problems occasioned by the participation of scientists in the determination of high policy are not nearly so novel as is generally supposed. The scientist has been brought into the councils of government because he possesses specialized skills and information believed relevant to the identification and resolution of particular policy problems. His relationship to the policy process is therefore a familiar one, that of an expert. Just as Sputnik I precipitated the establishment of a Special Assistant to the President for Science and Technology, so the earlier problems of fighting World War II and insuring postwar employment had brought the Joint Chiefs of Staff and the Council of Economic Advisers into the Offices of the President.

The central problems in policy-making posed by the entry of scientists into the policy process are thus formally no different from those associated with any other expert involved in the determination of national security policy. In particular, four such problems can be noted. (1) Like all experts, scientists will at times disagree, and the non-scientist (be he politician, administrator, or an expert in some other field) will confront the problem of choosing a course of action in the face of conflicting scientific advice. (2) Like all experts, scientists will at times evince certain predispositions toward the resolution of the policy problems on which their advice is sought, and the non-scientist will confront the problem of identifying the policy pre-dilections peculiar to scientists and being on his guard against them. (3) The non-scientist and scientist will confront one problem in common, and that is how to organize themselves to maximize the contribution that science can make to the government's programs, opportunities, and choices. Finally, (4) the scientist will confront a problem common to all experts who participate in the American policy process, and that is how to engage in politics without debasing the coinage of his own expertise.

II

The difficulties the non-scientist confronts in choosing a course of action in the face of conflicting scientific advice seem inherently no more formida-ble than those a non-expert would face in deciding what to do in the event of conflicting advice from economists, soldiers, or specialists on Soviet foreign policy. There are at least seven procedures that the non-expert can follow in such circumstances, singly or in combination, and they appear to have about the same promise, for better or for worse, regardless of the kind of experts involved.[8]

The first step the non-scientist can take is to make certain that it is really conflicting *scientific* advice he is receiving. In the fall of 1949 Presi-dent Truman asked Secretary Acheson to look into the disputes then current within the Atomic Energy Commission and elsewhere about the consequences of undertaking an intensive effort to make an H-bomb. Upon investigation the Secretary of State concluded that the scientists involved were not really very far apart except on the foreign policy issues that were his and Truman's responsibility to decide.[9]

Procedures two and three are simple: the non-scientist may be guided by quantitative or qualitative features of the division (he can side with the majority, or with that side whose past record is the more confidence-inspiring). Failing these, there is, four, the "principle of least harm" and, five, the "principle of minimal choice." In the former, one chooses that course of action which appears to involve the least cost if the technical premise on which it is based proves to be wrong. Thus in World War II, given the American belief that the Germans were hard at work on an A-bomb, it seemed more sensible to spend $2 billion on the assumption that the bomb could be made than to do little or nothing on the assump-

---

[8] *Cf.* the implication in the following remarks of Glenn T. Seaborg, the Chairman of the Atomic Energy Commission: "Scientists don't necessarily have to make the final political decisions, but it might be easier to let a capable scientist learn political reality than to teach a politician science." Quoted in the *Bulletin of the Atomic Scientists* (February 1961), p. 79.

[9] In this and subsequent undocumented references the present writer has drawn upon personal interviews during 1956–1958 with participants in the H-bomb decision.

tion that it could not. In the case of the "principle of minimal choice," one chooses that course of action which seems to close off the least number of future alternatives. This was the character of President Truman's first decision on the H-bomb. He decided to go ahead in the effort to explore the feasibility of an H-bomb, but nothing was decided about technical steps of a greater political or military consequence (for example, testing a device if one were fabricated, or preparing to produce the materials that would be required for weapons production in the event of a successful test).[10]

In the case of procedure six the non-scientist can make his choice among conflicting scientists on the basis of whichever technical estimate is most in accord with policy on which he was already intent. (In contrast to the first procedure, where the non-scientist endeavors to factor out of the conflict the policy preferences of the scientists, here he is factoring into the conflict his own policy preferences.) In the spring of 1942, the British scientists Henry Tizard and F. A. Lindemann (Lord Cherwell) diverged greatly in their estimates of the destruction that could be accomplished by an intensive bombing of the homes of the German working class. There was general agreement among the soldiers and politicians involved that if the lower estimate were correct there were better military uses for the resources the bombing campaign would require, but in the end the campaign was made in the expectation that the higher estimate would prove to be the more accurate (which it did not). This choice was clearly influenced by Churchill's interest in presenting the Russians with a dramatically visible contribution to the war against Germany and by the fact that British air doctrine had long presumed the efficacy of strategic bombing.[11]

In procedure seven the non-scientist is guided by his own sense for the scientific and technical problems involved. In the 1949 H-bomb debate, some of the politicians involved were little deterred by the fact that the scientists were by no means confident that they could make such a weapon and by the possibility that an all-out but failing effort might entail very high costs for the A-bomb program. These politicians were willing to press ahead in part because of their belief that the scientists were not really aware of their own potential. Similarly, when the German soldiers, scientists, and engineers engaged in the development of the V-2 divided on the question of whether it should be launched from mobile or fixed

---

[10] For the "principle of least harm," see Bernard Brodie, "Strategy as a Science," *World Politics* (July 1949), p. 479n. On the H-bomb choice, see the present writer's "The H-Bomb Decision: How to Decide Without Actually Choosing," *Political Science Quarterly* (March 1961), pp. 37–38.

[11] See C. P. Snow, *Science and Government* (Cambridge: Harvard University Press, 1961), pp. 47–51, the review of this book by P. M. S. Blackett in *Scientific American* (April 1961), pp. 192–194, and Winston S. Churchill, *The Second World War: The Hinge of Fate* (Boston: Houghton Mifflin Company, 1950), p. 281. For British air doctrine see also Herbert S. Dinnerstein, "The Impact of Air Power on the International Scene, 1933–1940," *Military Affairs* (Summer 1955), pp. 67–68.

batteries, Hitler's own technical enthusiasm for large, hardened bunkers led him, unwisely as it turned out, to decide on behalf of the latter.[12]

In concluding this survey of the problem of conflicting advice, it should be noted that one of the more likely outcomes is that the actions of the contending scientists may prove much more influential than the procedures followed by the non-scientists. Divided experts will not always be equal in their physical or personal access to the decision-maker, in the persistence with which they state their case, or in the force and clarity of their arguments. Thus, in the H-bomb debate, there were instances where equally qualified scientists differed greatly in the time and energy they spent circulating their views of the technical (and political) prospects, and such differences were by no means without consequence for the judgments of others.[13]

III

The discussion of the policy predispositions displayed by scientists must be entered with considerable caution. The major theoretical premise involved is that all experts will evidence certain predilections with regard to policy and policy-making which are the result of the character of their expertise: their skills, knowledge, and experience. Since experts differ in the skills, knowledge, and experience they command (or in the responsibilities with which they are charged), they will differ in the biases they characteristically exhibit. Thus scientists, soldiers, and diplomats jointly concerned with a policy problem are likely to approach the question of how and in what manner it should be resolved with rather dissimilar predispositions.

These points, however, are easier stated than demonstrated. To begin with, it should be clear that, insofar as policy is concerned, "the scientific mind" is as much a chimera as "the military mind." Scientists, like soldiers

[12] Maj. Gen. Walter Dornberger, V-2 (New York: Ballantine Books, 1954), pp. 97, 158–160, and Lt. Gen. James M. Gavin, *War and Peace in the Space Age* (New York, 1958), pp. 76–77.

[13] Note should also be taken of the problem the policy-maker faces when all his experts are *agreed*. The present writer is unable to suggest a useful procedure here (other than variations on numbers five, six, and seven above); but that the problem is a real one can be seen in the conclusion of the German physicists that it would be infeasible for any Power to develop an atomic bomb during World War II. Some of the German scientists later stated that political considerations were partly responsible for their advice and for the fact that they made so little progress themselves on an A-bomb (*cf.* procedure one).

The German work on the A-bomb during World War II is described in Samuel A. Goudsmit, *Alsos* (New York: Henry Schuman, Inc., 1947). For various appraisals of the influence exercised by political considerations, see Robert Jungk, *Brighter than a Thousand Suns* (New York: Harcourt, Brace and Company, 1958), pp. 88–104, Hans Bethe in the *Bulletin of the Atomic Scientists*, December 1958, p. 427, and William L. Laurence, *Men and Atoms* (New York: Simon and Schuster, 1959), pp. 90–93.

and the rest of us, differ greatly in the ideas they have about the political world and the things that will (or ought to) happen in it, and their views on foreign policy matters are far more likely to be reflective of these differences than conditioned by their common professional skills and interests. Moreover, even if differences in expertise or responsibility were the only factors determining the views of policy-makers (and they certainly are not), one would still have to take account of the fact that scientists are as varied in their professional skills and pursuits as soldiers. The perspectives of a theoretical physicist engaged in basic research are no more to be equated with those of an organic chemist engaged in applying extant knowledge to the improvement of an industrial product than is the outlook of a staff officer in Washington drafting a war plan to be considered identical with that of a general in charge of a theatre of operations.

In addition to these difficulties, analysis must also contend with the fact that it is directed toward a moving target. The policy perspectives that a physicist may have developed as a result of two decades in a university laboratory are unlikely to endure without change after a few years on a Washington advisory committee. Many American scientists are well along the same route that transformed the policy perspectives of large numbers of the American military profession during the war and immediate postwar years. As a result of new problems and new responsibilities, these soldiers acquired new skills, knowledge, and experience. In consequence, with regard to their approach to foreign policy, some are, for all practical purposes, interchangeable between the Pentagon and the State Department, and one could wish that there were more diplomats equally well equipped to work on both sides of the Potomac.

With these reservations in mind, six policy perspectives will be presented here which seem moderately characteristic of many scientists, most of them physicists, who have participated in national security policy in recent times. Most of these predispositions were first evidenced during their work with the military during World War II, and the extent and manner in which they have been later operative in reference to larger foreign policy issues is not always easy to document, since most of the sources are still classified. Needless to say, in outlining these predispositions, one is presenting a cross between a caricature and a Weberian ideal type, not describing real people. In discussing these predispositions, the present writer does not mean to convey the impression that they are either "good" or "bad" from the point of view of policy or policy-making, or that one or another of these predispositions may not also be evidenced by groups other than scientists. The point to this discussion is that if certain orders of scientists are indeed prone to these or other policy predispositions, the non-scientist will be wise to be alert to them, even if in the event he should conclude that they are all for the good.

Naïve Utopianism or Naïve Belligerency. C. P. Snow has described the scientist as an impatient optimist in his approach to social wrongs; he is quick to search for something to do and inclined to expect favorable results.[14] Certainly, the scientist's profession inclines him to look at problems in terms of searching for a solution to them. When this perspective is turned to problems of international politics, however, the scientist's approach often appears open to the characterization of "naïve utopianism or naïve belligerency."[15] His approach to international relations appears simplistic and mechanistic. It is almost as if he conceives of policy being made primarily by forward-looking, solution-oriented, rational-thinking types like himself.

In these perspectives the scientist is likely to find little in common with the diplomat (who is inclined to believe that most of his problems have no solution, and who is in any event too busy with the crises of the day to plan for tomorrow), or with the politician (whose approach to problems is so spasmodic as to seem neither analytical nor rational, and whose policy positions are anyway soon blurred by his efforts to accommodate to the positions of others), or with the professional student of international politics (who, when the opportunity permits, lectures the scientist on the elegant complexity of the political process, but who never seems, to the scientist at least, to have any really good ideas about what to do). It is perhaps these differences in perspective that lead the scientist on occasion to seem "intellectually arrogant"; it is as if he concludes that those who have no promising solutions or are not seeking them cannot be very bright. In his predisposition toward action and solutions, the scientist comes closest to sharing the predilection of the soldier for decision, which may be one reason why their partnership has been so spectacularly successful.

The whole problem approach. The first grant made by the United States Government for experimental research was in 1832 to the Franklin Institute. The scientists were asked to investigate the reasons for explosions in steamboat boilers. They reported back not only with a technical explanation but with a draft bill to provide for Federal regulation of steamboats.[16] In this they evidenced the scientist's predilection for the "whole problem approach." The reluctance of scientists to apply their expertise to mere fragments of the total problem, especially under conditions where those who prescribe the fragments do not reveal the whole of which they are a part, was evident in the work of both British and American scientists during World War II. Military officials initially approached the scientists

---

[14] C. P. Snow, *The Two Cultures and the Scientific Revolution* (New York: Cambridge University Press, 1959), pp. 9–11.

[15] I am indebted to Hans Speier for the phrasing of this point.

[16] Don K. Price, *Government and Science* (New York: New York University Press, 1954), pp. 10–11.

with requests for the development of particular weapons and devices without revealing the military problems or reasoning responsible for their requests. The scientists objected to this procedure, and they were eventually able to persuade the soldiers to inform them of the general military problems involved in order that the scientists might reach their own conclusions about the kinds of weapons and devices the military would need to meet those problems.[17]

In 1952, in connection with an Air Force project on air defense, a group of American scientists were asked to review the prospects for improving the nation's continental air defense. The scientists concluded that some new and promising systems were possible, and they submitted an estimate of what the developments might cost. They also recommended that the money be spent. The Air Force did not approve the recommendation, and as is customary in Washington the disputants on both sides began to search for allies and to leak their cases to the press. Certain Air Force officials, who feared that additional funds for air defense would come at the expense of dollars otherwise available for the Strategic Air Command and who were convinced that this would be militarily undesirable, charged that the scientists by entering into matters of military strategy and budget policy had exceeded both their assignment and their expertise. Commenting on this charge, one of the scientists involved later explained that he would have little interest in working on a study project that did not have the potential for leading into the question of whether the conclusions should be acted upon.[18]

The predisposition to want to be told and to deal with the whole problem no doubt has its base in the professional experience of scientists (and one of the central credos of science) that good ideas on a problem may

---

[17] This persuasion was largely accomplished through demonstrations of the military utility of the scientists' taking such an approach, although in the early history of the M.I.T. Radiation Laboratory a certain amount of polite bargaining was apparently practiced. One scientist involved, whenever told that the reason for a request was a problem for Washington, not him, to worry about, adopted the practice of working on something else until he was given a description of the problem involved. For a brief summary of the British experience, see Alexander Haddow, "The Scientist as Citizen," *Bulletin of the Atomic Scientists* (September 1956), p. 247.

[18] *Cf.* the following exchange between Gordon Gray and Jerrold Zacharias during the Oppenheimer hearing. Gray: "If you were directing a study which had to do with electronics, a pretty clearly defined field, and it started to come up with recommendations with respect to foreign policy, would you feel that an official of the Defense Department who urged that you stick to electronics was acting with impropriety?" Zacharias: "I think I would not direct a project that was as restrictive as that, sir, as to be restricted only to electronics." U. S. Atomic Energy Commission, *In the Matter of J. Robert Oppenheimer, Transcript of Hearing before Personnel Security Board*, Washington, 1954, p. 930.

For some of the issues involved in the 1952 air defense study, see *ibid.*, pp. 598–99, 749–50, 763–65, 923–24, 930–31, 935, 938, and also the account in Price, *Government and Science*, pp. 136–38.

come from the most unexpected quarters and that the widest possible dissemination of information about a problem will significantly enhance its chances for an early solution.[19] Still, there are problems and problems; some are open to determinate solutions, and others can be resolved only through the exercise of political power. The point about the "whole problem approach," as the air defense example illustrates, is that it not only helps propel the scientists from an advisory to a political role but it serves to make the scientist somewhat blind to the fact that he is so moving. In its most extreme form, the "whole problem approach" coupled with the "intellectual arrogance" perspective can lead to such instances as when, on one high-level advisory committee concerned with several areas of national security policy, a scientist whose formal claim to participation was a knowledge of infra-red ray phenomena was reportedly quite free with his proposals for what political policies should be adopted with regard to the United Nations.

Quantum Jumps versus Improvements. A number of scientists have advanced the proposition that the military tend to be more interested in improving existing weapons than in developing radically new ones, and they have urged that a separate civilian agency be established to undertake such development. Both scientists and soldiers have explained this difference in their approach to military research and development, "quantum jumps versus improvements," with the hypothesis that the soldier's interest in developing entirely new weapons must always be inhibited by his concern for the possibility that war may come in the near future, since in this event his interests are best served by improving existing weapons. It has also been suggested that military leaders, who must be prepared at any time to ask others to take up the weapons at hand and fight with them, cannot afford to let themselves or others become too impressed with the deficiencies of those weapons as compared with others that might have been had.[20]

An explanation less flattering to the military for this difference is the occasional assertion by scientists that theirs is a profession which stimulates original and creative thought, while that of the military tends to develop minds which accept the existing situation without too much question. As indicated in the discussion of the first predilection, this is a judgment which

---

[19] General Leslie Groves, who directed the Manhattan project, was especially sensitive to the scientists' tendency to take on the whole problem. (Some even advised him on how the garbage should be collected at Los Alamos, an act which may possibly have reflected self- rather than scientific interest.) One reason for his effort to compartmentalize the work scientists were doing was his fear that "if I brought them into the whole project, they would never do their own job. There was just too much of scientific interest, and they would just be frittering from one thing to another." *Oppenheimer Transcript*, p. 164.

[20] See, for example, Lloyd V. Berkner, "Science and National Strength," *Bulletin of the Atomic Scientists* (June 1953), pp. 155, 180.

the scientists may extend to the diplomat and the politician as well. The structure of both the domestic and the international political process is normally such as to make "quantum jumps" in policy infeasible. Diplomats and politicians are accustomed to seeing the same old policy problems come around year after year, and they are generally intent on policies which promise only slow and modest change. Scientists, on the other hand, have been demanding and searching for quantum jumps in foreign policy ever since the end of World War II. It is symptomatic that the first proposal developed by the Advisory Committee on Science and Technology to the Democratic National Advisory Council, established in 1959, was for the creation of a new scientific agency, independent of the State and Defense Departments, whose function would be "to face all the problems of disarmament." [21]

Technology for its own sweet sake. In the summer of 1945, after the A-bomb had been tested but before the first drop on Japan, the Director of the Los Alamos Laboratory, J. Robert Oppenheimer, suggested to his superior, General Leslie Groves, that if some improvements were made in the design of the bomb it would be more effective. Groves decided against the improvements because he did not want to incur any delay in the use of the bomb, which he expected would end the war with Japan. In the summer of 1943, after the Director of the German V-2 project, General Dornberger, had finally secured a first-class priority for the use of the weapon, those responsible for producing it in quantity were increasingly handicapped by the scientists and engineers who kept improving but changing its design. Dornberger was finally obliged to issue a flat order against any further improvements.[22]

There was nothing irresponsible in these scientists' actions. Charged with the technical development of weapons, they would have been remiss in their responsibilities if they had failed to call attention to the prospects for improvement. The point to the examples is that scientists and engineers, in the pursuit of their own responsibilities and interests, may easily lose sight of those of the policy maker.

The scientists on the General Advisory Committee to the Atomic Energy Commission who recommended against the development of an H-bomb in 1949 did so in part because of their concern for the foreign-policy consequences of introducing a weapon of such destructive power into the world. Oppenheimer, the Chairman of the Committee, later stated that the thermonuclear design developed by Edward Teller in 1951 was "technically so sweet" that, if it had been available in 1949, the Committee would probably not have made the recommendation that it did. Since, with a technically more promising design at hand, one might suppose that the Committee's foreign-policy concerns would have been all the greater, some observers

21 See the *Bulletin of the Atomic Scientists* (December 1959), p. 412.
22 *Oppenheimer Transcript*, p. 33, and Dornberger, V-2, pp. 134–137.

have concluded that in the pursuit of his technical interests the scientist can also easily lose sight of his own policy concerns.[23]

Such a judgment ignores the complexity of the Committee's position. For example, one of the reasons why the Committee thought the United States should take the initiative in renouncing the H-bomb was precisely because the device then in view seemed likely to be both difficult to make and of dubious military value. It was thought that for this reason the Russians might be willing to follow the American example and that, if they did not, the United States would not have risked much by the delay. These were considerations which obviously would have been changed if a technically more promising design had been available in 1949.[24] Still, the comments of several scientists close to these events are not without relevance. It is their feeling that there are times when the technician does take over, that when the scientist is faced with an interesting and challenging problem his inclination is to get to work on it, and that under these circumstances he should not be the first person to be expected to keep larger policy considerations in balance.

This predisposition, "technology for its own sweet sake," appears to have its roots in two more of science's central credos: the belief in the value of pursuing knowledge for its own sake, and the belief that the best motivation for the direction of research is the strength and character of individual curiosities. But the direction and strength of scientific interests and curiosities is not necessarily coincident with the requirements of military or foreign policy. One of the most recent examples of the scientist's capacity to get caught up in a challenging problem (assigned, to be sure, by policy-makers) is afforded by the ingenious techniques scientists conceived for evading nuclear-test detection systems and for the design of new systems to meet those evasions. In the light of the later course of negotiations, an American statesman who believed there was considerable foreign-policy gain in a test-ban treaty and who believed that the Russians were at one time seriously interested in such a treaty might well conclude that the formula developed by Watson-Watt, the scientist who fathered radar, with reference to the problem of meeting wartime military requirements was not without its implications for meeting peacetime foreign policy requirements: "Give them the third best to go with; the second comes too late, the best never comes." [25] This observation is not intended as an argument that the interests of the United States would have been better served by a test-ban treaty with a "third best" detection system than by no treaty at all.

---

[23] *Oppenheimer Transcript*, p. 251. For an extreme judgment, see Jungk, *Brighter Than a Thousand Suns*, p. 296.

[24] See Oppenheimer's statements in *Oppenheimer Transcript*, pp. 81, 251, 897, and "The H-Bomb Decision: How to Decide Without Actually Choosing," *loc. cit.*, pp. 30–36.

[25] Sir Robert Watson-Watt, *Three Steps to Victory* (London: Odhams, 1957), p. 74.

The point is that the policy maker must be sensitive to the prospect that, because of the constant advance of technology, his only real choices may be of this order.

The Sense for Paradise Lost. This predisposition is likely to be more characteristic of the scientists who had their graduate training and early professional experience in the years before World War II than of those who have known only war or Cold War conditions.[26] The prewar scientists took it as an article of faith that certain conditions were essential for the progress of science, in particular that scientists be free to select their research problems and that both scientists and scientific information be free to move among as well as within nations.[27] All of these conditions were violated during World War II, and as a result of the Cold War they were never fully re-established. The nuclear physicists had had perhaps the most highly developed sense of international community. They were relatively few in number, had intimate personal relationships at home and abroad, and had been experiencing an exciting exchange of discoveries since Rutherford identified the nucleus in 1911. They also lost the most, for theirs was militarily the most sensitive knowledge, and the pages of the *Bulletin of the Atomic Scientists* offer eloquent testimony to their ideological disturbance.

The result is that the senior scientists tend to be especially sensitive to possibilities which hold some promise for restoring the former order. They may usually be found on the side (or in front) of those urging freer exchange of scientific and military information with allied governments, less secrecy in the circulation of scientific (and sometimes military) information, and more extensive cultural, and especially scientific, exchanges with the Soviet Union. Similarly, the major activities of the Foreign Policy Panel of the President's Science Advisory Committee and of the Office of the Science Adviser to the Secretary of State have been in connection with the Science Attaché program, the facilitation of international scientific programs and conferences, and the exchange of scientists with the Soviet Union.[28]

26 In 1955 slightly more than half of the active research physicists in the United States were under forty years of age and had received their doctorates after December 7, 1941. Lee A. DuBridge, "The American Scientist: 1955," *Yale Review* (September 1955), p. 1.

27 These assumptions are excellently set forth in Margret Smith Stahl, "Splits and Schisms: Nuclear and Social," unpublished doctoral dissertation (Madison: University of Wisconsin, 1946), Ch. 4.

28 For the activities of the Panel and the Office, see James R. Killian, "Science and Public Policy," Address to the American Association for the Advancement of Science, December 29, 1958, as printed in *Science Program—86th Congress*, Report of the Senate Committee on Government Operations, 86th Cong., 1st sess. (1959), pp. 12–13, and *The Science Adviser of the Department of State*, Department of State Publication 7056 (Washington, 1960).

Science serves mankind. For at least 300 years the western scientific tradition has assumed that the unrestricted generation of new knowledge about the world was a social good. Over these years science in its purest form (the discovery of the facts of nature for knowledge's sake alone) became increasingly an autonomous social institution; research scientists were largely disassociated from the practical applications of their discoveries, but they took it for granted that these discoveries would ultimately benefit mankind.[29] The advent of nuclear and bacteriological weapons systems which have the potential of destroying so much of mankind and his works has called this faith sharply into question. It does not take much imagination to wonder if man, in view of his apparent inability to escape from the order of conflicts which have historically resulted in war, would not be better off in a world where the knowledge that has made the new weapons possible did not exist. For some of the senior nuclear physicists this is more than a philosophical question. They are unable to avoid a sense of real personal responsibility; they reason from the premise that they were few, and if they had acted differently weapons development might not have taken the turn it did.

In the immediate postwar years, the apparent contradiction between the good of science and the evil of war was resolved by the expectation that the very destructiveness of the new weapons would lead man to renounce at last the folly of war. The course of foreign policy in later years has weakened these expectations but not destroyed them, as the recent flurry of arms-control proposals premised on the rational self-interest of both sides in avoiding mutual destruction testifies.

The need to preserve their sense of service to mankind led some American scientists to refuse to work on weapons. Similarly, there are reports that several Russian scientists were imprisoned, exiled, or placed under surveillance for refusing to participate in weapons work between 1945 and 1953, and in 1957 a number of Germany's elite physicists announced that they would have no part in nuclear weapons work.[30] Such cases are dramatic, but nowhere have they prevented the development of weapons on which governments were determined. The more consequential resolutions have been those in which scientists have simply identified the good of mankind with the strength of their nation or have endeavored to develop new weapons systems which would be as effective as the old in promoting national policy but which would result in less slaughter if used. This was part of the rationale behind the recommendation made by a group

---

[29] See Stahl, *op. cit.*, Ch. 4.

[30] See Arnold Kramish, *Atomic Energy in the Soviet Union* (Stanford: Stanford University Press, 1959), p. 105. Kramish states that it is not certain whether the objections of the Russian scientists were technical or political. For the declaration of the German physicists, see the *Bulletin of the Atomic Scientists* (June 1957), p. 228.

of American scientists in 1951 that the government undertake the development and production of a large number of A-bombs for tactical use in the ground defense of Western Europe. Their hope was that such an innovation would relieve the United States of the burden of having to rely solely on the threat of strategic bombing to contain the Red Army.[31]

The failure of the United States to orbit a satellite before the Soviet Union did was the result of the State Department's insensitivity to the political implications of the event and the decision of the President and the Secretary of Defense not to let a satellite program interfere with military missile programs. A small part of the story, however, is to be found in the reluctance of some of the American scientists involved in the programming of the International Geophysical Year to see an American IGY satellite propelled by an operational military weapon. Their preference for the less developed but non-military Vanguard over the Army's Redstone appears to have reflected a combination of the "sense for paradise lost" and the "science serves mankind" predispositions, in this case an interest in showing the world the peaceful side of science and in demonstrating that the scientists of the world could cooperate in the interests of knowledge as well as compete in the interests of nations.[32]

IV

With regard to the two remaining problems to be discussed—how to organize relations between science and government, and how the scientist can participate in policy-making and still keep his expert standing—four points seem deserving of special emphasis: (A) the problem of organization, especially in the area of foreign policy, is still very much in the research and development stage, and so it may long remain, considering the precedent set by the problem of how to relate military experts and foreign policy; (B) in many areas of policy it will never be possible to specify what constitutes "the best" organization; the way in which policy-makers are organized is not without influence on the kind of policies they will produce, and so long as there are differences over policy there will be no agreement about organization; (C) in the American political system, at least, the science expert at the high-policy level has no real hope of keeping out of politics; his only choice is in the character of his political style; and finally, (D) it should not be forgotten that organization and policy-making are not the same as policy; successful instances of foreign policy capitalizing on or guiding developments in science and technology will not automatically follow just because scientists have been liberally injected into the policy-making process.

[31] *Oppenheimer Transcript*, pp. 584, 594–95, 891–94.
[32] See Walter Sullivan, *Assault on the Unknown* (New York: McGraw-Hill, 1961), pp. 79–81.

Organization. Current American organization in the area of science and foreign policy still reflects the emergency responses to the Russian ICBM and Sputnik I. One effect of these events was that scientists were rushed to the most important single center of power, the Office of the President, by means of the creation of the Special Assistant to the President for Science and Technology and the President's Science Advisory Committee.

The President certainly needs men around him sensitive to the areas of interaction between science and foreign policy. But a case can be made for the proposition that the center of gravity for the input of scientific advice into the policy-making process should be at a lower level than the White House. The President's political interests lie in keeping the staff about him small and generalized. Well-developed plans and programs will have a better chance of maturing in the larger and more diversified facilities that departments and agencies can provide. Secondly, as C. P. Snow concludes in his account of the differences between Tizard and Lindemann, there are risks in having a single science adviser sitting next to the center of political power. Although it should be noted that Churchill fared better with a single science adviser than Hitler did with none ("The Führer has dreamed," Dornberger was told, "that no [V-2] will ever reach England"), Snow's point has merit and it holds for institutions as well as for individuals.[33] The President will generally find his choices facilitated by the existence of multiple and independent sources of scientific advice.

This is a condition that already prevails in the case of many of the departments and agencies whose actions have significant foreign policy consequences, especially in the use of scientists by the Department of Defense, the Atomic Energy Commission, and the National Aeronautics and Space Administration. It is, however, a condition notably absent in the case of the Department of State. As it now stands, the President has more scientists to advise him on the scientific and technical aspects of various foreign policy issues, particularly in the national security field, than has the Secretary of State.

Excluding the science attachés overseas, the Department of State's Office of the Science Adviser numbers six people of whom three, including the director are professional scientists. There are no scientists, full or part-time, in the Department's offices for policy planning, space and atomic energy, or political-military affairs. As might be inferred from these arrangements, many of the policy-makers concerned believe that their needs for scientific advice are adequately met through formal and informal communication with scientists employed in the operating agencies and departments and with the President's own Science Advisory Committee. (It should also be noted that in at least one office the need for additional political personnel is clearly more urgent than the need for scientists.) The

---

[33] Snow, *Science and Government*, pp. 66–68, and Dornberger, V-2, p. 87.

Department's Science Adviser, who participates in the work of both the President's Committee and the Federal Council on Science and Technology, serves to facilitate such communication; otherwise both the demands placed on the Office and its own interests have limited its activity, as previously noted, to a relatively narrow range of foreign policy problems.[34]

Whether the interests of the Department of State would be better served by a larger "in-house" scientific competence is a question that an outside observer cannot easily answer. Much depends on the validity of the expectations that the Department can rely on the scientists of the operating agencies to alert it to developments and information relevant to foreign policy. Even more depends on how determined the Department is to play an active and influential part in shaping the scientific and technical programs of the government to conform to its own conception of national needs and priorities.[35] Should this determination be high, it is difficult to avoid the hypothesis that if the President has found it useful to have a relatively large science advisory body to help him monitor and direct the course of science and technology as they affect foreign and domestic policy, so too might the Secretary of State in the area of his own more limited but still extensive responsibilities.

Organization and Purpose. Since administrative organizations exist for the purpose of serving policy goals and implementing policy programs, it is to be expected that those who differ on the goals and programs of policy will differ about the proper design of administrative organizations. The desire of many scientists in 1945 to see atomic energy used for peaceful rather than military purposes was one of the reasons for their political campaign to place the postwar atomic energy program in the hands of a civilian commission instead of the War Department. Similarly, more recent differences about how to organize the government's space effort reflect, in part, policy differences about whether space will or should be an area for major military operations.

[34] There are eighteen scientists on the President's Science Advisory Committee; its working panels also contain participants from outside the committee. In December 1958 the Committee and the Office of the Special Assistant for Science and Technology had together some 75 scientists and engineers serving part time. See Killian, "Science and Public Policy," *loc. cit.*, p. 8. The work of the Committee and the Office are additionally described and appraised in *Science Organization and the President's Office*, Staff Study of the Subcommittee on National Policy Machinery, Senate Committee on Government Operations, 87th Cong., 1st sess. (1961).

The information presented about the Department of State is based on U. S. Department of State, *The Science Adviser of the Department of State*, and interviews with several Department officials in February 1962. Needless to say, the description and interpretation made above are entirely the present writer's responsibility.

[35] These two conditions are not unrelated. The more influence the Department exercises in determining the goals and programs of other agencies, the more confident it can be that scientists in those agencies will call the Department's attention to goals and programs which they believe to be receiving too much or too little attention.

The same point can be seen in the proposal to create a Department of Science and Technology which would include the variety of "little" science programs now scattered throughout the Executive structure (for example, those of the Weather Bureau, National Bureau of Standards, the Antarctic Office) but would exclude those of the Department of Defense, the Atomic Energy Commission, and the Space Administration. The hope behind this proposal is that, combined together, the "little" programs would be able to compete more effectively in the struggle for government dollars with the "big" science programs of the military, atomic energy, and space organizations.[36]

The question of the "best" science organization is thus inescapably tied to the question of what is the "best" science policy. But who can demonstrate whether science and foreign policy would be better served by allocating dollars to a program to control weather or to a program to explore Mars? There are no determinate solutions to problems of this order. Neither, for that matter, is there any "one right amount" of the nation's scientific resources that should be allocated to basic as compared to applied research. Differences on policy questions such as these are unavoidable among scientists and non-scientists alike, and they can be resolved in but one manner: through the interplay of power and interest in a political arena.

This condition, plus the increasing dependence of scientific programs and research on government funds, plus the increasing consequences of the choices the government makes in allocating those funds, all promise to put the politicians and the scientists under increasing pressure. As the opportunities for further development in each of a thousand different scientific fields mushroom with the acceleration of scientific knowledge, whatever the government decides to support, it will be deciding *not* to support more. Indeed, it is not too difficult to see the scientists becoming practiced advocates and lobbyists for the government's support of their cherished fields and projects, or to imagine the day when the politicians start to complain about "interscience rivalry" and begin to fancy that, if only there were a single Chief of Science, competition and duplication could be ended and the nation could have an integrated science policy.

Scientists in Politics. The American political system is not one that insulates its experts from the politics of choice.[37] The scientist involved in high-policy matters is likely to find himself propelled into the political arena, either by a push from behind or by his own interest in seeing that

---

[36] See Lloyd V. Berkner, "National Science Policy and the Future," Address at Johns Hopkins University, December 16, 1958, as printed in *Science Program—86th Congress*, pp. 116–18.

[37] This point, especially as it relates to science experts, is discussed in Price, *Government and Science*, pp. 61–62, and in Herman Finer, "Government and the Expert," *Bulletin of the Atomic Scientists* (November 1956), pp. 331–32.

the "right" choices are made. Some of the incentives the scientist may have, to follow up his advice with an effort to see that it is accepted (and to take a hand in a few other matters while he is at it), were outlined and illustrated in the preceding section. It is equally important to recognize that the scientist may find himself on the political firing line, placed there by a politician interested in using the scientist's prestige as an "expert" to disarm the critics of his (the politician's) choices.

Thus, prior to the moratorium on nuclear tests, the Eisenhower administration appeared to be using scientists and their scientific facts on fall-out as a means of justifying and defending a policy that was obviously compounded of a variety of considerations besides that of the radiological hazard. The comparison with Truman's use of the prestige of the Joint Chiefs of Staff to defend his choices in the Korean War comes easily to mind. So, too, do the statements of various Republican leaders that they had lost confidence in the Joint Chiefs and their determination, when they came to power, to get rid of the "Democratic" Chiefs and to appoint Chiefs in sympathy with Republican policies.

The scientist, in short, is not likely to orbit the centers of political power emitting upon request "beeps" of purely technical information. He will inevitably be pulled into the political arena. If his participation there is to be either productive or personally satisfying, both the scientist and the non-scientist need to be highly conscious of the character of their activity and the problems involved. The scientist (and many a non-scientist) must learn that the making of foreign policy is not a quest for the "right" answers to the problems of our time. There are only hard choices, the consequences of which will be uncertain and the making of which will often seem interminable in time and irrational in procedure.

The debate and disagreement over these choices will be heated and confused under the best of circumstances, but emotion and misunderstanding can be eased if scientists and non-scientists are both alert to the limits as well as the potential of the scientist's contribution. On the scientist's part, there is the obvious need to exercise the utmost care in making clear to himself and to others the areas where he speaks as a concerned citizen and those where he speaks as a professional expert. More difficult will be the task of learning how and to whom to address himself in each of these capacities when he is dissatisfied with the outcome of a policy decision in which he has participated. There is, as Don Price has pointed out, no clear code in Washington to govern the conduct of dissenting experts, only a "flexible" set of possible relationships with one's immediate superiors and those whose authority competes with or exceeds that of one's superiors. In contrast to the soldier, who can find some although not complete guidance in the doctrine of "civilian control," the very nature of the scientist's intellectual habits and many of his policy predispositions may make especially difficult his task in determining the limits to which he can stretch his dissent.[38]

On their part, the non-scientists need to recognize that scientists can hardly be expected to remain politically indifferent or inactive about the policy issues with which they are involved (especially when no one else in Washington practices such restraint). It was the naiveté of this expectation that was so appalling in the conclusion of the Gray Board that Oppenheimer was a security risk because (among other reasons) "he may have departed his role as scientific adviser to exercise highly persuasive influence in matters in which his convictions were not necessarily a reflection of technical judgment, and also not necessarily related to the protection of the strongest offensive military interests of the country." [39] It is unlikely that "civil-scientist" relations will ever get any worse than this. With time and experience one can expect many of these problems to be eased, but it would be unrealistic to expect them to disappear. Military experts have participated in the making of foreign policy far longer than scientists, and the question of how they can best do so is still the subject of more than a little disagreement.

Policy Processes and Policy. In closing this discussion of scientists and the problems of their organizational and political relationships to others engaged in the determination of foreign policy, it is important to remember that the policy process can bring minds together but it cannot make them think. It is worth noting that, in the political and administrative structure of the Soviet Union, no scientist is as institutionally close to the Premier as is the Special Assistant for Science and Technology to the President of the United States and that there is no equivalent of the Science Advisory Office in the Russian Ministry of

[38] See the discussion in Price, *Government and Science*, pp. 131, 133, 138–42. The point about the scientists' lacking a tradition of "civilian control" was suggested by William T. R. Fox.

[39] U. S. Atomic Energy Commission, *In the Matter of J. Robert Oppenheimer, Texts of Principal Documents and Letters* (Washington, 1954), pp. 19–20. Note the policy predisposition in the phrase "strongest offensive military interests."

It should not be comfortable for an American to reflect on the career of Peter Kapitsa, a Soviet physicist who was a student of Rutherford and who worked in England from 1922 to 1934 and then returned to the Soviet Union. Kapitsa was placed under house arrest in 1947 and remained there until after Stalin's death. Kapitsa has told western scientists and newsmen that his arrest was the result of his refusal to work on nuclear energy for military purposes. Kramish believes that his arrest was due to the government's dissatisfaction with his advice on certain technical approaches to weapons development. In either event, it is noteworthy that Kapitsa is believed to have recently been, on an informal basis, one of Khrushchev's main science advisers.

On the matter of his arrest, see the report by Harrison Salisbury in the *New York Times*, July 11, 1956; the *Bulletin of the Atomic Scientists* (January 1957), p. 38; and Kramish, *Atomic Energy in the Soviet Union*, pp. 109–110. The information on his recent activity was supplied by the staff of the Subcommittee on National Policy Machinery, Senate Committee on Government Operations.

Foreign Affairs.[40] Yet one would not say that the foreign policy of the Soviet Union has appeared either ineffectual or insensitive in its response to developments in science and technology.

The circumstances attendant on the development of radar by the British from 1935 to 1940 provide a useful insight into both the potential and the limits of effective organization. Essential, obviously, were the scientific and technical ideas that Watson-Watt and his colleagues had in mind in 1935, ideas which in turn were the result of the earlier years of research they had been free to conduct in the facilities of a government laboratory. Certainly, it was important that there were administrative scientists in the Air Ministry who were so alert to the military problems of the Air Force that they could see on their own initiative the need to establish a special scientific committee for the study of air defense (the Tizard Committee) and who were so alert to the work of the scientific community that they made their first request for information to Watson-Watt.[41] Of consequence, too, was the fact that the personal and political relations of the members of the Tizard Committee with the members of the military, administrative, and political hierarchies whose interest and cooperation were vital for the subsequent progress of the research and development program were relations characterized by mutual ease, respect, and understanding.

But these conditions would not have led from the formation of the Tizard Committee in 1935 to a chain of operational radar stations by 1940 and a Fighter Command practiced in their use if it had not been for the military ideas of members of the Royal Air Force. It was they who first thought of the formation of a committee to look specifically into the problem of detection, they who recommended more funds than those first proposed by the Tizard Committee for the development of an electromagnetic detection system, and they who were responsible for the decision to start constructing the stations and training the personnel while the equipment was still under development.[42] The explanation for this interest and sup-

40 On Soviet government and science organization, see *National Policy Machinery in the Soviet Union*, Report of the Subcommittee on National Policy Machinery, Senate Committee on Government Operations, 86th Cong., 2d sess. (Washington, 1949), pp. 24–35, 59–62, and Nicholas DeWitt, "Reorganization of Science and Research in the U.S.S.R.," *Science* (June 23, 1961), pp. 1981–91. The points made above were additionally confirmed by the staff of the Subcommittee on National Policy Machinery.

41 The circumstances provide an interesting variation of the "whole problem approach." The Tizard Committee was initially interested in techniques for destroying aircraft or their crews, and Watson-Watt was asked in 1935 to investigate the possibility of using electromagnetic radiation for this purpose. He reported that such a use was apparently infeasible. In any event, he went on to note, the aircraft would first have to be located, and if anyone was interested electromagnetic radiation might be useful for this. Watson-Watt, *Three Steps to Victory*, pp. 81–83.

42 For the development of radar, see *ibid.*, pp. 108–09; C. P. Snow, *Science and Government*, pp. 24–38, 60–61, 74–75; P. M. S. Blackett, "Tizard and the Science of War," *Nature* (March 5, 1960), pp. 648–49; and Basil Collier, *The Defense of the United Kingdom* (London: H.M.S.O., 1957), pp. 33, 36–39.

port is to be found in their theories about the next World War. They believed the Germans were planning to engage in the strategic bombing of Great Britain, and they wished to be prepared for it.[43]

The point is obvious but important. British scientists and science organization were in the final measure but ready tools. They were good tools, but the use to which they were put was the result of the kind of ideas the military men had about war. The same will hold in the other areas in which science may affect foreign policy. The contributions that science and technology will bring to international politics will largely turn, not so much on the particular arrangements of scientists in the policy-making process, but on the purposes of statesmen and the theories they have about the political world in which they live.

Saul Friedman

THE RAND CORPORATION
AND OUR POLICY MAKERS

For nearly a generation the United States has labored through an age of warlike peace. Because of the possibility of thermonuclear annihilation, it is inevitable that the nation's leading thinkers, scientists, and scholars should be preoccupied, as never before, with the study of the weaponry, strategy, economics, psychology, and politics of conflict.

During World War II thousands of talented scientists and technicians came to industry and government to create the means to win the war. Their contributions were decisive, but rarely did the scientist or scholar take part in the making of military and political strategy. In 1945, at the height of the war which gave birth to the atom bomb, radar, and jet power, the federal government spent $513 million for research and development of weapons. This year the federal government expects to spend more than $7 billion on defense research and development and nearly $4 billion more on atomic energy and space research. (In contrast, about $1 billion will

---

[43] Ironically, the British were mistaken in their theory. The German Air Force had no such strategy in mind, and in 1940 when it tried to improvise a strategic bombing campaign it had neither the equipment nor the doctrine with which to conduct the campaign effectively. See Herbert Dinnerstein, "The Impact of Air Power on the International Scene: 1933–1940," *Military Affairs* (Summer 1955), pp. 65–71; Telford Taylor, *The March of Conquest* (New York: Simon and Schuster, 1958), pp. 24–30; and Adolf Galland, *The First and the Last* (New York: Ballantine Books, 1954), Chs. 2–5.

FROM *The Atlantic Monthly*, 212 (September 1963). Reprinted by permission of the author.

be spent on all other—peaceful—research paid for by government.) It is estimated by the National Science Foundation that the federal budget finances about 65 percent of the total national expenditure for research and development, and 92 percent of that money is invested in defense research. Since 1945 the budget for defense research has increased more than twentyfold, and it continues to rise.

Figures in the billions become blurred in the consciousness, but the comparisons serve to show that research and development for defense have become a giant new industry. The scientist, the technologist, and the scholar have enlisted in the paramilitary, the branch of the nation's defense establishment which is neither military nor civilian but both, and which exerts astonishing influence. It gives rationality and intellectuality to foreign policy and military strategy and to possible wars, ranging from anti-guerrilla combat in the jungles of Southeast Asia to global thermonuclear holocaust.

The Department of Defense draws its paramilitary personnel from more than three hundred universities and nonprofit institutions in the nation. Universities have created—on and off the campus—centers and institutions to do research for defense. These university-associated research centers actively compete for consultation contracts with the Defense Department, the State Department, or the military services. If the special research center on the campus does not have a contract, then the individual member of the faculty who has become noted in his field consults with the government on the technological or the political problems of strategy. The Boston *Globe* reported recently that five thousand academics from the Cambridge area serve as consultants in Washington.

The single most influential research organization, however, is not directly associated with a university. The Rand Corporation of Santa Monica, California, is the oldest among more than one hundred and fifty nonprofit organizations which have been created to do specialized strategic research. It is to the other research groups what West Point, Annapolis, and the Air Force Academy are to the army, navy, and air force. The Rand Corporation is the paramilitary academy of United States strategic thinking.

Achieving a remarkable degree of intradisciplinary research, the Rand Corporation does the basic thinking behind the weapons systems, the procurement policies, and the global strategy of the United States. Unlike any strategic research organization anywhere else in the world, the Rand Corporation has become internationally famous, and controversial, for bringing a new mode of thought to problems of cold war strategy. (The Soviets, incidentally, have called Rand "The Academy of Death and Destruction.") In bringing about his revolution of the Defense Department, Secretary Robert McNamara acknowledged his debt to the Rand approach by naming Rand researchers and supporters to top posts in his department.

On November 7, 1944, a few months after D-day, General H. H. ("Hap") Arnold, head of the army air forces, issued a memorandum briefly recounting the important role research and development had played in the war, especially for the air forces, and expressing the need for the air force to retain organized brainpower after the war "to assist in avoiding future national peril and winning the next war." Officials of Rand (a contraction of the words "research and development") point to this memo as the origin of their organization.

In hearings last year before a House subcommitte on military operations, Rand President Franklin R. Collbohm recounted the early planning for what became Project Rand. In late 1945, Collbohm, assistant to Arthur Raymond, vice president of engineering for the Douglas Aircraft Company at Santa Monica, spoke to General Arnold about "ways in which we could save these scientific and industrial resources for the service of the Government. There was general agreement that there was no procurement agency in the Government existing at the time that was suitable for buying brains rather than bolts and nuts," Collbohm said, "and the discussion then was that a new high-level procurement agency that was really designed and staffed to buy brains would have to be set up. At that time it was recognized that it was not going to be suitable to use contract negotiation procedures that are typical of industrial negotiations."

In late 1945, without congressional approval and without taking bids, General Arnold signed a contract with the Douglas Aircraft Company to create Project Rand. Air Force Regulation 20-9 gave it official status, and on March 9, 1946, General Curtis E. LeMay, who was to become commander of the Strategic Air Command, said that the objectives of Project Rand were to engage in "a program of study and research on the broad subject of intercontinental warfare other than surface, with the objective of recommending to the Army Air Forces preferred techniques and instrumentalities for this purpose." The contradictions that were later to cause severely strained relations between Rand and the air force were inherent in Regulation 20-9, which defined Project Rand as an agency to furnish information and "independent, objective advice" in order to "assist in the formulation and implementation of Air Force plans, policies and programs."

Douglas, the fifth-largest contractor during the war, cooperated fully to create Project Rand. Collbohm was placed in charge. Rand was given space at the Santa Monica plant. Douglas furnished accounting services and security guards, and Rand became a subsidiary division of the aircraft company. However, in search of autonomy, Collbohm said, Rand moved from the Douglas plant, when it was justified, to rented quarters in downtown Santa Monica, still retaining some of Douglas' services. Nevertheless, other aircraft companies were somewhat nervous about the relationship between Rand, the air force, and Douglas. So Collbohm decided to "alleviate that problem" by setting up a Rand Advisory Council, a most un-usual move, since Rand was an air force project. Members of the council included Collbohm's former boss, Raymond, Douglas president Donald Douglas, and top executives from North American Aviation, Boeing Air-craft, and Northrop Corporation. The council, said Collbohm, "sat as a board over us, meeting regularly, knew what we were doing and so on."

By 1948 Rand set out for a wider range of thinkers. As Collbohm testified, "World War II weapons and concepts were rendered obsolete by advancing technology; the military, economic and political considera-tions have become indissolubly linked. Project Rand was formed out of the conviction by General Arnold that the Air Force should support this new effort to assist in its reaching decisions concerning air war of the future—decisions which must include economic and political, as well as scientific, engineering and military insights." To obtain men capable of such research, it was evident that Rand would have to abolish its rather thinly disguised association with the aircraft industry and seek autonomy also from the air force. "Actually," said Collbohm frankly, "we thought that pretty well at the beginning but we did not publicize it. But it was obvious that if something like this [Rand] was expected to survive, it would have to be completely independent. Otherwise it would never be thought to be completely objective and unbiased, whether or not it was."

Enter now the man who breathed the kind of life into Rand that made it the influence it is today. He was the late H. Rowan Gaither, Jr., a peripatetic San Francisco attorney and former chairman of the Ford Founda-tion who established a great reputation during World War II as a research and development administrator and logistics expert with the Radiation Laboratories of Massachusetts Institute of Technology. These were the laboratories at which the uses and appplications of radar were developed. Gaither worked there with Karl Compton, then president of M.I.T., and Arthur Raymond of Douglas Aircraft Company.

In 1948, about the time Rand began casting about for aid in setting up an autonomous shop, Gaither had been asked by Compton to undertake a study of possible programs and policies of what was to become the Ford Foundation. This was known to Raymond and to L. J. Henderson, Jr., a Harvard-trained attorney and banker then at Rand who had worked with Gaither at the Radiation Laboratories. Henderson and Collbohm ap-proached officials of the nascent Ford Foundation and received the promise of a loan of $500,000, which later became an outright grant of $1,000,000.

On May 14, 1948, with Collbohm, Henderson, and Gaither as the in-corporators, California granted the Rand Corporation a charter "to further and promote scientific, educational and charitable purposes, all for the public welfare and security of the United States of America." Collbohm became president, Henderson was named vice president, and Gaither was elected the first chairman of the board of trustees. Rand was incorporated as a nonprofit, nonstock organization owned by the member-trustees. With the exception of officers like Collbohm and Henderson, members of the board were elected to five-year terms, not to exceed two consecutive terms. The board meets twice a year for two or three days to ratify general policies of Rand. The day-to-day research work and policy are under the guidance of the full-time administrators and eminent Rand scholars who are on the corporation's research council. Under the terms of its contract with the air force, Rand's work is subject to the formal approval of an advisory group of air force officers. This became an impediment to independence as Rand research began to run counter to the purely military outlook of air force policies.

Once the Articles of Incorporation gave Rand *de jure*, if not *de facto*, autonomy from the air force and the aircraft industry, Rand's next job was to build its image and influence through an impressive new board of trustees. It included Dr. Lee A. DuBridge, a physicist, then president of California Institute of Technology; Charles Dollard, an educator, a former member of the General Staff Corps in World War II, and then president of the Carnegie Corporation; Philip M. Morse, a physicist who was director of Brookhaven National Laboratories; and J. A. Hutcheson, vice president and director of research for Westinghouse Electric.

The names of succeeding trustees indicate the evolution of Rand as a crucial research link in a chain which includes a powerful military service, educational institutions, and industries that are all heavily committed to a rather like-minded and single-minded view of this nation's role in the world. They therefore come naturally to the necessity of multibillion-dollar arms budgets. Rand has shown, to the occasional distaste of the air force, much remarkable objectivity and independence in its research, but rarely is it an objectivity which has *qualitatively* differed from the air force's view of the cold war, as Collbohm testified before Congress. "Whatever we take on," he said, "should mesh in with our ongoing program, which is primarily the Air Force program."

The present trustees include Mark W. Cresap, Jr., president of Westinghouse Electric Corporation; Don K. Price, Jr., dean of Harvard's Graduate School of Public Administration; David A. Shepard, executive vice president, Standard Oil Company (New Jersey); Kenneth S. Pitzer, president of Rice University; Charles A. Thomas, board chairman, Monsanto Chemical Company; J. A. Stratton, president of M.I.T.; William Webster, president of the New England Electric System; Edwin E. Huddleson, Jr., an attorney with Gaither's former law firm; William R. Hewlett, executive vice president and partner in Hewlett-Packard Company, an electronics firm; and Philip L. Graham, president of the Washington *Post* and *Newsweek*. Since Gaither's death in 1961, Frank Stanton, president of the Columbia Broadcasting System, has been chairman of the board.

Each year since 1948 Rand has grown by 10 percent. In 1953, with an assist from the Ford Foundation and a mortgage, Rand left its rented offices and built, around six inner courtyards, a two-story, two-million-dollar, palm-studded building overlooking the Pacific Ocean. In 1961 Rand spent about $4 million to put up an attached five-story building for more office space.

Rand makes most of its money by charging the air force 6 percent of the estimated cost of the contracts which the air force lets to private industry as a result of Rand's work. Rand, in recent years, has received relatively small grants and contracts from private foundations and other government agencies, and some money has come in from the publication of books written under Rand auspices. The air force, however, has accounted for more than 80 percent of Rand's earnings in the past few years and all of Rand's earnings in earlier years. In 1948 Rand earned about $3.5 million. By 1962 Rand was earning about $20 million and had spawned two subsidiary nonprofit organizations, Analytic Services, Inc. (Anser), earning more than $1 million a year, and Systems Development Corporation (SDC), earning more than $50 million a year. Rand, like all nonprofit research organizations working on defense contracts, reinvests the "profits" for independent research and new equipment.

Rand created Anser at the request of the air force, to do the detail work with which Rand did not want to bother. Systems Development Corporation, which did the studies of actual hardware needs of the air force, began as a division of Rand. It soon became apparent that SDC's work was going to make it much larger than Rand. Rand decided to let its child out of the house for fear the offspring would control the parent.

Since Rand, Anser, and SDC are not stock companies, Rand cannot control Anser or SDC through stock holdings. However, J. R. Goldstein, a Rand vice president, attorney Huddleson, and David Packard, a business partner with Rand trustee Hewlett in the Hewlett-Packard Company, are among those on the board of SDC. Collbohm, Goldstein, and Huddleson incorporated SDC in California, and it makes its main offices in Santa Monica. Anser, also incorporated in California by Collbohm, Huddleson, and Rand treasurer J. S. King, Jr., includes the latter two and Rand vice president Henderson on its board. In the event of the dissolution of SDC or Anser, the assets revert to Rand.

There is little doubt that much of Rand's original influence was generated by its close association with the air force, government, and industry. But, paradoxically, its greatest influence and its reputation as the innovator of strategic thinking have come because of its stubborn independence from the air force, government, and industry. This independence rests, of course, with the people who have come to Rand and the work they have done, sometimes in spite of the efforts of Rand's administrators, to maintain harmony with the air force, government, and industry.

The Rand Corporation began in 1948 with a base of about 255 people

—young Ph.D.'s with new ideas, and older scientists who had become intellectual or industrial gadflies. They were recruited quietly and slowly, through a scouting system, from the science and university centers of the West Coast and the Northeast. Today, recruiting in much the same way, Rand has nearly 1100 employees, of whom about 730 are researchers, almost all holding a Ph.D.

At first Rand was divided into four research departments. Now there are eleven: aero-astronautics, computer sciences, cost analysis, economics, electronics, logistics, mathematics, physics, planetary sciences, social sciences, and systems operations. Even the detractors of Rand, like Harvard's social scientist David Riesman, admit that Rand succeeded in bringing disciplines together in a working relationship as no university in the country has. "Rand has succeeded where universities have failed," says Riesman. "They have learned how to mobilize various disciplines, seemingly unrelated, to move with a problem from the seedling of theory to application."

One of Rand's distinguished alumni, Harvard professor Thomas C. Schelling, an economist turned strategist, calls Rand the perfect place for an intellectual prima donna. "University professors go to Rand because the salaries are good, the climate is ideal, there is much prestige in the job, and they can think and write without the nuisance of having to teach." Some go there for another reason, one which is beginning to influence many aspiring scholars—the desire to take part in power and policy making. "Rand is an ivory tower that is part of the real world," says Schelling. "You're part of a researching community, but you know your work is going to have an effect on things that are happening in the world."

Schelling gained his reputation through Rand, and so did men like Albert J. Wohlstetter, a logician who made a fortune building prefabricated houses; Herman Kahn, an intellectual iconoclast with a crackling-fast brain; Bernard Brodie, a grandfatherly political scientist from Yale who now gives learned lectures on "the residual possibility of general nuclear war"; Hans Speier, an historical sociologist famous for his studies of Nazi propaganda techniques; Charles Hitch, an economist, former Rhodes Scholar, and the author of a book which revolutionized defense policies; and Dr. Alain C. Enthoven, a brilliant, eclectic economist who came to Rand at age twenty-six with a new doctorate and now, at thirty-two, holds a top job under Hitch, helping to apply economic principles to strategy in the Department of Defense.

Rand is not monolithic, however, and should not be judged by a few thinkers. Hundreds of researchers have contributed to the quiet work of Rand. Until the mid-1950s Rand was doing a competent, sometimes spectacular job of providing the air force with reasons and workable ideas for hardware and new weapons systems, and the strategic rationalizations for weapons for which the air force was seeking appropriations. An air force spokesman said one of Rand's "oblique" accomplishments was to give "prestige type support for favored Air Force proposals to the Department of Defense and the Congress."

In-flight refueling was a Rand innovation which gave the Strategic Air Command its global capability. Rand scientists, like Richard and A. L. Latter, helped solve theoretical problems in the design of the hydrogen bomb. This work to create the relatively light H-bomb led to proposals for an intercontinental ballistic missile. Rand scientists largely solved the heat and re-entry problems, and thus made the ICBM a reality.

But for Rand the air force might not have "naturally" come by the hegemony it has over intercontinental missile weaponry; the army and navy research programs were left far behind. Rand established offices in Washington under Henderson, where a large staff keeps in constant liaison with the Pentagon, and in Dayton, Ohio, near Wright-Patterson Air Base. After scoffing for some years at the Rand boondoggle, the other services resurrected their stagnant research programs and established their research organizations—the army's Research Analysis Corporation at Bethesda, Maryland, and the navy's Institute for Naval Analysis at Franklin Institute of Pennsylvania. The Defense Department established its Institute for Defense Analysis.

Rand's most far-reaching contribution, in research which affected long-range policies of the entire Defense Department, exerted great influence on political leaders, but parted with short-range air force interests.

In the late 1950s, when the ICBM was becoming a reality, Albert Wohlstetter headed a Rand study of strategic air force bases scattered throughout the United States and around the world. Wohlstetter concluded very quickly, to SAC's horror, that if the Russians struck first with a surprise attack, American air bases, many of them close to the Soviet Union, would be obliterated and the planes would never leave the ground. Asking the question, "What would happen if the Russians struck at this moment?", Wohlstetter was forced to conclude we would lose a war in a matter of hours. Therefore, Wohlstetter said, our deterrent was no deterrent at all, and in view of our vulnerability we were not a retaliatory power but a first-strike power, and, therefore, we were giving the Russians good reason to surprise our forces.

In 1957, a committee headed by Rand board chairman Gaither made a report to the National Security Council on the state of American defense; and the same year the Soviet Union proved it had a workable ICBM when it orbited Sputnik. The Gaither Report, details of which remain secret, demolished the defense strategy of massive retaliation by pointing out that, with an effective ICBM which could reach to any part of the United States, the Soviet Union could destroy SAC bases and soft missile sites, and thus America's ability to retaliate. Our deterrent threat to retaliate was empty. Following the logic of deterrence, the United States was *not* a retaliatory or second-strike power, since we would have no second strike once the Russians hit us. Therefore the United States had, by its weakness, been thrust into the position of having become a first-strike power, of having to think seriously of making a pre-emptive attack on the Soviet Union. Worse than that, the Soviets were given good reason to make a surprise pre-emptive attack on the United States at any moment. One former Rand researcher reported at the time that Rand had come to be so sure of its logic that it was gloomily predicting the imminence of a Soviet surprise attack.

Wohlstetter, still worrying about the problem of vulnerability versus invulnerability, saw the coming world situation as a "delicate balance of terror." He suggested that if both sides achieved weapons which were immune to attack, then each side would have an "invulnerable second strike force." In that event neither side would want to attack the other for fear of being obliterated by the retaliatory blow. Wohlstetter felt this would bring stability to the cold war. This line of reasoning was one facet of systems analysis, the Rand brand of thinking that has had so much influence on the present Administration and on McNamara.

There was another strand of systems analysis which came largely from the economics department of Rand, headed by Charles Hitch, now Defense Department comptroller. It was called "cost effectiveness," and it applied traditional input-output methods of economics to defense weaponry and then to strategy. One of McNamara's "wizards of odds," Deputy Assistant Secretary of Defense Enthoven, worked at Rand under Hitch and Wohlstetter. Now in charge of systems analysis for Hitch's office, Enthoven explains it this way: "The problem was how to allocate economic and strategic resources most effectively in a world situation where strategies must change with changing conditions. We have a given amount of resources. What is the best weapons system in which to invest these resources? We have a given world situation with limited political 'resources.' What is the best strategy to invest in this situation?"

Under the leadership of the logician Wohlstetter and the economists headed by Hitch and Enthoven, Rand sought to quantify strategic problems, the better to deal with them; to quantify the effectiveness of American striking strength, the better to know what we need; to quantify even uncertainties, the better to be prepared for all possibilities. The Rand strategists categorically deny that they use computers to give the United States its strategy, but they attempt as nearly as possible to attain the same level of superhuman machine rationality.

The kind of superrational quantitative analysis being applied to strategy and nuclear war in the Defense Department is shown by this excerpt from a recent Enthoven speech: "By 1961, a great deal of progress had been made in the development of an economic theory for our posture for thermonuclear war. . . . Although there is obviously much more to the problem of thermonuclear war than economic analysis of efficient and inefficient postures . . . we have made a great deal of progress in the translation of our broad objectives into specific quantitative criteria that can be applied in a systematic and practical way to the evaluation of proposed forces and postures. . . . The economic theory of our posture for nuclear war can be described in terms very similar to the economic theory of a multi-product firm."

Following the precepts of Wohlstetter and the systems analysts, Mc-Namara built his Defense Department revolution around "controlled response," or the "controlled use of force," applying—in economic terms—an input of force to obtain the best possible output of results. This was cost effectiveness in strategy. Cost effectiveness in weapons procurement soon had the services howling at McNamara and Rand. With the building of Minuteman, McNamara saw no need for producing more manned bombers. If the navy had Polaris, there was no need for more expensive and more vulnerable aircraft carriers. It had to follow that the day of the big manned bomber and the big carrier was coming to an end. McNamara's application of systems analysis and cost-effectiveness brought the cancellation of Skybolt, the end of the RS-70 bomber program, and it may bring the end of Dyna-Soar. In McNamara's view, they were unnecessary for our strategy.

As contract-renewal time came around, the air force made threats about cutting down Rand's funds. A Defense Department official who came from Rand says many on the Rand staff were in favor of looking elsewhere for contracts. Others felt they ought to remain working for the air force. The Rand administrators promised to curb some of the more independent and anti-air-force thinkers at Rand. Rand vice president Henderson, based in Washington, obviously annoyed by the strained air force–Rand relations, partly blames top Rand men who went to work for McNamara. He says he can sympathize with the air force criticism that Rand men are "end running" to the Secretary of Defense to sell their positions or realize ambitions for a glamorous Washington job. "We watch carefully to see that the Rand researcher doesn't do too much consulting at the Defense Department," Henderson said. "I don't think a man can do his proper research job for the Air Force if he's constantly at the Pentagon trying to sell his proposals."

As the Rand front office sought to satisfy some of the air force complaints, Rand personnel began to resign. One long-time Rand worker is now at M.I.T. Herman Kahn formed his own research unit, the Hudson Institute in New York.

It is debatable whether Rand consciously undermined the air force position in the American defense establishment, or whether the logic of strategic thinking in a thermonuclear world led Rand into an unavoidable and unwanted conflict with its biggest customer. But premeditated or not, once the battle was joined, Rand thinkers used their elaborately gained skills in strategy to go over the head of the air force to the Department of Defense, or woo young junior officers to their position in an attempt to isolate the bluff and blunt top brass, who did not take kindly to professorial planning of a war.

Rand has helped revolutionize strategy and put the war-making power and the military under civilian authority; it has also had more intangible but nonetheless disturbing, contradictory, and far-reaching influences elsewhere. The Rand strategy, Harvard political scientist Henry Kissinger says, may lead to the breakup of any effective NATO alliance. McNamara's downgrading of thermonuclear threats and tactical nuclear capability in Europe has given impetus to France's desire to acquire its own deterrent threat with an independent nuclear force. Somehow, McNamara's staff of human computers cannot understand France's reluctance to place its nation's most vital interests in systems analysis.

"I have a great deal of respect for the intellectual contribution of Rand in bringing systematic and sophisticated study to strategic problems," Kissinger said. "But there is a fantastic intellectual arrogance for all traditional forms and all those facets of human beings and nations which are not rational. As a result there is a terrible lack of knowledge of men as they are in the real world. Rand looks upon general war and foreign policy from a point of view of cost effectiveness and efficient management. They would have Europeans fit into this scheme, but Europeans do not see themselves as men on the Rand chessboard. They know there is more to men than systems analysis."

More immediate, however, has been Rand's effect on American higher education. As Rand and other nonprofit research groups raided campuses to lure the best minds, many colleges and universities sponsored nonprofit institutions on or near their educational plants to take on various jobs in defense research and hold on to eminent scholars. The Bell Committee report on government contractors for research and development said, "Well over half of the research budgets of such universities as Harvard, Brown, Columbia, Massachusetts Institute of Technology, Stanford, California Institute of Technology, University of Illinois, New York University, and Princeton, for illustration, is supported by Federal funds." Many colleges, the report went on to say, have established research organizations related to but separated from the universities, to vie for government research and development contracts. At M.I.T. two such facilities, Lincoln Laboratories and Instrumentation Laboratories, have operating budgets which, when combined, are more than twice the total budget of M.I.T.

Harvard President Nathan Pusey indicated the uneasiness in the minds of many educators when he reported to the university's faculties and governing board in 1961 that, "At least 80 per cent of the institutions of higher education in the United States now receive federal funds, and Harvard is one of those heavily involved in federal programs. Federal research programs make it all the more difficult to preserve the proper balance among various schools and departments, or within each of them between research and teaching. There is danger that the total program of the university could be affected."

Congressmen have been bothered by the effects the nonprofit research organizations are having on industry. California Representative Chet Holifield, chairman of the military operations subcommittee, which has been keeping track of government-sponsored research and development, has expressed alarm that private industry has been enriching itself through the taxpayer-financed work of nonprofit corporations. He argued in Congress for an amendment to the defense appropriations bill which would protect, for the government, the patents on discoveries made by nonprofit research organizations. In the debate over the amendment Holifield wanted to know "whether the Defense Department is going to continue to give away windfall patent benefits to its contractors which have been paid for by money of American taxpayers." The amendment was defeated.

Industry spokesmen frankly admit that new weapons and hardware devised by nonprofit companies like Rand have helped in their nongovernment business. Arthur Raymond of Douglas Aircraft says his company could not have built the DC-8 without government-sponsored research on swept-wing bombers. The Boeing 707 virtually duplicates the government-financed designs for the jet tankers now in use. As the government puts more and more money into defense research, private industry decreases the amount of money it spends on research for nondefense products.

Controls over research and development programs, such as those recommended by the Bell Report, by Congress, and by educators, can ameliorate the deleterious effects of Rand and its kin in the areas of government, business, and education. Problems like conflict of interest and empire building are being watched by the responsible people in government, in education, and the scientific community. Yet the most disturbing influence emanating from Rand and other organizations of its type is less tangible, for it affects ordinary people, most of whom think Rand makes typewriters, and have become resigned to the cold war and the billions spent each year.

Roger Hagan, a Harvard historian and a contributor to the *Bulletin of the Atomic Scientists*, believes Rand has "increased public acceptance of nuclear war as a part of national policy. Rand thinking has always been negative in presupposing an eternal, ever spiraling conflict between the United States and the Soviet Union. Rand has done nothing to exert effort in thinking about reasons, alternatives and the way to end thermonuclear confrontation."

The little research Rand has done on disarmament or toward reaching an understanding with the Soviet Union has, in fact, been negative. Rand researchers, for example, have devised the presently used "Command and Control" systems to help prevent the accidental outbreak of war. They have analyzed disarmament proceedings to show why negotiations will probably continue to be fruitless. They have studied nuclear-test-ban proposals, but always with an eye to show the flaws. Once Rand issued a scholarly report entitled "Strategic Surrender" and suppressed it because of a congressional outcry.

Rand has done little positive research toward ending nuclear confrontation because of the belief of Rand's leading thinkers that the theory of "mutual invulnerability" is a positive way to peace. Its research, therefore, is founded on the ability of the United States and the Soviet Union each to maintain power enough to discourage the other from starting a war. Mutual invulnerability, however, is a foundation built upon the sand of an interminable cold war and an onward and upward arms race.

Once we had to have only enough weapons to render the Soviet Union a "massive and crushing blow" should it ever decide to attack the United States. Now, both sides are protecting their missile forces by putting them in submarines or in concrete underground silos. The Rand strategist has thus invented the words "overkill" and "megadeath" to work out in computer fashion the even greater potential destructive force which the United States must have in order to win a nuclear duel. In short, an overkill capacity is needed because a kill capacity will not suffice. Because the "winning" of such an exchange would be meaningless if the civilian population perished, Rand strategists call for a massive shelter program. Yet, paradoxically, if the United States or the Soviet Union was to embark upon mass shelter programs, each side would be tempted to assume that the other was preparing for attack.

In 1957, when the Russians launched the first Sputnik, Rand predicted the Soviet Union would embark on a crash ICBM program which would leave the United States on the short end of an intercontinental missile gap by 1961. As a result the United States began a crash ICBM program. As it developed, the Russians did not increase production of their ICBM until 1961, when it became evident to them that the United States had an overwhelming superiority. The Rand prediction, wrong, as it turned out, precipitated another round of the arms race.

Now limitless space beckons to the strategist for what may become a new round of the struggle for mutual invulnerability. Almost resigned to the loss of the prestigious manned bomber, the air force has opened its campaign for the military exploitation of space. The *Air Force and Space Digest*, a publication of air force supporters, has taken the offensive against McNamara for dropping the Skybolt and the B-70 bomber program, while it has simultaneously demanded for the air force a greater role in space. The air force, an old hand in the art of interservice rivalry, has been quietly exerting pressure to build up its own potential for space exploration while denigrating the role of civilian-controlled NASA. Rand strategists and researchers have been at work devising weapons systems for space and constructing the rationale. The Russians, they say, are already at work attempting to use earth-orbiting satellites as launching pads for nuclear missiles. Therefore, the Rand researchers believe, it is only a matter of time before the Soviets accomplish this. To maintain mutual invulnerability it is thus necessary that the United States immediately begin a program to exploit space for military purposes.

Largely because of the influence of Rand, the United States now has a rationale for an interminable cold war. Rand's new mode of thinking has led fascinated scholars to the theory of games in warfare and the "rationality of the irrational." Studied seriously, for example, is the prospect of taking certain strategic decisions out of the hands of statesmen and putting them into computers whose course could not be changed. Thus, if we give the computer a set of instructions to "push the button" under certain circumstances, any enemy will surely be deterred, since the possibility of turning back from war will be out of our hands. And so the rationality of Rand becomes a closed rational system which negates humanity and takes an exclusively intellectualist world view.

It is clear that the cold war has become a Frankenstein monster which toys precariously with the weapons for the world's obliteration. And until now, political leaders, military minds, strategists, scientists, and scholars have labored to keep the monster leashed, lest it bring doom to hundreds of millions of people.

The thousands of scientists and scholars influenced by Rand have given powerful demonstrations of their ability to create. But do they step back from the fascinating process of creation to see what it is they have wrought? Can these thinkers who have given of their talents seek the way to stop the mechanism and the will of the monster? Or must we hang on to its leash as it pulls us now across the threshold of infinity into space?

Gene M. Lyons

THE PROFESSIONALIZATION OF CIVILIAN LEADERSHIP

THE importance of continuity and stability in government is emphasized when the nature of the policy process is clearly understood; it is likelier to be appreciated more toward the end than at the beginning of any particular Administration. Policies are usually developed with a long history of conjecture, false starts and negotiation. Very often they take shape from a series of operational responses or the byplay of a number of viewpoints

FROM *The American Political Science Review*, LV, 1 (March 1961). Reprinted by permission of the author and The American Political Science Association.

rather than from a single breakthrough of brilliant analysis. Within such situations, the influence of careerists, military and civilian, is enormous. It is equally impressive in moments of crisis when only professionals have the background and experience to respond quickly. The military professionals wield their greatest influence within the military departments; a large and burgeoning staff of civilian careerists exert similar powers in the Department of Defense. They perform staff work in connection with establishing budgetary and manpower priorities, supply the background material for new programs and have usually developed a network of informal contacts that make them invaluable in inter-departmental negotiations. Indeed, General Gavin recalled (perhaps with some bitterness) that ". . . the Civil Service employees . . . in the Department of Defense . . . probably have more impact on decision-making . . . than any other individual or group of individuals, military or civilian." [1]

The hazy line that divides policy from administration and the influence of career professionals on decision-making are familiar themes in the literature of public administration.[2] In the Defense Department, professional influence has been increased by the tendency to seek solutions to problems at a technical level in order to minimize differences over vital matters of policy. In such cases, the guides for policy become efficiency and empirical verification rather than intuition and inspiration; and in any such atmosphere technicians and arbitrators play a critical role. Such tactics often reduce policy to a compromise between opposing positions, a practice that is often stultifying. In many cases it is nevertheless an inevitable consequence of policy-making within the democratic process, particularly in the field of national security. For within the goldfish bowl of American politics, there is a limit to the risks a political leader is willing to take in approving defense programs that can be argued in terms of national survival and for which there is no indisputable solution.

But like the "depoliticalization" of appointive posts, there are limits to the contribution that increased civil service influence can make to the professionalization of civilian leadership in the Pentagon. Some of these limits have already been suggested. For one thing, few civil servants possess the degree of specialized expertise that is required for technical staff work in fields such as research and engineering. Nor, for that matter, does the bureaucracy offer the environment in which careful study and reflection on basic problems, such as strategic doctrine, is encouraged and indeed rewarded. At the same time, there is little chance that the top layer of the American civil service can be transformed into an administrative class like

---

[1] James N. Gavin, *War and Peace in the Space Age* (New York: Harper & Row, 1958), p. 166.
[2] See, for example, Paul H. Appleby, *Policy and Administration* (University of Alabama Press, 1949). For an earlier statement on this issue, see Carl J. Friedrich, "Public Policy and the Nature of Administrative Responsibility," *Public Policy* (1940, Cambridge: Harvard University Press), p. 3 ff.

that in Great Britain; neither the social structure nor the political system to support such a class is present.[3]

Within the special context of American governmental institutions, a series of innovating techniques have therefore been developed to bring professional competence to bear on matters of public policy where neither political nor career executives can fully meet the demands. They include *ad hoc* and standing advisory committees, contractual arrangements for consultative services, the assignment of broad investigations or actual operations to outside institutions, and government-financed independent agencies set up outside the formality of the bureaucracy.[4] These administrative techniques perform a number of functions. They bring creativity to the public service in areas where it is often discouraged by the routinization of bureaucratic procedures or the dangers of interservice and political disagreement. They offer political executives (and congressional leaders) alternative sources of expert advice to the career services, civilian and military. They permit the kind of experimentation, reflection, flexibility, and deep probing that the complex problems of national security require but that the regular federal service cannot completely accommodate because of its size, its need for standardization, and its emphasis on current operations.

The strides taken in recent years to develop new modes of government administration have largely been forced by the demands of technology. The scientific programs during the second world war and the industry-based programs of the Air Force in the postwar years established precedents for government contracting in areas that now extend beyond technological projects to projects in the social and behavioral sciences. Each of the services has created a "think" organization to which it can farm out problems—the RAND Corporation of the Air Force, the Operations Research Office of the Army and the Operations Evaluation Group of the Navy. Within the Department of Defense a variety of advisory panels are available to the Secretary and his assistants—on research and development, on psychology and the social sciences and on education and manpower. In addition, the Institute of Defense Analyses has been established "to create machinery for putting a segment of the nation's intellectual resources more effectively at the disposal of the national security effort." [5] Originally established in connection with the evaluation of competing weapons systems, the

---

[3] Several of the essays in J. E. McLean (ed.), *The Public Service and University Education* (Princeton, 1949) are concerned with this issue. See particularly Rowland Egger, "A Second View: An American Administrative Class?" pp. 205 ff.

[4] For a general discussion of the development of such innovations in government administration, see Don K. Price, "Creativity in the Public Service," *Public Policy*, **IX** (Cambridge: Harvard University Press, 1959), p. 3 ff. For a discussion of some of the aspects of Defense Department contracting for advisory and consultative services, see Hearings, Subcommittee of the House Committee on Appropriations, 86th Cong., 2d sess., *Department of Defense Appropriations for 1961*, Pt. 7, pp. 164–196.

[5] *Annual Report II*, Institute of Defense Analyses, 1958, p. 1.

scope of the Institute now encompasses broad areas of military strategy where the support for judgments on weapons evaluation is very often to be found. Indeed the close connection with strategic issues has been the link that has extended research on military operations into the far reaches of national policy.

These innovations in administration project the professionalization of civilian leadership in defense far beyond the confines of government itself. That they extend as widely as they do is, in many ways, an indication of the response of industry, science and private scholarship to the problems of national security. Like government-sponsored research, research in industry has begun to go beyond technical subjects. General Electric, for example, publishes a *Defense Quarterly* that is devoted to the broad issues of technology and foreign and military policy. It has also established a "think" group of its own, as have other corporations such as General Dynamics, IBM and many of the large aircraft companies. While most of these "in house" divisions are set up for scientific research and development, many of them dig into military and social problems affected by technological advances. At the same time, many industrial companies contract out their research activities with institutions such as the Stanford Research Institute, a nonprofit corporation which has moved into the fields of military and foreign policy in the wake of its primary interest in the frontiers of technological change.

In addition, since 1950 there has been an out-pour of books and articles on national security from scholarly sources.[6] Some have actually been made possible through association with Defense Department projects or under contract with congressional groups investigating various aspects of the defense program. But a very high number of these efforts have been undertaken on private initiative, with or without foundation or university support. The subjects of these studies have ranged from the broadest issues of military strategy to more specialized problems of military organization and education. They include Kissinger's *Nuclear Weapons and Foreign Policy*, Osgood's *Limited War*, Huntington's *The Soldier and the State*, Brodie's *Strategy in the Missile Age*, the books by Walter Millis, the monographs of the Princeton Center of International Studies, the studies of the Rockefeller Brothers Fund and the volumes that have come out of the research projects conducted at the Center for International Studies at the Massachusetts Institute of Technology. In all cases, these works have plunged deep into military problems. Indeed there are indications that some military leaders are concerned that "there has been too little solid contribution from military pens to national security policy thinking for this new age . . ."[7]

[6] See Laurence I. Radway, *The Study of Military Affairs*, prepared for delivery at the 1958 Annual Meeting of the American Political Science Association (mimeographed).
[7] Col. George A. Lincoln and Col. Richard G. Stilwell, "Scholars Debouch Into

The practical consequence of all of these activities is that professional advice, studies and investigations on complex military issues are being made available to responsible officials from sources other than the military themselves. Civilian leaders need no longer rely entirely on the military services for the bases for policy decisions. Their own experience in service, the solid contribution of career professionals and the wide new sources of research and reflection, together with the multi-dimensional nature of defense problems, permit them to be more critical, more questioning and more constructive in their own right. Needless to say, all that has been discussed are tendencies, trends that can be perceived as we analyze the course of civil-military relations during the last ten years. Nevertheless, it seems safe to predict that these trends will continue to gain momentum—the "depoliticalization" of appointive posts, the influence of career executives, innovations in government administration and an interest in military affairs among writers, scientists and scholars. They are also bound to contribute to a growing professionalization of civilian leadership in military affairs and, in turn, this professionalization will have important repercussions on the nature of civil-military relations.

Strategy," *Military Review*, 40 (July 1960), p. 70. See also Captain Robert P. Beebe, "Guardians of Sea Power," United States Naval Institute *Proceedings*, 86 (June 1960), pp. 27 ff. The trend suggested here seems to contradict Bernard Brodie's thesis that "any real expansion of strategic thought . . . will . . . have to be developed largely within the military guild itself." *Strategy in the Missile Age* (Princeton, 1959), p. 9. Indeed, one might say that Brodie's own pioneering work refutes his prognosis.

V

The Overseas Administration
of American Foreign Policy

INTRODUCTION

UNITED STATES representation overseas has undergone a series of note-worthy changes since the end of World War II. The first two selections in Part V illuminate some of these changes. The selection from *The Overseas Americans* points out that American diplomacy is no longer confined to the capital city and is no longer restricted to relations with a small elite in the host country. It also notes the growing need for many kinds of specialized knowledge and skills not possessed by the normal Foreign Service officer. An American embassy in the 1960's will usually include economic counselors, foreign aid personnel, military advisers, Information Agency officers, intelligence and special operations personnel, and a variety of attachés, in such areas as labor, military affairs, treasury, and agriculture. Most of these people are not concerned with political tasks, in the narrow sense of that term. Nevertheless, they use their specialized knowledge and skills in communicating with individuals and groups in other countries that had previously been quite beyond the reach of the traditional Foreign Service officer.

The second selection offers excerpts from the study entitled "The Operational Aspects of United States Foreign Policy." It reveals somewhat the same perspective as the first selection, since it is based on the same research and involves overlapping personnel. The report emphasizes that it is the foreign *operations* of the United States Government, and not the increase in diplomatic activities, that has led to the exraordinary growth of America's overseas establishments. The United States is no longer restricted to *relations with* countries; to an unprecedented extent it now has *activities within* countries. This change radically alters the functioning of its embassies.

To be effective, an ambassador must be not only a skilled diplomat but a skilled administrator as well. He must be able to administer a sizeable establishment and coordinate a large number of programs. His task is vastly complicated by the fact that many persons who are formally under his jurisdiction in the host country look to Washington agencies—USIA, AID, Defense—for guidance, for recognition, and for promotion. The selection entitled "The Ambassador and the Country Team" deals with some of these problems of coordination.

The increase in overseas operations that has changed the role of the Ambassador has been reinforced by the impact of improved communications and improved physical mobility. As his administrative burdens have increased his immediate impact on the decision-making process has declined, so that the ambassador as diplomat is almost overshadowed by the diplomat as executive. Decision-making has tended to gravitate to Washington for a variety of reasons. That is where the President and Congress are located, the Secretaries of States and Defense, and, not to be forgotten, the Bureau of the Budget. Washington is the place where policies of significance can be discussed and assessed in the light of all competing obligations and demands and can then be decided authoritatively.

The rapidity and security of present communications has further acted to modify, if not seriously to diminish, the role of ambassadors as decision-makers. It is technically feasible to refer all difficult or sensitive matters to the home office; therefore Washington is in a position to insist that this be done. In addition, when a thorny issue comes up or a delicate negotiation is in order, the ambassador may find that he is scheduled to receive a visit from a White House assistant, an Under Secretary, a fact-finding "task force," one or more departmental secretaries, or, not infrequently, a Congressional delegation. It is safe to predict that the present pattern of centralization in decision-making will not be significantly altered despite the oft-repeated demands that greater latitude should be granted to the field. This is not to say, of course, that certain types of routine decisions might not profitably be devolved to the field.

The final selection consists of excerpts from the testimony of William Crockett, Deputy Under Secretary of State for Administration, before the Senate Subcommittee on National Security Staffing and Operations.* It provides information on the working of the Foreign Service today—recruitment, promotion policy, assignment practices, internal management, and related matters. The question of personnel has become increasingly acute in recent years. The number of overseas establishments has increased sharply as new functions and operating activities have been assumed. Moreover, the increase in the number of international and regional organizations, and the growth in the size of the United States

* November 21, 1963.

delegations to most of them, have created still further personnel demands.

In their study of "The Operational Aspects of United States Foreign Policy," the authors conclude that five personal characteristics are particularly important in achieving effective overseas performance:

1. Technical skill.
2. Belief in mission.
3. Cultural empathy.
4. A sense for politics.
5. Organizational ability.

The list helps explain why it has proved so difficult in the past to find a sufficient number of able and adaptable men and women for overseas work. The response to Peace Corps recruiting efforts during the last few years suggests, however, that there is in the United States a reservoir of talent, energy, and interest in overseas service that has only begun to be tapped. The increase in overseas study and travel also hints that the time may not be far off when the supply of talent for foreign employment may cease to lag so far behind the demand.

Harlan Cleveland, Gerard J. Mangone, John Clarke Adams
GOVERNMENT PERSONNEL OVERSEAS

1

THE three main groups of civilians overseas—the government people, the missionaries, and the businessmen—share the obligation to involve themselves deeply in the culture and the political economy of the alien peoples among whom they live. But the tasks they perform vary greatly and are strikingly different, too, from what these same groups were doing a generation ago. It will be useful to spend a few moments with each group to bring up to date our somewhat outmoded conceptions about Americans at work abroad.

"I began my job forty-seven years ago," wrote the British career diplomat Lord Vansittart in a *Foreign Affairs*[1] article not long ago, "and it was a

[1] *Foreign Affairs* (January, 1950).

fairly gentlemanly one on the surface. 'The rapine underneath' was there, but it was war . . . in lace." International government representation, until the beginning of the twentieth century, had changed little from the time modern diplomacy was invented during the Renaissance by the Most Serene Republic of Venice. Its purpose was to represent and to report— including the more genteel forms of spying.

It was part of this tradition that the foreign representative must above all be well versed in the aristocratic arts of social behavior. To appear to be a gentleman was the first requisite of diplomacy; and the higher the rank, the more importance that appearance assumed. Ideally the diplomat would have brains and education as well as a socially felicitous choice of parents; thus endowed, he could use his social entrée to carry out his reporting function. The nature of this function, however, and the restricted number of persons who made use of his reports, caused it to be subordinate to the splendidly conspicuous one of representation, not only in the eyes of the general public but also in those of many governments less wily, less sober, and less consistently well informed than that of fifteen-century Venice.

The well-dressed diplomat thus had to be able to charm over a cup of tea and scintillate at a court ball, precisely because his rounds of formal parties kept him in touch with the level of society containing nearly all the people who "mattered" in each country. His companions at these parties ran the country to which he was accredited; and they were also the same people whom visiting American dignitaries might want or need to know. It was by intimate and long social contact with a reasonably stable in-group that the United States diplomat could win the confidence of the rulers, pick up useful intelligence about changes in the power structure, and gain, if not always sympathetic consideration, at least a hearing for the American position on major international issues, and small favors for American residents and tourists, traders and seamen.

It is not our purpose here to assess the degree of proficiency attained in this essentially rarefied art by the long list of Americans who have served their nation without benefit of titles, pedigrees, or fancy-dress uniforms. It is enough to note an ironic twist: just as the United States began to take its international position seriously enough to add to its traditional consular service a body of career diplomats, the whole foundation of arm's-length capital-city aristocrat-level diplomacy began to crumble away.

Rapid communications between capitals made it increasingly possible to bypass or supersede ambassadors. The function of representation vis-à-vis the Foreign Office became more and more ceremonial as the practice developed of having ministers and experts meet and negotiate directly on trade agreements, arrangements for military installations, technical assistance, radio monitoring, atomic energy, and a host of other specialized activities beyond the possible knowledge of the "generalist" Foreign Service officer.

The rise of democracy and the breakdown of the power monopolies formerly in the hands of aristocracies of birth or wealth gradually robbed the teas and court balls of much of their pertinence to government. The function of representing America to whole societies, rather than just to an élite, placed a premium on different qualities. Political reporting began to require the widest imaginable range of contacts with all elements of real power in each society; after all, in a time of rapid political change it might be more relevant to get along with the next government than with the current one.

The expanded range of political reporting accounts, moreover, for less than half of the news reporting that our representatives are called on to submit. Today, in order to keep abreast of the developments in foreign countries, several government agencies in Washington need expert economic reporting as well. The political section of an embassy with its first, second, and third secretaries, which used not only to be the focal point of an embassy's activity but to perform almost all of the embassy's functions, is now overshadowed and overpowered by the economic counselors, the treasury representatives, and the attachés (agricultural, labor, commercial, mining, press, and scientific).

The advent of the labor attaché is an interesting case in point. The United States appointed its first labor attaché in the early 1940s when labor emerged as the predominant political force in some European countries. The men at the political desks at the embassies and in Washington had suddenly found they had no contacts with the upstarts who were ruling the countries to which they were accredited or on which they were specialists. In the few cases where we were lucky enough to have competent ones, the labor attachés, for the most part relatively humble and recently created pariahs of the service, quickly became indispensable links between the U.S. Government and some of the new rulers of Europe.

Most important of all, American *foreign operations* came increasingly to dominate the diplomatic landscape. The subject matter of foreign affairs, from the sixteenth century until World War II, was mostly "international" in the stricter sense of dealing with questions that arose among nations or their sovereigns: dynastic rivalries, territorial claims, commercial exchange, shifting alliances for attack or defense, and the like. Until World War II, America had no foreign aid program and no organized world-wide United States information program. Not only were we not engaged in "operations" abroad, but it would have been contrary to the "no entanglement" doctrine for American government officials to "operate" within foreign countries.

2

Before World War II virtually all overseas United States civilian personnel worked for the State Department; today even the recently enlarged

Foreign Service accounts for only about one in five of the 32,805 government people working abroad. The 331 American civilians working in foreign countries for the War and Navy Departments in 1938 had by 1958 become the 20,926 Defense Department civilian employees abroad.

A generation ago the great majority of government people abroad would have been found in Europe. Less than 40 per cent of the United States overseas civilians are now assigned to Europe; there are today almost as many American civilians working for government agencies in the Far East as there are in Europe. The 1958 figures show a drop, for the first time in recent years, in the total number of American civilians working for the U.S. Government abroad:

> March 1954   29,583
> March 1955   31,821
> June 1956   33,644
> March 1957   34,844
> June 1958   32,805

This drop reflects the reduction of 2,500 civilian employees of the Department of Defense, partially offset by small increases in the overseas personnel of the nonmilitary agencies.

The explosion of numbers (see Table) reflects not so much the ex-

PAID U.S. CIVILIAN EMPLOYEES OF THE FEDERAL GOVERNMENT IN FOREIGN COUNTRIES, BY AGENCY AND AREA (JUNE 30, 1958)

Areas	All Areas	Africa	Latin America	Europe	Near and Middle East, South Asia	Far East and Southeast Asia	Undis- tributed
Agencies							
All Agencies	32,805	1,840	2,548	13,837	3,172	11,335	73
State	6,462	361	1,096	2,666	1,187	1,149	3
ICA	3,338	349	771	136	893	1,119	70
USIA	1,168	55	134	361	287	331	
Defense	20,926	990	325	10,395	614	8,602	
Treasury	122		10	87	4	21	
Commerce	434	47	103	118	114	52	
HEW	191	24	47	27	49	44	
Agriculture	164	14	62	47	24	17	

Source: "Improvement in Standards of Language Proficiency and in Recruiting for the Foreign Service," Senate Foreign Relations Committee on S.1243, April 16, 1959, page 59.

pansion of reporting and of embassy-level negotiation as the addition of major new functions to the still-surviving tasks of professional diplomacy. It is our foreign operations—the postwar reliance on overseas bases and military aid to other nations' forces, the spreading of clandestine operations, the increased functions of the United States Information Service, and the new programs of economic and technical assistance—that largely account for the presence of U.S. Government offices in more than one hundred countries and territories.

Massive garrison forces have placed United States troops semi-permanently in Germany, England, and Japan, reflecting a decision in each of these countries that its domestic "self-defense" cannot be carried on without American soldiers, sailors, and airmen. A recent report of the U.S. Operations Coordinating Board showed one-quarter of all overseas Americans to be in Germany. In many other countries, such as Turkey, Iran, Pakistan, Thailand, Taiwan, and South Korea, American military strength takes the form of equipment and training personnel, but it is no less crucial to the defensive development of the nations concerned. The ring of bases around the Soviet periphery creates large and often essentially insoluble problems of public relations for the United States, notably in Morocco and Okinawa as this is written.

In all of these cases, and others too, the military build-up has massive political implications. Everywhere it strengthens the hands of the political "ins"; outside Western Europe military aid helps develop military officers in their expanding role as a new and often revolutionary middle class.

In Ethiopia, as in some of the Latin American nations, the military-aid mission has a primarily political function; its role (sometimes unknown to the American officers who are doing the job) is that of organizing an officer corps that will have the technical knowledge of weaponry and the sense of modern military organization to become a major factor in the politics of succession when existing leaders die or otherwise lose their grip.

Until twelve years ago the United States had no continuing civilian intelligence agency—and the military ones were not notably efficient when it came to nonmilitary information. Early in World War II, just before the invasion of that island from bases in North Africa, a group of economists was trying to put together some advice for the Army on civil government in Sicily. A member of the Washington research team was dispatched to the Office of Naval Intelligence to look up Sicily in their files; the latest entry (this was in 1943) was an unclassified consular report on commercial trends dated 1924!

Since its establishment in 1947 as the successor to the wartime Office of Strategic Services, the Central Intelligence Agency has been absorbing a constantly growing proportion of the foreign reporting and operating tasks of government—and tucking them behind a security curtain that obscures both successes and failures from foreign eyes and from serious Congressional review. Its expanding work, which until 1958 required a larger overseas staff in each successive year, would add to Table 2 several thousand overseas Americans. The exact number is an official secret.

Like other foreign operations, the Government's clandestine intelligence operations represent an unannounced revision of the principle of "noninterference." So, for that matter, does the intelligence work of other nations in the United States. One reason why a growing proportion of our foreign relations is being carried on in clandestine channels, perhaps, is that we need to hide what we are doing not only from others but also (in view of verbal adherence to "noninterference") from ourselves.

3

The spread of equalitarian enthusiasm has also led our foreign representatives deep into a function that hardly existed in our government at all a generation ago, that of propaganda and political advertising. It is no longer enough to impress only those who attend official receptions; the masses must be impressed too, and a number of new jobs have been created specifically for this purpose—press attachés, cultural attachés, librarians, technical specialists in the media of modern communication, and a growing number of researchers (some of them on government contracts) who take continuous soundings of foreign attitudes toward "the image of America."

The function of the United States Information Service in more than eighty countries consists of an effort to use the nation's communication network to get across certain ideas and attitudes. Those segments of foreign populations that are least favorably impressed by our efforts have often found in USIS buildings and American libraries a convenient target for brickbats.

The current involvement of whole societies in each other's daily lives is far beyond the control of government, if not beyond its concern. American-produced movies occupy more than 50 per cent of the *total* screen time in *each* of the world's major regions. American fast communication media pour forth each day between one and two million words for foreign consumption; the United States produces about 10 per cent of the world's books each year.[2] According to a recent compilation by the State Department, every year some 4,421,000 American tourists travel abroad; the United Nations says there are 64 million international tourists in all each year.

Considering its limitations—$100 million a year and only 1,168 overseas American employees—the problem for the U.S. Information Service is to make itself heard at all in the midst of this hubbub of international interaction. Its daily output is impressive: the USIA wireless file is 40,000 to

---

[2] The Soviet Union produces about 18 per cent.

50,000 words a day, or 4 to 5 per cent of the million words a day produced by the world's major wire services. The Voice of America is on the air for a little more than 5 per cent of the international total of 10,000 weekly hours of radio broadcasting. USIA maintains libraries in 77 countries with 2,542,275 books and about 1,100 program films on display, produces 68 foreign magazines or editions of magazines (18 in English and 50 in other languages), and maintains 225 permanent exhibits.

Compared to Soviet propaganda or even to private business operations, this output is less impressive than it seems at first glance. Soviet efforts, reputed to cost billions of dollars, reflect the Soviet view that the whole government apparatus is a propaganda vehicle; it employs 370,000 propagandists full time, according to a Senate Foreign Relations Committee report in 1958. In the field of American private enterprise, as Edward L. Bernays has noted, one company (Unilever) spent approximately $232,000,-000 in 1957 for advertising, to communicate with 1,800,000,000 consumers in the free world.

But the chief limitation of any United States propaganda operation is that it represents a wildly pluralistic society in which it is not anybody's official business to say authoritatively what America's purposes are and how they will be pursued. An accurate reflection of such a society is a multiple image. An undistorted echo of its politics is not a Voice but a babel of voices raised in democratic argument. It is hard for the government to "sell America," because the American people have not delegated to their government the authority to put it up for sale. Increasingly, therefore, the function of USIS in every country is to seek out all elements of the population and try to make sure they understand the nature of American society and have a sound basis for an understanding of American foreign policy from day to day. Other countries do the same work in the United States: the nations' intervention in each other's opinion-making processes is energetically reciprocal.

4

On the economic side of the government's overseas establishment, it is even clearer that a technical-assistance and public-investment program implies the deepest kind of involvement in the internal affairs of other nations—with their permission and within limits which their governments ultimately must set.

"There are some people," said the late Reverend A. Powell Davies, a Unitarian minister in Washington, D.C., "who still trot out the trite canard that loving our neighbor means what we do in direct relationship with him and that we cannot love him through acts of Congress. This is just a tired platitude. In the modern world we cannot even do our ordinary duty to our neighbor except through acts of Congress. This is true within our own country, as we have begun to recognize, and it is also true of our duty to the world."

Technical assistance, which the historian Arnold Toynbee has called "the greatest single idea in foreign policy to emerge from the twentieth century," brings Americans into contact with thousands of local and provincial leaders and with specialists in many fields who are far removed from the recipient nation's Foreign Office. These Americans deal with a society at its most sensitive point, at the very center of its rising expectations —teaching people to recognize their needs, helping them to be more articulate in demanding what they want from their own political leaders. By demonstrating what people can do for themselves once they set their minds to the task, technical assistance in the first instance increases the very gap between reality and expectations which is a prime cause of political ferment in every "underdeveloped" area. An investment program, moreover, requires attention to the whole of a nation's most sovereign process—the decisions as to how the nation's resources will be used, how the national budget will be allocated among purposes, what changes in the structure of public administration will be required to accomplish the modernization on which the leaders of the newly developing countries have generally set their hopes.

In 1958 the International Cooperation Administration, which administers most of the United States economic and technical aid abroad, had 3,338 Americans on its own payroll in more than 60 countries. In addition, there were more than 2,235 Americans overseas, representing private business firms and universities under contract to the ICA. Ten years ago, when the first of these figures was much smaller and the use of government contracts had barely started, nearly all the foreign-aid people had an arm's-length relationship with the governments to which they were accredited. But in Latin America the *servicios*—agreements by which Americans were placed as operating personnel inside Latin American governments—had already suggested a principle which the intervening years have dramatized again and again: that the more "underdeveloped" the country, the more inappropriate is mere cool advice, the more necessary an active role by the advisers in actual operations. As more countries emerge from colonial rule, especially in Africa, the need for operators rather than advisers becomes more acute, and is accompanied by the need for a clearer understanding on our own part of the role that Americans in the foreign-aid program actually play in foreign countries. In Ghana, first of the new African republics, there were, at the time of independence in 1957, just 80 architects of whom only 4 were Africans; only 20 to 30 per cent of all the engineers in Ghana were African; and hardly any of the young Ghanaians studying in Europe or America were taking any kind of technical course. In these circumstances the first job of a "technical adviser" often is to get something started; the next job to train nationals to perform subordinate tasks; the third stage is to select and train an "opposite number" who can gradually take over operating responsibility; then and only then can the American retire to a truly advisory role.

It is a slow business, and hundreds of foreign-aid officials have learned that it cannot be rushed. As an ICA man in the Middle East explained:

> At first we tried to do much more than they could assimilate here. I'm afraid some of our newer technicians don't understand this. They come out dewy-eyed and want to get things done. But the technical assistance program is a long-term program. Maybe you could say each project will go through three periods—the first five years getting started, the second five years of helping them, and the third five years of getting out of here.

This overseas veteran's time sense is wholly consistent with the original concept of technical assistance as a U.S. Government activity. "We are here embarking," President Truman said in his first message to Congress about the Point Four program, "on a venture that extends far into the future. We are at the beginning of a rising curve of activity, private, governmental and international, that will continue for many years to come." In a remarkable outcropping of administrative courage, an Assistant Secretary of State later told an inquiring Congressman in a public hearing that technical aid might go on for fifty years or more. The program, indeed, made no sense except in very long-range terms.

Yet today, with the first ten years of world-wide technical assistance behind us, the continuity of United States interest in economic development in the less-developed nations can be deduced from the fact that it continues, somehow, from year to year. That continuity is not yet formalized in our foreign-aid legislation, in the status of the government agency that administers foreign aid, or in the method of providing most of the investment funds and all of the technical services.

The foreign-aid program, financed though it is by year-to-year appropriations to an agency which would expire unless authorization were renewed each year, is a permanent aid program *de facto* if not *de jure*. The most striking evidence of ICA's permanence can be seen in the agency's own personnel policies.

Visiting the U.S. Operations Mission in Djakarta, we learned that more than a third of that 96-member mission had been on a field assignment with the foreign-aid program for more than four years—in other words, already at least on their third tour of duty. More than a quarter of all ICA employees in Indonesia had been in the field for more than five years. Other missions seemed to have comparable records; and percentages like these are the more remarkable since these missions typically include a good many short-term technicians sent out on spot assignments outside of the regular ICA employment system and an uncertain number of secretaries whose career ambition—to find a man—is fulfilled during their first tour of overseas duty.

The facts in the field are in the process of being institutionalized at headquarters. In the absence of cabinet-level leadership in the matter, the civil servants in the International Cooperation Administration began in 1957 a wholesale reform of personnel procedures designed to create in fact, in the absence of legislation, a viable career system for ICA's field staff. The scope of this undertaking was impressive: it meant, as ICA's personnel director put it to his staff at the time, "staffing some 4,200 positions in 60-odd countries encompassing a diversity of economic, cultural and political situations to stagger the imagination." In fashioning careers for its staff, ICA was encouraged by the parallel decision in the U.S. Information Agency to build a foreign information service on a career basis; USIA has been seeking for the last two years to get a Congressional imprimatur on the system it has already established by administrative action.

In short, ICA and USIA are not agencies which regard themselves as temporary aberrations from a norm of nineteenth-century diplomacy. The overseas Americans who make up the bulk of their staffs already know what the Budget Bureau and Congress do not yet officially admit: that foreign operations, enveloping and complicating United States foreign relations, are here to stay.

5

From this quick inventory of overseas government activity, it is once again evident that the United States already has its fingers in the political pastry of many countries, whether the American people like it or not, or, indeed, whether they know it or not. Judging from our interviews—and from the chronic malaise in our own country about United States foreign policy —these fingers are partly paralyzed by official reluctance to admit that the United States is interested in "domestic" political developments beyond our own shores.

The military-aid program is an example: The generals and colonels in charge of most military-assistance advisory groups abroad, many of them able soldiers with excellent records as combat leaders and peacetime administrators, usually believe their function to be limited to the training of troops in the use of modern weapons and advising on military organization and tactics. Yet in a dozen countries or more the foreign military officers we have trained are almost bound to have a powerful (or as we have recently seen in the Middle East, a controlling) voice in determining the political composition of their own civilian government, its foreign-policy posture, and the direction of its economic-development programs.

Similarly, United States technical and economic aid has very important

impacts on the domestic politics of several dozen nations. In this progress-conscious era, a Minister of Health may ride to the premiership not on a white horse but on a malaria-eradication program or a network of carefully placed rural health clinics. Yet if you ask civilian technicians or economic-aid officials to describe the central purpose of their mission, they will most often formulate it either in vague clichés about soliciting friendship or in the narrow language of the official's specialty.

Pressed to define the object of his work, one United States information officer at a small African post summed it up this way: "To create among these people an understanding of Americans by allaying their suspicions of the United States and getting them to give full support to their own government, which is pro-Western." Members of ICA missions typically pin their faith on "economic development" or "economic growth" or "improvement in living standards" or "getting people better educated" or "getting our aid out to the village level." Too seldom do they make the connection between these intermediate goals and the development of political institutions strong enough to survive in a turbulent world and free enough to be compatible with our own institutions in a peaceful world order. A typical statement of purpose follows.

> I suppose the general purposes of U.S. policy here in Mexico are to make Mexico a better prospect to sell or buy from. We're probably interested, out of every $100 spent, in $1 of brotherly love and $99 to benefit the U.S. Of course, in benefiting us we will also benefit the Mexicans. That's the way I'd sum up the purpose of our foreign policy as it applies to Mexico. Our job is that of being technicians in trying to give them some help.

On the military side the responses are equally devoid of political content; there are many references to foiling Russian aggression, a few mentions of internal security, and silence on political institution-building —although in most of the non-European countries in which we have military-aid programs, the actual priority of significance is precisely the opposite. If you ask directly about political impacts, you will generally be told that these are matters for the "political people" over at the embassy. The jurisdictional sensitivity thereby displayed is charming, but the referral is simple evasion. It is not the "political people" who are in day-to-day contact with the rising "middle class" of Army officers and economic planners. Moreover, some of our ambassadors are ill-equipped by training or inclination to provide the executive leadership to United States elements outside the embassy proper that would be necessary if the operation of military, economic, and information programs were to be shifted to the shoulders of the ambassadors. Nor is it clear that the President or Congress want our ambassadors to assume any such responsibility. In United States foreign operations to date, pluralism is still the order of the day.

The many overseas programs the United States sponsors—information and intelligence agencies, military and economic aid, international and private philanthropy, business and educational contacts by the thousands—give our government an unmatched opportunity to bring the United States into close and friendly touch with the coming leadership of all but a dozen nations in the world. But, while the government does many admirable things around the globe, it has yet to relate them effectively to each other and to the central purposes of American foreign policy.

The rapid changes in United States foreign operations have, moreover, not been accompanied by a bold enough look at the place of the diplomatic service itself in the scheme of things. Deep United States involvement in the internal affairs of other societies, for example, has called seriously into question the historic policy of sending most men for only two, three, or four years to each post. The acute need for people who can become intimately familiar with the language, culture, politics and administrative workways of every country is so great that the old policy, which was based on a fear that Foreign Service officers might "go native" if left in one place too long, is under widespread attack within, as well as outside of, the State Department's career service.

The need for specialists in the Foreign Service has forced a wholesale reorganization in which the career men, who have resisted the lateral entry of economists, labor and agricultural experts, and professional administrators, found themselves engulfed by the sudden merger of the Foreign Service with the civil servants in the State Department's Washington headquarters. Having strained at a series of gnats, the career officers finally had to swallow a camel; and it is altogether possible that two or more large groups of officials, the career people in USIA and ICA, will likewise be merged with the Foreign Service before the ferment about the government's overseas-personnel policy quiets down.

Above all, the new facts of diplomatic life have raised serious questions about a system which projects men whose main experience has been in reporting and negotiation into most of the nation's ambassadorships, just when the ambassador's task has come to be that of a large-scale public executive. In the era of foreign operations that is now upon us, the ambassador's constitutional position as the President's man abroad is now being reinterpreted to include the task of presiding over the whole range of United States governmental activities in the country to which he is assigned.

The effective ambassador, therefore, needs not only diplomatic but also executive qualities of the first order. If the trend of filling all but the "rich men's posts" (like Paris and London) from the career service continues, the career service will have to make sure that its members have been given ample opportunity to acquire executive experience by working in the foreign-operations agencies.

THE ADMINISTRATION
OF FOREIGN AFFAIRS

It is our foreign operations that largely account for the mushroom growth of U.S. Government activities and establishments abroad; and they also pose the most worrisome problems of administrative policy and relationships. The subject matter of foreign affairs, from the 16th century until just the last decade or so, was mostly "international" in the stricter sense of dealing with the questions that arose *between* nations or their sovereigns: dynastic rivalries, territorial claims, commercial exchange, shifting alliances for attack or defense, and the like. But now we are participating in a wide range of concerns largely *within* foreign countries—military budgets and organization, public health and education, agricultural extension, labor conditions, fiscal and monetary policies, the planning of public investments, and many, many others—for reasons and purposes which have already been indicated.

The involvement of our Government in the essentially domestic affairs of another nation entails grave risks of friction and enmity. This danger is especially great in the vitally important field of promotion of economic development, in view of the inevitable infringement of essential development policy decisions on touchy domestic interests and questions of sovereignty. As suggested in the earlier discussion, the problem could be substantially reduced, and our policy objectives furthered more effectively, by organizing our efforts in a multilateral context.

·   ·   ·

The administrative problems of our own Government's foreign operations are perhaps more complex, because our purposes are more diverse. But we can start with a simple fact: that the objects of foreign policy are located abroad—in the 86 countries where we maintain diplomatic or other missions, whose policies and actions may significantly affect our political, economic, or security interests, with whose governments we are negotiating, whose people we are seeking to influence, and whose national purposes we are trying to reconcile with our own. The test of the effective-

FROM *The Operational Aspects of United States Foreign Policy,* Study Number 6 in *United States Foreign Policy: Compilation of Studies,* prepared under the direction of the Senate Committee on Foreign Relations by the Maxwell Graduate School of Citizenship and Public Affairs, Syracuse University, November 1959.

ness of any nation's foreign policy administration is how well it works in the field.

This truism suggests that, within the framework set by our global objectives and strategy as defined by the President and Secretary of State, the day-to-day (and even, for most purposes, the year-to-year) conduct of foreign relations with each country should largely be determined by the complex of aspirations, interests, and forces at work in each society with which we have dealings. The shifting factors can best be appraised, the tactical situation most accurately judged, and the use of our various instruments of foreign policy most flexibly coordinated in the field. Further, the responsibility for coordination of U.S. bilateral activity in each country should be centered, insofar as possible, in the U.S. Ambassador in each country. In practice, however, the emphasis in making of policy, and of many detailed decisions, has tended in recent years to gravitate toward Washington. The effect has been to introduce distortions and irrelevancies into some programs, notably those for promoting economic development, and generally to make our policy excessively rigid and cumbersome.

The causes of this defect are complex, and include the following:

(*a*) Modern communications make it possible to exchange messages, at great length and detail, and get a quick reply. (To be sure, the ease of communications is partly self-defeating. The volume of messages swamps the recipients, requires more staff to draft replies, and hence further slows and complicates the decisionmaking progress. Even the mechanics of handling cables—coding, for example—are affected by the glut; American cables notoriously take much longer to reach their addressee than parallel messages through British channels.)

(*b*) Our main foreign policy concerns are global in character, and this appears to necessitate more coordination of specific decisions in the light of worldwide considerations. Before World War II, our policies in the Caribbean, China, and Czechoslovakia were, by and large, in separate compartments. We can no longer so regard them.

(*c*) There has been an extraordinary proliferation of U.S. agencies concerned in some way with foreign affairs, requiring more coordination both at headquarters and in the field. But since the final word rests with Washington, a very large number of questions involving interagency differences or understandings, rather than real policy, get referred to Washington for interagency brokerage.

(*d*) There has been a striking growth in congressional intervention in general, especially through its appropriations and investigative processes. This is a government-wide phenomenon; but the foreign affairs agencies, because their operations are well publicized, are particularly sensitive to detailed congressional review.

1. *The Executive Ambassador.* The ambassador represents in his person the authority of the President. In the era of foreign operations that is now upon us, his constitutional position must now be reinterpreted to include the task of presiding over the whole range of U.S. governmental activities in the country to which he is assigned. The most important and difficult parts of his job are likely to be not the traditional State Department functions of *foreign policy* and *foreign relations,* but *foreign operations* which in some countries are virtually as broad as those of the government to which he is accredited.

The effective ambassador must have, then, not only diplomatic but also executive qualities of the first order. Although the presumption in filling top embassy posts should certainly favor the career service, it would be a mistake to regard ambassadorships as its exclusive prerogative. It cannot be assumed that the experienced diplomat, however able in his field, will always have executive abilities, any more than an experienced administrator will necessarily possess the diplomatic qualities that are required—or that a successful politician will necessarily have either.

On the other hand, an increasing share of our foreign relations is now conducted in various international frameworks—the U.N. organs, the specialized agencies, NATO and other treaty organizations, the Organization of American States, etc. The duties of our representatives in these bodies are not mainly the coordination of operations but diplomatic negotiation, considerably complicated by the multilateral context in which it is conducted. Here is where the experienced Foreign Service officer can show to best advantage. Yet the major posts in our delegation to the U.N. General Assembly—and many other positions requiring special background in international politics and experience of diplomatic infighting—are often filled with estimable Americans trained in such dubiously relevant specialties as manufacturing, scientific research, teaching, singing, or organizing civic clubs.

Some of the amateur diplomats soon develop the requisite political sense and some FSO's make first-rate executives. But we could enhance the prospects of success by using men with demonstrated diplomatic skill for professional diplomacy and appointing as country chiefs of mission men with proven capacity as Government executives, as well as extensive overseas experience—from the career service if available, from outside if not. Perhaps the prime qualification for an effective ambassador, career or noncareer, is a strong sense of policy: an understanding of the objectives that the United States is trying to achieve in the country to which he is assigned, the ability to grasp the significance of the politico-economic-social forces at work there, and the imagination to see how some of our specific aims might be adapted to harmonize with local aspirations without prejudice to our essential interests.

The pool of potential executives, from which a sufficient number of ambassadorial candidates can be selected in the future, might be enlarged in several ways:

(*a*) By widening the Foreign Service to take in more of the "generalists" (e.g., the program officers and general administrators) from ICA and USIA.

(*b*) By insuring that members of such a combined Foreign Service have opportunities during their careers not only to handle visas and do politico-economic reporting but also, for example, to work in a foreign aid program, as a public affairs officer, with the ICA or as liaison with a MAAG.

(*c*) By urging our national political party leaders to endorse for Presidential and congressional consideration only those political candidates for embassy service who have already had successful executive and international experience.

The modern embassy is not, of course, concerned only with coordination of field operations. No less important is the characteristic foreign relations function—of negotiating, reporting, "keeping in touch." But the nature of this function has also changed; as indicated above, it involves making sure that we have some U.S. elements in close and friendly contact with all important forces in the country. The effective use of our plural contacts, official and nonofficial, in each country, however, requires that ambassadors and embassies recognize, as regards the diverse unofficial contingent, the inexpediency of trying to impose conformity to the current official line out of fear that deviations might "embarrass the United States." Coordination in this regard can better be informal rather than explicit, by leadership rather than by direction.

If recent history is a guide to the future, there is a good chance in many countries that the "next government" will be a military or a military-dominated one. The closest previous contacts that these new rulers are likely to have had with Americans are with the military personnel attached to our diplomatic missions and to MAAG's. This fact should be an important consideration in our selection and training of officers for such posts abroad. Apart from their competence in their several military specialties, the key members of our military aid missions should above all possess a "sense for politics," and be encouraged, under the ambassador's supervision, to cultivate politically minded leaders of the local armed forces, who may control the next regime. For this purpose it may be useful to call up for MAAG assignments some civilians experienced in Government who happen to be reserve officers.

In summary: The flexible, effective administration of foreign affairs requires a true delegation of responsible authority to the field. Within broad limits we need to get back to the concept that the ambassador is the President's representative, that he is "plenipotentiary." But such a delegation is acceptable only if we revert, in the selection of ambassadors, to standards closer to those observed in the earliest days of the Republic. Then our foreign relations were vital to survival, and we were on occasion represented by men of the caliber of Benjamin Franklin, Thomas Jefferson, John Jay, and John Quincy Adams. In this time of rapid change and deep involvement, the challenges we face cannot be met with money or armed power or technical skills alone; statesmanlike leadership is needed, and scope for its exercise.

2. *Training for Overseas Service.* An examination of Americans at work abroad reveals some uncommon qualities of mind and spirit which seem to be common to most of our citizens who have made successful careers abroad, whether in Government or with private business firms and voluntary agencies. These elements of effective oversea performance appear to be generally applicable to Americans in responsible positions abroad regardless of the kind of work the American is doing or in what foreign country he is doing it. Five of these elements stand out:

1. Technical skill: The versatility and willingness to improvise that requires both a thorough knowledge of a specialized field, but the attitude toward it of a general practitioner rather than a narrow specialist.

2. Belief in mission: A dedication to his work regardless of geography that enables a man to survive repeated frustrations and still retain zest for the job.

3. Cultural empathy: The curiosity to study and the skill to perceive the inner logic and coherence of the other fellow's way of thinking; and the restraint not to judge it as bad just because it is different from the American way.

4. A sense for politics: The sensitivity to see oneself as a "political man" whose action (or inaction) affects the power structure around him; the ability to do one's work despite being conspicuously the object of curiosity, envy, or opprobrium; and the understanding of American civilization that qualifies a man to represent not only himself but the culture and society from which he comes.

5. Organization ability: A tolerance for large-scale organization and an understanding of complicated headquarters-field relationships; and a special talent for building social institutions and teaching others to manage them.

No individual can be expected to possess, all by himself, just the proper "mix" of all the ingredients of effective oversea performance. But every American organization which operates abroad can be guided by these qualifications in trying to locate the proper people to mix together in carrying out its mission.

Now that nearly one percent of the U.S. population lives and works abroad, it is clear that the American educational system is not providing a sufficient number of Americans who, in addition to their vocational skills, have the necessary attitudes and kinds of understanding for useful oversea service. The best recruiting device is an educational program. If the colleges and universities can be induced to do more preparation for oversea life and work, the hiring agencies (in and out of Government) will be able to recruit from a pool of tested professionals, instead of (as at present) doing most of the weeding out of misfits and most of the relevant training for oversea service on the job, after the American has arrived at his post abroad.

The new importance of our deep involvement with other societies calls for some shifts in educational emphasis. For example:

(*a*) Immersion in an alien culture prior to the first oversea assignment is so important that colleges and universities should make it a live option for every interested student to spend at least a semester abroad under competent academic supervision.

(*b*) University area and language programs should be expanded to serve all three of the markets for regional studies. The first of these is the scholar who plans to make a career as an area expert. But the professional in a subject matter field who expects to work in the area also needs an academic haven to which he can repair for intensive language training closely associated with the study of cultural history and contemporary social and economic trends, geographic and military facts—a training that can help him face frankly, before he goes abroad, the nature of his role in speeding and influencing rapid social change. Area programs might also take on the task of organizing, for regular undergraduate and graduate students, a brief but intensive exposure in one country, as a practical introduction to cultural empathy.

(*c*) Every professional school, and graduate program in the social sciences, should reflect in its curriculum the certainty that some of its students will practice their profession abroad. In every American professional and graduate school the next revision of the curriculum should give prominent place to that disturbing and useful question: "What is universal about the rules and standards of our profession, and what is merely American practice?"

THE AMBASSADOR AND
THE COUNTRY TEAM

> In regard to your personal authority and responsibility, I shall count on you to oversee and coordinate all the activities of the United States Government in _____.
>
> You are in charge of the entire U.S. Diplomatic Mission, and I shall expect you to supervise all of its operations. The Mission, includes not only the personnel of the Department of State and the Foreign Service, but also the representatives of all other U.S. agencies which have programs or activities in
>
> . . . As you know, the U.S. Diplomatic Mission includes service attachés, military assistance advisory groups, and other military components attached to the Mission. It does not, however, include U.S. military forces operating in the field where such forces are under the command of a U.S. area military commander. The line of authority to these forces runs from me, to the Secretary of Defense, to the Joint Chiefs of Staff in Washington to the area commander in the field.
>
> Although this means that the Chief of the American Diplomatic Mission is not in the line of military command, nevertheless, as Chief of Mission, you should work closely with the appropriate area military commander to assure the full exchange of information. If it is your opinion that activities by the U.S. military forces may adversely affect our overall relations with the people or government of _____, you should promptly discuss the matter with the military commander and, if necessary, request a decision by higher authority.
>
> PRESIDENT JOHN F. KENNEDY, letter to American Ambassadors, May 29, 1961

IN the postwar years the United States greatly expanded its overseas operations. Alongside the old diplomatic missions large, semi-independent organizations for economic and military aid and cultural and information programs grew up. Labor, Agriculture and other agencies sent representatives abroad. American military bases and installations, with sizeable American forces, were established in many countries. Many of these organizations and representatives had their own lines of reporting to Washington and had statutory authority and responsibilities defined by Congress.

The volume and variety of American business with foreign countries dramatically increased. The texts of international agreements between the United States and foreign governments concluded in the 12 years between

FROM "Basic Issues," A study submitted by the Subcommittee on National Security Staffing and Operations to the Senate Committee on Government Operations, January 18, 1963.

1950 and 1962 fill 30 large volumes occupying 7 feet of shelf space! Many of these agreements dealt with highly technical matters and had to be negotiated with the help of experts from Washington.

All of these developments placed the authority and prestige of the ambassador in doubt and put great strains on the old diplomatic machinery. In 1951 President Truman took steps to support the ambassador's primacy. The concept of the country team, with the ambassador at its head, was initiated. Further steps in this direction were taken by President Eisenhower. President Kennedy's letter of May 29, 1961, is the most recent attempt to confirm the ambassador's leading position.

But in the field, as in Washington, the task of coordination has grown more complex as the instruments of national policy have multiplied. The major elements of the modern diplomatic mission are State, AID, USIS, the service attachés (Army, Navy, and Air Force), military assistance advisory groups (MAAGS), and CIA. Often there is also an area military commander.

Although all members of the country team acknowledge the ambassador's position, respect his precedence as chief of mission, tell him about their work, show him their cables, and invite his comments, their dependence on him and their desire to be coordinated by him differ greatly. As a general rule, their readiness to accept his right of decision varies with the degree to which they are involved in operational matters, such as the conduct of aid programs, and have their own reporting lines to Washington.

The political counselors and other old-line members of the diplomatic staff are most dependent on the ambassador and have the greatest interest in supporting him. They have no line of reporting except through the ambassador—and informal letters to colleagues in Washington. At the other end of the spectrum is the MAAG. Its work is highly operational, it has its own lines to the Pentagon, and it tends to take a restricted view of the ambassadors' right to interpose himself between it and the Pentagon on budgetary, programing, and operational decisions. The other groups fall somewhere between these positions. CIA is closer to the MAAG model, while USIS falls closer to the diplomatic model and AID somewhere in the middle.

Country team processes have, therefore, quite different meanings for the several participants, seeming almost a waste of time to those heavily involved in day-to-day operations. The fact that the deadlines and other decision-spurring pressures seldom hit the participants at the same time contributes to the unevenness of interest in the work of the country team. What is usually involved is action by one group at a time on a matter of great moment to it and of little immediate interest to the others. In the eyes of, say, a MAAG chief preparing his budget, the other members seem at best to be little more than spectators and at worst a threat. On particular issues, however, the ambassador's support may be helpful and this strengthens his position. But in general each group of operators would be happy to be left alone by the others.

To a degree the primacy of the ambassador is a polite fiction, especially when budgetary and programing decisions are concerned. Most elements of the country team do not, in other words, regard themselves as parts of the ambassador's staff—rather they look outside the country, to intermediate headquarters or Washington, for guidance and support and their loyalties tend to run in the same direction. Nevertheless, it is apparent that a strong ambassador can pull a team together and exert great influence.

Some suggest that an ambassador should have responsibility for preparing a complete country program and for reviewing and approving all parts of it, so that the final program would be his and so that he would be put by the nature of the process in the role of umpire and adjudicator of competing claims for resources. Because of the way agency programs are prepared in Washington, however, this would present great difficulties. A consequence is that decisions on military and economic aid and other programs are pulled toward the Presidential level in Washington and that the competition for resources tends to run between overall appropriations for military versus economic aid, and so forth, rather than between the need for military aid in comparison with economic aid in a particular country.

Despite these observations the field is refreshingly free of interagency strife. In general the deep jurisdictional clashes evident in Washington are absent. Divisions are present but are watered down, partly, no doubt, because the team acquires a certain solidarity by virtue of common experiences in dealing with the local government, on the one hand, and with Washington, on the other.

One of an ambassador's problems is that the country team is an interdepartmental organization which has no corresponding organization to which it is responsible or to which it can look for guidance, direction, and support. In Washington the decision-making process is, so to speak, vertical —up departmental lines which converge only at the Presidential level. In the field, coordination is horizontal, with differences being resolved and policies harmonized by the ambassador.

The Planning Function in the Field

Ideally, one would suppose, the country team should be the chief source of country plans. It is on the spot and should be familiar with the obstacles to the accomplishment of U.S. objectives. Yet with few exceptions little planning is in fact done in the field and what is done is patchy.

The operational groups are so deeply involved in day-to-day operations that they have little time for planning, even if they have officers with the training and experience for the planning task. And they seldom do. There is, furthermore, no stated requirement for a coordinated country plan or program, in which economic and military aid, cultural and information programs, and other elements of American policy are drawn together and focused on U.S. objectives. There is no place in the embassy where this task could now be done.

Among the best people in the field are some of the political and economic counselors and their staffs. But the reporting content of their jobs and the burden of representation and negotiation is so great that they have little time for thinking about what the United States is trying to accomplish in the country and what combination of activities would best serve American purposes.

Increasingly, the United States is seeking to accomplish its goals through regional programs and international organizations, but it has not yet taken adequate steps to relate country missions to regional planning.

As things stand in the field, apart from exceptional cases, Washington cannot rely on the country team for planning. Yet satisfactory arrangements for preparing coordinated country and regional plans are still to be devised in Washington also. This is one of the major problems of staffing and organizing for national security. Whether efforts should be made to staff the missions for planning, or whether country and regional planning groups should be organized in Washington, or whether some combination of the two should be found are questions that demand attention.

The Reporting Function

Reporting occupies a very large part of a mission's time and energies. The volume of messages between Washington and the field has reached almost astronomical proportions. The daily volume of telegraphic traffic alone between State and the embassies is more than 300,000 words! Much is necessary but much is of doubtful usefulness.

Despite the volume of reporting Washington often feels and is poorly informed. The reason is largely that the decision-making process is not well enough understood so that headquarters can identify a need until it arises. Reporting requirements are therefore not clear. No one knows how to issue general instructions on who should be told what and when. As a result the rule seems to be: Report Everything. The field tries to cover every base and to anticipate every requirement in the hope that any information Washington may need will be available when wanted. The resulting flood of information swamps Washington's absorptive capacities.

This reporting is of very uneven quality. Some is brilliant, but the top executives seldom have time to look at it. Most is routine. But all of it must be read by someone—a fact which accounts for a great deal of employment in Washington. Some of this talent could, one is confident, be employed in more useful ways.

Moreover the whole personnel system encourages reporting. Young officers get credit for writing reports, especially voluntary reports on matters outside their assigned responsibilities. An officer's reports are an important basis for evaluating his performance and recommending promotions. This may be sound personnel practice but it burdens the system with too much reporting and encourages wrong ideas about the proper allocation of time between direct observation and study of a country's problems and report writing.

Good reporting is essentially operational, directly serving the needs of men who must make decisions and direct operations. Much reporting at present is remotely related, if at all, to the decision-action process. Top executives are so heavily occupied that they have virtually no time for reading anything not immediately relevant to the day's problems.

Many countries are deeply involved in far-reaching political, economic, social, and military programs. The United States is assisting these programs of modernization and reform in many ways. Analysis of great depth and sophistication is needed as a basis for planning. What strains are these programs putting on the political system? Can they be carried without political collapse? What groups are gaining power and influence and which are losing? What political adjustments would strengthen the system? Are they feasible? How can the United States assist the process of adjustment?

The kind of knowledge and understanding needed to produce answers to such questions is not likely to be gained at a desk, reading second-hand accounts of what is happening in a society. Direct observation and study and a wide acquaintance in many social groups are needed.

But in addition the analyst needs to know his audience and its requirements. Scholarly analyses of great brilliance will be of little use unless they point to operationally significant conclusions. The definition of reporting requirements depends therefore on a clear location of responsibility for policy planning, and close contact between the analyst and the planner.

The reporting function should be carefully reviewed. Some suggest the reporting relevant to day-to-day decisions should be provided on a day-to-day basis in response to requests from the ambassador or Washington. The feasibility of this suggestion depends on the technical adequacy of the Government's communications system, and especially on the disciplined restraint of both the senders and the receivers of messages. Without such restraint, even the best communications system will soon be overloaded.

Some suggest that the kind of analysis needed for planning and programing should be a joint undertaking of teams consisting of members from Washington and the field and linked closely to the planning and programing process. This would require more frequent travel between Washington and the field, but might cost less and produce better results than present practices.

Whatever changes are made, intensive efforts are needed to develop officers who can produce the kind of political and economic analyses that are basic to the radically new nature of American foreign policy. There are now very few officers who have shown an ability to make "depth analyses" of the forces at work in society.

Personnel for the Country Team

Every mission has some first-rate people. But the number of big jobs is far larger than the number of able people available to fill them. With over 100 missions to be staffed—more than double the number only a few years ago—every personnel system has been strained. Every Washington head-quarters is evidently robbing Peter to pay Paul, trying to cover the most critical spots by shifting its best people around. There is no prospect that recruiting will overcome the deficiency of good people in the near future.

It is therefore all the more important that good people be well used. But under present practices each department and agency must staff its own overseas posts. All too often the result is that an ambassador cannot use his best people in his most important spots. He needs freedom with respect to his own mission to move his good people where they are most needed.

Obviously, however, this runs headlong into existing practice. Personnel systems are organized by departments and agencies. Promotions, assignments, career development programs, organizational loyalties—all work against it. Whether the conflicting needs of the ambassador and of the career services can be reconciled is a serious dilemma of personnel administration.

The Division of Labor

The personnel problem is intensified by the problem of the division of labor between Washington and the field.

There is little doubt that the abilities of most missions are under-employed. The country team is familiar with local issues and problems—from important questions of policy to minor details of mission housekeeping. Many matters could be handled locally, with action being reported to, but not cleared with, Washington. Ironically, "Washington clearance" often means that a junior officer in Washington is second-guessing a senior officer in the field—and second-guessing him on matters the latter is better qualified to decide than an equally experienced officer in Washington.

Some progress has recently been made in delegating authority to the field for administrative decisions on such matters as housing, travel, and hospitalization. This shift is desirable and should be encouraged.

No similar trend is evident in policy matters. In fact, the contrary is true. More and more issues are being referred to Washington, or handled by officers sent from Washington, or settled in Washington in negotations with visiting foreign officials.

Washington can of course assert its authority in any matter. But it should not assert it in every matter. There is a need to re-examine the division of labor between the two.

A proposal worth consideration is that issues might be left to the ambassador unless they are of such sensitivity, complexity, or importance that they demand attention of an Assistant Secretary or officer of higher rank. That is, an ambassador might indicate to Washington that he intends to act in a certain way by a certain date unless otherwise instructed. And Washington might exercise greater self-restraint in issuing instructions—with the philosophy that it may be better to act a little less than perfectly rather than employ the time of Washington officials in a search for perfection. Some may even doubt that the sun always shines more brightly in Washington than in the field.

A shift of greater action-responsibility to the field by such rules of thumb might lead to important economies. Too much time is spent in Washington on matters that could be left to the mission, thus double-teaming talent when there is not enough talent to go around. This tendency shows itself in the habit of Washington and the field to "live on the cables"—to keep each other busy debating points on which it might have been better to let the mission act by itself under its general instructions.

Obviously there are no iron rules for dividing responsibility. What seems to be called for is more respect in Washington for the judgment of ambassadors and more restraint in second-guessing them.

Military Advice

Today's ambassador frequently has to make decisions and give his views on military questions.

Every mission has three service attachés. Many have a MAAG chief. A few must work with an area military commander. To which of these should an ambassador turn for military advice?

A reorganization of the military advisory function seems to be needed. The number of military representatives reporting directly to the ambassador is too large—a fact which tends to reduce rather than increase their influence in the mission. Partly in order to deal with these representatives and with an area military commander, if any, a new politico-military post has been established in many missions. This officer, usually a career foreign service officer with some special training, assists the ambassador with the coordination of political and military activities. In some cases he serves as the executive secretary of the country team.

A suggestion meriting serious consideration is that a single defense attaché might be designated by the Department of Defense, with such assistants as necessary from the three services. Presumably the defense attaché would be an officer of the U.S. military service that was also the most important service in the country—an Army officer in countries where the Army is the principal military organization, and so forth.

Another proposal is that the functions of the MAAG chief and of the attachés might be combined in a single officer, who might be called the defense attaché. The objection that the military aid program should be clearly separate from the normal attaché functions needs to be reexamined. The combination has been successful in some places.

Where there is an area commander of U.S. forces, the possibility of placing the MAAG under the joint supervision of the ambassador and the commander might be considered. In any event, where there is such a commander, an ambassador tends to rely primarily on him for military advice.

Regional Organizations

There are now four American Ambassadors in Paris: the Ambassadors to France, NATO, OECD (Organization for Economic Cooperation and Development), and DAC (Development Assistance Committee). This is the extreme case. But it illustrates the growing importance of regional organizations in the conduct of American policy.

The task of an ambassador to an international organization is more confining and limited than is generally understood.

He is, of course, constantly involved in promoting or opposing particular actions by the organization which may have an important bearing on U.S. national security policies. But if he is not to commit the United States to positions inconsistent with our national security requirements, he must remain closely tied to Washington. The President and the Secretary of State require information and advice from him. But he is dependent on them not only to set policy lines but also to give him his major assistance in carrying out those policies. He can expect to get results when the United States, working with its allies through bilateral discussions or in other small groups, has developed a position which can command support in the organization.

At the present stage international organizations are more decision-ratifiers than decision-makers. Things go well in NATO, or the United Nations, for example, when the United States and other key countries have reached a common position.

The growth of international organizations is one of the powerful forces pulling decision-making into Washington. Rational, effective negotiation on complex and critical matters, like a multilateral NATO nuclear deterrent or the reduction and control of armaments, requires unified guidance and instruction to those conducting the negotiations. This is a basic principle of sound administration and avoids the dangers of crossed lines.

The unified source of instructions can only be the President himself (not others in the White House or the Executive Office), or the Secretary of State, acting for the President, or, in appropriate cases, an Assistant Secretary of State acting for the Secretary. In this connection, the post of Assistant Secretary of State has achieved a new importance in the policy process.

Certainly U.S. missions to regional and other international organizations should not, and cannot successfully, operate as little foreign offices. Such confusion of responsibility reinforces a tendency to give undue weight in policy formulation to considerations that necessarily seem more important in Paris or New York, for example, than they seem to the President.

The Government has not yet fully faced the problem of adjusting its organization and procedures to the problems created by the growth of international organizations, particularly the United Nations and the regional organizations in Europe and Latin America. This is one of those emotionally charged areas that needs careful study.

STATEMENT OF WILLIAM J. CROCKETT

It is a privilege to appear before this committee which has rendered such distinguished service in the area of national security. Your findings will be most beneficial to the country at large and certainly to the Department of State. I wish to express our indebtedness to you.

I value also the chance to comment on the ideas and criticisms that have already been expressed before this committee, to identify a number of problems with which we are dealing and, finally, to explain certain measures we have taken and are contemplating taking in the Department of State to meet our obligations toward the national security of our Nation. . . .

First of all, I would like to say that those who framed the Foreign Service Act of 1946—the organic act governing the present-day Service—were wise indeed. The objectives of that legislation, as stated in title I, were to develop and strengthen the Foreign Service of the United States of America so as:

    1. to enable the Foreign Service effectively to serve abroad the interests of the United States;

Presented before the Subcommittee on National Security Staffing and Operations of the Senate Committee on Government Operations, November 21, 1963.

2. to insure that the officers and employees of the Foreign Service are broadly representative of the American people and are aware of and fully informed in respect to current trends in American life;

3. to enable the Foreign Service adequately to fulfill the functions devolving on it by reason of the transfer to the Department of State of functions heretofore performed by other Government agencies;

4. to provide improvement in the recruitment and training of the personnel of the Foreign Service;

5. to provide that promotions leading to positions of authority and responsibility shall be on the basis of merit and to insure the selection on an impartial basis of outstanding persons for such positions;

6. to provide for the temporary appointment or assignment to the Foreign Service of representative and outstanding citizens of the United States possessing special skills and abilities;

7. to provide salaries, allowances, and benefits that will permit the Foreign Service to draw its personnel from all walks of American life and to appoint persons to the highest positions in the Service solely on the basis of their demonstrated ability;

8. to provide a flexible and comprehensive framework for the direction of the Foreign Service in accordance with modern practices in public administration; and

9. to codify into one Act all provisions of law relating to the administration of the Foreign Service.

The Congress gave us a concept that provided, in my opinion, an excellent Foreign Service personnel capability at that time—and still does. The authors of the act of 1946 established a Foreign Service Officers Corps founded upon several basic ordinances that have changed but little over the intervening years.

I would like to emphasize my personal conviction that the corps concept is as valid today as it was in 1946. It is also my conviction that the Foreign Service Act, as conceived by its framers—Foreign Service officers, officers of the Department of State and other Government agencies concerned with the Foreign Service, and Members of Congress—is broad enough today to encompass the personnel needs of all agencies operating in the foreign policy field.

There are many people, both inside and outside the Service, who say "Leave the Service alone, let it get over the various pruning and graftings that have been made over the past few years before new ideas are tried." As a matter of fact, things we plan for the months ahead are not intended to change the basic concepts of the Service. All they attempt is to improve and update techniques designed to strengthen the operation of the Service. Therefore, we do propose to move ahead.

The things that make the Service strong and unique, in my opinion, are the following:

1. *Competitive Intake.* We have had, for a number of years, a college relations program designed to acquaint representative colleges and univer-

sities across the land of the career opportunities in the Foreign Service and to encourage outstanding young men and women to interest themselves in taking the Foreign Service examinations.

The majority of our Foreign Service officers enter the Service at the bottom through examinations that are held semiannually across the country.

There are no quotas by state, no official endorsements or nominations are required, and there is no stipulation regarding formal level of education. We want only the best. And when only a few hundred are accepted out of several thousand applicants in a given year, then it might be assumed that we are meeting our standards. Yet we are not certain. Are enough people taking the exams? And are we attracting a proper cross section of our society or do we appeal only to those who feel they can afford the Service?

We therefore are making intensive efforts to publicize the Foreign Service and the examinations with the hope that we not only get more applicants but that they come from all quarters of our society and from all parts of our Nation.

We are looking at the examination itself, which consists of a day-long written general examination, followed—for the successful—by an hour and a half oral examination, which is then followed by physical, security, and suitability examinations. We hope to develop an examination that not only evaluates the intellectual breadth of an applicant but also searches for potentials of managerial and executive ability and leadership.

2. *Personal Grades.* Another basic strength of the Foreign Service is the concept of personal grades. In a system where personnel attain personal grades and carry with them their grades and salaries, we have a greater mobility and flexibility in the assignment and movement of people, enabling us to demand more of the individual because, whatever the circumstances of the job, or the location, or the environment, we can still expect the officer to perform in accordance with his personal grade.

3. *Worldwide Service.* Although we do have regional specialists, language specialists, and other kinds of specialists, the Foreign Service is based upon the concept that the individual is available to serve anywhere that he is needed in the Foreign Service. This enables us to have a highly mobile operation. It enables us to share equitably hardship posts as well as the better posts.

4. *Disciplined Service.* This, of course, goes hand in hand with worldwide service. Members of the Foreign Service pride themselves on being disciplined, on being available for service anywhere for the benefit of the United States. Certainly, the desire of the individual is taken into consideration, as well as the problems of family, family health, schooling needs of children, and the career development opportunities for the officer himself, but in the end an officer goes where he is assigned.

5. *Service in Washington.* Prior to 1954 relatively few of our officers had any period of service in the United States and became virtual expatriates with the result that they lost contact with the flow of life here. The present

concept is that an officer serves about 40 percent of his Foreign Service career in the United States, enabling him to be current on what we are doing in the fields of social improvement, culture, art, business, et cetera. I believe this duty at home is vital to the Foreign Service and, although we have been criticized occasionally for having too many officers in Washington at one time, the United States will be better represented by officers who know and understand the United States as it is today rather than as it was when they left school 15 or 20 years ago.

6. *Competitive Promotion.* Again, job level and job assignment are not as important in this as in the ability and the initiative of the individual in developing himself for greater and greater responsibility. We give a great deal of attention to our promotion system, to the selection of officers who serve on promotion panels, to the precepts that we expect these panels to follow in judging officers competitively, and in the selection of prominent private citizens to serve as public members on these boards.

Competition is an important motivating factor in any corps and it is particularly so in the Foreign Service. This is not inconsistent with nor detrimental to the esprit de corps of the Service.

Each year, officers of the same class are rated and ranked in relation to each other. Each year the promotion panels sift through each officer's personnel file and come up with recommendations regarding promotion, retention in grade, or selection out of the Service. I am convinced that this is a system that can operate effectively to assure the upward flow of our capable officers and the outward flow of the less capable.

In this regard we are giving considerable thought to revising the techniques of performance ratings and the standards by which the promotion panels operate.

We are aware that the value of an officer's efficiency rating depends as much on the capabilities of the rating officer as it does on the officer being rated. We are looking for ways to assure greater objectivity in this rating procedure.

We also have instructed the promotion panels to emphasize the promotion of outstanding officers and to disregard the outdated concept which required an officer to spend a specified time in his grade before being promoted.

I believe any body of people over a long period of time will identify those who do not measure up with their colleagues. Abilities diminish, motivations change, and people's abilities to keep up with their jobs also change. As a result, we expect to have a vigorous selection out of people at all grades who somehow have lost the physical or mental ability to maintain the high level that is expected of the Foreign Service. The act of 1946 provides generous retirement and selection out benefits for the purpose of insuring a vigorous administration of the act.

I would like to make my statement to the promotion panels and the precepts for this year's promotion panels a part of this record.

Hand in hand with competitive promotion goes selection out and retirement. To my knowledge, this is the only civilian agency in the Federal
Government whose philosophy is "up or out." . . .

7. *Efficiency Ratings and Inspection.* A system of personal evaluation
by supervisors, checked at frequent intervals by the inspection corps, is
the backbone of the Department's promotion and selection out system.
Obviously, there are many problems with a system that depends upon the
frailty of one person's evaluation of another but nevertheless until business,
as well as Government, can devise a better system, this is the only means
we have on which to base promotions and selection out. One of the problems with our efficiency rating system at present is the requirement we
impose that supervisors discuss their efficiency ratings with their subordinates and that the subordinate can read the efficiency rating only upon
his first return to the United States. In the regular elements of the day's
activities, supervisors can be and are critical and make suggestions for the
improvement of the work of their subordinates. There is no difficulty in
this. The problem arises when the superior talks with his subordinate
about his intellectual capacity or integrity, his personal conduct, the conduct of his family, and any impact that his subordinate's family may have
on his official life.

I personally believe that we must continue to strive for improvements in
this whole efficiency rating business—a process which perplexes and be-
devils management in both the public and private sector. Our goal must
be to insure that the Department gets valid, objective ratings that can be
used as a basis for further development, assignment, promotion, and
selection out. We are working on this and hope that we will have some
answers before the next efficiency rating period comes around in the spring.

Hand in hand with efficiency ratings is the Department's inspection
process. Inspectors have a broad range of responsibilities but one of the
most important is their evaluation of personnel and the evaluations of the
ratings that have been made on officers of the Service by their superiors.
Certainly it is difficult for an inspector spending only a few weeks in a city
to give an exhaustive and comprehensive rating on an individual, but it is
possible for him to read the reports that others have written and to come
to some conclusions about the validity of the reports.

8. *Specialization.* One of the areas that received the special attention of
the Committee on Foreign Affairs Personnel (the Herter committee) concerned the need for the development within the Foreign Service of specialist
capabilities.

In the past a belief persisted within the Service that the only way to become an Ambassador was by a series of assignments to the political sections
of our embassies. Good political reporting was supposed to be the path to
the top.

Many people inappropriately applied the title of generalist to officers
who spent their careers doing political reporting and assumed that a

person versed in any other aspect of our foreign affairs operations was a specialist. Specialists specialized but generalists became Ambassadors.

This belief in turn encouraged disdain for many of the new activities in foreign affairs that developed during and after the Second World War. The problem of generalists versus specialists has been with us for a long time.

However, I think we have made some inroads. What we are contemplating, what we are implementing, is a personnel system that recognizes and encourages the role of specialization in the Foreign Service, that establishes a number of clearly defined career management fields, and that offers a tailored career development program for each Foreign Service officer.

These career management fields will cover all of the functions in which the Foreign Service has responsibility, including area and language specialties as well as the highly technical specialties. This system is intended to formalize the concept of specialties but at the same time we intend to avoid rigidity.

There will be an interchange of personnel among functional areas and an effort to have our officers develop competence in more than one field. However, we want to enable our officers to develop within their specialties and we intend to encourage this by offering the specialist a challenging, rewarding, and satisfying career.

The specialist will be able to reach the senior grades within his functional competence. Moreover, he will be able to compete for DCM and Ambassador assignments since the incumbents of these exalted positions will be chosen on the basis of demonstrated ability, breadth of vision, and executive capacity.

We are seeking also means to allow our officers to develop a breadth of vision, a greater professionalism. We are planning to have some of our officers spend a year in residence on campuses across the country.

Although they are not going primarily to teach they will of course lecture on the Foreign Service and on the areas in which they have served. In turn they and the Foreign Service will have an opportunity to catch up on the developments of our Nation. Also, to date, too few of our officers have made serious contributions in the field of political science. We will encourage our officers to write and will give them the opportunity to do so.

9. *Lateral Entry.* A great deal of discussion has been generated about the philosophy of lateral entry. There are those in the Service who would say that excessive exercise of lateral entry will discourage people interested in the Service—that it will diminish the intake at the bottom because young people will feel that they can get ahead faster by entrance in the middle range and that lateral entry in general is a violation of the career concept.

There are others who state that a career service can maintain its vigor only if it has the competition provided by lateral entry—people coming into the Service in the middle and upper grades from other walks of life.

Lateral entry was a concept that was provided for in the act of 1946 but there was little use of this procedure for some years. The largest influx, of course, occurred as a result of the Wriston program, but in a sense this was not lateral entry because people already involved in State Department activities were moved from one personnel system to another.

True lateral entry, as I see it, is bringing people into the Foreign Service from other agencies of Government and from outside the Government. It is my belief that most thinking people in the Foreign Service and outside it would say that a bona fide, well-administered, commonsense lateral-entry program is essential to the well-being of the Service. To deny lateral entry is a presumption that we have within the Service all of the specialties and knowledge that are needed. Actually, seldom is there a day when we don't find the need for a new specialty or a new technique. Lateral entry can provide vital experience and knowledge and specialization.

We also realize that an infusion of fresh talent at the middle grades is necessary to maintain the dynamism of the Service. I do not want to be caught in a contradiction here since someone may ask whether our basic recruiting and training procedures are at fault if we are forced to bring people in at some point in order to rejuvenate the Service. There is also the question that recruitment of outside talent will demoralize those officers who came in from the bottom and are subjected to the disciplines and slow movement upward in the Service.

Let me emphasize that lateral entry is engineered so as to bring into the Service those talents that do not exist within it and, also, to allow a limited infusion of outstanding people who are interested in a career in the field of foreign affairs. Lateral entry is a supplement and not an alternative to our basic recruitment program.

10. *Assignment.* There is no more complicated administrative problem than the assignment of Foreign Service personnel. The responsibilities are great. We strive to place the right officer in the right place at the right time, but there is the factor of an officer's family and an officer's career to keep in mind. Language ability, specialization, availability of housing and schools, medical complications, not to mention the officer's personal desires, all have to be taken into consideration in making asignments. This imposes a deep responsibility on those making assignments because assignments made arbitrarily may leave little possibility for the assigned officer to achieve success in his job and therefore may be equivalent to forcing failure and eventual selection out.

We are concerned in the Department about the continuity that we can establish at our oversea operations and therefore have given much attention to tour of duty policies in an attempt to achieve longer assignments compatible both with national interests and the employees' personal interests.

There is no general agreement as to how long a person should stay at a post and much depends upon the job and the officer.

Officers should have a deep and sympathetic understanding of the people of the host country—their history, their social development, their aspirations. This is essential if an officer is to analyze properly the political and economic effort. On the other hand, objective appraisal is often blurred as knowledge and sympathy increases and we must insure that officers do not remain at a post so long that they lose their objectivity.

In addition to these substantive problems, there is the consideration of health and living conditions at posts where either isolation or climate makes a long period of duty undesirable. Through legislation we have achieved wide assignment flexibility ranging from 18 months to 5 years, coupled with authority to send employees and their families on rest and recuperation leave which permits us to custom tailor tours of duty. We are trying to make sensible assignments in terms of the job and the individual.

This committee has heard testimony concerning the tours of duty of ambassadors. Ambassadors, of course, are appointed by the President and serve at his pleasure.

There is no such thing as a normal tour of duty for Ambassadors at the diplomatic missions of the United States.

Ideally, we would like to see an Ambassador remain at a post for at least 4 years.

Depending upon various factors such as experience, adaptability, local political conditions, language, and the state of relations between the United States and the country concerned, an Ambassador can be expected to spend most of his first year learning the country and his job and to reach maximum effectiveness during his second year. He should be able to maintain his effectiveness for at least 2 or 3 years more. Some can continue longer but others may tend to take on a tinge of parochialism.

The President and the Secretary of State need to make a judgment in each individual case as to when an Ambassador's service in a country passes the point of full effectiveness.

Apart from the quality of an Ambassador's performance, other factors have to be taken into account in deciding on the length of tours of duty. Perhaps the most limiting factor is climate. There are a number of posts where climatic and health conditions make it undesirable for an Ambassador to serve more than 2 or 3 years.

As of November 1, 1963, the average length of tours of duty of Ambassadors was approximately 2 years and 10 months. The average is based on the length of service of all Ambassadors who resigned or otherwise completed their tours of duty since the beginning of the current administration in January 1961. . . .

Before concluding this discussion about personnel as being the most important factor in a successful Foreign Service, I would like to mention two other things.

The first is the place and importance of Foreign Service wives in the conduct of our foreign affairs. If it meets the pleasure of your committee, I would like to have inserted in the record a recent statement by Secretary Rusk. In the Foreign Service, to an extent not known in most other fields of work, the wife is almost as important as the officer. The Foreign Service is in fact a way of life. This commitment on the part of an officer includes his wife and family. Wives not only provide the stability for family life in difficult situations, but are also at their husband's elbows at all kinds of official receptions and other gatherings. Because of their important role, we now offer wives language training and orientation courses to prepare them for their oversea tasks.

The second item is the support given to our people serving abroad—medical care, housing, schools, allowances, representation, and so forth. Support has greatly improved in the past 10 years, thanks to the help we have received from Congress. I think it would be useful here to insert a chart showing the growth of these support activities.

Support Activities

Quarters allowance:		Temporary lodging allowance:	
1954	$2,292,449		
1964	3,841,316	1954	$244,127
Education allowance:		1964	449,137
1954	0	Home service allowance:	
1964	691,718	1954	0
Medical benefits:		1964	64,900
1954	171,619	Representation allowance:	
1964	395,793	1954	500,000
Official residence allowance:		1964	996,000
1954	414,577	Communications:	
1964	887,100	1954	2,826,018
Training:		1964	5,951,330
1954	768,451		
1964	4,796,400		

I feel compelled to say, however, that there are still some deficiencies. More money is needed if we are to provide the housing and allowances which our people need. I say this without any intention of minimizing the assistance that Congress has given to the Foreign Service.

Complementary to our efforts in the personnel field is our current concept of the role of the State Department in the formulation and implementation of foreign policy in today's world.

I hardly need to remind the members of this committee of the profound changes that have taken place in the conduct of foreign affairs since the end of World War II. Neither do I have to point out the impact these changes have had on the manner in which the U.S. Government is structured to carry on foreign affairs. With this in mind, I would like to speak briefly about some new approaches to our problems of coping with change and managing the new diplomacy.

A good starting place is to describe a new way of classifying the many and varied acivities of modern-day foreign affairs.

In a recent study made on the work of a typical U.S. mission in Latin America, we have identified some 25 separate tasks performed by mission personnel. For convenience sake, we have grouped these activities in three broad categories that I believe fairly well describe the purposes of our oversea effort: The first of these categories, which we have named internal development, consists of the various activities undertaken by the United States to encourage and assist other countries to modernize their own institutions.

More than the assistance programs of AID, this includes military assistance programs, the activities of the Peace Corps, and the efforts of other sections of U.S. missions designed to promote attitudes and actions conducive to the development of the host society.

The second category, which we have called international relations, covers the more traditional diplomatic activities that take place on a formal government-to-government basis between the United States and more than 100 other nations around the world.

Today, even the so-called traditional area is vastly enriched by a complexity of substantive concerns—trade promotion, mutual defense, vital negotiations in transportation and communications, and many other fields, policies in the United Nations and other multilateral bodies, commodity and tariff policies, and tourism.

The third category consists of a number of miscellaneous service and support activities including routine reporting, consular services, and general support and overhead.

The essential task of top management is to set the context for these varied activities by defining objectives and stating priorities, and then to balance resources to obtain the proper mix within and among the three broad categories.

The task is enormously complicated by the fact that each of the three clusters of activities cuts across the responsibilities of many executive departments and agencies.

This multiagency aspect of modern diplomacy—the fact that it does not fall entirely within the confines of any one agency—is one of its most difficult administrative problems. Again it is not necessary for me to recite to this group the many attempts in the past to construct effective machinery for dealing with multiagency concerns in foreign affairs. It is enough to say that the effort has had more than its share of trial and error, that the road has been rocky, and that I believe we are finally on at least one track that offers better possibilities than some of those that have been tried in the past.

SUGGESTED READINGS

THIS brief bibliography is intended to be merely suggestive and not exhaustive. It should be noted that none of the works from which selections have been taken for this book are included. The serious student of the foreign policy process will find it worthwhile to examine two exceptionally helpful bibliographies compiled by the staff of the Senate Subcommittee on National Policy Machinery.

The first is found in that subcommittee's volume *Organizing for National Security*, Vol. 2, *Studies and Background Material* (Washington: Government Printing Office, 1961), pp. 27–111; and a second compilation is *Administration of National Security: A Bibliography* (Washington: Government Printing Office, 1963). These are comprehensive, extremely well-organized, and many of the entries are annotated.

The fact that these are publications of a committee of Congress is worth noting. Students of the history of American foreign policy have always been deeply conscious of the crucial importance of the official collections of documents (such as the series *Foreign Relations of the United States*) in their research. Not as commonly recognized, however, is the great value that the study of the records of hearings before Congressional committees can have for the student, not only in understanding the substance of policy problems but in furnishing insights into the problems of policy formulation and decision-making. To be sure, the hearings are not organized for the benefit of the scholar. Many are not indexed, and even fewer are indexed adequately. The student must resort to his own devices and persevere if he is to extract the pertinent data from irrelevancies and repetitions, but the labor will be rewarding if the hearings are intelligently used.

Part I
UNITED STATES FOREIGN POLICY AND THE WORLD REVOLUTION

BASIC HISTORIES OF UNITED STATES FOREIGN POLICY:

BAILEY, THOMAS A. *Diplomatic History of the American People*. 6th ed. New York: Appleton-Century-Crofts, 1958.

BEMIS, SAMUEL FLAGG. *A Diplomatic History of the United States*. 4th ed. New York: Henry Holt and Co., 1955.

DECONDE, ALEXANDER. *American Foreign Policy*. New York: Charles Scribner's Sons, 1963.

PRATT, JULIUS W. *A History of United States Foreign Policy*. Englewood Cliffs, N.J.: Prentice-Hall, 1955.

INTERPRETATIONS AND COMMENTARIES ON THE HISTORY OF U.S. FOREIGN POLICY:

GRAEBNER, NORMAN (ed.). *An Uncertain Tradition: American Secretaries of State in the Twentieth Century*. New York: McGraw-Hill, 1961.

KENNAN, GEORGE F. *American Diplomacy, 1900–1950.* Chicago: University of Chicago Press, 1951.

OSGOOD, ROBERT E. *Ideals and Self-Interest in America's Foreign Relations.* Chicago: University of Chicago Press, 1953.

PERKINS, DEXTER. *The American Approach to Foreign Policy.* Cambridge, Mass.: Harvard University Press, 1952.

WORLD WAR II:

FEIS, HERBERT. *The China Tangle: The American Effort in China from Pearl Harbor to the Marshall Mission.* Princeton: Princeton University Press, 1953.

———. *Churchill, Roosevelt and Stalin: The War They Waged and the Peace They Sought.* Princeton: Princeton University Press, 1957.

———. *Between War and Peace: The Potsdam Conference.* Princeton: Princeton University Press, 1960.

———. *Japan Subdued: The Atomic Bomb and the End of the War in the Pacific.* Princeton: Princeton University Press, 1961.

LANGER, WILLIAM L., and S. EVERETT GLEASON. *The Challenge to Isolation* and *The Undeclared War.* New York: Harper and Brothers, 1952, 1953.

SNELL, JOHN L. *Illusion and Necessity: The Diplomacy of Global War, 1939–1945.* Boston: Houghton Mifflin Co., 1963.

GENERAL STUDIES OF THE DEVELOPMENT OF U.S. FOREIGN POLICY
SINCE WORLD WAR II:

CARLETON, WILLIAM G. *The Revolution in American Foreign Policy: Its Global Range.* New York: Random House, 1963.

CRABB, CECIL V. *American Foreign Policy in the Nuclear Age.* Evanston: Row, Peterson and Company, 1960.

IRISH, MARIAN D. (ed.). *World Pressures on American Foreign Policy.* Englewood Cliffs, N. J.: Prentice-Hall, 1964.

Part II
THE POLICY-MAKING ENVIRONMENT

ALSOP, JOSEPH, and STEWART ALSOP. *The Reporter's Trade.* New York: Reynal, 1958.

BAILEY, THOMAS A. *The Man in the Street: The Impact of American Public Opinion on Foreign Policy.* New York: Macmillan, 1948.

BAKER, ROSCOE. *The American Legion and American Foreign Policy.* New York: Bookman Associates, 1954.

BELOFF, MAX. *Foreign Policy and the Democratic Process.* Baltimore: Johns Hopkins Press, 1955.

BUCK, PHILIP W. (ed.). *Control of Foreign Relations in Modern Nations.* New York: W. W. Norton, 1957.

CATER, DOUGLASS. *The Fourth Branch of Government.* Boston: Houghton Mifflin, 1959.

CHEEVER, DANIEL S., and H. FIELD HAVILAND. *American Foreign Policy and the Separation of Powers.* Cambridge, Mass.: Harvard University Press, 1952.

COHEN, BERNARD. *The Press and Foreign Policy.* Princeton: Princeton University Press, 1963.

GRAEBNER, NORMAN A. *The New Isolationism: A Study in Politics and Foreign Policy Since 1950.* New York: Ronald Press, 1960.

HERO, ALFRED O. *Americans in World Affairs.* Boston: World Peace Foundation, 1959.

———. *Opinion Leaders in American Communities.* Boston: World Peace Foundation, 1959.

KENNAN, GEORGE F. *Realities of American Foreign Policy.* Princeton: Princeton University Press, 1954.

MILLIS, WALTER. *The Constitution and the Common Defense.* New York: Fund for the Republic, 1959.

WESTERFIELD, H. BRADFORD. *Foreign Policy and Party Politics: Pearl Harbor To Korea.* New Haven: Yale University Press, 1953.

WINDMULLER, JOHN P. *Foreign Affairs and the AFL-CIO.* Ithaca: New York State School of Industrial and Labor Relations, 1956.

Part III

THE CONGRESS AND FOREIGN POLICY

ACHESON, DEAN G. *A Citizen Looks at Congress.* New York: Harper and Brothers, 1957.

BROWN, MACALISTER. "The Demise of State Department Public Opinion Polls: A Study in Legislative Oversight," *Midwest Journal of Political Science,* **V** (1961), pp. 1–17.

BURNHAM, JAMES. *Congress and the American Tradition.* Chicago: Henry Regnery, 1959.

CARROLL, HOLBERT N. *The House of Representatives and Foreign Affairs.* Pittsburgh: University of Pittsburgh Press, 1958.

CHEEVER, DANIEL S., and H. FIELD HAVILAND, JR. *American Foreign Policy and the Separation of Powers.* Cambridge, Mass.: Harvard University Press, 1952.

COHEN, BERNARD C. *The Political Process and Foreign Policy: The Making of the Japanese Peace Settlement.* Princeton: Princeton University Press, 1957.

CRABB, CECIL V., JR. *Bipartisan Foreign Policy: Myth or Reality?* Evanston: Row, Peterson and Co., 1957.

DAHL, ROBERT A. *Congress and Foreign Policy.* New York: Harcourt, Brace and Co., 1950.

FARNSWORTH, DAVID N. *The Senate Committee on Foreign Relations.* Urbana: University of Illinois Press, 1961.

GRASSMUCK, GEORGE. *Sectional Biases in Congress on Foreign Policy.* Baltimore: Johns Hopkins University Press, 1951.

GREEN, HAROLD P., and ALAN ROSENTHAL. *Government of the Atom.* New York: Atherton Press, 1963.

HAVILAND, H. FIELD, JR. "Foreign Aid and the Policy Process, 1957," *American Political Science Review,* **LII** (1958), pp. 689–724.

JEWELL, MALCOLM. "The Senate Republican Policy Committee and Foreign Policy," *Western Political Quarterly,* **XII** (1959), pp. 966–980.

KESSELMAN, MARK. "Presidential Leadership in Congress on Foreign Policy," *Midwest Journal of Political Science,* **V** (1961), pp. 284–289.

MATTHEWS, DONALD R. *United States Senators and Their World.* Chapel Hill: University of North Carolina Press, 1960.

NELSON, RANDALL H. "Legislative Participation in the Treaty and Agreement Making Process," *Western Political Quarterly,* **XIII** (1960), pp. 154–172.

ROBINSON, JAMES A. *The Monroney Resolution: Congressional Initiative in Foreign Policy Making.* New York: Henry Holt and Co., 1959.

ROSENAU, JAMES N. *The Nomination of "Chip" Bohlen.* New York: Henry Holt and Co., 1959.

SHAPIRO, MARTIN. "Bipartisanship and the Foreign Policy Making Process," in Carl J. Friedrich and Seymour Harris (eds.), *Public Policy, 1960.* Cambridge, Mass.: Harvard University Press, 1960.

WESTPHAL, ALBERT C. F. *The House Committee on Foreign Affairs.* New York: Columbia University Press, 1942.

WESTERFIELD, H. BRADFORD. *Foreign Policy and Party Politics: Pearl Harbor to Korea.* New Haven: Yale University Press, 1955.

Part IV

THE EXECUTIVE ESTABLISHMENT

THE PRESIDENCY, THE SECRETARY OF STATE, AND THE DEPARTMENT OF STATE

BARNES, WILLIAM, and JOHN H. MORGAN. *The Foreign Service of the United States.* Washington: Government Printing Office, 1961.

COFFEY, JOSEPH I., and VINCENT P. ROCK. *The Presidential Staff.* Washington: National Planning Association, 1961.

CORWIN, EDWARD S. *The President, Office and Powers.* 4th rev. ed. New York: New York University Press, 1957.

DeCONDE, ALEXANDER. *The American Secretary of State: An Interpretation.* New York: Frederick A. Praeger, 1962.

ELDER, ROBERT E. *The Policy Machine: The Department of State and American Foreign Policy.* Syracuse: Syracuse University Press, 1960.

FENNO, RICHARD F., JR. *The President's Cabinet.* Cambridge, Mass.: Harvard University Press, 1959.

FINER, HERMAN. *The Presidency: Crisis and Regeneration.* Chicago: University of Chicago Press, 1960.

GRAEBNER, NORMAN S. (ed.). *An Uncertain Tradition: American Secretaries of State in the Twentieth Century.* New York: McGraw-Hill, 1961.

HELLER, FRANCIS H. *The Presidency: A Modern Perspective.* New York: Random House, 1960.

HOPKINS, FRANK S. "Planning for Foreign Policy Leadership," *Foreign Service Journal,* **XXXIX** (March 1962), pp. 21–23.

HOSKINS, HAROLD B. "Are American Foreign Service Officers Adequate?" *The Annals,* **CCCXXX** (July 1960), pp. 22–28.

KENNAN, GEORGE F. "Diplomacy as a Profession," *Foreign Service Journal,* **XXXVIII** (May 1961), pp. 23–26.

MARTIN, JAMES V. "The Quiet Revolution in the Foreign Service," *Foreign Service Journal*, **XXXVII** (February 1960), pp. 19–22.

MAY, ERNEST R. *The Ultimate Decision: The President as Commander in Chief.* New York: George Braziller, Inc., 1960.

NEUSTADT, RICHARD E. *Presidential Power: The Politics of Leadership.* New York: John Wiley & Sons, 1960.

NITZE, PAUL H. "The Modern President as a World Figure," *The Annals*, **CCCVII** (September 1956), pp. 114–123.

PENFIELD, JAMES K. "Is the Foreign Service a Profession?" *Foreign Service Journal*, **XXXVII** (March 1960), pp. 21–23.

PRICE, DON K. (ed.). *The Secretary of State.* Englewood Cliffs, N. J.: Prentice-Hall, 1960.

ROSSITER, CLINTON. *The American Presidency.* New York: Harcourt, Brace and Co., 1960.

RUSK, DEAN. "The President," *Foreign Affairs*, **XXXVIII** (April 1960), pp. 353–369.

TRUMAN, HARRY S. "My View of the Presidency," *Look*, **XXII** (November 11, 1958), pp. 25–31.

THE NATIONAL SECURITY COUNCIL, POLICY PLANNING,
AND THE BUDGETARY PROCESS

CUTLER, ROBERT. "The Development of the National Security Council," *Foreign Affairs*, **XXXIV** (April 1956), pp. 441–458.

DOWNS, ANTHONY. "Why the Government Budget Is Too Small in a Democracy," *World Politics*, **XII** (July 1960), pp. 541–563.

GUMZ, DONALD G. "The Bureau of the Budget and Defense Fiscal Policy," *U.S. Naval Institute Proceedings*, **LXXXV** (April 1959), pp. 80–89.

HALPERIN, MORTON H. "The Gaither Committee and the Policy Process," *World Politics*, **XIII** (April 1961), pp. 360–384.

HILSMAN, ROGER. "Planning for National Security: A Proposal," *Bulletin of the Atomic Scientists*, **XVI** (March 1960), pp. 93–96.

JACKSON, HENRY M. "Organizing for Survival," *Foreign Affairs*, **XXXVIII** (April 1960), pp. 446–456.

KATZENBACH, EDWARD L. "Bubud's Defense Policy," *The Reporter*, **XXII** (June 23, 1960), pp. 25–27.

KISSINGER, HENRY A. *The Necessity for Choice.* New York: Harper and Brothers, 1961.

LINDBLOM, CHARLES A. "The Science of 'Muddling Through,'" *Public Administration Review*, **XIX** (1959), pp. 79–88.

LINDSAY, F. A. "Planning in Foreign Affairs: The Missing Element," *Foreign Affairs*, **XXXIX** (January 1961), pp. 279–290.

MORGAN, GEORGE A. "Planning in Foreign Affairs: The State of the Art," *Foreign Affairs*, **XXXIX** (January 1961), pp. 271–278.

ROSTOW, WALT W. "Ideas and Action," *Department of State Building*, **XLVII** (July 9, 1962), pp. 59–63.

ROWEN, HOBART. "Washington's Unseen Powerhouse: David Bell and His Budgeteers," *Harper's Magazine*, **CCXXV** (July 1962), pp. 45–52.

STANLEY, TIMOTHY W. *American Defense and National Security.* Washington: Public Affairs Press, 1956.

U. S. Senate, Committee on Government Operations, Subcommittee on National Security Policy Machinery. *Organizing for National Security.* 3 vols. Hearings, Reports and Studies. Washington: Government Printing Office, 1961.

———, ———, Subcommittee on National Security Staffing and Operations. *Administration of National Security.* Hearings and Reports. Washington: Government Printing Office, 1962–1963.

THE MILITARY, THE INTELLIGENCE COMMUNITY, AND SCIENCE AND RESEARCH

BRODIE, BERNARD. *Strategy in the Missile Age.* Princeton: Princeton University Press, 1959.

———. *The Scientific Strategists.* Monograph No. 7, Council for Atomic Age Studies. Columbia University, 1962.

COFFIN, TRISTAM. *The Passion of the Hawks.* New York: The Macmillan Co., 1963.

COLLINS, J. LAWTON. "Our Modern Military Establishment," *Military Review,* XLII (September 1962), pp. 17–30.

DULLES, ALLEN W. *The Craft of Intelligence.* New York: Harper and Row, 1963.

DUPRE, STEFAN J., and S. A. LAKOFF. *Science and the Nation: Policy and Politics.* Englewood Cliffs, N. J.: Prentice-Hall, 1962.

ENTHOVEN, ALAIN C. "Systems Analysis and Decision Making," *Military Review,* XLIII (January 1963), pp. 7–17.

EVANS, ALLAN. "Intelligence and Policy Formation," *World Politics,* XII (October 1959), pp. 84–91.

FOX, WILLIAM T. R. "Representativeness and Efficiency: Dual Problem of Civil-Military Relations," *Political Science Quarterly,* LXXVI (September 1961), pp. 354–366.

HAMMOND, PAUL Y. *Organizing for Defense: The American Military Establishment in the Twentieth Century.* Princeton: Princeton University Press, 1961.

HUNTINGTON, SAMUEL P. *The Common Defense: Strategic Programs in National Politics.* New York: Columbia University Press, 1961.

KAPLAN, NORMAN. "The Role of the Research Administrator," *Administrative Science Quarterly,* IV (June 1959), pp. 20–42.

McCAMY, JAMES L. *Science and Public Administration.* University, Ala.: University of Alabama Press, 1960.

McGOVERN, WILLIAM M. *Strategic Intelligence and the Shape of Tomorrow.* Chicago: Henry Regnery, 1961.

RANSOM, HARRY H. *Central Intelligence and National Security.* Cambridge, Mass.: Harvard University Press, 1958.

SCHILLING, WARNER, PAUL Y. HAMMOND, and GLENN SNYDER. *Strategy, Politics and Defense Budgets.* New York: Columbia University Press, 1962.

STEIN, HAROLD (ed.). *American Civil-Military Decisions: A Book of Case Studies.* University, Ala.: University of Alabama Press, 1963.

TAYLOR, MAXWELL D. *The Uncertain Trumpet.* New York: Harper and Brothers, 1959.

WASSERMAN, BENNO. "The Failure of Intelligence Prediction," *Political Studies,* VIII (June 1960), pp. 156–169.

ZUCKERMAN, SIR SOLLY. "Judgment and Control in Modern Warfare," *Foreign Affairs,* XL (January 1962), pp. 192–212.

Part V

UNITED STATES ACTIVITIES OVERSEAS

The American Assembly. *The Representation of the United States Abroad.* New York: Columbia University, 1956.

BINGHAM, JONATHAN B. *Shirt-Sleeve Diplomacy: Point 4 in Action.* New York: John Day, 1953.

BLACK, EUGENE R. *The Diplomacy of Economic Development.* Cambridge, Mass.: Harvard University Press, 1960.

BLUM, ROBERT (ed.). *Cultural Affairs and Foreign Relations.* Englewood Cliffs, N. J.: Prentice-Hall, 1963.

HOLT, ROBERT T., and ROBERT W. VAN DE VELDE. *Strategic Psychological Operations and American Foreign Policy.* Chicago: University of Chicago Press, 1960.

JORDAN, AMOS A. *Foreign Aid and the Defense of Southeast Asia.* New York: Frederick A. Praeger, 1962.

LISKA, GEORGE. *The New Statecraft: Foreign Aid in American Foreign Policy.* Chicago: University of Chicago Press, 1960.

MONTGOMERY, JOHN D. *The Politics of Foreign Aid.* New York: Frederick A. Praeger, 1962.

President's Committee to Study the United States Military Assistance Program. *Composite Report, and Annexes.* Washington: Government Printing Office, 1959.

RAUSCHENBUSH, STEPHEN. *The Challenge to the Alliance for Progress.* Washington: Public Affairs Institute, 1962.

TAYLOR, PHILIP B., JR. "The Guatemalan Affair: A Critique of United States Foreign Policy," *American Political Science Review,* L (September 1956).

TEAF, HOWARD M., and PETER G. FRANCK. *Hands Across Frontiers: Case Studies in Technical Cooperation.* Ithaca: Cornell University Press, 1956.

WOLF, CHARLES. *Foreign Aid: Theory and Practice in Southern Asia.* Princeton: Princeton University Press, 1960.